SPEEDWAY YEARBOOK 1991

Edited by Peter Oakes

THE SPEEDWAY public responded magnificently to the re-introduction of the Speedway Yearbook series last year when the 1990 Speedway Yearbook was an instant success.
And, as we promised last year, we are delighted to be able to present you with the second issue of the new-style publication.
We are pleased to say that our decision to produce a book of some style and substance was entirely vindicated by your reaction to its availability.
We have decided to maintain both the style and format of the 1990 edition for the 1991 Speedway Yearbook and they should nestle sweetly together on any bookshelf or coffee table.
There have, though, been improvements and refinements, some suggested by readers (and if you have any thoughts please do let us know).
Among many new features is an expanded at-a-glance match-by-match section. Now you can not only find who scored what and where but you can also see who was your favourite team's captain, which riders were making their League debut and which riders were making their first appearance for the club. Another addition is a complete list of past winners of all last season's individual meetings.
We have also, in response to many requests, expanded the junior section which now gives the full end of season averages of all officially recognised Junior Leagues.
There are many other additions, some subtle, some obvious, and as a result of the extra information we have increased the pagination from last year's 160 to 192 pages.
Bearing this in mind we have also managed to keep the selling price of the 1991 Speedway Yearbook to a cost of living increase and this has been made possible by the support of some hand-picked advertisers who have offered their backing this year.
We ask you to support those advertisers wherever possible as it is only with their assistance that we have been able to maintain the price of this book at an affordable level for most speedway followers.
We have already started work on preparing next year's 1992 Speedway Yearbook – and look forward to a long and happy partnership with our readers.
Once again the volume covers the whole of the year – from January 1, 1990 until December 31, 1990.

FRONT PAGE BOOKS

1991 SPEEDWAY YEARBOOK Contents

1990 World Championship 5

Individual 5
Team Cup 21
Pairs 26
Long Track 29
Under 21 32

1990 Day by Day Diary 34

International Scene 59

England v Denmark 59
USSR National League Tour 61
Slangerup National League Tour 62
Major Internationals 63
USSR Australian Tour 191

SWAPA Awards 63

Champions Cup 65

The Majors 66

BLRC & Coastal Windows British Under 21 Championship 66
NLRC & Speedway Star NL Pairs Championship 69
NL Team Championship 71

Sunbrite League Section 73

Tables 73
Speedway Star Knock Out Cup 74
Gold Cup 77
Averages 80
Individual & Pairs Meetings 82
Challenge Matches 83
Club Reviews: Belle Vue-Wolverhampton 85

National League Section 116

Tables and Silver Helmet 116
National Series 118
National League Knock Out Cup 120
Club Reviews: Arena Essex-Wimbledon 123
Averages 177
Individual & Pairs Meetings 181
Challenge Matches 183

Junior Section 186

Tables 186
Averages 187
Individual Meetings 189

Subscribers & Acknowledgements 190

Australian season 1990-91 191
Legend: Key to the 1991 Speedway Yearbook 191

1991 Diary Dates 192

EDITED BY

Peter Oakes

Photographs by Mike Patrick

▲ **The 1991 SPEEDWAY YEARBOOK was first published in Great Britain, 1991, by Front Page Books, PO Box 251, Warrington, Cheshire, WA5 5AY, England. Tel: 0925-59484. Fax: 0925-58047.**

▲ The 1991 Speedway Yearbook was published by Front Page Books, printed by The Bath Press, Bath, England, from film prepared by Pinegen Limited, 95, Brighton Road, Surbiton, Surrey, KT6 5NF (081-399-0012) and is distributed by Front Page Books and Ruskin Book Services Limited, Marlborough House, Marlborough Street, Kidderminster, Worcestershire, DY10 1BJ (0562-515151).

▲ The dust jacket was printed by Nightingale Press (Baldock) Limited, Newark Close, Royston, Hertfordshire, SG8 5HL (0763-248393).

ISBN 0-948882-20-4. **£11.95.**

Star of 90

PER JONSSON

World Champion

IT'S SHOCKS GALORE AT THE WORLD FINAL

IN PER-FECT HARMONY

BRADFORD set a table fit for a King. But it wasn't the Coronation that everyone expected.

For Hans Nielsen, the shortest priced World Final favourite for many a long day, didn't even take part in the walk up the aisle.

Instead he had to settle for a view from the pews as three new contenders were installed as the heirs apparent.

PER JONSSON, the cool as a cucumber antagonist who was bidding to become Sweden's first World Champion since the early seventies.

SHAWN MORAN, the flamboyant American determined to prove his point against officialdom.

TODD WILTSHIRE, the first season Sunbrite Leaguer who had defied all his critics in his debut term in the top flight.

As the first British-staged World Final since 1985 unfolded it was obvious that this night would not belong to the defending champion.

No-one could get the odds on Nielsen making it four wins and when he won the opening race ahead of his Oxford team-mate Martin Dugard there was a sense of Here We Go Again from the spectators bathing in a balmy September evening.

Wiltshire, whose career was saved when Reading moved in with a last-ditch bid for his services after he had been ignored by most of the other senior tracks, streaked from the gate for a tape to flag win that left him totally unruffled and showing no discernible signs of first night nerves.

Jonsson had to fight for his three points, finally diving under his fellow Swede Jimmy Nilsen on the last bend for a dramatic on the line win which left Nilsen shaking his head in disbelief that he had left such an inviting gap in a World Final.

And, making it a glorious introduction to the individual big-time, Henrik Gustafsson, in because of yet another unfortunate accident suffered by Jan O. Pedersen, gave Sweden a second heat winner in heat four in the fastest time to date, three fifths of a second outside Nielsen's year-old track record as he relegated British and Commonwealth Champion Kelvin Tatum and Inter Continental Final winner Shawn Moran to the minor placings.

Those first four heats proved one thing: track curator Eric Boothroyd had prepared a perfect racing surface for the world's best.

The big shock came in the second batch of races when the blue helmeted title-holder was relegated to third position – the first time since his opening ride of the first day of the 1987 World Final at Amsterdam that he had been out of the first two.

It had been a long time. Three years, short of four days, and a total of 21 races since he had last finished with only one point from a World Final heat.

Everyone knew that an upset was on the cards at the end of that race as Nielsen now had only four points and he had been beaten by the two Swedes Jonsson and the dynamic debutant Gustafsson.

The Great Dane was pushed even further down the order as Todd Wiltshire made it two wins out of two and the England skipper revived British hopes with his first win of the night.

How would Nielsen react to his totally unexpected setback?

Like a champion was the swift answer as he came out, steely-faced, for a heat nine confrontation with the by-now confident Tatum and the in-form Wiltshire.

Tatum surges into the first turn and there is a groundswell of astonishment from the supporters as Nielsen is, once again, pegged back to third as he is taken wide by the young Aussie.

As the three challengers go down the back straight Nielsen realises his reign is over...unless!

He takes that reckless chance that is sometimes needed on the biggest night of the year, blasts past the white-leathered Wiltshire and then drives defiantly underneath Tatum who is sent sliding

Star of 90

KELVIN TATUM

British & Commonwealth Champion

towards the pits turn fence.

In that one full-blooded title-rescuing move Nielsen has revived his title dream – but Tatum's is shattered for another year as he drops back to fourth place behind Wiltshire and debutant Richard Knight, both of whom follow through the gap left by Nielsen.

Tatum, so desperate to become an English World Champion, admitted: "At that precise moment my World Final was over. It wasn't just the end of the championship but an end to all the hard work, physically and mentally, that goes into it. I honestly felt at the back of my mind that this was my best possible chance to be World Champion."

Nielsen walked back to his corner in the pits, deep in thought, convinced he could still retain his crown.

And the very same thought must have been running through the minds of those riders who were in line to succeed him.

Moran didn't let it affect him as he won heat 10, but perhaps that was why Jonsson suffered his first defeat of the evening in the following race after missing the start, catching and passing Toni Kasper but running out of time in his chase of American Rick Miller, another in his first World Final.

Gustafsson maintained his unexpected challenge with a second chance to win his third ride after Dutch referee Henny Van Den Boomen excluded Ronnie Correy as he tried to challenge the Swede.

The interval gave everyone time to draw breath with the huge video scoreboard recording the top six: Jonsson 8, Wiltshire 8, Gustafsson 8, Moran 7, Nielsen 7, Miller 7.

Eight races to go and, on a track built for action, it was anyone's World Final.

The next four races were to end so many hopes.

Nielsen dropped another point to Nilsen. Miller and Gustafsson (puncture) blew it as they finished behind Armando Castagna and Richard Knight.

Wiltshire could only add one point to his tally with a third place behind Moran and Jonsson which left the leaderboard looking like this as each rider looked towards his last programmed ride: Jonsson 10, Moran 10, Nielsen 9, Wiltshire 9, Nilsen 8, Gustafsson 8, Tatum 8, Miller 8.

Moran, Nielsen and outsider Miller would meet. So would Wiltshire, Nilsen and Gustafsson.

But Jonsson must have reflected on the luck of the draw as his last race brought him out against three riders, Castagna, Tatum and Correy who were out of it...but still dangerous opponents.

Showdown time. And it was Moran's nerve which held as he inflicted a third defeat on the now resigned ex-champion.

Moran waited, knowing that he would be World Champion if Jonsson failed to win heat 18. The Swede never looked like cracking as he made the swiftest of gates and had time to glance back although it is doubtful if he realised that the man most likely to wreck his night, Tatum, was initially back in fourth place.

Moran, four successive wins and mounted on an engine prepared by former World Champion Michael Lee, against Jonsson, beaten twice in his five outings.

Moran the extrovert v Jonsson the introvert.

It's Jonsson who exploded out of the start and the 1990 World Final is over as he pulls further and further away from his rival.

Todd Wiltshire adds a bronze medal to the silver he won with Leigh Adams in the World Pairs Final and Nielsen, the dethroned champion, accepts fourth place with dignity: "I've been in this situation before and, of course, I'm dejected but I'll get over it. I didn't get the breaks on the night and I wasn't getting out of the starts as well as I should have done."

Third placed Wiltshire claimed: "I couldn't have realistically asked for more in my opening Final. I don't think I was ready to become World Champion."

And the new King of the Track Jonsson said: "I have come the hard way up because I started without any money. I had to work for everything. It's been a long road and now that I'm there I can't believe it."

Ruthlessly, he had forced open the door to untold riches but even a newly-crowned World Champion can find there is no room at the inn as Jonsson, and his family, had to drive the 250 miles to their home in Swindon after being turned away from a handful of fully-booked hotels around Odsal.

For Shawn Moran, so near yet so far, his best-ever World Final was to have even more dramatic repercussions.

It was later revealed he had failed a drugs test at the Overseas Final (he had been taking pain-killers prescribed by a Swedish doctor) and he was subsequently stripped of his silver medal by the FIM and banned for 12 months, six months of which were suspended.

But the FIM didn't upgrade those riders who had finished behind him so the 1990 World Final

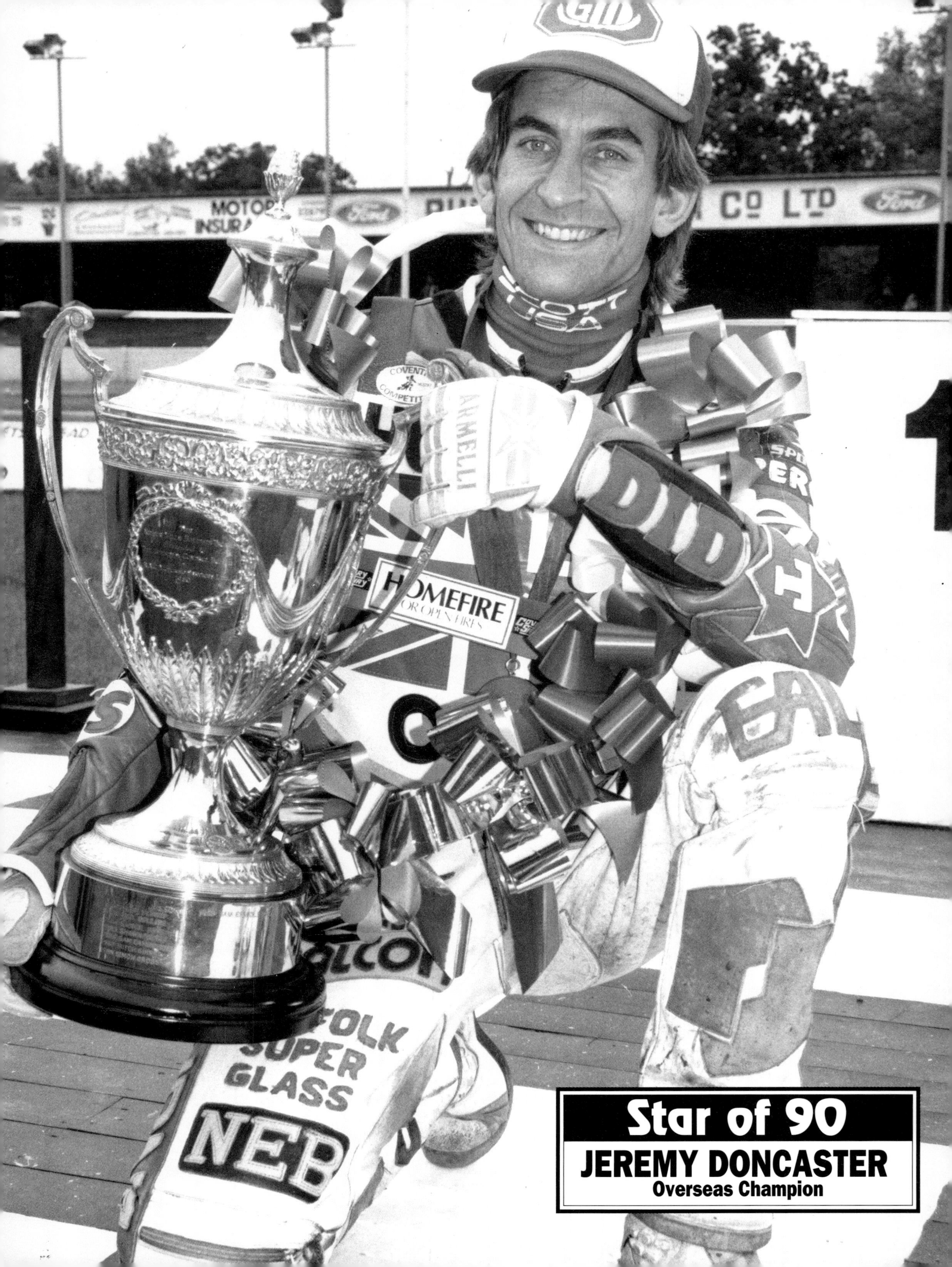

Star of 90

JEREMY DONCASTER

Overseas Champion

will forever be the meeting with no runner-up!

There were other victims of fate, denied ambitions strewn alongside the road that was the 1990 World Championship.

Two, in particular, evoked the sympathy of every speedway supporter.

Sam Ermolenko, his thigh and knee so badly smashed in a qualifying round of the 1989 World Long Track Championship that he hadn't ridden for nearly a year, applied to be seeded through to the Overseas Final instead of having to defend in the American Final.

His plea was turned down and then he had the misfortune to blow an engine while leading his opening race.

He hit deep dirt in his second and, realising he couldn't make the top four, quit to return to convalescence.

Shawn Moran, Billy Hamill, Rick Miller and Greg Hancock filled those top four places (all on 18 points) but in a run-off for placings, Hancock fell and suffered a broken left arm which was put in plaster and was to allow fifth-placed Ronnie Correy an Overseas Final reprieve.

The curse of Cradley Heath had claimed it's first – but not last – victim.

Simon Cross picked his way gingerly through the minefield that is the British qualification system and was preparing for the Inter Continental Final when he was so seriously injured in the World Pairs' Final that he has not ridden since.

He was the biggest of the British names to go out but was joined, from that Inter Continental Final at Fjelsted, by one of his England team-mates Jeremy Doncaster who had gone to Denmark as Overseas Champion.

But at least Donkey had failed where it mattered – on track.

Gert Handberg, Cradley's World Under 21 Champion, thought he had done enough to stay in the title race when he finished seventh in the Danish Final and was told he had qualified for the next round.

Hours later he heard the news that Coventry's John Jorgensen, who finished one place behind him, had been seeded to the next qualifier and his World Championship days were over!

It led to an angry protest from his Cradley promoter Colin Pratt who put forward the proposal that, in future, no country should be allowed to seed a rider.

Sweden dominated the Scandinavian Final even though it was Jan O. Pedersen who won the meeting with 14 points.

Five of the seven Inter Continental places were filled by the Swedes with Pedersen and Hans Nielsen providing the only other Scandinavian interest in the next stage.

Shawn Moran, unaware of the result of his drugs test at Coventry, qualified for his third World Final as he completed a hat-trick of Inter Continental Championships; Nielsen made it to his 11th World Final; and Pedersen had made amends for missing out on the 1989 World Final because of injury by making it through to the last 16 again.

Or so he thought....

In Norden, West Germany, the last Continental Final saw a home victory for Gerd Riss but elimination for King's Lynn's Bohumil Brhel and ex-Bradford favourite Antal Kocso.

The World Final line-up was known and included a handful of debutants: Rick Miller, Richard Knight, Martin Dugard, Todd Wiltshire and Zdenek Tesar.

But Lady Luck had another cruel hand to deal.

Little Jan O. went to watch a friend race karts in Birmingham only 17 days before the World Final, slipped, put out his hand to stop his fall, and heard the rifle shot that told him he had cracked the bone in his right arm.

He admitted: "It's shattering. The break isn't a serious break and it is something that is going to heal without any problem. But it has just come at the wrong time.

"I knew as soon as it happened that it was broken."

Pedersen officially withdrew six days later after Dr. Carlo Biagi told him there was no way he could be fitted up to race in the World Final and, a few days later, he was joined on the sidelines by another qualifier. West Germany's Gerd Riss had crashed in the World Long Track Final and was still in hospital nursing four broken ribs and head injuries when official practice was staged at Bradford.

Pedersen's tragic lightning-strikes-twice place was taken by Sweden's Henrik Gustafsson and Czechoslovakian Toni Kasper replaced the unlucky Riss.

Jan O., the third Cradley star to be ruled out of the World Championship because of injury, went along to the World Final simply to watch.

He would have been forgiven if he had shed a private tear for his stolen dream.

"I was confident about this year. I felt I had a much better chance than ever before because Bradford is a brilliant track for me because you can pass there."

Star of 90

SHAWN MORAN

Intercontinental Champion

FACTS & FIGURES...

GREAT BRITAIN

BRITISH QUARTER FINAL 1 (Ipswich, Thursday, April 5): **Alan Mogridge 13, Chris Louis 12 (+3), Mark Loram 12 (+x), Martin Goodwin 11 (+3),** Andy Galvin 11 (+2), Dean Standing 11 (+1), Carl Blackbird 9, Steve Schofield 8, Neville Tatum 8, Paul Whittaker 7, David Norris 6, Rob Tilbury 4, Nathan Simpson 4, Roger Johns 2, Paul Woods 1, Colin White, reserve, 1, Andy Buck 0.

David Norris replaced David Smart.

BRITISH QUARTER FINAL 2 (Middlesbrough, Thursday, April 5): **Gary Havelock 15, Les Collins 14, Mark Courtney 12, David Blackburn 12,** Darren Sumner 11, Jamie Luckhurst 10, Andy Hackett 8, Kenny McKinna 6, Martin Dixon 6, Steve Lawson 6, Sean Courtney 5, Bryan Larner 5, David Walsh 5, Duncan Chapman, reserve, 2, Tony Richardson, reserve, 2, Mike Lewthwaite 1, Mark Robinson 0.

Peter Carr (injured) withdrew; Sean Courtney replaced Andy Campbell after being overlooked in original draw; Gary Havelock replaced Andy Phillips after the Speedway Control Board ruled Havelock could not be seeded to the British semi-finals as he had not competed in the 1989 league.

BRITISH QUARTER FINAL 3 (Stoke, Saturday, April 21): **Nigel Crabtree 14, Dean Barker 13, Alun Rossiter 12, Louis Carr 10 (+3),** Andy Grahame 10 (+2), Alastair Stevens 9, Richard Green 9, Eric Monaghan 8, Ray Morton 8, Ian Barney 5, Carl Stonehewer 5, Paul Dugard 4, Gary Chessell 4, Peter Jeffery 4, Michael Coles 3, Ritchie Davidson 1, Jon Hughes, reserve, 1, Garry Stead, reserve, 0.

The meeting was originally scheduled for Saturday, April 14, but abandoned after 8 heats because of heavy rain. Scorers were: Monaghan 6, Barker 6, Crabtree 5, Grahame 5, Chessell 5, Carr 4, Stevens 4, Stonehewer 3, Green 2, Dugard 2, Gordon Kennett 2, Morton 2, Jeffery 1, Coles 1, Jolly 0, Barney 0, Ritchie Davidson, reserve, 0.

Michael Coles replaced Melvyn Taylor (injured). Gordon Kennett withdrew from the second staging because of injury, Kevin Jolly failed to arrive.

SEMI FINAL 1 (Cradley Heath, Sunday, May 6): **Gary Havelock 14, Simon Cross 13, Andrew Silver 12 (+3), Kelvin Tatum 12 (+2), Les Collins 9, Nigel Crabtree 9, Graham Jones 8, Paul Thorp 7 (+3),** Neil Collins 7 (+2), Alun Rossiter 7 (+1), Sean Wilson 6, Alan Grahame 6, Andy Phillips 4, Andy Grahame 4, Marvyn Cox 1, Martin Goodwin 0, David Haynes, reserve, 0, Rob Homer, reserve, 0.

David Blackburn withdrew because of injury.

SEMI FINAL 2 (King's Lynn, Sunday, May 6): **Jeremy Doncaster 15, Richard Knight 12 (+3), Andy Smith 12 (+2), John Davis 10, Chris Louis 10, Martin Dugard 9, Mark Loram 9, Simon Wigg 8 (+3),** Neil Evitts 8 (+2), Dean Barker 6, Joe Screen 6, Louis Carr 5, Alan Mogridge 4, Chris Morton 3, David Mullett 2, Mark Courtney 0, Tom Grinstead, reserve, 0.

HOMEFIRE BRITISH FINAL (Coventry, Sunday, May 20): **Kelvin Tatum 13, Simon Cross 11 (+3), Jeremy Doncaster 11 (+2), Gary Havelock 10, Martin Dugard 9, Mark Loram 9, Graham Jones 7, Simon Wigg 6 (+3), John Davis 6 (+2), Richard Knight 6 (+1),** Paul Thorp 6 (+0), Chris Louis 5, Les Collins 5, Andy Smith 5, Andrew Silver 5, Neil Collins 5, Paul Bromwich, reserve, 1.

Nigel Crabtree withdrew because of injury.

AUSTRALIA

NORTHERN TERRITORY FINAL (Darwin, Saturday, November 4, 1989): **Glen Baxter 12, Jamie Fagg 11,** David Jackson 10, Wayne Lorymer 8, Kelvin Willis 7, Brent Nott 7, Wayne Bridgeford 5, Dean Pierce 5, Robbie Wark 5, Pip Scholte 3, Stuart Cassidy 1, Bert Condon 1, Mark O'Cass 1, Dean Cottier, reserve, 0.

QUEENSLAND FINAL (Townsville, Saturday, December 2, 1989): **Troy Butler 15, Steve Regeling 14,** Alan Rivett 11, Steve Langdon 10, Darren Winkler 9, Gary Davey 9, Wayne Freeman 9, Mark Carlson 8, Peter Christopher 7, Mark Pearce 7, John Reid 4, David Thompson 4, Clint Butler 3, Glen Tregea 3, Gary Richards 3, Peter Byrne 2, Stafford Galvin 1, Keith Palfrey 0.

WESTERN AUSTRALIAN FINAL (Claremont, Perth, Friday, December 8, 1989): **Glenn Doyle 28, Glyn Taylor 24,** Ian Russell 22, Frank Smart 18, Guy Wilson 16, Mick Gardner 13, Clayton Isbel 12, Scott Fisher 11, Chris Lee 10, David Cheshire 7, Michael Carter 7, David Hedington 5, Peter Conroy 3, Ross Townsend 3.

Contested over nine heats, six riders per heat; two semi-finals and a Final, scoring throughout 7-5-4-3-2-1.

SOUTH AUSTRALIAN FINAL (North Arm, Adelaide, Friday, December 15, 1989): **Scott Norman 15, Shane Parker 13,** Shane Bowes 13, Damon Richardson 12, Phil Medson 11, Brett Tomkin 10, Billy Lellman 9, Paul Cooper 8, Neil Perry 8, Ross Noble 6, Lee Schooling 5, Shaun Sampson 3, Alex Pickl 2, Barry Golding 2, Roy Miller 1, Ivan Clothier 1, Dave Hartley 0, Gary Davies 0.

NEW SOUTH WALES FINAL (Newcastle, Tuesday, December 26, 1989): **Todd Wiltshire 15, Sean Willmott 13,** Chris Watson 10, Mick Poole 9, Stephen Davies 9, Rod Colquhoun 9, Mick Holder 8, Ian Wedgwood 8, Tony Primmer 8, Scott Humphries 6, Jamie Plumb 6, Dave Edwards 6, Dave Hamnett 5, Brian Nixon 3, Darren Etheridge 3, Warren Taggart 0, Paul Slade 0, Danny Jordan 0.

VICTORIAN FINAL (Myrtleford, Saturday, January 6): **Leigh Adams 14, Phil Crump 13,** Nigel Alderton 11, Anthony Key 11, Mark Lemon 10, Jason Lyons 10, Glen Bowles 10, Ricky Watson 9, Matt McWilliam 7, Justin Thomas 6, Jody Mason 5, Darren Wade 4, Corey Alderton 3, Chris Barton 3, Gavin Sedgman 3, Mike Futter 1.

Shane Bowes, Stephen Davies, Steve Langdon, Mick Poole and Chris Watson were seeded to the Australian Final.

AUSTRALIAN FINAL (Brisbane, Saturday, January 13): **Glenn Doyle 14,** Leigh Adams 14, Stephen Davies 13, Phil Crump 12, Shane Bowes 10, Mick Poole 9, Jamie Fagg 8, Glen Baxter 7, Steve Regeling 6, Steve Langdon 5, Shane Parker 5, Sean Willmott 4, Scott Norman 4, Troy Butler 4, Chris Watson 2, Glyn Taylor 1, Darren Winkler, reserve, 0, Clinton Butler, reserve, 0.

Todd Wiltshire withdrew from the re-arranged meeting to attend his sister's wedding. Leigh Adams, Troy Butler and Todd Wiltshire were seeded to the Commonwealth Final.

NEW ZEALAND

NEW ZEALAND FINAL (Ruapuna Park, Christchurch, Saturday, February 3): Larry Ross 14 (+3), Mark Thorpe 14 (+2), Craig Wilkie 14 (+x), James Martin 11, Justin Monk 10, Mike Long 9, Stephen Rose 8, Darrin Wilson 8, Mark Jamieson, reserve, 8, Max Brown 5, Philip Barakat 4, Kenny Webley 3, Rhys Hamburger, reserve, 3, Alan Mason 3, Greg Fisher 2, Gary Marsh 0, Trevor Chapman 0, John Tuffley, reserve, 0.

David Bargh and Gary Allan were seeded to the Commonwealth Final.

COMMONWEALTH

ANCIT COMMONWEALTH FINAL (Belle Vue, Sunday, June 10): **Kelvin Tatum 14, Martin Dugard 13, Simon Cross 12, Jeremy Doncaster 11, Richard Knight 11, Todd Wiltshire 10, Gary Havelock 8, Leigh Adams 7, David Bargh 6, Simon Wigg 6, Mark Loram 6, Troy Butler 5 (+3).** John Davis 5 (+2), Graham Jones 3, Glenn Doyle 3, Gary Allan 0.

UNITED STATES OF AMERICA

AMERICAN FINAL (Long Beach, California, Saturday, June 2): **Shawn Moran 18 (+3), Billy Hamill 18 (+2), Rick Miller 18 (+1), Greg Hancock 18 (+f),** Ronnie Correy 16 (+3), Kelly Moran 16 (+2), Bobby Schwartz 14, Mike Faria 12, Robert Pfetzing 12, Lance King 11, Steve Lucero 8, Jim Sisemore 8, Josh Larsen 7, Brad Oxley 5, Tony Bienert 5, Charles Ermolenko 3, Shawn McConnell, reserve, 3, Ed Castro 3, Sam Ermolenko 2, Don Odom, reserve, 2, John Kehoe (Canada) 1, Fred Legault (Canada) 0.

OVERSEAS

HOMEFIRE OVERSEAS FINAL (Coventry, Sunday, June 24): **Jeremy Doncaster 15, Todd Wiltshire 13, †Shawn Moran 10, Ronnie Correy 9, Martin Dugard 9, Kelvin Tatum 8, Rick Miller 8, Simon Cross 7, Troy Butler 7,** Richard Knight 6 (+3), Gary Havelock 6 (+2), Mark Loram 6 (+1), Simon Wigg 6 (+0), Leigh Adams 5, Billy Hamill 4, David Bargh 1.

Greg Hancock withdrew because of injury. †Shawn Moran gave a positive drugs test after this meeting – see World Final results.

SCANDINAVIA

DANISH FINAL (Holsted, Sunday, May 20): **Jan O. Pedersen 13, Hans Nielsen 12, Bo Petersen 11 (+3), Jens Henry Nielsen 11 (+2), Jan Petersen 10 (+3), Brian Karger 10 (+2),** Gert Handberg 10 (+x), **John Jorgensen 10 (+ef),** Per Sørensen 6, Henrik Kristensen 5, Ole Hansen 5, Allan Jensen 4, Peter Ravn 4, Kenneth Arnfred 3, John Eskildsen 3, Jens Peter Nielsen 3, John Pedersen, reserve, 0.

Allan Johansen withdrew through injury. John Jorgensen was seeded to the Scandinavian Final.

SWEDISH QUALIFYING ROUND (Målilla, Sunday, April 29): **Per Jonsson 13 (+3), Henrik Gustafsson 13 (+2), Dennis Löfqvist 12, Claes Ivarsson 12, Erik Stenlund 9, Tony Richardsson 9, Mikael Teurnberg 8, Stefan Dannö 8,** Kenny Nyström 7 (+3), Jörgen Johansson 7 (+2), Christer Jonsson 6, Mikael Löfqvist 5, Thomas Karlsson 4, John Jensen 3, Jan Bergqvist 3, Pier Karlsson 1.

SWEDISH QUALIFYING ROUND (Visby, Sunday, April 29): **Jimmy Nilsen 14, Tony Olsson 13, Niklas Karlsson 11, Mikael Rittervall 11, Conny Ivarsson 10, Peter Nahlin 10, Kenneth Lindby 10,** Christer Karlsson 9, Patrik Karlsson 8, Jimmy Engman 7, Tommy Nilsson 4, Tony Samuelsson 4, Raymond Smedh 4, Kent Rickardsson 2, Kori Vierte 2, Joachim Messing 0.

Peter Karlsson seeded to the championship rounds.

SWEDISH FINAL (Round 1, Vetlanda, Tuesday, May 15): Peter Nahlin 14, Conny Ivarsson 13, Per Jonsson 12, Jimmy Nilsen 12, Claes Ivarsson 9, Henrik Gustafsson 9, Dennis Löfqvist 9, Peter Karlsson 8, Niklas Karlsson 8, Mikael Rittervall 6, Tony Richardsson 6, Tony Olsson 5, Mikael Teurnberg 4, Erik Stenlund 4, Kenneth Lindby 1, Stefan Dannö 0.

SWEDISH FINAL (Round 2, Norköping, Wednesday, May 16): Per Jonsson 13, Jimmy Nilsen 12, Dennis Löfqvist 12, Henrik Gustafsson 11, Conny Ivarsson 9, Niklas Karlsson 9, Peter Nahlin 8, Claes Ivarsson 6, Peter Karlsson 6, Mikael Rittervall 6, Erik Stenlund 6, Tony Olsson 5, Tony Richardsson 5, Mikael Teurnberg 4, Kenneth Lindby 4, Stefan Dannö 2, Krister Karlsson, reserve, 1.

SWEDISH FINAL (Round 3, Avesta, Thursday, May 17): Per Jonsson 13, Dennis Löfqvist 13, Henrik Gustafsson 13, Conny Ivarsson 11, Jimmy Nilsen 10, Peter Nahlin 10, Tony Richardsson 10, Niklas Karlsson 8, Erik Stenlund 7, Mikael Teurnberg 7, Peter Karlsson 6, Stefan Dannö 4, Kenneth Lindby 3, Mikael Rittervall 2, Krister Karlsson 2, Kenneth Nyström, reserve, 1.

Tony Olsson and Claes Ivarsson withdrew because of injury.

SWEDISH FINAL OVERALL SCORERS: **Per Jonsson 38, Jimmy Nilsen 34, Dennis Löfqvist 34, Henrik Gustafsson 33, Conny Ivarsson 33, Peter Nahlin 32,** Niklas Karlsson 25, Tony Richardsson 21, Peter Karlsson 20, Erik Stenlund 17, Mikael Teurnberg 15, Claes Ivarsson 14, Mikael Rittervall 14, Tony Olsson 10, Kenneth Lindby 8, Stefan Dannö 6, Krister Karlsson, reserve, 3, Kenneth Nyström, reserve, 1.

*FINLAND seeded **Olli Tyrvainen** and **Kai Niemi** to the Scandinavian Final. **Vesa Ylinen** to the pre-meeting race-off.*

*NORWAY seeded **Einar Kyllingstad** and **Arnt Førland** to the Scandinavian Final. **Lars Gunnestad** to the pre-meeting race-off.*

SCANDINAVIAN FINAL (Linköping, Sweden, Saturday, June 9): **Jan O. Pedersen 14, Per Jonsson 12, Henrik Gustafsson 11 (+3), Conny Ivarsson 11 (+2), Jimmy Nilsen 11 (+1), Hans Nielsen 11 (+E), Dennis Löfqvist 9 (+3),** Brian Karger 9 (+2), Bo Petersen 6, Kai Niemi 6, Peter Nahlin 5, Einar Kyllingstad 5, Jens Henry Nielsen 3, Jan Pedersen 2, Arnt Førland 2, Olli Tyrvainen 2, Vesa Ylinen, reserve, 1, John Jorgensen, reserve, 0.

A qualifying race after practice on Friday, June 8, resulted: Peter Nahlin (Sweden), Vesa Ylinen (Finland), John Jorgensen (Denmark) and Lars Gunnestad (Norway) for the 16th qualifying place in the meeting.

EUROPE

SUNBRITE INTER CONTINENTAL FINAL (Fjelsted, Denmark, Sunday, August 12): **Shawn Moran 14, Per Jonsson 12, Hans Nielsen 11 (+3), Jan O. Pedersen 11 (+2), Rick Miller 10, Kelvin Tatum 9, Ronnie Correy 9, Richard Knight 8, Martin Dugard 7, Jimmy Nilsen 7, Todd Wiltshire 6,** Henrik Gustafsson 5, Dennis Löfqvist 4, Troy Butler 3, Conny Ivarsson 2, Jeremy Doncaster 2.

Simon Cross withdrew through injury. Brian Karger, who was scheduled to be reserve, withdrew through injury.

THE CONTINENT

PRELIMINARY ROUND 1 (Czestochowa, Poland, Saturday, May 5): **Jacek Wozniak (Poland) 13 (+3), Tommy Dunker (West Germany) 13 (+2), Jacek Rempala (Poland) 12, Dariusz Sledz (Poland) 11, Slawomir Drabik (Poland) 11, André Pollehn (West Germany) 10, Jaroslaw Szymkowiak (Poland) 10, Arkadij Kononiec (Soviet Union) 7,** Fabrizio Vesprini (Italy) 6 (+3), Mike Ott (East Germany) 6 (+2), Daniel Bohac (Czechoslovakia) 6 (+1), Andrej Korolev (Soviet Union) 5, Ralf Peters (East Germany) 5, Rene Elzinga (Holland) 4, Christoph Hilaire (France) 1, Henk Bangma (Holland) 0.

PRELIMINARY ROUND 2 (Krsko, Yugoslavia, Sunday, May 6): **Valentino Furlanetto (Italy) 15, Vladimir Kalina (Czechoslovakia) 13, Maciej Jaworek (West Germany) 12, Robert Funk (Autria) 12, Riccardo Salamon (Italy) 9, Gregor Pintar (Yugoslavia) 9, Andreas Bössner (Austria) 9, Borivoj Hadek (Czechoslovakia) 8 (+3),** Zdravko Jordanov (Bulgaria) 8 (+2), Martin Peterca (Yugoslavia) 7, David Ochocki (France) 5, Nikolaj Manev (Bulgaria) 4, Thomas Stadler (Austria) 4, Caba Lazar (Yugoslavia) 3, Patrice Blondy (France) 1, Rudi Spitaler (Yugoslavia) 1, Darko Tominac (Yugoslavia), reserve, 0.

PRELIMINARY ROUND 3 (Neustadt-Donau, West Germany, Sunday, May 6): **Alois Bachhuber (West Germany) 15, Lubomir Jedek (Czechoslovakia) 12, Jan Schinagl (Czechoslovakia) 12, Andrea Maida (Italy) 11, Walter Nebel (Austria) 10, †Vladimir Trofimov (Soviet Union) 10, Mariano Castagna (Italy) 9, Carsten Pelzmann (West Germany) 9,** Toni Pilotto (Austria) 8, Oleg Kurguskin (Soviet Union) 7,

Eugeniusz Skupien (Poland) 5, Peter Hehlert (West Germany) 4, Andreas Schapfl (West Germany) 3, Jacek Gomolski (Poland) 3, Ronnie Koppe (Holland) 2, Patrik Pino (Holland) 0.

†See Preliminary Round C.

PRELIMINARY ROUND 4 (Rovno, Soviet Union, Sunday, May 6): **Tomasz Gollob (Poland) 15, Igor Marko (Soviet Union) 13, Laszlo Bodi (Hungary) 12, Viktor Gaidym (Soviet Union) 11, Robert Csillik (Hungary) 11, Marius Soaita (Romania) 9, Rinat Mardanshin (Soviet Union) 9, René Aas (Soviet Union) 9,** Janusz Kapustka (Poland) 7, Sergei Kuzin (Soviet Union) 5, Georgi Petranov (Bulgaria) 5, Mircea Agrisan (Romania) 4, Galin Velichkov (Bulgaria) 3, Valery Christov (Bulgaria) 3, Zoltan Kovacs (Hungary) 2, Siegfried Eder (Austria) 2, Alexander Ganov (Soviet Union), reserve, 0, Sergei Tershak (Soviet Union), reserve, 0.

QUALIFYING ROUND A (Abensberg, West Germany, Monday, June 4): **Zoltán Adorján (Hungary) 14 (+3), Sándor Tihanyi (Hungary) 14 (+2), Klaus Lausch (West Germany) 12 (+3), Gerd Riss (West Germany) 12 (+2), Roman Matousek (Czechoslovakia) 11, Armando Castagna (Italy) 10, Bohumil Brhel (Czechoslovakia) 9, André Pollehn 9,** Armando dal Chiele (Italy) 7, Fabrizio Vesprini 6, Tommy Dunker 6, Jaroslaw Szymkowiak 3, Arkadij Kononiec 2, Slawomir Drabik 2, Jacek Rempala 2, Jacek Wozniak 1.

Dariusz Sledz did not ride.

QUALIFYING ROUND B (Miskolc, Hungary, Sunday, June 3): **Zoltán Hajdú (Hungary) 13, Piotr Swist (Poland) 11 (+3), Rif Saitgareev (Soviet Union) 11 (+2), Vladimir Kalina 11 (+1), Pavel Karnas (Czechoslovakia) 11 (+0), Petr Vandírek (Czechoslovakia) 9, Sándor Ujhelyi (Hungary) 8, Zsolt Böszmörményi (Hungary) 8,** Robert Funk 6 (+3), Valentino Furlanetto 6 (+2), Riccardo Salamon 6 (+1), Gregor Pintar 5, Igor Dubinin (Soviet Union) 5, Borivoj Hadek 4, Andreas Bössner 4, Ryszard Franczyszyn (Poland) 1.

Maciej Jaworek did not ride.

QUALIFYING ROUND C (Natschbach-Loipersbach, Austria, Saturday, June 2): **Antal Kocso (Hungary) 13, Zdenek Tesar (Czechoslovakia) 12, Heinrich Schatzer (Austria) 12, Robert Nagy (Hungary) 10, Wojciech Zaluski (Poland) 9, Antonin Kasper (Czechoslovakia) 9, Lubomir Jedek 9, Walter Nebel 9,** Andreas Marynowski (West Germany) 8 (+3), Toni Pilotto 8 (+2), Alois Bachhuber 6, Jan Schinagl 4, Jacek Krzyzaniak (Poland) 3, Mariano Castagna 3, Andrea Maida 2, Carsten Pelzmann 2, Oleg Kurguskin, reserve, 1.

Vladimir Trofimov was withdrawn under article 073.11 of the FIM code which states: "All riders having participated in the Continental semi-finals the previous year are not permitted to participate in the Preliminary rounds but must start in the Qualifying rounds." See Qualifying Round D.

QUALIFYING ROUND D (Rzeszow, Poland, Saturday, June 2): **Ryszard Dolomisiewicz (Poland) 15, Jozsef Petrikovics (Yugoslavia) 12 (+3), Jan Krzystyniak (Poland) 12 (+2), Zdenek Schneiderwind (Czechoslovakia) 11, Vladimir Trofimov 11, Viktor Gaidym 9, Igor Marko 9, Laszlo Bodi 9,** Tomasz Gollob 8, Vaclav Milik (Czechoslovakia) 7, Robert Csillik 6, René Aas 5, Rinat Mardanshin 2, Gianni Famari (Italy) 2, Gregori Harchenko (Soviet Union) 2, Marius Soaita 0.

CONTINENTAL SEMI FINAL 2 (Bydgoszcz, Poland, Saturday, June 23): **Antonin Kasper 14, Jan Krzystyniak 13, Tomasz Gollob 12 (+3), Zdenek Tesar 12 (+2), Antal Kocso 9, József Petrikovics 8, Wojciech Zaluski 7 (+3), Heinrich Schatzer 7 (+2),** Igor Marko 7 (+1), Lubomir Jedek 6, Robert Nagy 6, Laszlo Bodi 6, Ryszard Dolomisiewicz 5, Vladimir Trofimov 5, Walter Nebel 2, Viktor Gaidym 1.

Zdenek Schneiderwind withdrew because of injury.

CONTINENTAL SEMI FINAL 1 (Zarnovica, Czechoslovakia, Sunday, June 24): **Zoltán Adorján 15, Klaus Lausch 11 (+3), Armando Castagna 11 (+2), Gerd Riss 11 (+1), Sándor Tihanyi 10, Roman Matousek 9, Bohumil Brhel 9, Vladimir Kalina 9,** Petr Vandírek 8, André Pollehn 7, Rif Saitgareev 7, Zoltán Hajdú 6, Pavel Karnas 3, Sándor Ujhelyi 2, Robert Funk 1, Zsolt Böszörményi 1.

Piotr Swist withdrew because of injury.

▲ ***Riders in bold type qualified for the next stage of the 1990 World Championship although they did not necessarily compete in the next round.***

CONTINENTAL FINAL (Norden West Germany, Sunday, August 12): **Gerd Riss 13, Zoltán Adorján 12 (+3), Armando Castagna 12 (+2), Roman Matousek 11, Zdenek Tesar 10 (+3),** Antonin Kasper 10 (+2), Sándor Tihanyi 9, Wojciech Zaluski 7, Antal Kocso 7, Klaus Lausch 6, Bohumil Brhel 5, Vladimir Kalina 5, József Petrikovics 5, Tomasz Gollob 4, Heinrich Schatzer 3, Jan Krzystyniak 1.

WORLD FINAL

Odsal Stadium, Bradford, England

Saturday, September 1, 1990

1	**PER JONSSON**	**3**	**3**	**2**	**2**	**3**	**13 +3**
†2	*Shawn Moran*	*1*	*3*	*3*	*3*	*3*	*13 +2*
3	Todd Wiltshire	3	3	2	1	3	12
4	Hans Nielsen	3	1	3	2	2	11
5	Jimmy Nilsen	2	1	2	3	2	10
6	Henrik Gustafsson	3	2	3	0	1	9
6	Kelvin Tatum	2	3	0	3	1	9
8	Armando Castagna	F	2	1	3	2	8
8	Rick Miller	2	2	3	1	X	8
10	Richard Knight	1	2	1	2	1	7
11	Martin Dugard	2	0	1	0	3	6
12	Roman Matousek	1	R	0	2	2	5
13	Zoltán Adorján	1	R	0	1	0	2
13	Zdenek Tesar	0	0	2	0	R	2
15	Ronnie Correy	0	1	X	1	0	2
15	Antonin Kasper	0	1	1	0	0	2

Reserves: Dennis Löfqvist and Sándor Tihányi, did not ride.

Jan O. Pedersen qualified but was forced to withdraw with a broken arm. Gerd Riss qualified but was forced to withdraw with serious head injuries.

†Shawn Moran was subsequently stripped of second place after pleading guilty to a positive drugs test at the 1990 Overseas Final. The FIM decided the remaining placings should stay as they were and did not upgrade riders.

▲ *THE spelling of names throughout the International sections of the 1991 Speedway Yearbook are normally taken from official FIM records as are the finishing positions from all World Championship meetings.*

LOOKING BACK...

1936 (Wembley, England)
1 LIONEL VAN PRAAG 26 (14:12), 2 Eric Langton 26 (13:13), 3 Bluey Wilkinson 25 (15:10), 4 Cordy Milne 20 (11:9), 5 Frank Charles 20 (8:12), 6 Dick Case 17 (8:9), 7 Jack Ormston 17 (8:9), 8 Vic Huxley 17 (7:10), 9 George Newton 16 (4:12), 10 Jack Milne 15 (6:9), 11 Bob Harrison 15 (5:10), 12 Morian Hansen 15 (5:10), 13 Wal Phillips 12 (5:7), 14 Ginger Lees 11 (4:7), 15 Arthur Atkinson 9 (3:6), 16 Bill Pitcher 8 (2:6) 17 Norman Parker, reserve, 7 (1:6).
Balzer Hansen, reserve, did not ride.
Jack Parker (12 BP) and Joe Abbott (7 BP) qualified for World Final. Ron Johnson (7BP) should have stepped up from reserve but was unfit to ride.

1937 (Wembley, England)
1 JACK MILNE 28 (15:13), 2 Wilbur Lamoreaux 25 (13:12), 3 Cordy Milne 23 (12:11), 4 Jack Parker 21 (10:11), 5 Ginger Lees 19 (9:10), 6 Frank Charles 17 (7:10), 7 Lionel Van Praag 17 (6:11), 8 Bill Kitchen 16 (9:7), 9 George Newton 16 (5:11), 10 Eric Langton 16 (4:12), 11 Morian Hansen 15 (8:7), 12 Eric Chitty 15 (4:11), 13 Joe Abbott 14 (6:8), 14 Arthur Atkinson 14 (6:8), 15 Frank Varey 11 (3:8), 16 Tommy Croombs 2 (2:0), 17 Alec Statham, reserve, 0 (0:0).
Ron Johnson, reserve, did not ride.
Bob Harrison (7BP) qualified for World Final. Stan Greatrex qualified as reserve.

1938 (Wembley, England)
1 BLUEY WILKINSON 22 (14:8), 2 Jack Milne 21 (14:7), 3 Wilbur Lamoreaux 20 (13:7), 4 Lionel Van Praag 18 (11:7), 5 Bill Kitchen 15 (9:6), 6 Cordy Milne 15 (8:7), 7 Alec Statham 13 (8:5), 8 Eric Langton 13 (8:5), 9 Benny Kaufman 12 (7:5), 10 Jack Parker 10 (6:4), 11 Arthur Atkinson 10 (5:5), 12 Tommy Price 8 (4:4), 13 Tommy Croombs 8 (4:4), 14 George Newton 7 (2:5), 15 Geoff Pymar 7 (2:5), 16 Jack Ormston, reserve, 5 (5:0), 17 Frank Varey 4 (0:4).
Jimmy Gibb, reserve, did not ride.

1939 (Wembley, England)
Meeting abandoned because of the outbreak of war. Finalists with their qualifying points and bonus points were: Cordy Milne 53:8, Eric Langton 51:7, Wilbur Lamoreaux 50:7, Bill Kitchen 47:7, Vic Duggan 45:6, Lionel Van Praag 44:6, Arthur Atkinson 40:6, Jack Milne 40:6, Alec Statham 36:5, Jack Parker 34:5, Benny Kaufman 33:5, Eric Chitty 32:5, Ron Johnson 32:5, Frank Varey 31:4, Eric Collins 30:4, Aub Lawson 30:4. Reserves: Gil Craven 26:3, Frank Goulden 24.3.

Pre-war finalists carried forward bonus points based on their qualifying totals and these were included in their overall World Final score. Bonus points are listed in the results above after the World Final score.
From 1937-1938 bonus points were NOT carried forward by riders who did not finish among the 16 World Final qualifiers therefore, in 1937, Tommy Croombs and Alec Statham had no bonus points on World Final night and a similar situation applied to Jack Ormston in 1938.

1949 (Wembley, England)
1 TOMMY PRICE 15, 2 Jack Parker 14, 3 Louis Lawson 13, 4 Norman Parker 10, 5 Wilbur Lamoreaux 9, 6 Bill Kitchen 9, 7 Ron Clarke 8, 8 Aub Lawson 8, 9 Bill Longley 8, 10 Cyril Roger 7 11 Bill Gilbert 6, 12 Graham Warren 5, 13 Ken Le Breton 4, 14 Lloyd Goffe 2, 15 Cliff Watson 1, 16 Oliver Hart, reserve, 1, 17 Dent Oliver 0.
Alec Statham, reserve, did not ride.

1950 (Wembley, England)
1 FREDDIE WILLIAMS 14, 2 Wally Green 13, 3 Graham Warren 12, 4 Aub Lawson 10, 5 Tommy Price 8, 6 Jack Parker 8, 7 Split Waterman 8, 8 Ronnie Moore 7, 9 Jack Young 7, 10 Cyril Brine 7, 11 Dent Oliver 6, 12 Cyril Roger, reserve, 5, 13 Danny Dunton 5, 14 Vic Duggan 4, 15 Jack Biggs 3, 16 Ron Clarke 3,17 Arthur Payne 0, 18 Mike Erskine, reserve, 0.
Arthur Forrest qualified as first reserve.

1951 (Wembley, England)
1 JACK YOUNG 12, 2 Split Waterman 12, 3 Jack Biggs 12, 4 Ronnie Moore 11, 5 Jack Parker 10, 6 Louis Lawson 10, 7 Eddie Rigg 8, 8 Bob Leverenz 7, 9 Freddie Williams 7, 10 Aub Lawson 7, 11 Jeff Lloyd 6, 12 Eric Williams 6, 13 Cyril Brine 3, 14 Norman Parker 3 ,15 Dick Bradley, reserve, 2, 16 Ernie Roccio 2, 17 Alan Hunt 2.
Geoff Mardon, reserve, did not ride.

1952 (Wembley, England)
1 JACK YOUNG 14, 2 Freddie Williams 13, 3 Bob Oakley 12, 4 Ronnie Moore 10, 5 Dick Bradley 9, Dan Forsberg 9, Arthur Payne 9, 8 Arthur Forrest 7, 9 Henry Long 7, 10 Jeff Lloyd 7, 11 Brian Crutcher 6, 12 Split Waterman 6, 13 Graham Warren 5, 14 Derek Close 4, 15 Cyril Roger 2 ,16 Ron How 0.
Trevor Redmond and Basse Hveem, reserves, did not ride.
Bert Roger and Alan Hunt qualified.

1953 (Wembley, England)
1 FREDDIE WILLIAMS 14, 2 Split Waterman 13, 3 Geoff Mardon 12, 4 Olle Nygren 12, 5 Jack Young 10, 6 Ronnie Moore 9, 7 Jeff Lloyd 8, 8 Arthur Forrest 7, 9 Aub Lawson 7, 10 Brian Crutcher 6, 11 Rune Sörmander 5, 12 Graham Warren 5, 13 Eric Williams 4, 14 Alan Hunt 3, 15 Dick Bradley 2, 16 Jack Biggs 2, 17 Dent Oliver, reserve 1.
Arthur Payne, reserve, did not ride.

1954 (Wembley, England)
1 RONNIE MOORE 15, 2 Brian Crutcher 13, 3 Olle Nygren 13, 4 Jack Young 11, 5 Split Waterman 9, 6 Barry Briggs 9, 7 Eddie Rigg 7, 8 Fred Brand 7, 9 Jack Biggs 7, 10 Arthur Forrest 5, 11 Tommy Price 5, 12 Geoff Mardon 5, 13 Trevor Redmond 5, 14 Aub Lawson 4, 15 Peter Craven 3, 16 Ove Fundin 2.
Alan Hunt and Freddie Williams, reserves, did not ride.

1955 (Wembley, England)
1 PETER CRAVEN 13, 2 Ronnie Moore 12, 3 Barry Briggs 12, 4 Eric Williams 12, 5 Brian Crutcher 10, 6 Jack Young 10, 7 Ove Fundin 10, 8 Olle Nygren 9, 9 Arthur Forrest 7, 10 Arthur Wright 6, 11 Billy Bales 6, 12 Ron Johnson 6, 13 Kjell Carlsson 3,14 Phil Clarke 2,15 Henry Andersen 2, 16 Cyril Roger 0.
Ken McKinlay and Gerry Hussey, reserves, did not ride.

1956 (Wembley, England)
1 OVE FUNDIN 13, 2 Ronnie Moore 12, 3 Arthur Forrest 11, 4 Peter Craven 11, 5 Peo Söderman 10, 6 Ken McKinlay 10, 7 Barry Briggs 10, 8 Brian Crutcher 9, 9 Peter Moore 8, 10 Eric Boothroyd 7, 11 Alan Hunt 6, 12 Dick Fisher 5, 13 Doug Davies 4,14 Olle Andersson 2, 15 Ulf Ericsson 2, 16 Gerry Hussey 0.
Jack Biggs and Nigel Boocock, reserves, did not ride.

1957 (Wembley, England)
1 BARRY BRIGGS 14, 2 Ove Fundin 14, 3 Peter Craven 11, 4 Aub Lawson 11, 5 Rune Sörmander 11, 6 Ron Johnston 9, 7 Ken McKinlay 8, 8 Bob Roger 8, 9 Peo Söderman 7, 10 Jack Geran 7,11 Ron How 7, 12 Aage Hansen 4, 13 George White 4,14 Ian Williams 3, 15 Dan Forsberg 2, 16 Josef Hofmeister 0.
Brian Crutcher and Jack Biggs, reserves, did not ride.

1958 (Wembley, England)
1 BARRY BRIGGS 15, 2 Ove Fundin 13, 3 Aub Lawson 11, 4 Peter Craven 11, 5 Ken McKinlay 11, 6 Ronnie Moore 9, 7 Olle Nygren 9, 8 Ron Johnston 8, 9 Gerry Hussey 7, 10 Ron How 7, 11 Peter Moore 5, 12 Mike Broadbank 5, 13 Rune Sörmander 4, 14 Jack Geran 3, 15 Josef Hofmeister 2, 16 Joel Jansson 0.
Brian Crutcher and Peo Söderman, reserves, did not ride.

1959 (Wembley, England)
1 RONNIE MOORE 15, 2 Ove Fundin 13, 3 Barry Briggs 11, 4 Olle Nygren 11, 5 Aub Lawson 11, 6 Brian Crutcher 10, 7 Arne Carlsson 8, 8 George White 7, 9 Peter Craven 7, 10 Geoff Mardon 6, 11 Rune Sörmander 6, 12 Mieczyslaw Polukard 5, 13 Josef Hofmeister 4, 14 Peter Moore 3, 15 Ron How 3, 16 Cyril Roger 0.
Ken McKinlay and Florian Kapala, reserves, did not ride.

1960 (Wembley, England)
1 OVE FUNDIN 14, 2 Ronnie Moore 14, 3 Peter Craven 14, 4 Peter Moore 12, 5 Ron Johnston 10, 6 Barry Briggs 9, 7 Stefan Kwoczala 8, 8 Josef Hofmeister 6, 9 Ken McKinlay 6, 10 Jack Young 6, 11 Chum Taylor 5, 12 Rune Sörmander 5, 13 Henryk Zyto 4, 14 Aub Lawson 4, 15 Bob Andrews, reserve, 2, 16 Marian Kaiser 1, 17 Bryan Elliott 0.
Mieczyslaw Polukard, reserve, did not ride.

1961 (Malmö, Sweden)
1 OVE FUNDIN 14, 2 Björn Knutsson 12, 3 Göte Nordin 12, 4 Barry Briggs 12, 5 Ronnie Moore 10, 6 Bob Andrews 10, 7 Florian Kapala 8, 8 Rune Sörmander 7, 9 Ron How 7, 10 Peter Craven 6, 11 Ken McKinlay 5, 12 Cyril Maidment 4, 13 Igor Plechanov 4, 14 Ray Cresp 3, 15 Stanislaw Tkocz 3, 16 Mike Broadbank 2.
Jack Young and Leif Larsson, reserves, did not ride.
Josef Hofmeister qualified.

1962 (Wembley, England)
1 PETER CRAVEN 14, 2 Barry Briggs 13, 3 Ove Fundin 10, 4 Björn Knutsson 10, 5 Ronnie Moore 9, 6 Bob Andrews 9, 7 Ken McKinlay 9, 8 Göte Nordin 9, 9 Sören Sjösten 8, 10 Igor Plechanov 7, 11 Rune Sörmander 7, 12 Ron How 6, 13 Arne Carlsson 3, 14 Mike Broadbank 2, Ron Mountford 2, Pawel Waloszek 2.
Nigel Boocock and Henryk Zyto, reserves, did not ride.

LOOKING BACK...

1963 (Wembley, England)
1 OVE FUNDIN 14, 2 Björn Knutsson 13, 3 Barry Briggs 12, 4 Boris Samorodov 11, 5 Göte Nordin 10, 6 Sverre Harrfeldt 10, 7 Nigel Boocock 8, 8 Leo McAuliffe 7, 9 Ron How 7, 10 Peter Craven 6, 11 Peter Moore 6, 12 Peo Söderman 5, 13 Dick Fisher 5, 14 Jim Lightfoot 4, 15 Per Tage Svensson 1, 16 Arne Carlsson 1.
Tadeusz Teodorowicz and Ron Mountford, reserves, did not ride.
Antonin Kasper (sen), qualified as reserve.

1964 (Gothenburg, Sweden)
1 BARRY BRIGGS 15, 2 Igor Plechanov 13, 3 Ove Fundin 13, 4 Boris Samorodov 11, 5 Björn Knutsson 10, 6 Ron How 10, 7 Cyril Maidment 8, 8 Gennady Kurilenko 7, 9 Mike Broadbank 6, 10 Nigel Boocock 6, 11 Ken McKinlay 6, 12 Andrzej Wyglenda 4, 13 Bob Andrews 4, 14 Zbigniew Podlecki 3, 15 Jaroslav Volf 3, 16 Dick Fisher 1.
Jim Lightfoot and Gote Nordin, reserves, did not ride.

1965 (Wembley, England)
1 BJÖRN KNUTSSON 14, 2 Igor Plechanov 13, 3 Ove Fundin 13, 4 Barry Briggs 10, 5 Bengt Jansson 10, 6 Brian Brett 9, 7 Sören Sjösten 9, 8 Nigel Boocock 8, 9 Andrzej Pogorzelski 7, 10 Antonin Woryna 6, 11 Leif Larsson 5, 12 Reg Luckhurst 5, 13 Ken McKinlay 4, 14 Jimmy Gooch 3, 15 Andrzej Wyglenda 2, 16 Lubos Tomicek 2.
Mike Broadbank and Marian Rose, reserves, did not ride.

1966 (Gothenburg, Sweden)
1 BARRY BRIGGS 15, 2 Sverre Harrfeldt 14, 3 Antonin Woryna 13, 4 Ivan Mauger 11, 5 Torbjörn Harrysson 10, 6 Göte Nordin 9, 7 Leif Enecrona 8, 8 Igor Plechanov 8, 9 Stanislaw Tkocz 7, 10 Björn Knutsson 5, 11 Marian Kaiser 5, 12 Andrzej Pogorzelski 5, 13 Mike Broadbank 4, 14 Leif Larsson 3, 15 Nigel Boocock 2, 16 Peo Söderman 1.
Bengt Brannefors and Ken McKinlay, reserves, did not ride.

1967 (Wembley, England)
1 OVE FUNDIN 14, 2 Bengt Jansson 14, 3 Ivan Mauger 13, 4 Igor Plechanov 12, 5 Barry Briggs 11, 6 Anders Michanek 9, 7 Eric Boocock 9, 8 Ray Wilson 7, 9 Andrzej Pogorzelski 6, 10 Bernt Persson 6, 11 Antonin Woryna 5, 12 Rick France 5, 13 Colin Pratt 4, 14 Jerzy Trzeszkowski 3, 15 Andrzej Wyglenda 2, 16 Jochen Dinse 0.
Mike Broadbank and Jan Holub, reserves, did not ride.

1968 (Gothenburg, Sweden)
1 IVAN MAUGER 15, 2 Barry Briggs 12, 3 Edward Jancarz 11, 4 Gennady Kurilenko 11, 5 Pawel Waloszek 10, 6 Torbjörn Harrysson 10, 7 Anders Michanek 9, 8 Hasse Holmkvist 9, 9 Ove Fundin 7, 10 Gunnar Malmkvist 7, 11 Martin Ashby 5, 12 Antonin Woryna 5, 13 Reidar Eide 3, 14 Jerzy Trzeszkowski 3, 15 Nigel Boocock 1, 16 Bernt Persson 1.
Bengt Jansson and Igor Plechanov, reserves, did not ride.

1969 (Wembley, England)
1 IVAN MAUGER 14, 2 Barry Briggs 11, 3 Sören Sjösten 11, 4 Nigel Boocock 10, 5 Hasse Holmkvist 10, 6 Edward Jancarz 9, 7 Ove Fundin 9, 8 Ken McKinlay 7, 9 Andrzej Pogorzelski 7, 10 Jan Mucha 7, 11 Ronnie Moore 6, 12 Henryck Glucklich 5, 13 Valeri Klementiev 4, 14 Torbjörn Harrysson 4, 15 Zbigniew Podlecki, reserve, 3, 16 Andrzej Wyglenda 2, 17 Howard Cole 1.
Arnold Haley, reserve, did not ride.

1970 (Wroclaw, Poland)
1 IVAN MAUGER 15, 2 Pawel Waloszek 14, 3 Antonin Woryna 13, 4 Sören Sjösten 9, 5 Henryck Glucklich 9, 6 Valeri Klementiev 8, 7 Barry Briggs 7, 9 Andrzej Wyglenda 7, 9 Anders Michanek 7, 10 Ole Olsen 6, 11 Jan Mucha 6, 12 Hans Jurgen Fritz 5, 13 Vladimir Gordeev 5, 14 Edmund Migos, reserve, 4, 15 Zygfryd Friedek 2, 16 Gennady Kurilenko 2, 17 Trevor Hedge 0.
Juri Dubinin and Jerzy Szczakiel qualified.
Ronnie Moore qualified as reserve.

1971 (Gothenburg, Sweden)
1 OLE OLSEN 15, 2 Ivan Mauger 12, 3 Bengt Jansson 12, 4 Ray Wilson 11, 5 Anders Michanek 11, 6 Bernt Persson 9, 7 Jim Airey 8, 8 Sören Sjösten 8, 9 Nigel Boocock 6, 10 Ronnie Moore 5, 11 Eric Boocock 4, 12 Leif Enecrona 4, 13 Jiri Stancl 3, 14 Tommy Jansson 1, 15 Jerzy Szczakiel 0.
Tony Lomas and Göte Nordin, reserves, did not ride.
■ *Vladimir Gordeev finished fifth on 11 points but was subsequently disqualified by the FIM after tests showed he had used the banned fuel additive nitro-methane.*

1972 (Wembley, England)
1 IVAN MAUGER 13, 2 Bernt Persson 13, 3 Ole Olsen 12, 4 Christer Löfqvist 11, 5 John Louis 11, 6 Alexander Pavlov 8, 7 Anders Michanek 8, 8 Pawel Waloszek 6, 9 Viktor Trofimov 6, 10 Nigel Boocock 6, 11 Viktor Kalmykov 6, 12 Antoli Kuzmin 4, 13 Grigori Khlinovski 4, 14 Barry Briggs 3, 15 Eric Boocock 2, Jan Simensen, reserve, 2, 17 Valeri Gordeev 2, Jim McMillan, reserve, 2.

1973 (Katowice, Poland)
1 JERZY SZCZAKIEL 13, 2 Ivan Mauger 13, 3 Zenon Plech 12, 4 Ole Olsen 11, 5 Grigori Khlinovski 10, 6 Vladimir Paznikov 8, 7 Pawel Waloszek 8, 8 Valeri Gordeev 7, 9 Jan Mucha 7, 10 Anders Michanek 6, 11 Edward Jancarz 6, 12 Peter Collins 6, 13 John Boulger 6, 14 Ray Wilson 5, 15 Vladimir Zapleczny 2, 16 Tommy Jansson, reserve, 0, Andrzej Wyglenda, reserve, 0, Bernt Persson 0.

1974 (Gothenburg, Sweden)
1 ANDERS MICHANEK 15, 2 Ivan Mauger 11, 3 Soren Sjösten 11, 4 John Louis 9, 5 Bengt Jansson 9, 6 Peter Collins 9, 7 Tommy Johansson 8, 8 Zenon Plech 8, 9 Christer Löfqvist 8, 10 Grigori Khlinovski 6, 11 Dag Lövaas 6, 12 Terry Betts 6, 13 Dave Jessup 5, 14 Tommy Jansson, reserve, 3, 15 Mikhail Krasnov 3, 16 Ole Olsen 2, 17 Edward Jancarz, reserve, 1, 18 Vladimir Gordeev 0.

1975 (Wembley, England)
1 OLE OLSEN 15, 2 Anders Michanek 13, 3 John Louis 12, 4 Ivan Mauger 12, 5 Peter Collins 10, 6 Phil Crump 10, 7 Malcolm Simmons 10, 8 Viktor Trofimov 8, 9 Tommy Jansson 7, 10 Bernt Persson 5, 11 Ray Wilson 5, 12 Edward Jancarz 4, 13 Valeri Gordeev 4, 14 Zenon Plech 4, 15 Marek Cieslak 1, 16 Vladimir Gordeev, reserve, 0, Henryck Glucklich 0.
Martin Ashby, reserve, did not ride.

1976 (Katowice, Poland)
1 PETER COLLINS 14, 2 Malcolm Simmons 13, 3 Phil Crump 12, 4 Ivan Mauger 11, 5 Zenon Plech 11, 6 John Louis 9, 7 Doug Wyer 8, 8 Egon Müller 8, 9 Scott Autrey 7, 10 Jiri Stancl 6, 11 Chris Morton 6, 12 Edward Jancarz 5, 13 Marek Cieslak 4, 14 Jerzy Rembas 3, 15 Anders Michanek 2, 16 Valeri Gordeev 1, 17 Vladimir Gordeev 0.
Grigori Khlinovski, reserve, did not ride.

1977 (Gothenburg, Sweden)
1 IVAN MAUGER 14, 2 Peter Collins 13, 3 Ole Olsen 12, 4 Michael Lee 12, 5 Finn Thomsen 10, 6 Bengt Jansson 9, 7 Egon Müller 8, 8 Anders Michanek 8, 9 Billy Sanders 6, 10 Tommy Nilsson 6, 11 Bernt Persson 6, 12 John Boulger 5, 13 Edward Jancarz 4, 14 Jiri Stancl 3, 15 Jan Mucha 1, Jan Verner 1.
John Davis, Soren Karlsson and Boguslaw Nowak, reserves, did not ride.
Vladimir Rozanczuk qualified as reserve.

1978 (Wembley, England)
1 OLE OLSEN 13, 2 Gordon Kennett 12, 3 Scott Autrey 11, 4 Dave Jessup 11, 5 Jerzy Rembas 11, 6 Malcom Simmons 10, 7 Michael Lee 9, 8 Ivan Mauger 8, 9 John Titman 7, 10 Anders Michanek 7, 11 Ilkka Teromaa 6, 12 Marek Cieslak 5, 13 Jan Verner 5, 14 Jan Andersson 3, 15 Jiri Stancl 2, 16 Petr Ondrasik 0.
Steve Bastable, Zdenek Kudrna and Bernt Persson, reserves, did not ride.
Hans Wassermann qualified.

1979 (Katowice, Poland)
1 IVAN MAUGER 14, 2 Zenon Plech 13, 3 Michael Lee 11, 4 Kelly Moran 11, 5 Billy Sanders 11, 6 Ole Olsen 11, 7 Zdenek Kudrna 8, 8 Dave Jessup 8, 9 Edward Jancarz 7, 10 Finn Thomsen 6, 11 Peter Collins 6, 12 John Titman 6, 13 Mikhail Starostin 3, 14 Robert Slabon 2, Christoph Betzl 2, 16 Alois Wiesböck 1.
Petr Ondrasik and Larry Ross, reserves, did not ride.

1980 (Gothenburg, Sweden)
1 MICHAEL LEE 14, 2 Dave Jessup 12, 3 Billy Sanders 12, 4 Jan Andersson 11, 5 Bruce Penhall 9, 6 John Davis 9, 7 Kai Niemi 8, 8 Chris Morton 8, 9 Peter Collins 8, 10 Finn Thomsen 7, 11 Hans Nielsen 7, 12 Ales Dryml 5, 13 Jiri Stancl 5, 14 Egon Müller 4, 15 Zenon Plech 1, 16 Petr Ondrasik 0.
Hasse Danielsson, Ole Olsen and Vaclav Verner, reserves, did not ride.

1981 (Wembley, England)
1 BRUCE PENHALL 14, 2 Ole Olsen 12, 3 Tommy Knudsen 12, 4 Erik Gundersen 11, 5 Kenny Carter 11, 6 Jan Andersson 9, 7 Egon Müller 9, 8 Dave Jessup 7, 9 Hans Nielsen 6, 10 Michael Lee 5, 11 Chris Morton 5, 12 Edward Jancarz 5, 13 Larry Ross 4, 14 Ales Dryml 3, 15 Zenon Plech 3, 16 Jiri Stancl 3, 17 Henryck Olszak, reserve, 0.
Preben Eriksen, reserve, did not ride.

1982 (Los Angeles, United States of America)
1 BRUCE PENHALL 14, 2 Les Collins 13, 3 Dennis Sigalos 12, 4 Kelly Moran 11, 5 Kenny Carter 10, 6 Dave Jessup 8, 7 Hans Nielsen 8, 8 Jan Andersson 8, 9 Jiri Stancl 7, 10 Edward Jancarz 7, 11 Georg Hack 6, 12 Kai Niemi 5, 13 Peter Collins 5, 14 Phil Crump 4, 15 Vaclav Verner 2, 16 Mikhail Starostin 0.
Andy Grahame and Emil Sova, reserves, did not ride.

LOOKING BACK...

1983 (Norden, West Germany)
1 EGON MÜLLER 15, 2 Billy Sanders 12, 3 Michael Lee 11, 4 Erik Gundersen 10, 5 Kenny Carter 10, 6 Ole Olsen 10, 7 Hans Nielsen 9, 8 Dennis Sigalos 8, 9 Karl Maier 8, 10 Chris Morton 7, 11 Mitch Shirra 7, 12 Lance King 4, 13 Phil Collins 4, 14 Antonin Kasper (jun) 3, 15 Zenon Plech 1, 16 Jiri Stancl 1.

Henny Kroeze and Peter Ravn, reserves, did not ride.

Petr Ondrasik qualified.

1984 (Gothenburg, Sweden)
1 ERIK GUNDERSEN 14, 2 Hans Nielsen 13, 3 Lance King 13, 4 Kelly Moran 11, 5 Mitch Shirra 10, 6 Simon Wigg 9, 7 Bo Petersen 9, 8 Shawn Moran 7, 9 Karl Maier 7, 10 Jan Andersson 6, 11 Alan Grahame, reserve, 5, 12 Billy Sanders 5, 13 Kai Niemi 4, 14 Petr Ondrasik 3, 15 Egon Müller 3, 16 Jiri Stancl 1, 17 Vaclav Verner 0.

Tommy Nilsson, reserve, did not ride.

Edward Jancarz qualified.

1985 (Bradford, England)
1 ERIK GUNDERSEN 13, 2 Hans Nielsen 13, 3 Sam Ermolenko 13, 4 Kai Niemi 10, 5 Shawn Moran 10, 6 Tommy Knudsen 10, 7 John Cook 9, 8 Kelvin Tatum 8, 9 Jan O. Pedersen 7, 10 Jan Andersson 7, 11 Lance King 6, 12 Egon Müller 5, 13 Armando Castagna 4, 14 Zoltán Adorján 2, 15 Viktor Kuznetsov 2, 16 Karl Maier 1.

Phil Collins and Grzegorz Dzikowski, reserves, did not ride.

1986 (Katowice, Poland)
1 HANS NIELSEN 14, 2 Jan O. Pedersen 13, 3 Kelvin Tatum 12, 4 Jimmy Nilsen 11, 5 Tommy Knudsen 10, 6 Viktor Kuznetsov 10, 7 Sam Ermolenko 9, 8 Chris Morton 8, 9 Neil Evitts 8, 10 Erik Gundersen 7, 11 Ryszard Dolomisiewicz 6, 12 Marvyn Cox 3, 13 Karl Maier 3, 14 Antonin Kasper (jun) 2, 15 Armando Castagna 2, 16 Mitch Shirra 1, 17 Petr Vandirek, reserve, 1.

Jan Andersson, reserve, did not ride.

1987 (Amsterdam, Holland)
1 HANS NIELSEN 27 (12:15), 2 Erik Gundersen 24 (13:11), 3 Sam Ermolenko 24 (13:11), 4 Jimmy Nilsen 22 (9:13), 5 Per Jonsson 22 (11:11), 6 Jeremy Doncaster 20 (12:8), 7 Jan O. Pedersen 19 (10:9), 8 John Cook 15 (7:8), 9 Mitch Shirra 12 (7:5), 10 Gerd Riss 12 (4:8), 11 Simon Cross 10 (7:3), 12 Antonin Kasper (jun) 9 (5:4), 13 Chris Morton 9 (5:4), 14 Roman Jankowski 8 (0:8), 15 Roman Matousek 5 (3:2), 16 Henny Kroeze 1 (1:0), 17 Peter Ravn, reserve, 1 (1:N).

Vladimir Trofimov and Peter Seur, reserves, did not ride.

1988 (Vojens, Denmark)
1 ERIK GUNDERSEN 14, 2 Hans Nielsen 14, 3 Jan O. Pedersen 13, 4 Sam Ermolenko 12, 5 Per Jonsson 9, 6 Simon Wigg 9, 7 Roman Matousek 8, 8 Kelvin Tatum 8, 9 Conny Ivarsson 7, 10 Chris Morton 6, 11 Antal Kocso 6, 12 John Davis 3, 13 John Jorgensen 3, 14 Zenon Kasprzak 3, 15 Sándor Tihanyi 3, 16 Roman Jankowski 2.

Simon Cross and Andrzej Huszcza, reserves, did not ride.

1989 (Munich, West Germany)
1 HANS NIELSEN 15, 2 Simon Wigg 12, 3 Jeremy Doncaster 12, 4 Erik Gundersen 11, 5 Kelvin Tatum 10, 6 Mitch Shirra 10, Andy Smith 10, 8 Tony Olsson 8, 9 Gerd Riss 5, 10 Roman Matousek 5, 11 Karl Maier 5, 12 Troy Butler 4, Olli Tyrvainen 4, 14 Ronnie Correy 4, 15 Zoltán Adorján 4, 16 Bohumil Brhel 1.

József Petrikovics and Peter Ravn, reserves, did not ride.

Jan O. Pedersen qualified. Andy Grahame qualified as reserve but did not travel.

1990 (Bradford, England)
1 PER JONSSON 13, 3 Todd Wiltshire 12, 4, Hans Nielsen 11, 5 Jimmy Nilsen 10, 6 Henrik Gustafsson 9, 6 Kelvin Tatum 9, 8 Armando Castagna 8, 8 Rick Miller 8, 10 Richard Knight 7, 11 Martin Dugard 6, 12 Roman Matousek 5, 13 Zoltán Adorján 2, 13 Zdenek Tesar 2, 15 Ronnie Correy 2, 15 Antonin Kasper 2.

Dennis Löfqvist and Sándor Tihanyi, reserves, did not ride.

Jan O. Pedersen and Gerd Riss qualified.

■ *Shawn Moran competed in the World Final, scored 13 points and lost a run-off for the title. He was subsequently stripped of his placing after giving a positive drugs test at the Overseas Final. The FIM decided not to upgrade the remaining finalists and the records will show no silver medal issued.*

1990 NATIONAL CHAMPIONS

	Individual	*Pairs*	*Team*
AUSTRALIA	Glenn Doyle (Western Australia)	–	–
AUSTRIA	Heinrich Schatzer	††Speedway Szeged (Hungary) *(Antal Kocso/Robert Nagy)*	–
CZECHOSLOVAKIA	Antonin Kasper (Olymp Prague)	Olymp, Prague *(Petr Vandirek/Bohumil Brhel/Jan Holub)*	Olymp Prague
DENMARK	Hans Nielsen (Brovst)	–	Brovst
EAST GERMANY	Mike Ott (Neubrandenburg)	MSC Neubrandenburg *(Mike Ott/Wolfgang Buske/Bernhard Nicolas)*	MC Güstrow
GREAT BRITAIN	Kelvin Tatum (Coventry)	†Hackney *(Steve Schofield/Andy Galvin)*	Reading
HOLLAND	Robert Jan Munnecomb	–	–
HUNGARY	Zoltán Adorján (VC Hajdu)	†† Speedway Szeged *(Antal Kocso/Robert Nagy)*	SC Tisza
ITALY	Armando Castagna (MC La Favorita)	MC Lonigo *(Armando dal Chiele/Valentino Furlanetto)*	–
NEW ZEALAND	Larry Ross (Christchurch)	–	
NORWAY	Lars Gunnestad (NMK Drammen)	NMK Drammen *(Lars Gunnestad/Robert Langeland)*	NMK Drammen
POLAND	Zenon Kasprzak (Unia Leszno)	Polonia Bydgoszcz *(Ryszard Dolomisiewicz/Tomasz Gollob)*	Apator Torun
SWEDEN	Tony Richardsson (Stockholm United)	Stockholm United *(Per Jonsson/Jimmy Nilsen)*	Indianerna
UNITED STATES OF AMERICA	Mike Faria	–	–
WEST GERMANY	Klaus Lausch	–	Diedenbergen

▲ *The above details cover Championship meetings staged in 1990. † In Great Britain there was no national pairs championship held for the First Division clubs and the result relates to the 1990 Second Division (National League) competition. †† The Austrian Pairs Championship was held in conjunction with Hungary with five teams from Hungary and two from Austria.*

Stars of 90

AMERICA

World Team Cup Champions Billy Hamill, manager John Scott, Rick Miller, Shawn Moran, Sam Ermolenko and Kelly Moran

IT'S AN AMERICAN TEAM TRILOGY

YANKEE DOODLE DANDEES

SEVEN points separated the first three nations in the 1990 World Team Cup Final.

But Czechoslovakia were a Continent apart from the Big Three – both in the final result and their track preparation.

For the hosts provided a track that was fiercely criticised by England joint manager Eric Boocock and condemned by leading FIM official Günter Sorber in his official report of the World Final.

It became simply a follow-your-leader procession and, for once, the Yankee Doodle Dandees had their gating boots strapped on.

The retirement of Eric Gundersen and the injury to Simon Cross made it anyone's final...the most open competition for many years as England defended gold for the first time since 1981!

The Danes produced the first joker in their team selection when they recalled Tommy Knudsen and Brian Karger to their squad.

Both had been out with injuries. Knudsen had two comeback meetings in two seasons under his belt and Karger a couple of Danish warm-ups after breaking his leg.

Then American manager John Scott joined the game. He discarded World Finalist Ronnie Correy, drew youngster Billy Hamill and explained that the European rookie was more adept at coming from behind than his more illustrious countryman.

Certainly that ruled out any thoughts that the Californians had advance warning of track conditions!

England brought back Simon Wigg, included Marvyn Cox, ignored World Finalists Martin Dugard and Richard Knight, and called up Gary Havelock for his first World Team Cup appearance since he had top-scored as reserve in the 1988 Long Beach Final.

The Americans, who had qualified from a tough Group A by winning in Sweden, were slow out of the traps and had only two points from the first three heats to trail Denmark (7), England (6) and Czechoslovakia (3).

After eight heats they had overhauled the Czechs but were still merely interested on-lookers as England and Denmark fought for the lead with only a point between them.

But, inspired by the Moran brothers, America hit back, provided five winners in the next six heats, to hit the front and never looked back with Hamill replacing out of sorts Rick Miller to claim four valuable points.

England and Denmark had thrown their reserves in early as Cox and Bo Petersen struggled but they were left fighting for silver rather than gold.

For the five Californians it was a welcome return from the trophy-winning wilderness and America's first FIM gold medal since Bruce Penhall announced his retirement on the World Final rostrum at Los Angeles' Coliseum.

It also meant that the four major speedway World Finals had been won by four different countries: Sweden (individual), America (team), Denmark (pairs) and England (Under 21).

After the long-term Danish domination that can't be a bad thing.

And there are increasing signs that it won't be long before Australia are battling it out for real honours.

They stormed to a record qualifying total in Group B and then were far from disgraced in Group A where Sweden went into their home round with a one-point lead but were beaten by the eventual champions.

The new season should see a battle royal between Sweden and Australia for the last place in the 1991 World Team Cup Final.

And there was another welcome addition to the list of countries competing with East Germany, freed from the shackles of Communism, entering the World Team Cup for the first time and finishing runners-up to Austria in Group D.

The low spot? That has to be West Germany's performance in Sweden. They didn't get a single point and that, too, was a record!

FACTS & FIGURES...

WORLD TEAM CUP GROUP D

ROUND 1 (Güstrow, East Germany, Sunday, April 22): Austria 37 (Heinrich Schatzer 17, Toni Pilotto 14, Walter Nebel 6) East Germany 32 (Mike Ott 13, Thomas Diehr 11, Ralf Peters 8) Holland 19 (Ron Koppe 11, Rene Elzinga 6, Henk Bangma 2) Bulgaria 18 (Nikolai Manev 9, Zdravko Jordanov 6, Rudolf Valentinov 3) Yugoslavia 14 (Martin Peterca 7, Gregor Pintar 6, Kreso Omerzel 1).

ROUND 2 (Ljubljana, Yugoslavia, Tuesday, May 1): Austria 32 (Toni Pilotto 15, Heinrich Schatzer 11, Walter Nebel 6) East Germany 28 (Thomas Diehr 13, Mike Ott 12, Ralf Peters 3) Bulgaria 27 (Zdravko Jordanov 12, Nikolai Manev 11, Galin Velickov 4), Yugoslavia 19 (Gregor Pintar 11, Martin Peterca 4, Kreso Omerzel 4) Holland 14 (Rene Elzinga 6, Bob Dolman 5, Ron Koppe 3).

Aggregate: ***AUSTRIA 69,*** *East Germany 60, Bulgaria 45, Holland 33, Yugoslavia 33.*

Austria progress to Group C.

East Germany were admitted into the competition at a late stage and the ADMV agreed to hold an extra round at Güstrow. It is the first time the East Germans have competed in the competition.

WORLD TEAM CUP GROUP C

ROUND 1 (Lonigo, Italy, Sunday, May 20): Norway 44 (Einar Kyllingstad 13, Lars Gunnestad 13, Arnt Førland 9, Tor Einar Hjelm 9, Odd Pettersen 0) Finland 43 (Vesa Ylinen 14, Kai Niemi 13, Olli Tyrvainen 10, Juha Moksunen 6, Ari Koponen 0) Italy 24 (Armando dal Chiele 10, Valentino Furlanetto 8, Armando Castagna 3, Fabrizio Vesprini 2, Andrea Maida 1) Austria 8 (Toni Pilotto 4, Heinrich Schatzer 3, Walter Nebel 1, Franz Leitner 0, Siegfried Eder 0).

ROUND 2 (Karhula, Finland, Monday, May 28): Finland 45 (Kai Niemi 14, Juha Moksunen 13, Olli Tyrvainen 10, Vesa Ylinen 6, Roy Malminheimo 2) Norway 35 (Einar Kyllingstad 13, Arnt Førland 12, Lars Gunnestad 7, Tor Einar Hjelm 3, Odd Pettersen 0) Italy 24 (Valentino Furlanetto 8, Armando dal Chiele 7, Armando Castagna 6, Fabrizio Vesprini 3, Andrea Maida 0) Austria 16 (Heinrich Schatzer 6, Walter Nebel 4, Toni Pilotto 3, Franz Leitner 3).

Aggregate: ***FINLAND 88,*** *Norway 79, Italy 48, Austria 24. Finland progress to Group B. Austria relegated to Group D in 1991.*

WORLD TEAM CUP GROUP B

ROUND 1 (Szeged, Hungary, Sunday, July 8): Australia 49 (Todd Wiltshire 14, Troy Butler 13, Leigh Adams 11, Craig Boyce 6, Stephen Davies 5) Hungary 40 (Zoltán Adorján 14, Zoltán Hajdú 10, Sándor Tihanyi 8, Róbert Nagy 7, Jószef Petrikovics 1) Finland 22 (Vesa Ylinen 8, Olli Tyrvainen 7, Roy Malminheimo 5, Juha Moksunen 2, Kai Niemi, did not arrive) Poland 9 (Jan Krzystyniak 5, Tomasz Gollob 2, Eugeniusz Skupien 2, Jacek Gomolski 0, Tomasz Fajfer 0).

ROUND 2 (Gorzow, Poland, Saturday, July 14): Australia 55 (Todd Wiltshire 15, Leigh Adams 15, Troy Butler 13, Stephen Davies 9, Craig Boyce 3) Hungary 29 (Zoltán Adorján 10, Zoltán Hajdú 8, József Petrikovics 6, Laszlo Bodi 3, Sándor Tihanyi 2) Finland 24 (Olli Tyrvainen 10, Vesa Ylinen 7, Juha Moksunen 5, Roy Malminheimo 2, Kai Niemi, did not arrive) Poland 11 (Tomasz Gollob 4, Krzysztof Okupski 3, Dariusz Sledz 2, Ryszard Franczyszyn 1, Jan Krzystyniak 1).

Aggregate: ***AUSTRALIA 104,*** *Hungary 69, Finland 46, Poland 20. Australia progress to Group A. Poland relegated to Group C, 1991.*

WORLD TEAM CUP GROUP A

ROUND 1 (Olching, West Germany, Sunday, July 29): Sweden 38 (Jimmy Nilsen 13, Henrik Gustafsson 11, Per Jonsson 9, Conny Ivarsson 5, Dennis Löfqvist 0) United States of America 37 (Rick Miller 14, Kelly Moran 8, Ronnie Correy 8, Sam Ermolenko 7, Shawn Moran 0) Australia 23 (Troy Butler 7, Stephen Davies 6, Craig Boyce 6, Leigh Adams 4, Craig Hodgson 0) West Germany 22 (Klaus Lausch 10, André Pollehn 8, Tommy Dunker 2, Carsten Pelzmann 2, Alois Bachhuber 0).

ROUND 2 (Mariestad, Sweden, Saturday, August 25): United States of America 44 (Shawn Moran 15, Sam Ermolenko 14, Rick Miller 7, Kelly Moran 6, Ronnie Correy 2) Sweden 40 (Peter Nahlin 11, Per Jonsson 10, Henrik Gustafsson 10, Jimmy Nilsen 9, Conny Ivarsson) Australia 36 (Craig Boyce 12, Troy Butler 9, Todd Wiltshire 7, Leigh Adams 6, Stephen Davies 2) West Germany 0 (Klaus Lausch 0, Hans Otto Pingel 0, André Pollehn 0, Tommy Dunker 0).

Aggregate: ***UNITED STATES OF AMERICA 81,*** *Sweden 78, Australia 59, West Germany 22.*

USA progress to World Team Cup Final. West Germany relegated to Group B, 1991.

WORLD TEAM CUP FINAL

Pardubice, Czechoslovakia, Sunday, September 16

1 UNITED STATES OF AMERICA 37 (Kelly Moran 12, Sam Ermolenko 11, Shawn Moran 10, Billy Hamill 4, Rick Miller 0)
2 England 34 (Kelvin Tatum 11, Simon Wigg 8, Jeremy Doncaster 8, Gary Havelock 5, Marvyn Cox 2)
3 Denmark 30 (Hans Nielsen 13, Brian Karger 5, John Jorgensen 4, Bo Petersen 4, Tommy Knudsen 4))
4 Czechoslovakia 19 (Zdenek Tesar 6, Bohumil Brhel 6, Roman Matousek 3, Antonin Kasper 3, Vladimir Kalina 1).

Czechoslovakia relegated to Group A, 1991.

Denmark (hosts), United States of America (champions) and England seeded to World Team Cup Final, 1991.

LOOKING BACK...

1960 (Gothenburg, Sweden)
1 SWEDEN 44 (Ove Fundin 12, Olle Nygren 12, Rune Sörmander 11, Björn Knutsson 9) 2 Great Britain 30 (Peter Craven 8, Ken McKinlay 8, Ron How 7, George White 6, Nigel Boocock 1) 3 Czechoslovakia 15 (Antonin Kasper 5, Lubos Tomicek 4, Jaroslav Machac 3, Frantisek Richter 3) 4 Poland 7 (Konstanty Pociejkowicz 3, Marian Kaiser 2, Mieczyslaw Polukard 2, Jan Malinowski 0, Bronislaw Rogal 0).

1961 (Wroclaw, Poland)
1 POLAND 32 (Marian Kaiser 10, Henryk Zyto 7, Florian Kapala 6, Mieczyslaw Polukard 5, Stanislaw Tkocz 4) 2 Sweden 31 (Ove Fundin 11, Rune Sörmander 10, Björn Knutsson 7, Per Tage Svensson 3) 3 Great Britain 21 (Peter Craven 8, Bob Andrews 6, Ken McKinlay 4, Ron How 3) 4 Czechoslovakia 12 (Lubos Tomicek 7, Antonin Kasper 4, Bohumil Bartonek 1, Stanislav Svoboda 0).

1962 (Slany, Czechoslovakia)
1 SWEDEN 36 (Björn Knutsson 10, Sören Sjösten 10, Ove Fundin 9, Göte Nordin 4, Rune Sörmander 3) 2 Great Britain 24 (Ronnie Moore 10, Barry Briggs 8, Peter Craven 6, Ron How 0, Cyril Maidment 0) 3 Poland 20 (Marian Kaiser 9, Florian Kapala 5, Joachim Maj 4, Pawel Waloszek 2, Mieczyslaw Polukard 0) 4 Czechoslovakia 16 (Lubos Tomicek 7, Bedrich Slany 4, Jaroslav Volf 3, Karel Prusa 2).

1963 (Vienna, Austria)
1 SWEDEN 37 (Björn Knutsson 11, Peo Söderman 10, Ove Fundin 7, Göte Nordin 6, Rune Sörmander 3) 2 Czechoslovakia 27 (Antonin Kasper 10, Stanislaw Kubicek 7, Miroslaw Smid 5, Lubos Tomicek 5) 3 Great Britain 25 (Barry Briggs 12, Peter Craven 8, Dick Fisher 4, Peter Moore 1) 4 Poland 7 (Henryk Zyto 4, Marian Kaiser 1, Stanislaw Tkocz 1, Joachim Maj 1, Andrzej Pogorzelski 0).

1964 (Abensberg, West Germany)
1 SWEDEN 34 (Björn Knutsson 11, Göte Nordin 10, Rune Sörmander 7, Ove Fundin 6, Sören Sjösten 0) 2 Soviet Union 25 (Igor Plechanov 8, Gennady Kurilenko 8, Yuri Czekranov 6, Boris Samorodov 3) 3 Great Britain 21 (Barry Briggs 9, Ken McKinlay 7, Nigel Boocock 3, Ron How 2, Brian Brett 0) 4 Poland 16 (Andrzej Wyglenda 8, Andrzej Pogorzelski 3, Zbigniew Podlecki 3, Marian Rose 2, Marian Kaiser 0).

1965 (Kempten, West Germany)
1 POLAND 38 (Andrzej Wyglenda 11, Andrzej Pogorzelski 11, Antonin Woryna 9, Zbigniew Podlecki 7) 2 Sweden 33 (Björn Knutsson 11, Ove Fundin 8, Bengt Jansson 8, Göte Nordin 6) 3 Great Britain 18 (Ken McKinlay 7, Nigel Boocock 6, Jimmy Gooch 3, Barry Briggs 1, Charlie Monk 1) 4 Soviet Union 7 (Vladimir Sokolov 2, Yuri Czekranov 2, Gennady Kurilenko 2, Igor Plechanov 1, Viktor Trofimov 0).

1966 (Wroclaw, Poland)
1 POLAND 41 (Andrzej Wyglenda 11, Antonin Woryna 11, Marian Rose 11, Andrzej Pogorzelski 8, Edmund Migos 0) 2 Soviet Union 25 (Boris Samorodov 9, Viktor Trofimov 6, Igor Plechanov 6, Zarid Szajnurow 4) 3 Sweden 22 (Björn Knutsson 11, Leif Enecrona 4, Göte Nordin 3, Ove Fundin 2, Leif Larsson 2) 4 Great Britain 8 (Nigel Boocock 4, Ivan Mauger 3, Barry Briggs 1, Terry Betts 0, Colin Pratt 0).

1967 (Malmö, Sweden)
1 SWEDEN 32 (Göte Nordin 11, Bengt Jansson 9, Ove Fundin 6, Torbjörn Harrysson 6) 2 Poland 26 (Antonini Woryna 10, Andrzej Wyglenda 9, Jerzy Trzeszkowski 4, Zbigniew Podlecki 3, Andrzej Pogorzelski 0) 3 Great Britain 19 (Barry Briggs 8, Eric Boocock 5, Ray Wilson 4, Ivan Mauger 2, Colin Pratt 0) and Soviet Union 19 (Igor Plechanov 9, Viktor Trofimov 4, Boris Samorodov 3, Gabdrahman Kadirov 2, Farid Szajnurow 1).

1968 (Wembley, England)
1 GREAT BRITAIN 40 (Ivan Mauger 12, Nigel Boocock 10, Martin Ashby 8, Barry Briggs 7, Norman Hunter 3) 2 Sweden 30 (Ove Fundin 11, Bengt Jansson 7, Anders Michanek 7, Olle Nygren 3, Torbjörn Harrysson 2) 3 Poland 19 (Edmund Migos 8, Edward Jancarz 6, Andrzej Wyglenda 2, Henryck Glucklich 2, Pawel Waloszek 1) 4 Czechoslovakia 7 (Antonin Kasper 3, Lubos Tomicek 2, Jaroslav Volf 1, Jan Holub 1).

1969 (Rybnik, Poland)
1 POLAND 31 (Andrzej Wyglenda 11, Edward Jancarz 11, Stanislaw Tkocz 4, Henryck Glucklich 3, Andrzej Pogorzelski 2) 2 Great Britain 27 (Ivan Mauger 9, Barry Briggs 8, Nigel Boocock 5, Martin Ashby 5) 3 Soviet Union 23 (Vladimir Smirnov 9, Gennady Kurilenko 8, Valeri Klementiev 5, Yuri Dubinin 1, Viktor Trofimov 0) 4 Sweden 12 (Anders Michanek 7, Ove Fundin 2, Sören Sjösten 2, Bengt Jansson 1).

1970 (Wembley, England)
1 SWEDEN 42 (Ove Fundin 11, Bengt Jansson 11, Anders Michanek 10, Sören Sjösten 10) 2 Great Britain 31 (Barry Briggs 11, Ivan Mauger 9, Eric Boocock 5, Ray Wilson 4, Nigel Boocock 2) 3 Poland 20 (Jan Mucha 6, Antonin Woryna 5, Edmund Migos 4, Henryck Glucklich 3, Pawel Waloszek 2) 4 Czechoslovakia 3 (Vaclav Verner 3, Miroslav Verner 0, Jiri Stancl 0, Zdenek Majstr 0, Jan Holub 0).

1971 (Wroclaw, Poland)
1 GREAT BRITAIN 37 (Ray Wilson 12, Ivan Mauger 10, Jim Airey 9, Barry Briggs 6) 2 Soviet Union 22 (Grigori Khlinovski 8, Vladimir Smirnov 7, Vladimir Gordeev 4, Anatoli Kuzmin 3) 3 Poland 19 (Pawel Waloszeki 5, Henryck Glucklich 4, Antonin Woryna 4, Edward Jancarz 4, Andrzej Wyglenda 2) 4 Sweden 18 (Anders Michanek 9, Sören Sjösten 3, Bengt Jansson 3, Leif Enecrona 3, Bernt Persson 0).

1972 (Olching, West Germany)
1 GREAT BRITAIN 36 (Ivan Mauger 11, John Louis 9, Ray Wilson 8, Terry Betts 8) 2 Soviet Union 21 (Anatoli Kuzmin 6, Grigori Khlinovski 5, Viktor Trofimov 5, Viktor Kalmykov 5) 3 Poland 21 (Zenon Plech 7, Henryck Glucklich 6, Pawel Waloszek 5, Zdislaw Dobrucki 3, Marek Cieslak 0) 4 Sweden 18 (Christer Löfqvist 6, Anders Michanek 4, Tommy Jansson 4, Jan Simensen 3, Göte Nordin 1). *I n two races to decide second place the Soviet Union scored 7 points and Poland 5. Individual scorers: Kalmykov 3, Kuzmin 2, Khlinovski 1, Trofimov 1; Waloszek 3, Plech 2, Glucklich 0, Dobrucki 0.*

1973 (Wembley, England)
1 GREAT BRITAIN 37 (Peter Collins 12, Terry Betts 9, Malcolm Simmons 8, Ray Wilson 8) 2 Sweden 31 (Anders Michanek 11, Bernt Persson 9, Bengt Jansson 6, Tommy Jansson 5) 3 Soviet Union 20 (Vladimir Gordeev 7, Vladimir Paznikov 5, Grigori Khlinovski 4, Alexander Pavlov 2, Viktor Trofimov 2) 4 Poland 8 (Zenon Plech 5, Edward Jancarz 2, Pawel Waloszek 1, Jerzy Szczakiel 0).

1974 (Chorzow, Poland)
1 ENGLAND 42 (Peter Collins 12, John Louis 12, Dave Jessup 10, Malcolm Simmons 8) 2 Sweden 31 (Sören Sjösten 10, Anders Michanek 9, Tommy Jansson 7, Christer Löfqvist 5) 3 Poland 13 (Zenon Plech 4, Jan Mucha 4, Andrzej Jurczynski 3, Andrzej Tkocz 2, Jerzy Szczakiel 0) 4 Soviet Union 10 (Mikhail Krasnov 5, Valeri Gordeev 4, Viktor Kalmykov 1, Anatoli Kuzmin 0).

1975 (Norden, West Germany)
1 ENGLAND 41 (Peter Collins 12, Malcolm Simmons 11, Martin Ashby 10, John Louis 8) 2 Soviet Union 29 (Valeri Gordeev 8, Viktor Trofimov 8, Grigori Khlinovski 8, Vladimir Gordeev 5) 3 Sweden 17 (Anders Michanek 8, Tommy Jansson 4, Bernt Persson 2, Sören Sjösten 2, Sören Karlsson 1) 4 Poland 9 (Marek Cieslak 4, Henryck Glucklich 2, Jerzy Rembas 2, Edward Jancarz 1, Zenon Plech 0).

1976 (White City, England)
1 AUSTRALIA 31 (Phil Crump 11, Billy Sanders 7, Phil Herne 7, John Boulger 6) 2 Poland 28 (Edward Jancarz 9, Marek Cieslak 7, Zenon Plech 6, Jerzy Rembas 5, Boleslaw Proch 1) 3 Sweden 26 (Anders Michanek 11, Bernt Persson 8, Lars-Ake Andersson 5, Bengt Jansson 1, Christer Löfqvist 1) 4 Soviet Union 11 (Valeri Gordeev 5, Grigori Khlinovski 2, Vladimir Gordeev 2, Vladimir Paznikov 2, Viktor Trofimov 0).

1977 (Wroclaw, Poland)
1 ENGLAND 37 (Peter Collins 10, Michael Lee 9, Dave Jessup 9, John Davis 6, Malcolm Simmons 3) 2 Poland 25 (Edward Jancarz 10, Jerzy Rembas 6, Boguslaw Nowak 6, Marek Cieslak 2, Ryszard Fabiszewski 1) 3 Czechoslovakia 23 (Jiri Stancl 8, Vaclav Verner 5, Jan Verner 5, Ales Dryml 5) 4 Sweden 11 (Anders Michanek 5, Bernt Persson 4, Bengt Jansson 2, Tommy Nilsson 0, Sören Karlsson 0).

1978 (Landshut, West Germany)
1 DENMARK 37 (Hans Nielsen 11, Ole Olsen 10, Mike Lohmann 9, Finn Thomsen 7) 2 England 27 (Malcolm Simmons 8, Peter Collins 6, Dave Jessup 5, Michael Lee 5, Gordon Kennett 3) 3 Poland 16 (Edward Jancarz 6, Marek Cieslak 5, Jerzy Rembas 3, Zenon Plech 1, Andrzej Huszcza 1) 4 Czechoslovakia 16 (Jiri Stancl 7, Jan Verner 5, Vaclav Verner 2, Ales Dryml 2).

Jancarz beat Stancl in a run-off for third place.

1979 (White City, London)
1 NEW ZEALAND 35 (Larry Ross 11, Mitch Shirra 10, Ivan Mauger 9, Bruce Cribb 5) 2 Denmark 31 (Ole Olsen 12, Hans Nielsen 9, Mike Lohmann 6, Finn Thomsen 4, Bo Petersen 0) 3 Czechoslovakia 19 (Jiri Stancl 6, Ales Dryml 5, Zdenek Kudrna 4, Vaclav Verner 4) 4 Poland 11 (Piotr Pyszny 4, Zenon Plech 4, Robert Slabon 2, Marek Cieslak 1, Andrzej Tkocz 0).

LOOKING BACK...

1980 (Wroclaw, Poland)
1 ENGLAND 40 (Michael Lee 11, Chris Morton 11, Peter Collins 10, Dave Jessup 8) 2 United States of America 29 (Bruce Penhall 12, Scott Autrey 9, Dennis Sigalos 5, Bobby Schwartz 3, Ron Preston 0) 3 Poland 15 (Roman Jankowski 5, Zenon Plech 5, Edward Jancarz 3, Andrzej Huszcza 2, Jerzy Rembas 0) 4 Czechoslovakia 12 (Jiri Stancl 4, Vaclav Verner 3, Petr Ondrasik 3, Ales Dryml 1, Zdenek Kudrna 1).

1981 (Olching, West Germany)
1 DENMARK 36 (Hans Nielsen 11, Erik Gundersen 9, Tommy Knudsen 9, Ole Olsen 6, Finn Thomsen 1) 2 England 29 (Chris Morton 11, Kenny Carter 9, John Davis 5, Dave Jessup 3, Gordon Kennett 1) 3 West Germany 28 (Egon Müller 10, Karl Maier 8, Georg Hack 5, Georg Gilgenreiner 5) 4 Soviet Union 3 (Viktor Kuznetsov 2, Anatoli Maximov 1, Valeri Gordeev 0, Mikhail Starostin 0, Nikolai Kornev 0).

1982 (White City, London)
1 UNITED STATES OF AMERICA 37 (Kelly Moran 10, Bruce Penhall 10, Bobby Schwartz 9, Shawn Moran 8, Scott Autrey 0) 2 Denmark 24 (Hans Nielsen 11, Erik Gundersen 7, Preben Eriksen 4, Tommy Knudsen 1, Ole Olsen 1) 3 West Germany 18 (Karl Maier 7, Egon Müller 5, Georg Hack 5, Georg Gilgenreiner 1, Alois Wiesböck 0) 4 Czechoslovakia 17 (Ales Dryml 7, Vaclav Verner 6, Jiri Stancl 4, Petr Ondrasik 0, Antonin Kasper [jun] 0).

1983 (Vojens, Denmark)
1 DENMARK 37 (Erik Gundersen 12, Hans Nielsen 11, Ole Olsen 7, Peter Ravn 7, Finn Thomsen 0) 2 England 29 (Michael Lee 11, Kenny Carter 8, Chris Morton 7, Dave Jessup 2, Peter Collins 1) 3 United States of America 27 (Dennis Sigalos 9, Bobby Schwartz 6, Kelly Moran 6, Lance King 6) 4 Czechoslovakia 3 (Jiri Stancl 2, Vaclav Verner 1, Antonin Kasper [jun] 0, Petr Ondrasik 0, Ales Dryml 0).

1984 (Leszno, Poland)
1 DENMARK 44 (Erik Gundersen 12, Bo Petersen 12, Hans Nielsen 11, Preben Eriksen 9) 2 England 24 (Simon Wigg 9, Phil Collins 7, Chris Morton 4, Peter Collins 2, Neil Collins 2) 3 United States of America 20 (Shawn Moran 6, Kelly Moran 5, Lance King 5, Bobby Schwartz 2, John Cook 2) 4 Poland 8 (Zenon Plech 4, Leonard Raba 2, Roman Jankowski 1, Zenon Kasprzak 1, Boleslaw Proch 0).

1985 (Long Beach, United States of America)
1 DENMARK 37 (Tommy Knudsen 12, Erik Gundersen 10, Hans Nielsen 10, Preben Eriksen 5, Bo Petersen 0) 2 United States of America 35 (Shawn Moran 11, Bobby Schwartz 11, Lance King 9, Sam Ermolenko 3, John Cook 1) 3 England 13 (Jeremy Doncaster 6, Kelvin Tatum 3, Phil Collins 2, Richard Knight 2, John Davis 0) 4 Sweden 10 (Jan Andersson 5, Tommy Nilsson 3, Jimmy Nilsen 2, Per Jonsson 0, Pierre Brannefors 0).

1986 (Vetlanda, Sweden)
1 DENMARK 39 (Erik Gundersen 11, Hans Nielsen 10, Jan O. Pedersen 10, Tommy Knudsen 8) 2 Sweden 35 (Jan Andersson 11, Per Jonsson 10, Jimmy Nilsen 9, Tommy Nilsson 5) 3 England 29 (Chris Morton 8, Neil Evitts 8, Simon Wigg 7, Kelvin Tatum 4, Jeremy Doncaster 2) United States of America 17 (Shawn Moran 9, Bobby Schwartz 4, Sam Ermolenko 3, Lance King 1).

1986 (Vojens, Denmark)
1 DENMARK 48 (Erik Gundersen 14, Hans Nielsen 13, Tommy Knudsen 12, John Jorgensen 8, Jan O. Pedersen 1) 2 United States of America 29 (Sam Ermolenko 11, Shawn Moran 10, Lance King 7, Rick Miller 1, Bobby Schwartz 0) 3 England 23 (Simon Wigg 10, Kelvin Tatum 7, Chris Morton 5, Jeremy Doncaster 1, Neil Evitts 0) 4 Sweden 19 (Per Jonsson 8, Jan Andersson 7, Jimmy Nilsen 2, Tommy Nilsson 2, Erik Stenlund 0).

1986 (Bradford, England)
1 DENMARK 42 (Tommy Knudsen 13, Hans Nielsen 12, Jan O. Pedersen 9, Erik Gundersen 8) 2 United States of America 30 (Lance King 11, Sam Ermolenko 9, Shawn Moran 8, Bobby Schwartz 1, Rick Miller 1) 3 England 29 (Kelvin Tatum 8, Chris Morton 7, Simon Wigg 7, Jeremy Doncaster 7, Marvyn Cox 0) 4 Sweden 19 (Jan Andersson 10, Jimmy Nilsen 5, Per Jonsson 3, Erik Stenlund 1, Tony Olsson 0).

In 1986 the competition was extended to 20 heats and World Final placings were decided on a league points basis 3-2-1-0 and the final finishing positions were as follows: 1 DENMARK 9, 2 United States of America 4, 3 England 3, 4 Sweden 2.

1987 (Fredericia, Denmark)
1 DENMARK 47 (Hans Nielsen 15, Jan O. Pedersen 12, Erik Gundersen 10, Tommy Knudsen 10) 2 England 37 (Jeremy Doncaster 13, Simon Wigg 9, Simon Cross 8, Kelvin Tatum 7) 3 United States of America 24 (Sam Ermolenko 9, Rick Miller 8, Shawn Moran 4, Lance King 3) 4 Czechoslovakia 12 (Antonin Kasper [jun] 4, Lubomir Jedek 4, Roman Matousek 3, Petr Vandirek 1, Zdenek Schneiderwind 0).

1987 (Coventry, England)
1 UNITED STATES OF AMERICA 43 (Shawn Moran 14, Sam Ermolenko 11, Rick Miller 9, Lance King 5, Kelly Moran 4) 2 Denmark 37 (Hans Nielsen 11, Jan O. Pedersen 10, Erik Gundersen 9, Tommy Knudsen 7) 3 England 33 (Simon Wigg 11, Kelvin Tatum 9, Jeremy Doncaster 6, Simon Cross 5, Marvyn Cox 2) 4 Czechoslovakia 7 (Antonin Kasper [jun] 3, Roman Matousek 2, Petr Vandirek 1, Lubomir Jedek 1, Zdenek Scheiderwind 0).

1987 (Prague, Czechoslovakia)
1 DENMARK 46 (Erik Gundersen 14, Hans Nielsen 12, Jan O. Pedersen 10, Tommy Knudsen 10) 2 England 31 (Kelvin Tatum 9, Simon Wigg 9, Simon Cross 8, Jeremy Doncaster 5, Marvyn Cox 0) 3 United States of America 26 (Kelly Moran 10, John Cook 6, Rick Miller 5, Shawn Moran 5) 4 Czechoslovakia 17 (Roman Matousek 9, Zdenek Schneiderwind 3, Antonin Kasper [jun] 3, Petr Vandirek 2, Lubomir Jedek 0).

World Final 1987 placings were decided on aggregate race points and the final finishing positions were as follows: 1 DENMARK 130, 2 England 101, 3 United States of America 93, 4 Czechoslovakia 36.

1988 (Long Beach, United States of America)
1 DENMARK 44 (Hans Nielsen 14, Jan O. Pedersen 12, Erik Gundersen 8, Tommy Knudsen 8, John Jorgensen 2) 2 United States of America 32 (Sam Ermolenko 13, Shawn Moran 8, Lance King 6, Kelly Moran 5, Rick Miller 0) 3 Sweden 22 (Per Jonsson 9, Jimmy Nilsen 5, Tony Olsson 4, Henrik Gustafsson 4, Conny Ivarsson 0) 4 England 22 (Gary Havelock 8, Kelvin Tatum 7, Chris Morton 4, Simon Cross 3, Simon Wigg 0). *Jonsson beat Tatum in a run-off for third place.*

Sweden relegated to Group A in 1989 as England are seeded as hosts to the 1989 World Final.

1989 (Bradford, England)
1 ENGLAND 48 (Jeremy Doncaster 13, Paul Thorp 12, Kelvin Tatum 12, Simon Wigg 11, Simon Cross 0) 2 Denmark 34 (Hans Nielsen 11, Gert Handberg 9, John Jorgensen 7, Brian Karger 7, Erik Gundersen 0) 3 Sweden 30 (Mikael Blixt 10, Per Jonsson 8, Tony Olsson 7, Erik Stenlund 5, Jimmy Nilsen 0) 4 United States of America 8 (Kelly Moran 6, Greg Hancock 2, Ronnie Correy 0, Rick Miller 0, Lance King 0).

Sweden and United States of America relegated to Group A in 1990 as Czechoslovakia are seeded as hosts to the 1990 World Final.

1990 (Prague, Czechoslovakia)
1 UNITED STATES OF AMERICA 37 (Kelly Moran 12, Sam Ermolenko 11, Shawn Moran 10, Billy Hamill 4, Rick Miller 0) 2 England 34 (Kelvin Tatum 11, Simon Wigg 8, Jeremy Doncaster 8, Gary Havelock 5, Marvyn Cox 2) 3 Denmark 30 (Hans Nielsen 13, Brian Karger 5, John Jorgensen 4, Bo Petersen 4, Tommy Knudsen 4) 4 Czechoslovakia 19 (Zdenek Tesar 6, Bohumil Brhel 6, Roman Matousek 3, Antonin Kasper [jun] 3, Vladimir Kalina 1).

Czechoslovakia relegated to Group A in 1991.

DID YOU KNOW?

▲ *THE 1990 World Final was the second closest in the competition's history with only seven points separating the winners and the third placed nation. The tightest of all was in 1976 when Australia won with 31 points, Poland were runners-up with 28 and Sweden were third on 26 – only five points behind the winners.*

▲ *WEST GERMANY became the first nation to fail to score a point in a World Team Cup round when they finished bottom of the Group A second qualifying round at Mariestad, Sweden, in 1990.*

▲ *HANS NIELSEN is the only rider to have scored a 15 point maximum in a World Team Cup Final since the formula was changed to 20 heats in 1986.*

Stars of 90

DENMARK

World Pairs Champions
Hans Nielsen
and Jan O. Pedersen

IT'S GOOD RIDDANCE TO 6 RIDER RACES

UNLUCKY SIMON BREAKS BACK

A five-year experiment with six-rider heats ended in tragedy, recriminations and a dramatic about-turn by the FIM.

Leading delegates to the world governing body had decided even before the carnage of the World Final that they would end the gamble that six riders a race would make for more exciting speedway and bigger crowds.

Within 24 hours of Poland's Piotr Swist being rushed to hospital and put on a life support machine after an horrific crash in the semi-final at Wiener Neustadt, Austria, when he ended up in the sixth row of the concrete terracing, FIM Track Commission President Günter Sorber had decided the time had come to revert to the conventional four-man races for the 1991 World Pairs Championship.

Sadly, that decision came too late to save England's Simon Cross and West Germany's Gerd Riss from being admitted to a Landshut Hospital suffering from injuries sustained in two divorced crashes in the opening two heats.

Cross came down while trying to pass a couple of rivals on the first turn of the opening lap of the World Final and was subsequently transferred by road from Landshut to a Munich Hospital where he was operated on after fracturing one vertebra and displacing two others.

Riss was a little luckier, but still spent a time in hospital with a chipped ankle after a first bend mêlée in the second heat.

It left both England and West Germany down to one rider and prompted England co-manager Eric Boocock to ask the FIM to allow nations to carry a reserve in future competitions.

The two early accidents, and a rare exclusion for World Champion Hans Nielsen, opened up the competition and after the first 15 heats – when all nations had completed five rides – only four points separated leaders Australia and third-placed Hungary as they went into the final round.

Holders Denmark had struggled early on but kept one hand on the crown with a breathtaking last to second ride by Jan O. Pedersen in heat five when Nielsen also missed the gate.

When Aussies Todd Wiltshire and Leigh Adams nosed in front going into the first bend of the final race it looked as if they could pull off the biggest upset in the competition's history.

But the experience of Nielsen and Pedersen was decisive and by the time all six riders went into the third turn the two dashing Danes were in front.

That's where they stayed and with the youthful Aussies consolidating their third and fourth place, Hungary had to be content with third place - in itself a record as Zoltán Adorján and Sándor Tihanyi were the first Magyars to claim an FIM medal in any shale event.

They deserved their bronze with a string of stirring performances in the early heats but lost their nerve – and vital points – in each of their last two rides when the occasion got the better of them.

Contrastingly, the tougher it got the better the Danes competed and in the final analysis it was their experience at international level that kept them heading for a record-equalling seventh success which sees them tied with England for all time victories.

For Nielsen a sixth gold medal – the best individual tally of all time.

But it was the young Aussies who captured the hearts of the sweltering 12,000 Bavarian crowd.

Neither of them were well-known names on the Continent and manager James Easter had suffered a backlash from Australia when he overlooked 1989 World Finalist Troy Butler in his selection.

How his faith was repaid.

They finished third in the opening semi final – won, at a canter, by England – and they internationally came of age at Landshut as they led for most of the meeting...at least, until it came to the crunch.

And that was when we saw, for the first time, the best of the Danes!

WORLD PAIRS

Semi Finals

Wiener Neustadt, Austria, Saturday, June 16
1 ENGLAND 45 (Simon Cross 24, Kelvin Tatum 21) 2 Sweden 40 (Per Jonsson 20, Jimmy Nilsen 20) 3 Australia 39 (Todd Wiltshire 25, Leigh Adams 14) 4 New Zealand 41 (Mitch Shirra 24, David Bargh 17) 5 Austria 28 (Heinrich Schatzer 17, Toni Pilotto 11) 6 Italy 21 (Armando dal Chiele 11, Armando Castagna 10) 7 Soviet Union 27 (Rif Saitgareev 17, Valdimir Trofimov 10) 8 Yugoslavia 14 (Gregor Pintar 8, Martin Peterca 6) 9 Poland 9 (Piotr Swist 5, Ryszard Dolomisiewicz 4). *Meeting reserves: Walter Nebel 2, Rainer Selb 1.*

Prague, Czechoslovakia, Sunday, June 17
1 DENMARK 50 (Hans Nielsen 25, Jan O. Pedersen 25) 2 United States of America 44 (Ronnie Correy 24, Kelly Moran 20) 3 Hungary 37 (Zoltán Adorján 22, Sándor Tihanyi 15) 4 Czechoslovakia 38 (Roman Matousek 21, Antonin Kasper 17) 5 Finland 31 (Olli Tyrvainen 19, Kai Niemi 12) 6 Norway 24 (Lars Gunnestad 15, Arnt Førland 9) 7 Bulgaria 21 (Nikolai Manev 12, Zdravko Jordanov 9) 8 Holland 18 (Ronnie Koppe 9, Rene Elzinga 9) 9 France 7 (David Ochocki 7, Patrice Blondy 0).

WORLD FINAL

Landshut, West Germany, Saturday, July 21, 1990

1 DENMARK 43 (Hans Nielsen 19, Jan O. Pedersen 24)
2 Australia 41 (Todd Wiltshire 25, Leigh Adams 16)
3 Hungary 33 (Zoltán Adorján 21, Sándor Tihanyi 12)
4 Sweden 33 (Per Jonsson 15, Jimmy Nilsen 18)
5 New Zealand 32 (Mitch Shirra 23, David Bargh 9)
6 United States of America 28 (Ronnie Correy 15, Kelly Moran 13)
7 Czechoslovakia 21 (Roman Matousek 10, Antonin Kasper 11)
8 England 20 (Kelvin Tatum 20, Simon Cross 0)
9 West Germany 15 (Klaus Lausch 15, Gerd Riss 0).
Meeting reserve: Alois Bachhuber (West Germany) 3.

LOOKING BACK...

***1969 (Stockholm, Sweden)**
1 NEW ZEALAND 28 (Ivan Mauger 18, Bob Andrews 10) 2 Sweden 27 (Ove Fundin 14, Göte Nordin 13) 3 England 21 (Nigel Boocock 11, Martin Ashby 10) 4 Denmark 17 (Ole Olsen 13 Bent Norregaard Jensen 4) 5 Czechoslovakia 15 (Jan Holub 9, Zdenek Majstr 6) 6 East Germany 9 (Gerhard Uhlenbrock 8, Jochen Dinse 1) 7 Bulgaria 8 (Petr Petkov 6, Petr Iliev 2).

1970 (Malmö, Sweden)
1 NEW ZEALAND 28 (Ronnie Moore 16, Ivan Mauger 12) 2 Sweden 25 (Ove Fundin 15, Bengt Jansson 10) 3 England 19 (Eric Boocock 13, Nigel Boocock 6) 4 Scotland 18 (Jim McMillan 10, Bert Harkins 8) 5 Czechoslovakia 11 (Jiri Stancl 6, Vaclav Verner 5) 6 Yugoslavia 8 (Drasko Orsic 5, Ivan Kos 3).
Denmark 17 (Ole Olsen 12, Bent Norregaard Jensen 5) replaced Poland but their points did not count in final placings.

1971 (Rybnik, Poland)
1 POLAND 30 (Jerzy Szczakiel 15, Andrzej Wyglenda 15) 2 New Zealand 25 (Barry Briggs 13, Ivan Mauger 12) 3 Sweden 22 (Anders Michanek 13, Bernt Persson 9) 4 Czechoslovakia 17 (Vaclav Verner 9, Pavel Mares 8) 5 Scotland 16 (Jim McMillan 11, George Hunter 5) 6 Yugoslavia 10 (Drasko Orsic 5 Ivan Molan 5) 7 Austria 6 (Josef Haider 3, Heinz Zimmerman 3).

1972 (Borås, Sweden)
1 ENGLAND 24 (Ray Wilson 15, Terry Betts 9) 2 New Zealand 24 (Ivan Mauger 14, Ronnie Moore 10) 3 Sweden B 22 (Bernt Persson 13, Hasse Holmkvist 9) 4 Sweden A 22 (Anders Michanek 15, Bengt Jansson 7), 5 Poland 15 (Zbigniew Marcinkowski 13, Wiktor Jastrzebski 2) 6 Czechoslovakia 12 (Jiri Stancl 7, Jan Holub 5) 7 Hungary 6 (Ferenc Radacsi 6, Pal Perenyi 0).
Wilson beat Mauger in a run-off for first place; Persson beat Michanek in third place run off.

1973 (Borås, Sweden)
1 SWEDEN 24 (Anders Michanek 15, Tommy Jansson 9) 2 Denmark 21 (Ole Olsen 18, Kort Bøgh 3) 3 Poland 21 (Zenon Plech 14, Zbigniew Marcinkowski 7) 4 Soviet Union 20 (Vladimir Gordeev 10, Anatoli Kuzmin 10) 5 Norway 17 (Reidar Eide 9, Dag Lovaas 8) 6 Czechoslovakia 11 (Jiri Stancl 9, Petr Ondrasik 2) 7 New Zealand 10 (Ivan Mauger 8, Graeme Stapleton 2).
Olsen beat Plech in run off for second place.

1974 (Belle Vue, Manchester, England)
1 SWEDEN 28 (Anders Michanek 14, Sören Sjösten 14) 2 Australia 23 (Phil Crump 14, John Boulger 9) 3 New Zealand 21 (Ivan Mauger 17, Barry Briggs 4) 4 England 20 (Peter Collins 12, Dave Jessup 8) 5 Poland 18 (Zenon Plech 12, Edward Jancarz 6) 6 Soviet Union 10 (Grigori Khlinovski 6, Vladimir Gordeev 4) 7 Czechoslovakia 6 (Jan Holub 3, Jan Hadek 3).

1975 (Wroclaw, Poland)
1 SWEDEN 24 (Anders Michanek 17, Tommy Jansson 7) 2 Poland 23 (Edward Jancarz 15, Piotr Bruzda 8) 3 Denmark 20 (Ole Olsen 18, Jan Henningsen 2) 4 England 20 (John Louis 12, Peter Collins 8) 5 Australia 19 (Phil Crump 10, John Boulger 9) 6 West Germany 10 (Christoph Betzl 7, Frits Baur 3) 7 Austria 10 (Adi Funk 6, Herbert Szerecz 4).
Olsen beat Louis in run off for third place.

1976 (Eskilstuna, Sweden)
1 ENGLAND 27 (John Louis 17, Malcolm Simmons 10) 2 Denmark 24 (Ole Olsen 16, Finn Thomsen 8) 3 Sweden 22 (Bengt Jansson 11, Bernt Persson 11) 4 Australia 16 (Phil Crump 10, Billy Sanders 6) 5 New Zealand 15 (Ivan Mauger 8, Barry Briggs 7) 6 Scotland 12 (Jim McMillan 10, George Hunter 2) 7 Poland 10 (Edward Jancarz 7, Zenon Plech 3).

1977 (Belle Vue, Manchester, England)
1 ENGLAND 28 (Peter Collins 15, Malcolm Simmons 13) 2 Sweden 18 (Anders Michanek 16, Bernt Persson 2) 3 West Germany 18 (Egon Muller 11, Hans Wassermann 7) 4 Czechoslovakia 17 (Jiri Stancl 11, Jan Verner 6) 5 New Zealand 17 (Ivan Mauger 16, Larry Ross 1) 6 Finland 14 (Ilkka Teromaa 7, Kai Niemi 7) 7 Australia 12 (Phil Crump 10, Billy Sanders 2).

1978 (Chorzow, Poland)
1 ENGLAND 24 (Malcolm Simmons 15, Gordon Kennett 9) 2 New Zealand 24 (Ivan Mauger 12, Larry Ross 12) 3 Denmark 21 (Ole Olsen 16, Finn Thomsen 5) 4 Czechoslovakia 18 (Jiri Stancl 9, Jan Verner 9) 5 Poland 15 (Edward Jancarz 13, Boleslaw Proch 2) 6 West Germany 13 (Georg Hack 8, Hans Wassermann 5) 7 Sweden 11 (Jan Andersson 10, Börje Klingberg 1).
Simmons beat Mauger in run off for first place.

1979 (Vojens, Denmark)
1 DENMARK 25 (Ole Olsen 15, Hans Nielsen 10) 2 England 24 (Michael Lee 15, Malcolm Simmons 9) 3 Poland 20 (Edward Jancarz 13, Zenon Plech 7) 4 Australia 19 (Phil Crump 13, John Titman 6) 5 United States of America 14 (Bruce Penhall 14, no partner) 6 New Zealand 12 (Ivan Mauger 6, Larry Ross 6) 7 Finland 7 (Kai Niemi 7, Ilkka Teromaa 0).

1980 (Krsko, Yugoslavia)
1 ENGLAND 29 (Dave Jessup 15, Peter Collins 14) 2 Poland 22 (Edward Jancarz 15, Zenon Plech 7) 3 Denmark 21 (Ole Olsen 13, Hans Nielsen 8) 4 Sweden 18 (Jan Andersson 9, Richard Hellsen 9) 5 New Zealand 16 (Ivan Mauger 11, Larry Ross 5) 6 Finland 14 (Ilkka Teromaa 8, Kai Niemi 6) 7 Yugoslavia 6 (Stefan Kekec 6, Vlado Kocuvan 0).

1981 (Katowice, Poland)
1 UNITED STATES OF AMERICA 23 (Bruce Penhall 14, Bobby Schwartz 9) 2 New Zealand 22 (Ivan Mauger 12, Larry Ross 10) 3 Poland 21 (Zenon Plech 15, Edward Jancarz 6) 4 Czechoslovakia 18 (Ales Dryml 12, Jan Verner 6) 5 Denmark 17 (Ole Olsen 10, Hans Nielsen 7) 6 England 17 (Chris Morton 10, Dave Jessup 7) 7 West Germany 3 (Egon Müller 2, Georg Gilgenreiner 1).

1982 (Liverpool, Australia)
1 UNITED STATES OF AMERICA 30 (Dennis Sigalos 18, Boby Schwartz 12) 2 England 22 (Peter Collins 15, Kenny Carter 7) 3 Denmark 21 (Hans Nielsen 11, Ole Olsen 10) 4 Australia 16 (Billy Sanders 11, Gary Guglielmi 5) 5 Finland 16 (Kai Niemi 12, Ari Koponen 4) 6 New Zealand 13 (Mitch Shirra 8, Larry Ross 5) 7 Czechoslovakia 8 (Jiri Stancl 5, Ales Dryml 3).

1983 (Gothenburg, Sweden)
1 ENGLAND 25 (Kenny Carter 15, Peter Collins 10) 2 Australia 24 (Billy Sanders 15, Gary Guglielmi 9) 3 Denmark 19 (Hans Nielsen 11, Erik Gundersen 8) 4 United States of America 18 (Dennis Sigalos 10, Bobby Schwartz 8) 5 Sweden 16 (Jan Andersson 11, Pierre Brannefors 5) 6 West Germany 12 (Egon Müller 6, Karl Maier 6) 7 New Zealand 11 (Ivan Mauger 7, Larry Ross 4).

1984 (Lonigo, Italy)
1 ENGLAND 27 (Chris Morton 14, Peter Collins 13) 2 Denmark 25 (Hans Nielsen 15, Erik Gundersen 10) 3 New Zealand 25 (Mitch Shirra 15, Ivan Mauger 10) 4 United States of America 19 (Bobby Schwartz 11, Shawn Moran 8) 5 Australia 14 (Gary Guglielmi 8, Billy Sanders 6) 6 Czechoslovakia 10 (Ales Dryml 5, Jiri Stancl 5) 7 Italy 6 (Armando Castagna 5, Armando dal Chiele 1).
Nielsen beat Shirra in run off for second place.

1985 (Rybnik, Poland)
1 DENMARK 29 (Erik Gundersen 16, Tommy Knudsen 13) 2 England 27 (Kenny Carter 14, Kelvin Tatum 13) 3 United States of America 22 (Shawn Moran 13, Bobby Schwartz 9) 4 New Zealand 15 (Ivan Mauger 8, Mitch Shirra 7) 5 Sweden 14 (Jan Andersson 10, Per Jonsson 4) 6 Australia 11 (Steve Regeling 6, Phil Crump 5) 7 Poland 8 (Andrzej Huszcza 4, Grzegorz Dzikowski 4).

1986 (Pocking, West Germany)
1 DENMARK 46 (Hans Nielsen 27, Erik Gundersen 19) 2 United States of America 46 (Kelly Moran 23, Sam Ermolenko 23) 3 Czechoslovakia 32 (Antonin Kasper 22, Roman Matousek 10) 4 Sweden 32 (Jan Andersson 17, Tommy Nilsson 15) 5 New Zealand 32 (Larry Ross 20, Mitch Shirra 12) 6 West Germany 27 (Karl Maier 22, Klaus Lausch 5) 7 England 23 (Jeremy Doncaster 12, Simon Wigg 11) 8 Italy 15 (Valentino Furlanetto 8, Armando Castagna 7) 9 Australia 15 (Phil Crump 10, Steve Regeling 5).
Nielsen beat Moran in run off for first place.

1987 (Pardubice, Czechoslovakia)
1 DENMARK 52 (Erik Gundersen 26, Hans Nielsen 26) 2 England 44 (Kelvin Tatum 24, Simon Wigg 20) 3 United States of America 36 (Sam Ermolenko 18, Kelly Moran 18) 4 New Zealand 36 (David Bargh 20, Mitch Shirra 16) 5 Czechoslovakia 30 (Roman Matousek 16, Antonin Kasper 14) 6 Finland 19 (Olli Tyrvainen 11, Kai Niemi 8) 7 Australia 21 (Steve Baker 16, Steve Regeling 5) 8 Italy 18 (Armando Castagna 11, Valentino Furlanetto 7) 9 Poland 14 (Wojciech Zabialowicz 8, Roman Jankowski 6).

1988 (Bradford, England)
1 DENMARK 45 (Hans Nielsen 27, Erik Gundersen 18) 2 England 41 (Kelvin Tatum 21, Simon Cross 20) 3 United States of America 39 (Shawn Moran 23, Sam Ermolenko 16) 4 New Zealand 32 (Mitch Shirra 24, Alan Rivett 8) 5 Sweden 29 (Jimmy Nilsen 17, Per Jonsson 12) 6 Hungary 25 (Antal Kocso 15, Zoltán Adorján 10) 7 Italy 21 (Armando Castagna 17, Valentino Furlanetto 4) 8 West Germany 21 (Gerd Riss 17, Tommy Dunker 4) 9 Poland 17 (Piotr Swist 9, Roman Jankowski 8).

1989 (Leszno, Poland)
1 DENMARK 48 (Hans Nielsen 28, Erik Gundersen 20) 2 Sweden 44 (Jimmy Nilsen 23, Per Jonsson 21) 3 England 37 (Kelvin Tatum 21, Paul Thorp 16) 4 West Germany 36 (Karl Maier 22, Gerd Riss 14) 5 Finland 31 (Kai Niemi 18, Olli Tyrvainen 13) 6 Hungary 22 (Antal Kocso 14, Zoltán Adorján 8) 7 Czechoslovakia 25 (Bohumil Brhel 14, Zdenek Tesar 11) 8 Italy 15 (Armando dal Chiele 9, Valentino Furlanetto 6) 9 Poland 11 (Piotr Swist 11, Roman Jankowski 0).

1990 (Landshut, West Germany)
1 DENMARK 43 (Jan O. Pedersen 24, Hans Nielsen 19) 2 Australia 41 (Todd Wiltshire 25, Leigh Adams 16) 3 Hungary 33 (Zoltán Adorján 21, Sándor Tihanyi 12) 4 Sweden 33 (Jimmy Nilsen 17, Per Jonsson 16) 5 New Zealand 32 (Mitch Shirra 23, David Bargh 9) 6 United States of America 28 (Ronnie Correy 15, Kelly Moran 13) 7 Czechoslovakia 21 (Antonin Kasper 11, Roman Matousek 10) 8 England 20 (Kelvin Tatum 20, Simon Cross 0) 9 West Germany 15 (Klaus Lausch 15, Gerd Riss 0). Reserve: Alois Bachhuber 3.

■ *The 1969 World Final is no longer recognised by the FIM even though official FIM medals were issued to the three top nations.*

Star of 90

SIMON WIGG

World Long Track Champion

World Long Track Championship

Herxheim, West Germany, Sunday, August 19, 1990

DREAMING OF A WONDERFUL WORLD

GOLDEN dreams came true again for Simon Wigg...

It had been a troubled year for the Oxford star who had been in the wars with injuries and axed by the England management team for the second successive summer.

He put all those worries and niggling doubts about his commitment behind him when it really mattered to become the first Englishman to successfully defend the World Long Track title.

He had shale legend Ivan Mauger, over from his new home in Australia, alongside him in the pits – and pop legend John Lee Hooker whispering into his ear!

For Wigg ensured he was in the right psychological mood for his vital last race by listening to 'Dreaming' – the song written by the veteran bluesman and which has become a moving and personal favourite as Wigg has chased that golden dream.

He explained: "I'm one of the world's biggest dreamers and I'll never forget the first time I heard that song. I've been playing it over and over and it just sums up everything for me. It all comes down to how much you want something. And I know how much I wanted this."

He *had* to beat Hans Otto Pingel to prevent a new champion taking the rostrum.Wigg and Pingel were level on 30 points after the preliminaries.

The Englishman made the start and while his nerve remained intact, Pingel lost his cool and after two uncharacteristic bends he ended up on the centre green...able only to watch Wigg the Wonder complete another memorable weekend.

1990 Results

PRELIMINARY ROUND (Vilshofen, West Germany, Sunday, May 13): **Thomas Diehr (East Germany) 32, Stefan Dannö (Sweden) 30, Bernd Diener (West Germany) 30, Mark Loram (England) 28, Pavel Karnas (Czechoslovakia) 28, Markus Jans (West Germany) 28,** Craig Boyce (Australia) 27, Olli Tyrvainen (Finland) 26, Heinrich Diener (West Germany) 17, Robert Langeland (Norway) 12, Gary Allan (New Zealand) 10, Christoph Hilaire (France) 10, Klaus-Peter Gerdemann (West Germany) 10, Jens-Peter Nielsen (Denmark) 7, Mora Massimo (Italy) 6, Erik Drayer (Holland) 2, Roland Kolros (West Germany), reserve, 0.

SEMI FINAL 1 (Scheeßel, West Germany, Sunday, July 1): **Karl Maier (West Germany) 40, Klaus Lausch (West Germany) 39, Simon Wigg (England) 33, Marcel Gerhard (Switzerland) 30, Erik Stenlund (Sweden) 25,** Walter Scherwitzki (West Germany) 24, Pavel Karnas 20, John Pedersen (Denmark) 19, Stefan Dannö 16, John Bostin (England) 16, Ole Madsen (Denmark) 10, Kenneth Nyström (Sweden) 9, Ari Koponen (Finland) 8, Patrice Blondy (France) 8, André Haltermann (West Germany) 7, Jörg Janssen (West Germany), reserve, 2, Arnt Førland (Norway) 1.

SEMI FINAL 2 (Marianske-lazne, Czechoslovakia, Sunday, July 1): **Mario Trupkovic (West Germany) 37, Georg Limbrunner (West Germany) 33, Ales Dryml (Czechoslovakia) 32, Petr Vandirek (Czechoslovakia) 32, Mark Loram 25,** Uwe Gessner (West Germany) 25, Finn Rune Jensen (Denmark) 22, Kai Niemi (Finland) 22, Zoltán Hájdu (Hungary) 15, Thomas Diehr 14, Gaspar Forgac (Czechoslovakia) 13, Martin Hagon (England) 11, Franco Mozzato (Italy) 10, Frank Leonhardt (East Germany) 7, Clayton Williams (England) 5, Vaclav Maxim (Czechoslovakia) 3.

SEMI FINAL 3 (Mühldorf, West Germany, Sunday, July 1): **Jan O. Pedersen (Denmark) 40, Marvyn Cox (England) 36, Gerd Riss (West Germany) 29, Borivoj Hadek (Czechoslovakia) 25, Steve Schofield (England) 24,** Alois Bachhuber (West Germany) 21, Kelvin Tatum (England) 20, Hans Otto Pingel (West Germany) 18, Markus Jans 18, Jens Henry Nielsen (Denmark) 18, Troy Butler (Australia) 17, Bernd Diener 14, Jan Holub (Czechoslovakia) 9, Rickard Röseby (Sweden) 8, Andreas Bössner (Austria) 5, Roger Söderberg (Sweden) 0.

WORLD FINAL

Herxheim, West Germany, Sunday, August 19, 1990

1 SIMON WIGG 37, 2 Karl Maier 30 (+3), 3 Hans Otto Pingel 30 (+2), 4 Marcel Gerhard 28, 5 Klaus Lausch 28, 6 Marvyn Cox 23, 7 Erik Stenlund 21, 8 Borivoj Hadek 19, 9 Georg Limbrunner 15, 10 Mark Loram 15, 11 Petr Vandirek 14, 12 Ales Dryml 10, 13 Gerd Riss 9, 14 Steve Schofield 9, 15 Pavel Karnas 8, 16 Mario Trupkovic 4, 17 Jens Henry Nielsen, reserve, 3, 18 Finn Rune Jensen, reserve, 2.

Jan O. Pedersen qualified but did not ride because of injury.

Roll of Honour

A full list of FIM World Championships is listed on page 30. Prior to 1971 an European 1,000 Metre Sand Track Championship was held with the following results:

1957 1 Basse Hveem 2 Josef Hofmeister, 3 Egil Bratvold
1958 1 Josef Hofmeister 2 Auis Touminen 3 Josef Kamper
1959 1 Josef Hofmeister 2 Antti Pajari 3 Olle Nygren
1960 1 Josef Hofmeister 2 Josef Seidl 3 Josef Sinzinger
1961 1 Timo Laine 2 Ove Fundin 3 Erling Simonsen
1962 1 Bertil Strid 2 Josef Seidl 3 Timo Laine
1963 1 Bertil Strid 2 Kurt Petersen 3 Manfred Poschenrieder
1964 1 Kurt Petersen 2 Olavi Turunen 3 Manfred Poschenrieder
1965 1 Björn Knutsson 2 Timo Laine 3 Josef Seidl
1966 1 Manfred Poschenrieder 2 Kurt Petersen 2 Jon Odegard
1967 1 Manfred Poschenrieders 2 Don Godden 3 Jon Odegard
1968 1 Manfred Poschenrieder 2 Don Godden 3 Kurt Petersen
1969 1 Don Godden 2 Jon Odegard 3 Kurt Petersen
1970 1 Jon Odegard 2 Don Godden 3 Hans Zierk

LOOKING BACK...

1971 (Oslo, Norway)
1 IVAN MAUGER 27, 2 Manfred Poschenrieder 26, 3 Runo Wedin 22, 4 Jan Kater 15, 5 Bent Norregaard Jensen 13, 6 Barry Briggs 10, 7 Don Godden 10, 8 Hans Siegl 9, Sven Sigurd 9, Willihard Thomsson 9, 11 Josef Unterholzner 8, 12 Kurt Petersen 7, 13 Bernt Hornfeld 6, Jan Holm Nielsen 6, Jon Odegard 6, 16 Walter Matl 4, 17 Reijo Koski 3, 18 Hans Zierk 0.

1972 (Mühldorf, West Germany)
1 IVAN MAUGER 30, 2 Manfred Poschenrieder 23, 3 Jon Odegard 18, 4 Hans Siegl 17, Bent Norregaard Jensen 17, 6 Antonin Svaab 14, 7 Hans Zierk 13, 8 Josef Angermuller 11, Willihard Thomsson 11, 10 Don Godden 9, Rudi Kastl 9, 12 Jan Kater 6, 13 Heinrich Sprenger 4, 14 Gottfried Schwarze 3, Henning Hansen 3, 16 Matti Olin 2, 17 Nils Haraldsen 1, Runo Wedin 1.

1973 (Oslo, Norway)
1 OLE OLSEN 24, 2 Hans Siegl 20, 3 Manfred Poschenrieder 20, 4 Don Godden 19, 5 Jan Kater 15, Josef Angermuller 15, 7 Runo Wedin 11, Willihard Thomsson 11, 9 Egon Muller 10, 10 Milan Spinka 7, 11 Einar Egedius 6, Sture Lindblom 6, 13 Zdenek Majstr 3, Bernt Hornfeld 3, 15 Bent Norregaard Jensen 2, 16 Jon Odegard 0, Conny Samuelsson 0, Hakan Storm 0.

1974 (Scheeßel, West Germany)
1 EGON MULLER 30, 2 Ivan Mauger 26, 3 Alois Wiesböck 21, 4 Anders Michanek 15, 5 Don Godden 13, Josef Angermuller 13, 7 Peter Collins 11, Jon Odegard 11, 9 Mafred Poschenrieder 10, 10 Preben Bollerup 9, Jiri Stancl 9, 12 Christoph Betzl 8, 13 Preben Rosenkilde 5, 14 Milan Spinka 4, 15 Hans Zierk 3, 16 Stanislaw Kubicek 2, 17 Gottfried Schwartze 1, 18 Edgar Stangeland 0.
Jan Kater and Ole Olsen qualified, did not ride.

1975 (Radgona, Yugoslavia)
1 EGON MULLER 27, 2 Ivan Mauger 22, 3 Ole Olsen 19, 4 Barry Briggs 19, 5 Christoph Betzl 17, 6 Anders Michanek 13, 7 Hans Wassermann 11, Don Godden 11, Peter Collins 11, 10 Manfred Poschenrieder 9, Jiri Stancl 9, 12 Vaclav Verner 8, 13 Hans Zierk 5, 14 Joachim Kall 4, Vlado Kocuvan 4, 16 Runo Wedin 2, 17 Kristian Praestbro 1, 18 Stefan Kekec 0.
Zdenek Kudrna and Edgar Stangeland, reserves, did not ride.

1976 (Marianske-lazne, Czechoslovakia)
1 IVAN MAUGER 26, 2 Ole Olsen 25, 3 Egon Muller 21, 4 Alois Wiesböck 21, 5 Jiri Stancl 16, 6 Zdenek Kudrna 14, 7 Anders Michanek 12, 8 Christoph Betzl 10, 9 Josef Angermuller 9, 10 Vaclav Verner 8, 11 Barry Briggs 7, 12 Don Godden 5, 13 Emil Sova, reserve, 5, 14 Hans Wassermann 4, Wilhelm Duden 4, 16 Edgar Stangeland 3, 16 Conny Samuelsson 1, Stanislaw Kubicek 1, 18 Jan Verner, reserve, 0.

1977 (Aalborg, Denmark)
1 ANDERS MICHANEK 20, 2 Hans Siegl 18, 3 Ole Olsen 18, 4 Jiri Stancl 15, 5 Joachim Kall 14, 6 Alois Wiesböck 13, 7 Ales Dryml 12, 8 Ivan Mauger 12, Kristian Praestbro 12, 10 Georg Hack 11, 11 Christoph Betzl 9, 12 Zdenek Kudrna 8, 13 Hans Wassermann 5, 14 Jan Verner 4, 15 Vaclav Verner 3, 16 Jan Kater 2, 17 Otto Lantenhammer 2, 18 Egon Muller 0.
Peter Collins and Hans Zierk, qualified, did not ride.
Francesco Biginato, reserve, did not ride.

1978 (Mühldorf, West Germany)
1 EGON MULLER 26, 2 Alois Wiesböck 26, 3 Peter Collins 24, 4 Ivan Mauger 24, 5 Ole Olsen 23, 6 Georg Hack 19, 7 Karl Maier 17, 8 Jiri Jirout 12, 9 Jiri Stancl 11, 10 Ales Dryml 10, 11 Scott Autrey 9, Kristian Praestbro 9, Jan Verner 9, 14 Don Godden 8, 15 Zdenek Kudrna 7, 16 Wilhelm Duden, 17 Otto Lantenhammer, reserve, 1.
Anders Michanek, reserve, did not ride.

1979 (Marianske-lazne, Czechoslovakia)
1 ALOIS WIESBöCK 21, 2 Anders Michanek 20, 3 Ole Olsen 19, 4 Jiri Stancl 17, 5 Georg Hack 16, 6 Karl Maier 13, 7 Egon Muller 12, 8 Kristian Praestbro 11, 9 Michael Lee 9, 10 Ales Dryml 8, Ivan Mauger 8, 12 Peter Collins 7, 13 Christoph Betzl 6, Wilhelm Duden 6, 15 Alf Busk 3, 16 Zdenek Kudrna 2, 17 Francesco Biginato 1, Walter Grubmuller 1.
Don Godden and Hubert Sprenger, reserves, did not ride.

1980 (Scheeßel, West Germany)
1 KARL MAIER 23, 2 Egon Muller 18, 3 Josef Aigner and Christoph Betzl 16, 5 Georg Hack 14, 6 Wilhelm Duden 11, 7 Ivan Mauger 9, 8 Zdenek Kudrna 9, 9 Ole Olsen 8, 10 Michael Lee 8, 11 Peter Collins 7, 12 Jiri Stancl 6, 13 Chris Morton 5, 14 Milan Spinka 5, 15 Frits Koning 3, 16 Anders Michanek 2, 17 Bruce Penhall 0.
Alois Wiesböck scored 18 points to finish third but was later disqualified after it was found his engine was over the prescribed limit. The FIM awarded bronze medals to both Aigner and Betzl.
Kai Niemi and Erik Pedersen, reserves, did not ride.

1981 (Radgona, Yugoslavia)
1 MICHAEL LEE 23, 2 Christoph Betzl 20, 3 Anders Michanek 19, 4 Georg Gilgenreiner 19, 5 Egon Muller 16, 6 Phil Collins 14, 7 Josef Aigner 13, 8 Hans Otto Pingel 12, 9 Peter Collins 10, 10 Ivan Mauger 6, 11 Jiri Stancl 6, 12 Georg Hack 5, 13 Karl Maier 5, 14 Zdenek Kudrna 4, 15 Stefan Kekec 3, 16 Alois Wiesböck 1, Vlado Kocuvan 1, 18 Wilhelm Duden 0.
Bruce Penhall and Steve Bastable, reserves, did not ride.

1982 (Korskro, Denmark)
1 KARL MAIER 24, 2 Alois Wiesböck 22, 3 Egon Muller 21, 4 Georg Gilgenreiner 15, 5 Peter Collins 15, 6 Ivan Mauger 14, 7 Ole Olsen 11, 8 Anders Michanek 9, 9 Hans Nielsen 8, 10 Christoph Betzl 7, Georg Hack 7, 12 Marcel Gerhard 6, 13 Simon Wigg 5, 14 Bobby Schwartz 4, 15 Jiri Stancl 4, 16 Chris Morton 4, 17 Josef Aigner 4, 18 Phil Collins 0.
Petr Ondrasik and Hans Otto Pingel, reserves, did not ride.

1983 (Marianske-lazne, Czechoslovakia)
1 SHAWN MORAN 22, 2 Jiri Stancl 20, 3 Karl Maier 18, 4 Alois Wiesböck 16, 5 Finn Rune Jensen 16, 6 Ales Dryml 15, 7 Simon Wigg 11, 8 Egon Muller 11, 9 Ivan Mauger 10, 10 Georg Hack 9, 11 John Titman 9, 12 Hans Nielsen 7, 13 Bobby Schwartz 4, 14 Les Collins 3, 15 Marcel Gerhard 3, 16 Ole Olsen 3, 17 Hans Otto Pingel 2, 18 Heinrich Diener 1.
Klaus Lausch and Michael Lee, reserves, did not ride.

1984 (Herxheim, West Germany);
1 ERIK GUNDERSEN 23, 2 Egon Muller 19, 3 Karl Maier 17, 4 Peter Collins 16, 5 Finn Rune Jensen 16, 6 Gerd Riss 13, 7 Ales Dryml 10, 8 Jiri Stancl 9, 9 Marcel Gerhard 9, 10 John Titman 8, 11 Jeremy Doncaster 7, 12 Hans Nielsen 7, 13 Ivan Mauger 5, 14 Josef Aigner 5, 15 Hans Otto Pingel 4, 16 Kai Niemi 4, 17 Les Collins 4, 18 Shawn Moran 3.
Günter Bünning and Bo Petersen, reserves, did not ride.

1985 (Korskro, Denmark)
1 SIMON WIGG 22, 2 Jiri Stancl 19, 3 Peter Collins 18, 4 Shawn Moran 17, 5 Egon Muller 17, 6 Bobby Schwartz 15, 7 Martin Hagon 12, 8 Gerd Riss 11, 9 Jeremy Doncaster 9, 10 Georg Hack 7, 11 Klaus Lausch 6, 12 Finn Rune Jensen 5, 13 Vaclav Verner 5, 14 Ivan Mauger 4, 15 Ales Dryml 4, Petr Ondrasik 4, 17 Heinrich Diener 2, 18 Brian Jakobsen, reserve, 2, 19 Marcel Gerhard 0, Chris Morton, reserve, 0.

1986 (Pfarrkirchen, West Germany)
1 ERIK GUNDERSEN 25, 2 Peter Collins 18, 3 Marcel Gerhard 18, 4 Gerd Riss 17, 5 Hans Nielsen 14, 6 Karl Maier 11, 7 Bern Diener 10, 8 Kai Niemi 10, 9 Petr Vandirek 9, 10 Shawn Moran 8, 11 Hans Otto Pingel 8, Emil Sova 8, 13 Phil Collins 5, 14 Roland Dannö 4, 15 Pavel Karnas 4, 16 Heinrich Diener 4, 17 Trevor Banks 3, 18 Alois Wiesböck 0.
Ari Koponen and Jiri Svoboda, reserves, did not ride.

1987 (Mühldorf, West Germany)
1 KARL MAIER 22, 2 Simon Wigg 21, 3 Shawn Moran 19, 4 Martin Hagon 19, 5 Egon Müller 15, 6Heinz Huber 14, 7 Erik Gundersen 10, 8 Steve Baker 10, 9 Gerd Riss 9, 10 Lubomir Jedek 9, 11 Finn Rune Jensen 6, 12 Alois Wiesböck 6, 13 Trevor Banks 5, 14 Klaus Lausch 4, 15 Kai Niemi 3, 16 Erik Stenlund 3, 17 Pavel Karnas 2, Simon Cross, reserve, 2, 19 Chris Morton 2, 20 Petr Vandirek, reserve, 0.

1988 (Scheeßel, West Germany)
1 KARL MAIER 42, 2 Klaus Lausch 32, 3 Chris Morton 31, 4 Hans Nielsen 27, 5 Gerd Riss 26, 6 Heinrich Diener 26, 7 Roland Dannö 24, 8 Simon Wigg 21, 9 Jens Henry Nielsen 15, 10 Egon Müller 15, 11 Sam Ermolenko 13, 12 Petr Vandirek 9, 13 Kai Niemi 9, 14 Steve Schofield 6, 15 Antonin Kasper 4, 16 Simon Cross 3.
Steve Baker and Ari Koponen, reserves, did not ride.

1989 (Marianske-lazne, Czechoslovakia)
1 SIMON WIGG 38, 2 Ales Dryml 37, 3 Karl Maier 33, 4 Erik Stenlund 28, 5 Egon Müller 22, 6 Hans Nielsen 20, 7 Andre Pollehn 19, 8 Mario Trupkovic 19, 9 Marcel Gerhard 17, 10 Marvyn Cox 16, 11 Gerd Riss 12, 12 Steve Schofield 12, 13 Borivoj Hadek 12, 14 Petr Vandirek 9, 15 Chris Morton 8, 16 Klaus Lausch 1.
Finn Rune Jensen and Antonin Kasper, reserves, did not ride.

1990 (Herxheim, West Germany)
1 SIMON WIGG 37, 2 Karl Maier 30, 3 Hans Otto Pingel 30, 4 Marcel Gerhard 28, 5 Klaus Lausch 28, 6 Marvyn Cox 23, 7 Erik Stenlund 21, 8 Borivoj Hadek 19, 9 Georg Limbrunner 15, 10 Mark Loram 15, 11 Petr Vandirek 14, 12 Ales Dryml 10, 13 Gerd Riss 9, 14 Steve Schofield 9, 15 Pavel Karnas 8, 16 Mario Trupkovic 4, 17 Jens Henry Nielsen, reserve, 3, 18 Finn Rune Jensen, reserve, 2.
Jan O. Pedersen, qualified, did not ride.

Star of 90

CHRIS LOUIS

World Under 21 Champion

World Junior Championship
Lvov, Soviet Union, Sunday, September 9, 1990

WITCHES' HALLE-LOUIS-A

CHRIS LOUIS struggled to control his horse-power... on the way to being crowned King!

For the young Ipswich star's most nerve-wracking lap of the Russian track came once he had clinched the World Under 21 title and was asked to make his celebratory circuit on the back of a huge black Cossack stallion!

He had kept a cool head throughout the more important part of what was the Soviet Union's first-ever staging of a pukka speedway World Final.

His experience 12 months earlier when he finished runner-up in Italy, stood him in good stead as he went to the tapes for his fifth ride knowing that he needed to win to be spared another nerve-tingling run-off for the crown.

His nearest challenger, René Aas, who had completed his National Service at Lvov, was leaning over the pits wall with 13 points already in the bag as Louis prepared for his final race.

If it was any comfort, his Ipswich team-mate Shane Parker, was alongside him at the line with two Poles for company. A win for either Parker or Jaroslaw Olszewski would put them on the rostrum and Louis admitted: "I knew I had to do it from the tapes. In the conditions there was no point trying to race from behind as you would get filled in."

His father John, former British Champion, World Finalist and manager at Ipswich, claimed: "Chris proved that he can do it in all conditions."

It was a neat ending to a season in which the youthful Ipswich squad also proved their worth on the international market with three in the World Final and a fourth, David Norris, forced to pull out of the semi final because of a back injury.

1990 Results

QUALIFYING ROUND 1 (Brokstedt, West Germany, Tuesday, May 1)
Henrik Gustafsson (Sweden) 14, Peter Karlsson (Sweden) 11 (+3), Tommy Dunker (West Germany) 11 (+2), Chris Louis (England) 11 (+1), Jörg Pingel (West Germany) 11 (+0), Shane Parker (Australia) 10, André Pollehn (West Germany) 9 (+3), Gary Hicks (America) 9 (+2), David Norris (England) 9 (+1), Shane Bowes (Australia) 9 (+0), Markus Jans (West Germany) 5, Mick Powell (Australia) 3, Stefan Dannö (Sweden) 3, Scott Norman (Australia) 2, Mark Thorpe (New Zealand) 2, Volker Maassen (West Germany), reserve, 1, Henk Bangma (Holland) 0, Björn Danielcik (West Germany), reserve, 0.

QUALIFYING ROUND 2 (Targovishte, Bulgaria, Sunday, May 27):
Massimo Mora (Italy) 13, Zsolt Böszörményi (Hungary) 12, Jaroslav Olszewski (Poland) 11, René Aas (Soviet Union) 11, Csaba Hell (Hungary) 10, Andrej Korolev (Soviet Union) 9, Georgi Petranov (Bulgaria) 9, Martin Rybensky (Czechoslovakia) 8 (+3), Jacek Rempala (Poland) 8 (+2), Christoph Dubernard (France) 8 (+1), Sergei Kuzin (Soviet Union) 7, Rostislav Bures (Czechoslovakia) 7, Jacek Wozniak (Poland) 3, Matthias Backmeyer (East Germany) 2, Galin Velitchkov (Bulgaria) 1, Jan Hadek (Czechoslovakia) 0.

QUALIFYING ROUND 3 (Nyiregyhaza, Hungary, Sunday, May 27):
Attila Kovács (Hungary) 13, Tomasz Gollob (Poland) 12 (+3), Jaroslaw Szymkowiak (Poland) 12 (+2), Viktor Gaidym (Soviet Union) 10, Dariusz Sledz (Poland) 10, Thomas Hopp (East Germany) 9, Jiri Hurych (Czechoslovakia) 8, Jan Fejfar (Czechoslovakia) 8, Vladimir Malakhov (Soviet Union) 7 (+3), Zsolt Kovács (Hungary) 7 (+2), Csaba Csobán (Hungary) 7 (+1), Roland Kolros (West Germany) 6, Luca Taccini (Italy) 5, Igor Hauptmann (Yugoslavia) 3, René Rudolph (East Germany) 2, René Kühr (Austria) 1, Gábor Melicher (Hungary), reserve, 0, Zsolt Bencze (Hungary), reserve, 0.

QUALIFYING ROUND 4 (Elgane, Norway, Thursday, May 24)
Tony Richardsson (Sweden) 13, Lars Gunnestad (Norway) 12 (+3), Claus Jacobsen (Denmark) 12 (+R), Dean Barker (England) 11, Brian Andersen (Denmark) 10, Dean Standing (England) 9, Joakim Karlsson (Sweden) 9, Jacob Olsen (Denmark) 8 (+3), Odd Pettersen (Norway) 8 (+2), Hans Clausen (Denmark) 8 (+1), Petri Kokko (Finland) 7, Magnus Oscarsson (Sweden) 6, Esa Einola (Finland) 3, Petri Nurmesniemi (Finland) 2, Neil Varhaug (Norway) 1, Stefan Lardner (Sweden) 1.

SEMI FINAL 1 (Tarnow, Poland, Saturday, June 30)
Massimo Mora 13, René Aas 12 (+3), Jaroslaw Szymkowiak 12 (+2), Zsolt Böszörmányi 12 (+1), Atilla Kovács 10, Dariusz Sledz 10, Georgi Petranov 9, Jaroslaw Olszewski 8 (+3), Andrej Korolev 8 (+2), Viktor Gaidym 7, Csaba Hell 7, Martin Rybensky 4, Thomas Hopp 3, Vladimir Malakhov 2, Jan Fejfar 1, Jiri Hurych 1.
Tomasz Gollob withdrew because he qualified for the Continental Final of the World Championship.

SEMI FINAL 2 (Elgane, Norway, Sunday, July 1)
Chris Louis 14, Tony Richardsson 12, Lars Gunnestad 11 (+3), Dean Standing 11 (+2), Shane Parker 10, Peter Karlsson 10, Shane Bowes 9, Jacob Olsen 6 (+3), Brian Andersen 6 (+2), Dean Barker 5, Mick Powell 5, Tommy Dunker 5, Gary Hicks 3, André Pollehn 2, Claus Jacobsen 2, Joakim Karlsson 0.
Henrik Gustafsson withdrew because he qualified for the Inter Continental Final of the World Championship. Jörg Pingel, David Norris and Markus Jans withdrew because of injury.

WORLD FINAL

Lvov, Soviet Union, Sunday, September 9, 1990

1 CHRIS LOUIS 14, 2 René Aas 13, 3 Tony Richardsson 10 (+3), 4 Jaroslaw Olszewski 10 (+2), 5 Shane Parker 9, 6 Lars Gunnestad 9, 7 Brian Andersen 8, 8 Shane Bowes 7, 9 Jaroslaw Szymkowiak 6, 10 Dean Standing 6, 11 Massimo Mora 6, 12 Dariusz Sledz 5, 13 Zsolt Böszörmányi 5, 14 Georgi Petranov 4, 15 Andrej Korolev, reserve, 3, 16 Viktor Gaidym, reserve, 2, 17 Attila Kovács 1, 18 Peter Karlsson 0.
Jacob Olsen, qualified, did not ride through illness.

LOOKING BACK...

WORLD JUNIOR CHAMPIONSHIP

1988 (Slany, Czechoslakia)
1 PETER NAHLIN 14, 2 Henrik Gustafsson 11, 3 Brian Karger 11, 4 Kenneth Arnfred 11, 5 Krister Karlsson 10, 6 Niklas Karlsson 10, 7 Tommy Dunker 9, 8 Piotr Swist 9, 9 Troy Butler 8, 10 Waldemar Ciesewicz 8, 11 Rusian Koval 6, 12 Zbigniew Blazejczak 4, 13 Jan Schinagl 3, 14 Slawomir Dudek 3, 14 Jaroslaw Olszewski 3, 16 Vladimir Kalina 0.

1989 (Lonigo, Italy)
1 GERT HANDBERG 13, 2 Chris Louis 13, 3 Niklas Karlsson 12, 4 Henrik Gustafsson 11, 5 Mark Loram 10, 6 Freddy Schøtt 9, 7 Leigh Adams 9, 8 Claus Jacobsen 6, 9 René Aas 6, 10 Craig Hodgson 5, 11 Kenneth Lindby 5, 12 Dean Standing, reserve, 5, 13 Jan Holub, reserve, 4, 14 Peter Karlsson 4, 15 Piotr Swist 3, 16 Jaroslaw Olszewski 2, 17 Slawomir Dudek 1, 18 Riccardo Salamon 0.

1990 (Lvov, Soviet Union)
1 CHRIS LOUIS 14, 2 René Aas 13, 3 Tony Richardsson 10, 4 Jaroslaw Olszewski 10, 5 Shane Parker 9, 6 Lars Gunnestad 9, 7 Brian Andersen 8, 8 Shane Bowes 7, 9 Jaroslaw Szymkowiak 6, 10 Dean Standing 6, 11 Massimo Mora 6, 12 Dariusz Sledz 5, 13 Zsolt Böszörmányi 5, 14 Georgi Petranov 4, 15 Andrej Korolev 3, 16 Viktor Gaidym 2, 17 Attila Kovács 1, 17 Peter Karlsson 0.

▲ *1980 title-winner Tommy Knudsen*

▲ *First World Champion Peter Nahlin*

▲ *The 1989 number one Gert Handberg*

EUROPEAN JUNIOR CHAMPIONSHIP

1977 (Vojens, Denmark)
1 ALF BUSK 9, 2 Joe Owen 8, 3 Les Collins 7, 4 Lars Ericsson 6, Zytun Gafurov 6, Hans Nielsen 6, Peter Lempenauer 6, 8 Lillebror Johansson 4, Marek Okoniewski 4, 10 Alexander Chaljavin 3, Jiri Svoboda 3, Andrzej Huszcza 3, Franz Kreimoser 3, 14 Rudi Muts 2, Nikolai Manev 2, 16 Paolo Noro 0.
Meeting abandoned after 12 heats. Result to stand.

1978 (Lonigo, Italy)
1 FINN RUNE JENSEN 13, 2 Kevin Jolly 12, 3 Neil Middleditch 12, 4 Steve Finch 12, 5 Erik Gundersen 11, 6 Hans Nielsen 10, 7 Josef Juza 8, Pavel Karnas 8, 9 Henryk Olszak 6, Ryszard Romaniak 6, 11 Fausto Birbini 5, Leif Johansson 5, 13 Nikolai Manev 4, Mieczyslaw Kmieciak 4, 15 Armando Giglioli 2, Roman Jankowski 2.

1979 (Leningrad, Soviet Union)
1 RON PRESTON 13, 2 Airat Faljzulin 12, 3 Ari Koponen 11, 4 Knud Ellegaard 10, 5 Anders Eriksson 9, Stanislav Urban 9, 7 Trond Skretting 8, Marek Kempa 8, 9 Zbyszek Holy 7, Vladimir Pankin 7, 11 Jaromir Bartos 6, Hans Albert Klinge 6, 13 Stefan Berec 5, 14 Josef Aigner 4, 15 Jan Eriksson 3, 16 Fausto Birbini 1.

1980 (Pocking, West Germany)
1 TOMMY KNUDSEN 14, 2 Tony Briggs 12, 3 Dennis Sigalos 11, 4 Erik Gundersen 11, 5 Ari Koponen 9, Marek Kepa 9, Neil Collins 9, 8 Nigel Flatman 8, 9 Antonin Kasper 8, 10 Josef Aigner 6, 11 Lars Hammarberg 5, Christian Brandt 5, Rif Saitgareev 5, 14 Hans Albert Klinge 4, 15 Miroslav Berlinski 3, 16 Shawn Moran 2.

1981 (Slany, Czechoslovakia)
1 SHAWN MORAN 15, 2 Antonin Kasper 14, 3 Jiri Hnidak 13, 4 Roman Matousek 10, 5 Mark Courtney 10, 6 Piotr Podrzycki 9, Kent Noer 9, 8 Miroslav Berlinski 8, Lubomir Jedek 8, 10 Georg Greif 5, 11 Hans Albert Klinge 4, Peter Ravn 4, 13 Anders Eriksson 3, 14 Zoltán Hajdú, reserve, 2, 15 Roger Gustafsson 1, Flemming Pedersen 1, Peter Nieder, reserve, 1, 18 Zoltán Adorján 0.

1982 (Pocking, West Germany)
1 ANTONIN KASPER 14, 2 Mark Courtney 12, 3 Peter Ravn 12, 4 Lance King 11, 5 Jan O. Pedersen 10, 6 Zoltán Hajdú 9, Oleg Volokhov 9, John Jorgensen 9, 9 David Bargh 8, 10 Giorgio Zaramella 6, Zoltán Adorján 6, 12 Georg Greif 4, 13 Vladimir Trofimov 3, Klaus Lausch 3, Brian Jacobsen 3, 16 Sándor Tihanyi 0.

1983 (Lonigo, Italy)
1 STEVE BAKER 13, 2 David Bargh 12, 3 Marvyn Cox 11, 4 John Jorgensen 10, Oleg Volokhov 10, Neil Evitts 10, 7 Jozsef Petrikovics 9, 8 Valentino Furlanetto 8, 9 Peter Carr 7, 10 Zenon Kasprzak 6, 11 Sándor Tihanyi 5, Jan O. Pedersen 5, Vladimir Trofimov 5, 14 Heinz Huber 4, 15 Andras Kovacs 3, 16 Giorgio Zaramella 1.

1984 (King's Lynn, England)
1 MARVYN COX 12, 2 Neil Evitts 11, 3 Steve Lucero 11, 4 Hans Wahlstrom 11 5 Jozsef Petrikovics 10, Andy Smith 10, Frank Andersen 10, 8 Lars Andersson 9, 9 Armando Castagna 8, 10 Oleg Volokhov 6, 11 Leif Wahlmann 5, 12 Giorgio Zaramella 5, 13 Flemming Rasmussen 4, 14 Valentino Furlanetto 3, 15 Wojciech Zaluski 2, 16 Klaus Lausch 1, Kurt Hansen, reserve, 1, 18 Jiri Broz, reserve, 0, Paul Clarke, reserve, 0.
†Leif Wahlmann died of injuries received in a Heat 13 crash.

1985 (Abensberg, West Germany)
1 PER JONSSON 15, 2 Jimmy Nilsen 13, 3 Ole Hansen 11, 4 Kenneth Nyström 11, 5 Gerd Riss 9, Juha Moksunen 9, Roman Matousek 9, 8 Valentino Furlanetto 8, Kurt Hansen 8, 10 Miroslav Prager 6, Igor Marko 6, 12 Einar Kyllingstad 5, 13 Mikael Teurnberg 4, Heinz Huber 4, 15 Barnabas Gyepes 1, Peter Schroeck, reserve, 1, Peter Hehlert, reserve, 0.
Michael Datzmann qualified, did not ride.

1986 (Rovno, Soviet Union)
1 IGOR MARKO 13, 2 Tony Olsson 12, 3 Brian Karger 11, 4 Bohumil Brhel 10, 5 Jan Jakobsen 10, Conny Ivarsson 10, 7 Jan Staechmann 8, 8 Mikael Teurnberg 8, 9 Andrew Silver 7, 10 Zbigniew Blazejczak 7, 11 Nigel De'ath 5, David Cheshire 5, 13 Gerd Riss 4, 14 Allan Johansen 3, 15 Jan Holub, reserve, 3, 16 Robert Nagy 2, 17 Igor Zverev 1, Josef Fejfar, reserve, 1.

1987 (Zielona Gora, Poland)
1 GARY HAVELOCK 13, 2 Piotr Swist 11, 3 Sean Wilson 11, 4 Bo Arrhen 11, 5 Tommy Dunker 11, 6 Peter Nahlin, reserve, 9, 7 Gaspar Forgac 8, 8 Vladimir Kalina 7, 9 Niklas Karlsson 6, 10 Tor Einar Helm 6, 11 Ronnie Correy 5, 12 Borivoj Hadek 5, 13 Cezary Owizyc 5, 14 Oleg Kurguskin 4, 15 Torben Hansen 4, 16 Slawomir Drabik 2, Allan Johansen 2.

▲ *Before 1988 the competition was officially recognised as the European Junior Championship.*

Diary JAN

DAY BY DAY

1 BRILLIANT teenager David Norris is lined up to join Ipswich - as there are fresh doubts over the future of his 1989 track Eastbourne where promoter Gareth Rogers is poised to quit after failing to find backers willing to invest £30,000 in the club...Former World Finalist Marvyn Cox sends in a written transfer request to Oxford...Peter Ravn agrees terms with Belle Vue for his testimonial season...Mark Courtney wants to leave National League Cup holders Berwick...Exeter's Colin Hill agrees a new 3-year lease at the County Ground...Middlesbrough want £15,000 for transfer-seeking skipper Martin Dixon... England's shell-shocked tourists go down 41-67 in the sixth unofficial test at Brisbane Exhibition Ground.

2 BELLE VUE boss John Perrin ends doubts over Kelly Moran's future by declaring: "There's a team place for him this season"...Newcastle give Australian star Rod Hunter a mid-January deadline to decide whether he will accept a lucrative two-year deal that will include a 1991 testimonial...England international Sean Wilson brushes aside an offer to drop down into the National League insisting he wants to stay with Sunbrite British League Coventry.

3 *NEWCASTLE are considering a swoop for former British Under-23 international Sean Willmott, now a naturalised Australian - and they open negotiations with Bradford to sign youngster Simon Green...Milton Keynes take the unusual step of announcing the 1990 squad they want to sign! It includes Preben Eriksen (Mildenhall) and Kevin Jolly (Peterborough)...In the final match of their tour England's unofficial test side go down 50-58 at Parramatta to lose the series 5-1 with the 2nd drawn.*

4 MARTIN DUGARD and Chris Louis are top targets for West German League side Landshut although they admit they will have to wait for the British fixtures before making any positive move...Milton Keynes officially list five of last season's squad: Trevor Banks (£5,000), Tony Primmer (£8,000), Mark Lyndon (£6,000), Rob Fortune (£4,000) and Glenn Allan (for loan).

5 SWINDON ban stock cars from Blunsdon after complaints throughout 1989 about the damage to the race strip...Sam Ermolenko now hopes to be fit for the start of the new season after recuperating in Australia...Sweden's Mikael Blixt still wants to join Cradley Heath, but promoter Colin Pratt stalls as he considers his overall options.

6 *SCOTT NORMAN agrees terms to return to Peterborough for a third season at Alwalton...Berwick promoter Davie Fairbairn is locked in talks with a prospective buyer...But it's pessimism at Arlington where Eastbourne's future appears doomed as promoter Gareth Rogers makes little progress in finding new financial backing...Leigh Adams retains his Victorian Championship.*

7 PETER THOROGOOD, Arena Essex promoter, has three hours of talks with unsettled Simon Wolstenholme...Mark Courtney changes his mind about his future and says he is happy to stay at Berwick after peace talks with co-promoter Dick Barrie...Milton Keynes put in a firm approach for Peterborough's Kevin Jolly...Long Eaton deny interest in Exeter skipper Steve Regeling, claiming that his terms would be too expensive for the club.

8 WIMBLEDON'S young whizzkid Todd Wiltshire withdraws from the World Championship because the re-arranged Australian Final date clashes with his sister's wedding...The Russians name their touring party to visit National League tracks in the Spring. It includes double World Finalist Mikhail Starostin, former World Final reserve Vladimir Trofimov - son of old-time racer Viktor - and ex-European Under-21 Champion Igor Marko.

9 *EX-WORLD Champion Michael Lee, anxious to resume his racing career, makes an impassioned plea to the Speedway Control Board to be allowed to ride again. He even offers to undergo a drugs test at EVERY meeting claiming: "I'm totally clean now - and I swear that I have never raced under drugs. I was a bad boy in my private life but I've paid for that."*

10 BERWICK'S riders are given the news they wanted to hear - the track's future is assured after a take-over bid is accepted by long-time promoter Davie Fairbairn. But the identity of the new owner is kept secret and won't be revealed until he returns from a holiday in Lanzarote...Former Hackney, Bradford and Sheffield rider Randy Green is hoping to find himself a team place in Sweden with Stockholm United...Per Jonsson now seems certain to return to the Sunbrite British League in 1990 with his old club Reading although he would prefer to link up with Swindon...World Long Track Champion Simon Wigg confirms he will be staying at Oxford despite having talks with other tracks.

11 WOLVERHAMPTON decide to release American Robert Pfetzing and circulate his name to all other senior tracks...Edinburgh's Mick Powell, badly injured at Mildenhall towards the end of last season, is given the medical all-clear and told he can start racing again in February...Kiwi David Bargh, out of racing for two seasons, contacts Coventry and tells promoter Charles Ochiltree that he wants to ride again although it is unlikely there will be a team place at Brandon for him.

12 *BRAVE Erik Gundersen takes yet another step forward as he convinces specialists at Pinderfields General Hospital that he is fit enough to return home...Kenny McKinna says he will retire rather than leave Glasgow to squash rumours that he is unsettled at Shawfield. He also insists he has agreed terms for the new season with new promoter Peter McBride.*

13 GLENN DOYLE retains his Australian Championship, the first rider to do so since Billy Sanders won it four years in a row at the start of the eighties. He beats teenager Leigh Adams in a run-off after they had tied on 14 points, with Stephen Davies third on 13 points...Oxford plan a clear-out and put juniors Alastair Stevens, Nigel Sparshott, Nigel De'ath, Jon Surman, Peter Lloyd and Spencer Timmo on the transfer list and are willing to sell outright all but Timmo. All six spent the 1989 season on loan to National League clubs.

14 JOE SCREEN, the most exciting youngster in British speedway, has agreed terms to stay with Belle Vue for his second season...Six-time World Champion Ivan Mauger advises teenager Leigh Adams: "You must go into the Sunbrite British League." Mauger had a close hand view of Adams at his Australian training schools and in the Australian Championship.

WORLD ICE SPEEDWAY CHAMPIONSHIP

BRITS ON THE SKIDS

BRITAIN'S two World Ice-Speedway challengers Graham Halsall and John Walmsley failed to make it beyond the opening qualifying round.

The pair, both drawn at Deventer, finished way down the field in a meeting dominated by the powerful Swede Per Olof Serenius who relegated defending World Champion Nikolai Nischenko to second place in the round.

Walmsley, who had spells on the shale with Workington, Glasgow and Barrow, finished 12th with his team-mate one place behind.

Russians filled the top three places in the Italian qualifier and had two of the three on the rostrum in Holland.

Qualifying Round 1 (Madonna de Campiglio, Italy, January 13-14, 1990):
1 Vladimir Suchov 28 2 Stanislaw Kuznetsov 25 3 Mikhail Duplev 23 4 Peter Nybo 23 5 Bronislav Franc 20 6 Eskil Jonsson 20 7 Anton Hoerl 17 8 Erwin Walch 16 9 Luca Ravagnani 14 10 Magnus Karlien 14 11 Jiri Horeysi 10 12 Benny Winniger 8 13 Michel Masnada 8 14 Fabrizio Vesprini 7 15 Michael Neumeier 4 16 Thomas Kainz 1.

Qualifying Round 2 (Deventer, Holland, January 13-14,1990):
1 Per Olof Serenius 28 2 Nikolai Nischenko 25 3 Sergei Ivanov 23 4 Goran Yllner 21 5 Michael Lang 20 6 Stanislav Dyk 20 7 Tommy Lindgren 17 8 Roman Matousek 16 9 Robert Jan Munnecom 15 10 Ulrich Wehrle 12 11 Tjitte Bootsma 12 12 John Walmsley 9 13 Graham Halsall 8 14 Wiebe Vochteloo 7 15 Christian Reit 5 16 Huber Frommknecht 0.

DAY BY DAY

Diary JAN

15 *GARETH ROGERS ends all the winter doubts about Eastbourne's future when he announces he has found the financial support needed to keep speedway alive at Arlington...Former Milton Keynes manager Brian Penrose offers £10 million to buy Sheffield's Owlerton Stadium as he fights to reintroduce the sport at the greyhound venue...Sam Ermolenko gets good news from his doctors - he should be fit to race again in May.*

16 ROGER BROWN, the doctor who was first to Erik Gundersen after his World Team Cup crash, reveals that the three-time World Champion twice stopped breathing. First time was as he lay critically injured on the track and the second in the ambulance on his way to hospital...New promoters take over at Mildenhall. Skid Parish is joined by Dave Hunting - boss of the company that sponsored Ipswich in 1989 - former supermarket owner Stuart Norton and an anonymous benefactor. Their first decision is that they won't be asking Danish test star Preben Eriksen to stay for a second season...Rod Hunter turns down a two-year deal to return to Newcastle even though it would take him through to a testimonial...Kevin Price surprises Exeter by saying he wants to make a comeback after a two-season retirement.

17 WIMBLEDON, still debating their future, line up Australian Leigh Adams and Hackney's Andy Galvin as targets if they do move into the Sunbrite British League...Mildenhall make an approach for Rye House's unsettled Melvyn Taylor...Belle Vue stun their fans by agreeing to release American Gary Hicks and English teenager Carl Stonehewer, both of whom had successful 1989 seasons at Kirkmanshulme Lane.

18 *WORLD Long Track Champion Simon Wigg ends all the speculation about his future - by agreeing terms to stay at Oxford...Newcastle get in touch with Coventry asking for permission to talk with David Bargh.*

19 LONG EATON make their first signing of the winter - buying Peter Lloyd, 27, from Oxford...Bradford Corporation face a £230,000 bill if they are to meet Safety of Grounds specifications for Odsal Stadium....Mildenhall turn their attentions to former Fen Tigers Richard Green and Kevin Jolly as the new owners set about rebuilding a side...Poole skipper Alun Rossiter reveals plans to stage an ice-hockey match for speedway riders in aid of charity. It will be held at the Swindon rink at the end of February and half of the profits will go to Erik Gundersen's Stepping Stones Appeal.

20 BRIAN KARGER, third in the 1989 British League Riders' Championship, settles terms with Swindon. He is the fourth of last season's squad to sign new contracts at Blunsdon. John Davis, Jimmy Nilsen and Peter Nahlin have already put pen to paper.

21 *POOLE slap a record-breaking £25,000 fee on the head of their Australian sensation Leigh Adams. It will be a world record price for a teenager...Bradford are given the okay to talk with Oxford's unsettled Marvyn Cox who is anxious to move to a bigger home track...Berwick make a £5,000 offer for David Walsh, who spent 1989 on loan to them from Cradley Heath...Milton Keynes are keen on signing Frenchman Thierry Hilaire who failed to make the grade with Long Eaton...Eric Monaghan and Louis Carr agree terms to return to Stoke.*

22 COMPUTER whizzkid Terry Lyndon is Berwick's new promoter. The Liverpool-born ex-University graduate makes history as the sport's first black promoter...Five tracks, Belle Vue, Bradford, Cradley Heath, Swindon and Wolverhampton, declare an interest in Leigh Adams but Oxford pull out of the chase because the price is too high...Wimbledon delay a decision on their future and seek a written guarantee that they will be allocated a universally recognised number one if they join the Sunbrite British League...Glasgow line up Australian teenager Jason Lyons...Wolverhampton transfer-list Chris Cobby at £6,000 while Neil Collins agrees a new contract to stay at Monmore Green.

23 EX-WORLD Champion Peter Collins launches an astonishing attack on his old promoting partners as he slams their decision to release Hicks and Stonehewer. He claims had they been in charge when he was riding he would probably not have been given the chances he was...Steve Regeling agrees to return to Exeter...Ipswich close in on another young Australian, Billy Lellman...Mike Lewthwaite turns down the number seven berth with Belle Vue, saying he wants to return to National League Poole...Simon Wolstenholme has optimistic talks with Arena Essex after originally asking for a change of track.

24 *ERIK GUNDERSEN is given the best news of the year. Specialists at the Swedish Clinic where he is receiving treatment say he will, in time, recover full movement...Bradford begin talks with Marvyn Cox...King's Lynn transfer list Adrian Stevens.*

25 OLE OLSEN will conduct negotiations for his old club Coventry with Czechoslovakian Roman Matousek - because both speak fluent German...Mildenhall is close to closure - following the shock break-up of the new consortium...King's Lynn apply for four work permits - for Dennis Löfqvist, Stephen Davies, Lance King and Czechoslovakian World Finalist Bohumil Brhel...Australian specialists remove the plates and screws from Sam Ermolenko's broken leg.

26 BELLE VUE promoters John Perrin and Don Bowes accuse Peter Collins of "sour grapes" after his attack on their decision-making...Promoter Skid Parish formally notifies the National League HQ he will be withdrawing from the league...Fire and police object to issuing a new safety certificate for speedway to return to Sheffield's Owlerton Stadium...Stephen Davies breaks a bone in his wrist in the Australia Day Gold Cup at Parramatta and is to face an operation.

27 *MICHAEL LEE'S lawyer receives notification from the Speedway Control Board that he won't be able to start racing again until March 20, 1993. They explain that it took three years, eight weeks to pay an outstanding fine and he is suspended for a similar length of time under SCB regulations.*

28 ALAN RIVETT contacts Exeter to say he wants to return to National League racing after his premature retirement. He was allowed to join Long Eaton on loan last summer but returned home to Australia early and has recaptured his zest for the sport...Middlesbrough have been in touch with Australian international David Cheshire and offer him a 1990 team place at Cleveland Park.

WORLD ICE SPEEDWAY CHAMPIONSHIP

IRISH ON THE ROCKS

IRELAND'S sole representative in ice-racing bowed out of the title-chase...after a week-end he will want to forget.

All-rounder Tony Carey pulled out of the two day meeting at Frankfurt pointless as the Russians once again performed their one-nation assault on the competition.

Their three qualifiers all sailed through the round while, the same week-end, there were four Russkies in the top five in Finland.

Overall it meant that all twelve Soviet entrants had scored enough points to qualify for the semi-finals at Berlin and Assen...as they prepared for yet another assault on the World Final.

Qualifying Round 3 (Oulo, Finland, January 20-21, 1990): 1 Juri Ivanov 27 2 Igor Jakovlev 26 3 Valeri Ivanov 26 4 Jarmo Hirvasoja 23 5 Aleksei Jeremkin 22 6 John Fredriksson 21 7 Stefan Svensson 21 8 Ola Westlund 16 9 Geir Lilletvedt 14 10 Hannu Larronmaa 12 11 Mike Baldwin 7 12 Jari Ahlbom, reserve, 7 13 Henry Nielsen 6 14 Ilkka Perttunen, reserve, 5 15 Stephen Smith 3 16 Aapo Rijkonen, reserve, 2 17 Robert Irving 1 17 Jorma Reima 1 19 Tapio Leppämäki 0

Qualifying Round 4 (Frankfurt, W.Germany, January 20-21, 1990): 1 Sergei Kasakov 27 2 Sven-Erik Bjoerklund 25 3 Helmut Weber 25 4 Valeri Martemianow 20 5 Juri Beresin 19 6 Franz Schiefer 18 7 Harald Baumann 18 8 Antonin Klatovsky 14 9 Jiri Petrasek 14 10 Joakim Karlsson 12 11 Peter Hehlert 8 12 Werner Weinhart, reserve, 8 13 Erkki Aakko 7 14 Eddy Norrmark 6 15 Erich Soir, reserve, 6 16 Raimond Strobl 5 17 Franz Mayerbeuchler 4 18 Tony Carey 0.

Diary JAN

DAY BY DAY

29 MITCH SHIRRA is banned for five years after the Speedway Control Board find him guilty of bringing the sport into disrepute as a result of his conviction by the FIM of a drugs offence. Three years of the ban is suspended but the decision rules him out of British racing for 1990 and 1991.

SHIRRA AFFAIR

MITCH SHIRRA'S racing number (2) was drawn out of the hat as one of the three riders to be drug-tested at the 1988 Overseas Final of the World Championship at Coventry on the evening of Tuesday, July 12.

Nineteen days later – at the World Pairs Final – he was again chosen at random to give a sample.

Subsequently it was announced that both samples had been tested positive in the laboratory of the King's College Drugs Centre, Chelsea.

On Sunday, November, 27, 1988, at an FIM Tribunal the three-man CCP Executive Committee of President Jos Vaessen and Vice-presidents Renzo Giannini and Janos Nadasdi found Shirra guilty as charged and banned him from international competition for two years.

Early in February, 1989, an FIM Judicial hearing in Geneva, Switzerland, ordered the case to be reheard because of doubts that the correct procedure was carried out at the November Tribunal.

A reconvened Tribunal, again meeting in Geneva, reheard the two cases on August 8, 1989, and found Shirra guilty on one of the two charges but made no judgement on the other.

He was again banned for two years but gave notification of appeal.

On October 12, 1989, his appeal was considered in Geneva and the following morning the FIM announced that he is guilty but remit the sentence to a one-year suspended ban.

Following that confirmation of the New Zealander's guilt the Speedway Control Board decide to charge him with bringing the sport into disrepute under Regulation 9 (vii) which reads: "Any proceeding or act prejudicial to the interests of the SCB., the sport of speedway racing and motorcycling generally."

The case was heard on January 29, 1990 by members of the Speedway Control Board who find him guilty as charged although Shirra gives immediate notification that he will take the case to the Stewards of the R.A.C.

30 *TOP-SCORER Craig Boyce agrees to spend another season with National League Poole...Rob Tilbury asks Arena Essex for a move and says he wants to try and break into the Sunbrite British League...Czechoslovakians Zdenek Tesar and Vaclav Milik confirm they will be coming to Britain for the Telford Ice Spectacular.*

31 KING'S LYNN join the chase for Marvyn Cox...Coventry promoter Charles Ochiltree calls in his local MP after an inspection of Brandon by Safety Officers leaves him with a £100,000 bill for improvements if he is to continue holding speedway's big meetings.

1 WIMBLEDON announce they are staying in the National League - after the 11th hour breakdown of talks with the Sunbrite British League. They make their decision after BSPA chairman Maurice Ducker says he cannot guarantee that Jeremy Doncaster will join them following a Reading protest...Marvyn Cox agrees to join Bradford...Mildenhall officially withdraw from the National League.

2 IN a dramatic about-turn Skid Parish decides he wants to stay on as Mildenhall promoter and withdraws his resignation. Even so it is too late to be included in the draw for either the Knock Out Cup or the Fours tournament...Russell Lanning admits he is considering his own future.

3 EASTBOURNE finally clinch the signing of Tony Primmer. They will pay Milton Keynes £6,000 for the Australian...Garage chain Walker Jackson decide they won't take up their option on team sponsorship with Swindon...Danish League side Slangerup are to tour National League tracks in the Spring...Middlesbrough, Stoke and Ipswich will be venues for the World Championship qualifying rounds...Larry Ross wins the New Zealand Championship - and Leigh Adams takes the Australian Under-21 title.

4 RUSSELL LANNING is leaving Wimbledon. He won't be signing a new contract after the track's failure to join the Sunbrite British League...Rob Tilbury, already on the transfer list, confirms he wants to leave Arena Essex, even if there's no Sunbrite British League place.

5 MIDDLESBROUGH unveil their first major signing of the winter – Australian David Cheshire...King's Lynn and Bradford are locked in a signing tug-of-war over World Finalist Andy Smith...And Andy's younger brother Paul is talking with Wolverhampton...Rye House snap up veteran Roger Johns (Wimbledon).

6 SWINDON emerge as firm favourites to sign Leigh Adams and put in a concrete offer for the teenager...Berwick eye up Australian Damon Richardson...Oxford decide to use transfer-listed Alastair Stevens in their 1990 line-up...Only three days after winning the national crown, Larry Ross announces his retirement.

7 *OXFORD complete their new-look squad by finally signing Dean Barker...Long Eaton swoop for Poole's Kevin Smart...Rye House are in the market again: this time they sign Nigel Sparshott from Oxford.*

8 MORE good news for Rye House fans as Melvyn Taylor withdraws his transfer request and signs a new contract. It means there's no place at Hoddesdon for Paul Woods, Carl Chalcraft, Kevin Brice or Peter Schroeck...Dane Frank Andersen agrees terms to return for another season with Exeter...Carl Blackbird decides he wants to return to the National League and Peterborough are the first track to make inquiries.

9 *WORLD Finalist Andy Smith decides to stay at Bradford despite a counter offer from King's Lynn...Todd Wiltshire, top of the 1989 Wimbledon averages, confirms that he wants to leave Plough Lane for a Sunbrite British League career.*

10 THREE clubs, Swindon, Wolverhampton and Bradford are left in the chase for Leigh Adams...Peterborough and Milton Keynes agree terms for the transfer of Kevin Jolly.

11 KING'S LYNN open talks with American Gary Hicks...Bradford transfer-list three riders: Michael Graves, Henrik Kristensen and Antal Kocso.

WORLD ICE SPEEDWAY INDIVIDUAL CHAMPIONSHIP

RUSSIAN SWEEP

THANK heaven for Sweden's Sven-Erik Bjoerkland.

At least he was able to momentarily halt the Russians march towards total domination of the World Ice Speedway Championship by winning the first of the two semi-finals.

Bjoerklund's superb performance in Berlin exposed at least a tiny chink in the Soviet armour as they dominated the two semis by providing five of the six riders who filled the top three places.

Semi-Final (Berlin, West Germany, February 10-11, 1990):
1 Sven-Erik Bjoerklund 29 2 Sergei Kasakov 29 3 Juri Ivanov 24 4 Jarmo Hirvasoja 20 5 Helmut Weber 19 6 Harald Baumann 17 7 Stefan Svensson 14 8 Igor Jakovlev 14 9 Antonin Klatovsky 12 10 Valeri Martemianow 11 Juri Beresin 9 12 Aleksei Jeremkin 8 13 Ola Westlund 8 14 Valeri Ivanov 6 15 John Fredriksson 4 16 Franz Schiefer 1. Reserves: Jiri Petrasek 11, Geir Lilletvedt 4, Michael Pape 3.

Semi-Final (Assen, Holland, March 3-4, 1990):
1 Vladimir Suchov 28, 2 Sergei Ivanov 27, 3 Nikolai Nischenko 26, 4 Bronislav Franc 24, 5 Michael Lang 21, 6 Per-Olof Serenius 20, 7 Stanislav Dyk 14, 8 Eskil Jonsson 14, 9 Mikhail Duplev 13, 10 Robert Jan Munnecom 12, 11 Anton Hoerl 10,12 Peter Nybo 10, 13 Tommy Lindgren 6, 14 Erwin Walch 3, 15 Goran Yllner 0, 16 Stanislaw Kuznetsov, did not ride.

TEAM **Qualifying round (Inzell, West Germany, January 27-28, 1990)**
TEAM 1 FINLAND 74 (Jarmo Hirvasoja 34, Peter Nybo 28, Hannu Larronmaa 12) 2 West
TEAM Germany 72 (Helmut Weber 32, Harald Baumann 20, Michael Lang 20) 3 Czechoslo-
TEAM vakia 53 (Stanislav Dyk 20, Antonin Klatovsky 18, Bronislav Franc 15) 4 Austria 25
TEAM (Erwin Walch 11, Anton Hoerl 10, Walter Wartbichler 4) 5 Holland 16 (Robert Jan
TEAM Munnecom 7, Tjitte Bootsma 6, Wiebe Vochteloo 3).
TEAM **WORLD FINAL (Medeo, Alma-Ata, Soviet Union, February 24-25, 1990)**
TEAM **1 *SOVIET UNION 86 (Juri Ivanov 34, Nikolai Nischenko 27, Sergei Kasakov 25)*** 2
TEAM Sweden 52 (Sven-Erik Bjoerklund 23, Per Olof Serenius 22, Stefan Svensson 7) 3 West
TEAM Germany 50 (Harald Baumann 22, Helmut Weber 20, Michael Lang 8) 4 Czechoslovakia
TEAM 46 (Antonin Klatovsky 20, Stanislaw Dyk 16, Bronislav Franc 10) 5 Finland 5 (Hannu
TEAM Larronmaa 2, Erkki Aakko 2, Peter Nybo 1).

DAY BY DAY

Diary FEB

12 SWINDON win the race to sign Leigh Adams. Gary Chessell goes to Poole on loan...King's Lynn axe Lance King claiming he is too expensive...Arena Essex sign Adrian Stevens from the Zetor Stars.

13 *SUNBRITE British League boss Maurice Ducker hits back over Wimbledon claims they were let down by the senior league. And he reveals that the Montine Dons listed six riders they wouldn't have at Plough Lane: Kelvin Tatum, Simon Wigg, Peter Ravn, Bobby Schwartz, Kelly Moran and John Cook...American Billy Hamill, 19, agrees terms with Cradley Heath...Carl Stonehewer joins Wolverhampton...Doctors give Paul Woods the all-clear to ride again.*

14 THE 1993 World Final will definitely be held at Berlin's Olympic Stadium...Newcastle and Bradford agree terms for Simon Green to move from Odsal to Brough Park...Ice promoters Ian Thomas and Graham Drury come back from an exhibition tour of the Middle East with a contract to return with 20 riders next year.

15 ROBERT PFETZING, transfer-listed by Wolverhampton, is to take a year away from British racing...Hackney appeal to the Sunbrite British League promoters to be allowed to sign Danish veteran Bo Petersen even though his last BL average was above six points a meeting...Stoke are close to signing Australian Mark Carlson...Exeter transfer-list Michael Coles.

16 *CRADLEY HEATH make preliminary moves to sign Andy Galvin - as Gert Handberg turns down terms...Edinburgh lose their team sponsors Belmont Garages...Wolverhampton recall Lars Munkedal...Kevin Jolly agrees to join Milton Keynes.*

17 GLASGOW stave off the threat of a shock closure by agreeing to switch race-night from a Friday to Wednesday after an ultimatum by the Shawfield Stadium owners...Bob Burchett takes over as Wimbledon promoter and golf professional Peter Brown returns as team manager.

18 ICE promoters Ian Thomas and Graham Drury reveal they are talking to interested parties in Japan...Deon Prinsloo, nephew of ex-rider Peter, signs for Wimbledon.

19 GERT HANDBERG ends his dispute and signs for Cradley Heath...Coastal Windows are to be Swindon's new team sponsors...Australian Brian Nixon, 27, arrives in Britain and hopes to break into a National League side...Stephen Davies agrees to return to King's Lynn.

20 *ROMAN MATOUSEK will be back at Coventry...Poland offer Sunbrite British League tracks the pick of their best riders and say, in return, they'll let any junior riders spend the summer learning in Poland...Rye House claim Eastbourne are jumping the gun in announcing that Paul Woods is likely to rejoin the Eagles.*

21 JAN O. PEDERSEN is back with Cradley Heath...Reading are the second club to have talks with American Gary Hicks...Swindon add David Smart to their 1990 squad...Chris Morton is going into promotion with ex-Poole boss Terry Chandler - at Malta's Ta Qali Stadium.

22 *BRIAN PENROSE, who has seen his hopes of reviving speedway at Sheffield flounder, agrees to take over at Mildenhall and meets the National League Management Committee to outline his plans...Exeter transfer-list Dane Frank Andersen even though he had already signed a 1990 contract as they announce that Richard Green is returning to the County Ground...Long Eaton capture another former Milton Keynes rider, Nigel De'ath, who joins Keith White, Peter Lloyd and Kevin Smart at Station Road.*

23 CHANGE of heart sees Brian Penrose pull out of his proposed Mildenhall take-over. He claims his decision was based on a careful look at the track's 1989 books...Australians are to be allowed to compete in the National League's junior competition.

24 DENMARK are to set up a National Training Centre at Broust...Michael Coles is willing to return to Edinburgh.

25 KING'S LYNN name an eight-man squad and include both Gary Hicks and Michael Lee with the ex-World Champion at number eight...Newcastle re-open transfer talks with Middlesbrough over Martin Dixon...Skid Parish sets a 24-hour deadline to save Mildenhall.

HANDY ANDY!

SWEDISH Ice King Jan Andersson finally cracked...beaten by pretender to the throne Andy Campbell.

But it didn't take too long before Jan had slipped back into top form with a run-off victory as he ended Campbell's hopes of a spectacular ice double.

The Berwick star charged to a 15-point maximum to retain his British Open title (won last year in the absence of Andersson) as promoters Ian Thomas and Graham Drury had to turn fans away from the door as Telford's rink was turned into an ice speedway for the fifth successive winter.

The British Open was the afternoon diet while during the evening Telford hosted the third round of the European Ice Masters which went to a thrilling climax.

Campbell had looked certain of victory when he won his first three rides but was then relegated to third behind Lawson and Glanz before clinching a run-off with the sliding Swede by beating him in heat 20.

He couldn't repeat the victory in the race-off as Andersson rounded off his comeback with the victory he yearned for in what he announced was going to be his last ever meeting in Britain.

BRITISH OPEN CHAMPIONSHIP (Telford, Sunday, February 18, 1990)

1 ANDY CAMPBELL	**3 3 3 3 3**	**15**
2 Richard Hellsén	3 2 3 3 2	13
3 Alun Rossiter	3 2 2 2 3	12
4 Tony Olsson	2 1 2 3 2	10
5 Simon Cross	X 3 1 2 3	9
6 Jan Andersson	3 1 3 2 0	9
7 Steve Lawson	E N 2 3 3	8
8 Graham Jones	1 3 0 2 1	7
9 Peter Glanz	X 3 3 R 0	6
10 Allan Johansen	F 2 2 1 0	5
11 Zdenek Tesar	2 R 1 1 1	5
12 Keith White	2 X N 0 2	4
14 Andy Smith	0 1 0 1 2	4
13 Neil Evitts	2 0 1 1 X	4
15 Alastair Stevens	1 X N 0 1	2
16 Vaclav Milik	X N 1 0 1	2

EUROPEAN ICE MASTERS (Telford, Sunday, February 18, 1990)

1 JAN ANDERSSON	**2 3 3 3 2**	**13**	**3**
2 Andy Campbell	3 3 3 1 3	13	2
3 Simon Cross	3 2 3 3 1	12	3
4 Peter Glanz	2 2 3 2 3	12	2
5 Tony Olsson	3 1 2 2 2	10	
6 Steve Lawson	N 3 1 3 2	9	
7 Richard Hellsén	1 3 2 2 1	9	
8 Keith White	2 0 0 3 3	8	
9 Alun Rossiter	1 X 2 1 3	7	
10 Graham Jones	1 2 2 X 2	7	
11 Allan Johansen	3 1 0 1 1	6	
12 Vaclav Milik	X 2 1 2 1	6	
13 Zdenek Tesar	2 1 X 0 0	3	
14 Alastair Stevens	1 X 1 0 0	2	
15 Andy Smith	X 1 0 0 0	1	
16 Neil Evitts	F R R N N	0	

INTER NATIONS CHAMPIONSHIP (Telford, Sunday, February 18, 1990)
1 SWEDEN 8 (Richard Hellsén 6, Jan Andersson 2)
2 England 7 (Andy Campbell 5, Simon Cross 2)
3 Denmark 1 (Allan Johansen 1, Peter Glanz 0)
4 Czechoslovakia 1 (Vaclav Milik 1, Zdenek Tesar 0)

TOP OF THE POLL: National League promoters held their annual awards ballot and produced the following results: *Rider of the Year:* Steve Schofield (Hackney). *Promoters of the Year:* John Louis and Mike Western (Ipswich). *Best Newcomer:* Leigh Adams (Poole). *Best Programme:* Edinburgh. *Best Race Jacket:* Rye House. *Best Prepared Track:* Ipswich. *Best Stadium:* Wimbledon. *Best Supported Visiting Team:* Arena Essex. *Referee of the Year:* Stan Green.

DAY BY DAY

Diary FEB

26 ANDY GRAHAME, left out of the Oxford line-up, shelves his retirement plans and says he will ride in the National League if no Sunbrite British League track offers him a team place...Mark Crang, a £6,000 Belle Vue signing in 1985, is making a comeback after a three-season gap.

27 DANISH test star Peter Glanz is to join Milton Keynes...British League promoters turn down appeals by David Bargh and Bo Petersen to be allowed to step down into the National League...Mildenhall say they will definitely compete in the 1990 National League after stadium owner Terry Waters revises the £28,000 a year rent...Gary Hicks, who has also agreed terms with Reading, is told he must sign for King's Lynn or be barred from the Sunbrite British League.

28 COVENTRY agree an £18,000 fee to sign Sean Wilson whose contract is still owned by ex-Sheffield promoter Maurice Ducker...The Sunbrite British League 1990 fixtures are officially released.

1 *MITCH SHIRRA loses the latest - and final - round of his battle with officialdom. The Stewards of the Royal Automobile Club uphold the five-year suspension but do vary the punishment. Four years of the ban will be suspended meaning Shirra only has to sit out the 1990 domestic season...Andy Galvin, who has been seeking a move to the Sunbrite British League, has pledged his 1990 future to his National League track Hackney after surprisingly lukewarm interest from senior grade tracks...Berwick sign Australian Steve Widt from Ipswich, on the recommendation of former World Finalist John Titman. They agree to pay the princely sum of £65 to the Witches.*

2 THE FIM Spring Congress opens in Geneva and among items on the agenda is the plan to reorganise the individual World Championship...Three National League tracks, Peterborough, Milton Keynes and Mildenhall, have sought permission to talk to Exeter's transfer-listed Dane Frank Andersen. The Skoda Panthers switch to Andersen after negotiations with Chris Shears over the possible purchase of Carl Blackbird's contract hit major snags.

3 NEWCASTLE finally get their man - former Middlesbrough skipper Martin Dixon. The two clubs agree a near £12,000 transfer fee and Dixon is introduced to his new fans at a Supporters' Club function...Dave Younghusband, who won 10 major titles during his time as the Diamonds' team manager, is to take over a similar role at Berwick. He hasn't been actively involved in speedway since the end of the 1984 season.

4 *THE World Championship is to have it's biggest shake-up for years. In 1991 British riders will have to race in Russia to qualify for the World Final as the FIM agree to fundamental changes in the World Championship. There will now be two semi-finals - one in Russia and the other in West Germany - with 20 qualifiers from the Scandinavian and Overseas Finals being joined by 12 riders from the Continental rounds in a draw for the two semis. The FIM Track Commission throw out an even more revolutionary proposal that would have seen three semi-finals and another proposal to have a World Final with 24 riders and six-rider races...Berwick's Mark Courtney raises more than £2,600 for Cancer Research by staging the Redpath Cars Beach Classic at Cocklaw Beach, near Berwick. Around 500 fans gather to see the racing on 250 cc or 350 cc bikes around a 90-yard sand track. New Newcastle signing Martin Dixon beats Glasgow's Geoff Powell in a run-off (see right).*

Redpath Cars Beach Classic, Cocklaw Beach, Berwick, Sunday, March 4, 1990:

1 Martin Dixon	**3 3 3 3 1**	**13**	**3**
2 Geoff Powell	**3 3 2 2 3**	**13**	**2**
3 Ian Atkinson	**3 3 1 3 2**	**12**	
4 Paul Bentley	3 0 1 3 3	10	
5 Phil Jeffrey	2 2 3 2 R	9	
6 Kenny McKinna	2 R 3 1 2	8	
7 Charlie McKinna	R 1 3 3 R	7	
8 Mark Crang	2 2 2 0 1	7	
9 Ian Rae	2 2 2 1 0	7	
10 Sean Courtney, res	R 1 2 3	6	
11 Kevin Little	1 3 0 0 2	6	
12 Graeme Robertson	1 0 2 1 2	6	
13 Rob Grant	0 2 1 1 1	5	
14 Jason Straughan	R 1 0 R 3	4	
15 Brett Saunders	R R 1 2 0	3	
16 Paul McCarten	1 1 X 0 1	3	
17 Mark Courtney	R N N N N	0	
18 Steve Widt, res	did not ride		

5 OVERSEAS Finalist Andy Phillips is scheduled to have team talks with Coventry later this week....Gordon Kennett could miss the start of the season after crashing at an unofficial Eastbourne practice. A visit to his doctor confirms he has damaged the ball joint in his left shoulder...Middlesbrough inquire about Rye House's transfer listed West German Peter Schroeck.

6 PAUL WOODS is rejoining his old club Eastbourne. The Groombridge Eagles agree a £5,000 fee with Rye House...Mildenhall talk to former British Finalist Andy Grahame who is surplus to Oxford's requirements...Controversial British referee Frank Ebdon has been elected to the FIM International A grade list of officials and can now handle a World Final.

7 *COAL Products Limited are to invest around £250,000 in speedway over the next two years. And the Sunbrite British League is to be renamed the Sunbrite League as part of the package ...A limit of 27,491 has been set for the Sunbrite World Final at Bradford's Odsal Stadium...National League bosses make a fresh plea for Bo Petersen, David Bargh and Andy Grahame to step down. They write to each member of the Speedway Control Board asking them to overturn the ruling which bars the trio from racing because their last British League averages were above 6 points a match...Wimbledon join the race to sign Andy Grahame.*

8 LES COLLINS agrees terms to rejoin Edinburgh...Australian Shane Parker makes an immediate impact in Ipswich's pre-season practice...Oxford give Eastbourne first refusal on teenager Paul Dugard, if he fails to make Sunbrite League grade this coming season...Ambitious Berwick are to build a mini-track at Berrington Lough for Under 16s.

9 BELLE VUE sack Kelly Moran after he makes extravagant financial demands...Edinburgh snap up teenage Australian Nigel Alderton...Dane Frank Andersen agrees terms with Peterborough.

10 *ARENA ESSEX are to be sponsored by their own promoter Chick Woodroffe through his Promotasport company...Belle Vue talk with Lance King as they seek a replacement for Kelly Moran.*

11 ANDY PHILLIPS signs for Coventry, to complete the Bees' 1990 squad.

WORLD ICE SPEEDWAY CHAMPIONSHIP

BRAVO JARMO!

JARMO Hirvasoja brought delight and joy to the travelling Finnish fans...as he became his country's first-ever World Champion in a speedway discipline.

Hirvasoja, equally adept on the shale as the ice, had looked anything but World Champion material in his qualifying rounds.

But when it really mattered he turned in a superlative performance to outfox and outrace the perennial Russian favourites.

On the opening session of the two-day final he was tied on 14 points with defending title-holder Nikolai Nischenko and after they had both finished eight rides they were still locked together.

But Nischenko's dreams of retaining the crown were shattered when he lost control while trying to overtake the Finn in heat 34 of the marathon.

That left the way clear for Hirvasoja who safely got the third place he needed in his last race to become only the fourth non-Soviet to win the championship in its 25th staging.

Ex-champion Vladimir Suchov broke his right leg in three places when he fell in only his second ride; 1986 winner Sergei Ivanov was again on the rostrum; while two other former title-winners Sergei Kasakov and Juri Ivanov finished out of the top placing.

WORLD FINAL (Gothenburg, Sweden, March 10-11, 1990) 1 JARMO HIRVASOJA 27, 2 Nikolai Nischenko 24, 3 Sergei Ivanov 23, 4 Per Olof Serenius 23 5 Sergei Kasakov 21 6 Michael Lang 19 7 Igor Jakovlev 17 8 Stanislav Dyk 15 9 Bronislav Franc 14 10 Helmut Weber 12 11 Juri Ivanov 11 12 Sven-Erik Bjoerklund 10 13 Stefan Svensson 9 14 Harald Baumann 3 15 Eskil Jonsson 2 16 Vladimir Suchov 0. Reserves: Antonin Klatovsky 6 Robert Jan Munnecom 3.

Roll of Honour

1966 Gabdrahman Kadirov
1967 Boris Samorodov
1968 Gabdrahman Kadirov
1969 Gabdrahman Kadirov
1970 Antonin Svaab
1971 Gabdrahman Kadirov
1972 Gabdrahman Kadirov
1973 Gabdrahman Kadirov
1974 Milan Spinka
1975 Sergei Tarabanko
1976 Sergei Tarabanko
1977 Sergei Tarabanko
1978 Sergei Tarabanko
1979 Anatoli Bondarenko
1980 Anatoli Bondarenko
1981 Vladimir Lioubich
1982 Sergei Kasakov
1983 Sergei Kasakov
1984 Erik Stenlund
1985 Vladimir Suchov
1986 Sergei Ivanov
1987 Juri Ivanov
1988 Erik Stenlund
1989 Nikolai Nischenko
1990 Jarmo Hirvasoja

DAY BY DAY

Diary
MAR

...RESULTS...RESULTS...RESULTS...

GOLD CUP: Coventry 46 Belle Vue 44.
CHALLENGE: Belle Vue 47 Oxford 43; Cradley Heath 44 King's Lynn 46.
HL1 TROPHY, 1st leg: Ipswich 55 Hackney 41; 2nd leg: Hackney 51 Ipswich 45. *Ipswich win 100-92.*

12 NEW Coventry signing Andy Phillips is told he will miss the first three weeks of the season by surgeons who have taken the plate out of the thigh he smashed in 1987...Cradley Heath are ready to hand a golden career chance to Mark Robinson, 22, a junior who used to help put the covering sheets on the Dudley Wood track while still at school...Peter Chapman is transfer-listed by Peterborough...Arena Essex are still debating whether to make a concrete move for Rye House's on-offer Kevin Brice.

13 JAN ANDERSSON agrees to return to Reading...Mildenhall sack long-serving team manager Maurice Everett and replace him with 1989 junior team boss Chris Gould...Newcastle are poised to sign Essex-based youngster John Wainwright - despite a 500 mile round trip to Brough Park...Belle Vue's Paul Smith agrees to attend Middlesbrough's practice and promises to make up his mind on a contract offer then.

14 *WORLD Champion Hans Nielsen and Sunbrite League champions Oxford have parted company after a breakdown in contract talks...Rebel David Bargh agrees to temporarily shelve his planned legal action against the Speedway Control Board for 24 hours as they still ponder Newcastle's bid to use him in their team.*

15 KELLY MORAN could still end up in Belle Vue's colours after a dramatic peace move. He offers to rejoin the Aces on reduced financial terms after further talks with promoter John Perrin...Oxford offer Andy Grahame a full team place as they contemplate life without Hans Nielsen...David Bargh instructs his lawyers to take legal proceedings against the Speedway Control Board as he still awaits an answer...Ipswich's two Australian newcomers impress on their debuts. Both Shane Parker and Billy Lellman are paid 10 points against Hackney who track their two European imports Tim Korneliussen and Uwe Gessner...Andy Phillips gets good news from a specialist who cuts back his out of action time to a fortnight...Dianetics renew their Wolverhampton sponsorship - and tyre giants Goodyear back the juniors...Paul Smith signs for Middlesbrough.

16 CRISIS talks find a solution to the Hans Nielsen dispute and he signs a new contract with Oxford...Rob Tilbury ends a winter of unrest by putting his signature to a 1990 contract at Arena Essex's practice day...Edinburgh sign Mark Blackbird on loan from Long Eaton...Reading hit an unexpected snag in their negotiations to sign Australian Todd Wiltshire from National League Wimbledon over his assessed Sunbrite League average...Joe Screen is cleared to stay at Belle Vue after a contract dispute. His father finally agrees to give his parental permission...Roman Matousek (Coventry) is stuck in Czechoslovakia awaiting his work permit. American Gary Hicks (King's Lynn) is similarly affected.

17 DAVID BARGH is to issue a writ against the Speedway Control Board in his battle to be allowed to join Newcastle...Australian Stephen Davies misses King's Lynn's opener, still suffering from a winter hand injury. Also absent from the Zetor Stars' line-up are Gary Hicks and new Czechoslovakian signing Bohumil Brhel who is still awaiting his entry visa to Britain..David Jackson has confirmed he won't be returning to Mildenhall.

18 SWINDON complete their team planning for the new campaign when Andrew Silver agrees terms...Mildenhall, anxious to meet the National League minimum points limit, are to approach Hackney to sign Danish test star Bo Petersen on loan if he's cleared to ride in the Division...Gordon Kennett is likely to miss the opening of the season with his damaged shoulder as a specialist reports little improvement in movement.

19 *THE Speedway Control Board uphold appeals on behalf of Andy Grahame, Bo Petersen and David Bargh to join National League clubs...Hans Nielsen is to press for a new agreement between riders and promoters that will see contract negotiations completed by January 1 - with riders being free agents if a deal cannot be concluded...Swedish rider Kent Danielsson (Vetlanda) is killed in a road accident while on holiday in Austria....Todd Wiltshire officially joins Sunbrite League Reading...Neville Tatum re-signs for Wimbledon...New Cradley capture Billy Hamill reveals that he was threatened by a gun-carrying woman while being driven to Los Angeles Airport...Colin Cook takes a tumble at Exeter's pre-season practice and aggravates an old collar bone injury.*

20 THE British Speedway Promoters' Association announce ticket prices for the 1990 World Final at Bradford. It will cost a highest-ever £30 for a grandstand seat and £17.50 for a terrace ticket...Mildenhall reveal why they dropped their plans to sign Denmark's Bo Petersen. Promoter Skid Parish claims to have done so would have cost £1,000 a week....Edinburgh pull out of negotiations to sign Peterborough's transfer-listed Peter Chapman because of transport difficulties.

21 EDINBURGH are poised to make a sensational eve-of-season signing: they've reached agreement with deadly rivals Glasgow to take Phil Jeffrey on loan for a month...Bradford boss Bobby Ham predicts the Coalite Dukes will take the Sunbrite League title at their Press Day...Belle Vue promoter John Perrin offers American Gary Hicks practice facilities at Kirkmanshulme Lane - even though they have let him go on loan to King's Lynn. Hicks hasn't ridden since damaging his shoulder in the States...National League champions Poole put back their opening date by a week while repairs are carried out to the grandstand.

...RESULTS...RESULTS...RESULTS...

GOLD CUP: Reading v Swindon, postponed, waterlogged track; Belle Vue 46 Coventry 44; Coventry 53 Wolverhampton 37; Cradley Heath 41 Bradford 49; King's Lynn 44 Reading 46; Swindon 38 Oxford 51.
CHALLENGE: Wolverhampton v Oxford, postponed, waterlogged track; Long Eaton 53 Milton Keynes 42; Ipswich 64 Poole 32; Middlesbrough 54 Long Eaton 42; Oxford 53 Wolverhampton 37; Peterborough 59 Milton Keynes 37; Rye House 57 Poole 37; Edinburgh 54 Glasgow 42; Newcastle 34 Ipswich 62.
LONEX TROPHY, 1st leg: Hackney 62 Arena Essex 34; 2nd leg: Arena Essex 43 Hackney 52. *Hackney win 114-77*.

22 MILDENHALL are thrown out of the National League after declaring a team which is under the 42 point minimum...New Edinburgh signing Nigel Alderton puts his shoulder out at the club's official practice....Ex-Stoke rider Ian Stead is admitted to hospital in Dewsbury after damaging his neck when he fell from a moto-cross bike...Frank Andersen claims a 15-point maximum on his debut for Peterborough.

23 MILDENHALL plan to fight the National League Management Committee decision to expel them from the 1990 programme - and the first shot in the campaign to stay open is to agree terms with Bo Petersen...Hackney axe their West German newcomer Uwe Gessner...Doctors order Ipswich's Australian signing Billy Lellman to rest. He is suffering from depression.

24 COLIN PRATT orders his Cradley Heath team in for a special practice after they go down to their second successive home defeat, this time against Bradford. Ex-skipper Erik Gundersen offers to take charge of the session...Hackney have been invited to tour Poland later in the summer...Alan Rivett fails to agree terms with Exeter and is open to offers from any other track...Milton Keynes call off their scheduled opening meeting against Peterborough because they have still not completed essential work demanded by the Speedway Control Board.

25 *EDINBURGH snap up trackless Australian Mark Pearce...Australia's summer tour of the Soviet Union has been scrapped because Sunbrite League riders Glenn Doyle, Troy Butler and Stephen Davies have been refused their release.*

DAY BY DAY

Diary MAR

26 IN Australia, former rider Carl Askew admits that he was a drug addict and often raced in the National League while stoned. He makes his startling confession in *Peter White's Speedway World* as a warning to young riders...Gert Handberg breaks his hand during Cradley's practice.

27 GARY HAVELOCK is banned from beginning his 1990 World Championship challenge in the British semi finals. He was originally among the 32 seeds but under a Speedway Control Board rule he must race in the National League rounds because he did not compete in the 1989 league competition...Peter Carr is told to take a break by his doctors. He broke his shoulder during the winter but kept the injury a secret until it was obvious he was in pain while riding at Newcastle...Legends Jack Parker and Vic Duggan have been voted into the Speedway Hall of Fame - the first of the annual enrollees joining the 22 World Champions and sport's father Johnnie Hoskins..Berwick pay £200 to sign Alan Rivett from Exeter.

28 *LOCAL radio station Fox FM agree to sponsor Oxford's junior league side who will be known as the Fox FM Cubs...Swindon boss Ron Byford wants a rule change to allow riders to switch between Barum and Dunlop tyres during a meeting.*

29 MIDDLESBROUGH pull off one of the signings of the season by tempting Rod Hunter back to the National League. They announce the coup after losing at home to his old club Newcastle...Gordon Kennett will definitely miss the opening of the new season.

30 TEENAGER Paul Smith could face the chop at Middlesbrough after only one match for the club. To accommodate new signing Rod Hunter the Bears must re-shape their side and that seems certain to mean no long-term team places for either Smith or fellow reserve Max Schofield...National League announce the starting line-ups for all 17 tracks and the official 1-7s create one or two surprises. Berwick leave out young prospect Scott Robson and Glasgow have no room for Martin McKinna...Sweden's 1989 World Team Cup top-scorer Mikael Blixt retires because he can't find enough sponsorship to carry on racing.

31 *CRADLEY HEATH win the Premiership - for the sixth time in the competition's nine season history with a ten point win in the second leg at Dudley Wood. One of their heroes is American newcomer Billy Hamill with paid 11...Australian Stephen Davies is admitted to hospital after inadvertently swallowing methanol while siphoning his fuel tank in readiness for the meeting at Swindon. He is kept in overnight on a drip...Ipswich's Australian newcomer Billy Lellman is to return home on medical advice because he is suffering from severe depression...And Hackney's West German signing Uwe Gessner has walked out on the HL1 Kestrels after a miserable start to his National League career.*

...RESULTS...RESULTS...RESULTS...

PREMIERSHIP: Oxford 45 Cradley Heath 45; Cradley Heath 50 Oxford 40, *Cradley Heath win 95-85.*
SUNBRITE LEAGUE: Coventry 42 Reading 48.
GOLD CUP: Reading 46 King's Lynn 44; Wolverhampton 47 Coventry 43; Belle Vue 48 Bradford 42; Bradford 47 Belle Vue 43; Swindon 51 King's Lynn 39; King's Lynn 47 Swindon 43.
INDIVIDUAL: Maslens Classic (Wimbledon): Andy Grahame.
TYNE TEES TROPHY, 1st leg: Middlesbrough 45 Newcastle 51; Newcastle 52 Middlesbrough 44. *Newcastle win 103-89.*
EUROPEAN SPECIAL OLYMPIAD: Stars 57 Stripes 39 (at Glasgow).
CHALLENGE: Exeter 72 Long Eaton 24; Long Eaton 42 Peterborough 54; Peterborough 55 Long Eaton 40, *Peterborough win 109-82;* Ipswich 48 Kangaroos 48; Hackney 50 Wimbledon 46; Arena Essex 46 Eastbourne 50; Eastbourne 50 Arena Essex 46, *Eastbourne win 100-92;* Stoke 54 Milton Keynes 42; Berwick 59 Edinburgh 37; Edinburgh 45 Berwick 51, *Berwick win 110-82.*

1 HANS NIELSEN creates his own slice of history - by riding for Polish League side Lublin...Melvyn Taylor breaks his arm in a last heat fall during Rye House's home defeat against Ipswich.

2 *DANISH starlet Freddy Schøtt is offered a contract by Edinburgh...Berwick's Scott Robson is told he has cracked a bone in his elbow after a weekend crash at Edinburgh...Wolverhampton's injured skipper Sam Ermolenko arrives back in Britain but is not yet ready to start racing again even though he reveals he has had eight tentative laps at Ascot Park Raceway in his native Los Angeles...Surgeons operate on Melvyn Taylor's badly smashed arm.*

3 EASTBOURNE approach the Speedway Control Board for permission to run a benefit meeting for long-serving Gordon Kennett, now in his 20th season...Andy Grahame is furious that he's been left out of the 24 seeds for the British semi-finals of the World Championship claiming he should have been included in the draw based on his 1989 British League average.

4 SIMON WIGG is axed but Gary Havelock is recalled to a 12-rider England squad from which the side to face Denmark in the opening Sunbrite test will be picked. Also in - Oxford's Dean Barker...The Speedway Control Board consider Michael Lee's plea to be allowed to race again but refuse to reveal their verdict claiming: "We have to write to Lee first."

...RESULTS...RESULTS...RESULTS...

WORLD CHAMPIONSHIP: British quarter finals (Ipswich): Alan Mogridge. (Middlesbrough): Gary Havelock.
SUNBRITE LEAGUE: Reading v Coventry, postponed, track waterlogged.
SPEEDWAY STAR KNOCK OUT CUP, preliminary round, 1st leg: Coventry 45 Oxford 45.
GOLD CUP: Oxford 39 Swindon 51; Bradford 51 Coventry 39; Cradley Heath 52 Belle Vue 38; King's Lynn 39 Oxford 51; Swindon 47 Reading 42.
NATIONAL LEAGUE: Poole v Peterborough, postponed, grandstand unsafe; Long Eaton 54 Arena Essex 42; Hackney 67 Milton Keynes 29; Peterborough 41 Ipswich 55; Arena Essex 62 Exeter 34; Berwick 51 Middlesbrough 45; Newcastle 50 Stoke 46; Rye House 47 Peterborough 49.
INTERNATIONAL TOUR: Eastbourne 39 Slangerup (Denmark) 57.
CHALLENGE: Wolverhampton 41 Oxford 49; Exeter 61 Stoke 35; Milton Keynes 46 Long Eaton 50, *Long Eaton win 103-87;* Glasgow 53 Edinburgh 43, *Glasgow win 97-95;* Wimbledon 55 Hackney 41, *Wimbledon win 101-91;* Stoke 59 Long Eaton 37.
FOUR TEAM TOURNAMENT: Belle Vue B 37 Middlesbrough 31 Belle Vue A 24 Long Eaton 15.
BENEFIT: Doug Wyer Night Best Pairs (Edinburgh): Joe Screen and Les Collins.

5 EX-RIDER Steve Sant takes over as Stoke's team manager...Troy Butler and Stephen Davies apply to be Australia's representatives in the World Long Track Championship...The National League's two top riders Steve Schofield and Andy Galvin are both out of the World Championship after failing to finish in the top four in the qualifier at Ipswich, where home rider Alan Mogridge takes the honours. But there are no problems for Bradford's Gary Havelock as he cruises to a 15 point maximum at his old track Middlesbrough.

6 *EXETER sign French teenager Phillipe Berge after bright second half performances at the County Ground...The Speedway Control Board refuse Reading's plea to stage a special benefit meeting for Malcolm Holloway, who retired at the end of last season...Simon Wigg signs for Swedish League side Indianerna as a replacement for the retired Mikael Blixt.*

7 DANISH star Allan Johansen breaks his leg and Martin Dugard fractures his ankle in separate crashes during King's Lynn's match with Oxford....Arena Essex's Kevin Brice is fined £25 by referee Lew Stripp for failing to leave the track after he had been excluded for going outside the 'safety fence' at the Purfleet circuit.

8 MORE injury problems for Rye House as Glen Baxter and Jens Rasmussen are hurt. Rasmussen has a suspected broken leg and Baxter has broken bones in his hand.

DAY BY DAY

Diary APR

9 AMERICAN Rick Miller has a lucky escape when he's involved in a road accident and his van is a write-off. Doctors confirm that Martin Dugard has fractured his ankle and broken a bone in his wrist after his week-end spill at King's Lynn...Danish tourists Slangerup draft in Tim Korneliussen to replace the injured Per Sørensen...Rye House are told they cannot use a guest at Exeter even though they are without all three heat leaders because of injury. It is agreed to turn the National League match into a challenge and they use former Falcon Frank Andersen and Andy Galvin as replacements...Keith White is to retire.

10 *FINALLY Michael Lee receives a letter from the Speedway Control Board - but it's bad news. They have refused his plea for a licence but tell him they will hear a personal appeal at the beginning of next season when he must prove he is a fit and proper person to hold a speedway licence...Chris Louis, David Norris (both Ipswich), Dean Barker and Mark Loram are picked to represent Britain in the World Under 21 Championship.*

11 BO PETERSEN is to race in Britain after all. But it's with Sunbrite League Wolverhampton who want him as a short-term replacement for their injured captain Sam Ermolenko...King's Lynn have approached Carl Blackbird about staying in the Sunbrite League but he is still considering offers from National League Edinburgh, Arena Essex and Rye House...Jamie Habbin makes his debut for Long Eaton after being signed to replace the retired Keith White.

12 EDINBURGH make a daring double swoop - they sign Danish Under 21 international Freddy Schøtt and agree a £12,000 fee with Reading for Carl Blackbird.

13 PETER RAVN is the latest early season casualty, cracking his collar bone in a tumble during Belle Vue's Gold Cup match against his old club Wolverhampton...Alun Rossiter returns to lead the Poole side against Exeter but Tony Langdon breaks his wrist.

14 *TOP referee Frank Ebdon fails to arrive to take charge of a meeting at Arena Essex...Belle Vue are banned from using Troy Butler as a guest for the injured Peter Ravn when Swindon point out Butler is due there the following week with Oxford and is in breach of the eight day rule...Billy Hamill is hit by a flu bug and misses Cradley Heath's visit to Bradford where they go down 27-63 in the Gold Cup..Richard Knight (King's Lynn), suffers concussion in a fall at his home track.*

15 **JAN STAECHMANN breaks his arm guesting for Danish tourists Slangerup at Edinburgh who have Carl Blackbird in their side.**

...RESULTS...RESULTS...RESULTS...

WORLD CHAMPIONSHIP: British quarter final (Stoke): abandoned after 8 heats, rain.
SUNBRITE LEAGUE: Reading 46 Coventry 44; Swindon v Bradford, postponed, waterlogged track; Coventry 52 King's Lynn 38; Swindon 55 Belle Vue 35.
SPEEDWAY STAR KNOCK OUT CUP, preliminary round, 2nd leg: Oxford v Coventry, postponed, waterlogged track; 1st round, 1st leg: King's Lynn v Reading, postponed, waterlogged track.
GOLD CUP: Wolverhampton 45 Cradley Heath 45; Belle Vue 42 Wolverhampton 48; Bradford 63 Cradley Heath 27.
INTERNATIONAL TOUR: Poole 43 Slangerup (Denmark) 53; Glasgow 51 Slangerup (Denmark) 45; Middlesbrough 55 Slangerup (Denmark) 41; Edinburgh 53 Slangerup (Denmark) 41.
NATIONAL LEAGUE: Wimbledon 46 Peterborough 49; Ipswich v Middlesbrough, postponed, waterlogged track; Peterborough 74 Eastbourne 22; Newcastle 50 Long Eaton 46.
NATIONAL LEAGUE KNOCK OUT CUP: 1st round, 1st leg: Long Eaton 57 Berwick 39; 1st round, 2nd leg: Berwick 62 Long Eaton 33, *Berwick win 101-90.*
CHALLENGE: Exeter 59 Rye House 37; Milton Keynes 40.5 Stoke 55.5, *Stoke win 109.5-82.5;* Eastbourne 32 Wimbledon 63.
EASTER TRIANGLE: 1st leg (at Hackney): postponed, waterlogged track; 1st leg: Arena Essex 18 Hackney 21 Rye House 8, abandoned after 8 heats; 1st leg: Rye House 39 Hackney 38 Arena Essex 31.
EASTER TROPHY: Poole 50 Exeter 46.

...RESULTS...RESULTS...RESULTS...

WORLD CHAMPIONSHIP: British quarter final (Stoke): Nigel Crabtree.
SUNBRITE INTERNATIONAL: England 63 Denmark 45 (1st test at Oxford); England 62 Denmark 46 (2nd test at Bradford).
SPEEDWAY STAR KNOCK OUT CUP, 1st round, 1st leg: King's Lynn 47 Reading 42.
SUNBRITE LEAGUE: King's Lynn 52 Bradford 38; Swindon 57 Oxford 31.
GOLD CUP: Cradley Heath 52 Coventry 38; Coventry 40 Cradley Heath 50; Oxford 53 Reading 37; Reading 40 Oxford 26, abandoned after 11 heats, regional power failure; Wolverhampton 47 Belle Vue 43; Belle Vue v Cradley Heath, postponed, waterlogged track; Coventry 46 Bradford 44; Cradley Heath v Wolverhampton, postponed, waterlogged track.
NATIONAL LEAGUE: Peterborough 67 Glasgow 29; Milton Keynes 44 Ipswich 49; Poole v Arena Essex, postponed, waterlogged track; Glasgow 13 Berwick 10, abandoned after 4 heats, heavy rain; Wimbledon 62 Long Eaton 34; Ipswich 67 Rye House 28; Middlesbrough 60 Glasgow 36; Hackney v Eastbourne, postponed, waterlogged track; Peterborough v Arena Essex, postponed, waterlogged track; Arena Essex 52 Peterborough 43; Berwick 46 Hackney 47; Edinburgh 40 Hackney 56; Newcastle 39 Wimbledon 57; Peterborough 67 Arena Essex 29; Rye House 45 Stoke 49.
CHALLENGE: Eastbourne 50 Poole 46.
EASTER TROPHY: Exeter 56 Poole 40, *Exeter win 102-90.*

16 READING'S Gold Cup match against Oxford comes to a black finish - it has to be abandoned when a regional electricity sub-station plunges Smallmead into darkness...Andy Hackett (Coventry) is taken to hospital with back injuries after being brought down by out-of-control opponent Gert Handberg (Cradley Heath)...Poole move in with an offer for Carl Blackbird even though he has already made his debut for Edinburgh.

17 *THE Danes want Michael Lee to race in their league - but only if he can get ACU approval to take out a Danish licence.*

18 ENGLAND win the first Sunbrite test against Denmark with the Simon Cross-Marvyn Cox partnership dropping only two points...Dean Barker and Mark Loram make their international debuts as Martin Dugard and Richard Knight pull out with injuries.

19 *SHANE BOWES breaks a bone in his ankle during Glasgow's defeat at Middlesbrough.*

20 NATIONAL LEAGUE Management Committee order Carl Blackbird to stay at Edinburgh - even though he now wants to join Poole...Newcastle sign teenager Paul Smith on loan from Middlesbrough for a month.

21 *BERWICK lose their first home match since August 23, 1986, when Hackney end a run of 53 without defeat. There is a controversial ending to the match as referee Gus McLeod agrees to a re-run of heat 15 after Berwick claims of a faulty green light. He changes his mind after counter protests from Hackney and declares the original result..Former British Champion Andy Grahame goes out of the World Championship after losing a run-off against Peter Carr in the Stoke round...David Bargh has to return home to New Zealand after his father is taken seriously ill...Paul Thorp and John Jorgensen clash - after the end of heat 13 of Coventry's match against Bradford. Thorp rides into the Dane who falls on the slow-down lap and the England international needs a police escort out of Brandon after angry fans threaten his family.*

22 ENGLAND clinch the three-match Sunbrite series against Denmark with victory at Bradford where Simon Cross is again top-scorer. In a selection surprise the Danes team Hans Nielsen and Jan O. Pedersen together to gain experience for the World Pairs Championship...Carl Blackbird fails to turn up at Powderhall for his second match for the Monarchs - instead he is spectating with Poole at Eastbourne.

DAY BY DAY

Diary APR

23 THE touring Russians make a disastrous start to their National League tour going down 78-18 at Exeter. Only Viktor Gaidym beats an opponent as the Soviets arrive two riders short...Michael Lee decides against taking any legal steps against the Speedway Control Board...Bradford's Andy Smith crashes heavily at Wolverhampton and damages his back.

24 *THE National League Management Committee block Poole's bid to sign Carl Blackbird and tell the rider he either has to honour his commitment to Edinburgh or retire...Mildenhall apply to hold a series of open meetings during the summer...Danish Under 21 international Tom Knudsen has after the meeting rides at Poole. He's in action after the Russians, augmented by the arrival of Igor Zverev and Grigori Harchenko, score 37 against the National League champions.*

25 ENGLAND give a first cap to Wolverhampton's Graham Jones. He's named at reserve for the final test against Denmark...Carl Blackbird accepts the National League ruling on his future and agrees to return to Edinburgh...Poole reach agreement with his parent track Swindon to sign Tom Knudsen...In a shock move former World Champion Anders Michanek agrees to make a comeback with German League side Diedenbergen.

...RESULTS...RESULTS...RESULTS...

SPEEDWAY STAR KNOCK OUT CUP, 1st round, 2nd leg: Reading 54 King's Lynn 36, *Reading win 96-83.*
SUNBRITE LEAGUE: Belle Vue 48 Swindon 42; Coventry 43 Oxford 46; Cradley Heath 53 Belle Vue 37; Swindon 57 Wolverhampton 33.
GOLD CUP: Wolverhampton 61 Bradford 29; Cradley Heath 55 Wolverhampton 35; Oxford 46 King's Lynn 44.
INTERNATIONAL TOUR: Exeter 78 Soviet Union 18; Poole 59 Soviet Union 37; Ipswich 66 Soviet Union 30; Peterborough 67 Soviet Union 27; Newcastle 45 Soviet Union 51.
NATIONAL LEAGUE: Milton Keynes 46 Edinburgh 50; Long Eaton 52 Edinburgh 44; Wimbledon 66 Eastbourne 29; Middlesbrough 65 Edinburgh 31; Glasgow 46 Poole 49; Hackney 62 Eastbourne 33; Arena Essex 51 Long Eaton 43; Berwick 61 Poole 35; Stoke 40 Ipswich 56; Eastbourne 49 Long Eaton 47; Edinburgh 31 Ipswich 64; Rye House 47 Wimbledon 49.
SILVER HELMET: Kenny McKinna (Glasgow, holder) lost to Craig Boyce (Poole); Boyce beat David Blackburn (Berwick).
INDIVIDUAL: Coalite Classic (Bradford): Jan O. Pedersen.
CHALLENGE: King's Lynn 58 Michael Lee National League Select 32.

26 MICHAEL LEE is to make a fresh written appeal to the Speedway Control Board in the hope they'll reconsider his case...Glasgow have talks with West German Tommy Dunker after three successive league defeats.

27 SIMON WIGG, the defending champion, is to spearhead Britain's World Long Track challenge. He's one of eight riders named for the competition. The others are Marvyn Cox, Steve Schofield, Mark Loram, Kelvin Tatum and grass trackers Clayton Williams, Martin Hagon and John Bostin. All but teenager Loram are seeded through to the semi-finals on Sunday, July 1. Loram competes in the first qualifier...Acting host James Easter blasts referee Barry Bowles after he excludes two Russians under the two minute time limit during their match at Peterborough. He claims: "This is an international bridge-building exercise and it was very nearly ruined by one man."

28 *IPSWICH maintain their superb start to the new season with a 56-40 win at Stoke and have now won their first three away matches...Stoke's injured Ian M. Stead gives up all hopes of a racing comeback this year...Andrew Silver is named Swindon's Rider of the Month for April.*

29 CHRIS MORTON is hurt when he comes down in a run off at Bradford's Coalite Classic as Jan O. Pedersen goes on to win. Kelvin Tatum blows two engines and has to withdraw...Another week-end casualty is Long's Eaton's Nigel De'ath who breaks his toe at Eastbourne...Russia round off their British tour with a surprise win at Newcastle where Grigori Harchenko roars to a paid 15-point maximum.

30 ENGLAND make it a test match whitewash with their third in a row win over Denmark - the first time the Sunbrite Lions have won all tests in a rubber since 1984. Top scorer for the third match in a row is Simon Cross but debutant Graham Jones fails to finish in two rides...Wimbledon sign Peter Chapman on loan from Peterborough and their London rivals Hackney take Ian Humphreys on loan from Arena Essex.

1 *THE Auto-Cycle Union, worried by the increasing number of overseas riders taking out British licences, are to consider two barriers. ..that riders have to live in England for two years or they can't revert to their own national licence for three years...Berwick write to the Speedway Control Board over the refereeing of their home defeat against Hackney...Tom Knudsen wins three out of four races on his home debut for Poole...Milton Keynes win their first match - with the season seven weeks old...British-based stars Chris Louis, Shane Parker, Gary Hicks and David Norris make progress in the World Under 21 Championship, but Shane Bowes, Mick Powell, Scott Norman and Mark Thorpe miss the cut.*

...RESULTS...RESULTS...RESULTS...

WORLD CHAMPIONSHIP: British semi finals (Cradley Heath): Gary Havelock; (King's Lynn): Jeremy Doncaster.
SUNBRITE INTERNATIONAL: England 60 Denmark 47 (3rd test at Wolverhampton).
SUNBRITE LEAGUE: Coventry 46 Cradley Heath 44; Oxford 49 Bradford 41; Belle Vue 43 King's Lynn 46; Bradford 49 Swindon 41.
NATIONAL LEAGUE: Exeter 60 Glasgow 35; Milton Keynes 49 Newcastle 46; Poole 62 Glasgow 34; Glasgow 45 Stoke 51; Long Eaton 54 Newcastle 42; Wimbledon 55 Berwick 41; Ipswich 48 Berwick 48; Middlesbrough 58 Rye House 37; Edinburgh 51 Rye House 45; Hackney 62 Long Eaton 34; Peterborough 64 Berwick 32; Arena Essex 48 Middlesbrough 48; Berwick 61 Eastbourne 35; Stoke 47 Hackney 49; Eastbourne 42 Middlesbrough 54; Rye House 55 Exeter 40.
SILVER HELMET: Kenny McKinna (Glasgow) beat Craig Boyce (Poole, holder); McKinna beat Nigel Crabtree (Stoke).
INDIVIDUAL: Chris Prime Memorial Trophy (Newcastle): abandoned after five heats.
INTER LEAGUE FOUR TEAM TOURNAMENT: Reading 23 Poole 29 Wimbledon 25 Swindon 19.

2 JIM DORMER asks Wimbledon for a transfer in the wake of Ian Humphreys's arrival...Nigel Alderton (Edinburgh) has an operation on his damaged shoulder.

3 *TALKS between Glasgow and West German Tommy Dunker break down when he refuses to take out a British licence...Berwick shock Ipswich with a 45-45 draw at Foxhall Heath to dent their 100% National League record...Gary Havelock is to take over as Bradford's skipper as manager Allan Ham relieves Neil Evitts, struggling to find form, of the captaincy.*

4 KING'S LYNN win at Belle Vue - for the first time since they joined the British League in 1966...Ipswich are to sign another teenager - South Australian Damon Richardson who was fourth in the 1990 Australian Under 21 Championship...Marvyn Cox hurts his thigh in a crash at his old track Oxford...Only the prompt action of track medical staff save David Blackburn's life after he swallows his tongue in a crash at Peterborough. He is forced to withdraw from the World Championship...Dane Tim Korneliussen misses Hackney's match against Long Eaton with salmonella poisoning...Darren Sumner is given permission to ride for his club Middlesbrough at Eastbourne on Sunday instead of going to Cradley Heath as reserve for the World Championship British semi-final.

5 GLASGOW are to drop out of form Steve Lawson for the first time in his 13-year career with the Scottish club.

6 *INJURY victims Chris Morton and Marvyn Cox miss out in the World Championship British semi-finals. And the meetings claim two: qualifier Martin Dugard cracks a shoulder in a crash at King's Lynn but Martin Goodwin misses out and is detained in a Cradley Heath hospital with a neck injury.*

DAY BY DAY

Diary MAY

7 THE Speedway Control Board, after discussions with the Sports Council, are to launch a pilot alcohol testing at the Homefire British Final and all 16 riders will be given a breath test...Winter signing Nigel Sparshott is axed from the Rye House squad for the H.E.A.T. National League Four Team Championship rounds.

8 THREE-TIME winner of the American Final Sam Ermolenko has asked to be seeded through to the Homefire Overseas Final of the World Championship as he fears he won't be fully recovered to defend his title...The National League Management Committee turn down Glasgow's bid to bring in Tommy Dunker on a German licence...Western Australian Frank Smart signs for Exeter after a second half trial...King's Lynn are fined £250 by the British Speedway Promoters' Association for staging a match against a National League Select without permission...Glasgow are forced to recall dropped Steve Lawson when Martin McKinna cries off with flu - and he grabs 13 points against Exeter.

9 ROB WOFFINDEN breaks a couple of bones in his hand as Stoke go down at Wimbledon...Both Bradford and Swindon write letters of protest to the Speedway Control Board complaining that trainee referees should not be allowed to take control of league matches after an unqualified official took charge of two heats of their week-end match.

...RESULTS...RESULTS...RESULTS...

SUNBRITE LEAGUE: Reading 47 Wolverhampton 43; Wolverhampton 45 Reading 45; Belle Vue 56 Coventry 34; Coventry 45 Swindon 45; Cradley Heath 52 Reading 38; King's Lynn 45 Oxford 45.

GOLD CUP: Bradford 67 Wolverhampton 23.

NATIONAL LEAGUE: Exeter 45 Hackney 51; Ipswich 60 Middlesbrough 36; Poole 56 Milton Keynes 40; Glasgow 61 Exeter 35; Long Eaton 43 Ipswich 53; Wimbledon 55 Stoke 40; Middlesbrough 61 Exeter 34; Ipswich 60 Newcastle 36; Hackney 60 Newcastle 35; Peterborough 57 Wimbledon 39; Arena Essex 38 Eastbourne 58; Berwick 63 Exeter 32; Stoke 55 Milton Keynes 37; Eastbourne 54 Stoke 42; Edinburgh 66 Milton Keynes 30; Newcastle 50 Berwick 46.

SILVER HELMET: Kenny McKinna (Glasgow, holder) beat Steve Regeling (Exeter).

H.E.A.T. NATIONAL LEAGUE TEAM CHAMPIONSHIP: Rye House 19 Arena Essex 16 Hackney 31 Ipswich 30.

INDIVIDUAL: Peter Craven Memorial Trophy (Belle Vue); Billy Hamill; Soft Water Classic (Swindon): Jan O. Pedersen.

PAUL MUCHENE MEMORIAL TROPHY (Oxford): Martin Dugard's Elite 55 Simon Wigg's Wonders 52.

10 MILTON KEYNES are to face a Speedway Control Board charge after a scurrilous article in their match programme about the Michael Lee affair..New Zealander Mark Thorpe is dropped by Newcastle for two meetings as a disciplinary measure after team boss Tom Graham complains about his lack of professionalism.

11 DAMON RICHARDSON, Ipswich's latest Australian capture, is confirmed as arriving in Britain later this month.

12 *TROY PRATT breaks his collar bone and cracks a couple of ribs as Arena Essex, already without skipper Martin Goodwin, go down by 20 points at home to Eastbourne...Bradford's storming win over Wolverhampton means Cradley Heath now have to win the last Gold Cup Northern section match at Belle Vue to stop the Yorkshire side going through to the final...Frenchman Thierry Hilaire (broken ankle) and Kevin Jolly (sprained ankle) have to pull out of Milton Keynes' match at Stoke as the Knights lodge an official protest at the condition of the track. The meeting is delayed for 30 minutes while regrading takes place...Kelly Moran launches a bitter attack on any move to seed Sam Ermolenko in the World Championship claiming: "I was injured last year and no-one suggested I should be seeded."*

13 DAVID BARGH, back in Britain after a spell at home in New Zealand to see his sick father, smashes Ivan Mauger's 15-year-old Newcastle track record....And Jan O. Pedersen lowers Erik Gundersen's five-year-old Swindon fastest time...Jinxed Martin Dugard escapes serious injury when an oxy-acetylene bottle catches fire while he is brazing. He drags it outside and suffers third degree burns but saves further damage even though it is six hours before firemen leave.

14 EASTBOURNE reveal they have agreed terms with both Wolverhampton and the rider himself to sign Danish test star Bo Petersen...The Speedway Control Board agree to an official inquiry into the Berwick-Hackney match...Czechoslovakian Bohumil Brhel is warned he must improve or face the axe at King's Lynn...New Zealander Nathan Murray breaks his wrist in a crash at Reading...Rye House report a 22% increase in crowds this season.

15 PETER RAVN gets Castrol UK to back his forthcoming testimonial meeting in a sponsorship coup...Glasgow make hush-hush attempts to sign teenager Jacob Olsen, son of three-time World Champion Ole.

16 *THE Speedway Control Board act quickly on the complaints about trainee referees taking charge of league meetings and issue an instruction that it should not happen in the future...Stoke's Louis Carr clips half a second off the Long Eaton track record...The Danish Motor Union put the block on any more of their youngsters taking out British licences - at least until after a meeting with National League officials.*

17 MELVYN TAYLOR may have to face a bone graft on his broken arm after it fails to show real improvement...Satellite television channel Screensport announce they will show at least 14 meetings during the summer...1989 World Finalist Tony Olsson goes out of the World Championship in the three-round Swedish Final.

...RESULTS...RESULTS...RESULTS...

WORLD CHAMPIONSHIP: Homefire British Final (Coventry): Kelvin Tatum.

SPEEDWAY STAR KNOCK OUT CUP, preliminary round, 2nd leg: Oxford 44 Coventry 46, *Coventry win 91-89.*

SUNBRITE LEAGUE: Reading 57 Cradley Heath 33; Wolverhampton 53 Bradford 37; Bradford 44 Coventry 46; King's Lynn 48 Cradley Heath 42.

GOLD CUP: Belle Vue 44 Cradley Heath 43.

NATIONAL LEAGUE: Exeter v Peterborough, postponed, rain; Poole 38 Peterborough 28, abandoned, 11 heats; Milton Keynes 42 Wimbledon 53; Long Eaton 44 Stoke 52; Wimbledon 62 Milton Keynes 33; Stoke 54 Eastbourne 42; Eastbourne 66 Exeter 30; Rye House 59 Middlesbrough 37.

H.E.A.T. NATIONAL LEAGUE TEAM CHAMPIONSHIP: Edinburgh 32 Berwick 16 Glasgow 26 Newcastle 22; Glasgow 38 Berwick 23 Newcastle 22 Edinburgh 13 ; Berwick 26 Glasgow 29 Edinburgh 23 Newcastle 18; Ipswich 38 Hackney 26 Rye House 22 Arena Essex 10; Hackney 36 Ipswich 32 Rye House 15 Arena Essex 13; Arena Essex 18 Ipswich 35 Hackney 29 Rye House 13, *Aggregate: Ipswich 135 Hackney 122 Rye House 69 Arena Essex 57.*

CHALLENGE: Middlesbrough 56 Peterborough 39; Peterborough 55 Middlesbrough 40, *Middlesbrough win 96-94.* Swindon A 35 Swindon Select 34 Exeter 15 Poole 12; Newcastle 51 The Kangaroos 45.

18 BRADFORD qualify for their first national cup final when Cradley Heath go down by a single point at Belle Vue in the last match of the Northern Section of the Gold Cup...Teenager Paul Smith is to stay at Newcastle until the end of the season after an extension to his month's loan...The BBC2 show On Line are to investigate the Michael Lee affair.

19 BELLE VUE'S Kelly Moran and Wolverhampton hot-shot Ronnie Correy will be America's representatives in the World Pairs Championship semi-final...Stoke's Nigel Crabtree is taken to hospital with back injuries.

20 *KELVIN TATUM regains the British Championship he last won in 1987 and the National League World Championship challenge disappears as Chris Louis - despite five points from his first two rides - and Les Collins go out in the Homefire British Final. For the second successive round Simon Wigg needs a run-off before clinching his place in the next qualifier...In Denmark Jan O. Pedersen wins the domestic qualifier. Shock is the elimination of Peter Ravn. Gert Handberg is announced as the final qualifier in a post-meeting ceremony...Kai Niemi makes a comeback and helps Finland to second place, a point behind Norway, in the opening round of the Group C World Team Cup in Italy.*

DAY BY DAY

21 CRADLEY HEATH promoter Colin Pratt launches a bitter attack on the Danish Motor Union after they confirm that John Jorgensen has been seeded to the Scandinavian Final of the World Championship – displacing Gert Handberg who finished ahead of him in the Danish Final. Pratt claims: "It's disgusting and I will be asking our man at the FIM to try and have a rule introduced which forces countries to pick riders in the order they finish in a qualifying meeting"...Exeter junior Steve Hone is rushed to hospital with a broken thigh and the meeting is abandoned as the track doctor goes with him.

22 *KELVIN TATUM and Simon Cross are picked as England's representatives in the World Pairs Championship semi-final for the third year in a row ...Arena Essex sign Kevin Teager on loan from Rye House for a month...The Rockets name Linden Warner, out since 1987, as number eight for their forthcoming week-end match against league leaders Ipswich...Peter Glanz hurts his back and Trevor Banks damages his knee as both fall during Milton Keynes's defeat against Stoke...And Long Eaton's Jamie Habbin is taken to hospital with a leg injury at Poole.*

...RESULTS...RESULTS...RESULTS...

SPEEDWAY STAR KNOCK OUT CUP, first round, first leg: Wolverhampton 34 Belle Vue 56.

SUNBRITE LEAGUE: Belle Vue 48 Bradford 42; Oxford 52 Cradley Heath 38; Bradford 57 King's Lynn 33; Coventry 52 Wolverhampton 38; Cradley Heath 41 Oxford 49; Swindon 40 Reading 50.

GOLD CUP: Reading 51 Swindon 39.

NATIONAL LEAGUE: Exeter 65 Long Eaton 31; Milton Keynes 37 Stoke 59; Poole 56 Long Eaton 40; Wimbledon 52 Hackney 41; Glasgow 74 Arena Essex 22; Ipswich 65 Milton Keynes 31; Middlesbrough 53 Arena Essex 43; Edinburgh 56 Newcastle 40; Berwick 71 Arena Essex 25; Rye House 44 Ipswich 52.

SILVER HELMET: Kenny McKinna (holder) beat Rob Tilbury (Arena Essex).

H.E.A.T. NATIONAL LEAGUE TEAM CHAMPIONSHIP: Peterborough 35 Stoke 34 Middlesbrough 15 Long Eaton 12; Stoke 33 Peterborough 25 Middlesbrough 21 Long Eaton 16. Eastbourne 19 Wimbledon 28 Poole 25 Exeter 24; Newcastle 27 Berwick 28 Edinburgh 22 Glasgow 19. *Aggregate: Glasgow 112 Berwick 93 Edinburgh 90 Newcastle 89 .*

TESTIMONIAL: Peter Ravn (Belle Vue): Hans Nielsen.

CHALLENGE: Long Eaton 42 Ex-Leicester 42.

23 WIMBLEDON end Hackney's unbeaten run in a night of injuries at Plough Lane: Peter Chapman (broken ankle), Ray Morton (broken bone in hand), junior David Wolstenholme (broken arm and chipped elbow)...Steve Hone is moved into the Intensive Care Unit at the Royal Devon and Exeter Hospital with breathing problems.

24 SWINDON'S Jimmy Nilsen and Reading's Per Jonsson are Sweden's World Pairs choice - with Henrik Gustafsson as stand-by reserve...Brits Dean Barker and Dean Standing qualify for the semi-finals of the World Under 21 Championship at Elgane, Norway...Injured Steve Hone returns to a general ward...Ipswich's Damon Richardson breaks a couple of ribs in a second half crash.

25 *SHAWN MORAN misses Belle Vue's match against Bradford with an ear complaint...Jan O. Pedersen is ruled out of Cradley Heath's meeting at Oxford with a badly swollen foot after a crash in a West German meeting...Dover Customs officials refuse to let Roman Matousek into the country because he doesn't have a multi-entry visa.*

26 LARS MUNKEDAL fractures his left shin in a crash at Coventry...Jimmy Nilsen dislocates his thumb...Rob Tilbury is forced to pull out of a seventh race during Arena Essex's defeat at Berwick because he is suffering from arm cramp.

27 RYE HOUSE'S young Australian Jamie Fagg breaks his right leg in three places after hitting the fence during heat two of the National League match against Ipswich...Hans Nielsen wins the £1,250 first prize at Peter Ravn's Castrol-backed testimonial.

28 *NEW ZEALAND omit 5-time World Finalist Mitch Shirra from their two nominations. David Bargh (Newcastle) and Gary Allan (Poole) go into the Commonwealth Final as manager Trevor Redmond claims: "Mitch isn't race fit"...Oxford clinch their place in the Gold Cup Final despite a four-point defeat at Reading in the final match...Swedish Champion Peter Karlsson joins Wolverhampton.*

29 LEIGH ADAMS, Troy Butler and Todd Wiltshire will join national champion Glenn Doyle in the Commonwealth Final.

30 BAD news for Peterborough as Mick Poole breaks his thigh at Long Eaton...Australia team up youngsters Todd Wiltshire and Leigh Adams for the World Pairs semi-final...Colin Pratt warns two of his Cradley Heath team Alan Grahame and Gert Handberg that they will have to improve their scoring or he will bring in replacements.

31 *DEFENDING champions Peterborough are out of the H.E.A.T. National League Fours after having to track two local juniors at Middlesbrough. They were without injury victims Mick Poole and Scott Norman (swollen ankle)...In Australia John McNeill reveals he wants to stage the 1991 national championship at the Melbourne Showground...The Speedway Control Board turn down another plea to race again from Michael Lee.*

1 BELLE VUE'S Bobby Ott is suspended for a week by the American Motor Cycle Association after he refuses to return to the States for a series of domestic meetings...Kai Niemi is back on the World Championship trail after being seeded to the Nordic Final...Magistrates adjourn until July 13 an action brought by local residents against Milton Keynes for excessive noise...Bradford re-open negotiations with Henrik Kristensen...Phil Disney, on loan from Bradford, wins his first race for injury-hit Peterborough.

2 JIMMY NILSEN makes a remarkable return for Swindon only a week after dislocating his thumb...Greg Hancock breaks his arm in a run-off to decide the top four placings in the American Final of the World Championship.

3 *STADIUM owner Bob Dugard mixes 300 gallons of perfumed oil to combat a water shortage in Eastbourne - and it rains!..Dave Perks agrees another comeback for Long Eaton...Paul Bentley misses Middlesbrough's Knock out Cup match at Edinburgh - to race in the British Masters Grass Track qualifier at Bodiam, Sussex.*

...RESULTS...RESULTS...RESULTS...

SUNBRITE LEAGUE: Cradley Heath 53 Swindon 37; King's Lynn 42 Bradford 48; Swindon 46 Cradley Heath 44; Wolverhampton 48 Oxford 42; Belle Vue 41 Oxford 49; Bradford 53 Reading 37; Swindon 64 Coventry 26; Reading v Swindon, postponed, water logged track.

GOLD CUP: Reading 47 Oxford 43.

NATIONAL LEAGUE: Peterborough 61 Hackney 35; Hackney v Rye House, postponed, waterlogged track.

NATIONAL LEAGUE KNOCK OUT CUP: 1st round, 1st leg: Ipswich 60 Glasgow 36; Glasgow 54 Ipswich 41, *Ipswich win 101-90;* Peterborough 48 Stoke 48; Stoke 65 Peterborough 31, *Stoke win 113-79;* Arena Essex 41 Newcastle 55; Newcastle 61 Arena Essex 35, *Newcastle win 116-76;* Berwick 3 Poole 3, abandoned after two heats, rain; Edinburgh 51 Middlesbrough 45; Rye House v Milton Keynes, postponed, waterlogged track.

SILVER HELMET: Kenny McKinna (holder) beat David Norris (Ipswich); lost to Dean Standing (Ipswich).

H.E.A.T. NATIONAL LEAGUE TEAM CHAMPIONSHIP: Exeter 38 Poole 30 Wimbledon 16 Eastbourne 12; Poole v Eastbourne v Exeter v Wimbledon, postponed, waterlogged track; Wimbledon 39 Poole 27 Exeter 17 Eastbourne 13; Long Eaton 23 Middlesbrough 30 Stoke 30 Peterborough 13; Middlesbrough 42 Stoke 25 Peterborough 17 Long Eaton 12, *Aggregate: Stoke 122 Middlesbrough 108 Peterborough 90 Long Eaton 63.*

FOUR TEAM TOURNAMENT: Cradley Heath 26, Barum Stars 26 Oxford 22 Zetor Stars 22 (at King's Lynn).

CHALLENGE: Eastbourne 39 Oxford Select 57.

JUNIOR FOUR TEAM TOURNAMENT: Milton Keynes 39 Rye House 26 Long Eaton 18 Arena Essex 12 (at Milton Keynes).

DAY BY DAY

Diary JUN

4 **STEVE PAYNE, banned from racing in Britain in 1985 after being convicted of a drugs offence in Australia, is told the suspension has now been lifted...Greg Hancock has a plate inserted in his broken arm.**

5 *WOLVERHAMPTON call off their next Sunbrite League match against Coventry because Bull-mania hits the town. Everyone wants to watch soccer star Steve Bull in England's opening World Cup match against the Republic of Ireland and promoter Chris Van Straaten fears a poor crowd...Alun Rossiter injures his hand in a fall at Poole.*

...RESULTS...RESULTS...RESULTS...

WORLD CHAMPIONSHIP: Ancit Commonwealth Final (Belle Vue): Kelvin Tatum.
SUNBRITE LEAGUE: Wolverhampton 51 King's Lynn 39; Oxford 44 Belle Vue 45; King's Lynn v Swindon, postponed, waterlogged track.
NATIONAL LEAGUE: Glasgow v Edinburgh, postponed, waterlogged track; Ipswich 63 Peterborough 33; Berwick 54 Long Eaton 42; Edinburgh 71 Long Eaton 25; Newcastle 45 Glasgow 50; Stoke v Glasgow, postponed, waterlogged track.
NATIONAL LEAGUE KNOCK OUT CUP: 2nd round, 1st leg: Exeter 61 Wimbledon 35; 2nd leg: Wimbledon v Exeter, postponed, waterlogged track; Milton Keynes 56 Rye House 39; Rye House 51 Milton Keynes 45, *Aggregate: Milton Keynes 101 Rye House 90.* Hackney v Eastbourne, postponed, waterlogged track; Eastbourne 40 Hackney 56. Middlesbrough 51 Edinburgh 44, *Aggregate: Middlesbrough 96-95;* Poole 56 Berwick 40; .
SILVER HELMET: Dean Standing (holder) beat Craig Hodgson (Peterborough).
INDIVIDUAL: Essex Championship (Arena Essex): Jens Rasmussen.
INTER LEAGUE FOUR TEAM TOURNAMENT: Cradley Heath 30 Wimbledon 23 Poole 22 Ipswich 20; Bradford A v Bradford B v Newcastle v Middlesbrough Select, cancelled, waterlogged track.
PAIRS: East Midlands Pairs (Long Eaton): Paul Fry and Jon Surman; Best Pairs (Peterborough), cancelled, track waterlogged.

6 *SYDNEYSIDER Jack Stevens returns home after failing to break into Newcastle's National League side citing financial problems as the reason for his early departure.*

7 **DAVID BLACKBURN (Berwick), Martin Goodwin (Arena Essex) and Mick Poole (Peterborough) all withdraw from the Speedway Star National League Pairs because of injury...Mitch Shirra is told that he will be partnering David Bargh in the World Pairs semi-final at Wiener Neustadt, Austria.**

8 COVENTRY promoter Charles Ochiltree is in touch with the British Embassy in Prague - to try and sort out Roman Matousek's visa problems...King's Lynn's Mark Loram faces a club v country dilemma - as promoter Bill Barker says he won't release him from the Sunbrite League match against Reading the night before his World Long Track Championship semi-final in Czechoslovakia. Loram can't find a way of getting there by scheduled flights on the Sunday.

9 *JAN O. PEDERSEN is the new Scandinavian Champion but it is Sweden's night with five of their riders filling the top seven places...Ipswich's David Norris is back in the World Under-21 Championship. He will replace Sweden's Henrik Gustafsson. He withdraws after qualifying for the World Championship Inter Continental Final. No rider is allowed to compete in both. It also means Shane Bowes is now semifinal reserve.*

10 **KELVIN TATUM picks up his second World Championship trophy - adding the Commonwealth title to his British crown...Newcastle's David Bargh is flying high. He wins his first two races at the Commonwealth Final to qualify for the next round and is then airlifted by helicopter to Newcastle for the Debmat Diamonds match against Glasgow. The only hitch is the weather which forces the chopper to divert and Bargh doesn't arrive until heat 10 but still takes four rides...Sweden thrash Denmark in the first of three test matches. They win comfortably at Vestervik despite Hans Nielsen's six-rider maximum.**

...RESULTS...RESULTS...RESULTS...

SUNBRITE LEAGUE: Wolverhampton v Coventry, postponed to avoid a clash with the World Cup; Oxford 66 King's Lynn 24; Bradford 69 Wolverhampton 21; Swindon 59 King's Lynn 31; King's Lynn 45 Belle Vue 45.
SPEEDWAY STAR KNOCK OUT CUP, 1st round, 2nd leg: Belle Vue 61 Wolverhampton 29. *Aggregate: Belle Vue 117 Wolverhampton 63.*
SPEEDWAY STAR NATIONAL LEAGUE PAIRS CHAMPIONSHIP (Glasgow): Hackney (Steve Schofield & Andy Galvin).
NATIONAL LEAGUE: Exeter 67 Middlesbrough 29; Milton Keynes 45 Hackney 51; Poole 58 Middlesbrough 38; Long Eaton 48 Wimbledon 48; Ipswich 63 Eastbourne 33; Middlesbrough 60 Wimbledon 35; Peterborough 59 Milton Keynes 37; Arena Essex 47 Milton Keynes 49.
NATIONAL LEAGUE KNOCK OUT CUP: 2nd round, 2nd leg: Hackney 64 Eastbourne 32. *Aggregate: Hackney 120 Eastbourne 72.*
SILVER HELMET: Dean Standing (holder) beat Andy Buck (Eastbourne).
INTER SHIRES TROPHY: Coventry 44 Oxford 45.
SCOTTISH TEAM CHAMPIONSHIP, 1st leg: Edinburgh 41 Glasgow 49 Berwick 18.
MALCOLM HOLLOWAY FAREWELL (Reading): Reading 27 Oxford 27 Sunbrite League Select 25 Swindon 16.

11 POOLE are to stage two home meetings in 24 hours - to accommodate the final leg of their group H.E.A.T. Four Team Championship. They'll meet Ipswich on Tuesday, June 19, and Eastbourne, Exeter and Wimbledon the following evening...Sweden clinch the test series against Denmark with victory at Gothenburg's Ullevi Stadium but there is a poor crowd to see their win.

12 *BRADFORD promoter Eric Boothroyd launches a savage attack against the FIM and advocates Britain splitting from the world governing body and staging its own World Championship. He emphasises it is a personal view and not necessarily shared by the Bradford promotion or the British Speedway Promoters' Association even though he is vice-chairman.*

13 **GREG HANCOCK still hopes to race in the Homefire Overseas Final of the World Championship, despite his broken arm. He plans to ride with a special harness protecting the injury...Wolverhampton's Sam Ermolenko confirms he will make his British comeback at Monmore Green in the Ladbroke Olympique on Monday, June 18....Rye House's Melvyn Taylor has the plaster removed from his broken arm.**

14 ARENA ESSEX, Long Eaton and Exeter approach Peterborough to express an interest in transfer-seeking skipper Ian Barney...The Skoda Panthers opens talks with Milton Keynes to sign the unsettled Mark Lyndon...Bradford fail in a bid to sign Italian Armando Castagna.

15 *BELLE VUE join Reading in the last four of the Speedway Star Knock Out Cup after a double over Wolverhampton for whom debutant Peter Karlsson fails to score in five starts...Simon Wigg breaks his collar bone in a fall at Oxford. Berwick's Rob Grant breaks bones in his foot and Alan Rivett hurts his wrist at Edinburgh.*

16 **POLISH Under 21 Champion Piotr Swist is seriously hurt in the World Pairs semi-final at Wiener Neustadt, Austria. He is given oxygen at the track and taken to hospital with a broken jaw and serious head injuries...England (Kelvin Tatum and Simon Cross) win the semi...Simon Wigg has an emergency operation to insert a plate into his broken collar bone...Arena Essex are denied rider replacement for Troy Pratt because his name isn't in their programme after the absence of Martin Goodwin and Milton Keynes' Trevor Banks cancels out the facility. They lodge a protest.**

17 HACKNEY win the Speedway Star Pairs Championship at Glasgow...Exeter clinch the signing of Ian Barney...Denmark (Hans Nielsen and Jan O. Pedersen) are unbeaten in the World Pairs semi-final in Prague.

DAY BY DAY

Diary JUN

18 IPSWICH, the country's last unbeaten team, lose their record in a 53-43 defeat at Exeter where David Norris and Dean Standing end up in hospital. It ends a run of 13 National League matches without defeat for the East Anglians...Sam Ermolenko scores three points on his track return in the Ladbroke Olympique at Wolverhampton - his first British meeting for 11 months.

19 GREG HANCOCK is forced to withdraw from the World Championship because of a trapped nerve in his broken arm...Shawn Moran crashes heavily and hurts his hip in a Swedish meeting...Wolverhampton decide to release Swedish Champion Peter Karlsson after only two team matches after a BSPA ruling that they must release either Neil Collins or Jan Staechmann to accommodate him...And Belle Vue reveal they have turned down an offer from Wolverhampton for teenager Carl Stonehewer.

...RESULTS...RESULTS...RESULTS...

WORLD CHAMPIONSHIP: Homefire Overseas Final (Coventry): Jeremy Doncaster.
SUNBRITE LEAGUE: Cradley Heath v Coventry, postponed, waterlogged track; Belle Vue 50 Reading 40; Cradley Heath 47 Wolverhampton 43; King's Lynn 45 Coventry 45; Swindon 42 Belle Vue 48.
SPEEDWAY STAR KNOCK OUT CUP, 2nd round, 1st leg: Bradford v Cradley Heath, postponed, rain.
GOLD CUP FINAL, 1st leg: Oxford 47 Bradford 43; 2nd leg: Bradford 62 Oxford 27. *Aggregate: Bradford 106 Oxford 74.*
NATIONAL LEAGUE: Exeter 53 Ipswich 43; Newcastle 51 Rye House 44; Milton Keynes 46 Berwick 49; Poole 59 Ipswich 37; Long Eaton v Berwick, postponed, waterlogged track; Arena Essex v Berwick, postponed, waterlogged track; Ipswich v Stoke, postponed, waterlogged track; Middlesbrough 55 Newcastle 41; Hackney 51 Exeter 45; Peterborough 57 Rye House 39; Berwick 53 Wimbledon 42; Stoke 50 Glasgow 46; Eastbourne 53 Peterborough 43; Edinburgh v Wimbledon, postponed, waterlogged track; Glasgow 57 Middlesbrough 39; Rye House 36 Poole 60.
SILVER HELMET: Dean Standing (holder), unfit to defend at Exeter. Chris Louis (Ipswich) beat Steve Regeling (Exeter); lost to Craig Boyce (Poole). Boyce (holder) beat Jens Rasmussen (Rye House).
H.E.A.T. NATIONAL LEAGUE TEAM CHAMPIONSHIP: Poole 39 Eastbourne 14 Exeter 22 Wimbledon 21. *Aggregate: Poole 121 Wimbledon 104 Exeter 101 Eastbourne 58.*
INDIVIDUAL: Ladbroke Olympique (Wolverhampton): Ronnie Correy.
CHARITY MEETING: Newcastle v Joe Owen Jets, postponed, waterlogged track.

20 THE FIM are to scrap six rider races in the 1991 World Pairs Championship after the accident to Poland's Piotr Swist...A brain scan reveals no blood clot for a relieved Berwick star David Blackburn.

21 MILTON KEYNES are hit by a triple blow. New Zealander Mark Lyndon joins Peterborough and they receive transfer requests from David Clarke and junior Paul Atkins...Darren Standing agrees to rejoin Eastbourne...Mark Crang completes his first match for Middlesbrough since 1985.

22 GARY HAVELOCK and Bryan Larner are held up in Motorway traffic and are late for Bradford's Gold Cup Final first leg at Oxford...Milton Keynes grant David Clarke's transfer. The rider insists he will only move to a Sunbrite League track...Brian Karger is injured in Denmark. He breaks his jaw in four places and fractures his thigh...Ipswich's David Norris withdraws from the World Under 21 Championship with back injuries. Glasgow's Shane Bowes replaces him in the semi-final.

23 SAM ERMOLENKO scores 12 points at Cradley Heath in his first Sunbrite League match since July 10, 1989...David Blackburn makes a shock return for Berwick...Bradford win the Gold Cup - the first national trophy in their league history.

24 JEREMY DONCASTER is the new Homefire Overseas Champion - but World no 2 Simon Wigg goes out.

25 CRADLEY HEATH have to draft in untried novice Gary Frankum at Wolverhampton as Gert Handberg (kidney damage) and Mark Robinson (shoulder) withdraw because of injury...Oxford are stopped from using a guest for the injured Simon Wigg at Reading as the referee rules they haven't presented an updated medical certificate to cover his absence...Poole are to move tracks. A new circuit will be constructed on the current greyhound track to allow Poole Town FC to enlarge their soccer pitch following promotion to a higher grade. The work will be carried out next month.

26 KELVIN TATUM and Simon Cross are officially named as England's challengers for the World Pairs Final...Billy Hamill is called up for America's World Team Cup squad.

27 PETERBOROUGH promoter David Hawkins appeals for financial support from a co-promoter or a consortium...Steve Regeling (Exeter) breaks Hans Nielsen's Wimbledon track record...Kevin Smart (Long Eaton) sets a new fastest-ever four laps at Station Road before the National League match with Eastbourne is abandoned because of rain...Middlesbrough are fined £250 by the National League Management Committee because Paul Bentley raced in the British Masters grass track meeting instead of a cup match at Edinburgh.

28 SWINDON talk to Phil Crump about a Sunbrite League comeback and will seek permission to assess his average so that he can replace the injured Brian Karger...Andy Smith (Bradford) fractures his foot while guesting at King's Lynn.

29 BRADFORD agree terms with Denmark's Henrik Kristensen who agrees to return to Odsal...Milton Keynes ask former British Champion Malcolm Simmons to become full-time track man at Elfield Park.

30 CRADLEY HEATH object to the inclusion of Henrik Kristensen in the Bradford team - claiming the Coalite Dukes' management haven't complied with the rules governing the reintroduction of a rider in the previous season's official 1-7. Their protest is upheld by the meeting referee but the match is called off because of heavy rain...Graham Jones is taken to hospital with back injuries after falling at Swindon...Troy Pratt (Arena Essex) makes a successful return from a broken collar bone.

1 SIMON WIGG reaches the World Long Track Final by finishing third in his semi at Scheeßel, West Germany, despite his broken collar bone...Gary Hicks breaks his leg in the World Under 21 Championship semi-final at Elgane, Norway. Four British-based riders reach the World Final: Chris Louis, Dean Standing, Shane Parker (all Ipswich) and Glasgow's Shane Bowes.

...RESULTS...RESULTS...RESULTS...

SUNBRITE LEAGUE: Reading 51 Oxford 39; Wolverhampton 47 Cradley Heath 43; King's Lynn 46 Reading 44; Coventry 34 Belle Vue 56; Swindon 57 Wolverhampton 33.
SPEEDWAY STAR KNOCK OUT CUP, 2nd round, 1st leg: Cradley Heath v Bradford, postponed, rain.
NATIONAL LEAGUE: Exeter 53 Stoke 43; Milton Keynes 41 Eastbourne 55; Poole 57 Stoke 39; Glasgow 62 Ipswich 33; Long Eaton 10 Eastbourne 14, abandoned after four heats, rain; Middlesbrough 53 Ipswich 43; Hackney 68 Rye House 28; Peterborough 50 Middlesbrough 46; Arena Essex 51 Rye House 45; Stoke 8 Long Eaton 4, abandoned after two heats, track waterlogged; Eastbourne 54 Wimbledon 42; Newcastle 45 Poole 51; Rye House 43 Edinburgh 52.
NATIONAL LEAGUE KNOCK OUT CUP, 2nd round, 2nd leg: Wimbledon 62 Exeter 33. *Aggregate: Wimbledon 97 Exeter 94.* 2nd round, 2nd leg: Berwick v Poole, postponed, waterlogged track.
SILVER HELMET: Craig Boyce (holder) beat Eric Monaghan (Stoke); lost to David Bargh (Newcastle).
INDIVIDUAL: Oxford Junior Championship: Paul Dugard. Future Champions Chase (Edinburgh): Dave Edwards.

DAY BY DAY

Diary JUL

2 **EXETER equal their biggest-ever National League win with a 74-20 victory over Arena Essex who lose stand-in skipper Rob Tilbury with a foot injury after his second ride...Reading return to the top of the Sunbrite League with a win over King's Lynn...America confirm Kelly Moran and Ronnie Correy will continue in the World Pairs Championship after finishing runners-up in the semi-final.**

3 *THE 1993 World Final looks like heading for East Germany - at a 20-year-old, 60,000 capacity stadium in the old Eastern sector...Middlesbrough's Darren Sumner slices more than two seconds off the Milton Keynes' track record in the first meeting since track alterations....At their General Council meeting in Rugby Sunbrite League promoters agree to re-assess Phil Crump's 1986 average to 7.50 to allow Swindon to offer him a contract to replace injured Brian Karger; vote to let Henrik Kristensen rejoin Bradford; deny Wolverhampton a fresh plea to bring Peter Karlsson into their current squad...Belle Vue turn down a new transfer approach from Wolverhampton for teenager Carl Stonehewer.*

4 RYE HOUSE'S Roger Johns is told he has fractured his scaphoid after a fresh hospital examination...Ipswich boss Mike Western calls for a red card system in speedway for any rider who has been excluded three times for unfair or dangerous riding...Bradford's Andy Smith is told he will be out for a month with his broken foot.

5 **WOLVERHAMPTON announce they are to experiment with a 20-heat, ten rider formula in their Speedwaycall Trophy match against Cradley Heath later this month...Cradley Heath sign Belle Vue youngster Scott Smith who has asked for a transfer after failing to make the progress he expected at Kirkmanshulme Lane...Piotr Swist discharges himself from an Austrian Hospital and, against medical advice, is driven to his home in Gorzow to recover from his serious injuries sustained in the World Pairs semi-final...Darren Sumner continues his record breaking form - lowering David Bargh's two-week old Cleveland Park time.**

6 *CHRIS MORTON formally announces he will retire from Sunbrite League racing at the end of the season - and there is speculation he will join the promoting team at his only senior track. He has been riding for the Aces since 1973 and holds the all-time appearances and points-scoring records...There is a fresh protest about Bradford's signing of Henrik Kristensen as it is pointed out they did not have Speedway Control Board permission...Glasgow's Sean Courtney dislocates his shoulder in a fall against Rye House who lose Glen Baxter with a broken hand..*

...RESULTS...RESULTS...RESULTS...

SUNBRITE LEAGUE: Reading 57 King's Lynn 33; Wolverhampton 49 Swindon 41; Belle Vue 47 Cradley Heath 43; Oxford 41 Reading 48; Bradford 58 Belle Vue 32; Cradley Heath 42.5 Reading 47.5; King's Lynn 43 Oxford 47.

SPEEDWAY STAR KNOCK OUT CUP, 1st round, 1st leg: Swindon 56 Coventry 34.

NATIONAL LEAGUE: Exeter 76 Arena Essex 20; Milton Keynes 39 Middlesbrough 57; Long Eaton v Hackney, postponed, waterlogged track; Wimbledon v Middlesbrough, postponed, waterlogged track; Ipswich 50 Exeter 46; Middlesbrough 52 Stoke 44; Glasgow 60 Rye House 36; Hackney 52 Edinburgh 44; Peterborough 50 Exeter 46; Arena Essex 47 Newcastle 49; Berwick 68 Rye House 28; Stoke v Edinburgh, postponed, waterlogged track; Eastbourne 58 Berwick 38; Edinburgh 62 Peterborough 34; Rye House 39 Newcastle 57.

SILVER HELMET: David Bargh (holder) lost to Rob Tilbury (Arena Essex).

PAIRS: Echo Classic Pairs (Poole): Alun Rossiter & Craig Boyce.

7 PAUL DUGARD tells Oxford he is quitting as he has lost interest in speedway...Henrik Kristensen fails to turn up at Bradford.

8 *AUSTRALIA win the opening round of Group B in the World Team Cup - nine points in front of Hungary...Justin Walker breaks his arm in Eastbourne's big win over Berwick...Peterborough's Mick Poole (broken leg) reveals he hopes to race again before the end of the season.*

...RESULTS...RESULTS...RESULTS...

SUNBRITE LEAGUE: Reading 44 Cradley Heath 46; Wolverhampton 49 Coventry 41; Oxford 42 Coventry 48; Belle Vue 51 Wolverhampton 39; Coventry 42 Wolverhampton 47; King's Lynn 43 Belle Vue 47.

SPEEDWAY STAR KNOCK OUT CUP, 1st round, 1st leg: Cradley Heath 45 Bradford 45; 1st round, 2nd leg: Bradford 54 Cradley Heath 36. *Aggregate: Bradford 99 Cradley Heath 81.*

TEAM COASTAL UNDER 21 CHAMPIONSHIP OF GREAT BRITAIN (Wimbledon): Joe Screen.

NATIONAL LEAGUE: Exeter 56 Berwick 40; Newcastle 55 Peterborough 41; Poole 70 Berwick 26; Glasgow 53 Edinburgh 43; Ipswich 53 Wimbledon 43; Long Eaton 41 Eastbourne 55; Hackney 50 Glasgow 46; Arena Essex 44 Glasgow 52; Berwick 68 Newcastle 27; Stoke 61 Exeter 35; Eastbourne 53 Glasgow 42; Edinburgh v Exeter, postponed, waterlogged track; Rye House 51 Milton Keynes 45.

NATIONAL LEAGUE KNOCK OUT CUP, quarter final, 1st leg: Newcastle 35 Ipswich 18, abandoned after nine heats because of heavy rain.

SILVER HELMET: Rob Tilbury (holder) beat Steve Lawson (Glasgow).

PAIRS: Invitation Pairs (Middlesbrough): Steve Wilcock & Mark Thorpe.

INDIVIDUAL: Craig Featherby Memorial Trophy (Milton Keynes), postponed, due to vandalism at track.

9 ***IPSWICH'S Chris Louis agrees to ride in meetings for Polish League club Unia Tarnow next year...Oxford sign John Bostin on loan from Cradley Heath...Consortium members Chris Rance, Geoff Davies and Bernard Newton resign at Milton Keynes...Doctors confirm Glen Baxter (Rye House) will be out for a month with a broken bone in his hand. The Rockets talk to Reading about signing Italian Armando Castagna...James Easter quits as Australian team manager - giving six months' notice.***

10 *MORE troubles at Elfield Park where vandals have caused so much damage to the stadium and equipment that promoter Terry Cheney has to cancel the Craig Featherby Memorial meeting...Workmen rip up the Poole safety fence as soon as their National League match against Berwick is over - to start building the new 400 metre track on the site of the old greyhound circuit...Armando Castagna turns down a contract offer from Rye House - but recommends they sign fellow Roman Fabrizio Vesprini...Australia's five rider World Team Cup squad sign a petition pleading with manager James Easter to withdraw his resignation.*

11 JOE SCREEN beats 1988 champion Mark Loram in a run-off for the British Under 21 title at Wimbledon after both drop a single point...Martin McKinna (Glasgow) breaks a bone in his shoulder on his return to the Radio Clyde Tigers' line-up as a stand-in for the injured Sean Courtney!..Cradley Heath are held 45-45 in their Speedway Star Knock Out Cup tie against Bradford and are now in danger of losing for the first time since they were beaten by Ipswich in the 1985 semi-final!

12 *PHIL CRUMP accepts an offer to return to his old club Swindon - he'll be back on July 26...Newcastle take Ian Stead on loan from Stoke.*

13 **MORE injury woes for Wolverhampton who lose Jan Staechmann with a broken hand after a spectacular tumble at Belle Vue - he'll be out for between a month and six weeks.**

14 *BILLY HAMILL (Cradley Heath) is ordered to take a three-week break because of torn knee ligaments and Cradley bow out of the Knock-out Cup in his absence - their first defeat since 1985...Sean Wilson (Coventry, ankle) and Neil Collins (Wolverhampton, concussion) are taken to hospital after separate spills at Brandon...Martin Goodwin has a second half race at Arena Essex - his first competitive outing in 10 weeks.*

15 AUSTRALIA set a new points-scoring record as they get 55 in their World Team Cup Group B second round meeting to go through to the next group...Promoters Neil Macfarlane (Glasgow) and Gareth Rogers (Eastbourne) are banished from the Arlington centre green by controversial referee Frank Ebdon.

DAY BY DAY

16 EXETER's meeting is abandoned after an horrific crash during a sidecar demonstration. Driver Colin Watkins and passenger Clare Allen are taken to hospital...The Speedway Control Board ban Terry Cheney from holding a promoter's licence for two years but suspend the sentence for two years. He is ordered to pay £600 costs...SCB manager John Eglese flies to Poole and gives approval for their new look track...Long Eaton promoter Roger Jones is to press for a clamp-down on grass track organisers using speedway assets after he learns that Peter Lloyd will be out for two months after dislocating his shoulder in a freak accident while warming up his bike.

17 POOLE streak to their biggest win of the season on their new-look track, hammering Rye House by 50 points...Chris Morton is to be offered a managerial role at Belle Vue when he retires at the end of the season.

18 *SIMON CROSS wins the Speedwaycall Golden Hammer - and Hans Nielsen smashes the Dudley Wood track record...Geoff Powell falls off three times in five races during his testimonial at Glasgow...Stoke's Louis Carr misses the first leg of the Tee Mill Knock Out Cup quarter final at Wimbledon with food poisoning.*

...RESULTS...RESULTS...RESULTS...

SUNBRITE LEAGUE: Swindon 50 Bradford 40; Belle Vue 54 Swindon 36; Bradford 49 Reading 41.
SPEEDWAY STAR KNOCK OUT CUP, 1st round, 2nd leg: Coventry 37 Swindon 53. *Aggregate: Swindon 109 Coventry 71.* Semi final, 1st leg: Reading 53 Belle Vue 36.
NATIONAL LEAGUE: Exeter 63 Eastbourne 32; Poole 73 Rye House 23; Long Eaton 49 Hackney 47; Hackney 61 Berwick 35; Edinburgh 48 Wimbledon 48; Newcastle 55 Exeter 41; Rye House 46 Arena Essex 49.
NATIONAL LEAGUE KNOCK OUT CUP, 2nd round, 2nd leg: Berwick 50 Poole 44, *Aggregate: Poole 100 Berwick 90.* 3rd round, 1st leg: Milton Keynes 40 Middlesbrough 56; 2nd leg: Middlesbrough 69 Milton Keynes 27, *Aggregate: Middlesbrough 125 Milton Keynes 67.* Wimbledon 57 Stoke 37; Stoke 51 Wimbledon 45, *Aggregate: Wimbledon 102 Stoke 88.* 1st leg: Ipswich 61 Newcastle 35.
SILVER HELMET: Rob Tilbury (holder) lost to Jens Rasmussen (Rye House).
CHALLENGE: Oxford 59 Wimbledon 31; Peterborough 43 King's Lynn 35.
ZETOR CUP: King's Lynn 44 Wolverhampton 34.
SPEEDWAYCALL CUP: Wolverhampton 60 Cradley Heath 60.
PAIRS: Star Arena Pairs (Arena Essex): Rob Tilbury and Adrian Stevens.
INDIVIDUAL: Speedwaycall Golden Hammer (Cradley Heath): Simon Cross.
ARTHUR NUTLEY JUNIOR CHAMPIONSHIP (Eastbourne): Scott Humphries.
TESTIMONIAL: Geoff Powell (Glasgow): Glasgow 53 Leggy's Heroes 42.

19 *TRAVEL agency boss James Easter wants to buy out Peterborough promoter David Hawkins.*

20 BRITISH Under 21 Champion Joe Screen breaks his collar bone - while taking part in a Quad demonstration at Belle Vue.

21 SIMON CROSS crashes in the opening heat of the World Pairs Final and is taken to hospital with serious back injuries. Denmark win from Australia and Hungary. West Germany's Gerd Riss is also badly injured in a meeting sadly marred by accidents...Peterborough's new-look safety fence is approved by Speedway Control Board manager John Eglese...Tom Knudsen (Poole) breaks his left thigh at Berwick but the Echo Pirates go through to the quarter final after losing both the Dane and skipper Alun Rossiter (knee ligaments) in their opening rides..Martin Goodwin returns at Arena Essex.

22 *KELVIN MULLARKEY breaks a rib in Rye House's home defeat against Arena Essex. Rob Tilbury lowers the Hoddesdon track record - and then loses the Silver Helmet to Jens Rasmussen*

23 ENGLAND are to press the FIM to allow a reserve in future World Pairs events to cover for injury to one of the two nominated riders...Milton Keynes co-promoter Chris Rance is suspended for two years by the Speedway Control Board following comments on the Michael Lee affair in the official club programme. Terry Cheney is handed a similar sentence but in his case it is suspended for two years...Rye House step up their bid to sign Italian Fabrizio Vesprini.

24 *INJURED England star Simon Cross is ruled out for the rest of the season and his club Cradley Heath call off their match against King's Lynn because of the injury crisis...Sam Ermolenko is recalled to America's World Team Cup squad...Wayne Bridgeford is to have trials at Peterborough.*

25 PETER RAVN puts in a written transfer request to Belle Vue saying he won't ride for the club again...Martin Dugard has agreed to join Polish League side Rybnik in 1991.

26 CRADLEY HEATH approach Belle Vue but are turned down in a bid to take Peter Ravn on loan until the end of the season...Shawn Moran is relegated to reserve in the American World Team Cup quintet...Exeter youngsters Andy Sell and Scott Pegler announce their retirements.

27 *TODD WILTSHIRE withdraws from Australia's World Team Cup squad with a broken collar bone as he takes a tumble at Belle Vue and manager James Easter starts a frantic search for a replacement...Reading lodge a protest over the Aces's use of rider replacement for Peter Ravn in their Speedway Star Knock Out Cup semi-final. The Aces win by seven points on aggregate after the second leg....Peterborough promoter David Hawkins pays a £200 fine so that Australian Craig Hodgson (penalised after he failed to turn up for a meeting at Long Eaton earlier in the season) can race against the Invaders...Aussie Rod Colquhoun damages his shoulder as Poole go down to their third National League defeat of the season...Rob Woffinden asks to miss Stoke's National League against Middlesbrough because he claims to be suffering from a lack of confidence.*

...RESULTS...RESULTS...RESULTS...

SUNBRITE LEAGUE: Reading 56 Bradford 34; Wolverhampton 53 Belle Vue 36; Coventry 44 Bradford 46; Cradley Heath v King's Lynn, postponed, lack of riders.
SPEEDWAY STAR KNOCK OUT CUP, Semifinal, 2nd leg: Belle Vue 57 Reading 33. *Aggregate: Belle Vue 93 Reading 86.*
NATIONAL LEAGUE: Exeter 68 Peterborough 28; Milton Keynes 40 Glasgow 56; Poole 58 Peterborough 38; Long Eaton 45 Poole 51; Wimbledon 54 Glasgow 42; Ipswich 56 Glasgow 40; Middlesbrough 59 Poole 37; Edinburgh 53 Poole 43; Hackney 57 Stoke 39; Peterborough 52 Long Eaton 44; Arena Essex 50 Wimbledon 46; Berwick 49 Ipswich 47; Stoke 45 Middlesbrough 51; Eastbourne 39 Arena Essex 56; Glasgow 60 Berwick 36.
NATIONAL LEAGUE KNOCK OUT CUP, quarter final, 2nd leg: Newcastle 54 Ipswich 41. *Aggregate: Ipswich 102 Newcastle 89.*
INDIVIDUAL: Supporters' Club Trophy (Oxford): Simon Wigg; Barum Trophy (King's Lynn): Jan O. Pedersen; Herts Mercury Classic (Rye House): Steve Schofield.
CHALLENGE: Swindon 35 Belle Vue 12 Oxford 21 Wolverhampton 28.

28 BELLE VUE offer £20,000 for Hackney's Andy Galvin, and a similar sum for Ipswich's Chris Louis...Phil Crump scores six on his comeback for Swindon....Andy Grahame is taken to hospital with a hand injury after coming off at Arena Essex...Coventry are keen on Peter Ravn.

29 **CRADLEY HEATH have a second bid to sign Peter Ravn turned down by Belle Vue. They sound out American Lance King but are knocked back..Long Eaton want to sign Canadian Shawn Venables (Hackney) on a month's loan...Sean Courtney has to pull out after two rides on his comeback for Glasgow after a long spell out with a shoulder injury...Rye House sign Australian Scott Humphries from Wimbledon after he scored four points in the Herts Mercury Classic individual meeting at Hoddesdon.**

DAY BY DAY

Diary AUG

30 *ANDY PHILLIPS is axed by Coventry after a run of low scores...Injured Allan Johansen (out since April 7) is ordered to take at least a two month break after his broken leg is examined by doctors at Basildon Hospital.*

...RESULTS...RESULTS...RESULTS...

SUNBRITE LEAGUE: Reading 44 Belle Vue 45; Wolverhampton 48 Bradford 42; Oxford 44 Swindon 46; Bradford 47 Coventry 41; King's Lynn 45 Wolverhampton 45; Swindon 45 Reading 45.

HEAT NATIONAL LEAGUE TEAM CHAMPIONSHIP : Semi finals: Ipswich 16, Stoke 11, Wimbledon 11, Glasgow 10; Poole 16, Hackney 13, Berwick 10, Middlesbrough 9. FINAL: Stoke 16, Poole 13, Hackney 10, Ipswich 9.

NATIONAL LEAGUE: Exeter 56 Edinburgh 39; Milton Keynes 51 Peterborough 45; Poole 52 Edinburgh 43; Glasgow 63 Milton Keynes 32; Long Eaton 48 Exeter 48; Wimbledon v Newcastle, postponed, non-arrival of doctor; Edinburgh 43 Glasgow 52; Ipswich 48 Hackney 47; Middlesbrough 68 Milton Keynes 28; Hackney 59 Peterborough 37; Arena Essex 47 Ipswich 49; Berwick 51 Glasgow 44; Eastbourne 61 Rye House 34; Stoke 44 Long Eaton 52.

SILVER HELMET: Paul Woods (Eastbourne) beat Scott Humphries (Rye House). Holder Jens Rasmussen unable to defend title.

CHALLENGE: Cradley Heath 35 Belle Vue 29 Oxford 14.

31 PETERBOROUGH are upset that Milton Keynes are allowed to use rider replacement for the missing Trevor Banks after the Skoda Panthers become only the second side this season to lose at Elfield Park.

1 **PATIENT fans at Wimbledon wait for 90 minutes for the meeting to start - before it is called off because of the non-arrival of the track doctor...Milton Keynes sack Trevor Banks following his continued absence from their team even though he has raced in the European Grass Track Championship at the weekend...Belle Vue turn down Coventry's bid to sign Peter Ravn on loan until the end of the season and insist that if they want him they have to sign him outright...Shane Bowes scores his first ever maximum with 15 points against Milton Keynes...Swedish Champion Peter Karlsson can return to the Wolverhampton side after the issue of a new set of green sheet averages.**

2 *STEVE SCHOFIELD is controversially excluded by referee Lew Stripp as the HL1 Kestrels go down at Ipswich in a last race decider...Ove Fundin, five-times World Champion, agrees to turn out at his old track Long Eaton for Keith White's farewell meeting.*

3 WEST GERMAN Tommy Dunker turns down a chance to join Sunbrite League Belle Vue...Milton Keynes want to sign Jon Cooper...Swindon win at Oxford, the last Sunbrite League track to win away from home this season...David Clarke (Milton Keynes) turns down a move to Stoke...Martin Dixon says he would like to stay at Newcastle in 1991.

4 *JENS RASMUSSEN is rushed to hospital with a suspected broken leg after crashing at Eastbourne but x-rays reveal no fracture. He is unable to defend the Silver Helmet Match Race Championship and his place is taken by top scorer Scott Humphries on his debut for the Rockets. He loses the title to challenger Paul Woods...Glasgow District Council decide to honour Radio Clyde Tigers long-serving skipper Steve Lawson.*

5 **EASTBOURNE are considering a shock move back to the Sunbrite League and promoter Gareth Rogers canvasses fans for their views...Peter Carr asks Newcastle to move him from the number one slot because he believes his form is suffering by going out in the first race every meeting...Stoke win the HEAT National League Four Team Final after finishing second in their semi. There is a punch up in the pits after Poole's Gary Allan appears to take Middlesbrough's David Cheshire into the fence although the referee sees nothing wrong with his riding...Mark Courtney fails an alcohol test but is allowed to ride after a fault is discovered in the machine used to carry out the examination...Hans Nielsen wins his fourth Danish National Championship.**

6 NEIL MACFARLANE vows that Glasgow won't visit Berwick for anything other than official fixtures in protest about track conditions at Berrington Lough.

7 **PETERBOROUGH make inquiries about Coventry's Andy Phillips and Stoke's unsettled Rob Woffinden...Magistrates visit Milton Keynes to assess the nuisance factor at Elfield Park...Doctors rule out an immediate comeback for Bradford's Andy Smith who ius still recovering from a broken foot.**

8 *SWINDON'S Ron Byford is to press for a major rule reform to save clubs having to risk riders who aren't fully fit. He wants to see Sunbrite League clubs able to recall their on loan to the National League assets to replace injured riders rather than having to use a raw junior...Belle Vue offer transfer listed Peter Ravn a new chance to stay with the club...Simon Cross returns home to England after an 18-day stay in a German Clinic...Long Eaton promoter Roger Jones blasts his side after they go down by 16 points at home to Middlesbrough and accuses them of being unprofessional and not putting in effort.*

9 TODD WILTSHIRE turns down Ivan Mauger's offer of help at the Inter Continental Final of the World Championship...Coventry boss Charles Ochiltree slams proposals for a two-week summer break...Spencer Timmo (Newcastle) has the pin removed from the thigh he fractured at Mildenhall towards the end of 1989...Milton Keynes make an inquiry about Peterborough junior Paul Blackbird

10 **BELLE VUE are thrown out of the Speedway Star Knock Out Cup as the Speedway Control Board uphold Reading's appeal against their use of rider replacement for Peter Ravn on the basis that the Dane's name was not in the programme. After rider replacement points are deducted from the second leg score Reading go through to the final 91-87 on aggregate...Magistrates at Stoney Stratford dismiss a case brought by the local Environmental Health Officer claiming that speedway racing at Milton Keynes is a nuisance and award costs to promoter Terry Cheney...Andy Phillips turns down a move to National League Stoke...Poole sign Peter Schroeck from Wimbledon.**

...RESULTS...RESULTS...RESULTS...

SUNBRITE LEAGUE: Reading 49 Coventry 41; Wolverhampton 49 King's Lynn 41; Oxford 40 Wolverhampton 50; Bradford 58 Swindon 32; Coventry 43 Belle Vue 45.

NATIONAL LEAGUE: Exeter 62 Wimbledon 34; Newcastle 54 Edinburgh 42; Milton Keynes 53 Arena Essex 42; Glasgow 66 Eastbourne 30; Long Eaton 40 Middlesbrough 56; Wimbledon 61 Exeter 35; Middlesbrough 61 Eastbourne 35; Edinburgh 60 Eastbourne 36; Peterborough 51 Newcastle 45; Arena Essex 57 Edinburgh 36; Stoke 66 Peterborough 30; Eastbourne 62 Edinburgh 34; Newcastle 21 Hackney 21, abandoned after seven heats, rain; Rye House 56 Long Eaton 39.

NATIONAL LEAGUE KNOCK OUT CUP, quarter final, 1st leg: Hackney 47 Poole 48.

SILVER HELMET: Paul Woods (holder) lost to Steve Lawson (Glasgow).

INDIVIDUAL: Elfords Blue Riband (Poole): Chris Louis. Star of Anglia (Ipswich): Chris Louis. Stars of Tomorrow (Berwick): Mike McLuskey.

CHALLENGE: Belle Vue 59 Stoke 29; Swindon 44 Poole 40

11 *COVENTRY lose their fourth successive home meeting, an all-time record...Peterborough try to persuade former Danish international Preben Eriksen to make a comeback...Long Eaton ask Milton Keynes about their unsettled grass track star and former skipper Trevor Banks...Dane Freddy Schøtt is taken to hospital with damaged knee ligaments after crashing during Edinburgh's match at Arena Essex.*

12 OVERSEAS Champion Jeremy Doncaster goes out of the World Championship in the Inter Continental Final but three English riders, Kelvin Tatum, Martin Dugard and Richard Knight make it to the World Final. There will be big night debuts for Dugard, Knight, American Rick Miller and Australia's Todd Wiltshire. Swedish sensation Henrik Gustafsson will be reserve at Odsal.

Diary AUG

DAY BY DAY

13 *UNLUCKY American Gary Hicks is in the wars again. The King's Lynn rider breaks his collar bone at Reading...Wolverhampton include Graham Jones in their side for his first meeting since damaging his back at the end of June and he scores a couple of points in the Dianetics' Wolves Dudley-Wolves Trophy win over Cradley Heath...Hospital X-rays reveal that Nigel Flatman has a fractured bone in his foot after crashing at Stoke on Saturday night.*

14 RICHARD HELLSÉN (Long Eaton) breaks his collar bone in his second race at Milton Keynes...Retired schoolteacher Derek Howse is set to become a co-promoter at Hackney...Ex-World Final reserve Preben Eriksen turns down the chance of a late season comeback with Peterborough...Berwick pledge they will compete in the second leg of the Scottish Team Championship at Glasgow, despite the Radio Clyde Tigers' insistence they won't race at Berrington Lough.

15 AN EXTRA 5,000 World Final tickets go on sale...The draw for the Odsal meeting is announced with favourites Hans Nielsen and Jan O. Pedersen meeting in the fifth heat...Belle Vue lodge an official appeal against the Speedway Control Board decision that puts Reading into the final of the Speedway Star Knock Out Cup...Cradley Heath and Belle Vue agree terms for the loan of Peter Ravn to the Heathens – but the rider has to say yes to the move.

...RESULTS...RESULTS...RESULTS...

SUNBRITE LEAGUE: Reading 57 King's Lynn 30; Belle Vue 51 Coventry 39; Oxford 45 King's Lynn 45; Cradley Heath 38 Belle Vue 52; Bradford 45 Wolverhampton 45; Coventry 43 Reading 47; King's Lynn 44 Swindon 46.

NATIONAL LEAGUE: Exeter 55 Newcastle 41; Milton Keynes 59 Long Eaton 37; Poole 63 Newcastle 33; Long Eaton 40 Glasgow 56; Wimbledon 47 Rye House 49; Ipswich 70 Arena Essex 25; Middlesbrough 70 Peterborough 26; Hackney 53 Ipswich 42; Arena Essex 53 Rye House 43; Berwick 73 Peterborough 23; Stoke 41 Newcastle 55; Eastbourne v Milton Keynes, postponed, rain; Edinburgh 5 Exeter 0, abandoned after one heat, rain; Glasgow 64 Peterborough 32.

SILVER HELMET: Steve Lawson (holder) lost to Nigel De'ath (Long Eaton).

INDIVIDUAL: Golden Greats (Swindon), postponed, rain.

PAIRS: Diamond Reunion Pairs (Newcastle), postponed, waterlogged track.

DUDLEY-WOLVES TROPHY, 1st leg: Wolverhampton 50 Cradley Heath 39; 2nd leg: Cradley Heath 52 Wolverhampton 37. *Aggregate: Cradley Heath 91 Wolverhampton 87.*

HERTS-ESSEX TROPHY, 1st leg: Rye House v Arena Essex, postponed, waterlogged track.

16 TOMMY KNUDSEN is to make a track return after being out for more than a year with a back injury...World Finalist Jan O. Pedersen breaks his arm in a freak accident when he stumbles while watching kart racing...Mervyn Stewkesbury tells his fellow National League promoters that he won't be standing for reelection as chairman...Long Eaton are having talks with Rye House's out of favour Nigel Sparshott following impressive second half performances at Station Road...Stoke renew their bid to sign Milton Keynes' unsettled David Clarke and will offer Rob Woffinden in an exchange deal...Mark Crang (Middlesbrough) agrees to join Peterborough on a month's loan...Newcastle turn down Peter Carr's plea to be moved from the number one slot in their line-up.

17 BELLE VUE inquire about Milton Keynes' David Clarke...Kelvin Tatum breaks a bone in his foot when he comes off at Belle Vue.

18 *NEIL EVITTS and Wayne Carter are taken to hospital after separate crashes during the Bradford-Wolverhampton clash. Evitts has two fractured ribs and Carter back and leg injuries*

19 SIMON WIGG retains his World Long Track crown at Herxheim, West Germany, but World Finalist Gerd Riss is taken to hospital in a coma after a high-speed crash.

20 COVENTRY are refused permission to reintroduce the injured Tommy Knudsen to their side on an assessed six point average. The Sunbrite League Management Committee insist he returns on his 1988 10.1 figure...David Mullett breaks his left ankle and fractures a finger in top of the table Reading's Sunbrite League match against challengers Wolverhampton...Victory for the Goodyear Wolves means they are certain of the British League Division Two title...Glasgow are ordered to fulfil their Berwick commitment in the Scottish Team Championship.

...RESULTS...RESULTS...RESULTS...

SUNBRITE LEAGUE: Reading 45 Wolverhampton 45; Cradley Heath 53 King's Lynn 37; Swindon 46 Bradford 44.

NATIONAL LEAGUE: Ipswich 48 Stoke 48; Arena Essex 16 Poole 32, abandoned after eight heats, thunderstorm; Berwick 56 Stoke 40; Eastbourne 49 Newcastle 46; Edinburgh 67 Arena Essex 29; Rye House 52 Berwick 43.

NATIONAL LEAGUE KNOCK OUT CUP, quarter final, 2nd leg: Poole 62 Hackney 33. *Aggregate: Poole 110 Hackney 80.* Semi final, 1st leg: Wimbledon 36 Middlesbrough 59; 2nd leg: Middlesbrough 69 Wimbledon 27. *Aggregate: Middlesbrough 128 Wimbledon 63.*

INDIVIDUAL: Southern Riders' Championship (Hackney): Steve Schofield; Frank Barney Memorial Trophy (Peterborough): Wayne Bridgeford.

SCOTTISH TEAM CHAMPIONSHIP, 2nd leg: Glasgow 47 Edinburgh 37 Berwick 24.

CHALLENGE: Oxford 49.5 Sunbrite Select 40.5; Coventry 56 Belle Vue 34; White Knights 39 Black Knights 56 (at Milton Keynes)

MARTIN HEWLETT MEMORIAL TROPHY: Exeter 32 Swindon 24 Express and Echo Rangers 22.

KEITH WHITE FAREWELL (Long Eaton): Long Eaton 26 Stoke 25 Leicester 24 National League Select 20.

21 *AMERICAN Bruce Penhall turns down a plea from injury-hit Cradley Heath to make a full time track return...Jan O. Pedersen officially withdraws from the World Final...Peterborough's Mick Poole has a successful practice at the East of England Showground after recovering from a broken leg.*

22 FORMER World Finalist Tommy Knudsen confirms he will make a track comeback less than two years after specialists told him he would never race again. New scans reveal his injured back is as strong as it ever was...Stoke and Milton Keynes finally agree a rider exchange which takes David Clarke to Loomer Road and sees Rob Woffinden move in the opposite direction.

23 PETERBOROUGH are considering an approach from Belle Vue for their Australian Craig Hodgson...Brian Karger plans a racing comeback in Denmark at the weekend.

24 *PETER RAVN settles his differences with Belle Vue...Coventry lodge an appeal with the Speedway Control Board in their fight to reintroduce Tommy Knudsen to their squad...Shawn Moran is banned for two weeks by the American Motorcycle Association after refusing to return home for a compulsory rider return. It will start two days after the World Final and end on the eve of the World Team Cup Final so he is available for both.*

25 TONY OLSSON fractures his thigh and arm in a crash while guesting for Cradley Heath to leave Reading without two of their regular team members...Tommy Knudsen is back in action, in a challenge match against Belle Vue and scores a paid three points...America qualify for the World Team Cup Final...Long Eaton put in a firm approach for Peterborough second halfer Paul Blackbird.

26 *CONTINENTAL Champion Gerd Riss is officially withdrawn from the World Final. He is still in hospital with head injuries sustained in the World Long Track Final...Milton Keynes sign Jonathan Cooper from the old Mildenhall management...Simon Green misses Newcastle's match at Eastbourne – after coming off when his clutch lever snapped on the pre-meeting parade! He was taken to hospital with a back injury*

DAY BY DAY

Diary SEP

27 SIMON WIGG is recalled to the England set-up and is given a place in the Sunbrite Lions' World Team Cup squad after being ruled out of all other internationals this season. The rest of the squad is Kelvin Tatum, Marvyn Cox and Jeremy Doncaster with the reserve slot to be filled after the World Final...Andy Phillips tells Coventry he is retiring, at least until the end of the season...Reading strengthen their grip on the Sunbrite League title with a home and away Bank Holiday double over Oxford...Exeter's Peter Jeffery suffers a fractured leg...Carl Stonehewer (Wolverhampton) suffers three cracked vertebrae when he falls while riding against his parent club Belle Vue.

28 *BERWICK announce the year's richest meeting, the £3,500 Bonanza with a £1,000 first prize...Long Eaton are keen to sign Middlesbrough tail-ender Duncan Chapman on a month's loan...The World Final organisers spring a surprise by naming Bradford pair Gary Havelock and Paul Thorpe as supplementary reserves...Craig Hodgson tells Peterborough he is returning home to Australia at the weekend.*

29 COVENTRY appeal to the Speedway Control Board against a Management Committee refusal to re-assess Tommy Knudsen's average....Duncan Chapman makes his debut for Long Eaton – while Milton Keynes new boy Jon Cooper top scores and qualifies for a crack at Nigel De'ath's Silver Helmet.

30 ERIK GUNDERSEN tips Per Jonsson as an outsider to take the World crown at Odsal...Belle Vue promoter John Perrin tells BBC North TV viewers that he will quit at the end of the season...Andy Hines tells Milton Keynes he is ready to retire...Poole qualify for the second successive Knock Out Cup Final, beating Ipswich at Foxhall Heath to complete a semi final double.

31 *MILTON KEYNES sign Long Eaton youngster Michael Howe following an impressive second half display at Elfield Park...Berwick promoter Terry Lyndon has given up most of his footballing interests to concentrate on speedway...Exeter sign Deon Prinsloo on a month's loan from Wimbledon.*

1 PER JONSSON wins the 1990 World Final, beating Shawn Moran in a run-off with Australia's debutant Todd Wiltshire in third place. Racing is enthusiastically greeted by fans, officials and riders alike...Peterborough persuade Craig Hodgson to see out the season...King's Lynn want to talk to Swindon's Brian Karger with a view to him joining them on loan until the end of the season

2 HACKNEY skipper Andy Galvin is taken to hospital with his thigh fractured in three places after a crash involving Rye House's young Australian Scott Humphries...Glasgow's Kenny McKinna (broken left wrist) is another casualty...Eastbourne's Darren Grayling asks for a transfer and says he won't ride for the club again after being dropped for the National League match against Ipswich...AMA lift Shawn Moran's two-week ban.

...RESULTS...RESULTS...RESULTS...

WORLD FINAL (Bradford): Per Jonsson.
SUNBRITE LEAGUE: Cradley Heath 43 Coventry 47; King's Lynn 35 Swindon 55; Oxford 43 Reading 46; Coventry 45 Cradley Heath 45; Swindon 59 King's Lynn 31; Reading 47 Oxford 43; Wolverhampton 52 Belle Vue 37; Belle Vue 55 King's Lynn 35.
NATIONAL LEAGUE: Exeter 44 Poole 52; Newcastle 55 Arena Essex 41; Stoke 58 Berwick 38; Milton Keynes 48 Rye House 47; Long Eaton 56 Milton Keynes 40; Wimbledon v Ipswich, postponed, waterlogged track; Arena Essex 50 Stoke 46; Middlesbrough 62 Long Eaton 34; Glasgow 74 Long Eaton 22; Hackney 47 Poole 49; Peterborough 46 Stoke 49; Eastbourne 46 Ipswich 49; Newcastle 48 Middlesbrough 47; Rye House 50 Hackney 46; Stoke 54 Arena Essex 40.
NATIONAL LEAGUE KNOCK OUT CUP, semi final, 1st leg: Poole 60 Ipswich 36; 2nd leg: Ipswich 47 Poole 49, *Aggregate: Poole 109 Ipswich 83.*
SILVER HELMET: Nigel De'ath (Long Eaton, holder) beat Jon Cooper (Milton Keynes), lost to Darren Sumner (Middlesbrough). Sumner (holder) lost to David Bargh (Newcastle).
SCOTTISH CUP, 1st leg: Edinburgh 50 Glasgow 46.
INDIVIDUAL: Hillside Trophy (Peterborough): Steve Regeling.

3 ITALIAN Armando Castagna makes his 1990 debut for Reading after agreeing to rejoin them until the end of the season...The FIM are considering scrapping the World Under 21 Championship after the 1991 season...Gary Havelock is called up to fill the reserve berth in England's World Team Cup Final squad.

4 BARRY BRIGGS announces plans for a new production speedway machine, a 600 cc Yamaha with streamlining. He will unveil it at his re-arranged Golden Greats meeting at Swindon and has already had talks with the FIM about an official World Championship...Rye House have agreed to a transfer request from junior Colin Thorpe.

5 *INDOOR speedway is on it's way back to London. Dave Pavitt (Hackney), Gareth Rogers (Eastbourne) and John Louis (Ipswich) are to promote two meetings at the London Arena on Sunday, January 6, 1991 and have a three-year contract at the Docklands venue. It is the first Indoor meeting in England since the 1982 show at Birmingham's National Exhibition Centre and the first in London since the 1981 Wembley event.*

...RESULTS...RESULTS...RESULTS...

SUNBRITE LEAGUE: Wolverhampton 48 Reading 42; Oxford 51 Bradford 39; Bradford v Cradley Heath, postponed, waterlogged track; Belle Vue 55 Cradley Heath 35; Bradford 59 Belle Vue 31; Cradley Heath 53 Wolverhampton 37; Swindon 43 Oxford 47; King's Lynn v Reading, postponed because of injuries.
NATIONAL LEAGUE: Exeter 64 Milton Keynes 32; Milton Keynes 40 Exeter 56; Poole 63 Hackney 32; Wimbledon 50 Edinburgh 46; Ipswich 56 Edinburgh 40; Hackney 44 Arena Essex 50; Peterborough 53 Edinburgh 43; Berwick 68 Milton Keynes 27; Stoke 51 Wimbledon 45 Eastbourne v Hackney, postponed, injuries to Hackney; Edinburgh 46.5 Berwick 49.5; Glasgow 44 Wimbledon 52; Newcastle 63 Milton Keynes 33; Rye House 62 Eastbourne 33.
SILVER HELMET: David Bargh (Newcastle, holder) beat Peter Glanz (Milton Keynes).
INDIVIDUAL: British League Division Two Championship: Richard Musson.
CHALLENGE: Long Eaton 52 Exeter 44; Middlesbrough 65 Newcastle 54; Arena Essex 28 Rye House 40 Ipswich 14 Peterborough 14.

6 *OXFORD are asked to try and bring one of their young fans out of a coma. Dean Goldsmith, 10, was hurt in a cycling accident and co-promoter Peter York visits his bedside and plays a series of tapes of the youngster's speedway idols...Edinburgh lose skipper Brett Saunders (six broken ribs and internal injuries) and the badly bruised Freddy Schøtt after spills at Ipswich.*

7 POOLE sign schoolboy Justin Elkins...Newcastle's Gordon Whitaker will miss the rest of the season after pulling his shoulder out of joint pulling up a floorboard at home...Hackney, already without Andy Galvin and Gary Tagg (shoulder injury) finish the night with two more riders on the sidelines as Steve Schofield and Tim Korneliussen both suffer back injuries...Mick Poole wins two races and scores 12 (paid 13) on his return for Peterborough.

8 DEPOSED World Champion Hans Nielsen smashes the Swindon track record...Frenchman Thierry Hilaire falls off NINE times at Berwick and finishes only once after coming to the tapes on 11 separate occasions including re-runs...Eastbourne call off their National League match against Hackney because the HL1 Kestrels are without four first teamers through injury...And King's Lynn call off their clash with Reading because they cannot raise a team.

9 *CHRIS LOUIS wins the World Under 21 Championship at Lvov, Soviet Union...Former speedway rider Dick Partridge agrees to take over the motor sport rights at Mildenhall Stadium...Teenager Richard Musson, 17, wins the British League Division Two Riders' Championship despite an exclusion in his first race...There is a long delay at Glasgow when Wimbledon protest about a tyre being used by home skipper Steve Lawson...David Bargh agrees to return to Newcastle in 1991 but Martin Dixon dislocates a shoulder that will put him out for the rest of the year.*

Diary
SEP

DAY BY DAY

10 *DENMARK spring two major shocks in their World Team Cup Final selection by recalling Tommy Knudsen and Brian Karger even though both have been out of racing with serious injuries...New World Champion Per Jonsson is given a hero's welcome at Smallmead - dropping in by helicopter onto the centre green.*

11 AMERICA decide to axe World Finalist Ronnie Correy from their World Team Cup plans and draft in 20-year-old Billy Hamill...Reserves Gary Chessell and Rod Colquhoun grab a paid 26 points between them – as Poole thrash Eastbourne.

12 **CRADLEY HEATH and King's Lynn are given permission by Swindon to talk with Brian Karger, now back in action after breaking his leg at the end of June. The Team Coastal Robins cannot reintroduce him to their line-up because of the averages...Belle Vue lose their appeal against being thrown out of the Speedway Star Knock Out Cup Final...Aces' promoter John Perrin calls off this Friday's individual meeting claiming a lack of co-operation from riders and promoters...Another injury blow for Cradley Heath as Gert Handberg is taken to hospital for x-rays on a foot injury.**

...RESULTS...RESULTS...RESULTS...

NATIONAL LEAGUE RIDERS' CHAMPIONSHIP (Coventry): Andy Grahame.
SUNBRITE LEAGUE: Reading 59 Swindon 31; Wolverhampton 46 Coventry 44; Cradley Heath 58 Bradford 32; Oxford 50 Belle Vue 40.
SPEEDWAY STAR KNOCK OUT CUP, semi final, 1st leg: Bradford 51 Swindon 39.
NATIONAL LEAGUE: Exeter 64 Rye House 32; Poole 71 Eastbourne 25; Long Eaton 49 Rye House 47; Wimbledon 61 Arena Essex 35; Arena Essex 54 Hackney 42; Ipswich 55 Long Eaton 41; Middlesbrough 71 Berwick 25; Hackney 51 Wimbledon 45; Peterborough 29 Poole 67; Eastbourne 35 Poole 61; Edinburgh 45 Middlesbrough 51; Rye House 46 Glasgow 49; Stoke 61 Long Eaton 35.
INDIVIDUAL: Brett Alderton Memorial Trophy (Milton Keynes): Paul Blackbird. Golden Greats (Swindon): Fabulous Fifties: Roy Trigg. Swinging Sixties: Terry Betts.
SCOTTISH TEAM CHAMPIONSHIP, 3rd leg: Berwick 41 Glasgow 44 Edinburgh 23. *Aggregate: Glasgow 140 Edinburgh 101 Berwick 83.*
CHALLENGE: King's Lynn 29 Belle Vue 11 British League Select 19 Swindon 37.

13 *KING'S LYNN complete a deal to sign World Finalist Henrik Gustafsson but he will not make his debut until October 6...The Speedway Control Board confirm that one of this year's World Finalists failed a drugs test at the Overseas Final but refuse to name him...Exeter are to stage an end-of-season meeting for grass track riders...Newly-crowned World Under 21 Champion Chris Louis parades his trophy in front of a rapturous Ipswich crowd...Berwick's David Walsh is forced out of the match at Middlesbrough with back injuries after failing to finish a ride following a crash with team-mate Andy Campbell in the third heat.*

14 STEVE LAWSON is taken ill during Glasgow's Scottish Team Championship at Berwick. He has been suffering from flu and is violently sick, forcing him to withdraw after two rides...Peter Chapman misses Wimbledon's match at Hackney after a domestic accident. Jim Dormer, who hasn't ridden for two months, stands in...Travel firm Tee Mill go into bankruptcy...Martin Goodwin tells Arena he wants to move in 1991.

15 **ANDY GRAHAME is the new National League Riders' Champion. He drops his only point to runner-up Chris Louis in his opening ride...Graham Jones pulls out of a meeting at King's Lynn after his major sponsor Jim Davies is killed in a road crash.**

16 AMERICA are the shock World Team Cup winners on a slick Pardubice track...Andy Buck quits Eastbourne because of a post-viral infection...Rye House skipper Jens Rasmussen misses his first match of the season after crashing in the National League Riders' Championship the previous night. His place is taken by Kevin Teager who was called up so late he missed his opening ride.

17 *AUSTRALIAN promoter Trevor Harding and Tom Shirra, father of New Zealand international Mitch Shirra, are keen to revive speedway in Birmingham and have been looking at likely venues in the Second City.*

18 **THE General Council of the Sunbrite League veto a Management Committee decision to switch the 1990 British League Riders' Championship from Belle Vue to Bradford. But the start-time is now switched from evening to afternoon...The General Council decide they cannot overturn the Speedway Control Board decision on the Belle Vue cup drama.**

19 LONG EATON claim they have signed Paul Blackbird for 1991 – but it is disputed by Peterborough who still hold his contract.

20 *POOLE promoter Mervyn Stewkesbury denies the Echo Pirates are planning to apply for 1991 Sunbrite League membership after winning the National League Knock Out Cup for the first time.*

21 COASTAL WINDOWS threaten to withdraw from speedway as a protest over Bradford's use of Billy Hamill as a guest for Neil Evitts in their Speedway Star Knock Out Cup semi final win over Swindon. The American scored 15 points from six rides including four race wins.

...RESULTS...RESULTS...RESULTS...

SUNBRITE LEAGUE: Wolverhampton 44 Oxford 46; Belle Vue 45 Wolverhampton 45; Oxford 48 Cradley Heath 42; Cradley Heath 39 Oxford 51; Coventry 46 Bradford 44; King's Lynn 50 Coventry 40.
SPEEDWAY STAR KNOCK OUT CUP, semi final, 2nd leg: Swindon 50 Bradford 40. *Aggregate: Bradford 91 Swindon 89.*
NATIONAL LEAGUE: Newcastle 51 Eastbourne 45; Glasgow 51.5 Newcastle 44.5; Long Eaton 46 Berwick 50; Wimbledon 49 Ipswich 47; Arena Essex 58 Berwick 38; Stoke 62 Edinburgh 34; Eastbourne v Hackney, postponed, waterlogged track; Edinburgh 66 Exeter 29; Newcastle 47 Ipswich 49; Milton Keynes 44 Poole 52.
SILVER HELMET: David Bargh (Newcastle, holder) beat Gordon Kennett (Eastbourne). Bargh beat Steve Lawson (Glasgow). Bargh beat Chris Louis (Ipswich).
NATIONAL LEAGUE KNOCK OUT CUP FINAL, 1st leg: Poole 62 Middlesbrough 34; 2nd leg: Middlesbrough 51 Poole 45. *Aggregate: Poole 107 Middlesbrough 85.*
INDIVIDUAL: Craig Featherby Memorial Trophy (Milton Keynes): Steve Regeling.
INTER LEAGUE CHALLENGE: Reading 51 Ipswich 39. Ipswich 42 Reading 53.
CHALLENGE: Exeter 54 National League Select 35; Peterborough 29 Exeter 28 Stoke 28 National League Select 11; Berwick 22 Newcastle 20, abandoned after seven heats, generator fault.
HERTS-ESSEX CUP, 2nd leg: Rye House 49 Arena Essex 47. *Aggregate: Arena Essex 100 Rye House 92.*
AUTUMN TROPHY, 1st leg: Hackney 47 Arena Essex 29 Rye House 32.

22 **BERWICK'S Autumn Trophy match against Newcastle is abandoned after seven heats when the stadium generator refuses to start. Referee Will Hunter calls off the meeting after an attempt was made to carry on by driving cars, with headlights ablaze, onto the centre green..Stoke clinch the final place in the end of season National Series by beating Edinburgh...Sweden, led by World Champion Per Jonsson, are to make an official winter tour of Australia...Coventry end a run of six successive home matches without a win by defeating Bradford in a last heat decider.**

23 MICHAEL LEE has agreed to act as technical advisor to National League Hackney until the end of the season...World Under 21 Champion Chris Louis lowers the Newcastle track record...Berwick announce that fans holding tickets for the abandoned match against Newcastle will be allowed free admittance to either of their next two meetings at Berrington Lough...Gary Hicks misses his first ride at King's Lynn after being caught in a traffic jam en route to East Anglia...Aussie Mick Powell gives himself the best 21st birthday present – by scoring his first paid maximum of his career against Exeter only hours before officially getting the key of the door.

DAY BY DAY

Diary OCT

24 *WONDER Boy Ben Howe, the most sought after schoolboy in the country, says he will sign for either Hackney or Ipswich when he is 16 later in the year...The AMA reintroduce a 14-day ban on Shawn Moran following his refusal to return home for meetings and Belle Vue's hopes of overhauling Reading at the top of the Sunbrite League disappear with a 61-29 defeat at Smallmead.*

25 POOLE clinch their second successive National League title with a home win over Wimbledon...Peterborough promoter David Hawkins hits out at rumours that the track is about to close...Swindon promoter Ron Byford is to ask his fellow promoters to ignore bonus points when calculating team averages in 1991.

26 **SIMON WIGG is out of racing after x-rays reveal he crushed the fourth vertebra in a weekend crash in Italy. Doctors tell him it is a miracle he hasn't been paralysed as he has been walking about for three days with the injury...The Speedway Control Board adjourn Coventry's appeal against the refusal to reassess Tommy Knudsen's average...Hackney's young Dane Tim Korneliussen is taken to hospital after breaking his leg in a heat three crash at Glasgow.**

27 DAVID NORRIS breaks his collar bone when he takes a tumble as Ipswich lose at home to newly-crowned champs Poole...Michael Lee is with Hackney in his new role as technical advisor as they go down at Middlesbrough...Marvyn Cox wants to stay at Bradford next season after enjoying his loan term from Oxford...Poole will be given a Civic reception in recognition of their cup and league double...Greg Hancock comes through a private practice session after being out since June with a broken arm and is named in Cradley Heath's squad for the weekend's matches.

28 *COVENTRY axe Sean Wilson so they can use Tommy Knudsen for his first League match since the end of 1988. But he fails to score and breaks his thumb in his second ride. Andy Hackett is another casualty, he fractures his collar bone at Oxford...Injury-ravaged Hackney lose number one Steve Schofield with a back injury after a spectacular heat 11 crash.*

29 **STEVE REGELING, heading the Exeter averages, opens talks with promoter Colin Hill over a 1991 contract...Dean Barker (Oxford) and Kenny McKinna (Glasgow) join Martin Dugard as confirmed starters for the Indoor Speedway Spectacular at the London Arena....Eastbourne are unable to use Justin Walker as they fail to meet transfer payments to Cradley Heath...World Champion Per Jonsson will advise Berwick on track surface preparation for the £3,500 Bonanza.**

30 EASTBOURNE'S Keith Pritchard turns down an offer to become the Eagles' club manager as he wants to carry on riding...Jeremy Doncaster retains the Czechoslovakian Golden Helmet at Pardubice.

...RESULTS...RESULTS...RESULTS...

SUNBRITE LEAGUE: Reading 61 Belle Vue 29; Wolverhampton 8 Swindon 4, abandoned after two heats, rain; Belle Vue v Cradley Heath, postponed, waterlogged track; Oxford 51 Coventry 38; Cradley Heath v Swindon, postponed, waterlogged track; Bradford 46 Oxford 44; Coventry v King's Lynn, postponed, waterlogged track; King's Lynn v Cradley Heath, postponed, waterlogged track .

NATIONAL LEAGUE: Poole 54 Wimbledon 42; Glasgow 54 Hackney 42; Long Eaton 69 Peterborough 27; Wimbledon 47 Poole 48; Ipswich 44 Poole 51; Middlesbrough 58 Hackney 38; Hackney 43 Middlesbrough 53; Berwick 48 Edinburgh 45; Stoke 34 Rye House 26, abandoned after 10 heats, rain; Eastbourne 56 Milton Keynes 39; Edinburgh v Stoke, postponed, waterlogged track; Newcastle v Hackney, postponed, waterlogged track; Poole v Exeter, postponed, waterlogged track. .

INDIVIDUAL: Crown Craft South West Junior Championship (Exeter): Scott Swain; Supernational Marathon (Arena Essex): abandoned after 12 heats, rain.

ANGLIA-HERTS CUP, 1st leg: Peterborough 57 Rye House 39; 2nd leg, postponed, waterlogged track.

1 **STEVE SCHOFIELD is told he will miss the rest of the season with a knee injury that could require an operation...David Mullett returns to the Reading side after recovering from a broken left ankle.**

2 *WORLD Long Track Champion Simon Wigg sets himself a New Year comeback date and says he wants to race again in Australia towards the end of January...The first ever National Series meeting sees Exeter outscore Poole and Wimbledon although only five points separate all three teams...Alun Rossiter receives the National League Championship trophy as Poole celebrate with a big win over Arena Essex.*

3 JAMES GRIEVES, 16, makes his debut for Glasgow as number eight but crashes in his first ride...Ray Morton crashes out with an ankle injury as Wimbledon are held at home by Middlesbrough.

4 **TODD WILTSHIRE is voted Rider of the Year by the Speedway Writers' and Photographers' Association. Other award winners are Ipswich's Chris Louis (Young Rider of the Year), promoter Colin Pratt (Merit Award) and Speedway Yearbook Editor Peter Oakes (the inaugural Journalist of the Year)...The evening ends in disappointment for Jan O. Pedersen and Simon Cross – their cars are stolen from the Solihull Hotel where the Awards dinner is being held.**

...RESULTS...RESULTS...RESULTS...

SUNBRITE LEAGUE: Reading 53 Swindon 37; Wolverhampton 54 Cradley Heath 36; Coventry 58 King's Lynn 32; Oxford 49 Swindon 41; Bradford 47 Cradley Heath 43; Belle Vue v Oxford, postponed, waterlogged track; King's Lynn 43 Wolverhampton 47; Swindon v Coventry, postponed, waterlogged track; Cradley Heath 48 Bradford 42.

SPEEDWAY STAR KNOCK OUT CUP FINAL, 1st leg: Bradford v Reading, postponed, waterlogged track.

NATIONAL LEAGUE: Poole 61 Arena Essex 35; Wimbledon 48 Middlesbrough 48; Arena Essex 41 Poole 51; Eastbourne 51 Hackney 45.

NATIONAL SERIES, 1st leg: Exeter 39 Poole 35 Wimbledon 34. 1st leg: Middlesbrough 50 Glasgow 31 Berwick 27; 2nd leg: Berwick v Glasgow v Middlesbrough, postponed, waterlogged track. 1st leg: Stoke v Ipswich v Hackney, postponed, waterlogged track.

INDIVIDUAL: East Midlands Championship (Long Eaton): Nigel Crabtree; Fork Rent 16 Lapper (Ipswich): Craig Boyce; Scottish Open Championship (Edinburgh), postponed, waterlogged track.

CHALLENGE: Hackney Past and Present 35 Australian Select 31, abandoned after 11 heats, rain.

AUTUMN TROPHY, 2nd leg: Newcastle 43 Berwick 53. *Aggregate: Berwick 75 Newcastle 63.*

SCOTTISH CUP, 2nd leg: Glasgow 55 Edinburgh 40. *Aggregate: Glasgow 101 Edinburgh 90.*

ANGLIA-HERTS CUP, 2nd leg: Rye House 60 Peterborough 36. *Aggregate: Rye House 99 Peterborough 93.*

JUNIOR FOUR TEAM TOURNAMENT: Peterborough 15 Arena Essex 26 Ipswich 24 Long Eaton 28.

5 *MARK LORAM is told by the Sunbrite League Management Committee that he cannot race at National League Hackney as a guest for the HL1 Kestrels...The Soviet Union name their nine rider squad to tour Australia and it includes all their top riders...Ian Thomas and Graham Drury announce the British Open Ice Championship at Telford on Sunday, February 17, 1991.*

6 **HENRIK GUSTAFSSON makes his debut for King's Lynn and finishes off with a race win in the nominated riders' heat...Paul Blackbird confirms that he wants a move from Peterborough and says he wishes to join Milton Keynes or Long Eaton...the 1990-91 Australian season officially opens at Newcastle, New South Wales.**

7 IN FORM Mark Courtney equals Chris Louis' Newcastle track record...Jens Rasmussen equals his own Rye House track record...Glasgow finish in fourth place in the National League – their highest ever position...Eurosport, who provide a service for satellite television, agree to cover the Indoor meeting at the London Arena in the New Year.

DAY BY DAY

Diary OCT

8 *MICHAEL LEE seems set to be allowed to race again when he appeals for clemency at the Speedway Control Board in his bid to get his licence back.*

9 BILLY HAMILL and his girl-friend are taken to hospital after being involved in a Freeway car crash on their way to Los Angeles International Airport to return to Britain after a compulsory return home for the American Championship...Sean Wilson is made available by Coventry.

10 POOLE'S Australian star Craig Boyce, top of the National League averages, wants to move into the Sunbrite League next season...Edinburgh are told their future at Powderhall is secure despite take-over talks that would see local bookmaker Edgar Ramsey buy the stadium...Graham Jones (Wolverhampton) is to see a specialist after further problems with his injured back...Wimbledon's Andy Grahame takes the Silver Helmet off Newcastle's David Bargh and will hold the championship throughout the winter months.

11 *SEAN WILSON, released by Coventry to accommodate Tommy Knudsen, has joined King's Lynn on loan and makes his bow for them against Cradley Heath...Gary Muckley wants to take over as promoter at Mildenhall.*

12 READING clinch the 1990 Sunbrite League title by claiming a bonus point at Belle Vue while Wolverhampton, their last remaining challengers, go down at Oxford...Middlesbrough are ready to grant Darren Sumner's written transfer to be allowed to join a Sunbrite League club...Alan Grahame is considering dropping down to the National League after a 15-season Sunbrite League career that began at Birmingham in 1976...Peter York is told his services are no longer required at Oxford...Junior Phil Roberts, who broke his back 14 months ago, has an interval ride at Sandy Lane.

...RESULTS...RESULTS...RESULTS...

BRITISH LEAGUE RIDERS' CHAMPIONSHIP FINAL (Belle Vue): Hans Nielsen.

SUNBRITE LEAGUE: Wolverhampton 58 Swindon 32; Cradley Heath 41 Coventry 49; King's Lynn 47 Cradley Heath 43; Oxford 49 Wolverhampton 41; Belle Vue 51 Reading 39; Bradford 46 King's Lynn 43; Coventry 48 Oxford 42; Swindon 38 Cradley Heath 52.

SPEEDWAY STAR KNOCK OUT CUP FINAL, 1st leg: Reading 51 Bradford 39. 2nd leg: Bradford 43 Reading 47. *Aggregate: Reading 98 Bradford 82.*

NATIONAL LEAGUE: Wimbledon 57 Newcastle 39; Edinburgh v Stoke, postponed, waterlogged track; Poole 57 Exeter 39.

NATIONAL SERIES, 1st leg: Stoke 47 Ipswich 32 Hackney 29; 2nd leg: Ipswich 44 Stoke 35 Hackney 29. 3rd leg: Hackney 35 Ipswich 38 Stoke 34. *Aggregate: Stoke 116 Ipswich 114 Hackney 103.* 2nd leg: Glasgow 50 Berwick 33 Middlesbrough 25; 3rd leg: Berwick 40 Glasgow 35 Middlesbrough 33. *Aggregate: Glasgow 116 Middlesbrough 108 Berwick 100.* 2nd leg: Poole 42 Exeter 33 Wimbledon 33.

SILVER HELMET: David Bargh (Newcastle, holder) lost to Andy Grahame (Wimbledon).

INDIVIDUAL: Berwick £3,500 Bonanza (Berwick): David Walsh. Championship of Sussex (Eastbourne): Alan Mogridge.

CHALLENGE: Long Eaton 57 Simmons Select 39; Middlesbrough v Edinburgh, postponed, waterlogged track; Peterborough A 18 Peterborough B 19 Swindon A 28.5 Swindon B 30.5.

AUTUMN TRIANGLE, 2nd leg: Arena Essex 47 Rye House 31 Hackney 30. 3rd leg: Rye House 35 Hackney 41 Arena Essex 31. *Aggregate: Hackney 118 Arena Essex 107 Rye House 98.*

13 IT'S the double for Reading. They beat Bradford at Odsal in the second leg of the Speedway Star Knock Out Cup to become the seventh club to win both league and cup in the same season. Bradford's hopes were dashed when high-scoring reserve Glenn Doyle was taken to hospital with bad bruising.

14 *HANS NIELSEN wins his third British League Riders' Championship, scoring a 15 point maximum and finishing three points clear of defending title holder Shawn Moran who is runner-up...David Walsh wins the £1,000 first prize at Berwick's £3,500 Bonanza final meeting.*

15 STOKE face the threat of closure following an announcement by the stadium owners that they do not feel speedway and greyhound racing mix...Spencer Timmo ends the season on the injured list after breaking his arm as Newcastle go down to their fifth home defeat against Hackney, who are without three of their regulars through injury...Jan Staechmann puts in a written transfer request to leave Wolverhampton...A planned end-of-season tour of National League tracks by Czechoslovakia has been shelved...Programmed referee Reg Trott fails to appear at Reading and former Ipswich co-promoter Chris Shears takes over.

...RESULTS...RESULTS...RESULTS...

SUNBRITE LEAGUE: Reading 54 Bradford 36; Bradford 50 Cradley Heath 40; Swindon 54 Coventry 36; Belle Vue 59 Bradford 31; Cradley Heath 47 King's Lynn 43; Bradford 57 Oxford 33; Coventry 44 Swindon 46; King's Lynn 61 Reading 29.

NATIONAL LEAGUE: Newcastle 44 Hackney 52; Edinburgh v Stoke, postponed, waterlogged track; Stoke 50 Rye House 46; Edinburgh 49 Stoke 47.

NATIONAL SERIES, 3rd leg: Wimbledon 52 Poole 29 Exeter 27. *Aggregate: Wimbledon 119 Poole 106 Exeter 99.*

INDIVIDUAL: Stars of Tomorrow (Hackney), cancelled, waterlogged track; Nene Litho Trophy (Peterborough), postponed, waterlogged track; Supernational Marathon (Arena Essex): Alan Mogridge.

INTER LEAGUE CHALLENGE: Wolverhampton 56 Poole 34; Middlesbrough v King's Lynn, postponed, waterlogged track; Edinburgh 33 Belle Vue 63; Rye House 36 Wolverhampton 60.

CHALLENGE: King's Lynn 43 Sunbrite League Swedish Select 47; Newcastle 45 Joe Owen's Jets 33.

PAIRS: Devon Pairs Championship (Exeter): Richard Green and Rob Woffinden; Billy Sanders Memorial Pairs (Ipswich): Gary Tagg and Paul Whittaker.

INTER LEAGUE FOUR TEAM TOURNAMENT: Poole 16 Reading 38 Wimbledon 24 Wolverhampton 18.

JUNIOR CHALLENGE: Eastbourne 39 National League Select 57.

16 SHAWN MORAN is reported to the FIM after failing a drugs test at the Overseas Final. The papers have been forward to the World's governing body by the Speedway Control Board...Mildenhall's last promoter Skid Parish puts Jamie Habbin, who has spent the season on loan to Long Eaton, up for sale

17 *BRADFORD co-promoter Bobby Ham reveals he is seriously considering quitting speedway to put in more time on the family construction business...Glasgow are told they cannot hold their home leg of the National Series Final on Sunday, October 28, because it clashes with Edinburgh's Scottish Open Championship. The Radio Clyde Tigers respond by saying they have no other available date...Eastbourne want to switch their raceday from the traditional Sunday afternoon to a Friday night in 1991.*

18 EDINBURGH have their fourth successive home meeting called off because of the weather.

19 VETERAN Chris Morton rounds off his British League career with a paid maximum for Belle Vue and then wins the bonus point in a run-off against Bradford's Gary Havelock.

20 *IN a bizarre finish to the Odsal season, referee Angus McLeod has to call off the second leg of the British League Division Two Knock Out Cup Final after two legs when fog descends and obscures his view of the back straight...Nigel Crabtree is hospitalised with a back injury after being involved in a four rider pile-up – after the chequered flag...Chick Woodroffe announced that he is quitting as promoter at Arena Essex and puts the entire operation up for sale*

21 KING'S LYNN scorch to their biggest win of the season, against champions Reading...Paul Dugard makes a racing comeback in the last meeting of the year at Eastbourne and scores a paid maximum in a Junior meeting...Freddy Schøtt is injured in a race that never was. He crashes in heat nine of Edinburgh's challenge against Belle Vue but the race is later declared null and void as referee Bill Easton discovers Schøtt was only programmed because of a printer's error.

22 SUNBRITE League and National League Management Committee are to hold a joint meeting on the sport's future at Rugby on November 7...Peter Thorogood confirms he will stay on as co-promoter at Arena Essex if a buyer can be found willing to pay Chick Woodroffe's £70,000 price...Berwick's Mark Courtney announces his retirement...Glen Baxter stuns Rye House by saying he will be staying at home in Australia next season to recover from a shoulder operation.

23 *TOMMY KNUDSEN, who has now completed six matches, confirms that he plans to race full time next season. He says: "I am sure I can get back to what I was."*

24 BRIAN KARGER is to return to the Swindon team – at reserve in an end of season challenge against Reading with both teams using eight riders and operating under a 14-heat formula...Shawn Moran is ordered to fly to Budapest, Hungary, to appear before the FIM Track Commission to answer a charge of giving a positive drugs test at the Overseas Final of the World Championship...Wimbledon's Nathan Simpson puts in a transfer request as he wants to step up into the Sunbrite League next year...Paul Dugard reveals he would like to join King's Lynn in 1991...Simon Wigg is told he needs an urgent operation to save his racing career...Veteran Steve Wilcock is voted Middlesbrough's Rider of the Year.

25 THE FIM Track Commission ban Shawn Moran for 12 months although six months of that sentence is suspended...Other major decisions reached in Budapest are: Changes in the 1991 individual World Championship sees only nine riders qualify from the Overseas Final for the new semi finals. The 1991 World Final will be held on August 31 at Gothenburg and the referee will be Britain's Graham Brodie...The 1991 World Under 21 Final, originally allocated to Australia, will now be hosted by England...TV2 of Denmark have secured the exclusive TV rights to all major World Championship events until the end of 1993

26 *CHAOS at Belle Vue where Kelly Moran turns up for their final meeting of the season without a bike. And teenager Joe Screen, who lends one of his machines to the Californian, quits half way through the meeting after both machines are damaged. Belle Vue's defeat means they fail to snatch the runners-up spot from Wolverhampton...Ray Morton has been transfer-listed by Wimbledon. He wants a British League future.*

27 LONG EATON skipper Richard Hellsén could face a winter skin graft on a badly burnt arm...Screensport are to show a review of the 1990 season – through the eyes of World Champion Per Jonsson...World Finalist Martin Dugard is to go into hospital on November 7 for four separate operations, all as a result of crashes during the season...Wimbledon and Peterborough begin talks on a possible full transfer for Peter Chapman who has been on loan at Plough Lane.

28 GLASGOW win their first ever national trophy – the National Series – with a three point advantage over Wimbledon.

...RESULTS...RESULTS...RESULTS...

SUNBRITE LEAGUE: Cradley Heath 48 Swindon 42; Belle Vue 40 Oxford 49.

NATIONAL SERIES FINAL, 1st leg: Wimbledon 36 Glasgow 25 Stoke 16; 2nd leg: Stoke 28 Glasgow 42 Wimbledon 38. 3rd leg: Glasgow 40 Wimbledon 35 Stoke 32. *Aggregate: Glasgow 107 Wimbledon 104 Stoke 75.*

INDIVIDUAL: Denny Pyeatt Memorial Trophy (Reading): Per Jonsson; Stadium Trophy (Ipswich): Alan Mogridge. Nene Litho Trophy (Peterborough): Mark Blackbird; Pride of the East (King's Lynn): Kelvin Tatum; Scottish Open Championship (Edinburgh), postponed, waterlogged track.

INTER LEAGUE CHALLENGE: Poole 48 Swindon 48; Middlesbrough 43 King's Lynn 46.

CHALLENGE: Phonesport Fours: Hackney v Arena Essex v Ipswich v Wimbledon, cancelled, waterlogged track; Cradley Heath v Wolverhampton, postponed, waterlogged track.

PAIRS: Phil Bishop Lokeren Pairs (Arena Essex): Troy Pratt and Tommy Palmer.

29 RESULTS of a Supporters' Poll at Swindon show that 98% of fans want to see the two Leagues merge. Other findings include 60% for a total ban on the use of guests...Cradley Heath make a firm approach to try and sign Poole's transfer-listed Australian Craig Boyce...Coventry skipper Kelvin Tatum hands in an official transfer request.

30 OXFORD settle terms with Poole to sign Australian Craig Boyce who has agreed to join the Skol Cheetahs in 1991. A clause in the contract provides for a bonus payment if he finishes in the World Final top three in 1991, 1992 or 1993...Todd Wiltshire is voted Sports Star of the Year in his native Lake Macquarie.

31 *FORMER World Champion Hans Nielsen agrees terms to lead Oxford in 1991. It will be his eighth successive season at Sandy Lane since moving there from Birmingham in 1984...Cradley Heath beat Black Country rivals Wolverhampton in the last meeting of the 1990 season.*

...RESULTS...RESULTS...RESULTS...

CHALLENGE: Swindon v Reading, cancelled, waterlogged track; Cradley Heath 50 Wolverhampton 40.

...WINNERS...WINNERS...WINNERS...

SUNBRITE LEAGUE CHAMPIONS: *Reading.*
SPEEDWAY STAR KNOCK OUT CUP WINNERS: *Reading.*
GOLD CUP WINNERS: *Bradford.*
NATIONAL LEAGUE CHAMPIONS: *Poole.*
NATIONAL LEAGUE KNOCK OUT CUP WINNERS: *Poole.*
NATIONAL SERIES WINNERS: *Glasgow.*
NATIONAL LEAGUE PAIRS CHAMPIONS: *Hackney.*
H.E.A.T. NATIONAL LEAGUE FOUR TEAM CHAMPIONS: *Stoke.*
BRITISH LEAGUE DIVISION TWO CHAMPIONS: *Wolverhampton.*
BRITISH LEAGUE DIVISION TWO KNOCK OUT CUP WINNERS: *Wolverhampton.*
WORLD CHAMPION: *Per Jonsson (Sweden).*
WORLD TEAM CUP CHAMPIONS: *United States of America.*
WORLD PAIRS CHAMPIONS: *Denmark.*
BRITISH LEAGUE RIDERS' CHAMPION: *Hans Nielsen (Oxford).*
NATIONAL LEAGUE RIDERS' CHAMPION: *Andy Grahame (Wimbledon).*
BRITISH LEAGUE DIVISION TWO RIDERS' CHAMPION: *Richard Musson (Belle Vue).*

1 *THE Speedway Control Board find Mark Courtney (Berwick) and Gary Havelock (Bradford) guilty of bringing the sport into disrepute after complaints that they indecently exposed themselves at the 1990 National League Four Team Tournament at Peterborough. Both are fined £250 and ordered to pay £500 costs and are banned for a year. Courtney's sentence is suspended for two years but Havelock will be out of racing until January 5, 1994, after the Board reactivate his suspended sentence imposed after a positive drugs test at the 1988 British League Riders' Championship Final. Havelock, who pleaded not guilty, says he will appeal the decision.*

2 GLASGOW are to canvas for the scrapping of a maximum points limit in the National League...Ipswich win the race to sign talented schoolboy Ben Howe who agrees to sign for the Witches on his 16th birthday.

3 IT is revealed that another rider has given a positive drugs test, this time at a domestic meeting. The Speedway Control Board have written to him asking if he wants a second sample to be analysed...Injured Simon Cross is named as Cradley Heath's Rider of the Year in a supporters' poll...Eastbourne landlord Bob Dugard has talks with promoter Gareth Rogers about the possibility of returning to the Sunbrite League in 1991...Wolverhampton tell teenager Wayne Carter there is a 1991 team place for him in the senior side...The Russians open their Australian tour with a big win against Northern Territory at Darwin.

4 AUSTRALIAN David Jackson, who missed out on the 1990 season, confirms he wants to come back next year and is willing to rejoin his old club Rye House

DAY BY DAY

Diary NOV

5...STOKE promoter Eric Stead is asked to pay an extra £500 a meeting at Loomer Road...Glasgow are to stay at Shawfield Park despite talks with Glasgow Parks and Recreation Council about a new permanent site for the Tigers...Exeter's Peter Jeffery is to stay with the club...***6***...**MICHAEL LEE'S long-term ban is lifted by the Speedway Control Board...The Sunbrite League and National League Management Committees meet at Rugby and NL chairman Mervyn Stewkesbury outlines his blueprint with the new league operating a two Division set-up, with promotion and relegation, in 1992...*****7***...PETERBOROUGH want Stephen Davies...Wimbledon sign Jesper Olsen for 1991...Australian Trevor Harding is keen to buy Long Eaton...***8***...**SHAWN MORAN accepts the FIM ban...Sunbrite League promoters back the Stewkesbury plan and agree to further talks on amalgamation in 1991..*****9***...MILTON KEYNES want Rob Woffinden....Skid Parish, former promoter at Mildenhall, is having talks with David Hawkins with an eye to becoming co-promoter of the Skoda Panthers...***10***...**THE Soviet speedsters maintain their 100% tour record with a second successive win over North Queensland, this time at Cairns where local rider John Reid becomes the first Australian to score double figures against the tourists with 16 points (four wins) in six rides...*****11***...BELLE VUE approach Peterborough and want Mick Poole to join them on loan for 1991.

12...MARTIN DUGARD decides he won't have a winter operation on his damaged scaphoid...Roger Johns will have an operation for a similar injury...***13***...**RUSSIA are willing to send two of their most promising prospects to England in 1991...Berwick boss Terry Lyndon is told he cannot run Quads at Berrington Lough by the Speedway Control Board...*****14***...STOKE promoter Eric Stead dies of a heart attack while attending hospital in Sheffield...***15***...**CRADLEY HEATH promoter Colin Pratt opens negotiations to sign World Under 21 Final runner up René Aas...Simon Wigg has his bone graft operation...*****16***...LONG EATON want to sign Rye House's unsettled Melvyn Taylor...Bob Radford, announcer and PR man, reveals he is quitting the Russian tour of Australia claiming there have been problems over finance...***17***...**SUNBRITE LEAGUE promoters meet at Rugby and are wary over the Stewkesbury plan to abolish guests except when a team has three heat leaders out...Paul Whittaker agrees terms to stay at Hackney in 1991..*****18***...MERVYN STEWKESBURY, Maurice Ducker and Colin Pratt discuss guests and agree a compromise which means the amalgamation blueprint now has the full approval of the Sunbrite League Management Committee...Peterborough pull out of the race to sign Carl Blackbird, frightened off by Edinburgh's £13,000 asking price...Swindon unveil plans for a 175 metre training track inside the Blunsdon circuit.

BLUEPRINT FOR THE FUTURE

INTRODUCTION

I think few people would disagree that, at the moment, Speedway does not get the credibility, media coverage or sponsorship that it should. It is perhaps not surprising when you consider we have two Leagues both operating totally independently of each other with different rules and, as far as the public are concerned, little or no common ground between us. Speedway promoters effectively run the sport and it must be our responsibility if the sport is not being conducted attractively and in the most efficient manner.

The National League, which consists of 18 (sic) tracks, in my opinion conducts itself well but it is a fact that as far as riding standard is concerned we always have been, and will continue to be, looked upon as the Second Division. Therefore as long as there is a senior Division the progress of the National League will be restricted.

As regards the Sunbrite League I cannot comment in detail except to say that it consists of only 9 tracks and has decreased in numbers considerably over the years. To the best of my knowledge seven National League Tracks have had Sunbrite League experience within the last 10 years yet they have no desire to return to that League in its present form, despite a lucrative offer last winter of a share in the World Final. It is, therefore, reasonable to assume that the Sunbrite League (the senior League), in all the circumstances does not appear either, to have found the answers to speedway problems.

Quite clearly changes are needed and it is we, the Promoters, who have the power to make these changes. We all need each other but possibly for different reasons.

THE FUTURE OF SPEEDWAY

Doubtless the present Sunbrite League would like at least four of the National League tracks to join them and this could be achieved in one of two ways:

1 *Total amalgamation, or*

2 *Four tracks simply leaving the National League and joining the Sunbrite League.*

I do not believe the second option is a realistic possibility as I cannot concede any offer from the Sunbrite League which would tempt National League Tracks to leave the National League and join the present Sunbrite League.

I am of the opinion that for the future of British speedway there should be a complete amalgamation with two Leagues incorporating a promotion and relegation system. In my opinion promotion and relegation is essential to bring about an amalgamation as, without promotion and relegation, we will simply be two separate Leagues and therefore we may just as well remain as we are at present (certainly the National League). Furthermore without the offer of promotion and relegation there is little point in the National League voting to accept amalgamation. Remember amalgamation would require a change in the Constitution and therefore would require majority approval of both Leagues.

LEAGUE

If the principal of promotion and relegation is accepted I would propose the following:

1 The total number of teams available be divided equally between two Leagues called Division I and Division II (subject to agreement for the first year).

2 In the event of there being an odd number of teams the additional team should be in Division II.

3 All new entrants (regardless of any previous status) should enter Division II.

4 At the end of each year the winner of Division II would be promoted to Division I and the team who comes bottom of Division I would be relegated to Division II.

POINTS LIMIT

I wish to stress that the MAXIMUM points available for allocation is a mathematical equation and not arbitrarily based on personal preferences. I do not propose taking up time explaining how I arrive at these calculations but, of course, if necessary, will be happy to do so at some later stage.

The average number of bonus points taken from the 1990 Final Green Sheet averages of both Leagues are as follows:

Sunbrite League 4.87} SAY 5 POINTS
National League 4.92}

In any future reference to points I will give two figures, the first excluding bonus points and the second including bonus points, i.e. 42/47. The standard of the average Sunbrite League rider is accepted to be 1.5 times better than that of the average National League rider, i.e. a Sunbrite League rider with a 6 point average would be a 9 point rider in the National League of vice versa.

Division I

With four teams joining Division One the points limit mathematically could not be more than 37/42 but I would strongly recommend not more than 35/40 (35 without or 40 with bonus points).

Division II

This should remain as at present with a natural average of 42/47 points. The setting of the points limit at these levels would, after the first year, change the mathematical ratio of the difference between the standard of the two Leagues from 1.5 to 1.25 and this plays a very important part in the promotion and relegation dealt with later.

After the first year a Division I rider with an 8 point average would be a 10 point rider in Division II or vice versa.

NON BRITISH RIDERS

I recommend the complete adoption of the present British League system but with careful consideration being given to the assessment of incoming non-British riders to differentiate between Division One and Two. I now think this for many reasons, the two main ones being:

a) The National League can no longer continue to exclude EEC riders from their League as this would be illegal.

b) The National League, by restricting the entry of non-British riders, has greatly reduced the supply of SUITABLE riders which, in turn, increases demand and ultimately costs. Therefore I believe all Speedway riders should be entitled to ride in either League (subject, of course, to complying with any other Laws and Conditions of entry).

MANAGEMENT

My recommendation is complete amalgamation and therefore we must cease operating separately. There can only be one General Council consisting of all Members and one Management Committee, where Rules are made which will apply equally to both Leagues. One point immediately comes to mind, 15 or 16 heats – this and other matters would be resolved by a straightforward vote of all Tracks.

Chairman

In most organisations where the chairman holds a voluntary position his time in office is limited for many reasons and I believe this should apply to Speedway, restricting any one person to a maximum of two years at any one time (or 3 years in very special circumstances). I believe the chairmanship of the Association should alternate on a two-year cycle with one from one League followed by a chairman from the other League. Because no-one in the National League has a good knowledge of the workings of the FIM I recommend the first chairman should be one from the

DAY BY DAY

Diary DEC

19...COVENTRY'S Andy Hackett is anxious to find a team place on the Continent to supplement his British earnings...***20***...**SUNBRITE LEAGUE chairman Maurice Ducker announces that his promoters are wholeheartedly in favour of amalgamation and want to see two Division speedway - with promotion and relegation - in 1991...Mark Blackbird puts in a written transfer request as he wants to leave Long Eaton**...***21***...AMALGAMATION moves another vital step nearer as the National League promoters, on the opening day of their annual conference in Tenerife, vote, in principle, for the merging of the two leagues...Tony Langdon hurts his back during practice for the South Queensland-Soviet Union match...***22***...**TIM SWALES (Middlesbrough) is the new National League chairman. Neil Macfarlane (Glasgow) and Dave Pavitt (Hackney) join Peter Thorogood (Arena Essex) and Rye House's Ronnie Russell on the new-elected Management Committee**...***23***...NATIONAL League promoters agree: the points limit stays as it was in 1990 (42 points maximum, 38 points minimum); foreigners to be admitted; Eastbourne (Sunday-Friday), Edinburgh (Sunday-Friday) and Glasgow (Wednesday-Sunday) switch race-nights...Andy Galvin (Hackney) and Brett Saunders (Edinburgh) to get 1991 testimonials..***24***...**RUSSIA keep their unbeaten record with victory over South Queensland**...***25***...GORDON KENNETT learns his testimonial plea has been turned down by the National League.

26...IN a dramatic about-face National League promoters vote against promotion and relegation and demand one big League for 1991 at an extraordinary meeting of members in Tenerife...Long Eaton admit they are in danger of folding if Australian entrepreneur Trevor Harding pulls out of talks to join the promotion...***27***...**PETERBOROUGH open negotiations with an as yet unnamed Danish rider for 1991**..***28***...SWEDE Tony Olsson could be out until next June with his broken hip and knee...***29***...**EDINBURGH transfer list Mick Powell (at his own request) and Scott Lamb**...***30***...**EASTBOURNE Stadium owner Bob Dugard has talks with Maurice Ducker about rejoining the Sunbrite League in 1991 and makes an official application...Long Eaton agree a new rental deal at Station Road for next season**...***1***...STOCK CAR promoter David Mason agrees a deal for all motor sport rights at Stoke and says he wants speedway to remain at Loomer Road...Poole call off their New Year trip to Australia because they haven't been given a full itinery...Troy Butler retains his Queensland Championship to qualify for the Australian Final...Eastbourne officially announce they want to join the Sunbrite League and open negotiations to sign former Eagle Kelly Moran from Belle Vue...***2***...**KING'S LYNN want Dennis Löfqvist to return in 1991 even though his end of season average was below six points...Bohumil Brhel is keen to race in the Indoor meeting at the London Arena.**

STEWKESBURY'S PROPOSALS

present Sunbrite League.

Vice Chairman

I believe the vice chairman should always be from the opposite League than that of the chairman and therefore the first vice chairman should be from the present National League. There is also logic in selecting a vice chairman who is prepared to be the chairman during the next period.

Management Committee

I believe this should continue with a total of five persons with the chairman, plus two members from one League (including the vice chairman) together with two members from the other League. The Management Committee should continue as at present to administer the day to day business of speedway in accordance with the Speedway Control Board Regulations and the Constitution. The one Management Committee would administer both Leagues.

Offices & Administration

I think the ideal long term arrangement would be one central office but I do not believe this should be implemented immediately. Both offices at present seem to function very well and I think discussion should take place between all concerned with a view to consideration being given to the future. In the meantime, or in the long term, we can easily continue with both offices.

USE OF GUESTS

There is very little doubt that the decision of the National League to abolish guests gained more credibility than most other decisions. However, having seen one National League team during 1990 with all three heat leaders being injured and only being able to use one rider replacement, I personally believe that in such circumstances a guest facility should be offered for the number 1 heat leader only, together with one rider replacement facility. Even with careful selection of the guest in no way would it bring that team back to normal strength but it would make that team's performance more acceptable to the paying public.

I therefore propose that the only time a guest be permitted in either League should be when all three heat leaders are absent due to injury or other reason specified in the Speedway Control Board regulations in which case a guest facility be permitted for the number 1 heat leader only, together with one rider replacement facility.

This may cause concern to some Sunbrite League promoters due to international duty but, with the proposed points reduction, present Sunbrite League clubs should have less international riders in their team. Furthermore it has been found in the National League that because there is only one rider replacement facility available promoters with international riders pay more attention when arranging fixtures in order to avoid a clash of dates with international events.

PROMOTION AND RELEGATION

As I said earlier, after the first year of amalgamation the natural points limit at the start of each season would be a maximum of 42/47 points with, say, 38/43 minimum. This would, of course, apply to both Leagues but difference in standards between the two Leagues would then be 1.25.

Promotion 1991-92

The team who wins the Division II is the team that starts the season with around 42/47 points and increases in team strength by usually 5 to 6 points. If that team ends the season with 49/54 points they would immediately be eligible to compete in Division I without having to strengthen their team - Poole ended this year with 50-56 points.

Relegation 1991-92

Equally, the team coming bottom of the Division I will have become weaker in team strength than they started the season with and may well be able to take that same team to Division II.

Promotion or Relegation

Although it may be possible to change Divisions with the same team, at the very worst, it would only be necessary to change one rider.

I have heard arguments from Sunbrite League clubs of what would they do with their riders if they were relegated to Division Two. From the above, I hope Sunbrite League clubs can now see that if they came bottom of Division One they would have to do little or no shedding of riders to compete in Division Two.

Under the present system the club who comes bottom of the Sunbrite League and wishes to remain in the Sunbrite League must go to the expense of strengthening his team for the following year.

Equally, the common complaint from the team who wins the National League is "Why should I have to get rid of riders?" - with promotion he may not have to and, hopefully, with this in mind, all National League clubs will be able to see the benefits of winning the National League and gaining promotion. It is on this very point that I am hoping the National League will accept these proposals as the thought of gaining promotion and maintaining the same team should have great appeal to them.

CONSTITUTION

If these proposals are accepted clearly the Constitution would need to be altered once again as, at the moment, it is drawn for two separate Leagues but I do not see this as a problem.

If these proposals are accepted I would strongly recommend both Leagues to be only prepared to implement these proposals if certain items like promotion and relegation, one Management Committee and one General Council etc., are written into the Constitution. Unless this is done, at some time in the future, one Division or the other could go their separate way and start the whole cycle off again. With these major changes written into our Constitution no group of clubs could go their own separate way without stepping outside the jurisdiction of Speedway Control. Including these changes in the Constitution would not, of course, prevent changes being made in the future but it could only be done with the agreement of three quarters of all promoters, not just a minority. If these proposals are accepted I am prepared to redraw the Constitution.

CONCLUSIONS

I have tried to put forward proposals to improve the status and credibility of British Speedway for its long term future, at the same time doing my best to consider both Leagues and its members. I truly believe these proposals could work with the right will from everyone to make them work, which, in turn, could bring about a new dimension to speedway which is so badly needed. Some of you may be nervous about these proposals but just imagine the interest which would be generated, perhaps among new sponsors, from amalgamation with promotion and relegation, let alone from a Knock Out competition involving all clubs.

I personally am hoping this whole thing could rejuvenate speedway as a major sport once again.,

If we can find the will to make this work then I think there is only one challenge left to achieve and that is to show the same determination to make it possible to stage a World Final at Wembley.

M. STEWKESBURY
12 November 1990

Diary DEC

DAY BY DAY

3 *AMERICA will hold their United States Final – a World Championship qualifier – at the beginning of March because refurbishment work at regular venue Veterans' Stadium at Long Beach will rule out the traditional June date. It means suspended Shawn Moran could miss out...The two Management Committees meet for eight hours to discuss amalgamation. The Sunbrite League confirm they want no part of a Conference system and the NL track bosses agree to recommend promotion and relegation to their General Council.*

4 PAUL THORP has his licence suspended by the Auto-Cycle Union after racing abroad without permission...Belle Vue's Peter Ravn is considering retirement from British racing.

5 FORMER Crayford and Hackney promoter Terry Russell pulls out of talks to take over Milton Keynes, but retains an interest in buying Arena Essex.

6 *NATIONAL LEAGUE promoters back the Stewkesbury plan and agree to promotion and relegation. Poole, Ipswich, Berwick and Wimbledon are nominated to join the nine Sunbrite League tracks in the new First Division with the remaining tracks forming Division Two. Eastbourne are on stand-by for automatic promotion.*

7 EXETER promoter Colin Hill announces that he intends to give up as County Ground promoter because of pressure of other business interests and the decision to amalgamate.

8 DEVON businessman Dave Dart, who runs a car and van hire company, makes initial approaches about taking over Exeter...The Russian tourists suffer their first defeat in the ninth match of their Australian tour, going down 41-49 to New South Wales for whom Todd Wiltshire scored a 15 point maximum...Glenn Doyle wins the Western Australian Open Championship at Perth...Trevor Harding expresses fresh doubts about taking over at Long Eaton.

9 *RYE HOUSE agree to pay Wimbledon £2,000 for Australian Scott Humphries who joined the Rockets on loan during the 1990 season...Eastbourne is to close if they are not admitted to the new First Division....Glasgow offer £4,000 for Edinburgh's Mick Powell.*

10 GARY HAVELOCK and Paul Thorp are found not guilty of bringing the sport into disrepute following damage to a Czechoslovakian hotel but the Speedway Control Board warn they will not tolerate bad behaviour by British-based riders...Mark Crang is the third rider to be convicted of bringing the sport into disrepute after indecently exposing himself after the National League Four Team Championship at Peterborough. He is fined £250 and suspended for 12 months, the ban to be suspended for two years...The Sunbrite League Annual Conference opens.

11 TERRY CHENEY tells Milton Keynes' supporters he needs £25,000 to keep the track alive in 1991...Darren Sumner puts in a written transfer request in his bid to leave Middlesbrough...Tests of an unnamed rider's second sample are positive...Sunbrite League promoters confirm a 40 point limit in 1991 and Reading's Pat Bliss becomes the first woman to be elected to the Management Committee, taking over from Peter York. The SL tracks are also to propose a reintroduction of the League Cup competition in the new 1991 First Division.

12 *THERE will be a £7,000 purse at the New Year Indoor meeting at the London Arena...Rob Woffinden is to be charged with failing a drugs test. Samples showed traces of cannabis. Eric Monaghan, who has admitted taking night nurse for a cold, is also to be charged....Rye House want Wolverhampton's transfer-listed Dane Jan Staechmann...Colin Pratt and Eric Boocock are to continue as joint England team managers.*

13 THE 1991 World Under 21 Final is to be held at Coventry and the 1991 Commonwealth Final at King's Lynn....Berwick make inquiries about young Dane Brian Andersen.

14 *EDINBURGH announce they have signed Bundaberg's Darren Winkler for the 1991 season...Bradford are willing to release former skipper Neil Evitts...Australian Trevor Harding re-opens negotiations to take over Long Eaton...Milton Keynes sign Paul Blackbird from Peterborough...Glasgow sign young Australian Michael Carter for 1991.*

15 STOKE co-promoter Ray Sant discovers that there is a clause in the motor sports contract with stock car promoter David Mason which prohibits him from sub-letting the speedway rights at Loomer Road...It is revealed that Wolverhampton have taken over the contract of Danish international Allan Johansen who missed the whole of the 1990 Sunbrite League season with a broken leg...Russia lose a second successive meeting in Australia, this time to an Australian Select in the first-ever international in Tasmania...Edinburgh sign a one-year lease to stay at Powderhall.

16 *HACKNEY promoter Dave Pavitt is to hand over control of the London club to Ipswich schoolteacher Derek Howse who appoints former British Champion and World Finalist Malcolm Simmons as team manager and to be in charge of track preparation.*

17 GARY HAVELOCK will have his appeal against suspension heard on January 14, 1991...Wolverhampton team manager Peter Adams is to become America's joint manager alongside John Scott.

18 *AMERICAN riders vote in favour of a six point average limit on those British-based riders competing in the World Championship and it will rule out Greg Hancock...Poole to carry out research over switching race-night to a Wednesday to avoid clashes with soccer club Bournemouth*

19 BERWICK approach Belle Vue about the availability of American Kelly Moran...There are hush-hush negotiations by a consortium of promoters to take over Mildenhall and to staff the track with Eastbourne's 1990 National League riders to allow the Eagles to join the new First Division...John Eskildsen, 30, who hasn't ridden in Britain since 1987, wants to return in 1991.

20 AUSTRALIAN promoter John McNeill reveals he is considering ignoring solos in all future events because the red tape involved in getting official approval from the authorities...The Sunbrite League and National League Management Committees agree a new Constitution and call a General Council meeting on January 10...Milton Keynes chase ex-Wolverhampton rider Sam Nikolajsen who hasn't ridden in England since 1986.

21 *EASTBOURNE stadium owner Bob Dugard announces that the track is to close after being told he will have to wait until January 10 to find out if the Eagles will start 1991 in the First Division...Peterborough now switch their sights to Rye House's transfer-listed Melvyn Taylor.*

22 EASTBOURNE agree to wait until the next General Council before pulling out of speedway – after Milton Keynes promoter Terry Cheney reveals a round-robin check shows 22 promoters in favour of the Eagles joining the First Division...Dave Dart claims he has offered £80,000 to take over Exeter...Richard Knight travels to Berwick for talks with promoter Terry Lindon and agrees to join the Bandits in 1991.

23 SWINDON'S Leigh Adams wins the Victorian Final of the World Championship...Long Eaton give Trevor Harding a January deadline if he is to take over the club.

24 *ALLAN HAM guarantees Bradford's future by announcing he will stay on as promoter even though brother Bobby will spend more time concentrating on the family business.*

25 NEWCASTLE'S future is in doubt as owner Kevin Wilde contemplates putting the company into liquidation.

26 TODD WILTSHIRE is surprisingly beaten into second place in the New South Wales Championship, by Craig Boyce.

27 *KING'S LYNN agree to let Stephen Davies talk to Peterborough...Terry Russell continues take-over talks at Arena Essex and plans to sign Andy Galvin to spearhead a promotion drive if talks are successful.*

28 RICHARD BAILEY, a major shareholder in Spectate Limited, promoters at Newcastle, reveals he is trying to take over the club...Glenn Doyle retains his Western Australian title...Todd Wiltshire wins a brand new GM engine in the Billy Sanders Memorial Open.

29 SHANE BOWES misses the South Australian Championship because of a late nomination but is told he can compete in the final qualifier at Alice Springs.

30 *SIMON WIGG turns down an approach from Milton Keynes who offer him a major shareholding in the company to ride for the Knights in 1991...Wolverhampton are ready to release Neil Collins.*

31 BERWICK are given the go-ahead to talk to Swindon's World Finalist Jimmy Nilsen.

The International Scene

WHITEWASH

ENGLAND, the reigning World Champions, are back on top of the speedway world....

If tangible proof was ever needed it came at Oxford, Bradford and Wolverhampton.

For those were the three venues where the Sunbrite Lions roared loudly again to claim a first-ever series whitewash against Denmark.

A couple of seasons ago it would have been unthinkable. But fortunes can change swiftly in speedway where injuries and retirement can play such a major part in determining where collective, if not individual, honours lay.

The Danes have, in the last 12 months or so, lost the services of two of their Big Four: Tommy Knudsen and 3-time World Champion Erik Gundersen.

England had, as managers Eric Boocock and Colin Pratt have been quick to point out, experienced that sort of agony with the death of Kenny Carter and the career suicide of Michael Lee.

As Boocock points out: "You can't take two of the world's top riders out of a team and expect it to carry on as if nothing has happened."

The wisdom of those words were evident as the Danes succumbed to a confident Sunbrite Lions who set out in search of a first series win against the Danes since the summer of 1984 when, incidentally, the England spearhead included Peter Collins, Dave Jessup and John Louis – a statistic which perhaps illustrates how long ago that was!

Already pared to the bone there were even more eve of the series setbacks for the once invincible Scandinavians.

Belle Vue's Peter Ravn dislocated his collar bone and Wolverhampton's Jan Staechmann joined him on the injured list.

Countering that, former World Team Cup gold medallist Bo Petersen had returned to the Sunbrite League with the Dianetics' Wolves – and England's build-up was also fraught with non availability of selected riders.

ROLL OF HONOUR

1981			
1st Test	Hackney	June 12	England 62 Denmark 46
2nd Test	Reading	June 22	England 58 Denmark 50
3rd Test	Coventry	July 1	England 46 Denmark 62
1982			
1st Test	Halifax	June 13	England 60 Denmark 48
2nd Test	Leicester	June 15	England 66 Denmark 42
3rd Test	Hackney	August 6	England 40 Denmark 68
1983			
1st Test	Coventry	June 29	England 46 Denmark 62
2nd Test	Halifax	July 3	England 65 Denmark 43
3rd Test	Hackney	July 8	England 65 Denmark 43
1984			
1st Test	Reading	June 4	England 54 Denmark 54
2nd Test	Wimbledon	June 7	England 45 Denmark 63
3rd Test	Wolverhampton	June 8	England 59 Denmark 48
4th Test	Halifax	June 10	England 59 Denmark 49
1985			
1st Test	Coventry	April 20	England 47 Denmark 61
2nd Test	Oxford	April 28	England 58 Denmark 50
3rd Test	Cradley Heath	May 4	England 53 Denmark 55
1986			
1st Test	Cradley Heath	May 3	England 53 Denmark 55
2nd Test	Belle Vue	May 16	England 45 Denmark 63
3rd Test	Wolverhampton	May 23	England 41 Denmark 66
4th Test	Bradford	May 25	England 57 Denmark 51
5th Test	Oxford	May 30	England 49 Denmark 59
1987			
1st Test	King's Lynn	May 3	England 58 Denmark 50
2nd Test	Oxford	May 8	England 49 Denmark 59
3rd Test	Cradley Heath	May 10	England 54 Denmark 54
4th Test	Belle Vue	May 13	England 56 Denmark 52
5th Test	Wolverhampton	May 18	England 53 Denmark 55
1988			
1st Test	Cradley Heath	September 25	England 48 Denmark 60
2nd Test	Sheffield	October 2	England 46 Denmark 62
1990			
1st Test	Oxford	April 18	England 63 Denmark 45
2nd Test	Bradford	April 22	England 62 Denmark 46
3rd Test	Wolverhampton	April 30	England 60 Denmark 47

Overall Series Record
England 5 Denmark 3 Drawn 1
Overall Test Record
England 15 Denmark 14 Drawn 2

The above records relate only to official series in England. Other results between the two countries are as detailed below:

1988 (Diamond Jubilee Series)			
1st Test	Ipswich	May 1	England 47 Denmark 43
Final	King's Lynn	June 26	England 38 Denmark 52
IN DENMARK			
1979	Vojens	May 18	Denmark 40 England 37
1981	Vojens	June 26	Denmark 60 England 48
1982	Vojens	August 20	Denmark 73 England 35
1984	Fredericia	July 1	Denmark 59 England 49
1987	Outrup	April 19	Denmark 68 England 40
1987	Brovst	April 26	Denmark 67 England 41
1988	Hanherred	May 11	Denmark 74 England 34
1988	Slangerup	May 12	Denmark 71 England 37

The RESULTS

First Test, at Oxford, Wednesday, April 18

ENGLAND 63

1 †Kelvin Tatum	1 1 3 2 1 1	9	3
2 Gary Havelock	2 2 2 3 0 0	9	1
3 Simon Cross	2 3 1 3 2 3	14	3
4 Marvyn Cox	3 2 2 2 3 2	14	3
5 Andrew Silver	2 1 1 2 3 3	12	1
6 Jeremy Doncaster	1 2 0 N 1 N	4	1
7 §Mark Loram	0	0	
8 §Dean Barker	1	1	1

DENMARK 45

1 Brian Karger	3 0 2 1 0 2	8	1
2 Bo Petersen	0 1 3 0 1 1	6	1
3 Jan O. Pedersen	1 3 1 R 2 2	9	1
4 John Jorgensen	0 0 0 1 N 3	4	
5 †Hans Nielsen	3 3 3 3 2 1	15	1
6 Lars Munkedal	0 0 N N 3 0	3	
7 Gert Handberg	0 0 0	0	

Team Managers
England: Colin Pratt and Eric Boocock Denmark: Kjeld Lund

Second Test, at Bradford, Sunday, April 22

ENGLAND 62

1 †Kelvin Tatum	2 1 3 3 0 2	11	2
2 Andy Smith	3 0 N 2 2 3	10	1
3 Simon Cross	3 2 2 3 1 2	13	3
4 Jeremy Doncaster	1 3 3 2 2 1	12	2
5 Gary Havelock	1 3 2 1 3 3	13	
6 Paul Thorp	0 1 N fxN 0	1	
7 Marvyn Cox	0	0	
8 Sean Wilson	2 R	2	1

DENMARK 46

1 Brian Karger	0 N 3 1 3 1	8	1
2 Bo Petersen	1 1 1 0 R 2	5	
3 John Jorgensen	2 0 1 1 N N	4	
4 Gert Handberg	0 2 0 0 2 1	5	
5 †Hans Nielsen	3 3 0 3 3 0	12	
6 Jan O. Pedersen	2 2 1 2 1 3	11	3
7 Lars Munkedal	0 1 0	1	1

Third Test, at Wolverhampton, Monday, April 30

ENGLAND 60

1 †Kelvin Tatum	3 1 3 3 1 3	14	
2 Martin Dugard	1 fxN N N N	1	
3 Simon Cross	3 3 3 2 2 3	16	1
4 Jeremy Doncaster	2 1 fx3 1 R	7	2
5 Gary Havelock	2 1 2 1 2 2	10	3
6 Andrew Silver	1 2 0 2 3 R	8	1
7 §Graham Jones	fxF	0	
8 Marvyn Cox	1 3	4	

DENMARK 47

1 †ans Nielsen	2 2 3 2 3 3	15	
2 Gert Handberg	0 0 N N 0 N	0	
3 John Jorgensen	1 R 2 R 0 2	5	
4 Brian Karger	0 3 fxN N N	3	
5 Jan O. Pedersen	3 3 2 3 2 2	15	
6 Peter Ravn	0 2 1 0 0 N	3	2
7 Bo Petersen	1 0 1	2	
8 Lars Munkedal	1 1 1 1	4	2

The International Scene

British Under 21 Champion Martin Dugard was ruled out after he broke his ankle at King's Lynn.

In the same meeting Zetor Stars' Richard Knight, named at reserve for the opening Test, was also in the wars, suffering concussion but no serious damage.

But the biggest shock of all was of the management's own volition for when they pruned their squad down to 10 riders there was no place for World number two, British and Commonwealth Champion Simon Wigg.

And that was for the first of the three Sunbrite internationals on his own home track at Cowley.

Joint team boss Colin Pratt explained: "Our decision has nothing whatsoever to do with anything other than the way he is riding.

"He hasn't started the season very well and whenever we have seen him he has looked fine when he has been in front but has struggled when he has been behind."

The management even had a second chance to bring him into the camp when Dugard pulled out – but kept to their 10-rider squad which meant teenager Dean Barker stepping up closer to his England debut.

There was another scare for the Sunbrite Lions the night before.

Skipper Kelvin Tatum rang Pratt to tell him: "I can't ride - I've damaged my wrist."

King's Lynn's Mark Loram was brought in but on the morning of the opening Test Tatum was back on the 'phone - this time re-assuring Pratt that after a night's sleep and some extensive treatment he was ready to race.

Disappointment for Loram? Pratt had no sooner received the good news from Tatum than he was given the bad news.

Richard Knight hadn't fully recovered from his crash and had been advised to withdraw on medical advice so Loram was back in the squad at reserve.

ENGLAND	M.	R.	Pts.	BP	TPts.	Ave.
Simon Cross	3	18	43	7	50	16.667
Marvyn Cox	3	9	18	3	21	14.000
Andy Smith	1	5	10	1	11	13.200
Kelvin Tatum	3	18	34	5	39	13.000
Gary Havelock	3	18	32	4	36	12.000
Dean Barker	1	1	1	1	2	12.000
Andrew Silver	2	12	20	2	22	11.000
Jeremy Doncaster	3	16	23	5	28	10.500
Sean Wilson	1	2	2	1	3	9.000
Martin Dugard	1	2	1	0	1	3.000
Paul Thorp	1	4	1	0	1	1.500
Mark Loram	1	1	0	0	0	0.000
Graham Jones	1	2	0	0	0	0.000

DENMARK	M.	R.	Pts.	BP	TPts.	Ave.
Hans Nielsen	3	18	42	1	43	14.333
Jan O. Pedersen	3	18	35	4	39	13.000
Brian Karger	3	14	19	2	21	9.000
Lars Munkedal	3	11	8	3	11	6.000
Peter Ravn	1	5	3	2	5	6.000
Bo Petersen	3	15	13	1	14	5.600
John Jorgensen	3	15	13	0	13	5.200
Gert Handberg	3	12	5	0	5	2.500

Not the ideal build-up. But you wouldn't have known it as the Sunbrite Lions tore into the dethroned World Champions.

Brian Karger was a shock winner of the opening heat with Tatum back in third place but by the end of heat five the Sunbrite Lions were eight points up with the Simon Cross-Marvyn Cox pairing unbeaten in two rides together.

Hans Nielsen pegged them back in heat nine but that was to be their only defeat of the night and they had ample revenge when they crowned a magnificent English performance by relegating the World Champion to third place in the last race.

By then England had chalked up their biggest win over the Danes since 1983.

Denmark's plight hadn't been helped by the fact they could track only seven riders – even though there were another handful racing in the National League, but on British ACU licences which ruled them out of representing their country of birth.

England made three changes for the second Test at Bradford with Andrew Silver and the two young reserves Barker and Loram dropping out to accommodate World Finalist Andy Smith, his Bradford team-mate Paul Thorp and big track expert Sean Wilson.

It didn't make the slightest difference to either England – or the brilliant Cross.

The Cradley Heath star, partnered this time by Jeremy Doncaster, was again England top scorer and he beat Nielsen in both heats nine and 18!

The Danes weren't helped by their insistence of keeping Nielsen and their number two Jan O. Pedersen together as a pairing.

It left them totally unbalanced and while it was, no doubt, good practice for the World Pairs Championship, it left them with even less chance of saving the series.

Nielsen won four races and claimed a 5-1 in three of those. Pedersen won a race and shared in those maximums.

But the engine-room pairing of John Jorgensen and Gert Handberg conceded all five heats in which they were programmed together – a tactical naivety bordering on the absurd.

England were in no mood to be charitable and registered seven 5-1s on their way to another resounding victory.

The result of the third and final Test at Wolverhampton was academic but at least an opportunity for Denmark to regain some lost credibility as Peter Ravn declared himself fit again and they did have two home riders (Petersen and Lars Munkedal) at reserve.

England's selectors gave a first cap to 26-year-old Graham Jones and Martin Dugard came into the series for the first time with his injured ankle wrapped in a lightweight protective cast.

Sadly, the young Oxford rider fell in his second ride and had to withdraw from the meeting giving Jones his first tough taste of international combat.

There was no Roy of the Rovers-style debut for the former grass-tracker as over zealousness saw him fall in his two rides.

Simon Cross maintained his new-found international wings – and this time came stunningly close to a six-ride maximum.

He beat Nielsen at the first time of asking but finished behind him in heat 13 although he could look back on a series in which he had met the World number one on six occasions and come out on top four times.

Three wins in a row also saw England edge ahead of the Danes in overall victories in officially recognised Test matches in this country but, more important than that, it helped the Sunbrite Lions believe in themselves.

Co-manager Eric Boocock claimed: "We won the World Team Cup last year and now we've beaten the Danes three times out of three in Test matches.

"Who can deny us our right to be called World Champions now?"

The International Scene

SOVIETS HAMMERED!

THE Russians came, saw and were well and truly conquered!

Despite sending over a strong squad hand-picked from the best of the Ufa Bashkiria and Rovno Signal clubs their lack of competitive equipment told...from the opening heat of their first match at Exeter's County Ground Stadium.

National League tracks drew straws to see which five centres would entertain the Russkies on their first tour of Britain since 1976.

Coincidentally they started their 1990 visit where they had said their good-byes 14 years earlier - in Devon.

This time they were on an even more demoralising defeat than at the hands of a side led by Ivan Mauger and Scott Autrey!

Their plight wasn't helped when Rif Saitgareev, named in the original tour party, had to withdraw because of a conflicting World Championship commitment, and René Aas was another non-starter because of injury.

When Igor Zverev was also missing it did not bode well for the visit and the Soviets were duly dispatched from Exeter on the wrong end of a massive beating with only Viktor Gaidym beating an opponent in 16 heats of fairly dull and boring fare for the locals.

Fortunately things did pick up. Zverev and Grigori Harchenko arrived in time for the second meeting at Poole and no-one would begrudge the Russians their farewell victory at Newcastle where Harchenko was the star of the show with a paid maximum.

They made plenty of friends, notably Ipswich's Alan Mogridge, who took time out at Foxhall Heath to help them change to the Barum tyres midway through the meeting, a move which certainly improved their scoring over the last half dozen races.

One man who didn't appear to endear himself to the tourists was referee Barry Bowles, in charge at Peterborough.

The Russians' touring confidante James Easter, who had fixed up the visit in the first place, lodged an official protest at the East of England Showground complaining that the referee was not allowing enough time for the visitors to get ready for races.

Overall, while it was an international bridge-building exercise, other than at Brough Park, the Russians were far too weak even for run-of-the-mill National League sides and it would appear that they have lagged a long, long way behind the Best of the West – not especially in skills but certainly by way of high-speed equipment which was their major downfall on an otherwise pleasing return to our tracks.

▲ ***For details of the Soviet Union 1990 tour of Australia see page 191.***

AVERAGES

SOVIET UNION

	M.	R.	Pts.	BP	TPts.	Ave.
Vladimir Trofimov	5	29	41	2	43	5.931
Grigori Harchenko	4	19	26	2	28	6.105
Nikolai Kornev	5	20	19	3	22	4.400
Viktor Gaidym	5	26	24	4	28	4.308
Mikhail Starostin	5	25	22	1	23	3.680
Igor Marko	5	21	17	2	19	3.619
Igor Zverev	4	18	14	1	15	3.333
Sergei Tershak	1	2	0	0	0	0.000

Team Managers
Boris Judin and Grigori Khlinovski.

▲ *The above averages are based on the recognised four rides per meeting as the series was run under the 16-heat National League formula. Maximum average is 12.000.*

The RESULTS

First Match, at Exeter, Monday, April 23

EXETER 78			
1 †Steve Regeling	**2 3 3 3 3**	**14**	**1**
2 Steve Bishop	**3 2 3 2 3**	**13**	**2**
3 Richard Green	**3 3 2 3 2**	**13**	**2**
4 Colin Cook	2 3 3 2 2	12	2
5 Peter Jeffery	1 2 2 2 3	10	4
6 Andy Sell	**3 2 2 2**	**9**	**3**
7 Mark Simmonds	2 2 3	7	2
SOVIET UNION 18			
1 †Vladimir Trofimov	1 1 0 1 0 0 0	3	
2 Mikhail Starostin	0 0 0 0 0 T	0	
3 Igor Marko	1 0 1 0 1 0	3	
4 Daniel Kalodij	*rider replacement*		
5 Viktor Gaidym	3 1 1 0 1 1	7	
6 Nikolai Kornev	1 1 1 0 1 1	5	
7 Sergei Tershak	0 0 N	0	
8 Greg Daniels	did not ride		

Second Match, at Poole, Tuesday, April 24

POOLE 59			
1 Gary Chessell	2 3 3 2 fx	10	1
2 Gary Allan	1 2 2 1 2	8	2
3 †Alun Rossiter	**3 3 3 3 3**	**15**	
4 Craig Boyce	**3 3 3 3 3**	**15**	
5 Steve Langdon	0 R F 0 N	0	
6 Steve Leigh	2 1 2 1	6	2
7 Rod Colquhoun	0 1 2 2	5	3
SOVIET UNION 37			
1 †Vladimir Trofimov	3 2 3 1 2 1	12	1
2 Igor Marko	0 1 T 0 T	1	1
3 Mikhail Starostin	0 R 1 T 0	1	1
4 Nikolai Kornev	1 F 0 T N	1	1
5 Igor Zverev	2 1 2 0 3 1	9	
6 Grigori Harchenko	3 1 2 1 X 2	9	
7 Viktor Gaidym	1 2 0 1	4	1

Third Match, at Ipswich, Thursday, April 26

IPSWICH 66			
1 Chris Louis	**3 3 3 3 3**	**15**	
2 Robbie Fuller	1 2 3 2 1	9	2
3 Dean Standing	3 2 2 R 0	7	1
4 †Alan Mogridge	2 3 3 0 2	10	2
5 David Norris	3 2 2 2 3	12	2
6 Shane Parker	2 2 3 0	7	2
7 Colin White	3 2 1	6	2
SOVIET UNION 30			
1 †Vladimir Trofimov	2 1 1 3 3 1	11	
2 Grigori Harchenko	0 0 1 F T 1	2	1
3 Igor Marko	1 0 fx N T	1	
4 Viktor Gaidym	0 1 1 1 2 0	5	1
5 Mikhail Starostin	1 0 X 2 3 2	8	
6 Nikolai Kornev	1 1 T T	2	
7 Igor Zverev	0 0 0 1	1	1

Fourth Match, at Peterborough, Friday, April 27

PETERBOROUGH 67			
1 †Mick Poole	3 2 3 3 2	13	1
2 Craig Hodgson	1 3 3 1 2	10	1
3 Frank Andersen	**3 3 3 3 3**	**15**	
4 Ian Barney	3 2 1 2 1	9	3
5 Scott Norman	2 3 R 2 2	9	3
6 Nigel Flatman	3 fx 2 3	8	1
7 Sean Barker	1 2 F	3	1
SOVIET UNION 27			
1 †Vladimir Trofimov	2 R 2 1 3	8	
2 Grigori Harchenko	N 1 R R N	1	
3 Igor Marko	1 1 3 N R	5	1
4 Viktor Gaidym	1 1 0 0 0	2	
5 Mikhail Starostin	R R 2 1 R	3	
6 Nikolai Kornev	2 0 2 1	5	1
7 Igor Zverev	0 0 2 1 0 0	3	

Fifth Match, at Newcastle, Sunday, April 29

NEWCASTLE 45			
1 †Peter Carr	1 3 3 3 3	13	
2 Spencer Timmo	0 1 N T 0	1	
3 Martin Dixon	2 3 2 2 3 2	14	1
4 Mark Thorpe	0 2 2 1 0	5	
5 Simon Green	2 fx 0 0 F	2	
6 Paul Smith	2 1 0 2 1	6	2
7 John Wainwright	3 R 1	4	1
SOVIET UNION 51			
1 †Vladimir Trofimov	3 1 0 1 2	7	1
2 Grigori Harchenko	**2 3 3 3 3**	**14**	**1**
3 Igor Marko	3 R 3 0 1	7	
4 Viktor Gaidym	1 1 1 2 1	6	2
5 Mikhail Starostin	3 2 0 2 3	10	
6 Nikolai Kornev	0 2 1 1 2	6	1
7 Igor Zverev	1 0 N	1	

The International Scene

SIZZLING BO'S BOOSTER

TOURISTS Slangerup added the vastly experienced Bo Petersen to their squad – and what a difference it made.

After their 1989 experience when they lost all five matches against National League club sides, Klaus Lohmann's Kulsvierne riders were determined that they wouldn't suffer another humiliation in their warm-up to the Danish Super League season.

And their squad certainly had a familiar look about it with all but two of their seven rider party having had British League experience in the past.

Petersen was, by far, the most experienced of their starters – but Peter Glanz, Jan Staechmann, Lars Munkedal and Per Sørensen had all been regular members of First Division tracks in the past.

Completing the squad were last season's tourists Bo Sørensen and the highly promising Jesper Olsen who had at least three offers of National League contracts before the visit was over - from Exeter, Milton Keynes and Glasgow.

The trip began with a comfortable win at Eastbourne where the home side were without skipper Gordon Kennett who was still nursing a pre-season shoulder injury.

When they also won at National League champions Poole two nights later there were optimistic hopes that the tour could end in a 5-0 whitewash.

But the Danes hit a succession of problems which effectively reduced their chances.

Per Sørensen was the first to take a tumble at Arlington and he was to have only one further ride all tour before having to pull out again in the final match at Edinburgh.

The Danes drafted in new Hackney signing Tim Korneliussen but he was surprisingly out of touch in his outings.

Lars Munkedal, back in the Sunbrite League with Wolverhampton, was as enigmatic as he had been during his summer with Edinburgh, and recorded a paid maximum at Eastbourne – and a single point from four starts at Glasgow!

Throughout, though, Petersen was superb as befits a rider of his pedigree and his performances were of such a high calibre that you could only wonder what might have been for Mildenhall had they managed to complete his signing before they were ejected from the National League.

He was unbeaten by an opponent in his first two meetings, won five out of six rides at Glasgow, and had double figure returns at both Middlesbrough and Edinburgh to finish the tour with 78 points from only five matches.

It was certainly a far happier trip for the Danes than it had been 12 months earlier.

AVERAGES

SLANGERUP

	M.	R.	Pts.	BP	TPts.	Ave.
Bo Petersen	5	30	77	1	78	10.400
Lars Munkedal	5	26	46	6	52	8.000
Jan Staechmann	5	24	33	6	39	6.500
Jesper Olsen	5	28	34	4	38	5.429
Peter Glanz	3	13	17	2	19	5.846
Bo Sørensen	5	22	19	4	23	4.182
Per Sørensen	2	4	4	0	4	4.000
Tim Korneliussen	3	10	7	1	8	3.200

Team Managers
Klaus Lohmann and Sven Mortensen.

■ *The above averages are based on the recognised four rides per meeting as the series was run under the 16-heat National League formula. Maximum average is 12.000.*

ROLL OF HONOUR

1989			
1st Match	April 14	Hackney 62	Slangerup 34
2nd Match	April 15	Arena Essex 54	Slangerup 41
3rd Match	April 16	Eastbourne 63	Slangerup 33
4th Match	April 17	Exeter 65	Slangerup 31
5th Match	April 18	Poole 58	Slangerup 38
1990			
1st Match	April 8	Eastbourne 39	Slangerup 57
2nd Match	April 10	Poole 43	Slangerup 53
3rd Match	April 11	Glasgow 51	Slangerup 45
4th Match	April 12	Middlesbrough 55	Slangerup 41
5th Match	April 15	Edinburgh 53	Slangerup 41

The RESULTS

First Match, at Eastbourne, Sunday, April 8

EASTBOURNE 39			
1 †Keith Pritchard	3 1 R 1 1 3	9	2
2 Gordon Kennett	*rider replacement*		
3 Andy Buck	1 2 3 0 3 1 1	11	
4 Paul Woods	2 2 1 2 1 1	9	1
5 Tony Primmer	2 1 1 2 R 0	6	3
6 Darren Grayling	R 0 0 0	0	
7 Steve Masters	1 2 1	4	
8 John Cook	*did not ride*		
SLANGERUP 57			
1 Per Sørensen	1 3 F N N	4	
2 Peter Glanz	0 0 1 2 3	6	
3 †Bo Petersen	**3 3 3 3 2**	**14**	**1**
4 Jesper Olsen	fx2 2 2 0	6	2
5 Jan Staechmann	3 N 3 R 3	9	
6 Bo Sørensen	2 0 1 0 2 2	7	3
7 Lars Munkedal	**3 2 3 3**	**11**	**1**

Second Match, at Poole, Tuesday, April 10

POOLE 43			
1 Gary Chessell	E 2 2 0 1 3	8	
2 Gary Allan	1 3 1 0 2 1	8	1
3 †Craig Boyce	1 3 2 3 3 0 2	14	1
4 Alun Rossiter	*rider replacement*		
5 Tony Langdon	0 2 1 1 1	5	2
6 Steve Langdon	R fx0 2 0	2	1
7 Rod Colquhoun	2 2 2 0	6	1
8 Steve Leigh	*did not ride*		
SLANGERUP 53			
1 Per Sørensen	*rider replacement*		
2 Tim Korneliussen	2 0 1 0 3	6	1
3 †Bo Petersen	**3 3 3 3 3 3**	**18**	
4 Jesper Olsen	1 1 1 1 0 1	5	
5 Jan Staechmann	3 0 3 2 2	10	2
6 Bo Sørensen	1 0 0 2 0	3	1
7 Lars Munkedal	3 2 3 1 2	11	1
8 Alan Spencer	*did not ride*		

Third Match, at Glasgow, Wednesday, April 11

GLASGOW 51			
1 †Steve Lawson	3 1 0 1 1	6	2
2 Charlie McKinna	2 2 2 3 2	11	2
3 Kenny McKinna	2 3 2 1 3	11	
4 Shane Bowes	R 3 2 2 3	10	
5 Sean Courtney	1 1 1 R 2	5	2
6 Martin McKinna	3 1 0 0	4	1
7 Jason Lyons	1 3 0	4	
SLANGERUP 45			
1 Tim Korneliussen	1 0 N N 0	1	
2 Peter Glanz	0 2 1 T N	3	
3 †Bo Petersen	3 3 3 3 3 1	16	
4 Jesper Olsen	3 2 1 2 2	10	2
5 Jan Staechmann	2 1 2 R N	5	2
6 Bo Sørensen	2 0 X 0 3 3	8	
7 Lars Munkedal	R 0 N 1 E 1	2	

Fourth Match, at Middlesbrough, Thursday, April 12

MIDDLESBROUGH 55			
1 Darren Sumner	3 1 1 3 1	9	1
2 David Cheshire	2 3 2 2 3	12	1
3 †Jamie Luckhurst	0 1 1 3 2	7	1
4 Paul Bentley	1 3 2 0 fx	6	1
5 Rod Hunter	2 0 1 2 3	8	2
6 Steve Wilcock	**3 3 3 2**	**11**	**1**
7 Paul Smith	2 0 0	2	1
SLANGERUP 41			
1 Tim Korneliussen	0 T T N E	0	
2 Peter Glanz	1 1 3 2 1	8	2
3 †Bo Petersen	2 2 3 3 2 1	13	
4 Jesper Olsen	F 2 F 0 3	5	
5 Jan Staechmann	3 R 3 1 R	7	1
6 Bo Sørensen	1 0 0 0	1	
7 Lars Munkedal	R 1 2 1 1 2	7	2

Fifth Match, at Edinburgh, Sunday, April 15

EDINBURGH 53			
1 Les Collins	3 3 3 2 3	14	
2 Michael Coles	1 1 2 2 2	8	2
3 †Brett Saunders	R 3 1 1 1	6	1
4 Mark Blackbird	3 R 0 1 2	6	2
5 Carl Blackbird	2 3 E 3 2	10	1
6 Freddy Schøtt	2 2 R 1 0 3	8	
7 Nigel Alderton	1 F N	1	1
SLANGERUP 41			
1 Per Sørensen	R N T N N	0	
2 Peter Glanz	*rider replacement*		
3 †Bo Petersen	1 2 1 3 3 3 3	16	
4 Jesper Olsen	2 R 0 2 1 2 1	8	
5 Jan Staechmann	R R 1 X 1 0	2	1
6 Bo Sørensen	fxT N N	0	
7 Lars Munkedal	3 3 2 3 2 2	15	2

The International Scene

POLAND v SWEDEN

Gniezno, Poland, Tuesday, April 10
POLAND 36 (Tomasz Gollob 11, Jacek Gomolski 9, Ryszard Dolomisiewicz 8, Zbigniew Krakowski 4, Zenon Kasprzak 2, Szczepan Kulczak 1, Tomasz Fajfer 1, Piotr Pawlicki 0) **SWEDEN 71** (Tony Richardsson 15, Peter Karlsson 12, Joakim Karlsson 11, Jörgen Johansson 11, Mikael Teurnberg 10, Christer Karlsson 9, Thomas Karlsson 3)
Zielona Gora, Poland, Thursday, April 12
POLAND 60 (Jaroslaw Szymkowiak 12, Piotr Swist 11, Zenon Kasprzak 11, Slawomir Dudek 8, Andrzej Huszcza 8, Zbigniew Krakowski 5, Ryszard Franczyszyn 4, Zbigniew Blazejczak 1) **SWEDEN 46** (Tony Richardsson 16, Mikael Teurnberg 13, Jörgen Johansson 9, Joakim Karlsson 4, Peter Karlsson 3, Christer Karlsson 1, Thomas Karlsson 0)
Gorzow, Poland, Friday, April 13
POLAND 65 (**Piotr Swist 18**, Tomasz Gollob 16, Ryszard Dolomisiewicz 14, Jacek Wozniak 9, Jacek Gomolski 4, Ryszard Franczyszyn 2, Jan Krzystyniak 1, Cezary Owizyc 1) **SWEDEN 43** (Tony Richardsson 12, Christer Karlsson 11, Mikael Teurnberg 9, Thomas Karlsson 7, Peter Karlsson 3, Jörgen Johansson 1, Joakim Karlsson 0).

SWEDEN v DENMARK

Vestervik, Sweden, Sunday, June 10
SWEDEN 63 (Jimmy Nilsen 14, Dennis Löfqvist 13, Per Jonsson 11, Conny Ivarsson 11, Henrik Gustafsson 5, Peter Nahlin 3, Tony Olsson 3, Joakim Karlsson 3) **DENMARK 45** (**Hans Nielsen 18**, Jan O. Pedersen 13, John Jorgensen 5, Gert Handberg 4, Jens Henry Nielsen 2, Brian Karger 2, Bo Petersen 1, Jan Pedersen 0).
Gothenburg, Sweden, Monday, June 11
SWEDEN 62 (Jimmy Nilsen 15, Dennis Löfqvist 13, Per Jonsson 13, Henrik Gustafsson 11, Tony Olsson 4, Conny Ivarsson 3, Peter Nahlin 3, Niklas Karlsson 0) **DENMARK 46** (Jan O. Pedersen 16, Hans Nielsen 10, John Jorgensen 8, Gert Handberg 8, Jens Henry Nielsen 4, Brian Karger 0, Bo Petersen 0, Jan Pedersen 0)
Outrup, Denmark, Wednesday, June 13
DENMARK 50 (Hans Nielsen 16, Jan O. Pedersen 11, Brian Karger 10, Hans Clausen 7, Gert Handberg 5, John Jorgensen 1, Jens Henry Nielsen 0, Jan Pedersen 0) **SWEDEN 58** (Per Jonsson 13, Dennis Löfqvist 12, Jimmy Nilsen 11, Conny Ivarsson 8, Henrik Gustafsson 8, Peter Nahlin 3, Tony Olsson 3)

OTHER MAJOR INTERNATIONALS

Brisbane, Australia, Saturday, January 27
AUSTRALIA 49 (Phil Crump 14, Mick Poole 13, Leigh Adams 7, Glenn Doyle 6, Troy Butler 5, Steve Regeling 3, Alan Rivett 1) **REST OF THE WORLD 41** (Mitch Shirra [New Zealand] 10, Kelvin Tatum [England] 8, Hans Nielsen [Denmark] 8, Jimmy Nilsen [Sweden] 7, Simon Wigg [England] 6, Jan Staechmann [Denmark] 2, Bobby Schwartz [America] 0)

Castelmassa, Italy, Saturday, March 31
ITALY 60 (Armando dal Chiele 13, Armando Castagna 11, Fabrizio Vesprini 9, Luca Ravagnani 9, Gianni Famari 8, Massimo Mora 7, Valentino Furlanetto 2, Andrea Maida 1) **SOVIET UNION 47** (**Rif Saitgareev 18**, Oleg Kurguskin 10, Andrej Korolev 6, Rinat Mardanshin 4, Igor Dubinin 3, René Aas 2, Arkadij Kononiec 2, Grigori Harchenko 2).

Pocking, West Germany, Sunday, April 15
WEST GERMANY 36 (Karl Maier 11, Gerd Riss 11, Alois Bachhuber 8, Klaus Lausch 6, Carsten Pelzmann) **SWEDEN 32** (Henrik Gustafsson 9, Claes Ivarsson 8, Niklas Karlsson 8, Conny Ivarsson 7) **HUNGARY 18** (Robert Nágy 6, Zoltán Adorján 4, Jozsef Petrikovics 4, Zoltán Hajdü 3, Sándor Tihanyi 1) **CZECHOSLOVAKIA 10** (Antonin Kasper 7, Zdenek Tesar 2, Zdenek Schneiderwind 1, Petr Vandirek 0, Pavel Karnas 0).

Blijham, Holland
HOLLAND 29 (Ron Koppe 11, Henk Bangma 7, Erik Drayer 6, Rene Elzinga 5) **EAST GERMANY 25** (Matthias Beckmeyer 10, Thomas Kock 7, Herbert Musseh1 5, Raik Arnheim 3).
Miskolc, Hungary, Tuesday, August 21
HUNGARY A 46 (**Zsolt Böszörmányi 15**, Zoltán Hajdü 14, Sándor Uljhely 12, Istvan Osvath 5) **HUNGARY B 38** (Attila Kovacs 10, Zoltan Kovacs 10, Zsolt Kovacs 9, Jozsef Petrikovics 9) **SOVIET UNION 21** (Vladimir Trofimov 12, Boris Ignatov 5, Vladimir Rybnikov 2, *Csaba Csoban 2*) **AUSTRIA 15** (Andreas Bössner 7, Walter Nebel 5, Rainer Selb 3, Siegfried Eder 0).
Felixdorf, Austria
AUSTRIA 56 (Andreas Bössner 14, Walter Nebel 13, Toni Pilotto 12, Robert Funk 8, Thomas Stadler 7, Rainer Selb 1, Josef Bössner 1) **POLAND 51** (Janusz Kapustka 10, Piotr Styczynsky 10, Jacek Rempala 9, Slawomir Tronina 9, Zieba 7, Piotr Lesniowski 6).

NORDIC UNDER 21 CHAMPIONSHIP

Eskilstuna, Sweden, Saturday, August 4
SWEDEN 42 (Henrik Gustafsson 12, Joakim Karlsson 10, Jimmy Engman 9, Tony Richardsson 8, Robert Johansson 3) **DENMARK 31** (Brian Andersen 10, Jan Andersen 9, Robert Larsen 5, Johnny Jorgensen 4, Claus Jacobsen 3) **NORWAY 18** (Lars Gunnestad 11, Odd Pettersen 4, Ingvar Hvamstad 2, Rolf Netland 1, Nils Mellomstrand 0) **FINLAND 17** (Petri Nurmesniemi 5, Petri Kokko 4, Niklas Havu 4, Petri Vaatsio 3, Tomi Havu 1).

MAJOR UNDER 21 TESTS

Torun, Poland, Sunday, April 15
SWEDEN 44 (Peter Karlsson 12, Tony Richardsson 12, Joakim Karlsson 10, Tomas Karlsson 6, Stefan Dannö 4) **POLAND 31** (Dariusz Sledz 11, Tomasz Gollob 7, Jacek Rempala 7, Robert Sawina 4, Jacek Wozniak 2) **DENMARK 27** (Claus Jacobsen 8, Brian Andersen 7, Jacob Olsen 6, Jan Andersen 6, Johnny Jorgensen 0).
Gdansk, Poland, Monday, April 16
POLAND 43 (Dariusz Sledz 14, Tomasz Gollob 12, Jacek Rempala 9, Robert Sawina 7, Jacek Wozniak 1) **SWEDEN 27** (Tony Richardsson 10, Peter Karlsson 6, Stefan Dannö 6, Joakim Karlsson 5) **DENMARK 26** (Jacob Olsen 8, Claus Jacobsen 7, Jan Andersen 6, Brian Andersen 5) **FINLAND 9** (Petri Nurmesniemi 3, Jarmo Makinen 3, Tomi Havu 2, Petri Kokko 1).
Eskilstuna, Sweden, Saturday, May 19
SWEDEN 46 (Tony Richardsson 11, Jimmy Engman 11, Joakim Karlsson 9, Raymond Smedh 9, Robert Johansson 6) **DENMARK 29** (Brian Andersen 9, Claus Jacobsen 7, Hans Clausen 6, Jacob Olsen 4, Richard Juul 3) **POLAND 17** (Janusz Slaczka 7, Robert Sawina 4, Robert Kuzdzal 4, Marek Hucko 2, Jerzy Mordel 0) **FINLAND 16** (Petri Kokko 8, Petri Vaatsio 5, Petri Nurmesniemi 2, Jarmo Makinen 1, Esa Einola 0).
Vestervik, Sweden, Sunday, May 20
SWEDEN 35 (Jimmy Engman 10, Stefan Dannö 9, Joakim Karlsson 8, Stefan Lardner 4, Tomas Karlsson 4) **DENMARK 30** (Claus Jacobsen 8, Brian Andersen 8, Hans Clausen 6, Richard Juul 5, Jacob Olsen 3) **POLAND 24** (Robert Sawina 8, Janusz Slaczka 6, Robert Kuzdzal 5, Marek Hucko 3, Jerzy Mordel 2) **FINLAND 18** (Esa Einola 5, Petri Kokko 5, Jarmo Makinen 4, Petri Nurmesniemi 3, Petri Vaatsio 1).
Seinäjoki, Finland, Saturday, June 16
DENMARK 36 (Brian Andersen 10, Hans Clausen 10, Claus Jacobsen 9, Jacob Olsen 5, Johnny Jorgensen 2) **SWEDEN 31** (Tony Richardsson 12, Joakim Karlsson 7, Robert Johansson 6, Jimmy Engman 5, Raymond Smedh 1) **FINLAND 21** (Esa Einola 5, Jarmo Makinen 5, Petri Vaatsio 5, Tomi Havu 3, Petri Nurmesniemi 3) **POLAND 20** (Miroslaw Kowalik 8, Robert Kuzdzal 7, Janusz Slaczka 4, Jaroslaw Olszewski 1, Robert Sawina 0).
Seinäjoki, Finland, Sunday, June 17
SWEDEN 42 (Tony Richardsson 12, Joakim Karlsson 12, Robert Johansson 12, Raymond Smedh 6, Jimmy Engman 0) **DENMARK 34** (Hans Clausen 10, Jacob Olsen 9, Brian Andersen 7, Claus Jacobsen 6, Johnny Jorgensen 2) **POLAND 23** (Robert Kuzdzal 7, Tomasz Fajfer 6, Janusz Slaczka 4, Jaroslaw Olszewski 3, Miroslaw Kowalik 3).
Slangerup, Denmark, Saturday, June 23
DENMARK 37 (Jan Andersen 11, Claus Jacobsen 10, Brian Andersen 8, Hans Clausen 8, Jacob Olsen 0) **SWEDEN 32** (Tony Richardsson 12, Robert Johansson 7, Jimmy Engman 6, Joakim Karlsson 5, Goran Flood 2) **NORWAY 20** (Lars Gunnestad 11, Odd Pettersen 5, Jørn Årne Ardal 2, Nils Mellomstrand 2, Rolf Netland 0) **POLAND 19** (Janusz Slaczka 6, Tomas Fajfer 5, Jaroslaw Karskicwich 4, Miroslaw Kowalik 3, Robert Kuzdzal 1).
Copenhagen, Denmark, Sunday, June 24
DENMARK 40 (Claus Jacobsen 10, Jacob Olsen 9, Hans Clausen 9, Brian Andersen 8, Heinrich Nielsen 4) **POLAND 26** (Tomasz Fajfer 8, Robert Sawina 7, Jaroslaw Olszewski 7, Miroslaw Kowalik 4, Janusz Slaczka 0) **SWEDEN 25** (Joakim Karlsson 10, Jimmy Engman 7, Goran Flood 6, Robert Johansson 2, Tony Richardsson 0) **NORWAY 15** (Lars Gunnestad 9, Odd Pettersen 3, Jørn Årne Ardal 2, Rolf Netland 1, Nils Mellomstrand 0).
Stralsund, East Germany, Thursday, August 16
DENMARK 41 CZECHOSLOVAKIA 34 EAST GERMANY 21 OTHER NATIONS 6
Neubrandenburg, East Germany, Friday, August 17
DENMARK 42 (Claus Jacobsen 15, Kenneth Arnfred 12, Lars Henryk Jorgensen 10, Per Jensen 5) **CZECHOSLOVAKIA 29** (Gaspar Forgac 8, Vladimir Kalina 7, Jan Holub 7, Jiri Hurych 7) **OTHER NATIONS 20** (Jens Peter Nielsen 11, Mario Busch 5, Rostislav Bures 4, Frank Leonhardt 0) **EAST GERMANY 11** (Thomas Hopp 6, Raik Arnheim 2, Frank Biljuk 2, Matthias Beckmeyer 1)
Ludwigslust, East Germany, Saturday, August 18
CZECHOSLOVAKIA 40 (Vladimir Kalina 14, Gaspar Forgac 10, Jan Holub 9, Rostislav Bures 7) **DENMARK 35** (Claus Jacobsen 11, Lars Henryk Jorgensen 10, Kenneth Arnfred 9, Per Jensen 5) **OTHER NATIONS 20** (Johnny Jorgensen 9, Jiri Hurych 5, Ralf Baumann 3, Frank Biljuk 3) **EAST GERMANY 7** (Thomas Hopp 3, Matthias Beckmeyer 2, Raik Arnheim 1, Mario Busch 1, Thomas Kock 0)
Wolfslake, East Germany, Sunday, August 19
DENMARK 39 (Claus Jacobsen 15, Kenneth Arnfred 11, Lars Henryk Jorgensen 7, Johnny Jorgensen 6) **OTHER NATIONS 24** (Mario Busch 9, Per Jensen 6, Jiri Hurych 6, Frank Biljuk 2, Heuer 1) **CZECHOSLOVAKIA 21** (Jan Holub 13, Vladimir Kalina 7, Gaspar Forgac 1, Rostislav Bures 0, Jozef Lastovka 0) **EAST GERMANY 18** (Thomas Hopp 9, Thomas Kock 5, Matthias Beckmeyer 3, Ralf Baumann 1, Raik Arnheim 0)

The S.W.A.P.A. Awards

RIDER OF THE YEAR

1978 Ole Olsen 1979 Ivan Mauger 1980 Dave Jessup 1981 Bruce Penhall 1982 Les Collins 1983 Michael Lee 1984 Erik Gundersen 1985 Erik Gundersen 1986 Hans Nielsen 1987 Hans Nielsen 1988 Erik Gundersen 1989 Hans Nielsen **1990 Todd Wiltshire**

YOUNG RIDER OF THE YEAR

1983 Kelvin Tatum 1984 Lance King 1985 Kelvin Tatum 1986 Paul Thorp 1987 Jimmy Nilsen 1988 Mark Loram 1989 Joe Screen **1990 Chris Louis**

ORDER OF MERIT

1979 Barry Briggs 1980 Jack Parker 1981 Tommy Price 1982 Ove Fundin 1983 Freddie Williams 1984 Frank Varey 1985 Ivan Mauger 1986 Peter Collins 1987 Erik Gundersen 1988 Ole Olsen 1989 Chris Morton **1990 Colin Pratt**

GRAHAM BAKER AWARD

1988 Frank Maclean 1989 Barry Briggs

TRAVEL PLUS TOURS JOURNALIST OF THE YEAR

1990 Peter Oakes

▲ Rider of the Year, which is supported by British Airways, and Young Rider of the Year awards are voted for by members of the Speedway Writers' and Photographers' Association. The Order of Merit Award and the Graham Baker Award – in memory of the former SWAPA member – are at the discretion of the SWAPA Committee. Travel Plus Journalist of the Year is selected by James Easter, managing director of Travel Plus, Australian Team Manager and European Agent for the Soviet Union Speedway Federation. The 1990 Awards were announced at the annual SWAPA Dinner at the St. John's Hotel, Solihull, West Midlands, on Thursday, October 4.

Star of 90

HANS NIELSEN

BLRC Champion

Champions Cup

Lonigo, Italy, Sunday, April 29, 1990

HANS PICKS UP NEW CROWN

HANS Nielsen finally put the seal of approval on the competition that no-one wanted...by becoming the first rider to hold both the individual World Championship and the FIM's Champion of Champions.

The Great Dane suffered a shock defeat but then went on to victory - and his country's second win in a row - after a run-off with Hungarian Champion Zoltán Adorján, the only ex-title winner in the line-up.

America's Ronnie Correy actually set off for Italy but never arrived - after forgetting his passsport!

But he was the only non-starter in a meeting which has increased in status on an almost annual basis although the meeting is still widely shunned by British fans in particular.

British Champion Simon Wigg cast aside his cloak of Sunbrite League uncertainty to once again prove himself on a world stage - repeating his World Final rostrum placing, although, this time, he had to be content with third spot.

Most impressive of the relatively unknown riders were Norway's Arnt Førland - surely worth a chance in the UK? - and Swedish Champion Peter Karlsson who was excused duty in his domestic World Championship rounds to compete.

1990 Results

1 HANS NIELSEN (Denmark)	**14**	(+3)
2 Zoltán Adorján (Hungary)	**14**	(+2)
3 Simon Wigg (England)	**12**	
4 Klaus Lausch (West Germany)	11	
5 Arnt Førland (Norway)	11	
6 Peter Karlsson (Sweden)	10	
7 Rif Saitgareev (Soviet Union)	10	
8 Juha Moksunen (Finland)	8	
9 Petr Vandirek (Czechoslovakia)	7	
10 Wojciech Zaluski (Poland)	6	
11 Valentino Furlanetto (Italy)	5	
12 Toni Pilotto (Austria)	5	
13 Gregor Pintar (Yugoslavia)	3	
14 Nikolai Manev (Bulgaria)	2	
15 Gianni Famari (Italy*)	1	
16 Rene Elzinga (Holland)	1	

Ronnie Correy did not arrive and was replaced by Gianni Famari.

Roll of Honour

1986 (Pardubice, Czechoslovakia)
1 ERIK STENLUND 14, 2 Viktor Kuznetsov 13 (+3), 3 Antonin Kasper 13 (+2), 4 Armando Castagna 12, 5 Roman Matousek 10, 6 Zoltán Adorján 8, 7 Petr Vandirek 7, 8 Pavel Karnas 7, 9 Nikolai Manev 7, 10 Zenon Plech 6, 11 John Davis 6, 12 Siegfried Eder 6, 13 Kreso Omerzel 4, 14 Juha Moksunen 4, 15 Henny Kroeze 2, 16 Petr Kucera, reserve, 1, 17 Diethelm Triemer 0.

1987 (Miskolc, Hungary)
1 ZOLTAN ADORJAN 12 (+3), 2 Armando Castagna 12 (+2), 3 Antonin Kasper 11 (+3), 4 Neil Evitts 11 (+2), 5 Per Jonsson 11 (+1), 6 Erik Stenlund 10, 7 Gerd Riss 9, 8 Diethelm Triemer 8, 9 Jens Peter Nielsen 6, 10 Wojciech Zabialowicz 6, 11 Valeri Gordeev 5, 12 Heinrich Schatzer 5, 13 Nikolai Manev 4, 14 Juha Moksunen 3, 15 Henny Kroeze 2, 16 Artur Horvat 2.

1988 (Krsko, Yugoslavia)
1 PER JONSSON 14, 2 Gerd Riss 13 (+3), 3 Zoltán Adorján 13 (+2), 4 Heinrich Schatzer 11, 5 Per Sorensen 10, 6 Antonin Kasper 9, 7 Zenon Kasprzak 9, 8 Valentino Furlanetto 8, 9 Valeri Gordeev 8, 10 Kelvin Tatum 6, 11 Ari Koponen 5, 12 Zvenko Pavlic 4, 13 Henk Steman 3, 14 Nikolai Manev 3, 15 Artur Horvat 2, 16 Einar Tor Helm 2.

1989 (Natschbach-Loipersbach, Austria)
1 JAN O. PEDERSEN 15, 2 Mitch Shirra 13, 3 Kai Niemi 10, 4 Simon Wigg 9, 5 Sam Ermolenko 9, Roman Matousek 9, Zoltán Adorján 9, Klaus Lausch 9, 9 Lars Gunnestad 8, 10 Vladimir Trofimov 7, 11 Per Jonsson 5, Armando Castagna 5, 13 Nikolai Manev 4, 14 Robert Funk, reserve, 3, 15 Zenon Kasprzak 2, 16 Artur Horvat 1, Heinrich Schatzer 1.

1990 (Lonigo, Italy)
1 HANS NIELSEN 14 (+3), 2 Zoltán Adorján 14 (+2), 3 Simon Wigg 12, 4 Klaus Lausch 11, 5 Arnt Førland 11, 6 Peter Karlsson 10, 7 Rif Saitgareev 10, 8 Juha Moksunen 8, 9 Petr Vandirek 7, 10 Wojciech Zaluski 6, 11 Valentino Furlanetto 5, 12 Toni Pilotto 5, 13 Gregor Pintar 3, 14 Nikolai Manev 2, 15 Gianni Famari 1, 16 Rene Elzinga 1.

Ronnie Correy did not arrive and was replaced by a second Italian rider Gianni Famari.

European Grass Track Championship

Uithuizen, Holland, Saturday, August 4, 1990

BRITAIN'S grass track challenge melted away in the heat of a scorching summer.

And it was West Germany's defending champion Robert Barth who was the ice-cool winner of his second successive championship, beating former Birmingham, Exeter and Wolverhampton rider Kent Noer in a run-off.

Top placed Brit was Milton Keynes' Trevor Banks.

Roll of Honour

1978	1 Chris Baybutt	2 Franz Kolbeck	3 Don Godden
1979	1 Gerald Short	2 Gunther Brackland	3 John Britcher & Tjalle Reitsma
1980	1 Willi Stauch	2 Gerald Short	3 Sture Lindblom
1981	1 Neil Farnish	2 Bernie Leigh	3 Skjold Larsen
1982	1 Jeremy Doncaster	2 Mike Beaumont	3 Josef Maucher
1983	1 Christian Brandt	2 Erich Schafferer	3 Gerald Short
1984	1 Martin Hagon	2 Vaclav Verner	3 Kent Noer
1985	1 Clayton Williams	2 Harm Horstede	3 Tommy Broch
1986	1 Simon Cross	2 Steve Schofield	3 Joachim Reitzel
1987	1 Roman Matousek	2 Joachim Reitzel	3 Bob Dolman
1988	1 Frank Kehlenbeck	2 Will James	3 Kent Noer
1989	1 Robert Barth	2 Kent Noer	3 John Bostin
1990	1 Robert Barth	2 Kent Noer	3 Henk Snijder

1 ROBERT BARTH 24 (+3), 2 Kent Noer 24 (+2), 3 Henk Snijder 15, 4 Anne van den Helm 14, 5 Helmut Zapf 13, 6 Trevor Banks 13, 7 Richard Juul Sorensen 10, 8 Tommy Lindgren 10, 9 Will James 9, 10 Armando dal Chiele 8, 11 Tim Fey 8, 12 Tony Forward 7, 13 Vaclav Milik 6, 14 Andy Riley 5, 15 Robert Price 5, 16 Roland Comblon 4, 17 Thomas Meggle, reserve, 3, 18 Jan Schinagl 1, 19 Uppie Bos 0, 19 Benny Tøgersen, reserve, 0.
Frank Kehlenbeck, Bob Dolman and Christian Ianotto withdrew through injury.

The B.L.R.C.

HANS NIELSEN may have forfeited the World crown on an off-night at Bradford...but he's still the most consistent big-meeting winner in World speedway.

And he rounded off an otherwise disappointing domestic season by winning his third British League Riders' Championship.

But the revenge clash that everyone wanted to see – a re-match with World Champion Per Jonsson – was denied the fans as the Swedish star missed out of the qualifying ratings as he was only third in the Reading averages at the BLRC cut-off date.

Jan O. Pedersen, of course, was also missing, and that made Nielsen's task even easier.

He was one of the most comprehensive winners in the long history of the championship and his toughest moments came from trying to placate referee John Whitaker who was far from amused with his wheelie antics down the home straight.

Nielsen was warned he would be fined if he repeated the offence but spectator Chris Morton offered to meet any financial penalty explaining: "Speedway should be about entertaining the crowd and that was what Hans was doing!"

Nielsen was fined £20 and Mort, watching his last BLRC as a rider, stumped up.

There had been concerted moves during the season to move the meeting from its traditional Belle Vue home and there is no disguising the fact that what was once the biggest individual meeting of the year apart from the World Final, has now lost much of its gloss and appeal.

Tyre manufacturers Dunlop stepped in as late sponsors, along with local company Groundwork Landscapes Limited, and, fittingly, the meeting was won on the British-made tyres.

Martin Dugard and Greg Hancock began on Barums and when the Oxford rider asked to switch to Dunlop he was refused permission and withdrew from the meeting on a track where he had been a regular tall scorer.

It gave American Bobby Ott a chance of mixing it and he sneaked an enterprising second place in his one race, ahead of World Team Cup star Gary Havelock and World number three Todd Wiltshire.

Ott's form at reserve reflected the effort that the entire American party put into the meeting.

Kelly Moran, the most entertaining rider of the afternoon, won a run-off for second place and, overall, there were three Californians in the top five including Sam Ermolenko, crowning a remarkable return from injury with an admirable fifth place in a meeting that needs a new injection of life if it is to regain former status.

Belle Vue, Sunday, October 14

1 Hans Nielsen	**3 3 3 3 3**	**15**
2 Kelly Moran	2 3 2 3 2	12 (+3)
3 Ronnie Correy	3 2 3 2 2	12 (+2)
4 Marvyn Cox	1 3 3 2 3	12(+1)
5 Sam Ermolenko	0 3 2 3 3	11
6John Jorgensen	3 1 1 3 0	8
7 Andrew Silver	2 2 fx1 3	8
8 Jeremy Doncaster	1 1 3 2 1	8
9 Shawn Moran	3 2 2 0 0	7
10 Gary Havelock	2 1 1 1 2	7
11 Mark Loram	2 1 1 1 1	6
12 Todd Wiltshire	0 2 2 0 1	5
13 Jimmy Nilsen	1 0 0 0 2	3
14 Kelvin Tatum	1 0 1 1 0	3
15 Greg Hancock	0 0 0 0 1	1
16 Martin Dugard	0 0 0 NN	0
Track reserves		
17 Bobby Ott	2	2
17 Richard Musson	0	0

ROLL OF HONOUR

1965 Barry Briggs (Swindon) 14
1966 Barry Briggs (Swindon) 15
1967 Barry Briggs (Swindon) 15
1968 Barry Briggs (Swindon) 14
1969 Barry Briggs (Swindon) 14
1970 Barry Briggs (Swindon) 13
1971 Ivan Mauger (Belle Vue) 14
1972 Ole Olsen (Wolverhampton) 15
1973 Ivan Mauger (Exeter) 14
1974 Peter Collins (Belle Vue) 15
1975 Peter Collins (Belle Vue) 15
1976 Ole Olsen (Coventry) 15
1977 Ole Olsen (Coventry) 15
1978 Ole Olsen (Coventry) 13
1979 John Louis (Ipswich) 14
1980 Les Collins (Leicester) 14
1981 Kenny Carter (Halifax) 15
1982 Kenny Carter (Halifax) 15
1983 Erik Gundersen (Cradley Heath) 14
1984 Chris Morton (Belle Vue) 13
1985 Erik Gundersen (Cradley Heath) 14
1986 Hans Nielsen (Oxford) 15
1987 Hans Nielsen (Oxford) 14
1988 Jan O. Pedersen (Cradley Heath) 14
1989 Shawn Moran (Belle Vue) 15
1990 Hans Nielsen (Oxford) 15

British U21

TEENAGER Joe Screen, struggling to maintain his supersonic start in his second season of Sunbrite League racing, had never even seen Plough Lane – let alone ridden the famous London track.

You would never have guessed it as he smashed the track record in his first ride even though he had to come from behind to beat rival Simon Green.

Mark Loram later equalled the new time and after three rides each they were bracketed together on nine points while Chris Louis and home star Nathan Simpson had eight points apiece!

The first big crunch came in heat 14 when Screen lined up alongside – and was beaten by – Chris Louis.

Loram went into an overall lead as he made it four wins out of four in the following race as Simpson's hopes of a home victory disappeared as he trailed in behind the King's Lynn youngster.

Screen and Loram met in heat 18 and it was the Belle Vue starlet who was into the turn first.

But in a tangle of machinery, Darren Grayling came down and referee Mick Barnes ordered a re-run to offer 1988 winner Loram a chance to regain the crown, sponsored this year by Coastal Windows.

But Screen's extra sharpness from the tapes was again evident as he forced a run-off for the title.

Louis, out in heat 20, needed a win to make it a three-rider decider but in the hurley-burly of a first bend shunt, he was moved out towards the fence and had to start chasing from fourth place.

He overhauled Scott Robson and David Clarke but couldn't make up the leeway on Simpson and had to be content with the minor placing race-off rather than the major decider.

Louis raced away from the advantageous inside gate in the rostrum run-off and then Screen won the vital toss for choice of start positions in the more important match-race.

For the third successive time, he outgated Loram and he wasn't going to give him any unexpected opportunity to squeeze past.

And he became the sixth Belle Vue rider to win the British Under 21 Championship in 18 years.

Wimbledon, Wednesday, July 11

1 Joe Screen	**3 3 3 2 3**	**14 (+3)**
2 Mark Loram	3 3 3 3 2	14 (+2)
3 Chris Louis	3 3 2 3 2	13 (+3)
4 Nathan Simpson	3 3 2 2 3	13 (+2)
5 Dean Standing	2 2 3 1 X	8
6 Carl Stonehewer	1 1 3 0 2	7
7 Gary Tagg	1 1 1 3 1	7
8 Richard Musson	2 2 2 1 0	7
9 David Clarke	0 X2 3 1	6
10 Simon Wolstenholme	1 0 0 2 3	6
11 Chris Cobby	2 2 1 1 0	6
12 Simon Green	2 X0 F 3	5
13 Darren Grayling	F 1 1 2 1	5
14 Scott Robson	1 2 R1 0	4
15 Kevin Little	0 1 1 0 X	2
16 Mark Simmonds	0 0 0 0 2	2

ROLL OF HONOUR

1969 Graham Plant (Leicester)
1970 Barry Thomas (Canterbury) 14
1971 Ian Turner (King's Lynn) 15
1972 Allan Emmett (Rayleigh) 13
1973 Peter Collins (Belle Vue) 14
1974 Chris Morton (Belle Vue) 15
1975 Neil Middleditch (Eastbourne) 13
1976 Michael Lee (King's Lynn) 15
1977 Les Collins (Belle Vue) 15
1978 Phil Collins (Ellesmere Port) 15
1979 Kenny Carter (Halifax) 12
1980 Mark Courtney (Middlesbrough) 14
1981 Rob Lightfoot (Stoke) 14
1982 Peter Carr (Belle Vue) 12
1983 Keith Millard (Exeter) 13
1984 Marvyn Cox (Oxford) 13
1985 Carl Blackbird (Belle Vue) 15
1986 Gary Havelock (Middlesbrough) 15
1987 Darren Sumner (Stoke) 14
1988 Mark Loram (Hackney) 15
1989 Martin Dugard (Oxford) 15
1990 Joe Screen (Belle Vue) 14

In 1969 meeting was held as a second half event with a Final.

Star of 90

JOE SCREEN

British Under 21 Champion

Star of 90

ANDY GRAHAME

NLRC Champion

The N.L.R.C.

IN THE far distant years ahead of him when he looks back on his speedway career, Andy Grahame will fondly remember his nights of glory at Brandon.

It was there, on June 2nd, 1982, that he won the British Final with elder brother Alan his runner-up.

Grahame returned to Coventry for what he will probably remember as the second most memorable meeting of his life, to become the 1990 Jawa-Barum National League Riders' Champion.

He admitted: "Tonight has brought it all back."

As in the past, he dropped one point – this time in his opening ride when he had to give best to the brilliant World Under 21 Champion Chris Louis.

But, as in the past, his nerve held and four successive wins saw him finish a point in front of the Ipswich flier who was beaten by the Australian duo Rod Hunter and Steve Regeling in mid-meeting.

Those two setbacks were enough to prevent Chris completing what would have been an unique family double as father John had been crowned National League Riders' Champion in 1971.

And now that amalgamation is on the way it is one record that may never fall to the East Anglian fraternity.

But it was Louis who suffered most of the cruel breaks on the night.

He was leading heat five when it was stopped after Jens Rasmussen had fallen; and was again in front in heat 11 when referee John Whitaker had to call the riders back to the tapes after Shane Bowes came to grief on the pits bend.

If nothing else, Louis must now know that if you are going to win major meetings then you have to have that little bit of luck that makes all the difference between taking the title and having to settle for most of the glory!

Coventry, Saturday, September 15

1 Andy Grahame	**2 3 3 3 3**	**14**
2 Chris Louis	3 2 2 3 3	13
3 Craig Boyce	3 3 2 3 0	11 (+3)
4 David Bargh	2 3 3 1 2	11(+2)
5 Steve Regeling	1 2 3 2 2	10
6 Steve Schofield	3 1 2 1 2	9
7 Les Collins	3 0 R 2 3	8
8 Eric Monaghan	1 1 3 2 1	8
9 Martin Goodwin	2 1 1 3 1	8
10 Rod Hunter	2 3 0 0 1	6
11 Shane Bowes	1 2 X 1 2	6
12 Richard Hellsén	1 2 1 1 1	6
13 David Walsh	F F 2 0 3	5
14 Gordon Kennett	0 1 1 2 0	4
15 Mick Poole	X R 1 R 0	1
16 Jens Rasmussen	R F N N N	0
Track reserves		
17 Andy Meredith	0 0	0
17 Lee Coleman	0 0	0

ROLL OF HONOUR

1968 Graham Plant (Middlesbrough) 13
1969 Geoff Ambrose (Crayford) 14
1970 Dave Jessup (Eastbourne) 14
1971 John Louis (Ipswich) 14
1972 Phil Crump (Crewe) 12
1973 Arthur Price (Boston) 12
1974 Carl Glover (Boston) 13
1975 Laurie Etheridge (Crayford) 13
1976 Joe Owen (Newcastle) 14
1977 Colin Richardson (Eastbourne) 15
1978 Steve Koppe (Canterbury) 14
1979 Ian Gledhill (Stoke) 14
1980 Wayne Brown (Berwick) 14
1981 Mike Ferreira (Canterbury) 15
1982 Joe Owen (Newcastle) 14
1983 Steve McDermott (Berwick) 13
1984 Ian Barney (Peterborough) 14
1985 Neil Middleditch (Arena Essex) 14
1986 Paul Thorp (Stoke) 15
1987 Andrew Silver (Arena Essex) 15
1988 Troy Butler (Milton Keynes) 15
1989 Mark Loram (Ipswich) 14
1990 Andy Grahame (Wimbledon) 14

N.L. Pairs

THE two finest riders in the National League were rewarded – with their first major national trophy.

Steve Schofield and Andy Galvin started the Speedway Star Pairs Championship as the brightest of pre-meeting favourites.

After all Schofield was top of the national averages and his club skipper Galvin was also in the Top Ten and, between them, they boasted a combined average higher than any of their 15 rivals.

For a moment it looked as if their challenge might founder as Schofield struggled to hold onto third place in their opening outing at Glasgow's Shawfield Park, later explaining: "I never like riding in the first race. I don't know why - but I've always been the same."

Galvin equalled the track record, established a fortnight earlier by Chris Louis, but that was the only race he was to win all afternoon.

It was his partner who found the quickest way around the 332 metre track and collected four wins in a row, including the final victory over the previously unbeaten Steve Regeling (Exeter) to give Hackney their first success in the tournament.

Luckiest duo of all were Ipswich's Louis and Alan Mogridge who were gifted seven points in their opening heat when both the Poole riders failed to finish; got another break when Glen Baxter (Rye House) fell in their second race but they finally went out at the hands of Messrs. Schofield and Galvin in their third outing.

Until then most of their opponents were convinced that they would ride their good fortune all the way into the final!

Unluckiest? Probably Newcastle who looked to have Exeter beaten in the semi-final when David Bargh, who had been representing New Zealand in the previous day's World Pairs semi-final in Austria, was adjudged at fault as Peter Jeffery fell.

Surprisingly the Scottish challenge never materialised even though Les Collins was a classy contributor.

The former Inter Continental Champion won his three qualifying races but had no support at all from partner Carl Blackbird and the home pair, brothers Kenny and Charlie McKinna, couldn't provide a race win between them with the Radio Clyde Tigers actually finishing bottom of their group.

Glasgow, Sunday, June 17

GROUP A
HACKNEY 18 (Steve Schofield 2-4-4- 10, Andy Galvin 4-2-2- 8) **Ipswich 15** (Alan Mogridge **3**-**2**-3- 8, Chris Louis 4-3-0- 7) **Poole 10** (Craig Boyce R-3-**3**- 6, Gary Chessell fx-0-4- 4) **Rye House 9** (Jens Rasmussen 3-4-2- 9, Glen Baxter 0-F-0- 0).

GROUP B
NEWCASTLE 17 (Peter Carr 4-4-3- 11, David Bargh R-2-4- 6) **Long Eaton 13** (Richard Hellsén 3-4-4- 11, Kevin Smart 2-0-0- 2) **Wimbledon 12** (Nathan Simpson **2**-3-2- 7, Andy Grahame 3-**2**-0- 5) **Arena Essex 10** (Rob Tilbury 4-3-3- 10, Kevin Brice 0-0-0- 0).

GROUP C
EXETER 18 (Steve Regeling 4-4-**3**- 11, Peter Jeffery **3**-0-4- 7) **Stoke 18** (Nigel Crabtree 4-2-4- 10, Louis Carr 2-3-**3**- 8) **Peterborough 11** (Frank Andersen 2-**3**-2- 7, Craig Hodgson 0-4-0- 4) **Eastbourne 5** (Gordon Kennett 3-R-N- 3, Justin Walker 0-2-0- 2).

GROUP D
MIDDLESBROUGH 19 (Rod Hunter 4-3-4- 11, Darren Sumner **3**-**2**-**3**- 8) **Berwick 14** (Mark Courtney 3-4-2- 9, David Walsh **2**-**3**-0- 5) **Edinburgh 12** (Les Collins 4-4-4- 12, Carl Blackbird 0-0-0- 0) **Glasgow 9** (Kenny McKinna 0-2-3- 5, Charlie McKinna 2-fx-**2**- 4).

Semi Finals
HACKNEY 7 (Schofield 4, Galvin **3**) beat **Middlesbrough 2** (Sumner 2, Hunter 0)
EXETER 5 (Regeling 3, Jeffery **2**) beat **Newcastle 4** (Carr 4, Bargh fx).

FINAL
HACKNEY 6 (Schofield 4, Galvin 2) beat **Exeter 3** (Regeling 3, Jeffery 0).

ROLL OF HONOUR

1975 NEWCASTLE (Tom Owen & Brian Havelock)
1976 ELLESMERE PORT (John Jackson & Chris Turner)
1977 BOSTON (Rob Hollingworth & Colin Cook)
1978 ELLESMERE PORT (John Jackson & Steve Finch)
1979 MILTON KEYNES (Bob Humphreys & Andy Grahame)
1980 MIDDLESBROUGH (Steve Wilcock & Mark Courtney)
1981 CANTERBURY (Mike Ferreira & Denzil Kent)
1982 WEYMOUTH (Martin Yeates & Simon Wigg)
1983 WEYMOUTH (Martin Yeates & Simon Cross)
1984 STOKE (Nigel Crabtree & Tom Owen)
1985 ELLESMERE PORT (Louis Carr & Joe Owen)
1986 EDINBURGH (Les Collins & Doug Wyer)
1987 MILDENHALL (Melvyn Taylor & Dave Jessup)
1988 STOKE (Graham Jones & Steve Bastable)
1989 STOKE (Eric Monaghan & Nigel Crabtree)
1990 HACKNEY (Steve Schofield & Andy Galvin)

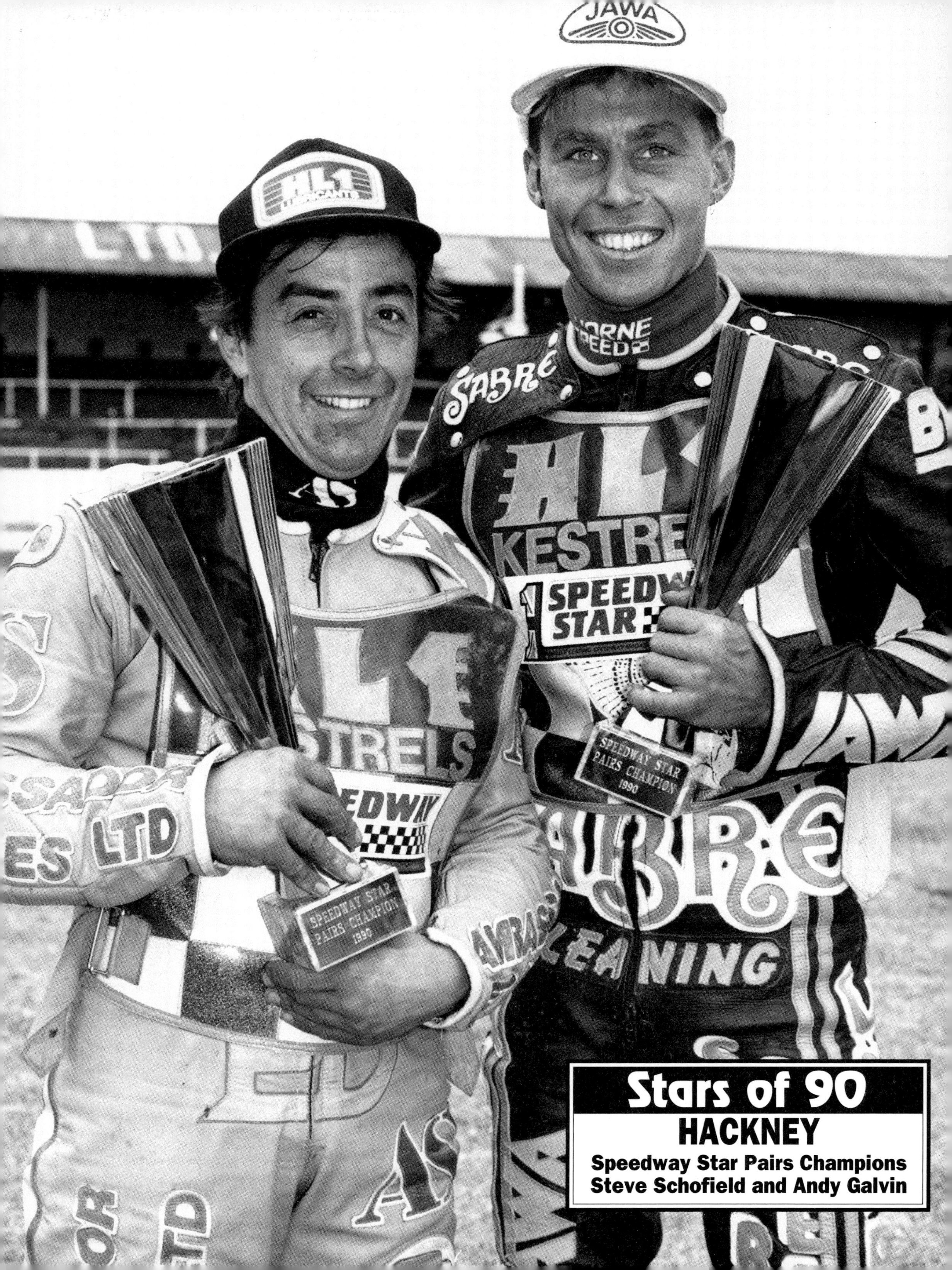

Stars of 90
HACKNEY
Speedway Star Pairs Champions
Steve Schofield and Andy Galvin

N.L. Team

STOKE took advantage of their good luck to defy the odds and win the newly sponsored H.E.A.T. National League Four Team Championship for the first time.

The Abacus Windows Potters only scraped through the first semi final through a slice of fortune and the meeting regulations.

Louis Carr took a fortunate three points in his opening ride when Wimbledon's Nathan Simpson stopped while leading and then they got through to the final because of their two heat wins against the Montine Dons' sole heat victory after the two teams had tied on 11 points.

But there was no doubting their supremacy in the final when they outraced favourites Poole, Hackney and Ipswich with Eric Monaghan unbeaten from his two starts and Louis Carr dropping a solitary point to Andy Galvin.

They overcame Nigel Crabtree's third place in the opening race and provided four heat winners in the eight-race final.

On the sadder side Poole's Gary Allan was involved in an unsavoury incident with David Cheshire and was then the victim of a fan's protest before the start of heat six.

Qualifying

First leg, Edinburgh, Thursday, May 17:
EDINBURGH 32 (Les Collins 3-3-2-3- 11, Michael Coles 2-0-N-N- 2, †Brett Saunders 3-1-3-0- 7, Carl Blackbird 2-2-R-3- 7, Freddy Schøtt 2-3- 5) **Glasgow 26** (Kenny McKinna 3-3-1-1- 8, Shane Bowes 2-2-2-fx- 6, Sean Courtney fx-0-N-N- 0, †Steve Lawson 1-2-3-3- 9, Charlie McKinna 1-2- 3) **Newcastle 22** (David Bargh 3-3-3-2- 11, Simon Green fn-N-N-N- 0, Mark Thorpe 0-1-0-1- 2, †Peter Carr 1-1-3-1- 6, Paul Smith 1-0-1-1- 3) **Berwick 16** (Mark Courtney 2-3-1-0- 6, David Walsh 0-2-2-2- 6, Andy Campbell 0-0-0-N- 0, †Rob Grant 1-1-0-2- 4, Alan Rivett 0- 0).
Second leg, Glasgow, Friday, May 18:
GLASGOW 38 (Sean Courtney 1-3-0-N- 4, **†Steve Lawson 3-3-3-3- 12**, Shane Bowes 2-3-2-3- 10, Kenny McKinna 3-2-2-3- 10, Charlie McKinna 2- 2) **Berwick 23** (Mark Courtney 2-1-2-1- 6, David Walsh 3-3-3-2- 11, Andy Campbell 3-0-0-0- 3, †Rob Grant 1-0-N-N- 2, Alan Rivett 1- 1) **Newcastle 22** (David Bargh fx-2-3-3- 8, Simon Green 1-R-1-0- 2, Martin Dixon 2-2-2-1- 7, †Peter Carr 2-R-1-2- 5, Paul Smith) **Edinburgh 13** (Les Collins R-1-3-R-4, †Brett Saunders 0-R-1-1- 2, Carl Blackbird 1-2-0-2- 5, Michael Coles 0-1-1-N- 2, Freddy Schøtt E- 0).
Third leg, Berwick, Saturday, May 19:
GLASGOW 29 (Charlie McKinna 3-3-2-1- 9, †Kenny McKinna 3-3-1-3- 10, Sean Courtney 1-1-3-fx- 5, Shane Bowes 3-2-R-0- 5, Jason Lyons) **Berwick 26** (Mark Courtney 2-2-1-3- 8, David Walsh 3-R-2-2- 7, Andy Campbell N-3-fx-2- 5, †Rob Grant 2-0-3-1- 6, Alan Rivett 0- 0) **Edinburgh 23** (Les Collins 1-2-1-2- 6, †Brett Saunders 1-1-2-1- 5, Carl Blackbird 1-2-2-3- 8, Michael Coles 2-0-1-1- 4, Freddy Schøtt) **Newcastle 18** (David Bargh 0-3-3-fx- 6, Simon Green R-0-0-N- 0, Martin Dixon 2-1-3-2- 8, †Peter Carr fx-1-R-3- 4, Paul Smith 0- 0).
Fourth leg, Newcastle, Sunday, May 27
BERWICK 28 (David Walsh 3-2-3-1- 9, †Rob Grant 0-1-0-2- 3, Andy Campbell 2-0-3-1- 6, Mark Courtney 3-2-2-3- 10, Alan Rivett) **Newcastle 27** (David Bargh 3-3-3-0- 9, †Peter Carr 1-0-1-3- 5, Simon Green 0-3-1-0- 4, Martin Dixon 2-3-1-3- 9, Paul Smith) **Edinburgh 22** (Les Collins 3-1-3-3- 10, †Brett Saunders 1-1-2-1- 5, Carl Blackbird 2-0-0-2- 4, Freddy Schøtt 1-0-0-N- 1, Scott Lamb 2- 2) **Glasgow 19** (Charlie McKinna 0-2-2-2- 6, Kenny McKinna 1-1-1-0- 3, Shane Bowes 2-3-0-0- 5, Sean Courtney 0-2-2-1- 5, †Steve Lawson).
Agg: GLASGOW 112 BERWICK 93 Edinburgh 90 Newcastle 89.

First leg, Rye House, Sunday, May 13:
HACKNEY 31 (Paul Whittaker fx-2-1-2- 5, Steve Schofield 3-3-1-3- 10, Gary Tagg 2-2-1-2- 7, †Andy Galvin 3-3-1-2- 9, Michael Warren) **Ipswich 30** (David Norris 3-2-2-3- 10, Chris Louis 2-3-3-0- 8, †Alan Mogridge 2-2-3-fx- 7, Dean Standing 2-0-fx-3- 5, Shane Parker) **Rye House 19** (Roger Johns N-0-R-0- 0, †Jens Rasmussen 3-1-3-2- 9, Jamie Fagg 0-N-2-0- 2, Glen Baxter 0-1-3-3- 7, Trevor O'Brien 0-1- 1) **Arena Essex 16** (Simon Wolstenholme 1-R-2-1- 4, †Rob Tilbury 1-3-2-1- 7, Adrian Stevens 1-0-0-1- 2, Wayne Garratt 1-N-0-N- 1, Kevin Brice 1-1- 2).
Second leg, Ipswich, Thursday, May 17
IPSWICH 38 (Chris Louis 3-1-3-2- 9, David Norris 1-3-2-2- 8, Dean Standing 3-3-2-3- 11, †Alan Mogridge 1-3-3-3- 10, Shane Parker) **Hackney 26** (Paul Whittaker 2-1-1-1- 5, **†Andy Galvin 3-3-3-3- 12**, Gary Tagg 0-0-N-N- 0, Steve Schofield 2-1-1-2- 6, Michael Warren 1-2- 3) **Rye House 22** (†Jens Rasmussen 2-2-3-3- 10, Jamie Fagg 1-0-2-1- 4, Roger Johns 0-2-0-R- 2, Glen Baxter 2-2-2-0- 6, Trevor O'Brien) **Arena Essex 10** (†Rob Tilbury 3-2-1-R- 6, Wayne Garratt 1-1-0-0- 2, Simon Wolstenholme 0-0-0-1- 1, Adrian Stevens 0-R-N-N- 0, Kevin Brice 0-1- 1).
Third leg, Hackney, Friday, May 18:
HACKNEY 36 (Steve Schofield R-2-3-3- 8, Gary Tagg 2-3-2-N- 7, Paul Whittaker E-3-1-3- 7, †Andy Galvin 3-3-2-3- 11, Michael Warren 1-2- 3) **Ipswich 32** (Chris Louis 1-2-3-1- 7, David Norris 2-2-2-3- 9, Dean Standing 2-1-2-2- 7, †Alan Mogridge 3-3-3-fx- 9, Shane Parker) **Rye House 15** (†Jens Rasmussen 1-0-3-0- 4, Jamie Fagg 3-R-0-1- 4, Roger Johns fx-1-0-1- 2, Glen Baxter 2-0-1-2- 5, Trevor O'Brien) **Arena Essex 13** (†Rob Tilbury 3-2-1-2- 8, Adrian Stevens 0-0-N-0- 0, Simon Wolstenholme 0-N-0-N- 0, Wayne Garratt 1-1-1-1- 4, Kevin Brice 1-0-0- 1).
Fourth leg, Arena Essex, Saturday, May 19:
IPSWICH 35 (David Norris 3-2-3-3- 11, †Alan Mogridge 1-E-2-3- 6, Dean Standing 3-1-3-3- 10, Shane Parker 3-3-2-0- 8, Damon Richardson fx-0) **Hackney 29** (†Andy Galvin 2-3-1-0- 6, Paul Whittaker 1-3-1-2- 7, Gary Tagg 2-1-1-1- 5, Steve Schofield 2-3-3-3- 11, Michael Warren) **Arena Essex 18** (†Rob Tilbury 3-2-3-1- 9, Wayne Garratt R-2-0-R- 2, Simon Wolstenholme R-2-2-1- 5, Adrian Stevens 1-1-0-R- 2, Kevin Brice) **Rye House 13** (†Jens Rasmussen 2-X-1-2- 5, Roger Johns 0-R-N-N- 0, Nigel Sparshott 1-1-0-2- 4, Glen Baxter 0-0-2-2- 4, Trevor O'Brien 0-X- 0).
Agg: IPSWICH 135 HACKNEY 122 Rye House 69 Arena Essex 57.

First leg, Peterborough, Friday, May 25
PETERBOROUGH 35 (Mick Poole 3-3-2-3- 11, †Ian Barney 2-N-N-N- 2, Scott Norman 1-1-3-2- 7, Frank Andersen 1-1-3-3- 8, Craig Hodgson 2-2-3- 7) **Stoke 34** (Louis Carr 0-3-2-2- 7, Chris Cobby 2-0-N-N- 2, †Nigel Crabtree 3-3-3-2- 11, Eric Monaghan 2-2-3-3- 10, Rob Woffinden 2-2- 4) **Middlesbrough 15** (†Darren Sumner 0-0-0-0- 0, Paul Bentley 1-0-0-1- 2, Rod Hunter 3-2-1-1- 7, David Cheshire 3-1-1-N- 5, Duncan Chapman 1- 1) **Long Eaton 12** (Kevin Smart R-2-0-1- 3, †Richard Hellsén 2-3-0-R- 5, Peter Lloyd 0-0-1-F- 1, Paul Fry 1-1-1-0- 3, Jon Surman).
Second leg, Stoke, Saturday, May 26:
STOKE 33 (Louis Carr 3-3-3-3- 12, Chris Cobby 2-0-0-N- 2, †Nigel Crabtree 3-3-1-1- 8, Eric Monaghan 1-3-3-2- 9, Rob Woffinden 2- 2) **Peterborough 25** (Mick Poole fx-2-3-2- 7, †Ian Barney 0-N-N-N- 0, Scott Norman 1-fx-N-N- 1, Frank Andersen 2-3-1-F- 6, Craig Hodgson 2-2-3-1-3- 11) **Middlesbrough 21** (†Darren Sumner 2-2-1-0- 5, Paul Bentley 0-F-2-1- 3, Rod Hunter 3-0-2-3- 8, David Cheshire 1-0-1-3- 5, Max Schofield) **Long Eaton 16** (†Richard Hellsén 3-1-2-1- 7, Gary O'Hare 0-1-0-0- 1, Kevin Smart 2-1-0-N- 3, Paul Fry 1-2-0-2- 5, Jon Surman 0- 0).
Third leg, Long Eaton, Wednesday, May 30:
STOKE 30 (Louis Carr 2-3-1-3- 9, Rob Woffinden 2-1-1-1- 5, †Nigel Crabtree 3-2-R-3- 8, Eric Monaghan 2-1-3-2- 8, Mark Carlson) **Middlesbrough 30** (†Darren Sumner 2-0-3-1- 6, Paul Bentley 1-1-2-0- 4, Rod Hunter 3-3-3-2- 11, David Cheshire 3-2-2-2- 9, Duncan Chapman) **Long Eaton 23** (†Richard Hellsén 1-0-1-2- 4, Paul Fry 1-3-3-3- 10, Kevin Smart 1-2-3-1- 7, Peter Lloyd F-1-0-1- 2, Jon Surman) **Peterborough 13** (Mick Poole 3-fx-N-N- 3, †Ian Barney 0-0-0-N- 0, Nigel Flatman 0-0-N-N- 0, Frank Andersen 0-3-2-fx- 5, Craig Hodgson 2-R-1-2-0- 5).
Fourth leg, Middlesbrough, May 31:
MIDDLESBROUGH 42 (**†Darren Sumner 3-3-3-3- 12**, Paul Bentley 3-3-2-3- 11, Rod Hunter 1-3-3-2- 9, David Cheshire 2-3-2-3- 10, Steve Wilcock) **Stoke 25** (Louis Carr 3-2-1-2- 8, Chris Cobby 2-1-2-2- 7, †Nigel Crabtree 2-2-0-2- 6, Eric Monaghan 2-fx-1-N- 3, Rob Woffinden 1- 1) **Peterborough 17** (*Dave Edwards 1-2-1-0- 4*, †Ian Barney 1-0-0-0- 1, Craig Hodgson 3-2-3-1- 9, Frank Andersen 1-1-F-N- 2, *Max Schofield 1-0-1*) **Long Eaton 12** (†Richard Hellsén R-2-3-1- 6, Kevin Smart 0-1-0-N- 1, Paul Fry E-1-fx-N- 1, Peter Lloyd 0-0-0-3- 3, Jon Surman 0-0-1- 1).
Agg: STOKE 122 MIDDLESBROUGH 108 Peterborough 90 Long Eaton 63.

First leg, Eastbourne, Sunday, May 27:
WIMBLEDON 28 (Nathan Simpson 2-3-3-0- 8, Neville Tatum 1-3-3-0- 7, Nigel Leaver 2-0-2-R- 4, Andy Grahame 1-2-3-3- 9, Deon Prinsloo) **Poole 25** (Gary Chessell 1-3-0-1- 5, Gary Allan 2-1-1-1- 5, Craig Boyce 3-2-1-1- 7, †Alun Rossiter 1-3-2-N- 6, Tom Knudsen 2- 2) **Exeter 24** (†Steve Regeling 3-3-2-3- 11, Peter Jeffery 0-2-2-3- 7, Richard Green 1-1-1-3- 6, Mark Simmonds 0-0-0-0- 0, Frank Smart) **Eastbourne 19** (†Gordon Kennett 3-1-0-2- 6, Andy Buck 3-0-F-2- 5, Justin Walker 0-N-1-N- 1, Paul Woods 0-0-N-N- 0, Tony Primmer 2-2-1-2- 7).
Second leg, Exeter, Monday, May 28:
EXETER 38 (**†Steve Regeling 3-3-3-3- 12**, Richard Green 3-0-3-2- 8, Peter Jeffery 3-3-2-3- 11, Andy Sell F-2-3-2- 7, Steve Bishop) **Poole 30** (Gary Chessell 2-2-2-1- 7, †Alun Rossiter 2-3-1-3- 9, Craig Boyce 2-1-3-3- 9, Tony Langdon 2-1-2-N- 5, Tom Knudsen R- 0) **Wimbledon 16** (Nathan Simpson F-1-0-0- 1, Neville Tatum R-1-0-1-2, Nigel Leaver 0-2-1-1- 4, Andy Grahame 3-3-2-1- 9, Deon Prinsloo) **Eastbourne 12** (†Gordon Kennett 1-2-1-2- 6, Andy Buck 1-0-1-R- 2, Paul Woods 1-0-N-0- 1, Justin Walker 1-0-N-N- 1, Tony Primmer 0-0-2- 2).
Third leg, Wimbledon, Wednesday, May 30:
WIMBLEDON 39 (Nigel Leaver 2-1-3-2- 8, Nathan Simpson 2-3-3-2- 10, Neville Tatum 3-2-1-3- 9, **Andy Grahame 3-3-3-3- 12**, Deon Prinsloo) **Poole 27** (Gary Chessell 2-1-2-0- 5, †Alun Rossiter 1-3-2-3- 9, Craig Boyce 3-3-2-2- 10, Tony Langdon fx-1-0-N- 1, Tom Knudsen 2- 2) **Exeter 17** (Steve Regeling 1-2-3-3- 9, Richard Green 1-1-0-0- 2, Peter Jeffery 1-2-2-0- 5, Mark Simmonds 0-0-1-N- 1, Steve Bishop 0- 0) **Eastbourne 13** (†Gordon Kennett 2-0-N-N- 2, Andy Buck 0-0-1-1- 2, Paul Woods 3-2-0-1- 6, Justin Walker 0-1-0-N- 1, Tony Primmer 0-1-1- 2).
Fourth leg, Poole, Wednesday, June 20:
POOLE 39 (Tony Langdon 2-3-3-0- 8, Craig Boyce 3-2-3-3- 11, †Alun Rossiter 2-3-3-3- 11, Gary Allan 3-2-1-3- 9, Tom Knudsen) **Exeter 22** (†Steve Regeling 3-3-2-3- 11, Richard Green 0-0-2-0- 2, Peter Jeffery 2-2-2-fx- 6, Ian Barney 0-1-N-N- 1, Steve Bishop 1-1- 2) **Wimbledon 21** (Nathan Simpson 1-0-2-2- 5, Neville Tatum 0-0-1-2- 3, Ray Morton 3-1-0-2- 6, Alan Grahame 0-2-3-2- 7, Nigel Leaver) **Eastbourne 14** (Tony Primmer 1-3-1-1- 6, Andy Buck 1-1-0-1- 3, Paul Woods 1-1-0-1- 3, Justin Walker 2-0-0-0- 2, John Cook).
Agg: POOLE 121 WIMBLEDON 104 Exeter 101 Eastbourne 58.

Semi Finals (Peterborough, Sunday, August 5)

IPSWICH 16 (Chris Louis 3-3- 6, Shane Parker 3-1- 4, Dean Standing 2-1- 3, †Alan Mogridge 1-2- 3, Robbie Fuller) **Stoke 11** (Louis Carr 3-R- 3, Mark Carlson 2-0- 2, †Nigel Crabtree 0-2- 2, Eric Monaghan 3-1- 4, Chris Cobby) **Wimbledon 11** (†Ray Morton 3-2- 5, Neville Tatum 1-2- 3, Andy Grahame 2-0- 2, Nathan Simpson 1-R- 1, Peter Chapman) **Glasgow 10** (†Steve Lawson 1-N- 1, Kenny McKinna 1-3- 4, Charlie McKinna 0-N- 0, Shane Bowes 2-3- 5, Jason Lyons 0-R- 0).

POOLE 16 (Craig Boyce 3-2- 5, †Alun Rossiter 3-0- 3, Tony Langdon 1-3- 4, Gary Allan 1-3- 4, Gary Chessell) **Hackney 13** (†Andy Galvin 2-3- 5, Gary Tagg X-2- 2, Paul Whittaker 1-1- 2, Steve Schofield 2-2- 4, Michael Warren) **Berwick 10** (†Mark Courtney 0-0- 0, David Blackburn 3-3- 6, Alan Rivett 0-3- 3, Andy Campbell 0-1- 1, Scott Robson) **Middlesbrough 9** (David Cheshire 2-0- 2, Paul Bentley 1-2- 3, Rod Hunter 1-1- 2, Darren Sumner 2-0- 2, †Jamie Luckhurst).

FINAL

STOKE 16 (Louis Carr 2-3- 5, Mark Carlson 0-N- 0, Nigel Crabtree 1-3- 4, Eric Monaghan 3-3- 6, Chris Cobby 1- 1) **Poole 13** (Craig Boyce 1-2- 3, Alun Rossiter 2-3- 5, Tony Langdon 2-2- 4, Gary Allan 0-1- 1, Gary Chessell) **Hackney 10** (Andy Galvin 0-3- 3, Gary Tagg 0-X- 0, Paul Whittaker 0-2- 2, Steve Schofield 3-2- 5, Michael Warren) **Ipswich 9** (Chris Louis 3-1- 4, Shane Parker 1-1- 2, Dean Standing 0-2- 2, Alan Mogridge 1-0- 1, Robbie Fuller).

ROLL OF HONOUR

1976 NEWCASTLE (Tom Owen, Joe Owen, Andy Cusworth, Phil Michelides, Ron Henderson)
1977 PETERBOROUGH (Ian Clark, Andy Hines, Kevin Hawkins, Brian Clark, Nigel Flatman)
1978 PETERBOROUGH (Nigel Couzens, Nigel Flatman, Tim Hunt, Dave Gooderham, Brian Clark)
1979 ELLESMERE PORT (John Jackson, Louis Carr, Steve Finch, Pete Ellams, Paul Embley)
1980 CRAYFORD (Les Rumsey, Paul Woods, Steve Naylor, Alan Sage, Laurie Etheridge)
1981 EDINBURGH (Dave Trownson, Neil Collins, Chris Turner, Ivan Blacka, Guy Robson)
1982 NEWCASTLE (Joe Owen, Bobby Beaton, Rod Hunter, Alan Emerson, Tom Owen)
1983 NEWCASTLE (Alan Emerson, Rod Hunter, Joe Owen, Bobby Beaton, Martin Scarisbrick)
1984 MILDENHALL (Ray Bales, Carl Blackbird, Robert Henry, Carl Baldwin, David Jackson)
1985 MIDDLESBROUGH (Geoff Pusey, Steve Wilcock, Martin Dixon, Mark Fiora, Gary Havelock)
1986 MIDDLESBROUGH (Jim Burdfield, Mark Courtney, Martin Dixon, Steve Wilcock, Glenn Hornby)
1987 MILDENHALL (Mel Taylor, Eric Monaghan, Dave Jessup, David Jackson, Glen Baxter)
1988 PETERBOROUGH (Ian Barney, Kevin Jolly, Mick Poole, Craig Hodgson, Jon Stokes)
1989 PETERBOROUGH (Ian Barney, Mick Poole, Kevin Jolly, Craig Hodgson, Scott Norman)
1990 STOKE (Louis Carr, Mark Carlson, Nigel Crabtree, Eric Monaghan, Chris Cobby)

▲ *MILTON KEYNES did not compete in the competition after finishing bottom of the 1989 National League.*

Stars of 90

STOKE

National League Team Champions
The late Eric Stead, Eric Monaghan, Ray Sant, Mark Carlson, Chris Cobby, Nigel Crabtree and Louis Carr

1990 SUNBRITE BRITISH LEAGUE FINAL TABLE

		Home					Away							
Team	*M*	*W*	*D*	*L*	*PtsF*	*PtsA*	*W*	*D*	*L*	*PtsF*	*PtsA*	*Pts*	*BP*	*TPts*
1 READING	32	13	1	2	827	609	6	2	8	686.5	751.5	41	13	54
2 Wolverhampton	32	14	1	1	794	644	3	4	9	652	787	39	10	49
3 Belle Vue	32	12	1	3	794	644	7	1	8	660	774	40	7	47
4 Oxford	32	9	1	6	764	677	8	1	7	703	733	36	10	46
5 Bradford	32	14	1	1	834	603	2	0	14	636	804	33	8	41
6 Swindon	32	11	1	4	812	626	4	1	11	650	790	33	8	41
7 Cradley Heath	32	10	0	6	756.5	683.5	2	1	13	669	771	25	7	32
8 Coventry	32	6	2	8	727	709	4	1	11	659	778	23	7	30
9 King's Lynn	32	6	4	6	734	706	1	1	14	581	854	19	2	21

Roll of Honour

1965	1 WEST HAM	2 Wimbledon	3 Coventry
1966	1 HALIFAX	2 Coventry	3 Swindon
1967	1 SWINDON	2 Coventry	3 West Ham
1968	1 COVENTRY	2 Hackney	3 Exeter
1969	1 POOLE	2 Belle Vue	3 Wimbledon
1970	1 BELLE VUE	2 Wimbledon	3 Coventry
1971	1 BELLE VUE	2 Leicester	3 Coventry
1972	1 BELLE VUE	2 Reading	3 King's Lynn
1973	1 READING	2 Sheffield	3 King's Lynn
1974	1 EXETER	2 Belle Vue	3 Ipswich
1975	1 IPSWICH	2 Belle Vue	3 Newport
1976	1 IPSWICH	2 Belle Vue	3 Exeter
1977	1 WHITE CITY	2 Exeter	3 Reading
1978	1 COVENTRY	2 Belle Vue	3 Hull
1979	1 COVENTRY	2 Hull	3 Cradley Heath
1980	1 READING	2 Hackney	3 Belle Vue
1981	1 CRADLEY HEATH	2 Ipswich	3 Swindon
1982	1 BELLE VUE	2 Cradley Heath	3 Ipswich
1983	1 CRADLEY HEATH	2 Ipswich	3 Coventry
1984	1 IPSWICH	2 Belle Vue	3 Cradley Heath
1985	1 OXFORD	2 Sheffield	3 Coventry
1986	1 OXFORD	2 Cradley Heath	3 Wolverhampton
1987	1 COVENTRY	2 Cradley Heath	3 Swindon
1988	1 COVENTRY	2 Belle Vue	3 Cradley Heath
1989	1 OXFORD	2 Wolverhampton	3 Cradley Heath
1990	1 READING	2 Wolverhampton	3 Belle Vue

All the '90 Results	Belle Vue	Bradford	Coventry	Cradley Heath	King's Lynn	Oxford	Reading	Swindon	Wolves
BELLE VUE		48-42 59-31	56-34 51-39	47-43 55-35	43-46 55-35	41-49 40-49	50-40 51-39	48-42 54-36	51-39 45-45
BRADFORD	58-32 59-31		44-46 47-41	47-43 50-40	57-33 46-43	46-44 57-33	53-37 49-41	49-41 58-32	69-21 45-45
COVENTRY	34-56 43-45	44-46 46-44		46-44 45-45	52-38 58-32	43-46 48-42	42-48 43-47	45-45 44-46	52-38 42-47
CRADLEY HEATH	53-37 38-52	58-32 48-42	43-47 41-49		53-37 47-43	41-49 39-51	52-38 42.5-47.5	53-37 48-42	47-43 53-37
KING'S LYNN	45-45 43-47	52-38 42-48	45-45 50-50	48-42 47-43		45-45 43-47	46-44 61-29	44-46 35-55	45-45 43-47
OXFORD	44-45 50-40	49-41 51-39	42-48 51-38	52-38 48-42	66-24 45-45		41-48 43-46	44-46 49-41	40-50 49-41
READING	44-45 61-29	56-34 54-36	46-44 49-41	57-33 44-46	57-33 57-30	51-39 47-43		59-31 53-37	47-43 45-45
SWINDON	55-35 42-48	50-40 46-44	64-26 54-36	46-44 38-52	59-31 59-31	57-31 43-47	40-50 45-45		57-33 57-33
WOLVERHAMPTON	53-36 52-37	53-37 48-42	49-41 46-44	47-43 54-36	51-39 49-41	48-42 44-46	45-45 48-42	49-41 58-32	

The PREMIERSHIP

SHOW Cradley Heath a piece of silverware and they are a team possessed.

How else can you explain their remarkable Premiership victory over reigning league champions Oxford?

The Heathens went into the tie having lost their first two matches of the new season – at home to King's Lynn and Bradford – but then snatched a dramatic draw as they came back from six points down with only three races to go.

Simon Cross rode in three of the last five heats but it was rookie Mark Robinson's third place ahead of Paul Dugard that swung the tie.

In the return 24 hours later Oxford's hopes nose-dived when a distraught Simon Wigg walked out after only two pointless, completed rides.

Cradley boss Colin Pratt admitted: "After two defeats everyone had written us off. But with the season only four matches old we have won our first trophy. That's what it is all about."

First leg, at Cowley, Friday, March 30

OXFORD 45			
1 †Hans Nielsen	2 3 3 3 2	13	
2 Dean Barker	0 **2** 3 **2**	7	2
3 Martin Dugard	3 3 2 R 0	8	
4 Troy Butler	0 2 2 0	4	
5 Simon Wigg	1 **1** **1** 2	5	2
6 Paul Dugard	**1** 0 N 0	1	1
7 Alastair Stevens	2 **2** R **1** 2	7	2
CRADLEY HEATH 45			
1 Simon Cross	3 3 3 **1** 3 1	14	1
2 Alan Grahame	1 F **1** N	2	1
3 Jan O. Pedersen	**1** 1 3 2 1 3	11	1
4 Greg Hancock	3 fx0 T	3	
5 Billy Hamill	**2** 1 1 T	4	1
6 Mark Loram	*3 2 0 2 0 3*	*10*	
7 Mark Robinson	F N N F 1	1	

Second leg, at Dudley Wood, Saturday, March 31

CRADLEY HEATH 50			
1 Jan O. Pedersen	3 3 2 2 **2**	12	1
2 Gert Handberg	*rider replacement*		
3 Simon Cross	3 1 2 2 3 3	14	
4 Alan Grahame	2 0 0 3	5	
5 Billy Hamill	**1** 2 3 **1** 1 1	9	2
6 Greg Hancock	**2** 3 1 **1** **1** 2	10	3
7 Mark Robinson	E N 0 0	0	
8 David Haynes	*did not ride*		
OXFORD 40			
1 †Hans Nielsen	1 3 3 3 2 R	12	
2 Dean Barker	0 1 0 1 0	2	
3 Martin Dugard	2 2 2 3 1 2	12	
4 Simon Wigg	0 0 T T	0	
5 Troy Butler	3 3 **1** 0 0	7	1
6 Paul Dugard	2 0 T 1	3	
7 Alastair Stevens	**1** R T 3	4	1

CRADLEY HEATH win 95-85 on aggregate

Roll of Honour

1982 CRADLEY HEATH 84 Ipswich 72
1983 BELLE VUE 79 Cradley Heath 77
1984 CRADLEY HEATH 82 *Belle Vue 74*
1985 *Cradley Heath 81* IPSWICH 75
1986 *Coventry 86* OXFORD 70
1987 OXFORD 82 Cradley Heath 73
1988 Cradley Heath 43* COVENTRY 47
1989 Cradley Heath 112 COVENTRY 67
1990 Cradley Heath 95 OXFORD 85

In 1988 the Premiership was awarded to Cradley Heath when Coventry failed to stage the second leg.

Teams in Capitals were the previous season's British League Champions; teams in italics won previous season's League Cup. In all other cases teams won the previous season's Speedway Star Knock Out Cup Final.

ACES DUMPED IN OFF TRACK RUMPUS

IT'S TROUBLE AT THE DOUBLE

READING became the seventh club to win both the British League and the Speedway Star Knock Out Cup in the same season...but it was the most controversial double in the sport's history.

For they achieved it after a boardroom ruling which saw Belle Vue thrown out of the competition even though they had qualified, on the track, for the Final against their Northern rivals Bradford.

The big argument centred around the Manchester club's use of rider replacement for their Danish international Peter Ravn in the semi final second leg. They had held the league leaders to a 17 point lead in the first leg and confidently set about reaching the final for the first time since 1984 as promoter John Perrin hoped to celebrate his first competition victory since taking over at the Greyhound Stadium.

During the build-up to the meeting Ravn, who had been in conflict with the club for several weeks, asked for a transfer and insisted he wouldn't turn out again for the Radio Piccadilly Aces.

The day before the meeting the Sunbrite League Management Committee agreed that Ravn was withholding his services and gave Belle Vue a facility. They chose to operate rider replacement on the night and continued to use it despite a pre-meeting protest by the visitors.

Belle Vue finished off the evening 24 points to the good - to go through to the final with a seven point winning margin.

But when the Speedway Control Board discussed the XXXX Racers' appeal they didn't give a XXXX for Belle Vue's case and ruled that because they hadn't included Ravn's name in the programme and had not named a number eight they were not entitled to have used rider replacement and amended the scores to give Reading a route into the final with an overall four point success!

It was hardly the ideal way to reach only their third ever Speedway Star Knock Out Cup Final and left not only Belle Vue fans, but all neutral supporters, fuming that such a decision could have been taken off the track.

It led to promoter Perrin announcing that he would quit at the end of the season, a spur-of-the-moment decision he later rescinded.

There was talk of Bradford and Belle Vue getting together and staging their own *alternative* Cup Final but that never came to anything and the Tribunal result ensured that there would be a new name on the trophy.

Reading, despite their long pedigree, had never won the Cup and for Bradford, who earlier in the season had won the first national trophy (the Gold Cup) in their history, it was a chance of making it two in a row.

En route to the final they had ended Cradley Heath's remarkable run of victorious ties – a sequence stretching back to the 1985 semi final! – with a fighting 45-45 draw at Dudley Wood and an easy second leg win against a somewhat lacklustre Heathens outfit missing their two Americans Greg Hancock and Billy Hamill.

Reading were installed as the favourites but the odds swung in the Coalite Dukes' favour when, inspired by a double figure return from reserve Glenn Doyle, they held the Berkshire club to 12 points in the opening leg at Smallmead.

But all Bradford's hopes disappeared in the second heat of the re-arranged second leg (the original staging had been a victim of the wet October weather) in an ugly-looking first bend pile-up.

First leg hero Doyle was the major victim, so badly shaken and bruised that the track doctor advised him not to take any further part in events and ordered him to hospital for X-rays.

Without Doyle, the fight was lost as Bradford had only out-of-touch Bryan Larner and number eight Stuart Parnaby to call upon to fill Doyle's place in his remaining programmed rides.

World number three Todd Wiltshire again showed his liking for the Odsal bowl and with reserve David Mullett in inspired form the XXXX Racers never looked like losing the tie and went on to win the second leg to make sure of the double for the first time in their history.

There had been earlier controversy in the other semi final also, when Bradford opted to use a guest, Billy Hamill, instead of Neil Evitts in the second leg at Swindon where they were defending a 12 point lead.

Evitts was actually in the pits helping his team-mates and saw the American win his first four rides on the way to a 15 point tally that gave Bradford an overall two point victory.

Swindon fans, including their sponsors Coastal Windows, saw it as an unsporting tactical decision by Bradford – and wasted no time in making their views widely known!

ROLL OF HONOUR

1965 WEST HAM 114 Exeter 78
1966 HALIFAX 113 Wimbledon 79
1967 COVENTRY 104 West Ham 88
1968 WIMBLEDON 119 Wolverhampton 98
1969 WIMBLEDON 94 Sheffield 62
1970 WIMBLEDON 80 Belle Vue 75
1971 HACKNEY 88 Cradley Heath 68
1972 BELLE VUE 82 Hackney 73
1973 BELLE VUE 78 Reading 78*
1974 SHEFFIELD 90 Ipswich 66
1975 BELLE VUE 86 Leicester 70
1976 IPSWICH 91 King's Lynn 63
1977 KING'S LYNN 79 Reading 77
1978 IPSWICH 92 Belle Vue 64
1979 CRADLEY HEATH 120 Hull 96
1980 CRADLEY HEATH 116 Belle Vue 100
1981 IPSWICH 110 Birmingham 92
1982 CRADLEY HEATH 81 Belle Vue 75
1983 CRADLEY HEATH 86 Coventry 70
1984 IPSWICH 92 Belle Vue 64
1985 OXFORD 79 Ipswich 76
1986 CRADLEY HEATH shared with OXFORD**
1987 CRADLEY HEATH 94 Coventry 86
1988 CRADLEY HEATH 100 Coventry 80
1989 CRADLEY HEATH 95 Wolverhampton 85
1990 READING 98 Bradford 82

**Peter Collins (Belle Vue) defeated Anders Michanek (Reading) in a run-off.*
***The first leg at Cradley Heath was drawn 39-39 and the second leg was never raced.*

INTER LEAGUE KNOCK OUT CUP

1975 BELLE VUE 90 Halifax 65
1976 HULL 96 Wolverhampton 60
1977 IPSWICH 81 Cradley Heath 75
1978 KING'S LYNN 94 Exeter 52
1979 CRADLEY HEATH 85 King's Lynn 71
1980 KING'S LYNN 83 Swindon 73

The Inter League Knock-out Cup was discontinued in 1981 although that season eight National League tracks were included in the Speedway Star Knock-out Cup.

Throughout the six years of the Inter League KO Cup and the 1981 Speedway Star Knock out Cup four National League sides defeated British League opposition.

They were: Boston (v Hackney), Edinburgh (v Sheffield), Peterborough (v Halifax) and Workington who achieved the feat twice in 1975, beating Ipswich and King's Lynn on their way to the semi-finals.

Boston also had a walk-over against Swindon to reach the 1975 semi-finals.

SPEEDWAY STAR CUP

1st Round

First leg, at Coventry, April 4

COVENTRY 45

1 †Kelvin Tatum	1 3 2 3 1	10	
2 Andy Phillips	0 1 1 N	2	
3 John Jorgensen	3 3 1 0 0	7	1
4 Rick Miller	1 0 1 0	2	2
5 Sean Wilson	2 1 2 2	7	
6 Roman Matousek	3 1 0 2	6	1
7 Andy Hackett	2 3 1 2 3	11	2

OXFORD 45

1 †Hans Nielsen	**2 3 3 3 2**	**13**	**2**
2 Dean Barker	3 2 2 0	7	1
3 Martin Dugard	2 2 3 1	8	1
4 Simon Wigg	3 1 3 1 3	11	1
5 Troy Butler	R 2 0 2	4	
6 Paul Dugard	0 0 N 0	0	
7 Alastair Stevens	1 0 0 0 1	2	

Second leg, at Oxford, April 13

OXFORD 44

1 †Hans Nielsen	3 2 3 3 2	13	
2 Dean Barker	1 1 2 1	5	2
3 Martin Dugard	1 2 0 0	3	
4 Troy Butler	1 2 2 0	5	2
5 Simon Wigg	2 3 0 1 0	6	
6 Paul Dugard	2 0 0 0	2	1
7 Alastair Stevens	3 3 1 3	10	

COVENTRY 46

1 †Kelvin Tatum	2 1 3 3 3 1	13	
2 Andy Phillips	0 0 1 T	1	
3 John Jorgensen	3 3 1 2 1 3	13	2
4 Rick Miller	3 1 0 2	6	1
5 Sean Wilson	0 3 2 2	7	
6 Glenn Doyle	*0 0 N 1*	*1*	*1*
7 Roman Matousek	1 2 0 2	5	1

COVENTRY win 91-89 on aggregate.

2nd Round

First leg, at King's Lynn, April 13

KING'S LYNN 47

1 †Richard Knight	3 3 3 2 1	12	1
2 Stephen Davies	0 2 F 0	2	1
3 Bohumil Brhel	F N 0 N	0	
4 Joe Screen	*F 0 N N*	*0*	
5 Gary Hicks	3 2 2 2 0	9	
6 Mark Loram	1 2 2 1 0 1	7	3
7 Dennis Löfqvist	2 3 3 3 3 3	17	

READING 42

1 †Jeremy Doncaster	2 3 2 3 3	13	
2 David Mullett	1 1 2 1	5	2
3 Per Jonsson	3 0 3 0 2	8	1
4 Tony Olsson	R 0 1 1	2	1
5 Jan Andersson	2 1 2 1	6	
6 Todd Wiltshire	3 1 1 1 N 2	8	1
7 Nathan Murray	0 N N 0 0	0	

Second leg, at Reading, April 23

READING 54

1 †Jeremy Doncaster	3 3 3 2 3	14	
2 David Mullett	2 1 0 0	3	1
3 Per Jonsson	3 N 1 3	7	1
4 Tony Olsson	3 1 3 1 2	10	2
5 Jan Andersson	2 0 0 2	4	2
6 Nathan Murray	0 N N 0 0	0	
7 Todd Wiltshire	3 2 3 3 2 3	16	1

KING'S LYNN 36

1 †Richard Knight	1 2 1 3 1 1	9	2
2 Stephen Davies	0 3 2 0 0	5	
3 Bohumil Brhel	0 0 T N	0	
4 Sean Wilson	*0 2 1 0*	*3*	*1*
5 Gary Hicks	1 1 N N	2	1
6 Mark Loram	2 2 1 2 0 2	9	1
7 Dennis Löfqvist	1 1 T 2 3 1	8	2

READING win 96-83 on aggregate.

2nd Round

First leg, at Wolverhampton, May 21

WOLVERHAMPTON 34

1 Ronnie Correy	2 3 fx 3 3 1	12	
2 Jan Staechmann	1 2 T 0	3	2
3 †Graham Jones	2 2 2 2 fx	8	
4 Carl Stonehewer	F 1 N F 1	2	
5 Neil Collins	2 R 0 T	2	
6 Dennis Löfqvist	*2 0 1 1 2 0*	*6*	*1*
7 Lars Munkedal	0 T 0 1	1	1

BELLE VUE 56

1 †Shawn Moran	**3 3 3 3 3**	**15**	
2 Joe Screen	0 2 1 1	4	1
3 Sean Wilson	*1 1 2 2*	*6*	*1*
4 Kelly Moran	3 3 1 2 2	11	3
5 Bobby Ott	1 0 2 1	4	1
6 Richard Musson	1 0 N 0	1	
7 Greg Hancock	***3 3 3 3 3***	***15***	

Second leg, at Belle Vue, June 15

BELLE VUE 61

1 Shawn Moran	2 1 2 2	7	2
2 Bobby Ott	1 3 2 3 3	12	2
3 †Chris Morton	3 3 2 2 1	11	
4 Kelly Moran	2 2 2 3	9	2
5 Joe Screen	3 1 3 1	8	2
6 Richard Musson	1 2 1 F	4	1
7 Paul Thorp	*3 3 1 3*	*10*	*1*

WOLVERHAMPTON 29

1 Ronnie Correy	3 3 1 3 3 2	15	
2 Jan Staechmann	0 0 1 0	1	
3 †Graham Jones	1 2 0 0 1	4	
4 Peter Karlsson	0 0 0 0 0	0	
5 Neil Collins	1 2 1 0	4	
6 Carl Stonehewer	2 0 T 1	3	1
7 Wayne Carter	0 0 T 2	2	

BELLE VUE win 117-63 on aggregate.

First leg, at Swindon, July 7

SWINDON 56

1 Jimmy Nilsen	3 3 2 3 0	11	1
2 Matthew Cross	0 0 N N	0	
3 Andrew Silver	2 3 2 2 3	12	1
4 Neil Collins	*3 2 0 2*	*7*	*1*
5 Jan Staechmann	*1 0 N N*	*1*	
6 †John Davis	2 1 2 3 3 2	13	4
7 Peter Nahlin	3 1 2 0 3 3	12	

COVENTRY 34

1 †Kelvin Tatum	1 1 2 3 3 1 1	12	2
2 Rick Miller	*rider replacement*		
3 John Jorgensen	2 3 2 0 1 1 2	11	
4 Andy Hackett	2 fx 0 0	2	
5 Sean Wilson	0 3 1 1 1 0	6	
6 Andy Phillips	0 1 T 0	1	1
7 Roman Matousek	1 0 T 1	2	

Second leg, at Coventry, July 21

COVENTRY 37

1 Shawn Moran	*1 3 3 3 3 1*	*14*	
2 Andy Hackett	0 1 1 E	2	1
3 John Jorgensen	0 1 0 1	2	
4 †Rick Miller	2 0 3 0 0	5	
5 Sean Wilson	0 1 0 0	1	
6 Andy Phillips	0 2 T E	2	
7 Alan Grahame	*3 2 2 1 3*	*11*	*1*

SWINDON 53

1 Peter Ravn	***2 3 2 3***	***10***	***2***
2 †John Davis	**3 2 3 3**	**11**	**1**
3 Andrew Silver	3 0 1 1 3	8	2
4 Simon Wigg	*1 0 0 2*	*3*	*1*
5 Peter Nahlin	3 2 1 2 2	10	1
6 Troy Butler	*1 2 2 2*	*7*	*1*
7 Richard Musson	*2 1 0 1*	*4*	*1*

SWINDON win 109-71 on aggregate.

2nd Round

First leg, at Cradley Heath, July 11

CRADLEY HEATH 45

1 Jan O. Pedersen	3 2 3 3 3	14	
2 Alan Grahame	0 0 2 1	3	
3 †Simon Cross	2 1 3 1 0	7	1
4 Richard Knight	*1 2 3 F*	*6*	*2*
5 Billy Hamill	2 3 1 0	6	
6 Mark Robinson	0 R N 0	0	
7 Gert Handberg	2 2 1 2 2	9	2

BRADFORD 45

1 Marvyn Cox	2 E 1 2	5	1
2 Neil Evitts	1 1 3 0	5	1
3 †Gary Havelock	3 1 2 1 1	8	2
4 Glenn Doyle	0 0 0 T	0	
5 Jimmy Nilsen	*3 3 2 2 3 2*	*15*	
6 Paul Thorp	3 R 3 0 N 3	9	
7 Stuart Parnaby	1 1 N 0 1	3	

Second leg, at Bradford, July 14

BRADFORD 54

1 Marvyn Cox	1 3 2 1 2 2	11	2
2 Neil Evitts	R 1 3 2 2	8	1
3 †Gary Havelock	3 3 1 2 3 1	13	1
4 Glenn Doyle	3 0 0 3 2	8	1
5 Andy Smith	*rider replacement*		
6 Stuart Parnaby	1 0 N 1	2	
7 Paul Thorp	3 2 3 1 3	12	2
8 Phil Disney	*did not ride*		

CRADLEY HEATH 36

1 Jan O. Pedersen	3 1 1 3 3 1 3	15	1
2 Greg Hancock	*rider replacement*		
3 †Simon Cross	2 2 1 2 3 1 0	11	2
4 Peter Nahlin	*2 2 1 0 0 0*	*5*	
5 Alan Grahame	0 0 T N	0	
6 David Haynes	0 0 T 0	0	
7 Gert Handberg	2 1 0 0 2	5	1

BRADFORD win 99-81 on aggregate.

Semi Finals

First leg, Bradford, September 13

BRADFORD 51

1 Marvyn Cox	1 1 0 N	2	
2 Andy Smith	fx 3 2 2	7	1
3 †Gary Havelock	**2 3 3 3 2**	**13**	**2**
4 Glenn Doyle	2 1 2 3	8	
5 Paul Thorp	0 3 1 2 3	9	2
6 Sean Wilson	*3 3 R 3 1 2*	*12*	
7 Bryan Larner	F N 0 0	0	

SWINDON 39

1 Jimmy Nilsen	3 2 1 2 0 0	8	
2 Peter Nahlin	2 0 R 1 1	4	2
3 Andrew Silver	1 2 0 0	3	
4 Phil Crump	1 1 T T	2	1
5 Leigh Adams	3 2 3 3 2 1	14	
6 David Smart	1 0 T 1	2	1
7 †John Davis	2 0 1 3	6	

Second leg, Swindon, September 20

SWINDON 50

1 Andrew Silver	2 1 1 2	6	2
2 Peter Nahlin	1 2 0 N	3	1
3 Jimmy Nilsen	1 3 3 2 3	12	1
4 Phil Crump	1 1 0 3	5	1
5 Leigh Adams	3 2 2 1 3 2	13	1
6 David Smart	1 0 N 1	2	1
7 †John Davis	2 2 2 0 N 3	9	1

BRADFORD 40

1 Marvyn Cox	3 3 2 1 1	10	
2 Glenn Doyle	0 0 1 0	1	
3 †Gary Havelock	2 0 3 1 0	6	1
4 Andy Smith	2 1 3 0	6	
5 Paul Thorp	0 0 2 N	2	1
6 Billy Hamill	*3 3 3 3 1 2*	*15*	
7 Bryan Larner	R N N 0 0	0	

BRADFORD win 91-89 on aggregate.

Semi Finals

First leg, Reading, July 16

READING 53

1 Todd Wiltshire	2 3 2 2 2	11	2
2 Jan Andersson	3 2 2 1	8	2
3 †Jeremy Doncaster	3 2 3 3 3	14	
4 Per Jonsson	3 1 3 1	8	2
5 Tony Olsson	1 2 1 1	5	
6 David Steen	2 1 N 0	3	
7 David Mullett	R 1 1 0 2	4	2

BELLE VUE 36

1 Shawn Moran	1 3 2 2 2 0	10	
2 Bobby Ott	0 0 3 1 3	7	1
3 †Chris Morton	2 0 0 T	2	
4 Peter Ravn	0 0 0 T	0	
5 Kelly Moran	2 3 3 0 0 1	9	
6 Richard Musson	fx 1 T 3	4	
7 Joe Screen	3 R 0 1	4	

Second leg, Belle Vue, July 27

BELLE VUE 51

1 Shawn Moran	3 3 3 2 2	13	1
2 Bobby Ott	F 2 2 2	6	2
3 †Chris Morton	3 2 3 3	11	
4 Kelly Moran	3 3 2 3 0	11	1
5 See note above right			
6 Richard Musson	2 1 N 1	4	2
7 Alan Grahame	*3 R 1 0 2*	*6*	*1*

READING 38

1 Todd Wiltshire	2 fx N N	2	
2 †Jan Andersson	1 2 0 1	4	2
3 Marvyn Cox	*2 1 3 3 1 3*	*13*	
4 Tony Olsson	2 1 0 1	4	
5 Per Jonsson	1 3 1 1	6	1
6 David Mullett	1 0 T 2 2 3 1	9	
7 David Steen	N fx T F	0	

†READING win 91-87 on aggregate.

ONE of the major controversies of the competition was the Speedway Control Board decision to uphold a Reading protest against Belle Vue's use of rider replacement in the second leg of the semi final.

The SCB ordered that points scored by the use of rider replacement should be deducted from the scores and riders' finishing positions upgraded where appropriate.

It turned an on-track 57-33 Belle Vue win into a 51-38 victory which, in turn, reversed the aggregate scores.

Listed below are the on-the-night scores with affected results underlined.

Second leg, Belle Vue, July 27

BELLE VUE 57

1 Shawn Moran	3 2 3 3 2 2	15	2
2 Bobby Ott	F 3 2 2 2	9	2
3 †Chris Morton	3 2 1 3 3	12	1
4 Kelly Moran	2 3 2 3 1 0	11	1
5 Peter Ravn	*rider replacement*		
6 Richard Musson	2 1 N 1	4	2
7 Alan Grahame	*3 R 1 0 2*	*6*	*1*

READING 33

1 Todd Wiltshire	2 fx N N	2	
2 Jan Andersson	1 1 0 1	3	2
3 Marvyn Cox	*2 1 3 3 1 3*	*13*	
4 Tony Olsson	1 1 0 0	2	
5 Per Jonsson	0 3 0 1 0	4	
6 David Mullett	1 0 T 2 2 3 1	9	
7 David Steen	N fx T F	0	

BELLE VUE win 93-86 on aggregate.

THE FINAL

BRADFORD'S dream of adding the Speedway Star Knock Out Cup to their first ever national trophy, the Gold Cup, disappeared on the first bend of heat two.

Their often potent reserve, Australian Champion Glenn Doyle, came down racing into the first turn and was forced to miss the rest of the Cup Final with severe bruising.

While he was on his way to the local hospital, the XXXX Racers were not only holding onto their 12 point first leg lead, but building on it.

They were four point down at heat eight - and only eight points in front overall – when Jan Andersson and in-form reserve David Mullett combined for a 5-1 that brought the scores level and a further heat maximum from skipper Jeremy Doncaster and Armando Castagna pushed them into a heat 10 lead they never sacrificed. And when Todd Wiltshire and the Italian shared the points in heat 13 there was no way that the Berkshire club could be beaten.

First leg, at Reading, October 8

READING 51			
1 Todd Wiltshire	**3 3 3 3 3**	**15**	
2 Jan Andersson	1 **2** 1 **2**	6	2
3 Per Jonsson	**1** 3 3 3 **2**	12	2
4 Armando Castagna	**2** R 2 1	5	1
5 †Jeremy Doncaster	3 2 0 1	6	
6 David Steen	2 N 0 0	2	
7 David Mullett	**1** 2 0 F 2	5	1

BRADFORD 39			
1 Marvyn Cox	2 3 3 2 R 1	11	
2 Neil Evitts	0 1 T N	1	
3 †Gary Havelock	3 1 **2** 3 2 0	11	1
4 Andy Smith	0 **1** 1 N	2	1
5 Paul Thorp	1 2 0 0	3	
6 Glenn Doyle	3 0 1 **1** 2 3	10	1
7 Bryan Larner	0 0 T 1	1	

READING win 98-82 on aggregate.

Second leg, at Bradford, October 13

BRADFORD 43			
1 Marvyn Cox	2 **2** 1 3 **1**	9	2
2 Neil Evitts	**1** 3 1 0	5	1
3 †Gary Havelock	3 3 3 0 2	11	
4 Andy Smith	3 2 **1** 1	7	1
5 Paul Thorp	**2** 0 2 3	7	1
6 Glenn Doyle	fnN N N	0	
7 Bryan Larner	2 0 0 0 0	2	
8 Stuart Parnaby	0 2	2	

READING 47			
1 Todd Wiltshire	3 3 2 2 3	13	
2 Jan Andersson	0 1 3 **1**	5	1
3 Per Jonsson	**1** E 3 0	4	1
4 Armando Castagna	1 2 **2** **1** 0	6	2
5 †Jeremy Doncaster	0 **1** 3 2	6	1
6 David Mullett	3 2 N 1 **2** N 3	11	1
7 David Steen	1 N 0 N 1	2	

▲ ***KINGS OF THE CUP...Reading celebrate after their Speedway Star Knock Out Cup Final victory at Odsal Stadium. Todd Wiltshire, David Mullett, Jeremy Doncaster, Armando Castagna and Per Jonsson acknowledge the cheers of their travelling fans***

DUKES WIN FIRST MAJOR TROPHY

GOLDEN NIGHTS FOR BRADFORD

TWENTY-FIVE seasons is a long time to wait for a first major national trophy.

But for Bradford it all became worthwhile as Andy Smith took the chequered flag at the end of heat 12 of the second leg of the Gold Cup Final against defending Cupholders Oxford.

By then there was absolutely nothing that even World Champion Hans Nielsen could do to prevent the Coalite Dukes polishing up their first piece of silverware since league racing was first introduced at Odsal in 1946.

They were 22 points ahead after 27 races – and even three races with only Oxford providing the finishers would not deprive them of their moment of glory.

It had been a long time coming: 12 seasons in the old National League, a disastrous 1960 in the Provincial League, another awful season at the city's Greenfields Stadium in the 1962 Provincial League, six years in the British League Division Two, and four trophy-less campaigns in the British League since the move from Halifax.

But, at last, in their silver jubilee league season, Bradford had reason to be proud of their side which had brought home a cup.

Yet, how thin was the thread that helped to stitch together their battle plans.

For Bradford owed their place in the Gold Cup Final to a shock 5-1 in the very last race of the predominantly Northern qualifying group.

Cradley Heath led Belle Vue 42-39 and had Jan O. Pedersen and Simon Cross come to the tapes for the nominated riders' heat in their match at Kirkmanshulme Lane.

Cradley needed two points to win the match and with it the group. But the Moran brothers, Kelly and Shawn, teamed up to send the Belle Vue fans, and the watching Bradford promoter Allan Ham, into a jig of delight as they headed the two Heathens in the closest possible finish to the group.

That lost point put Bradford into the final despite losing at home once (to Belle Vue) and being massacred 61-29 at Wolverhampton against whom they still grabbed the vital bonus point by virtue of a record 67-23 home win in their last group match.

Belle Vue's own hopes of reaching the final disappeared when they lost by six points at home to Wolverhampton who, in turn, dropped out of the reckoning when they picked up only one out of the four available bonus points.

If the Northern group had a dramatic finale then there was also a nail-biting race to the final in the South.

Swindon were in with a shout until losing both the match and the bonus point in their final meeting at Reading late in May.

King's Lynn had already been resigned to finishing at the bottom of the table – a four point win over Swindon provided their only points – and with Swindon also out of it everything hinged on the result of the final group match between Reading and Oxford.

The Skol Cheetahs knew they had to win the bonus point and to do that had to score at least 38 points at Smallmead. They made it with a few points to spare (43-47) thanks to three race wins from Martin Dugard and a spirited half dozen from reserve Alastair Stevens which made up for a lower than expected eight-point return from skipper Hans Nielsen.

Everything was set for Oxford to defend their title and they must have thought it was going to be plain sailing when, as the referee pressed the two-minute buzzer for the opening race of the first leg, Bradford were in apparent disarray.

Skipper Gary Havelock and reserve Bryan Larner hadn't arrived and neither had co-promoter Bobby Ham – all three trapped in a snarl-up on the M1.

The Coalite Dukes had only one rider in the reserves' race and Neil Evitts (down to number six) had to replace Havelock in heat four.

Both riders arrived subsequently but neither had any significant contribution to make. Havelock got one second place, a last and was replaced in his final programmed outing while Larner failed to score from the one ride that he finished, having broken the tapes and fallen in two others.

Encouragingly for their fans despite all the traumas Bradford lost by only four points and were confident of overcoming that slim deficit on their own track.

They did – with plenty to spare as they smashed in three quick 5-1s in heats three, four and five to wipe out the leeway and build a commanding lead.

Oxford had only three heat wins all night (Nielsen, twice, and Martin Dugard) and Bradford recorded seven maximums and never once surrendered heat advantage in the finest night of the track's 25 season history!

The waiting had been well worth it....

ROLL OF HONOUR

1989 OXFORD 102 Cradley Heath 78
1990 BRADFORD 106 Oxford 74

LEAGUE CUP

1981 COVENTRY 122 King's Lynn 70
1982 CRADLEY HEATH 83 Ipswich 73
1983 BELLE VUE 86 Coventry 70
1984 CRADLEY HEATH 80 Oxford 76
1985 COVENTRY 86 Oxford 70
1986 ◆CRADLEY 38 OXFORD 40
1987 COVENTRY 78 Belle Vue 78
COVENTRY 84 Belle Vue 72 (replay)

In 1981 and 1982 the competition was run on a regional basis with the two group winners meeting in the final.

In 1983 and 1984 the competition was run on a regional basis with the top two teams from each group meeting in the semi-finals.

In 1985, 1986 and 1987 the competition was run on a national basis with the top four teams qualifying for the semi-finals.

◆ In 1986 only the Cradley leg of the final was held and it was declared that the two finalists would share the trophy.

The competition was discontinued at the end of the 1987 season.

Belle Vue

Coventry (A), March 17, L44-46

1 Shawn Moran	1 3 1 3 1	9	3
2 †Chris Morton	2 0 3 2	7	
3 Peter Ravn	1 2 3 1 2	9	
4 Neil Evitts	*1 3 2 1*	*7*	
5 Joe Screen	0 0 1 0	1	1
6 Mike Lewthwaite	2 1 0 1	4	3
7 Bobby Ott	3 0 2 2	7	1

COVENTRY (H), March 23, W46-44

1 Shawn Moran	**3 3 3 2 3**	**14**	**1**
2 †Chris Morton	2 1 3 2	8	2
3 Peter Ravn	1 2 3 3 X	9	
4 Kelly Moran	3 R 1 3	7	
5 Joe Screen	fx1 0 2	3	1
6 Mike Lewthwaite	1 N F 0	1	
7 Bobby Ott	3 0 0 0 1	4	

Ravn beat Jorgensen for bonus point.

BRADFORD (H), March 30, W48-42

1 Shawn Moran	3 3 2 R 2 2	12	3
2 †Chris Morton	2 2 0 3	7	2
3 Peter Ravn	2 3 3 3 3	14	
4 Kelly Moran	2 0 3 3	8	
5 Joe Screen	0 1 T 0	1	
6 Mike Lewthwaite	0 0 N 1	1	1
7 Bobby Ott	2 0 1 0 2	5	

Bradford (A), March 31, L43-47

1 Shawn Moran	0 3 3 3 2 1	12	
2 Joe Screen	1 0 2 1 T	4	2
3 †Chris Morton	3 2 2 2 3 0	12	1
4 Peter Ravn	0 0 T N	0	
5 Kelly Moran	2 1 3 2 0	8	1
6 Mike Lewthwaite	1 T 0 3	4	
7 Bobby Ott	0 1 T 0 2	3	1

Cradley Heath (A), April 7, L38-52

1 Shawn Moran	3 1 1 T 0	5	1
2 †Chris Morton	1 0 1 2 2	6	
3 Peter Ravn	2 3 3 1 0 1	10	1
4 Kelly Moran	3 1 T 2	6	
5 Joe Screen	0 3 2 1 1	7	1
6 Mike Lewthwaite	1 T 0 1	2	1
7 Carl Stonehewer	*fx0 0 2*	*2*	

WOLVERHAMPTON (H), April 13, L42-48

1 Shawn Moran	2 3 1 2 1 R	9	
2 †Chris Morton	1 2 2 0 1	6	4
3 Peter Ravn	fx N T N	0	
4 Kelly Moran	2 2 3 2 3 2	14	1
5 Joe Screen	3 X 1 3	7	1
6 Mike Lewthwaite	1 N 1 0	2	
7 Bobby Ott	R 1 fxT T 2 1	4	1

Wolverhampton (A), April 16, L43-47

1 Shawn Moran	1 3 1 3 2	10	1
2 †Chris Morton	0 2 2 3 0 1	8	1
3 Peter Ravn	*rider replacement*		
4 Kelly Moran	3 3 2 1 3 fx	12	
5 Joe Screen	1 2 2 0 0	5	1
6 Mike Lewthwaite	0 0 N 0	0	
7 Bobby Ott	2 1 1 3 1	8	1

CRADLEY HEATH (H), April 20, W44-43

1 Shawn Moran	**3 3 3 3 2**	**14**	**1**
2 Joe Screen	2 0 2 2	6	3
3 †Peter Ravn	2 fx2 fx	4	
4 Kelly Moran	3 3 2 1 3	12	
5 Bobby Ott	X 1 R E	1	
6 Richard Musson	1 0 N fx	1	1
7 Carl Stonehewer	*2 F 3 0 1 F*	*6*	

Bradford

Cradley Heath (A), March 24, W 49-41

1 Paul Thorp	3 0 3 3	9	
2 Andy Smith	0 2 1 F	3	
3 †Neil Evitts	1 1 0 N	2	
4 Gary Havelock	0 3 2 2 2	9	3
5 Marvyn Cox	2 2 3 3 3	13	1
6 Bryan Larner	0 0 N 2	2	
7 Glenn Doyle	2 3 3 2 1 F	11	

Belle Vue (A), March 30, L42-48

1 Paul Thorp	1 3 2 1 0	7	1
2 Andy Smith	0 2 2 1	5	3
3 †Neil Evitts	1 1 1 0	3	
4 Gary Havelock	1 1 2 2	6	1
5 Marvyn Cox	3 2 1 1 1	8	1
6 Bryan Larner	1 0 N X	1	
7 Glenn Doyle	3 3 3 0 3	12	

BELLE VUE (H), March 31, W47-43

1 Paul Thorp	3 R R 1	4	1
2 Andy Smith	2 3 0 3 3	11	1
3 †Neil Evitts	2 2 1 1	6	
4 Gary Havelock	3 2 1 2	8	
5 Marvyn Cox	1 1 3 3 2	10	2
6 Bryan Larner	2 N 1 R	3	2
7 Glenn Doyle	3 0 1 0 1	5	

COVENTRY (H), April 7, W51-39

1 Paul Thorp	2 3 3 3	11	
2 Andy Smith	1 2 3 2 1	9	4
3 Gary Havelock	3 3 3 3 2	14	
4 †Neil Evitts	0 1 1 1	3	2
5 Marvyn Cox	1 2 2 1	6	
6 Bryan Larner	2 F N 1	3	
7 Glenn Doyle	R R 2 0 3	5	1

CRADLEY HEATH (H), April 14, W63-27

1 Paul Thorp	3 0 3 3	9	
2 Andy Smith	1 2 2 2	7	2
3 Gary Havelock	2 3 3 2 2	12	2
4 †Neil Evitts	2 2 2 1	7	3
5 Marvyn Cox	**3 3 3 3 3**	**15**	
6 Bryan Larner	3 1 0 2	6	2
7 Glenn Doyle	R 3 1 3	7	

Coventry (A), April 21, L44-46

1 Paul Thorp	1 3 3 1	8	1
2 Andy Smith	2 2 3 2 1	10	3
3 Gary Havelock	2 3 2 0	7	
4 †Neil Evitts	0 1 0 0	1	1
5 Marvyn Cox	3 2 3 2 2	12	
6 Bryan Larner	1 0 0 2	3	
7 Glenn Doyle	3 0 0 R	3	

Wolverhampton (A), April 23, L29-61

1 Paul Thorp	3 1 2 1 0 0	7	
2 Andy Smith	1 0 fxN	1	
3 Gary Havelock	2 0 2 1 0	5	
4 †Neil Evitts	0 0 T N	0	
5 Marvyn Cox	3 2 0 N 1 1	7	
6 Bryan Larner	1 N T 0 fx	1	1
7 Glenn Doyle	2 1 2 T 0 1 2	8	1

WOLVERHAMPTON (H), May 12, W 67-23

1 Paul Thorp	1 1 2 1	5	1
2 Andy Smith	**3 3 3 3 3**	**15**	
3 †Gary Havelock	3 1 1 3 2	10	1
4 Neil Evitts	**2 2 2 3**	**9**	**3**
5 Marvyn Cox	3 3 3 1	10	
6 Bryan Larner	2 fxN 2	4	2
7 Glenn Doyle	**3 3 2 3 3**	**14**	**1**

Coventry

BELLE VUE (H), March 17, W46-44

1 †Kelvin Tatum	**3 3 3 2 3**	**14**	**1**
2 Paul Bromwich	0 0 N N	0	
3 John Jorgensen	3 2 3 2 0	10	
4 Rick Miller	2 1 1 3	7	3
5 Sean Wilson	3 2 2 R	7	
6 Lee Coleman	1 N N 0 0 0 0	1	
7 Andy Hackett	F 2 1 1 N N 3	7	2

Belle Vue (A), March 23, L44-46

1 †Kelvin Tatum	0 3 2 1 1	7	1
2 Mark Loram	*1 2 1 1*	*5*	*3*
3 John Jorgensen	2 2 3 1 2	10	1
4 Rick Miller	2 3 R F	5	
5 Sean Wilson	1 1 1 N	3	1
6 Roman Matousek	2 0 N 2	4	1
7 Andy Hackett	F 3 2 2 0 3	10	1

Jorgensen lost to Ravn for bonus point.

WOLVERHAMPTON (H), March 24, W53-37

1 †Kelvin Tatum	2 3 3 3 1	12	
2 Andy Phillips	1 2 0 0	3	2
3 John Jorgensen	3 3 1 1	8	
4 Rick Miller	2 2 1 1	6	2
5 Sean Wilson	3 3 0 3 R	9	
6 Roman Matousek	2 2 1 3	8	2
7 Andy Hackett	3 2 0 2	7	1

Wolverhampton (A), March 26, L 43-47

1 †Kelvin Tatum	2 3 3 3 2	13	
2 Andy Phillips	1 1 1 0	3	2
3 John Jorgensen	2 2 3 2	9	
4 Rick Miller	0 1 0 N	1	1
5 Sean Wilson	3 2 2 1 1	9	2
6 Roman Matousek	2 0 0 F	2	
7 Andy Hackett	1 1 2 0 2	6	2

Bradford (A), April 7, L39-51

1 †Kelvin Tatum	3 3 2 N 2 3	13	
2 Andy Phillips	0 0 N T	0	
3 John Jorgensen	1 N 3 1 T	5	2
4 Rick Miller	2 1 0 0	3	2
5 Sean Wilson	3 2 1 2 0	8	
6 Roman Matousek	3 0 1 0 2	6	
7 Andy Hackett	1 2 1 R R 0	4	

Cradley Heath (A), April 16, L38-52

1 †Kelvin Tatum	3 3 3 3 3 0	15	
2 Andy Phillips	0 0 N T	0	
3 John Jorgensen	1 R 1 T	2	
4 Chris Morton	*1 1 0 0*	*2*	*1*
5 Sean Wilson	3 2 1 1 F 1	8	
6 Roman Matousek	1 fx1 R T 1	3	
7 Andy Hackett	3 N 1 1 3	8	

CRADLEY HEATH (H), April 16, L40-50

1 †Kelvin Tatum	3 fx2 3 3	11	
2 Andy Phillips	0 1 1 0	2	2
3 John Jorgensen	3 3 1 2 R 2	11	1
4 Rick Miller	*rider replacement*		
5 Sean Wilson	3 2 2 0 2 0	9	
6 Roman Matousek	R 0 0 2 1 2	5	1
7 Andy Hackett	2 R N fnN	2	
8 Andy Meredith	0	0	

BRADFORD (H), April 21, W46-44

1 †Kelvin Tatum	3 2 1 3 3	12	1
2 Andy Phillips	0 1 1 2	4	2
3 John Jorgensen	3 3 1 2 0	9	1
4 Rick Miller	2 1 1 1	5	
5 Sean Wilson	1 0 3 3	7	1
6 Roman Matousek	2 1 R 2 3	8	
7 Lee Coleman	0 N 0 1	1	

Cradley Heath

BRADFORD (H), March 24, L41-49

1 Simon Cross	2 2 2 1 0	7	1
2 Gert Handberg	*rider replacement*		
3 Jan O. Pedersen	1 2 1 2 0 1	7	1
4 Alan Grahame	3 1 3 3 2 0	12	
5 Billy Hamill	1 3 1 fx1	6	
6 Greg Hancock	3 0 0 F 3	6	
7 Mark Robinson	1 N 1 1	3	1
8 David Haynes	*did not ride*		

BELLE VUE (H), April 7, W52-38

1 Jan O. Pedersen	2 2 3 2	9	1
2 Gert Handberg	0 0 1 0	1	
3 Simon Cross	3 2 3 3 3	14	
4 Alan Grahame	1 3 1 3 2	10	3
5 Billy Hamill	2 2 2 0	6	1
6 Greg Hancock	3 1 0 3 3	10	
7 Mark Robinson	2 N 0 N	2	1
8 David Haynes	0	0	

Wolverhampton (A), April 9, D45-45

1 Jan O. Pedersen	**3 3 3 3 3**	**15**	
2 Gert Handberg	fx0 T 0	0	
3 Simon Cross	3 1 3 2 0 2	11	3
4 Alan Grahame	0 0 0 N	0	
5 Billy Hamill	1 2 2 1	6	
6 Greg Hancock	3 2 2 3 0 3	13	1
7 David Haynes	0 0 T F	0	

Bradford (A), April 14, L27-63

1 Jan O. Pedersen	2 0 1 2 1 0	6	
2 Gert Handberg	0 1 0 0	1	
3 Simon Cross	3 3 2 R 2 1	11	
4 Alan Grahame	1 1 1 0	3	1
5 Dean Child	0 T T 0	0	
6 Greg Hancock	2 1 1 0 fx	4	
7 David Haynes	1 0 T 1	2	1

COVENTRY (H), April 16, W52-38

1 Jan O. Pedersen	2 3 3 3 3	14	
2 Gert Handberg	1 2 3 2	8	3
3 Simon Cross	3 3 2 2 2	12	1
4 Alan Grahame	2 2 2 2	8	1
5 Billy Hamill	0 1 E 1	2	2
6 Greg Hancock	2 2 0 2 R 2	8	2
7 Mark Robinson	0 N 0 0	0	

Coventry (A), April 16, W50-40

1 Jan O. Pedersen	2 3 3 1 1	10	
2 Gert Handberg	1 1 3 fx	5	1
3 Simon Cross	2 3 3 2 3	13	
4 Alan Grahame	2 1 1 3	7	2
5 Billy Hamill	1 2 2 1	6	2
6 Greg Hancock	3 1 0 0 3	7	1
7 Mark Robinson	1 N 0 1	2	

WOLVERHAMPTON (H), April 25, W55-35

1 Jan O. Pedersen	**3 3 3 3 3**	**15**	
2 Gert Handberg	0 1 0 N	1	
3 Simon Cross	3 1 2 3	9	
4 Alan Grahame	0 1 2 2	5	3
5 Billy Hamill	3 2 3 N 2	10	1
6 Greg Hancock	3 2 3 2 2 3	15	2
7 Mark Robinson	0 N E F 0	0	

Belle Vue (A), April 20, L43-44

1 Jan O. Pedersen	F 2 3 2 1	8	1
2 Gert Handberg	fx0 1 1	2	
3 Simon Cross	3 2 3 2 3 0	13	
4 Alan Grahame	2 2 1 T	5	1
5 Billy Hamill	E 3 fxN N	3	
6 Greg Hancock	3 1 1 R 1 3	9	1
7 Mark Robinson	0 1 N N 0 2	3	2

Wolverhampton

Coventry (A), March 24, L37-53

1 Ronnie Correy	3 1 2 3 0 2	11	2
2 Jan Staechmann	0 R 1 2	3	1
3 Peter Ravn	*1 0 3 3 2 3*	*12*	
4 †Graham Jones	0 2 2 0 2	6	
5 Neil Collins	1 0 1 T	2	1
6 Carl Stonehewer	0 0 N T 0	0	
7 Lars Munkedal	1 N 1 T 1	3	

COVENTRY (H), March 26, W 47-43

1 Ronnie Correy	**3 3 3 3 3**	**15**	
2 Jan Staechmann	0 1 3 1	5	
3 Jimmy Nilsen	*3 3 2 1 0*	*9*	*1*
4 †Graham Jones	1 0 1 0	2	2
5 Neil Collins	2 2 2 2	8	
6 Carl Stonehewer	F 0 0 1	1	
7 Lars Munkedal	3 0 1 3	7	1

CRADLEY HEATH (H), April 9, D45-45

1 Ronnie Correy	2 3 3 3 0	11	
2 Jan Staechmann	1 F 0 N	1	1
3 Jimmy Nilsen	*2 3 2 1 1*	*9*	*1*
4 †Graham Jones	3 2 0 2	7	1
5 Neil Collins	2 1 1 2	6	2
6 Carl Stonehewer	1 1 1 1 2	6	2
7 Lars Munkedal	2 1 1 1	5	2

Belle Vue (A), April 13, W48-42

1 Ronnie Correy	3 3 3 1 3	13	
2 Jan Staechmann	0 1 0 N	1	
3 John Jorgensen	*2 1 3 0*	*6*	*1*
4 †Graham Jones	1 3 2 0	6	1
5 Neil Collins	0 2 3 2 1	8	1
6 Carl Stonehewer	2 0 0 2	4	2
7 Lars Munkedal	3 3 1 0 3	10	

BELLE VUE (H), April 16, W47-43

1 Ronnie Correy	3 3 R 3 2 2	13	2
2 Jan Staechmann	*rider replacement*		
3 Bo Petersen	2 3 1 1 2 0	9	1
4 †Graham Jones	0 0 2 3 3	8	
5 Neil Collins	2 1 1 0 1	5	
6 Carl Stonehewer	1 0 0 2	3	1
7 Lars Munkedal	3 2 1 3	9	1

BRADFORD (H), April 23, W61-29

1 Ronnie Correy	2 3 3 2 2	12	2
2 Carl Stonehewer	0 1 3 1	5	
3 Bo Petersen	0 1 2 3	6	1
4 †Graham Jones	1 3 3 3 3	13	1
5 Neil Collins	2 2 2 2	8	3
6 Leigh Adams	***3 3 3 3***	***12***	
7 Lars Munkedal	X 1 3 1	5	

Cradley Heath (A), April 25, L35-55

1 Ronnie Correy	1 3 3 R 3 2 R	12	1
2 Bo Petersen	*rider replacement*		
3 Marvyn Cox	*2 1 2 1 1*	*8*	
4 †Graham Jones	1 2 1 0 1 1	6	2
5 Neil Collins	2 0 0 1 0	3	
6 Carl Stonehewer	1 0 T 2	3	1
7 Lars Munkedal	2 0 T 1	3	1
8 Ade Hoole	*did not ride*		

Bradford (A), May 12, L23-67

1 Ronnie Correy	2 1 0 2 2 1	8	
2 Jan Staechmann	F 0 1 0	1	
3 Bo Petersen	2 2 1 0	5	
4 †Graham Jones	1 2 0 0	3	
5 Neil Collins	0 0 1 2 0	3	
6 Wayne Carter	0 0 T 1	1	
7 Lars Munkedal	1 1 0 0	2	1

GOLD CUP

King's Lynn

READING (H), March 24, L44-46

1 †Richard Knight	2 2 3 1 3	11	
2 Stephen Davies	0 1 3 N	4	1
3 Bohumil Brhel	0 0 N N	0	
4 Allan Johansen	1 3 1 0 F	5	
5 Gary Hicks	3 2 0 0	5	1
6 Mark Loram	3 3 3 3 3 R	15	
7 Dennis Löfqvist	1 0 0 1 2	4	

Reading (A), March 26, L 44-46

1 †Richard Knight	3 2 3 2 2 3	15	1
2 Stephen Davies	0 1 T T 1	2	2
3 Bohumil Brhel	1 N 0 T	1	
4 Allan Johansen	2 1 0 3 0	6	1
5 Gary Hicks	E 2 3 1 2	8	1
6 Mark Loram	3 0 1 2	6	
7 Dennis Löfqvist	R R 0 3 2 1	6	2

Swindon (A), March 31, L39-51

1 †Richard Knight	3 2 2 3 1 3	14	
2 Carl Stonehewer	*1 0 T T*	*1*	
3 Gary Hicks	1 1 1 1 T	4	
4 Allan Johansen	1 0 R 2 0	3	
5 Bohumil Brhel	0 T T 1	1	1
6 Mark Loram	2 0 3 1 3 0	9	
7 Dennis Löfqvist	1 3 0 1 2	7	2

SWINDON (H), April 1, W47-43

1 †Richard Knight	F 2 1 2 1	6	2
2 Mark Loram	3 0 1 2	6	
3 Bohumil Brhel	3 0 1 0	4	
4 Allan Johansen	2 1 0 T	3	2
5 Gary Hicks	3 2 2 3 3 3	16	
6 Roman Matousek	*1 1 N 2*	*4*	*1*
7 Dennis Löfqvist	3 2 0 0 3	8	

OXFORD (H), April 7, L39-51

1 †Richard Knight	2 3 2 2 3	12	
2 Stephen Davies	0 2 2 0 1 0	5	1
3 Bohumil Brhel	E 2 T 0	2	
4 Allan Johansen	fx N N T	0	
5 Gary Hicks	2 0 R 1	3	
6 Mark Loram	3 2 R 3 3 1	12	
7 Dennis Löfqvist	1 R 2 1 0 1	5	1

Oxford (A), April 27, L44-46

1 †Richard Knight	2 1 2 F 0	5	
2 Stephen Davies	E 0 2 1	3	2
3 Bohumil Brhel	fx N N 0	0	
4 Todd Wiltshire	*3 2 1 1 3*	*10*	
5 Gary Hicks	0 1 0 N	1	1
6 Mark Loram	0 2 1 3 2 3	11	1
7 Dennis Löfqvist	3 2 3 3 2 1	14	1

Oxford

Swindon (A), March 24, W51-38

1 †Hans Nielsen	**3 3 3 3 3**	**15**	
2 Dean Barker	2 1 0 1	4	1
3 Martin Dugard	2 3 R 2	7	
4 Simon Wigg	3 2 3 2 0	10	1
5 Troy Butler	2 1 2 1	6	4
6 Paul Dugard	1 0 N 0	1	
7 Alastair Stevens	3 0 3 fx2	8	

SWINDON (H), April 6, L39-51

1 †Hans Nielsen	2 0 0 2	4	
2 Dean Barker	1 2 1 3 0	7	1
3 Martin Dugard	3 3 2 2 2	12	
4 Simon Wigg	2 3 1 0	6	
5 Troy Butler	0 2 0 1	3	2
6 Paul Dugard	1 0 N 1	2	1
7 Alastair Stevens	2 0 3 R 0	5	

King's Lynn (A), April 7, W51-39

1 †Hans Nielsen	**3 3 3 2 3**	**14**	**1**
2 Dean Barker	1 1 3 1	6	
3 Martin Dugard	1 1 2 fx	4	
4 Simon Wigg	**3 3 3 3 2**	**14**	**1**
5 Troy Butler	1 1 1 2	5	
6 Paul Dugard	0 0 N 0	0	
7 Alastair Stevens	2 3 0 1 2	8	1

READING (H), April 16, W53-37

1 †Hans Nielsen	**3 2 3 2 3**	**13**	**2**
2 Dean Barker	0 3 F 0	3	
3 Jimmy Nilsen	*3 3 1 2*	*9*	
4 Simon Wigg	2 2 2 3 1	10	
5 Troy Butler	F 1 1 0	2	2
6 Paul Dugard	1 2 0 3	6	
7 Alastair Stevens	2 3 3 2	10	1

KING'S LYNN (H), April 27, W46-44

1 †Hans Nielsen	3 2 3 3 1	12	1
2 Dean Barker	1 0 1 T	2	
3 Martin Dugard	3 3 2 3 3 2	16	1
4 Simon Wigg	1 2 0 1	4	2
5 Troy Butler	2 3 1 2	8	1
6 Paul Dugard	1 1 N 2	4	
7 Alastair Stevens	fx 0 R 0 0	0	

Reading (A), May 28, L43-47

1 †Hans Nielsen	3 0 2 1 2	8	
2 Dean Barker	2 1 0 1	4	2
3 Martin Dugard	3 3 3 2 1	12	1
4 Simon Wigg	2 1 R 3	6	1
5 Troy Butler	3 F 2 0	5	
6 Paul Dugard	1 0 N 1	2	2
7 Alastair Stevens	2 1 1 0 2	6	

Reading

King's Lynn (A), March 24, W46-44

1 †Jeremy Doncaster	3 0 3 2 2 1	11	1
2 David Mullett	1 1 1 0	3	1
3 Per Jonsson	1 3 2 3 2	11	2
4 Tony Olsson	0 2 1 1	4	2
5 Jan Andersson	2 1 2 2	7	2
6 Nathan Murray	0 0 T 1	1	
7 Todd Wiltshire	2 2 2 3	9	

KING'S LYNN (H), March 26, W46-44

1 †Jeremy Doncaster	2 2 2 3 1	10	1
2 David Mullett	1 1 1 1	4	3
3 Per Jonsson	2 3 0 0	5	1
4 Tony Olsson	3 3 3 0 2	11	
5 Jan Andersson	1 0 2 1	4	1
6 Todd Wiltshire	2 3 N 0 3 3	11	
7 Nathan Murray	1 0 N N 0	1	1

Swindon (A), April 7, L42-47

1 †Jeremy Doncaster	3 3 1 3 fx	10	
2 David Mullett	0 1 0 0	1	
3 Per Jonsson	3 X 1 1	5	
4 Tony Olsson	2 2 2 0	6	2
5 Jan Andersson	1 3 3 3 2	12	1
6 Todd Wiltshire	2 1 2 R 2	7	
7 Nathan Murray	1 0 N 0	1	1

Oxford (A), April 16, L37-53

1 †Jeremy Doncaster	2 0 2 3 2	9	
2 David Mullett	1 3 1 0	5	2
3 Per Jonsson	1 1 0 N	2	
4 Tony Olsson	3 2 3 1 1 0	10	1
5 Jan Andersson	1 1 2 1	5	1
6 Todd Wiltshire	3 0 2 T 0 1	6	
7 Nathan Murray	0 0 N 0	0	

SWINDON (H), May 21, W51-39

1 †Jeremy Doncaster	3 3 3 X 3	12	
2 David Mullett	2 0 2 0	4	2
3 Per Jonsson	3 R 2	8	1
4 Tony Olsson	2 1 1 2	6	1
5 Jan Andersson	1 2 3 3 1	10	1
6 David Steen	0 N 0 0	0	
7 Todd Wiltshire	2 1 3 3 2	11	

OXFORD (H), May 28, W47-43

1 †Jeremy Doncaster	0 2 3 3 3	11	
2 David Mullett	1 1 3 1	6	1
3 Per Jonsson	R 2 3 R	5	1
4 Tony Olsson	0 2 2 1	5	1
5 Jan Andersson	1 3 3 1 2	10	1
6 David Steen	R N T 0 0	0	
7 Todd Wiltshire	3 2 2 N 3 0	10	1

Swindon

OXFORD (H), March 24, L38-51

1 Brian Karger	1 1 R 3	5	1
2 Peter Nahlin	0 2 2 1	5	
3 Andrew Silver	3 3 3 2 1 2	14	
4 †John Davis	1 0 T 0	1	
5 Jimmy Nilsen	0 2 2 0	4	1
6 David Smart	0 N 0 1	1	
7 Leigh Adams	2 1 1 0 3 1	8	2

KING'S LYNN (H), March 31, W51-39

1 Brian Karger	2 2 3 3 2	12	1
2 Peter Nahlin	fx 3 3 2	8	1
3 Andrew Silver	2 1 0 3	6	
4 †John Davis	2 1 fx N 1	4	2
5 Jimmy Nilsen	3 3 2 2	10	1
6 David Smart	0 0 N 0	0	
7 Leigh Adams	3 3 2 2 0 1	11	1

King's Lynn (A), April 1, L43-47

1 Brian Karger	2 0 3 1	6	1
2 Peter Nahlin	1 3 3 2 0	9	2
3 Andrew Silver	2 3 1 0	6	
4 †John Davis	1 3 0 2 2	8	
5 Jimmy Nilsen	0 1 3 1	5	
6 Leigh Adams	2 1 2 3 fx	8	1
7 David Smart	0 fx N 1	1	

Oxford (A), April 6, W51-39

1 Brian Karger	0 0 N 3	3	
2 Peter Nahlin	3 1 0 3	7	
3 Andrew Silver	2 3 2 1 1	9	1
4 †John Davis	1 2 2 0	5	
5 Jimmy Nilsen	3 1 1 3 3	11	2
6 Leigh Adams	3 1 2 3 1 3	13	
7 Matthew Cross	0 1 N 2	3	2

READING (H), April 7, W47-42

1 Brian Karger	2 3 0 0	5	
2 Peter Nahlin	1 2 3 1	7	2
3 Andrew Silver	2 1 2 1 3	9	2
4 †John Davis	3 2 3 2 R	10	
5 Jimmy Nilsen	0 0 2 2	4	1
6 Matthew Cross	0 N 0 1	1	
7 Leigh Adams	3 1 1 3 3	11	1

Reading (A), May 21, L39-51

1 Brian Karger	1 3 0 1 R	5	1
2 Peter Nahlin	0 0 0 T	0	
3 Andrew Silver	2 2 2 3 0	9	
4 †John Davis	0 2 1 1	4	1
5 Jimmy Nilsen	3 1 2 1 2	9	1
6 David Smart	1 0 N T 1	2	
7 Leigh Adams	3 N 1 1 2 3	10	1

The Tables

NORTH

	P	W	D	L	PtsF	PtsA	BP	Pts
1 BRADFORD	**8**	**5**	**0**	**3**	**392**	**328**	**3**	**13**
2 Cradley Heath	8	4	1	3	365	352	3	12
3 Wolverhampton	8	4	1	3	343	377	1	10
4 Belle Vue	8	3	0	5	348	369	2	8
5 Coventry	8	3	0	5	349	371	1	7

Bradford qualify for Gold Cup Final.

SOUTH

	P	W	D	L	PtsF	PtsA	BP	Pts
1 OXFORD	**6**	**4**	**0**	**2**	**283**	**256**	**3**	**11**
2 Reading	6	4	0	2	269	270	2	10
3 Swindon	6	3	0	3	269	269	1	7
4 King's Lynn	6	1	0	5	257	283	0	2

Oxford qualify for Gold Cup Final

The FINAL

First leg, at Oxford, June 22

OXFORD 47

1 †Hans Nielsen	3 3 1 3 2 3	15	
2 Dean Barker	1 2 0 2 1	6	
3 Martin Dugard	3 fx2 3 3 2 1	14	
4 Simon Wigg	*rider replacement*		
5 Alastair Stevens	0 1 T 1	2	1
6 Paul Dugard	1 1 0 3	5	1
7 Troy Butler	2 fx1 1 1	5	1
8 Kevin Pitts	*did not ride*		

BRADFORD 43

1 Marvyn Cox	2 3 2 3 2	12	
2 Glenn Doyle	0 2 1 0	3	1
3 †Gary Havelock	N 2 0 N	2	
4 Andy Smith	1 3 2 0	6	
5 Paul Thorp	3 1 0 3 0	7	
6 Neil Evitts	3 2 1 3 2 2	13	1
7 Bryan Larner	N E N fx0	0	

Second leg, at Bradford, June 23

BRADFORD 63

1 Marvyn Cox	2 1 1 1	5	1
2 Glenn Doyle	1 3 1 2	7	2
3 †Gary Havelock	3 1 3 3	10	
4 Andy Smith	2 3 3 3 1	12	1
5 Paul Thorp	**3 2 2 2 3**	**12**	**3**
6 Bryan Larner	0 fn N N	0	
7 Neil Evitts	3 2 3 2 2 3	15	2
8 Stuart Parnaby	2	2	1

OXFORD 27

1 †Hans Nielsen	3 0 2 3 1 R 2	11	
2 Dean Barker	0 1 0 0 0	1	
3 Martin Dugard	1 2 3 1 2	9	
4 Simon Wigg	*rider replacement*		
5 Alastair Stevens	0 0 0 0	0	
6 Paul Dugard	2 0 N 1	3	
7 Troy Butler	1 1 0 T F 1 R	3	1
8 Kevin Pitts	*did not ride*		

BRADFORD win 106-74 on aggregate.

AVERAGES

Sunbrite League

No.	Rider	Track	M.	R.	Pts.	BP.	TPts.	Average	1989Up/Down	
1	Hans Nielsen	Oxford	32	171	413.0	28	441.0	10.316	1	0
2	Jan O. Pedersen	Cradley Heath	13	67	148.0	7	155.0	9.254	2	0
3	Jeremy Doncaster	Reading	31	145	318.0	10	328.0	9.048	8	5
4	Simon Cross	Cradley Heath	14	70	148.0	10	158.0	9.029	7	3
5	Kelvin Tatum	Coventry	30	159	342.0	16	358.0	9.006	6	1
6	Marvyn Cox	Bradford	30	150	313.0	20	333.0	8.880	24	18
7	Sam Ermolenko	Wolverhampton	24	133	269.0	26	295.0	8.872	3	-4
8	Ronnie Correy	Wolverhampton	30	163	339.0	21	360.0	8.834	10	2
9	Jimmy Nilsen	Swindon	28	137	285.0	10	295.0	8.613	9	0
10	Todd Wiltshire	Reading	23	113	221.0	19	240.0	8.496		
11	Gary Havelock	Bradford	32	161	318.0	23	341.0	8.472		
12	Per Jonsson	Reading	31	148	286.0	26	312.0	8.432		
13	Martin Dugard	Oxford	30	143	290.0	10	300.0	8.392	17	4
14	Kelly Moran	Belle Vue	28	131	249.0	24	273.0	8.336	12	-2
15	John Jorgensen	Coventry	32	152	291.0	13	304.0	8.000	32	17
16	Brian Karger	Swindon	11	47	89.0	4	93.0	7.915	11	-5
17	Mark Loram	King's Lynn	29	160	294.0	20	314.0	7.850		
18	Andy Smith	Bradford	23	102	169.0	31	200.0	7.843	22	4
19	Shawn Moran	Belle Vue	24	114	193.0	27	220.0	7.719	5	-14
20	Simon Wigg	Oxford	24	106	187.0	13	200.0	7.547	15	-5
21	Andrew Silver	Swindon	32	145	244.0	29	273.0	7.531	21	0
22	Peter Nahlin	Swindon	31	143	213.0	50	263.0	7.357	35	13
23	Richard Knight	King's Lynn	32	164	280.0	19	299.0	7.293	13	-10
24	Jan Andersson	Reading	31	143	225.5	34	259.5	7.259		
25	Bobby Ott	Belle Vue	31	139	216.0	31	247.0	7.108		
	Henrik Gustafsson	King's Lynn	5	22	36.0	3	39.0	7.091		
26	Rick Miller	Coventry	27	130	207.0	19	226.0	6.954	27	1
27	Chris Morton	Belle Vue	28	122	192.0	19	211.0	6.918	39	12
28	Billy Hamill	Cradley Heath	27	129	200.0	20	220.0	6.822		
29	Paul Thorp	Bradford	32	145	222.0	25	247.0	6.814	16	-13
30	Leigh Adams	Swindon	29	141	218.0	22	240.0	6.809		
31	Joe Screen	Belle Vue	29	129	192.0	25	217.0	6.729	33	2
32	John Davis	Swindon	25	84	124.0	15	139.0	6.619	29	-3
33	Armando Castagna	Reading	6	24	30.0	9	39.0	6.500	47	14
34	Alan Grahame	Cradley Heath	32	145	198.5	33	231.5	6.386	42	8
35	Graham Jones	Wolverhampton	15	69	100.0	10	110.0	6.377	35	0
36	David Mullett	Reading	27	118	156.0	32	188.0	6.373	50	14
37	Tony Olsson	Reading	23	95	125.0	26	151.0	6.358	36	-1
38	Glenn Doyle	Bradford	27	132	191.0	18	209.0	6.333	58	20
39	Neil Evitts	Bradford	24	90	116.0	23	139.0	6.178	19	-20
40	Gert Handberg	Cradley Heath	28	135	187.0	20	207.0	6.133	30	-10
41	Peter Ravn	Belle Vue	24	97	128.0	16	144.0	5.938	20	-21
42	Roman Matousek	Coventry	27	119	152.0	23	175.0	5.882	49	7
43	Neil Collins	Wolverhampton	28	120	151.0	24	175.0	5.833	28	-15
44	Sean Wilson	Coventry/King's Lynn	31	136	170.0	28	198.0	5.824	37	-7
45	Gary Hicks	King's Lynn	15	54	67.0	11	78.0	5.778	23	-22
46	Jan Staechmann	Wolverhampton	20	77	90.0	21	111.0	5.766	25	-21
47	Tommy Knudsen	Coventry	6	23	32.0	1	33.0	5.739		
48	Stephen Davies	King's Lynn	29	131	154.0	33	187.0	5.710	55	7
49	Dean Barker	Oxford	31	127	153.0	28	181.0	5.701		
50	Phil Crump	Swindon	16	61	63.0	23	86.0	5.639		
51	Carl Stonehewer	Wolverhampton	21	100	120.0	19	139.0	5.560	45	-6
52	Alastair Stevens	Oxford	31	136	169.0	20	189.0	5.559		
53	Greg Hancock	Cradley Heath	18	77	102.0	4	106.0	5.506	41	-12
54	Bohumil Brhel	King's Lynn	30	137	172.0	16	188.0	5.489		
55	Dennis Löfqvist	King's Lynn	32	141	158.0	29	187.0	5.305	56	1
56	Andy Hackett	Coventry	22	89	105.0	13	118.0	5.303	44	-12
57	Peter Karlsson	Wolverhampton	13	50	58.0	7	65.0	5.200		
58	David Smart	Swindon	31	124	123.0	36	159.0	5.129	62	4
59	Troy Butler	Oxford	29	118	124.0	24	148.0	5.017	40	-19
60	Richard Musson	Belle Vue	29	113	105.0	28	133.0	4.708		
	Lars Munkedal	Wolverhampton	5	18	17.0	4	21.0	4.667		
61	Paul Dugard	Oxford	12	38	27.0	9	36.0	3.789	66	5
	Troy Smith	Reading	3	8	5.0	2	7.0	3.500		
62	Wayne Carter	Wolverhampton	19	63	46.0	9	54.0	3.492		
	Max Schofield	Belle Vue	4	12	8.0	2	10.0	3.333		
	Jon Surman	Oxford	1	4	3.0	0	3.0	3.000		
63	Andy Phillips	Coventry	19	65	38.0	10	48.0	2.954	43	-20
64	Nathan Murray	Reading	12	37	19.0	8	27.0	2.919		
	Bo Petersen	Wolverhampton	4	14	8.0	1	9.0	2.571		
65	Mark Robinson	Cradley Heath	28	97	50.0	12	62.0	2.557		
66	Bryan Larner	Bradford	23	73	28.0	13	41.0	2.247	46	-20
67	David Steen	Reading	19	65	28.0	6	34.0	2.092		
68	Phil Disney	Bradford	6	16	6.0	2	8.0	2.000		

AVERAGES Sunbrite League

No.	Rider	Track	M.	R.	Pts.	BP.	TPts.	Average	1989Up/Down	
	Kevin Pitts	Oxford	1	4	2.0	0	2.0	2.000	70	
	Sean McCullagh	Oxford	1	2	1.0	0	1.0	2.000		
69	Andy Meredith	Coventry	14	43	18.0	3	21.0	1.953		
70	John Bostin	Oxford	16	50	19.0	4	23.0	1.840	65	-5
	Stuart Parnaby	Bradford	5	16	5.0	1	6.0	1.500		
	Tom Grinstead	King's Lynn	3	8	2.0	1	3.0	1.500		
	Christian Howell	Reading	2	4	1.0	0	1.0	1.000		
71	Roger Horspool	King's Lynn	11	27	6.0	0	6.0	0.889		
	Lee Coleman	Coventry	5	16	3.0	0	3.0	0.750		
	David Haynes	Cradley Heath	5	14	1.0	1	2.0	0.571		
	Kieran McCullagh	Oxford	4	10	1.0	0	1.0	0.400		
	Mike Lewthwaite	Belle Vue	3	10	1.0	0	1.0	0.400		
	Paul Bromwich	Coventry	2	5	0.0	0	0.0	0.000		
	Gary Frankum	Cradley Heath	1	2	0.0	0	0.0	0.000		
	Scott Smith	Cradley Heath	1	3	0.0	0	0.0	0.000		
	Wayne Parker	Oxford	1	3	0.0	0	0.0	0.000		
	Listed below are the averages of the one rider who rode for more than one club.									
	Sean Wilson	Coventry	27	119	145.0	24	169.0	5.681		
		King's Lynn	4	17	25.0	4	29.0	6.824		

LEGEND

The 1990 Sunbrite League averages listed are taken from the official referee's marked programmes.

Reading from left to right the figures list the following: overall ranking; rider; track or tracks; matches; rides; points; bonus points; total points; calculated match average (out of 12.000), 1989 ranking; and movement up or down the rankings.

The calculated match average is taken by dividing the total number of points scored by the number of rides and multiplied by four.

Riders are only given an overall ranking if they rode in a minimum of six Sunbrite League matches during the 1990 season.

Guest appearances are not included in the figures but lists of guest riders are given on the appropriate club statistical pages which list scorers in all Sunbrite League matches in riding order.

DEBUTANTS

The averages of riders who made their debut in the 1990 Sunbrite League were:

Todd Wiltshire (Reading & Australia)	8.496
Henrik Gustafsson (King's Lynn & Sweden)	7.091
Billy Hamill (Cradley Heath & America)	6.822
Leigh Adams (Swindon & Australia)	6.809
Bohumil Brhel (King's Lynn & Czechoslovakia)	5.489
Peter Karlsson (Wolverhampton & Sweden)	5.200
Richard Musson (Belle Vue & England)	4.708
Max Schofield (Belle Vue & England)	3.333
Nathan Murray (Reading & New Zealand)	2.919
Mark Robinson (Cradley Heath & England)	2.557
Phil Disney (Bradford & England)	2.000
Sean McCullagh (Oxford & England)	2.000
Andy Meredith (Coventry & England)	1.953
Christian Howell (Reading & England)	1.000
Kieran McCullagh (Oxford & England)	0.400
Gary Frankum (Cradley Heath & England)	0.000
Scott Smith (Cradley Heath & England)	0.000
Wayne Parker (Oxford & England)	0.000

▲ *The highest average debutant in the 1989 British League was Gary Hicks (Belle Vue & America) on 7.171.*

CHART TOPPERS

The top rider from each nation represented in the 1990 Sunbrite League was:

Hans Nielsen (Denmark)	10.316
Jeremy Doncaster (England)	9.048
Sam Ermolenko (America)	8.872
Jimmy Nilsen (Sweden)	8.613
Todd Wiltshire (Australia)	8.496
Armando Castagna (Italy)	6.500
Roman Matousek (Czechoslovakia)	5.882
Nathan Murray (New Zealand)	2.919

▲ *Riders from eight nations competed in the 1990 Sunbrite League, two fewer than in 1989 when Finland and Hungary were also represented.*

BEST OF BRITISH

The ten best-placed British born riders in the 1990 Sunbrite League averages (with their 1989 rankings) were:

1 Jeremy Doncaster (Reading)	*3*	9.048
2 Simon Cross (Cradley Heath)	*2*	9.029
3 Kelvin Tatum (Coventry)	*1*	9.006
4 Marvyn Cox (Bradford)	*11*	8.880
5 Gary Havelock (Bradford)	–	8.472
6 Martin Dugard (Oxford)	*7*	8.392
7 Mark Loram (King's Lynn)	–	7.850
8 Andy Smith (Bradford)	*10*	7.843
9 Simon Wigg (Oxford)	*5*	7.547
10 Andrew Silver (Swindon)	*9*	7.531

The following riders (with their 1989-1990 rankings) have dropped out of the Top Ten British chart:

Richard Knight (King's Lynn)	*4-11*	7.293
Paul Thorp (Bradford)	*6-13*	6.814
Neil Evitts (Bradford)	*8-19*	6.178

BYE-BYE BOYS

The following riders appeared in at least six matches in the 1989 British League but did not ride in the 1990 Sunbrite League:

Erik Gundersen (retired), Lance King (remained in USA), Mitch Shirra (suspended), Andy Grahame (National League), Allan Johansen (injured), Robert Pfetzing (remained in USA), Carl Blackbird (National League), Bart Bast (remained in USA), Gary Chessell (National League), Henrik Kristensen (remained in Denmark), Armando dal Chiele (remained in Italy), Kai Niemi (retired), Antal Kocso (remained in Hungary), Malcolm Holloway (retired), Michael Graves (retired), Adrian Stevens (National League), Gordon Whitaker (National League), Paul Smith (National League).

INDIVIDUAL MEETINGS

Sunbrite League

COALITE CLASSIC
Bradford, Sunday, April 29
Jan O. Pedersen 14, Simon Cross 11 (+3), Marvyn Cox 11 (+2), Jeremy Doncaster 11 (+R), Chris Morton 11 (+fx), Gary Havelock 10, Paul Thorp 9, Neil Evitts 7, Shawn Moran 7, Sean Wilson 7, Kelly Moran 7, Leigh Adams 6, Mark Loram 4, Neil Collins 4, Glenn Doyle 1, Kelvin Tatum 0. *Meeting reserves:* Bryan Larner 0 (2), Phil Disney 0 (2).
Roll of Honour
1986 - Hans Nielsen; 1988 - Sam Ermolenko; 1989 - Sam Ermolenko; 1990 - Jan O. Pedersen.

PETER CRAVEN MEMORIAL
Belle Vue, Sunday, May 13
Billy Hamill 12 (+3), Shawn Moran 12 (+2), Neil Collins 12 (+1), Simon Cross 12 (+0), Kelly Moran 11, Paul Thorp 9, Peter Ravn 7, Gary Hicks 6, Andy Smith 6, Kenny McKinna 6, Greg Hancock 6, Ronnie Correy 6, Bobby Ott 5, Todd Wiltshire 5, Mick Poole 3, Richard Musson 2.
Roll of Honour
1967 - Ivan Mauger; 1969 - Ole Olsen; 1970 - Jim Airey; 1971 - Ole Olsen; 1974 - Chris Morton; 1975 - Chris Morton; 1978 - Peter Collins; 1980 - Dennis Sigalos; 1985 -Andy Smith; 1986 - Chris Morton; 1988 - Kelly Moran; 1989 - Shawn Moran; 1990 - Billy Hamill.

† Peter Theodore CRAVEN (B 21.6.1934 – D 24.9.1963). England's second World Champion, he won the title in both 1955 and 1962. He began riding at Liverpool in 1949 and after a brief spell at Fleetwood joined Belle Vue in 1954 and spent the rest of his career with the Aces. He died four days after crashing at Edinburgh's Meadowbank Stadium of severe head injuries sustained when he opted to ride into the safety fence to avoid a fallen opponent. His elder brother Brian was also a rider as was his son Robert.

SOFT WATER CLASSIC
Swindon, Sunday, May 13
1 Jan O. Pedersen, 2 Kelvin Tatum, 3 Andrew Silver, 4 Leigh Adams. *Losing semi-finalists:* Jimmy Nilsen, John Davis, Richard Knight, Jeremy Doncaster. *Qualifying scorers:* Jimmy Nilsen 13, Jan O. Pedersen 11, Andrew Silver 10, Leigh Adams 9, Richard Knight 9, Jeremy Doncaster 9, Kelvin Tatum 8, John Davis 8, Peter Nahlin 5, Dennis Löfqvist 5, David Smart 3, Neil Evitts 0. *Reserves:* Matthew Cross 0 (1), Wayne Freeman 0 (1).
Roll of Honour
1990 - Jan O. Pedersen.

LADBROKE OLYMPIQUE
Wolverhampton, Monday, June 18
Ronnie Correy 12 (+3), Leigh Adams 12 (+2), John Jorgensen 10 (+3), Jan O. Pedersen 10 (+2), Kelly Moran 9, Todd Wiltshire 9, Martin Dugard 8, Mark Loram 7, Gary Havelock 7, Kelvin Tatum 6, Graham Jones 6, Neil Collins 6, Carl Stonehewer 5, Jan Staechmann 4, Peter Karlsson 3, Sam Ermolenko 3. *Reserves:* Wayne Carter 3 (2), Ade Hoole, did not ride.
Roll of Honour
1966† - Barry Briggs; 1967† - Anders Michanek; 1970 - Ole Olsen; 1971 - Ole Olsen; 1972 - Ole Olsen; 1973 - Ole Olsen; 1974 - Ole Olsen; 1975 - Ole Olsen; 1976 - Peter Collins; 1977 - Billy Sanders; 1978 - Gordon Kennett; 1979 - Phil Crump; 1980 - Les Collins; 1984 - Hans Nielsen; 1987 - Sam Ermolenko; 1988 - Hans Nielsen; 1989 - Jan O. Pedersen; 1990 - Ronnie Correy.
†Staged at Newcastle Brough Park.

SUPERCALL GOLDEN HAMMER
Cradley Heath, Wednesday, July 18
Simon Cross 13, Ronnie Correy 12, Kelvin Tatum 11, Hans Nielsen 10, Jan O. Pedersen 10, Mark Loram 9, Gary Havelock 9, Jeremy Doncaster 8, Jimmy Nilsen 7, Richard Knight 6, Per Jonsson 6, Neil Evitts 5, Martin Dugard 5, Alan Grahame 4, Gert Handberg 3, Andrew Silver 2. *Reserve:* David Haynes 0 (1).
Roll of Honour
1977 - Ole Olsen; 1978 - Scott Autrey; 1979 - Bobby Schwartz; 1980 - Chris Morton; 1982 - Kenny Carter; 1983 - Lance King; 1984 - Alan Grahame; 1985 - Kenny Carter; 1986 - Erik Gundersen; 1987 - Erik Gundersen; 1988 - Hans Nielsen; 1989 - Jan O. Pedersen; 1990 - Simon Cross.

SKOL MASTERS TROPHY
Oxford, Wednesday, July 25
1 Simon Wigg, 2 Sam Ermolenko, 3 Kelly Moran, 4 Andrew Silver. *Qualifying scorers:* Wigg 13, Ermolenko 13, Moran 11, Silver 11, Martin Dugard 10, Mark Loram 9, Leigh Adams 8, Jimmy Nilsen 8, John Jorgensen 8, Troy Butler 7, Alastair Stevens 5, Marvyn Cox 5, Dean Barker 5, Stephen Davies 4, Sean McCullagh 2, John Bostin 1.
Roll of Honour
1980 - Martin Yeates; 1981 - Dave Perks; 1982- Martin Yeates; 1983 - Martin Yeates; 1984 - Jan Andersson; 1985 - Simon Wigg; 1986 - Erik Gundersen; 1988 - Jan O. Pedersen; 1989 - Hans Nielsen; 1990 - Simon Wigg. †Competition was incorporated with the Oxford Speedway Supporters' Club Trophy, winners of which are listed above.

BARUM TROPHY
King's Lynn, Sunday, July 29
1 Jan O. Pedersen, 2 Hans Nielsen, 3 Richard Knight, 4 Gary Havelock. *Losing semi finalists:* Cox, Brhel, Loram, Tatum. *Qualifying scorers:* Jan O. Pedersen 14, Hans Nielsen 13, Richard Knight 12, Kelvin Tatum 11, Marvyn Cox 8, Gary Havelock 6, Mark Loram 6, Bohumil Brhel 5, Bobby Ott 5, Roman Matousek 4, John Davis 3, Martin Dugard 2. *Reserves:* Roger Horspool 1 (2), Tom Grinstead 0 (1).
Roll of Honour
1989 - Hans Nielsen; 1990 - Jan O. Pedersen.

GOLDEN GREATS
Swindon, Sunday, September 16
FABULOUS FIFTIES: 1 Roy Trigg, 2 Barry Briggs, 3 Gote Nordin,4 Ove Fundin. *Qualifying scorers:* Nordin 8, Briggs 7, Fundin 7, Trigg 5, Mike Broadbank 4, Taffy Owen 3, Glyn Chandler 2, Col Smith 0, Barry Duke 0. **SWINGING SIXTIES:** 1 Terry Betts, 2 Finn Thomsen, 3 Anders Michanek, 4 Ray Wilson. *Qualifying scorers:* Betts 9, Thomsen 9, Michanek 7, Wilson 7, Bob Coles 5, Graham Plant 5, Alan Cowland 3, Mick Handley 3, Ian Turner 3, Bernie Leigh 2, Bert Harkins 1, Tom Leadbitter 0.
Roll of Honour
1988 (Coventry): Fabulous Fifties: Ove Fundin. Swinging Sixties: Peter Collins.
1989 (Landshut, West Germany): Fabulous Fifties: Barry Briggs. Swinging Sixties: Zenon Plech.
1990 (Swindon): Fabulous Fifties: Roy Trigg. Swinging Sixties: Terry Betts.

DENNY PYEATT MEMORIAL TROPHY
Reading, Monday, October 22
Per Jonsson 12, Todd Wiltshire 10 and Armando Castagna 10, Mark Loram 9, Jeremy Doncaster 9, David Mullett 8, Phil Crump 7, Billy Hamill 6, Peter Nahlin 6, Leigh Adams 5, Brian Karger 4, Dennis Löfqvist 4, Jan Andersson 4, David Steen 1, Greg Hancock 1, Christian Howell 0.
Roll of Honour
1982- Shawn Moran; 1983 - Shawn Moran; 1986 Jan Andersson/David Mullett; 1988 - Shawn Moran; 1989 - Troy Butler; 1990 - Per Jonsson.

†Dennis (Denny) PYEATT (B 15.11.1957 – D 17.7.1982). A young American who first came to Britain to join Reading at the beginning of the 1981 season. He spent two full seasons with the Racers before his death in hospital in the early hours of the morning following a track crash at Hackney. In all he had 79 official fixtures for Reading, scoring 383 points for an overall average of 4.53.

PRIDE OF THE EAST
King's Lynn, Sunday, October 27
Kelvin Tatum 14, Henrik Gustafsson 12 (+3), Ronnie Correy 12 (+2), Richard Knight 11, Todd Wiltshire 10, Hans Nielsen 9, Jimmy Nilsen 8, Sean Wilson 7, Martin Dugard 6, John Davis 6, Jan Staechmann 6, Mark Loram 6, Dennis Löfqvist 4, Bohumil Brhel 4, Billy Hamill 4, Roger Horspool 1. *Reserve:* Tom Grinstead, did not ride.
Roll of Honour
1957 - Ove Fundin; 1958- Peter Raven; 1959 - Peter Craven; 1960 - Björn Knutsson; 1961 - Barry Briggs; 1962- Björn Knutsson; 1963 - Björn Knutsson; 1966 - Colin Pratt; 1967 - Bengt Larsson; 1968 - Terry Betts; 1969 - Howard Cole; 1970- Ole Olsen; 1971 - Ole Olsen; 1972 - Ole Olsen; 1973 - Anders Michanek; 1974 - Ivan Mauger; 1975 - John Louis; 1976 - Peter Collins; 1977- Ole Olsen; 1978 - Ole Olsen; 1979- Dave Jessup; 1980 - Dave Jessup; 1981 - Michael Lee; 1982 - Tommy Knudsen; 1983 - Michael Lee; 1984 - Hans Nielsen; 1985 - Jan Andersson; 1986 - Sam Ermolenko; 1988 - Kelvin Tatum; 1989 - Martin Dugard; 1990 - Kelvin Tatum.
†Held at Norwich, 1957-1963.

Testimonial Meetings

PETER RAVN
Belle Vue, Sunday, May 27
1 Hans Nielsen, 2 John Jorgensen, 3 Simon Cross, 4 Bobby Ott, 5 Jan O. Pedersen. *Qualifying scorers:* Simon Cross 15, Jan O. Pedersen 13, Hans Nielsen 13, Bobby Ott 13, John Jorgensen 9 (+3), Richard Knight 9 (+2), Marvyn Cox 8, Leigh Adams 8, Paul Thorp 7, Carl Stonehewer 6, Graham Jones 6, Darren Sumner 4, Kelvin Tatum 3, Nigel Crabtree 2, Andy Galvin 2, Ronnie Correy 2.

Peter RAVN joined Belle Vue in 1981 and has remained on their books ever since although he has had loan spells with Cradley Heath and Wolverhampton. See Belle Vue roster.

MALCOLM HOLLOWAY FAREWELL
Reading, Monday, June 11
READING 27 (+3) (Jeremy Doncaster 12 +3, David Mullett, injured, did not ride, Todd Wiltshire 11, David Steen 3, Christian Howell 1)
OXFORD 27 (+2) (Martin Dugard 7+2, Dean Barker 9, Alastair Stevens 6, Paul Dugard 5, Troy Smith 0)
BRITISH LEAGUE SELECT 25 (Marvyn Cox [Bradford] 10, Graham Jones [Wolverhampton] 9, Jon Surman [Oxford] 5, Malcolm Holloway 1, Mark Seabright)
SWINDON 16 (*Jan Staechmann 5*, Leigh Adams 5, David Smart 4, *Andy Hackett 0*, Lance Sealey 2)

Malcolm Thomas HOLLOWAY (B 22.12.1956, Stratton St. Margaret, Wiltshire) joined Reading in 1984 after seven seasons at Swindon. He announced his retirement after crashing at Bradford on October 5, 1989.

CHALLENGE MATCHES

Sunbrite League

Friday, March 16
BELLE VUE 47 (Shawn Moran 14:1, Chris Morton 12:2, Peter Ravn 10, *rider replacement for Kelly Moran*, Joe Screen 2, Mike Lewthwaite 5:2, Bobby Ott 4:1)
OXFORD 43 (Hans Nielsen 12, Dean Barker 8:3, Martin Dugard 3, Simon Wigg 5:2, Troy Butler 7:1, Paul Dugard 1, Alastair Stevens 7:1)

Saturday, March 17
CRADLEY HEATH 44 (Gert Handberg 5, Billy Hamill 4:2, Jan O. Pedersen 10:2, Simon Cross 13:1, Alan Grahame 4:1, Greg Hancock 7, Mark Robinson 1:1)
KING'S LYNN 46 (Richard Knight 9, Mark Loram 5:2, *Tony Olsson 4:1*, Allan Johansen 8:1, *Troy Butler 8*, Roger Horspool 1, Dennis Löfqvist 11:1)

First leg, Monday, March 19
WOLVERHAMPTON v OXFORD, ***postponed, waterlogged track.***

First leg, Friday, March 23
OXFORD 53 (**Hans Nielsen 15**, Dean Barker 5:2, Martin Dugard 8, Troy Butler 6:1, Simon Wigg 5:1, Paul Dugard 3:1, Alastair Stevens 11)
WOLVERHAMPTON 37 (*Richard Knight 8*, Jan Staechmann 7, Ronnie Correy 5, Graham Jones 5:1, Neil Collins 8:1, Carl Stonehewer 2, Lars Munkedal 2)

Second leg, Monday, April 2
WOLVERHAMPTON 41 (Ronnie Correy 12, Jan Staechmann 2:2, *Peter Ravn 3:1*, Graham Jones 9:1, Neil Collins 4:2, Carl Stonehewer 5:1, Lars Munkedal 6:1)
OXFORD 49 (Hans Nielsen 11:1, Dean Barker 3:1, Martin Dugard 14, Simon Wigg 7, Troy Butler 4:1, Paul Dugard 0, Alastair Stevens 10)
Oxford win 102-78 on aggregate.

PAUL MUCHENE MEMORIAL

Oxford, Friday, May 11
MARTIN DUGARD'S ELITE 55 (Stephen Davies [King's Lynn] 12, David Clark [Milton Keynes] 6:1, Dean Barker 13:1, Paul Dugard 8:4, Troy Butler 11, Troy Pratt [Arena Essex] 5:5, Kevin Pitts, Wayne Parker)
SIMON WIGG'S WONDERS 52 (Simon Wigg 12, Thierry Hilaire [Milton Keynes] 1, Marvyn Cox [Bradford] 11, Tony Primmer [Eastbourne] 11:3, Alastair Stevens 16, Jon Surman 1:1, Sean McCullagh 0, Kevin Howse 0)

†Paul MUCHENE (B 7.1.1966 – D 4.7.1989) was an Oxford junior who had ridden in two official matches for the Skol Cheetahs – one in 1988 and another the following season. He died in hospital four days after suffering serious head and internal injuries in a track crash at Hackney.

King's Lynn, Saturday, June 2
BARUM STARS 26 (Gary Hicks 11, Stephen Davies 6, Dennis Löfqvist 8, Darren Spicer 1, Emerson Fairweather)
CRADLEY HEATH 26 (**Jan O. Pedersen 12**, David Haynes 2, Alan Grahame 8, John Bostin 4, Martin Cobbin)
ZETOR STARS 22 (Richard Knight 8, Mark Loram 6, Roger Horspool 5, Tom Grinstead 3, Emerson Fairweather)
OXFORD 22 (Martin Dugard 8, Troy Butler 9, Paul Dugard 4, Sean McCullagh 1, Martin Cobbin)

INTER SHIRES TROPHY

Saturday, June 16
COVENTRY 44 (*Chris Morton 7:1*, Paul Bromwich 1:1, John Jorgensen 13, Rick Miller 11:3, Andy Hackett 6:3, Andy Phillips 6:1, Sean Wilson 0, Lee Coleman 0)
OXFORD 45 (*Shawn Moran, did not arrive*, Dean Barker 11:2, Martin Dugard 15, *rider replacement for Simon Wigg*, Alastair Stevens 2, Paul Dugard 5, Troy Butler 12:2, *Kevin Pitts, did not ride*)

SPEEDWAYCALL TROPHY

Monday, July 16
WOLVERHAMPTON 60 (Ronnie Correy 15:1, *Rick Miller 8:1*, Sam Ermolenko 12:2, Carl Stonehewer 2:1, *rider replacement for Graham Jones, Andy Phillips 3:1*, Wayne Carter 10, Stephen Morris 0, Ade Hoole 5:1, Shane Cooper 5)
CRADLEY HEATH 60 (Jan O. Pedersen 8:1, Alan Grahame 6, Simon Cross 17:2, *Neil Evitts 8:1, rider replacement for Greg Hancock*, Gert Handberg 10, David Haynes 2, Steve Griffiths 2:1, Scott Smith 2, Mark Meredith 5).

Swindon, Saturday, July 28
SWINDON 35 (John Davis 10, Peter Nahlin 10, Andrew Silver 9, Phil Crump 6) **WOLVERHAMPTON 28** (Neil Collins 8, Peter Karlsson 8, Wayne Carter 6, Carl Stonehewer 6) **OXFORD 21** (Martin Dugard 11, Dean Barker 7, John Bostin 3, Sean McCullagh 0) **BELLE VUE 12** (Chris Morton 4, *David Smart 4*, Max Schofield 3, Richard Musson 0, *Steve Camden, reserve, 1*)

ZETOR CUP

Saturday, July 21
KING'S LYNN 44 (Mark Loram 12, Roger Horspool 0, Dennis Löfqvist 5:2, Tom Grinstead 0, Richard Knight 10, Stephen Davies 10, Bohumil Brhel 7)
WOLVERHAMPTON 34 (Sam Ermolenko 8:1, Peter Karlsson 7, *rider replacement for Graham Jones, Dean Barker 5:1*, Neil Collins 7:2, Carl Stonehewer 7, Wayne Carter 0)

Cradley Heath, Saturday, August 4
CRADLEY HEATH 35 (**Jan O. Pedersen 11:4, Alan Grahame 12,** Gert Handberg 4:1, *Bobby Ott 8*) **BELLE VUE 29** (Chris Morton 7:1, Kelly Moran 8:1, Shawn Moran 12, Richard Musson 2)
OXFORD 14 (Martin Dugard 6, Alastair Stevens 0, Troy Butler 7, John Bostin 1:1, *David Haynes, reserve, 0*)

DUDLEY WOLVES TROPHY

First leg, Monday, August 13
WOLVERHAMPTON 50 (Ronnie Correy 6:1, Peter Karlsson 3:1, Sam Ermolenko 12:2, Graham Jones 2:1, *Sean Wilson 9*, Carl Stonehewer 7:2, Neil Collins 11)
CRADLEY HEATH 39 (Jan O. Pedersen 1:1, Alan Grahame 14, *Kelvin Tatum 11*, Billy Hamill 7, *Bobby Ott 3:1*, Mark Robinson 1, Gert Handberg 2:1)

Second leg, Wednesday, August 15
CRADLEY HEATH 52 (Jan O. Pedersen 13:1, Alan Grahame 5:3, *Kelvin Tatum 12*, Billy Hamill 6:2, Jimmy Nilsen 8:2, Mark Robinson 2, Gert Handberg 6)
WOLVERHAMPTON 37 (Ronnie Correy 1, Peter Karlsson 1, Sam Ermolenko 9, Graham Jones 0, *Sean Wilson 12*, Carl Stonehewer 4:2, Neil Collins 10:1)
Cradley Heath win 91-87 on aggregate.

Friday, August 24
OXFORD 49.5 (**Hans Nielsen 15,** Alastair Stevens 5, Martin Dugard 9:1, Simon Wigg 9, Dean Barker 6:2, Kieran McCullagh 0, John Bostin 5.5:1)
SUNBRITE SELECT 40.5 (John Jorgensen [Coventry] 6:2, Bohumil Brhel [King's Lynn] 5, Phil Crump [Swindon] 3, Billy Hamill [Cradley Heath] 15, David Smart [Swindon] 0, Gert Handberg [Cradley Heath] 7.5, Andy Hackett [Coventry] 4:1)

Saturday, August 25
COVENTRY 56 (**Kelvin Tatum 15,** Roman Matousek 6:2, John Jorgensen 11:1, Tommy Knudsen 2:1, Sean Wilson 11, Andy Hackett 10:3, Andy Meredith 1)
BELLE VUE 34 (*Martin Dugard 4, Dean Barker 1:1*, Chris Morton 15:2, *rider replacement for Shawn Moran*, Joe Screen 4, Richard Musson 1, Peter Ravn 9)

Saturday, September 15
KING'S LYNN 29 (Mark Loram 8, Stephen Davies 6, Dennis Löfqvist 8, Richard Knight 7) **BELLE VUE 11** (Bobby Ott 5, Max Schofield 1, Richard Musson 0, Joe Screen 3, *Tom Grinstead, reserve, 2*) **BRITISH LEAGUE SELECT 19** (Ronnie Correy [Wolverhampton] 8, Roger Horspool [King's Lynn] 3, Alan Grahame [Cradley Heath] 6, Gary Hicks [King's Lynn] 2, Darren Spicer [King's Lynn], reserve, 0) **SWINDON 37** (Phil Crump 5, Leigh Adams 11, Peter Nahlin 9, **Jimmy Nilsen 12**)

Wednesday, October 17
KING'S LYNN 43 (Richard Knight 3:1, Sean Wilson 5, Ronnie Correy 11, Mark Loram 5:2, Jeremy Doncaster 7, Stephen Davies 3:1, Bohumil Brhel 9)
SWEDISH STARS 47 (Jimmy Nilsen [Swindon] 5:2, Peter Nahlin [Swindon] 4, **Per Jonsson [Reading] 14:1**, Henrik Gustafsson [King's Lynn] 11:1, Peter Karlsson [Wolverhampton]), Jan Andersson [Reading] 9:2, Dennis Löfqvist [King's Lynn] 4:1)

EUROPEAN SPECIAL OLYMPIAD

✯ GLASGOW began their third season at Shawfield Park playing a major part in the promotion of a special civic event.

The Strathclyde Regional Council asked the Tigers' to help launch the European Summer Games of the Special Olympics.

The event was part of a year-round programme of sports training for people with a mental handicap and the movement was founded in America by Eunice Kennedy Shriver, sister of the late President John F. Kennedy.

In July, more than 3,000 athletes gathered in Strathclyde for the 1990 European Games and it was decided to stage the speedway event – involving American riders – to both increase public awareness for the Special Olympics movement and to help raise some of the £3,000,000 needed to host the Games in Scotland.

Glasgow, Friday, March 30
STARS 57 (Ronnie Correy 10:1, Sean Courtney 9:3, Kenny McKinna 10:1, **Gary Hicks 13:2**, Mark Courtney 9, Martin McKinna 5:1, Jason Lyons 1)
STRIPES 39 (Rick Miller 4:2, Charlie McKinna 10, Steve Lawson 3, Shane Bowes 5:1, Les Collins 13:1, Phil Jeffrey 4:1, Geoff Powell 0)

CHALLENGE MATCHES

Inter League

PETERBOROUGH flattered to deceive throughout their National League campaign...but at least they had one major achievement to their name: they were the only National League side to defeat Sunbrite League opposition in a series of Inter League battles.

In all there were a dozen matches – interestingly enough five of them on Sunbrite League circuits – and the senior league side came out on top in 10 of those meetings, with National League double winners Poole holding Swindon to a 48-48 draw at Wimborne Road.

But what was evident throughout the clashes was that given a genuine international class heat leader, and the odds were most of the matches would have either seen the result reversed or the final scores a lot closer.

Impressively, National League stars Ray Morton, Nigel Crabtree, Craig Boyce, Gary Chessell and Chris Louis all managed to score double figures on Sunbrite League tracks while only six stars, Martin Dugard, Todd Wiltshire, Ronnie Correy, Armando Castagna, Henrik Gustafsson (all 1990 World Finalists) and Dean Barker were unbeaten against National Leaguers.

Saturday, April 28
KING'S LYNN 58 (Richard Knight 10:1, *rider replacement for Allan Johansen*, Bohumil Brhel 10:4, *Paul Thorp 1*, Gary Hicks 14, **Mark Loram 11:1**, Stephen Davies 12:4, Roger Horspool 0)
MICHAEL LEE NATIONAL LEAGUE SELECT 32 (Andy Galvin [Hackney] 13, Steve Schofield [Hackney] 0, Andy Grahame [Wimbledon] 5, Ray Morton [Wimbledon] 3:2, Mick Poole [Peterborough] 5:1, Craig Hodgson [Peterborough] 3:1, Scott Norman [Peterborough] 3)

Eastbourne, Sunday, June 3
EASTBOURNE 39 (Gordon Kennett 11, Justin Walker 2:1, Andy Buck 10, Paul Woods 5:2, Tony Primmer 1:1, Keith Pritchard 7, Darren Grayling 3:1)
OXFORD SELECT 57 (Alastair Stevens 12:2, Jon Surman 9:3, **Dean Barker 15, Martin Dugard 15,** Paul Dugard 4:1, Kevin Pitts 0, Wayne Parker 2)

Friday, July 20
OXFORD 59 (Troy Butler 6, Dean Barker 7:2, Martin Dugard 12, Alastair Stevens 9:3, Simon Wigg 12:1, *Andy Hackett 10,* John Bostin 3:1)
WIMBLEDON 31 (Nathan Simpson 3, Neville Tatum 6, Ray Morton 10:1, *rider replacement for Andy Grahame,* Nigel Leaver 8:2, Peter Chapman 1, Deon Prinsloo 3:1).

Sunday, July 22
PETERBOROUGH 43 (Frank Andersen 8, Nigel Flatman 5:2, Craig Hodgson 11, Scott Norman 9, Mark Lyndon 4:3, Sean Barker 4, Paul Blackbird 2:1)
KING'S LYNN 35 (Richard Knight 4:1, Stephen Davies 9:1, Dennis Löfqvist 9, Bohumil Brhel 9, Darren Spicer 1, Roger Horspool 3:1, Tom Grinstead 0)

Friday, August 10
BELLE VUE 59 (Bobby Ott 11, *Andy Phillips 7:3,* Chris Morton 10, *Gary Hicks 7:3,* Kelly Moran 11, Richard Musson 11:1, Max Schofield 2)
STOKE 29 (Louis Carr 6, Mark Carlson 0, Nigel Crabtree 13, Eric Monaghan 0, *David Blackburn 3,* Chris Cobby 6, Mark Pearce 1:1)

Sunday, August 12
SWINDON 44 (Malcolm Holloway 1, Phil Crump 8, Andrew Silver 9, Peter Nahlin 6:2, Leigh Adams 10, Wayne Freeman 3:1, David Smart 7:2)
POOLE 40 (Craig Boyce 10, Gary Allan 3:2, Alun Rossiter 4, Tony Langdon 8:1, *Chris Louis 4:1,* Gary Chessell 11:1, Peter Schroeck 0)

Monday, September 17
READING 51 (Todd Wiltshire 14:1, *Phil Crump 4:1,* Jan Andersson 6, **Armando Castagna 13:2,** Jeremy Doncaster 9:2, David Steen 5, Troy Smith 0)
IPSWICH 39 (Chris Louis 10, Shane Parker 9:3, Dean Standing 5, Alan Mogridge 2, David Norris 5:1, Robbie Fuller 5, Craig Hyde 3:1)

Thursday, September 20
IPSWICH 42 (Chris Louis 10:1, Shane Parker 7:2, Dean Standing 2, Alan Mogridge 8, David Norris 7:1, Robbie Fuller 7:2, Craig Hyde 1)
READING 53 (*Mark Loram 12:1,* Mark Seabright 0, **Todd Wiltshire 15,** Armando Castagna 8:2, Jeremy Doncaster 12:1, David Steen 2:1, Troy Smith 4)

Monday, October 15
WOLVERHAMPTON 56 (Ronnie Correy 14:1, Jan Staechmann 4, Sam Ermolenko 9:2, Neil Collins 7:1, *Alan Grahame 8:2,* Peter Karlsson 10, Wayne Carter 4:2)
POOLE 34 (Craig Boyce 7, Gary Allan 5, Alun Rossiter 8, Tony Langdon 3:2, *Andy Grahame 9,* Rod Colquhoun 2, Justin Elkins 0)

Sunday, October 21
EDINBURGH 33 (Les Collins 10:1, Michael Coles 7:1, Freddy Schøtt 4, Carl Blackbird 0, *Shane Bowes 7:1,* Scott Lamb 2, Mick Powell 3:2)
BELLE VUE 63 (Shawn Moran 12, *rider replacement for Chris Morton,* Bobby Ott 13:2, Kelly Moran 15:2, Joe Screen 11:3, Max Schofield 3:1, Richard Musson 9)

Sunday, October 21
RYE HOUSE 36 (Melvyn Taylor 9, Trevor O'Brien 4:2, Jens Rasmussen 10, Glen Baxter 1, *Troy Pratt 9:1,* Scott Humphries 3, Wayne Baxter 0)
WOLVERHAMPTON 60 (Ronnie Correy 18, Jan Staechmann 12:3, Sam Ermolenko 11:1, Neil Collins 8:1, *rider replacement for Graham Jones,* Peter Karlsson 6, Wayne Carter 5)

Tuesday, October 23
POOLE 48 (Craig Boyce 17, Gary Allan 2, Alun Rossiter 12:2, Tony Langdon 10:3, *rider replacement for Tom Knudsen,* Rod Colquhoun 7, Justin Elkins 0)
SWINDON 48 (Jimmy Nilsen 8:1, Peter Nahlin 10:1, Andrew Silver 5, John Davis 7:1, Leigh Adams 5:1, Phil Crump 9:1, David Smart 4)

Thursday, October 25
MIDDLESBROUGH 43 (Darren Sumner 10, Steve Wilcock 2, *Les Collins 2:2,* Paul Bentley 10:3, *Steve Regeling 11:1, Simon Green 7,* Duncan Chapman 1:1)
KING'S LYNN 46 (Stephen Davies 0, Dennis Löfqvist 3:1, Mark Loram 12, **Henrik Gustafsson 12,** Sean Wilson 4:2, Roger Horspool 1, Bohumil Brhel 14)

FOUR TEAM TOURNAMENTS

Belle Vue, Friday, April 6
BELLE VUE B 37 (Peter Ravn 12, Joe Screen 9, Chris Morton 11, Mike Lewthwaite 3, Richard Musson 2)
MIDDLESBROUGH 31 (Darren Sumner 7, David Cheshire 6, Jamie Luckhurst 4, Rod Hunter 6, Paul Bentley 8) **BELLE VUE A 24** (Shawn Moran 11, Scott Smith 0, Bobby Ott 3, Kelly Moran 9, Richard Smith 1) **LONG EATON 15** (Peter Lloyd 1, Gary O'Hare 2, Paul Fry 7, *Paul Smith 2,* Michael Howe 3)

Reading, Monday, April 30
POOLE 29 (Gary Chessell 7, Alun Rossiter 5, Craig Boyce 7, Tom Knudsen 10, *Troy Smith)* **WIMBLEDON 25** (Nathan Simpson 4, Neville Tatum 3, Ray Morton 10, Andy Grahame 8, Nigel Leaver) **READING 23** (*Billy Hamill 5,* David Mullett 8, Todd Wiltshire 10, David Steen 0, Christian Howell)
SWINDON 19 (*Bobby Ott 7,* David Smart 7, Leigh Adams 3, Matthew Cross 2, *Lance Sealey)*

Swindon, Saturday, May 19
SWINDON A 35 (Andrew Silver 10, John Davis 9, Leigh Adams 10, David Smart 6, Wayne Freeman) **SWINDON B 34 (Jimmy Nilsen 12,** Peter Nahlin 4, ***Ronnie Correy 12,*** Matthew Cross 6, Peter Byrne) **EXETER 15** (Steve Regeling 4, Richard Green 1, Peter Jeffery 7, Steve Bishop 3, *Andy Witts)*
POOLE 12 (Tony Langdon 3, Alun Rossiter 3, Craig Boyce 4, Tom Knudsen 2, Jon Gould)

Cradley Heath, Saturday, June 9
CRADLEY HEATH 30 (Simon Cross 9, Alan Grahame 9, Billy Hamill 6, *Andy Hackett 6,* David Haynes 0)
WIMBLEDON 23 (Nathan Simpson 2, Neville Tatum 4, Ray Morton 4, Andy Grahame 7, Nigel Leaver 6)
POOLE 22 (Gary Chessell 2, Craig Boyce 9, Tony Langdon 6, Gary Allan 3, Tom Knudsen 2) **IPSWICH 20** (Chris Louis 6, Shane Parker 5, *Carl Blackbird 5,* David Norris 4, Robbie Fuller)

Peterborough, Friday, October 12
SWINDON B 30.5 (Jimmy Nilsen 10, *Alan Grahame 11,* Martin Chessell 5.5, Matthew Cross 4) **SWINDON A 28.5** (Andrew Silver 8, Phil Crump 11, Wayne Freeman 3.5, David Smart 6)
PETERBOROUGH B 19 (*Carl Blackbird 6, Melvyn Taylor 4,* Wayne Bridgeford 6, *Adrian Stevens 3)*
PETERBOROUGH A 18 (Mick Poole 8, Nigel Flatman 7, Scott Norman 0, Sean Barker 2, Scott Birland 1)

Poole, Tuesday, October 16
READING 38 (Jan Andersson 9, Todd Wiltshire 10, Armando Castagna 8, David Mullett 11) **WIMBLEDON 24** (Nathan Simpson 4, Ray Morton 7, Neville Tatum 3, Andy Grahame 10)
WOLVERHAMPTON 18 (Sam Ermolenko 1, Ronnie Correy 7, Jan Staechmann 4, Peter Karlsson 5, *Steve Leigh, reserve, 1)* **POOLE 16** (Alun Rossiter 4, Tony Langdon 4, Gary Allan 2, Craig Boyce 6)

● Throughout the 1991 Speedway Yearbook a style has been adopted for all team results. Riders who have scored maximum points are always listed in **bold** type and riders who are making guest appearances are listed in *italics*.

Aces deal fans a pack of problems

Track Data

Promoters: Don Bowes and John Perrin.
Address: The Greyhound Stadium, Kirkmanshulme Lane, Gorton, Manchester M18 7BA.
Telephone: 061-223-7720.
Hotline: 0898 800 672
Track Length: 285 metres.
Track Record: 59.3 secs, Erik Gundersen (Cradley Heath), October 9, 1988, Heat 1, British League Riders' Championship Final.

YOU would never have guessed that Belle Vue had finished third in the Sunbrite League and only been knocked out of the Speedway Star Knock Out Cup on a deplorable technicality.

Such was the venom heaped upon promoter John Perrin that you would have thought they had finished bottom of the table and lost all interest in the cup competitions at the preliminary stage!

But even Perrin himself was bitterly disappointed and disillusioned at the end of a season in which he had the best team in the country – but didn't have the team spirit necessary to ensure a bountiful collection of silverware.

He admitted candidly: "We should have won everything!" He was probably right as the seven riders who regularly wore the most famous race jacket the sport has seen, showed, time after time, that they could not only defeat but demolish the best of the opposition.

They destroyed Cradley Heath at Dudley Wood; they beat champions Reading at Smallmead; they won comfortably at Coventry; and sneaked away wins at Oxford, King's Lynn and Swindon. That was the good side of Belle Vue. The bad side saw them lose at home to bottom of the table King's Lynn (the Zetor Stars ONLY away win of the season!), hand all FOUR home League points to Oxford and generally flatter to deceive whenever the going got tough.

They won only one of their first four matches; put together an unbeaten run of four successive away matches; clawed their way back into title contention and then threw it all away with four September matches in which they claimed only one point! It was a staggering season of contradiction which certainly wasn't helped by the internal bickering that saw Peter Ravn transfer-listed after complaining about track conditions and Kelly Moran turning up for the final match of the season without a bike.

No wonder promoter Perrin felt like quitting!

The season started badly for him when he was roundly condemned after deciding to release youngsters Carl Stonehewer and Gary Hicks on loan to accommodate Californian Bobby Ott.

Final statistics proved it was a wise decision as Ott was a sensational find in his first full season in the Sunbrite League.

But fans, and ex-promoting partner Peter Collins, wouldn't let him forget his original decision.

His case wasn't helped by a slump in Shawn Moran's form, the controversy surrounding Ravn and the time it took Joe Screen to adjust to new engines.

Throughout all the trauma one man rode his heart out every race: Chris Morton.

It was his last season and it ended with a paid maximum in his 703rd and last match for his only club.

It was precisely what he deserved!

Roll of Honour

Seasons in British League: 26 (1965-1987 [Hyde Road], 1988-1990 [Kirkmanshulme Lane]).
British League Record: Champions (4), 1970, 1971, 1972, 1982. Runners-up (7), 1969, 1974, 1975, 1976, 1978, 1984, 1988. Third (2), 1980, 1990.
Speedway Star Cup Record: Winners (3), 1972, 1973, 1975. Runners-up (5), 1970, 1978, 1980, 1982, 1984.
Best League Cup Record: Winners (1), 1983. Runners-up (2), 1984, 1987.
Inter League Cup Record: Winners (1), 1975.
Premiership: Winners (1), 1979. Runners-up (1), 1984.
Appearances: Chris Morton, 703 (1973-1990).
Points: Chris Morton, 7041 (1973-1990).
World Finalists: Joe Abbott (1937), Peter Collins (1973-74-75-76-77, 1979-80, 1982), Peter Craven (1954-55-56-57-58-59-60-61-62-63), Dick Fisher (1956-57, 1963-64), Ove Fundin (1967), Bob Harrison (1936), Ron Johnston (1955, 1958, 1960), Bill Kitchen (1937-38), Eric Langton (1936-37-38), Louis Lawson (1949, 1951), Henry Long (1952), Cyril Maidment (1964), Ivan Mauger (1969-70-71-72), Shawn Moran (1990), Chris Morton (1976, 1980-81, 1983, 1986-87-88), Dent Oliver (1949-50), Jack Parker (1949-50-51), Peter Ravn (1987), Larry Ross (1981), Sören Sjösten (1962, 1969-70-71, 1974), Frank Varey (1937-38).
BLRC Finalists: Cyril Maidment (1965-66), Ove Fundin (1967), Sören Sjösten (1968, 1973), Ivan Mauger (1969-70-71-72), Peter Collins (1974-75-76-77-78-79-80, 1985), Chris Morton (1981-82-83-84-85-86-87-88), Shawn Moran (1989-90), Peter Ravn (1989), Kelly Moran (1990).
Other Honours: National League (Division One) Champions, 1933, 1934, 1935, 1936, 1963. National League Champions (Division Two), 1968, 1969. National Trophy Winners, 1933, 1934, 1935, 1936, 1937, 1946, 1947, 1949, 1958. National League (Division Two) Cup Winners, 1969.

Star of 90

BOBBY OTT

Belle Vue

BELLE VUE

01...Swindon, April 14, L35-55

1 Shawn Moran	3 3 3 2 0 1	12	1
2 Peter Ravn	*rider replacement*		
3 †Chris Morton	2 2 1 2 T	7	
4 Kelly Moran	3 2 2 3 0 T R	10	1
5 Joe Screen	1 0 0 T 2 fx1	4	
6 §Bobby Ott	1 0 0 N 1	2	
7 Mike Lewthwaite	F 0 N 0 0	0	

02...SWINDON, April 27, W48-42

1 Shawn Moran	R 2 2 2 2	8	1
2 †Chris Morton	2 0 1 1	4	1
3 Peter Ravn	3 2 2 X	7	
4 Kelly Moran	3 3 2 3 0	11	
5 Joe Screen	2 2 R 2	6	2
6 Mike Lewthwaite	0 0 N 1	1	
7 Bobby Ott	3 1 3 1 3	11	2

03...Cradley Heath, April 28, L37-53

1 Shawn Moran	2 2 3 1 F	8	1
2 †Chris Morton	1 1 0 T 1 0	3	2
3 Peter Ravn	1 2 3 2 0	8	
4 Kelly Moran	3 2 1 1 3 3	13	
5 Joe Screen	1 0 0 T	1	
6 Mike Lewthwaite	0 0 T 0	0	
7 Bobby Ott	2 0 T 2	4	

04...KING'S LYNN, May 4, L43-46

1 Shawn Moran	R 1 2 2	5	1
2 Joe Screen	2 3 2 1	8	1
3 †Peter Ravn	F fnN N	0	
4 Kelly Moran	3 2 3 3 3	14	
5 Bobby Ott	2 1 0 1 2	6	3
6 Todd Wiltshire	*3 3 R 0 0*	*6*	
7 §§Richard Musson	0 1 1 1 0 1	4	1

05...COVENTRY, May 11, W56-34

1 Shawn Moran	3 3 0 3 3	12	
2 Joe Screen	2 fx2 1	5	1
3 †Peter Ravn	**3 3 3 2**	**11**	**1**
4 Kelly Moran	3 3 1 2 0	9	2
5 Bobby Ott	1 2 2 3	8	1
6 Richard Musson	0 1 0 3	4	
7 Leigh Adams	*3 1 1 2*	*7*	*2*

06...BRADFORD, May 25, W48-42

1 John Jorgensen	*2 3 3 1 1*	*10*	*1*
2 Joe Screen	1 1 1 2	5	2
3 †Peter Ravn	R R 0 N	0	
4 Kelly Moran	3 3 3 2 0	11	
5 Stephen Davies	*2 0 1 1*	*4*	*1*
6 Richard Musson	2 1 N 2	5	1
7 Bobby Ott	1 2 3 1 3 3	13	1

07...OXFORD, June 1, L41-49

1 Bobby Ott	1 2 0 2	5	1
2 †Chris Morton	2 1 2 2 1	8	1
3 Gary Havelock	*3 2 2 1 0*	*8*	
4 Graham Jones	*2 1 0 1*	*4*	*2*
5 Kelvin Tatum	*3 3 2 R*	*8*	
6 Richard Musson	2 2 0 0	4	1
7 Joe Screen	F 0 1 3	4	1

08...Oxford, June 6, W45-44

1 Shawn Moran	3 3 1 3 0	10	
2 †Chris Morton	N 1 0 0	1	
3 Simon Cross	*3 2 3 1 3*	*12*	*1*
4 Joe Screen	F 2 0 N	2	
5 Marvyn Cox	*2 X 1 2*	*5*	
6 Richard Musson	1 1 0 N 1	3	
7 Sean Wilson	*3 2 3 1 0 3*	*12*	*1*

09...King's Lynn, June 17, D45-45

1 Shawn Moran	1 3 2 2 1 2 1	12	4
2 Bobby Ott	0 fx0 2 2	4	
3 †Chris Morton	0 2 T 0 1	3	1
4 Andy Smith	*2 2 3 2 2 3 2*	*16*	*1*
5 Kelly Moran	*rider replacement*		
6 Richard Musson	1 1 T 1	3	2
7 Joe Screen	3 1 1 2	7	1
8 Scott Smith	*did not ride*		

10...READING, June 22, W50-40

1 Simon Cross	*3 2 3 0 2*	*10*	*1*
2 Bobby Ott	2 3 2 2 1	10	3
3 †Chris Morton	3 3 0 1	7	1
4 Kelly Moran	2 2 2 1	7	
5 Peter Ravn	0 0 1 2	3	1
6 Richard Musson	2 2 fx3	7	2
7 Joe Screen	3 0 1 2	6	1

11...Swindon, June 23, W48-42

1 Jan Andersson	*2 3 3 3 3*	*14*	
2 Bobby Ott	F 2 3 0	5	1
3 †Chris Morton	3 2 1 1	7	
4 Kelly Moran	3 2 1 2 2	10	3
5 Peter Ravn	0 3 0 0	3	
6 Richard Musson	3 0 0 1	4	1
7 Joe Screen	2 0 1 2	5	1

12...Coventry, June 30, W56-34

1 Jeremy Doncaster	*3 2 3 3*	*11*	
2 Bobby Ott	2 1 3 0 2	8	3
3 †Chris Morton	2 3 2 3 3	13	1
4 Kelly Moran	2 2 2 2	8	3
5 Peter Ravn	3 3 1 1	8	1
6 Richard Musson	1 1 0 fx	2	
7 Joe Screen	0 3 R 3	6	

13...CRADLEY HEATH, July 6, W47-43

1 Shawn Moran	3 3 2 2 E	10	1
2 Bobby Ott	0 2 1 3 2	8	2
3 †Chris Morton	0 3 1 2	6	
4 Kelly Moran	3 1 1 0	5	1
5 Peter Ravn	0 0 2 0	2	
6 Richard Musson	2 1 0 2	5	2
7 Joe Screen	3 2 3 3 0	11	

14...Bradford, July 7, L32-58

1 Shawn Moran	3 0 0 1 R	4	
2 Bobby Ott	1 1 1 0	3	
3 †Chris Morton	2 2 3 0 2 0	9	
4 Kelly Moran	3 1 1 3 1 1	10	
5 Peter Ravn	0 0 T N	0	
6 Richard Musson	R 0 T 1	1	1
7 Joe Screen	2 1 T 0 2	5	1

15...WOLVERHAMPTON, July 13, W51-39

1 Shawn Moran	3 2 2 2 1	10	1
2 Bobby Ott	1 0 0 N	1	
3 †Chris Morton	1 2 1 N	4	2
4 Peter Ravn	1 1 0 0	2	1
5 Kelly Moran	3 2 3 3 3	14	
6 Richard Musson	2 fx3 2	7	2
7 Joe Screen	3 2 3 2 0 3	13	

16...King's Lynn, July 14, W47-43

1 Shawn Moran	1 X 2 R	3	1
2 Bobby Ott	3 3 3 3 0	12	
3 †Chris Morton	3 1 1 2	7	1
4 Peter Ravn	1 1 1 1	4	2
5 Kelly Moran	2 0 2 1	5	1
6 Richard Musson	3 2 0 1	6	
7 Joe Screen	2 2 2 3 1	10	3

17...SWINDON, July 20, W54-36

1 Shawn Moran	**2 2 3 3 3**	**13**	**2**
2 Bobby Ott	3 3 1 2 2	11	3
3 †Chris Morton	2 3 1 1	7	1
4 Peter Ravn	3 1 1 N	5	2
5 Kelly Moran	2 2 2 2	8	1
6 Richard Musson	0 0 1 1	2	1
7 Joe Screen	2 2 0 2 2	8	1

18...Wolverhampton, July 23, L36-53

1 Shawn Moran	2 1 0 1	4	2
2 Bobby Ott	1 2 3 1 3 F	10	1
3 †Chris Morton	0 2 0 T	2	
4 Peter Ravn	0 0 0 T	0	
5 Kelly Moran	3 2 1 2 2 2	12	1
6 Richard Musson	fxF N 0	0	
7 Stephen Davies	*2 2 1 2 1*	*8*	

19...Reading, July 30, W45-44

1 Shawn Moran	2 1 1 1	5	2
2 Bobby Ott	3 2 3 0	8	
3 †Chris Morton	2 2 2 0	6	
4 Jimmy Nilsen	*3 3 2 3 0*	*11*	*1*
5 Kelly Moran	2 0 3 3 2	10	1
6 Richard Musson	fx0 0 1 fx	1	1
7 §§Max Schofield	2 1 N 1	4	1

20...Coventry, August 11, W45-43

1 Bobby Ott	3 3 3 fx2	11	
2 Neil Collins	*F 1 3 1*	*5*	
3 †Chris Morton	3 2 2 2	9	1
4 Gary Hicks	*1 0 1 2*	*4*	*1*
5 Kelly Moran	2 3 3 3 1	12	1
6 Richard Musson	R R 1 R 3	4	
7 Max Schofield	fxfxN fx	0	

21...COVENTRY, August 17, W51-39

1 Shawn Moran	**3 3 3 3 2**	**14**	**1**
2 Bobby Ott	2 1 2 0	5	1
3 †Chris Morton	2 2 0 0	4	1
4 Kelly Moran	2 2 0 1	5	1
5 Joe Screen	3 E 3 3 3	12	
6 Richard Musson	3 3 1 N 0 1	8	2
7 Max Schofield	0 0 N 1 2	3	

22...Cradley Heath, August 18, W52-38

1 Shawn Moran	1 2 3 2	8	3
2 Bobby Ott	2 3 3 2 1	11	1
3 †Chris Morton	**3 3 3 3 3**	**15**	
4 Kelly Moran	1 3 2 3	9	1
5 Joe Screen	2 0 R 1	3	
6 Max Schofield	0 N N 1	1	1
7 Richard Musson	2 1 0 0 2	5	

23...Wolverhampton, August 27, L37-52

1 Shawn Moran	2 2 1 3 2 0 0	10	
2 Bobby Ott	E 1 T 2 N	3	1
3 †Chris Morton	3 0 1 2 1 2	9	2
4 Kelly Moran	*rider replacement*		
5 Joe Screen	2 3 fxX 1 2	8	1
6 Peter Ravn	X 1 0 2 0 2	5	
7 Richard Musson	0 1 N T 1	2	1
8 Max Schofield	*did not ride*		

24...KING'S LYNN, August 31, W55-35

1 Shawn Moran	3 2 3 N	8	1
2 Bobby Ott	**2 3 3 2 2**	**12**	**3**
3 †Chris Morton	3 1 2 R	6	
4 Kelly Moran	3 2 3 2 3	13	
5 Joe Screen	2 1 1 2	6	2
6 Richard Musson	R N 0 1 fn	1	1
7 Peter Ravn	2 2 1 0 3	8	1
8 Max Schofield	1	1	

25...CRADLEY HEATH, September 7, W55-35

1 Shawn Moran	3 3 1 1 0	8	1
2 Bobby Ott	0 0 3 3	6	
3 †Chris Morton	2 3 2 0	7	
4 Kelly Moran	2 1 2 2	7	1
5 Joe Screen	3 3 1 3 3	13	1
6 Richard Musson	2 1 0 2	5	3
7 Peter Ravn	3 2 1 3	9	2

26...Bradford, September 8, L31-59

1 Shawn Moran	3 0 2 2 0	7	
2 Bobby Ott	0 1 1 0	2	1
3 †Chris Morton	2 X 1 2 0	5	
4 Kelly Moran	1 0 2 1	4	
5 Joe Screen	0 1 T 0 R	1	
6 Richard Musson	1 T 0 1	2	1
7 Peter Ravn	3 1 2 2 2	10	1

27...Oxford, September 12, L40-50

1 Shawn Moran	2 2 3 0 fn	7	
2 Bobby Ott	0 0 T 2	2	
3 †Chris Morton	1 3 2 2 0	8	2
4 Kelly Moran	3 2 3 1 1 3	13	1
5 Joe Screen	1 0 2 1 0	4	1
6 Richard Musson	0 0 T 2	2	
7 Peter Ravn	1 2 0 1	4	1

28...WOLVERHAMPTON, Sept. 21, D45-45

1 Shawn Moran	2 F 2 F	4	2
2 Bobby Ott	3 2 fx3	8	
3 †Chris Morton	0 0 1 0	1	
4 Kelly Moran	2 3 3 2 1	11	2
5 Joe Screen	3 2 2 3 2	12	2
6 Richard Musson	1 2 1 1	5	1
7 Peter Ravn	2 2 0 R	4	

29...Reading, September 24, L29-61

1 Paul Thorp	*R 0 T 2*	*2*	
2 Bobby Ott	1 1 0 E	2	
3 †Chris Morton	1 1 1 3 2 2	10	1
4 Kelly Moran	R R 0 0	0	
5 Joe Screen	1 2 1 N 0 1	5	1
6 Richard Musson	0 T 0 1	1	1
7 Peter Ravn	2 3 1 1 0 2	9	

30...READING, October 12, W51-39

1 Shawn Moran	0 3 1 0	4	1
2 Bobby Ott	3 0 3 2 2	10	1
3 †Chris Morton	3 2 3 2 3	13	
4 Kelly Moran	0 2 2 2	6	1
5 Joe Screen	2 3 1 0	6	1
6 Richard Musson	1 1 1 1	4	1
7 Peter Ravn	3 0 2 3	8	1

31...BRADFORD, October 19, W59-31

1 Shawn Moran	3 3 F 1	7	1
2 Bobby Ott	1 1 0 2	4	
3 †Chris Morton	**3 3 2 3**	**11**	**1**
4 Kelly Moran	3 2 2 2 0	9	2
5 Joe Screen	1 3 3 2 3	12	1
6 Richard Musson	1 1 1 3	6	
7 Peter Ravn	3 2 3 2	10	1

Morton beat Havelock for bonus point.

32...OXFORD, October 26, L40-49

1 Billy Hamill	*2 R 2 2 2 3 1*	*12*	*1*
2 Bobby Ott	1 fx1 3 3 3 0	11	2
3 †Kelly Moran	1 2 T N	3	
4 Shawn Moran	*rider replacement*		
5 Joe Screen	2 2 fxR N N	4	
6 Richard Musson	1 F T 0 1	2	2
7 Peter Ravn	2 0 1 2 1 2	8	1

'90 ROSTER

GRAHAM, Robert Ian (Bobby)
B 13.10.1973, Warrington, Cheshire. *Local junior.*

HAMPSON, Michael John
B 26.7.1973, Ashton-under-Lyne, Gt. Manchester. *Local junior.*

LEWTHWAITE, Michael Grant
B 1.12.1967, Rochdale, Greater Manchester.

MORAN, Kelly Michael
B 21.9.1960, Huntingdon Beach, Ca., USA.

MORAN, Shawn
B 19.11.1961, Lakewood, Ca., USA.

MORTON, Christopher John
B 22.7.1956, Davyhulme, Manchester.

MUSSON, Richard Neil
B 14.7.1973, Leeds, West Yorkshire. *Junior*

OTT, Robert William (Bobby)
B 17.11.1962, Inglewood, Ca., U.S.A. *Returned after five season absence.*

RAVN, Peter
B 16.3.1962, Bogense, Denmark.

SCHOFIELD, Max
B 10.3.1970, Leeds, West Yorkshire. *On loan from Middlesbrough.*

SCREEN, Joseph
B 27.11.1972, Chesterfield, Derbys.

SCOTT SMITH – *See Cradley Heath.*

Marvyn is Bradford's Cox's pippin

Track Data

Promoters: Northern Speedways Limited (Allan Ham, Bobby Ham and Eric Boothroyd).
Address: Odsal Stadium, Rooley Avenue, Bradford, West Yorkshire, BO6 1BS.
Telephone: 0274-729443.
Hotline: 0898 800 673.
Track Length: 338 metres.
Track Record: 58.8 secs, Hans Nielsen (Oxford), August 13, 1989, heat 4, Inter Continental Final.

BOBBY HAM proudly told a crowded eve of the season Press Conference: "This is the year when Bradford will win the Sunbrite League Championship."

He was wrong and the year ended with the former professional footballer quitting day to day involvement with the Coalite Dukes to concentrate more of his efforts into the family construction business.

But at least Bobby went out knowing that he and brother Allan, who will stay on as promoter in 1991, had provided West Yorkshire fans with their most successful side since Halifax did the League and Cup double nearly a quarter of a century ago.

For Bradford finished in their highest ever Sunbrite League placing (fifth); won their first ever national trophy (the Gold Cup); and reached the final of the Speedway Star Knock Out Cup.

So, much of that pre-season optimism had been well-founded and Odsal also had the major feather in their collective cap of staging the most thrilling World Final since Bruce Penhall won his first crown at Wembley in 1981.

How sad then that 1990 should finish with fresh doubts about the track's long-term future although, fortunately, those doubts were dispelled a couple of days before Christmas when co-promoter Allan Ham announced that he would be continuing in charge of the Coalite Dukes.

And his first New Year action was to open fresh negotiations with Oxford to ensure that 1990 newcomer Marvyn Cox would be staying at Odsal for at least another year.

Cox had arrived with his career at a watershed. He had been one of England's brightest prospects during his days at National League Rye House and, later, in his first seasons at Oxford, when he made his World Final debut. But his star had waned and he had seen his average drop successively in 1988 and 1989 and obviously needed a fresh challenge.

That challenge was to join Bradford and it worked. He had his best-ever season in the sport, established himself as England number four and won a place in the Sunbrite Lions' World Team Cup Final squad in Czechoslovakia. He also enjoyed himself with a new club and relished a fresh start at a big home track.

He took over as the Coalite Dukes' undisputed number one and his performances even overshadowed those of Gary Havelock who returned to the saddle after his enforced absence. Havelock wasted no time at all in settling back into a high-scoring groove and such was his overall influence on his team-mates that he was appointed captain early in the season when the incumbent Neil Evitts was going through a troubled period.

Evitts never recovered from his sluggish start and will probably benefit, as Cox has done, by a change of scenery. Certainly there were only the occasional glimpse of the form that took him to the 1986 British Championship and there must be now grave doubts whether he will ever recapture that exciting form.

Paradoxically, while as a team Bradford enjoyed their most successful ever season, several of the individual team members were far from their best. Paul Thorp, like Evitts, dropped back in the rankings and Bryan Larner, who had looked so sharp in pre-season practice, struggled throughout and made out a good case for a more sensible attitude towards the loaning out of tail-enders to National League tracks. Instead of being given a chance to regain his confidence, sapped by injury, in the Second Division, Larner had to battle on in the top flight.

Andy Smith, ruled out for a spell with a broken bone in his foot, progressed and Australian Champion Glenn Doyle was as enigmatic as ever.

Often he looks a major talent: occasionally he flatters to deceive.

Roll of Honour

Seasons in British League: 5 (1986-1990).
Best British League Season: Fifth, 1987, 1990.
Speedway Star Cup Record: Finalists, 1990.
Best League Cup Season: Seventh, 1986.
Inter League Cup Record: Never competed in the competition.
Gold Cup: Winners (1), 1990.
Appearances: Neil Evitts 178 (1986-1990).
Points: Neil Evitts, 1538 (1986-1990).
World Finalists: Jack Biggs (1950), Ron Clarke (1949-50), Neil Evitts (1986), Arthur Forrest (1952-53-54-55-56), Oliver Hart (1949), Dent Oliver (1953), Eddie Rigg (1951, 1954), Andy Smith (1989), Arthur Wright (1955).
BLRC Finalists: Neil Evitts (1986), Sean Willmott (1987), Gary Havelock (1988, 1990), Paul Thorp (1989), Marvyn Cox, 1990.

Star of 90
GARY HAVELOCK
Bradford

BRADFORD

01...King's Lynn, April 16, L38-52

1 Paul Thorp	3 3 R 0	6	
2 Andy Smith	2 1 F 2	5	1
3 Gary Havelock	1 3 3 2 2	11	
4 †Neil Evitts	0 1 0 T	1	
5 §Marvyn Cox	3 3 2 E 3 0	11	
6 Bryan Larner	0 0 N 0	0	
7 Glenn Doyle	1 0 2 0 0 1	4	

02...Oxford, May 2, L41-49

1 Paul Thorp	1 3 1 1	6	1
2 Leigh Adams	*3 0 2 2 0*	*7*	
3 †Gary Havelock	3 3 3 1 2	12	
4 Neil Evitts	3 2 0 fx	5	
5 Marvyn Cox	2 fx N N	2	1
6 Bryan Larner	R 1 N E R	1	
7 Glenn Doyle	3 1 0 1 1 2	8	

03...SWINDON, May 5, W 49-41

1 Paul Thorp	R 1 1 2	4	1
2 Andy Smith	3 3 2 2 3	13	1
3 †Gary Havelock	1 2 3 3 1	10	
4 Neil Evitts	2 1 0 1	4	1
5 Sean Wilson	*1 3 2 2*	*8*	*2*
6 Bryan Larner	fx0 N 0	0	
7 Glenn Doyle	3 1 3 1 2	10	1

04...Wolverhampton, May 14, L37-53

1 Paul Thorp	1 3 1 T 0	5	
2 Andy Smith	0 2 2 2 2 1	9	2
3 †Gary Havelock	1 2 3 1 0	7	1
4 Neil Evitts	0 1 0 T	1	1
5 Marvyn Cox	3 2 1 1 2 2	11	1
6 Bryan Larner	0 0 T 0	0	
7 Glenn Doyle	3 0 T 1	4	

05...COVENTRY, May 19, L44-46

1 Paul Thorp	2 1 R 0	3	1
2 Andy Smith	1 2 3 3 2	11	1
3 †Gary Havelock	3 2 1 2 1	9	2
4 Neil Evitts	0 1 3 1	5	1
5 Marvyn Cox	2 2 1 1	6	1
6 Bryan Larner	0 1 N R	1	
7 Glenn Doyle	3 0 2 2 2	9	1

06...Belle Vue, May 25, L42-48

1 Marvyn Cox	3 2 3 2 3	13	
2 Neil Evitts	fx 1 2 T	3	1
3 †Gary Havelock	2 2 2 2 3 2	13	3
4 Andy Smith	F 1 1 0	2	
5 Paul Thorp	1 3 F R	4	
6 Bryan Larner	F 0 N 1	1	
7 Glenn Doyle	3 3 0 fxfx	6	

07...KING'S LYNN, May 26, W57-33

1 Marvyn Cox	**3 3 3 3**	**12**	
2 Neil Evitts	2 R X 2 3	7	2
3 †Gary Havelock	3 3 2 3	11	
4 Andy Smith	2 3 3 fx2	10	2
5 Paul Thorp	**3 2 2 2**	**9**	**3**
6 Bryan Larner	1 0 N 0	1	1
7 Glenn Doyle	2 0 2 0 3	7	

08...King's Lynn, May 28, W48-42

1 Marvyn Cox	2 3 3 3 2	13	1
2 Neil Evitts	1 1 3 1	6	1
3 †Gary Havelock	3 2 0 1 3	9	1
4 Andy Smith	1 0 1 N	2	1
5 Paul Thorp	2 3 0 0	5	
6 Bryan Larner	0 0 N N 1	1	
7 Glenn Doyle	1 N 3 2 2 1 3	12	1

09...READING, June 2, W53-37

1 Marvyn Cox	1 2 1 2	6	2
2 Glenn Doyle	2 1 2 0	5	2
3 †Gary Havelock	3 3 2 0 R	8	1
4 Andy Smith	2 1 3 3 3	12	1
5 Paul Thorp	0 2 0 3	5	
6 Bryan Larner	1 E 0 2	3	1
7 Neil Evitts	**3 2 3 3 3**	**14**	**1**

10...WOLVERHAMPTON, June 16, W69-21

1 Marvyn Cox	2 3 3 3 2	13	1
2 Glenn Doyle	0 2 2 2	6	3
3 †Gary Havelock	3 3 3 1	10	
4 Andy Smith	**3 2 2 2**	**9**	**3**
5 Paul Thorp	**2 3 3 3 3**	**14**	**1**
6 Bryan Larner	2 R N 2	4	2
7 Neil Evitts	**3 2 3 2 3**	**13**	**2**

11...BELLE VUE, July 7, W58-32

1 Marvyn Cox	2 1 3 1 3 2	12	3
2 Neil Evitts	0 1 3 2 N	6	
3 †Gary Havelock	**3 3 3 3 3 3**	**18**	
4 Glenn Doyle	2 2 0 1 2	7	2
5 Andy Smith	*rider replacement*		
6 Stuart Parnaby	1 0 N 0	1	
7 Paul Thorp	3 2 2 2 2 3	14	3
8 Phil Disney	*did not ride*		

12...Swindon, July 19, L40-50

1 Marvyn Cox	2 2 3 3 2	12	
2 Glenn Doyle	fx1 2 T	3	1
3 †Gary Havelock	3 2 3 0 2 1	11	1
4 Neil Evitts	1 0 2 0	3	1
5 Jan Andersson	*2 3 0 1*	*6*	*1*
6 Paul Thorp	2 0 1 R 1	4	1
7 Stuart Parnaby	1 0 N 0	1	1

13...READING, July 21, W49-41

1 Marvyn Cox	1 3 2 0 1	7	1
2 Neil Evitts	R 3 1 0 3	7	1
3 †Gary Havelock	2 3 3 1 1 1	11	2
4 Glenn Doyle	2 2 0 2 2	8	2
5 Andy Smith	*rider replacement*		
6 Stuart Parnaby	0 0 N 0	0	
7 Paul Thorp	3 2 3 2 3 3	16	1
8 Phil Disney	*did not ride*		

14...Reading, July 23, L34-56

1 Marvyn Cox	2 2 2 2 2 2	12	
2 Neil Evitts	1 1 R T	2	2
3 †Gary Havelock	2 2 0 1 1 fx	6	1
4 Glenn Doyle	2 0 0 0	2	
5 Peter Nahlin	*0 1 T T*	*1*	
6 Paul Thorp	3 0 2 3 0 2	10	
7 §§Phil Disney	1 0 T fn	1	
8 Stuart Parnaby	0	0	

15...Coventry, July 28, W46-44

1 Marvyn Cox	2 3 2 2 1	10	1
2 Neil Evitts	1 2 1 1	5	3
3 †Gary Havelock	2 2 3 3 0	10	1
4 Glenn Doyle	3 0 2 3	8	
5 Bobby Ott	*0 1 1 N*	*2*	*1*
6 Paul Thorp	2 3 3 0 R 2	10	
7 Phil Disney	0 1 N 0	1	1

Cox lost to Tatum for bonus point.

16...Wolverhampton, July 30, L42-48

1 Marvyn Cox	3 0 2 3 2 0	10	1
2 Neil Evitts	0 1 T 1	2	
3 †Gary Havelock	3 0 2 3 3 3	14	
4 Glenn Doyle	1 0 R T	1	1
5 Leigh Adams	*2 3 0 1 N*	*6*	
6 Paul Thorp	3 1 1 T 1 2	8	1
7 Phil Disney	0 0 N 1	1	1

17...COVENTRY, August 4, W47-41

1 Marvyn Cox	2 3 3 2 2 3	15	1
2 Neil Evitts	1 2 1 2 3	9	2
3 †Gary Havelock	3 1 fx2 2 1	9	
4 Andy Smith	*rider replacement*		
5 Paul Thorp	1 0 2 R N	3	1
6 Phil Disney	F 1 N 1	2	
7 Glenn Doyle	3 0 3 0 0 3	9	
8 Stuart Parnaby	*did not ride*		

18...SWINDON, August 11, W58-32

1 Marvyn Cox	**3 2 3 3 3 3**	**17**	**1**
2 Andy Smith	*rider replacement*		
3 †Gary Havelock	2 2 1 3 3	11	2
4 Neil Evitts	3 2 3 2 0	10	2
5 Paul Thorp	0 R 3 3 0	6	
6 Glenn Doyle	3 3 3 X 3 1	13	
7 Phil Disney	0 1 N 0	1	
8 Stuart Parnaby	*did not ride*		

19...WOLVERHAMPTON, August 18, D45-45

1 Neil Evitts	fnN N N	0	
2 Marvyn Cox	*rider replacement*		
3 †Gary Havelock	3 2 3 3 3 1	15	1
4 Andy Smith	fx3 2 R 2	7	1
5 Paul Thorp	2 3 3 1 2 2	13	2
6 Glenn Doyle	1 3 1 2 1 1	9	1
7 Bryan Larner	0 0 1 0 0 0	1	1
8 Stuart Parnaby	*did not ride*		

20...Swindon, August 25, L44-46

1 Marvyn Cox	3 3 3 2 R	11	
2 Phil Disney	0 N 0 N	0	
3 †Gary Havelock	1 1 3 2	7	
4 Andy Smith	3 2 3 F	8	1
5 Paul Thorp	1 3 2 R 3	9	1
6 Glenn Doyle	3 2 fx1 F 3	9	1
7 Bryan Larner	0 R N 0 0	0	

21...Oxford, September 5, L39-51

1 Marvyn Cox	2 2 3 3 2 2	14	
2 Glenn Doyle	1 0 N N	1	1
3 †Gary Havelock	2 0 0 1	3	
4 Andy Smith	1 2 0 1 0	4	2
5 Paul Thorp	2 1 1 0	4	1
6 Sean Wilson	*3 1 2 1 1 3*	*11*	*1*
7 Bryan Larner	1 0 T 1	2	

22...BELLE VUE, September 8, W59-31

1 Marvyn Cox	2 3 1 1	7	
2 Rick Miller	*1 2 0 3*	*6*	*2*
3 †Gary Havelock	**3 3 3 3 3**	**15**	
4 Andy Smith	**2 2 3 3**	**10**	**2**
5 Paul Thorp	3 3 2 2 1	11	2
6 Glenn Doyle	2 N 1 3 1 3	10	
7 Bryan Larner	fx0 N N 0	0	

23...Cradley Heath, September 12, L32-58

1 Marvyn Cox	2 0 3 2 1 3	11	
2 Andy Smith	0 1 fxN	1	
3 †Gary Havelock	2 1 0 1	4	1
4 Glenn Doyle	1 1 1 0 0 R	3	
5 Paul Thorp	0 0 0 T	0	
6 Stephen Davies	*2 3 0 2 3*	*10*	
7 Bryan Larner	0 N T 1 2	3	2

24...Coventry, September 22, L44-46

1 Marvyn Cox	2 2 2 2	8	
2 Neil Evitts	1 0 1 N	2	1
3 †Gary Havelock	3 1 2 1	7	2
4 Andy Smith	2 1 2 1 1	7	4
5 Paul Thorp	3 2 3 0 0	8	
6 Glenn Doyle	3 2 0 3 0 3	11	
7 Bryan Larner	0 0 N 1	1	

25...OXFORD, September 29, W46-44

1 Marvyn Cox	2 2 3 1 1	9	1
2 Neil Evitts	0 1 2 N	3	1
3 †Gary Havelock	3 2 3 1 0	9	
4 Andy Smith	2 1 3 2	8	1
5 Paul Thorp	3 3 2 0	8	1
6 Glenn Doyle	2 1 1 0 0 2	6	1
7 Bryan Larner	1 1 N 1	3	3

26...CRADLEY HEATH, October 4, W47-43

1 Marvyn Cox	3 1 3 3 1	11	1
2 Neil Evitts	1 2 2 0	5	
3 †Gary Havelock	1 2 2 1	6	2
4 Andy Smith	3 2 2 0 0	7	
5 Paul Thorp	0 0 1 N	1	1
6 Glenn Doyle	3 R 3 3 3 3	15	
7 Bryan Larner	1 0 N 1	2	

27...Cradley Heath, October 7, L42-48

1 Marvyn Cox	3 1 0 0 2	6	1
2 Neil Evitts	1 R 0 T	1	
3 †Gary Havelock	1 2 2 3 3 3	14	
4 Andy Smith	2 1 1 3 0	7	2
5 Paul Thorp	3 3 2 0	8	
6 Glenn Doyle	2 0 1 T 2	5	
7 Bryan Larner	1 0 N 0	1	1

28...KING'S LYNN, October 13, W46-43

1 Marvyn Cox	**3 3 3 3 3**	**15**	
2 Neil Evitts	R 1 1 R	2	
3 †Gary Havelock	2 2 3 0	7	
4 Andy Smith	**2 2 3 2 2**	**11**	**4**
5 Paul Thorp	3 3 R 2	8	
6 Stuart Parnaby	1 0 0 0 0 2	3	
7 Bryan Larner	fxN N	0	

29...Reading, October 15, L36-54

1 Marvyn Cox	2 0 0 3	5	
2 Billy Hamill	*1 1 3 1 0*	*6*	*1*
3 †Gary Havelock	2 3 1 1	7	
4 Andy Smith	3 2 2 0 3	10	
5 Paul Thorp	0 1 1 0	2	2
6 Dean Barker	*3 0 N 0 0 2*	*5*	
7 Lance Sealey	*1 N 0 N 0*	*1*	

30...CRADLEY HEATH, October 17, W50-40

1 Marvyn Cox	3 3 2 3 3	14	
2 Neil Collins	*1 2 2 1*	*6*	*2*
3 †Gary Havelock	0 3 3 3 1	10	
4 Andy Smith	3 2 1 1	7	2
5 Paul Thorp	1 3 2 0	6	
6 Roman Matousek	*2 1 0 1 2*	*6*	
7 Bryan Larner	0 0 N 1	1	1

31...Belle Vue, October 19, L31-59

1 Marvyn Cox	2 1 3 0 1	7	
2 Gert Handberg	*0 0 T 0*	*0*	
3 †Gary Havelock	2 2 3 0 3 1	11	1
4 Andy Smith	0 0 T fx	0	
5 Paul Thorp	2 2 1 1 0 2	8	
6 Peter Karlsson	*2 fx1 T 1 1*	*5*	
7 Bryan Larner	0 0 N 0	0	

Havelock lost to Morton for bonus point.

32...OXFORD, October 20, W57-33

1 Marvyn Cox	**3 3 2 2 3**	**13**	**2**
2 Joe Screen	*2 1 2 3*	*8*	*1*
3 †Gary Havelock	3 3 3 2 2	13	1
4 Andy Smith	0 3 3 3	9	
5 Paul Thorp	1 2 1 0	4	1
6 Peter Ravn	*2 N 2 R 1 3*	*8*	*1*
7 Bryan Larner	1 0 N N 1	2	1

'90 ROSTER

COX, Marvyn
B 11.7.1964, Whitstable, Kent. *On loan from Oxford.*

DISNEY, Phillip Anthony
B 25.11.1970, Halifax, W. Yorks. *Local junior.*

DOUGLAS, Nigel Grant
B 6.2.1970, Perth, Australia. *Australians newcomer.*

DOYLE, Glenn
B 4.3.1965, Sydney, New South Wales, Australia.

EVITTS, Neil
25.9.1964, Birmingham, W. Midlands.

HAVELOCK, Robert Gary
B 4.11.1968, Eaglescliffe, Cleveland. *Returned after one year's suspension.*

LARNER, Bryan Patrick
B 6.6.1968, Bradford, West Yorkshire.

PARNABY, Stuart Graham
B 2.5.1970, Bradford, West Yorks.

SMITH, Andrew (Andy)
B 25.5.1966, York, North Yorkshire.

THORP, Paul
B 9.9.1964, Macclesfield, Cheshire.

Sting in the tail for the dizzy Bees

Track Data

Promoter: Charles Ochiltree (in Association with Midland Sports Stadiums Limited).
Address: Coventry Stadium, Rugby Road, Brandon, Near Coventry, CV8 3GJ.
Telephone: 0203-542395.
Clubcall: 0898 12 18 90.
Track Length: 335 metres.
Track Record: 61.3 secs, Peter Ravn (Denmark), June 29, 1983, heat 1, England v Denmark.

TOMMY KNUDSEN turned a wake into a Welcome Home! His comeback was a totally unexpected return at a time when Coventry were on the lookout for anything positive.

They were in the middle of the most depressing run of results in the club's British League history – five successive home League defeats and seven matches without a point – when Knudsen saw the surgeon who operated on his badly damaged back at the beginning of 1989 and was pronounced fit to resume his career.

It was a piece of news that had them dancing on the terraces at Brandon...but then in stepped Mr. Rule Book with the shock demand that if Knudsen did return to action then it would have to be at the expense of another of the Bees' top-liners.

He was told: "You have to go back to your old 1988 average." And, in Knudsen's case, that meant returning with an average higher than that of the World number one Hans Nielsen.

Coventry promoter Charles Ochiltree argued long and hard, took his battle to the Speedway Control Board but still didn't get any satisfaction and eventually had to accept the ruling and decide whether to risk Knudsen on his old average or wait another winter before he could strap on the fighting Bee race-jacket.

He opted for the sensible way out. He recalled Knudsen just in time for him to fit in six official fixtures (which means he starts next season with an advantageous 5.74 average) and to prove to himself that he is capable of making a successful comeback.

Knudsen took it easy in those matches (who could blame him?) but pointed out: "What pleased me was that in each of the six meeting I won a race. That proved to me that I can come back at the level I was."

To accommodate Knudsen, the popular Sean Wilson had to be sacrificed and he ended his season on loan to King's Lynn. That exposed yet another absurdity in some of the rules which governed team strength as Coventry had to release Wilson even though Andy Hackett was ruled out because of injury!

Just as Brandon fans were looking to the prospect of seeing Knudsen link up again at the top of the scorecard with his successor as captain, British Champion Kelvin Tatum, the England skipper stung the Bees by handing in a written transfer request.

He had been unhappy for much of the season – he felt Coventry had moved too slowly to cover for Tommy's long-term absence – and feels that his career is now at the stage where it needs fresh impetus after six summers with the Midlanders.

He had suffered the consequences of being left so isolated at the sharp end of the action for most of the season.

John Jorgensen climbed into the world's Top Twenty for the first time in his life and Rick Miller reached his first World Final.

But neither provided Tatum with the backing he desired and the rest of the team was a mish-mash of inconsistency with the club's only winter signing, 1989 Overseas Finalist Andy Phillips, having a disastrous run which prompted his retirement in the middle of August.

Roll of Honour

Seasons in British League: 26 (1965-1990).
British League Record: Champions (5), 1968, 1978, 1979, 1987, 1988. Runners-up (2), 1966, 1967. Third (5), 1965, 1970, 1971, 1983, 1985.
Speedway Star Cup Record: Winners (1), 1967. Runners-up (3), 1983, 1987, 1988.
League Cup Record: Winners (3), 1981, 1985, 1987. Runners-up (1), 1983.
Inter League Cup Record: Never competed in the competition.
Premiership: Winners (1), 1986. Runners-up (2), 1988, 1989.
Appearances: Nigel Boocock, 415 (1965-1976).
Points: Nigel Boocock, 4495.5 (1965-1976).
World Finalists: Nigel Boocock (1963-64-65, 1968-69, 1971-72), Rick France (1967), John Jorgensen (1988), Tommy Knudsen (1981, 1985-86), Jim Lightfoot (1963), Roman Matousek (1990), Ken McKinlay (1962, 1964), Rick Miller (1990), Ron Mountford (1962), Ole Olsen (1977-78-79, 1981, 1983), Jan Simensen (1972), Peo Söderman (1956), Jiri Stancl (1976), Kelvin Tatum (1985-86, 1988-89-90), Jack Young (1960), Henryk Zyto (1960).
BLRC Finalists: Nigel Boocock (1965-66-67-68, 1970-71-72, 1974), Garry Middleton (1973), Bob Valentine (1975), Ole Olsen (1976-77-78-79-80-81-82-83), Tommy Knudsen (1984-85-86-87-88), Kelvin Tatum (1985, 1987-88-89-90), John Jorgensen (1986, 1990), Rick Miller (1989).
Other Honours: National League (Division Two) Champions, 1953.

Star of 90

RICK MILLER

Coventry

COVENTRY

01...READING, March 31, L42-48

1 †Kelvin Tatum	3 1 1 3 3 R	11	1
2 §Andy Phillips	0 2 0 T	2	
3 John Jorgensen	3 3 2 1 2 2	13	2
4 Rick MIller	1 3 0 0 R	4	
5 Sean Wilson	F 0 T 2 3	5	
6 Roman Matousek	R R T 1	1	
7 Andy Hackett	2 1 T 3	6	

02...Reading, April 9, L44-46

1 †Kelvin Tatum	3 3 3 3 1 3 R	16	
2 Andy Phillips	0 0 0 N	0	
3 John Jorgensen	2 3 2 2 3 1	13	1
4 Rick Miller	*rider replacement*		
5 Sean Wilson	0 0 2 2 2	6	2
6 Roman Matousek	2 0 1 T 0 3	6	
7 Andy Hackett	1 1 0 1	3	2
8 Paul Bromwich	*did not ride*		

03...KING'S LYNN, April 14, W52-38

1 †Kelvin Tatum	3 2 3 2 3	13	
2 Andy Phillips	1 0 0 N	1	
3 John Jorgensen	3 1 2 3 0	9	
4 Todd Wiltshire	*3 3 3 1*	*10*	*1*
5 Sean Wilson	1 2 2 2	7	3
6 Roman Matousek	1 2 0 R	3	1
7 Andy Hackett	3 2 2 0 2	9	1

04...OXFORD, April 28, L43-46

1 †Kelvin Tatum	3 3 3 R R	9	
2 Andy Phillips	1 1 0 N	2	
3 John Jorgensen	3 3 2 3 2	13	
4 Rick Miller	0 2 2 2	6	
5 Sean Wilson	2 0 1 0	3	1
6 Roman Matousek	3 0 N 3 1 0 3	10	
7 Lee Coleman	0 0 N N 0	0	

05...CRADLEY HEATH, May 2, W46-44

1 †Kelvin Tatum	3 3 3 1 2	12	1
2 Andy Phillips	0 0 0 N	0	
3 John Jorgensen	2 3 3 3 1	12	1
4 Rick Miller	2 2 3 2	9	1
5 Sean Wilson	3 0 1 1	5	
6 Roman Matousek	3 fx 2 2 0 1	8	1
7 David Smart	*0 N 0 R*	*0*	

06...Belle Vue, May 11, L34-56

1 †Kelvin Tatum	1 1 0 0	2	
2 Andy Phillips	0 0 T T	0	
3 John Jorgensen	2 2 3 3 1	11	
4 Rick Miller	2 2 0 2 1 2	9	1
5 Sean Wilson	0 1 3 2 0 1	7	2
6 Lars Munkedal	*2 1 T 0*	*3*	*1*
7 Roman Matousek	1 0 0 1	2	1

07...SWINDON, May 12, D45-45

1 †Kelvin Tatum	3 3 3 3 0	12	
2 Andy Phillips	0 1 1 N	2	1
3 John Jorgensen	3 3 2 3 1	12	
4 Rick Miller	2 3 3 0	8	
5 Sean Wilson	0 R 0 0	0	
6 §§Paul Bromwich	0 0 N 0	0	
7 Roman Matousek	2 1 2 2 1 3	11	2

08...Bradford, May 19, W46-44

1 †Kelvin Tatum	**3 3 3 3 3**	**15**	
2 Andy Phillips	0 0 0 N	0	
3 John Jorgensen	2 3 2 3	10	
4 Rick Miller	1 3 2 R 0	6	
5 Sean Wilson	3 1 1 2	7	2
6 Richard Musson	*1 0 N 1*	*2*	*1*
7 Roman Matousek	2 0 1 R 0 3	6	

09...WOLVERHAMPTON, May 26, W52-38

1 †Kelvin Tatum	3 3 2 2 3	13	1
2 Andy Phillips	0 1 2 1	4	1
3 John Jorgensen	**3 3 3 3**	**12**	
4 Rick Miller	1 0 3 3 2	9	2
5 Sean Wilson	2 1 1 1	5	
6 Lee Coleman	1 N 0 0	1	
7 Andy Hackett	3 2 1 0 2	8	2

10...Swindon, June 2, L26-64

1 †Kelvin Tatum	3 2 2 2 1 2	12	
2 Rick Miller	*rider replacement*		
3 John Jorgensen	0 1 1 2 1 1	6	
4 Andy Hackett	1 0 0 1 R	2	1
5 Paul Bromwich	0 T N 0	0	
6 Andy Phillips	0 0 0 0 0	0	
7 Sean Wilson	3 0 R 2 0 1	6	

11...King's Lynn, June 23, D45-45

1 †Kelvin Tatum	**3 3 3 3 3**	**15**	
2 §§Andy Meredith	0 0 N N	0	
3 John Jorgensen	2 3 0 2	7	
4 Rick Miller	3 3 2 1 0	9	
5 Andy Hackett	E 0 0 0	0	
6 Andy Phillips	1 0 0 N 0 1	2	2
7 Sean Wilson	2 2 1 2 3 2	12	2

12...BELLE VUE, June 30, L34-56

1 †Kelvin Tatum	1 0 3 2	6	
2 Andy Meredith	0 T N 0	0	
3 John Jorgensen	1 1 2 N	4	
4 Rick Miller	1 3 0 1 0	5	
5 Andy Hackett	0 0 3 fx0	3	
6 Andy Phillips	2 0 T 1 1 1	5	3
7 Sean Wilson	3 2 2 1 2 1	11	1

13...Wolverhampton, July 9, L41-49

1 †Kelvin Tatum	1 3 3 0 3 2	12	
2 Andy Hackett	0 2 0 2	4	1
3 John Jorgensen	1 2 3 1	7	
4 Rick Miller	3 1 0 3 2 0	9	2
5 Sean Wilson	0 2 2 0	4	1
6 Andy Phillips	2 1 T 2	5	1
7 Roman Matousek	0 0 T 0	0	

14...Oxford, July 11, W48-42

1 †Kelvin Tatum	2 3 3 3 0	11	
2 Andy Hackett	fx0 0 N	0	
3 John Jorgensen	1 1 1 0	3	2
4 Rick Miller	1 1 1 1	4	2
5 Sean Wilson	2 2 3 3 3	13	
6 Andy Phillips	1 0 N 1	2	
7 Roman Matousek	3 2 3 2 2 3	15	1

15...WOLVERHAMPTON, July 14, L42-47

1 †Kelvin Tatum	0 0 3 3 2 2	10	1
2 Andy Hackett	1 1 0 T	2	
3 John Jorgensen	3 0 1 1 3	8	
4 Rick Miller	2 R 3 2 1 3	11	1
5 Sean Wilson	fxN T N	0	
6 Roman Matousek	3 2 2 0 X 3	10	1
7 Andy Phillips	R 1 T 0	1	

16...BRADFORD, July 28, L44-46

1 †Kelvin Tatum	3 0 3 3 2 3	14	
2 Andy Hackett	0 1 2 0	3	
3 John Jorgensen	3 2 3 0 2	10	2
4 Rick Miller	2 0 1 1	4	2
5 Sean Wilson	1 1 2 1	5	1
6 Roman Matousek	1 R T 3	4	
7 Andy Phillips	3 0 0 1	4	

Tatum beat Cox for bonus point.

17...Bradford, August 4, L41-47

1 †Kelvin Tatum	3 2 3 3 3 2	16	
2 Roman Matousek	R 1 1 T	2	1
3 John Jorgensen	2 2 3 1 1	9	
4 Rick Miller	3 2 R 1 0	6	1
5 Sean Wilson	0 3 1 T	4	
6 Andy Meredith	2 E N N 0	2	
7 Andy Hackett	N N 0 0 N 2	2	

18...Reading, August 6, L41-49

1 †Kelvin Tatum	3 3 3 3 1 1	14	1
2 Roman Matousek	0 0 T N	0	
3 John Jorgensen	1 1 E 1	3	1
4 Rick Miller	2 1 2 2 3 2	12	2
5 Sean Wilson	1 2 1 1 2	7	2
6 Lee Coleman	0 0 T 0	0	
7 Andy Hackett	3 0 0 0 2	5	

19...BELLE VUE, August 11, L43-45

1 Mark Loram	*2 1 2 1*	*6*	
2 Carl Stonehewer	*1 3 X 0*	*4*	*1*
3 †John Jorgensen	2 2 2 3 3	12	
4 Alan Grahame	*E 2 3 0*	*5*	
5 Sean Wilson	3 R 1 1 0	5	
6 Andy Hackett	3 1 1 0 R	5	2
7 Andy Phillips	2 0 2 N 2	6	1

20...Belle Vue, August 17, L39-51

1 †Kelvin Tatum	1 3 1 3 N	8	1
2 Roman Matousek	0 F 1 2	3	1
3 John Jorgensen	1 2 3 2 2 0	10	
4 Rick Miller	0 3 2 2	7	
5 Sean Wilson	1 1 1 R 1	4	1
6 Andy Hackett	2 0 T 1 3	6	1
7 Andy Phillips	1 0 T 0	1	1

21...READING, August 18, L43-47

1 Kelvin Tatum	*rider replacement*		
2 Roman Matousek	0 2 2 3 3 1	11	1
3 †John Jorgensen	2 1 1 0 T	4	1
4 Rick Miller	1 2 0 1 0	4	
5 Sean Wilson	R 2 3 3 1 1	10	
6 Andy Hackett	3 X 2 2 3 3	13	
7 Andy Phillips	1 R N 0	1	
8 Lee Coleman	*did not ride*		

22...Cradley Heath, August 27, W47-43

1 †Kelvin Tatum	3 2 3 3 2 2	15	2
2 Roman Matousek	1 1 1 1	4	1
3 John Jorgensen	3 3 1 0	7	
4 Rick Miller	1 3 3 3 3	13	
5 Sean Wilson	0 0 1 1	2	
6 Andy Meredith	0 0 T 0	0	
7 Andy Hackett	2 1 0 3	6	

23...CRADLEY HEATH, August 27, D45-45

1 †Kelvin Tatum	3 3 1 R 3 1	11	
2 Roman Matousek	0 1 T T	1	
3 John Jorgensen	1 2 3 3 3 3	15	
4 Rick Miller	2 2 3 1 2	10	1
5 Sean Wilson	1 0 0 1	2	1
6 Andy Hackett	3 R N 0 3	6	
7 Andy Meredith	0 0 N T F	0	

24...Wolverhampton, September 10, L44-46

1 †Kelvin Tatum	1 3 2 0	6	
2 Roman Matousek	0 1 2 1	4	1
3 John Jorgensen	1 2 0 3 F	6	
4 Rick Miller	3 2 3 1 1	10	
5 Sean Wilson	2 1 2 2	7	4
6 Andy Meredith	F 1 N 0	1	1
7 Andy Hackett	3 0 1 3 3	10	1

25...BRADFORD, September 22, W46-44

1 †Kelvin Tatum	3 3 1 3 3 2	15	1
2 Roman Matousek	R 0 3 0	3	
3 John Jorgensen	2 3 1 3 3	12	
4 Rick Miller	0 3 0 2	5	1
5 Sean Wilson	1 1 1 0	3	
6 Andy Hackett	2 1 N 2 2	7	2
7 Andy Meredith	1 0 N T 0	1	1

26...King's Lynn, September 23, L40-50

1 †Kelvin Tatum	2 3 3 0 2 1	11	2
2 Roman Matousek	0 0 0 2	2	
3 John Jorgensen	3 2 1 0	6	
4 Rick Miller	3 2 3 3 3 2	16	
5 Sean Wilson	1 1 0 1	3	1
6 Andy Meredith	0 0 N fx	0	
7 Andy Hackett	1 fxN N	1	
8 Lee Coleman	1	1	

27....Oxford, September 28, L38-51

1 †Kelvin Tatum	0 2 3 3 3 0	11	
2 Roman Matousek	2 X fxX	2	
3 John Jorgensen	1 2 1 3 2 1	10	2
4 Rick Miller	2 2 1 3 0	8	
5 Tommy Knudsen	0 0 T T	0	
6 Andy Meredith	0 0 2 T 1	3	
7 Andy Hackett	2 2 N N	4	
8 Lee Coleman	F	0	

28...KING'S LYNN, October 3, W58-32

1 †Kelvin Tatum	**2 3 2 2 3**	**12**	**3**
2 Roman Matousek	**3 2 3 3 2**	**13**	**2**
3 John Jorgensen	0 2 3 3	8	
4 Tommy Knudsen	3 1 2 3	9	
5 Sean Wilson	1 0 0 1	2	
6 Peter Karlsson	*3 3 0 2 2*	*10*	*2*
7 Andy Meredith	0 N 1 3	4	

29...Swindon, October 6, L36-54

1 †Kelvin Tatum	2 1 1 fx	4	1
2 Roman Matousek	0 2 1 R	3	
3 John Jorgensen	3 2 3 1 2 3	14	
4 Rick Miller	2 1 0 3	6	
5 Tommy Knudsen	0 3 3 E 0	6	
6 Lee Coleman	1 0 0 0	1	
7 Andy Meredith	0 1 T 0 1	2	

30...Cradley Heath, October 10, W49-41

1 †Kelvin Tatum	3 3 3 0 3	12	
2 Roman Matousek	2 1 3 2 2	10	3
3 John Jorgensen	2 3 1 3	9	
4 Rick Miller	3 0 1 1	5	1
5 Tommy Knudsen	1 3 2 0	6	
6 Andy Meredith	2 0 N N 1	3	1
7 Bohumil Brhel	*fxN R 2 0 2*	*4*	*1*

31...OXFORD, October 13, W48-42

1 †Kelvin Tatum	2 3 3 3 2	13	
2 Roman Matousek	1 2 3 2 1	9	4
3 John Jorgensen	3 2 3 1	9	
4 Rick Miller	1 X 2 0	3	
5 Tommy Knudsen	3 2 0 0	5	
6 Peter Karlsson	*3 0 0 2 3*	*8*	*1*
7 Andy Meredith	F N 0 1	1	

32...SWINDON, October 20, L44-46

1 †Kelvin Tatum	1 3 3 3 1	11	1
2 Roman Matousek	0 2 3 2 2	9	2
3 John Jorgensen	2 2 1 2	7	1
4 Rick Miller	R 3 3 1 2	9	2
5 Tommy Knudsen	3 0 2 1	6	1
6 Lee Coleman	0 0 T 1	1	
7 Andy Meredith	1 fx0 fx	1	

'90 ROSTER

BROMWICH, Paul Richard
B 26.8.1973, Coventry, W. Midlands. *Local junior.*

CLARENCE, Christopher
B 16.4.1973, Marston Green, West Midlands. *Local junior.*

COLEMAN, Lee John
B 6.12.1971, Leicester, Leics.

HACKETT, Andrew Justin
B 6.3.1970, Halesowen, West Midlands.

JORGENSEN, John
B 18.7.1962, Middelfart, Denmark.

KNUDSEN, Tommy
B 9.11.1961, Roager, Denmark. *Back from injury.*

MATOUSEK, Roman
B 23.5.1964, Slany, Czechoslovakia.

MEREDITH, Andrew Colin
B 28.12.1973, Bradford, W. Yorks. *Local junior.*

MILLER, Richard Leonard
B 12.1.1961, Reseda, Ca., USA.

PHILLIPS, Andrew David (Andy)
B 10.10.1968, Worcester, Hereford & Worcester. *On loan from Wolverhampton.*

TATUM, Kelvin Martin
B 8.2.1964, Epsom, Surrey.

WILSON, Sean
B 7.11.1969, York, North Yorkshire. *Loaned to King's Lynn.*

Heathens get all the bad breaks

Track Data

Promoters: Derek Pugh and Colin Pratt.
Address: Cradley Heath Stadium Limited, Dudley Wood Road, Dudley, West Midlands, DY2 0DH.
Telephone: 0384-69008/66604.
Clubcall: 0898 12 18 78.
Track Length: 338 metres.
Track Record: 60.7 secs, Hans Nielsen (Oxford), July 18, 1990, Heat 2, SpeedwayCall Golden Hammer.

COLIN PRATT did just about everything at Dudley Wood during 1990. He looked after the track, he handled all the administration, he acted as team manager – and for a spell he resumed his old role as the Cradley Heath skipper.

In fact the only thing he didn't do for the Heathens was get on a bike and race again – but there were times when he must have given it serious consideration!

After a traumatic 1989 in which Cradley Heath's world fell apart, no-one believed that the Black Country club could face another troublesome season. Yet, if it was possible, 1990 provided as much, if not more, ill luck than the previous year.

Number one Jan O. Pedersen missed the last 18 League matches with a broken arm that also kept him out of the Odsal World Final.

Number two Simon Cross spent a fortnight in a German clinic after breaking a couple of bones in his back in the World Pairs Final and rode in only 14 of the club's 32 Sunbrite League matches.

Number three Billy Hamill was marked absent five times in a sizzling debut season in Britain. Number five Gert Handberg missed a handful of early season Gold Cup matches after coming off in a practice session. Number six Greg Hancock smashed his arm in a run-off in the American Final and had to sit out 14 League matches, most of them at a time when both Pedersen and Cross were also sidelined.

And Mark Robinson, who used to help cover the greyhound track for meetings, took a knock or two in his first real stab at holding down a regular team-place after being offered the number seven race-jacket at the beginning of the season.

Only one rider, evergreen Alan Grahame, came through the season unscathed and things got so bad for the team that, at one stage, Pratt had to take over the captaincy as no-one else wanted it after a catalogue of misfortune for the incumbent.

If, as many people claim, green is an unlucky colour then perhaps it is time that the Heathens swapped their traditional colours for something a little less fateful!

Somehow battered pride and a shrewd long-term guest policy kept Cradley off the bottom of the Sunbrite League and for those who believe that speedway can do without guests under any circumstances then the supporters of the replacement regulation must ask: "What would have happened to Cradley without guests?"

It's a question that begs only one answer – the track's whole future would have been in question as they experienced the sort of season that should be reserved for nightmares.

Despite their problems, Cradley soldiered on and actually ended another painful season by winning three out of their last four matches, including a 14 point away win at Swindon.

Before then they had lost their proud unbeaten Speedway Star Knock Out Cup record with defeat in the second round at Bradford being the club's first overall loss since going down to Ipswich in the 1985 semi-final.

And they finished out of the top three for the first time in five seasons at the end of their worst season since they were bottom of the table in 1973!

Yet it could, and possibly should, have been even worse....

Roll of Honour

Seasons in British League: 26 (1965-1990).
British League Record: Champions (2), 1981, 1983. Runners-up (3), 1982, 1986, 1987. Third (4), 1979, 1984, 1988, 1989.
Speedway Star Cup Record: Winners (7*), 1979, 1980, 1982, 1983, 1987, 1988, 1989. Joint Winners (1), 1986. Runners-up (1), 1971.
League Cup Record: Winners (2*), 1982, 1984. Joint winners (1), 1986.
Inter League Cup Record: Winners (1), 1979. Runners-up (1), 1977.
Gold Cup: Runners-up (1), 1989.
Premiership: Winners (6), 1982, 1984, 1985, 1988, 1989, 1990. Losers (1), 1983.
Appearances: Alan Grahame, 504 (1978-1985, 1987-1990).
Points: Erik Gundersen, 4858.5 (1979-1989).
World Finalists: Phil Collins (1983), Simon Cross (1987), Alan Grahame (1984), Erik Gundersen (1981, 1983-84-85-86-87-88-89), Lance King (1983-84), Anders Michanek (1977), Jan O. Pedersen (1985-86-87-88), Bruce Penhall (1980-81-82), Bernt Persson (1971-72-73, 1975, 1977).
BLRC Finalists: George Major (1965), Brian Brett (1967), Roy Trigg (1968-69), Bernt Persson (1970, 1972), Howard Cole (1973), John Boulger (1974-75-76), Steve Bastable (1978), Bruce Penhall (1979-80-81), Erik Gundersen (1982-83-84-85-86-87-88), Phil Collins (1985), Jan O. Pedersen (1986-87-88), Alan Grahame (1989), Greg Hancock (1990).
Other Honours: Provincial League Cup Winners, 1961, 1963.

Star of 90

BILLY HAMILL

Cradley Heath

CRADLEY HEATH

01...BELLE VUE, April 28, W53-37

1 Jan O. Pedersen	3 3 2 2 2	12	2
2 Gert Handberg	0 1 1 3	5	1
3 †Simon Cross	3 3 3 1 1	11	2
4 Alan Grahame	0 0 0 3	3	
5 §§Billy Hamill	2 3 2 2	9	
6 Greg Hancock	3 2 1 2 3	11	1
7 §§Mark Robinson	1 N 0 1	2	

02...Coventry, May 2, L44-46

1 Jan O. Pedersen	2 3 2 2 3	12	
2 Gert Handberg	1 1 1 1	4	2
3 †Simon Cross	3 1 2 3 R	9	1
4 Alan Grahame	1 1 2 0	4	
5 Billy Hamill	0 0 1 R	1	1
6 Greg Hancock	2 2 3 0 3	10	
7 Mark Robinson	1 1 N 2	4	2

03...READING, May 12, W52-38

1 Jan O. Pedersen	2 3 3 3 2	13	1
2 Gert Handberg	3 0 0 1	4	
3 †Simon Cross	3 3 2 2	10	
4 Alan Grahame	0 1 2 1	4	1
5 Billy Hamill	3 3 3 1 1	11	2
6 Greg Hancock	2 2 0 1 3	8	1
7 Mark Robinson	0 N 1 1	2	1

04...Reading, May 14, L33-57

1 Jan O. Pedersen	1 3 3 1 3	11	
2 Gert Handberg	E 1 0 0	1	
3 †Simon Cross	3 2 2 0 1 2	10	1
4 Alan Grahame	0 T 0 0	0	
5 Billy Hamill	3 N 1 1 2 1	8	1
6 Greg Hancock	F N 0 0 T 2	2	
7 Mark Robinson	1 R T F	1	

05...King's Lynn, May 19, L42-48

1 Jan O. Pedersen	2 3 3 3 2 2	15	1
2 Gert Handberg	0 1 1 0	2	
3 †Simon Cross	3 3 2 2 0	10	1
4 Alan Grahame	0 0 2 3	5	
5 Greg Hancock	3 1 3 1 0	8	1
6 David Mullett	*R 0 T 1*	*1*	
7 Mark Robinson	1 0 T R	1	

06...Oxford,May 25, L38-52

1 Jan O. Pedersen	*rider replacement*		
2 Alan Grahame	1 0 N 1	2	1
3 †Simon Cross	fx3 3 2 2 1 3	14	1
4 Gert Handberg	0 2 0 1	3	
5 Billy Hamill	2 3 1 R 2 2 0	10	1
6 Greg Hancock	3 0 3 R 0 3	9	
7 Mark Robinson	0 0 N 0	0	

07...OXFORD, May 26, L41-49

1 Jan O. Pedersen	1 3 3 3 0	10	
2 Gert Handberg	0 1 2 0	3	1
3 †Simon Cross	3 3 2 1 1	10	
4 Alan Grahame	1 0 0 N	1	1
5 Billy Hamill	2 3 3 F	8	
6 Greg Hancock	3 1 0 3 0 2	9	
7 Mark Robinson	R N R 0	0	

08...SWINDON, May 28, W53-37

1 Jan O. Pedersen	2 3 3 3 2	13	1
2 Gert Handberg	3 0 1 1	5	1
3 †Simon Cross	2 3 3 3 0	11	1
4 Alan Grahame	2 0 1 2	5	1
5 Billy Hamill	fx3 3 0	6	
6 Greg Hancock	3 3 1 2 3	12	
7 Mark Robinson	0 N 1 0	1	

09...Swindon, May 28, L44-46

1 Jan O. Pedersen	3 3 2 R 2	10	1
2 Gert Handberg	0 2 fxR	2	1
3 †Simon Cross	3 2 X 2 3	10	1
4 Alan Grahame	2 2 1 1	6	1
5 Billy Hamill	0 R 2 1	3	1
6 Greg Hancock	2 3 3 3 2	13	
7 Mark Robinson	0 0 N 0	0	

10...WOLVERHAMPTON, June 23, W47-43

1 Jan O. Pedersen	3 2 3 3 1	12	
2 Gert Handberg	1 1 fxN	2	1
3 †Simon Cross	3 F N N	3	
4 Billy Hamill	0 0 1 0	1	
5 Per Jonsson	*3 2 3 3 0*	*11*	
6 Alan Grahame	**3 N 3 3 3 3**	**15**	
7 Mark Robinson	0 1 N 1 1 0 fx	3	

11...Wolverhampton, June 25, L43-47

1 Jan O. Pedersen	3 0 fx3 3	9	
2 Sean Wilson	*2 1 3 3*	*9*	*1*
3 †Simon Cross	3 3 3 2	11	
4 Billy Hamill	3 3 2 2 0	10	1
5 §§Gary Frankum	F 0 N N	0	
6 Alan Grahame	2 0 1 0 0 1	4	
7 §§David Haynes	R 0 N R 0	0	

Pedersen beat Correy for bonus point

12...Belle Vue, July 6, L43-47

1 Jan O. Pedersen	2 3 3 2 1 1	12	
2 Greg Hancock	*rider replacement*		
3 †Simon Cross	1 3 E 3 3 3	13	1
4 Billy Hamill	2 2 2 1 3 1	11	1
5 Alan Grahame	1 1 0 0 T	2	2
6 David Haynes	0 R N 0	0	
7 Gert Handberg	1 2 1 0 0 1	5	1
8 Mark Meredith	*did not ride*		

13...READING, July 7, L42.5-47.5

1 Jan O. Pedersen	2 3 2 0 0	7	1
2 Greg Hancock	*rider replacement*		
3 †Simon Cross	3 3 2 3 2 1	14	
4 Alan Grahame	2 1.5 0 2 1 3	9.5	
5 Billy Hamill	fxR 1 0	1	1
6 David Haynes	0 0 0	0	
7 Gert Handberg	3 1 1 2 1 3	11	1
8 Mark Robinson	*did not ride*		

14...Reading, July 9, W46-44

1 Jan O. Pedersen	3 3 1 3 2	12	
2 Alan Grahame	0 0 0 3	3	
3 †Simon Cross	3 3 3 2 1	12	1
4 Billy Hamill	3 0 0 1	4	
5 Jimmy Nilsen	*2 2 1 N*	*5*	*1*
6 Mark Robinson	1 0 N 1	2	1
7 Gert Handberg	2 0 3 0 0 3	8	

15...BELLE VUE, August 18, L38-52

1 Martin Dugard	*3 1 1 1 2 0*	*8*	*2*
2 Greg Hancock	*rider replacement*		
3 Alan Grahame	0 2 1 0 0	3	1
4 Billy Hamill	R 1 2 2 0	5	
5 Troy Butler	*3 R 1 1 2*	*7*	*1*
6 Mark Robinson	1 0 N R	1	
7 Gert Handberg	3 2 2 3 1 3	14	

16...KING'S LYNN, August 25, W53-37

1 Simon Wigg	***3 3 3 3 3 3***	***18***	
2 Greg Hancock	*rider replacement*		
3 Alan Grahame	2 2 3 1 3 2	13	3
4 Tony Olsson	*fxN N N*	*0*	
5 Billy Hamill	3 3 1 2 0	9	
6 Mark Robinson	2 0 0 0 0 1	3	1
7 Gert Handberg	3 0 1 1 2 3	10	

17...COVENTRY, August 27, L43-47

1 Chris Morton	*2 2 2 2 1*	*9*	*1*
2 Alan Grahame	0 1 2 0	3	2
3 Sam Ermolenko	*R 2 F N*	*2*	
4 Bobby Ott	*3 F R 3 0*	*6*	
5 Billy Hamill	2 3 2 1	8	1
6 Mark Robinson	1 2 N 1	4	1
7 Gert Handberg	3 1 3 2 0 2	11	1

18...Coventry, August 27, D45-45

1 Gary Havelock	*1 1 3 2 2 0*	*9*	*1*
2 Greg Hancock	*rider replacement*		
3 Alan Grahame	2 2 2 2 1 2	11	1
4 Billy Hamill	3 3 3 1 0	10	1
5 Paul Thorp	*R 1 2 0*	*3*	
6 Mark Robinson	1 0 N 1	2	2
7 Gert Handberg	2 3 2 1 fx2	10	2
8 David Haynes	*did not ride*		

19...Belle Vue, September 7, L35-55

1 Marvyn Cox	*1 2 0 3 2 2*	*10*	*1*
2 Sean Wilson	*2 0 1 T*	*3*	
3 Gary Havelock	*0 2 3 0 3 1*	*9*	*1*
4 Alan Grahame	1 1 0 N	2	1
5 Billy Hamill	F 1 2 2 0	5	1
6 Mark Robinson	1 T T 1 1	3	1
7 Andy Hackett	*R 3 F 0*	*3*	

20...WOLVERHAMPTON,Sept. 8, W53-37

1 Kelvin Tatum	*3 2 3 3 3 3*	*17*	
2 Greg Hancock	*rider replacement*		
3 John Jorgensen	*2 1 3 2 3*	*11*	*2*
4 Alan Grahame	0 2 2 2 2 1	9	4
5 Billy Hamill	2 3 1 3 1	10	1
6 Mark Robinson	0 N 0 1	1	
7 Gert Handberg	2 R 0 3 R	5	

21...BRADFORD, September 12, W58-32

1 Jimmy Nilsen	***3 2 3 2 2***	***12***	***3***
2 Alan Grahame	1 2 2 1 3 2	11	1
3 Todd Wiltshire	*0 2 2 3 3*	*10*	*2*
4 Greg Hancock	*rider replacement*		
5 Billy Hamill	3 3 3 3 2 1	15	2
6 Mark Robinson	1 1 N 1 0 1	4	1
7 Gert Handberg	3 3 fnN N	6	
8 Scott Smith	*did not ride*		
9 David Haynes	0	0	

22...Oxford, September 21, L42-48

1 Jimmy Nilsen	*3 3 2 3 3 1*	*15*	
2 Greg Hancock	*rider replacement*		
3 Marvyn Cox	*0 3 2 3 1 0*	*9*	
4 Alan Grahame	3 1 1 1 0	6	
5 Billy Hamill	1 1 3 F 0	5	
6 Mark Robinson	3 1 N 0 0 2	6	
7 David Haynes	0 N 0 N 1	1	1
8 Scott Smith	*did not ride*		

23...OXFORD, September 22, L39-51

1 Chris Morton	*2 2 1 2*	*7*	*1*
2 Alan Grahame	1 1 3 2 1	8	2
3 Shawn Moran	*2 2 3 2 0*	*9*	
4 Kelly Moran	*2 1 0 0*	*3*	
5 Billy Hamill	1 3 2 0	6	1
6 Mark Robinson	2 fx0 0	2	
7 Wayne Carter	*1 1 0 2*	*4*	*1*

25...Wolverhampton, October 1, L36-54

1 Kelvin Tatum	*2 3 2 1 0*	*8*	
2 Greg Hancock	0 0 1 0	1	
3 Billy Hamill	2 2 3 3 2 1	13	
4 Alan Grahame	3 1 1 0	5	1
5 Sean Wilson	*1 3 2 0*	*6*	
6 Mark Robinson	0 0 N 0	0	
7 Gert Handberg	1 0 T 0 2	3	

26...Bradford, October 4, L43-47

1 Leigh Adams	*2 1 1 0*	*4*	
2 Greg Hancock	0 3 1 F	4	
3 Mark Loram	*3 3 3 2 2*	*13*	*1*
4 †Alan Grahame	1 1 1 2 3	8	2
5 Neil Collins	*2 0 2 1*	*5*	*1*
6 Mark Robinson	F N 0 0	0	
7 Gert Handberg	2 2 0 3 2	9	1

27...BRADFORD, October 7, W48-42

1 Per Jonsson	*2 3 3 2 2*	*12*	
2 Greg Hancock	0 1 3 0	4	
3 Todd Wiltshire	*3 2 1 1*	*7*	*1*
4 Alan Grahame	1 2 1 1	5	2
5 Peter Ravn	*0 3 3 0*	*6*	
6 Mark Robinson	0 2 0 1	3	1
7 Gert Handberg	3 2 2 3 1	11	2

28...COVENTRY, October 10, L41-49

1 Jimmy Nilsen	*1 2 3 2 1*	*9*	
2 Greg Hancock	0 1 1 N	2	1
3 Jeremy Doncaster	*3 2 1 3 0*	*9*	
4 Alan Grahame	2 0 3 1	6	1
5 Sean Wilson	*R 2 2 2*	*6*	*2*
6 Mark Robinson	1 1 N 0	2	
7 Gert Handberg	3 1 X 0 0 3	7	1

29...King's Lynn, October 11, L43-47

1 Martin Dugard	*2 2 1 3 R*	*8*	*1*
2 Greg Hancock	0 0 T 1	1	
3 Marvyn Cox	*3 2 3 3 3 3*	*17*	
4 Alan Grahame	2 2 2 1 3 1	11	
5 Dean Barker	*0 1 0 T*	*1*	*1*
6 Mark Robinson	0 T 0 0	0	
7 Gert Handberg	1 0 2 2	5	1

30...Swindon, October 13, W52-38

1 Kelly Moran	*1 1 2 3*	*7*	*1*
2 Greg Hancock	fx0 R N	0	
3 Ronnie Correy	*3 3 3 1*	*10*	*1*
4 Alan Grahame	3 3 1 0 3	10	
5 Billy Hamill	2 2 3 2 1	10	2
6 Mark Robinson	0 0 N 0	0	
7 Gert Handberg	3 2 3 1 3 3	15	1

31...Bradford, October 17, L40-50

1 John Jorgensen	*2 1 2 2*	*7*	
2 Greg Hancock	0 0 1 N	1	
3 Leigh Adams	*2 1 3 0 2*	*8*	*1*
4 Alan Grahame	2 1 0 1	4	2
5 Billy Hamill	0 2 3 2 0	7	
6 Mark Robinson	1 0 N X	1	
7 Gert Handberg	3 3 3 0 R 3	12	

32...KING'S LYNN, October 20, W47-43

1 Billy Hamill	fx3 3 2 2	10	1
2 Greg Hancock	1 1 3 1	6	
3 Jeremy Doncaster	*2 3 2 3*	*10*	
4 Alan Grahame	1 2 1 1	5	3
5 Per Jonsson	*3 3 2 2 3*	*13*	*1*
6 §§Scott Smith	0 N 0 0	0	
7 Gert Handberg	1 1 0 0 1	3	1

Jonsson beat Löfqvist for bonus point

24...SWINDON, October 24, W48-42

1 Kelvin Tatum	*2 3 1 2 0*	*8*	*2*
2 Greg Hancock	0 1 0 N	1	
3 Todd Wiltshire	*3 2 2 R*	*7*	
4 †Alan Grahame	**3 3 3 3 3**	**15**	
5 Billy Hamill	1 0 2 1	4	1
6 Mark Robinson	0 N E 0 2	2	1
7 Gert Handberg	3 2 0 1 2 N3	11	1

▲ Where no captain is indicated Colin Pratt also acted as team captain.

'90 ROSTER

BOSTIN, John
B 23.2.1962, Stourbridge, W.Mids.
Loaned to Oxford.

CHILD, Dean Russell
B 2.11.1969, Morley, West Yorkshire.
Junior.

CROSS, Simon James
B 31.5.1965, Hereford, Hereford & Worcs.

FRANKUM, Gary
B 31.12.1964, Exeter, Devon.

GRAHAME, Alan William
B 5.2.1954, Birmingham, W. Mids.

HAMILL, William Gordon (Billy)
B 23.5.1970, San Marino, Ca., U.S.A.
American newcomer.

HANCOCK, Gregory Alan
B 3.6.1970, Whittier, Ca., U.S.A.

HANDBERG, Gert
B 30.5.1969, Brastrup, Denmark.

HAYNES, David
B 4.11.1969, Nuneaton, Warwickshire.

MEREDITH, Mark Stephen
B 11.2.1974, Krefeld, West Germany.
Local junior.

PEDERSEN, Jan Osvald
B 9.11.1962, Middlefart, Denmark.

ROBINSON, Mark
B 7.2.1968, Cradley Heath, W. Mids.

SMITH, Scott Anthony
B 29.9.1972, Sheffield, S. Yorkshire.
Signed from Sheffield.

Stars look to a bright new future ahead

Track Data

Promoters: William C. Barker.
Address: The Stadium, Saddlebow Road, King's Lynn, Norfolk, PE34 3AG.
Telephone: 0553-771111.
Hotline: 0898 800 644.
Track Length: 342 metres.
Track Record: 608. secs, Hans Nielsen (Oxford), July 1, 1989, Heat 5, Barum Individual Trophy.

WHEN you finish bottom of the Sunbrite League for the fifth time in six years there shouldn't be too much room for glowing optimism.

But King's Lynn fans ended 1990 in happier mood than they have been for many, many years. The reasons were threefold.

NUMBER ONE: the superb first season-long performances of £20,000 buy Mark Loram who came close to regular full England status in his first full campaign back in the First Division.

NUMBER TWO: the late season capture of World Finalist and Swedish sensation Henrik Gustafsson with a promise that he will be back in 1991.

NUMBER THREE: The Speedway Control Board decision to allow former World Champion Michael Lee to resume his racing career in 1991 back in the colours of his old club.

Those three unrelated events guaranteed a happy Christmas for all Zetor Stars fans as they eagerly look forward to a prosperous on-track future.

Loram edged out Richard Knight as the club number one and, indirectly, convinced the club that their former skipper could talke to newcomers Berwick; Gustafsson came storming in to make his late season debut and to score 39 points in five matches; and Lee proved that he is a reformed character by paying his own way to all but one of the club's League matches even though he was still suspended from taking out a British licence.

Since Bill Barker took over as promoter at the East Anglian track he has campaigned in his own unique style to win over the fans and he seems to be winning that particular battle. Certainly he escaped the hysterical criticism that one of two other track bosses faced over team affairs and the crowd remained loyal to the club despite the sequence of poor results which has seen them finish in the bottom three for each of the last six years.

There were other factors that brought satisfaction. Bohumil Brhel had a nightmarish start to his British career and was on the verge of being told to pack up all his belongings and head back to Prague when he suddenly found his feet and began scoring well, particularly when down at reserve. Dennis Löfqvist reached his first World Final (as a late replacement reserve) and, like the Czech, revelled in one of the reserve roles.

His problem was translating the sort of form which brought him a string of double figure scores when in that position to a place in the top five where, generally, he struggled to win a race. It was an odd contradiction as riders he could comfortably defeat when wearing the number seven race jacket were constantly his betters when he was in the main body of the side!

Gary Hicks, signed on loan from Belle Vue amidst opposition from Reading, had an unhappy second season in Britain and was plagued by injuries which kept him out. He damaged a knee competing in the World Under 21 Championship which not only ended his progress in that competition but also kept him out for weeks, and after his return he was again sidelined with shoulder problems.

He never really settled into his new life away from the North West and was finally replaced by another loanee signing Sean Wilson.

Another disappointment was Stephen Davies who survived a workshop accident when he swallowed methanol and had to be treated at hospital. Like Brhel and Löfqvist he found it too difficult to maintain his scoring rate when in the top five.

Roll of Honour

Seasons in British League: 25 (1966-1990).
British League Record: Third (2), 1972, 1973.
Speedway Star Cup Record: Winners (1), 1977. Runners-up (1), 1976.
League Cup Record: Runners-up (1), 1981.
Inter League Cup Record: Winners (2), 1978, 1980. Runners-up (1), 1979.
Appearances: Terry Betts, 471 (1966-1978).
Points: Terry Betts, 5017.5 (1966-1978).
World Finalists: Terry Betts (1974), Armando Castagna (1985), Howard Cole (1969), John Cook (1987), John Davis (1988), Dave Jessup (1979-80-81), Richard Knight (1990), Michael Lee (1977-78-79-80-81).
BLRC Finalists: Terry Betts (1966-67-68-69-70-71-72, 1974-75-76), Malcolm Simmons (1973), Michael Lee (1977-78-79-80), Dave Jessup (1981, 1985), Billy Sanders (1982), John Louis (1983-84), Andy Campbell (1986), Richard Knight (1987-88-89), Lance King (1989), Mark Loram (1990).

Star of 90

DENNIS LÖFQVIST

King's Lynn

KING'S LYNN

01..Coventry, April 14, L38-52
1 †Richard Knight 2 0 N N 2
2 Stephen Davies 0 1 1 1 3
3 §§Bohumil Brhel 1 1 0 0 2
4 Tony Olsson 2 3 N 1 0 2 8
5 §Gary Hicks R 2 0 3 1 6 2
6 Mark Loram 2 3 3 1 1 10
7 Dennis Löfqvist 0 0 T 3 1 3 7

02...BRADFORD, April 16, W52-38
1 †Richard Knight 1 1 N 3 3 8 1
2 Stephen Davies R 2 1 N 3
3 Bohumil Brhel 3 0 3 1 7 1
4 Leigh Adams 1 2 2 1 6 1
5 Gary Hicks 2 0 1 N 3 1
6 Mark Loram 3 2 2 3 2 3 15 1
7 Dennis Löfqvist 2 3 1 1 2 1 10 2

03...Belle Vue, May 4, W46-43
1 †Richard Knight 3 0 3 2 F 8 1
2 Bohumil Brhel R N 0 N 0
3 Stephen Davies 1 2 2 0 1 6 1
4 Alan Grahame 0 2 N N 2 1
5 Gary Hicks 1 3 F 1 5
6 Mark Loram 2 3 R 1 2 3 11 2
7 Dennis Löfqvist 1 2 3 3 3 2 14 2

04...OXFORD, May 12, D45-45
1 †Richard Knight 3 2 0 2 0 7 1
2 Bohumil Brhel 0 1 N N 1 1
3 Stephen Davies 1 1 1 0 3 1
4 Joe Screen 1 2 1 3 7
5 Gary Hicks 0 0 0 N 0
6 Mark Loram 3 3 3 2 3 1 15 1
7 Dennis Löfqvist 2 3 3 2 1 1 12 1

05...CRADLEY HEATH, May 19, W48-42
1 †Richard Knight 3 2 3 3 3 14
2 Bohumil Brhel 1 1 2 0 4 1
3 Stephen Davies 1 2 1 1 5 3
4 Todd Wiltshire 1 2 0 N 3 1
5 Gary Hicks 2 R 1 N 3
6 Mark Loram 2 2 3 1 3 1 12 1
7 Dennis Löfqvist 3 0 2 0 2 7 1

06...Bradford, May 26, L33-57
1 †Richard Knight 0 1 1 2 1 0 5
2 Bohumil Brhel 1 0 1 N 2
3 Stephen Davies 2 1 1 0 T 1 5 2
4 Joe Screen 1 2 1 1 0 5 1
5 Gary Hicks 0 T 0 T 0
6 Mark Loram 3 2 3 1 3 2 14
7 Dennis Löfqvist 0 1 N 1 2 2

07...BRADFORD, May 28, L42-48
1 †Richard Knight 3 1 1 2 3 1 11 1
2 Bohumil Brhel 0 N 0 N 0
3 Stephen Davies 2 2 0 0 4
4 Sean Wilson 0 2 3 2 0 7 1
5 Gary Hicks 3 0 T 2 5
6 Mark Loram 3 1 1 3 2 R 10 2
7 Dennis Löfqvist 2 0 1 N 2 5 1

08...Wolverhampton, June 4, L39-51
1 †Richard Knight 1 3 1 1 1 7 1
2 Dennis Löfqvist R fx0 0 T 0
3 Stephen Davies R R 0 T 0
4 Joe Screen 3 3 0 1 2 9 1
5 Mark Loram 2 1 3 3 2 1 12 1
6 Roger Horspool 1 N 1 T 0 2
7 Gary Hicks 3 1 fn2 3 0 9

09...Oxford, June 15, L24-66
1 †Richard Knight 1 2 R 1 1 5
2 Dennis Löfqvist 0 0 T 0 0
3 Mark Loram 2 0 1 1 1 5
4 John Davis 0 2 N R 2
5 Stephen Davies 1 1 1 fx0 3 1
6 Bohumil Brhel F N 0 1 1
7 Gary Hicks 3 1 1 3 0 X 8 1

10...Swindon, June 16, L31-59
1 †Richard Knight 3 3 1 2 1 0 10
2 Dennis Löfqvist 0 2 0 1 R 3 2
3 Mark Loram 2 1 R 1 4
4 Bohumil Brhel 3 2 3 0 fx1 9
5 Stephen Davies 0 0 N T 0
6 Alan Grahame 1 1 F T 1 2 5 1
7 Gary Hicks 0 fnT N 0
8 Roger Horspool 0 0

11...BELLE VUE, June 17, D45-45
1 †Richard Knight 2 3 3 3 3 14 1
2 Dennis Löfqvist 3 0 0 1 4
3 Mark Loram 2 1 3 0 0 6 1
4 Glenn Doyle 1 1 1 0 3
5 Stephen Davies 0 3 0 N 3
6 Bohumil Brhel 2 3 3 3 1 3 15
7 Roger Horspool 0 N 0 0 0

12...COVENTRY, June 23, D45-45
1 †Richard Knight 2 2 3 3 1 11 1
2 Stephen Davies 1 1 1 1 4 2
3 Mark Loram 3 2 1 2 2 10 1
4 David Mullett 0 2 2 1 5
5 Dennis Löfqvist E 1 1 0 2 2
6 Gary Hicks 3 0 1 3 2 3 12 1
7 Roger Horspool F 1 N N 0 1

13...READING, June 28, W46-44
1 †Richard Knight 2 1 1 1 3 2 10
2 Stephen Davies R 0 1 3 2 6 1
3 Dennis Löfqvist 3 fxN 1 4 1
4 John Davis 0 1 T T 1 1
5 Mark Loram 3 2 3 3 2 1 14 1
6 Alan Grahame 1 N N 1 3 5
7 Bohumil Brhel 3 F 1 T R 2 6 1

14...Reading, July 2, L33-57
1 †Richard Knight 2 0 R N 1 2 5
2 Allan Johansen rider replacement
3 Dennis Löfqvist 1 0 3 0 R 4
4 Tom Grinstead 0 N 0 N 0
5 Mark Loram 3 1 2 0 2 1 9
6 Stephen Davies 1 1 0 N 1 N 1 2 6 3
7 Bohumil Brhel 3 N 1 2 0 0 3 9
8 Roger Horspool did not ride

15...OXFORD, July 7, L43-47
1 Mark Loram 3 3 3 3 3 0 15
2 Allan Johansen rider replacement
3 Dennis Löfqvist 2 0 2 2 2 0 8 2
4 Roger Horspool 0 0 N N 0
5 †Richard Knight 2 2 1 2 1 2 10
6 Bohumil Brhel 0 3 1 E 1 3 8 2
7 Wayne Carter 0 1 T 1 N 0 0 2 1
8 Martin Cobbin did not ride

16...BELLE VUE, July 14, L43-47
1 Mark Loram R 3 1 2 3 3 3 15 1
2 Allan Johansen rider replacement
3 Dennis Löfqvist 0 R 2 R N 2 4 2
4 Tom Grinstead 0 1 T N 1 1
5 †Richard Knight 2 3 2 3 3 3 2 18 1
6 Roger Horspool 1 N T 1 0 2
7 Bohumil Brhel F 1 T R fxR 2 3
8 Martin Cobbin did not ride

17...WOLVERHAMPTON, August 4, D45-45
1 Mark Loram 2 2 2 1 3 1 11
2 Allan Johansen rider replacement
3 Dennis Löfqvist 1 3 2 1 0 1 8 2
4 Gary Hicks 1 1 T 2 3 2 9 3
5 †Richard Knight 2 2 1 3 3 1 12 2
6 Bohumil Brhel 1 0 N 2 3
7 Stephen Davies 0 0 T 1 1 2 1
8 Roger Horspool did not ride

18...Wolverhampton, August 6, L41-49
1 Mark Loram 2 3 2 2 2 0 11
2 Allan Johansen rider replacement
3 Dennis Löfqvist 0 3 0 1 4
4 Gary Hicks 1 2 0 R 0 3 2
5 †Richard Knight 3 2 2 2 3 1 13 1
6 Stephen Davies 3 1 1 3 1 0 9 1
7 Bohumil Brhel 0 N 0 1 1
8 Roger Horspool did not ride

19...Reading, August 13, L30-57
1 Mark Loram fx1 0 N 1 0 1 3 2
2 Allan Johansen rider replacement
3 Dennis Löfqvist 1 0 3 1 1 0 6
4 Gary Hicks N N N N 0
5 †Richard Knight 0 2 3 1 0 6
6 Tom Grinstead 1 X 0 0 1
7 Stephen Davies 3 1 3 1 1 2 11
8 Bohumil Brhel 0 2 1 3

20...Oxford, August 17, D45-45
1 Mark Loram 2 1 2 2 3 2 12 2
2 Allan Johansen rider replacement
3 Dennis Löfqvist 3 2 3 3 1 0 12 1
4 Roger Horspool 0 0 N N N 0
5 †Richard Knight 1 2 2 1 N 6
6 Bohumil Brhel 3 0 0 0 2 1 6 1
7 Stephen Davies 2 2 1 1 1 2 9 4

21...SWINDON, August 18, L44-46
1 †Richard Knight 2 3 3 3 3 2 16
2 Allan Johansen rider replacement
3 Dennis Löfqvist 2 1 1 1 2 0 7 1
3 Alastair Stevens 2 R R N 2
5 Dean Barker 1 1 1 N 0 3 2
6 Bohumil Brhel 0 N 3 1 1 1 1 7 1
7 Stephen Davies 2 3 N 2 0 2 9
8 Roger Horspool did not ride

22...Cradley Heath, August 25, L37-53
1 †Richard Knight 1 2 N 0 1 4
2 Allan Johansen rider replacement
3 Dennis Löfqvist 1 2 3 0 2 8
4 Bohumil Brhel 0 1 2 0 1 4 2
5 Mark Loram 2 1 2 2 3 1 R 11 2
6 Carl Stonehewer 0 3 1 1 2 2 9 1
7 Roger Horspool 1 0 0 1

23...SWINDON, August 27, L35-55
1 †Richard Knight 1 2 3 3 1 2 2 14
2 Allan Johansen rider replacement
3 Dennis Löfqvist 1 0 0 1 1 0 3
4 Roger Horspool N 0 0 0 0
5 Mark Loram 0 2 fnN 2
6 Bohumil Brhel 3 3 1 2 0 3 12
7 Stephen Davies 1 1 1 R 1 0 4 1
8 Tom Grinstead did not ride

24...Swindon, August 27, L31-59
1 †Richard Knight 2 2 1 3 1 1 0 10 1
2 Allan Johansen rider replacement
3 Dennis Löfqvist 1 0 0 0 1
4 Roger Horspool 0 N N 0 0
5 Andy Smith 1 0 1 1 1 4
6 Bohumil Brhel 1 2 T 1 2 3 1 10 1
7 Stephen Davies 1 0 3 1 0 1 6 1
8 Tom Grinstead did not ride

25...Belle Vue, August 31, L35-55
1 Sam Ermolenko 0 3 2 3 3 0 11
2 Alastair Stevens 1 R 0 N 1
3 Dennis Löfqvist 0 0 T 0 0
4 †Richard Knight 0 2 0 N 2 1
5 Billy Hamill 1 3 2 1 3 1 11
6 Bohumil Brhel 3 1 0 1 R 5
7 Stephen Davies 1 1 T 1 2 5

26...COVENTRY, September 29, W50-40
1 †Richard Knight 1 0 1 2 3 0 7
2 Gary Hicks N 3 1 fxN 4 1
3 Dennis Löfqvist 1 0 N 0 1 1
4 Allan Johansen rider replacement
5 Mark Loram 2 2 2 2 1 3 12 1
6 Bohumil Brhel 2 2 1 3 1 3 12 2
7 Stephen Davies 3 3 2 1 3 2 14 2
8 Roger Horspool did not ride

27...Coventry, October 3, L32-58
1 †Richard Knight 1 2 3 2 0 1 9 1
2 Peter Ravn 0 3 1 0 4
3 Dennis Löfqvist 1 1 T T 2 1
4 Jan Staechmann 2 1 1 0 2 0 6
5 Mark Loram 0 3 0 1 4
6 Bohumil Brhel 2 0 1 0 3
7 Stephen Davies 1 2 0 1 4 1

28...WOLVERHAMPTON, October 6, L43-47
1 †Richard Knight 2 0 2 3 1 8 2
2 Roger Horspool 0 N N T 0 0
3 Mark Loram 3 3 3 2 2 1 14
4 §§Henrik Gustafsson 0 E 2 1 3 6
5 Dennis Löfqvist 1 3 0 T 4
6 Stephen Davies 3 0 0 1 1 5 1
7 Bohumil Brhel 2 1 1 E T 2 6 1

29...CRADLEY HEATH, October 11, W47-43
1 †Richard Knight 3 3 3 fx2 11
2 §Sean Wilson 1 0 1 1 3
3 Mark Loram 1 3 2 2 0 8 1
4 Henrik Gustafsson 3 3 2 2 10
5 Dennis Löfqvist 1 1 1 1 4 2
6 Stephen Davies 2 2 0 3 7 1
7 Bohumil Brhel 3 0 0 1 4

30...Bradford, October 13, L43-46
1 †Richard Knight 2 0 1 1 4 1
2 Sean Wilson 1 1 2 2 6 2
3 Mark Loram 3 2 2 0 0 7
4 Henrik Gustafsson 1 3 2 3 1 10
5 Dennis Löfqvist 0 1 N N 1
6 Stephen Davies 2 0 1 3 6 2
7 Bohumil Brhel 3 1 3 1 1 X 9 1

31...Cradley Heath, October 20, L43-47
1 †Richard Knight 2 1 N 1 4 1
2 Dennis Löfqvist 3 fx1 1 5 1
3 Mark Loram 3 2 0 3 fx 8
4 Henrik Gustafsson 0 2 fx0 2
5 Sean Wilson 2 1 2 0 5 1
6 Bohumil Brhel 3 0 3 3 3 1 13
7 Stephen Davies 2 0 2 2 6 2
Löfqvist lost to Jonsson for bonus point.

32...READING, October 21, W61-29
1 †Richard Knight 2 3 2 2 9 1
2 Dennis Löfqvist 0 2 3 1 6 2
3 Mark Loram 2 3 3 3 3 14
4 Henrik Gustafsson 2 1 2 3 8 3
5 Sean Wilson 3 2 3 2 1 11 1
6 Bohumil Brhel 3 1 0 3 7 1
7 Stephen Davies 2 1 1 2 6 2

'90 ROSTER

BRHEL, Bohumil
B 10.6.1965, Gottwaldov, Czechoslovakia. *First season newcomer.*
COBBIN, Martin Jon
B 1.10.1971, Edmonton, London.
DAVIES, Stephen
B 31.1.1964, Newcastle, New South Wales, Australia.
FAIRWEATHER, Emerson John
B 18.8.1973, Ipswich, Suffolk.
FARTHING, Lee Roy
B 9.8.1969, Ipswich, Suffolk.
GRINSTEAD, Thomas Andrew
B 14.9.1972, Maldon, Essex.
GUSTAFSSON, Henrik Anders
B 14.8.1970, Kumla, Sweden. *First season newcomer.*
HICKS, Gary Thomas
B 24.4.1969, Pasadena, Ca., U.S.A. *On loan from Belle Vue.*
HORSPOOL, Roger John
B 21.10.1971, Wisbech, Cambs.
JOHANSEN, Allan
B 2.12.1966, Odense, Denmark
KNIGHT, Richard John
B 26.5.1959, Cambridge, Cambs.
LÖFQVIST, Dennis
B 5.1.1967, Visby, Sweden.
LORAM, Mark Royston Gregory
B 12.1.1971, Malta. *Signed from Ipswich.*
SPICER, DARREN
B 28.3.1974, Bromley, Kent.
SEAN WILSON – See Coventry.

Home, sour home for Hans & Co

Track Data

Promoters: Bernard Crapper, John Payne and Peter York.
Address: Oxford Sports & Leisure Centre, Sandy Lane, Cowley, Oxford, OX4 5LJ.
Telephone: 0865-778222.
Hotline: 0898 800 693.
Track Length: 297 metres.
Track Record: 56.2 secs, Hans Nielsen (Oxford), October 13, 1988, Heat 1, Oxford v Coventry (Speedway Star KO Cup).

OXFORD should have won the 1990 Sunbrite League and made it four title successes in the last six years.

They didn't – despite having the best side on the road. And the reason? They were far too vulnerable in front of their own fans. You only have to look at Oxford's travelling performances to realise that it was their home form which saw their League crown go sailing out of the window and along the A423 to Smallmead.

For Hans Nielsen's men had the best away record in the Sunbrite League, winning eight and losing only seven, superior figures to even the champions. Yet Oxford still finished eight points behind the title-winners and had to be content with fourth place in the Division because they lose six of their home matches. Only lowly Coventry lost more!

And what unlikely defeats some of them were. In a dreadful mid-summer spell the Skol Cheetahs went six home matches without a win, losing successively to Reading, Coventry, Swindon and Wolverhampton, before a draw against wooden spoonists King's Lynn, followed by a second League defeat against the XXXX Racers.

Things got better after that and the University city team actually won it's last six home matches but, by then, they were too far behind the pacesetters to have any real influence on the title outcome.

So why were Oxford so brittle at Sandy Lane? The riders and management would have totally different views on the reasons – and possibly their fans would have a third!

The riders claimed that their Cowley track was so poorly prepared for much of the season that it gave the visitors an automatic advantage as the home riders were taken by surprise by the differing conditions on a week by week basis.

The management would insist that inconsistent performances from most of their team members accounted for the up and down form which saw them lose their reputation as the most professional team in the land.

Certainly few reputations were made at Oxford during 1990 – and one or two were lost! Even Hans Nielsen struggled uncharacteristically at times and had his worst season since joining the club from Birmingham at the beginning of 1984. He claimed only four League maximums (his lowest seasonal tally since his debut year in Britain in 1977!) but he could hardly be blamed for the slump as he was still a full point ahead of anyone else at the top of the national averages and a full 81 point in front of his nearest challenger.

Martin Dugard upped his average by nearly half a point a meeting to establish himself as the undisputed number two and no-one could complain about the first season contribution of Dean Barker (181 points and a near six point average) or the return of Alastair Stevens (189 points and a 5.6 average).

The biggest disappointments lay among the other three team members who started off the season. Simon Wigg, troubled more than anyone by track conditions, clung onto a place in the Sunbrite League Top Twenty by the skin of his teeth but had only two double figure home scores before being ruled out with a neck injury.

Troy Butler slipped 19 places in the rankings, dropped more than a point a match on his average and simply failed to make the progress everyone thought he would after such a promising 1989 which included a World Final debut.

And Paul Dugard, a cut above everyone in junior League racing, was so despondent at his form which saw him averaging less than a point a ride, that he retired after a dozen matches to be replaced by the ineffective John Bostin who did even worse.

Roll of Honour

Seasons in British League: 18 (1965-1975, 1984-1990).
British League Record: Champions (3), 1985, 1986, 1989.
Speedway Star Cup Record: Winners (1*), 1985. Joint Winners (1), 1986.
League Cup Record: Joint winners (1), 1986. Runners-up (1), 1985.
Inter League Cup Record: Semi-finalists, 1975.
Gold Cup: Winners (1), 1989. Runners-up (1), 1990.
Premiership: Winners (1), 1987. Runners-up (2), 1986, 1990.
Appearances: Hans Nielsen 397 (1984-1990).
Points: Hans Nielsen, 3859 (1984-1990).
World Finalists: Troy Butler (1989), Marvyn Cox (1986), Martin Dugard (1990), Ronnie Genz (1961), Jimmy Gooch (1965), Ron How (1964), Hans Nielsen (1984-85-86-87-88-89-90), Simon Wigg (1984, 1988-89).
BLRC Finalists: Jimmy Gooch (1965-66), Roy Trigg (1967), Colin Gooddy (1969), Hasse Holmkvist (1970), Garry Middleton (1972), Gordon Kennett (1973), Bob Kilby (1974), Dag Lovaas (1975), Hans Nielsen (1984-85-86-87-88-89-90), Simon Wigg (1985-86, 1988-89), Martin Dugard (1989-90).
Other Honours: National League Champions, 1964. National League (Division Three) Champions, 1950. National League Cup Winners, 1964.

The most successful video company in speedway

MBI video

Star of 90

MARTIN DUGARD

Oxford

OXFORD

01...Swindon, April 21, L31-57

1 †Hans Nielsen	R 3 2 1 3 3	12	1
2 §§Sean McCullagh	1 0 T N	1	
3 Kelly Moran	*3 1 3 0 1*	*8*	
4 Simon Wigg	R 2 1 2 0 0	5	
5 Troy Butler	2 0 fx0	2	
6 Jon Surman	2 0 T 0 1	3	
7 §§Wayne Parker	0 0 T 0	0	

02...Coventry, April 28, W46-43

1 †Hans Nielsen	R 3 3 2 3	11	
2 §Dean Barker	2 1 2 1	6	
3 Martin Dugard	2 2 3 3 1	11	
4 Simon Wigg	1 2 2 1	6	1
5 Troy Butler	3 1 0 fx	4	1
6 Paul Dugard	1 N 0 1	2	2
7 Alastair Stevens	2 1 0 1 2	6	2

03...BRADFORD, May 2, W49-41

1 †Hans Nielsen	2 2 3 3 2 3	15	1
2 Dean Barker	fxR 1 T	1	
3 Martin Dugard	2 3 2 3 3 1	14	1
4 Simon Wigg	1 1 2 3	7	1
5 Troy Butler	0 2 1 0 2	5	1
6 Paul Dugard	1 0 T 1	2	1
7 Alastair Stevens	2 T 0 3	5	

04...King's Lynn, May 12, D45-45

1 †Hans Nielsen	2 3 3 3 2 2	15	2
2 Dean Barker	1 1 1 0	3	1
3 Kelly Moran	*2 3 2 0*	*7*	*1*
4 Simon Wigg	2 2 2 3 3	12	1
5 Troy Butler	3 0 1 1	5	1
6 Paul Dugard	0 0 T R	0	
7 Alastair Stevens	1 R 0 2	3	

05...CRADLEY HEATH, May 25, W52-38

1 †Hans Nielsen	3 2 3 3 1	12	1
2 Dean Barker	2 1 1 1	5	3
3 Martin Dugard	2 3 3 3 2	13	
4 Simon Wigg	3 2 3 0	8	
5 Troy Butler	1 1 1 2	5	2
6 Paul Dugard	1 1 0 1	3	3
7 Alastair Stevens	2 2 0 2	6	

06...Cradley Heath, May 26, W49-41

1 †Hans Nielsen	3 1 3 2 2	11	3
2 Dean Barker	2 2 0 1	5	1
3 Martin Dugard	2 2 2 2	8	
4 Simon Wigg	3 1 2 3 3	12	1
5 Troy Butler	0 2 1 1	4	2
6 Paul Dugard	2 0 N 1	3	
7 Alastair Stevens	1 0 1 1 3	6	2

07...Wolverhampton, May 28, L42-48

1 †Hans Nielsen	2 3 1 3 3	12	
2 Dean Barker	1 0 3 3	7	1
3 Martin Dugard	1 1 0 2	4	1
4 Simon Wigg	1 0 1 0	2	
5 Troy Butler	R 3 0 R	3	
6 Paul Dugard	1 0 N 1	2	
7 Alastair Stevens	3 2 2 2 3 0	12	1

08...Belle Vue, June 1, W49-41

1 †Hans Nielsen	3 2 3 3 2	13	1
2 Dean Barker	0 0 T 0	0	
3 Martin Dugard	1 3 3 3 3 3	16	
4 Simon Wigg	0 3 3 2	8	1
5 Troy Butler	1 1 1 0	3	
6 Paul Dugard	1 0 N 1	2	1
7 Alastair Stevens	3 0 1 1 2	7	

09...BELLE VUE, June 6, L44-45

1 †Hans Nielsen	fx3 3 3 1	10	1
2 Dean Barker	2 1 2 2	7	1
3 Martin Dugard	1 3 2 2 2	10	1
4 Simon Wigg	3 2 2 0	7	
5 Alastair Stevens	1 0 0 N	1	
6 Paul Dugard	0 0 N 0	0	
7 Troy Butler	2 F 1 3 1 2	9	2

10...KING'S LYNN, June 15, W66-24

1 †Hans Nielsen	**3 3 3 2 2**	**13**	**2**
2 Dean Barker	2 2 2 2	8	3
3 Martin Dugard	**3 3 3 3 3**	**15**	
4 Simon Wigg	2 3 3 fn	8	1
5 Alastair Stevens	3 1 2 2	8	2
6 Paul Dugard	1 0 0 2	3	2
7 Troy Butler	2 1 2 3 3	11	2

11...Reading, June 25, L39-51

1 †Hans Nielsen	3 3 2 3 2 1	14	1
2 Dean Barker	2 2 1 T	5	2
3 Martin Dugard	3 2 3 1 1 0	10	
4 Troy Butler	1 2 1 1	5	1
5 Alastair Stevens	0 R R R	0	
6 Paul Dugard	R 0 T 3	3	
7 Kevin Pitts	1 1 0 0	2	

12...READING, July 6, L41-48

1 †Hans Nielsen	3 3 2 3 3 1	15	
2 Dean Barker	0 1 2 1	4	1
3 Martin Dugard	3 X 2 1	6	
4 Simon Wigg	3 3 2 0 0	8	
5 Alastair Stevens	0 0 1 T	1	1
6 Paul Dugard	0 0 N 3	3	
7 Bohumil Brhel	*2 R 1 0 1*	*4*	*1*

13...King's Lynn, July 7, W47-43

1 †Hans Nielsen	1 3 3 2 1	10	2
2 Dean Barker	2 1 0 0	3	
3 Martin Dugard	3 2 3 2 3	13	
4 Simon Wigg	3 2 1 3	9	1
5 Alastair Stevens	1 3 0 1	5	1
6 Paul Dugard	2 0 N 2	4	
7 Carl Stonehewer	*1 0 1 0 1*	*3*	*2*

14...COVENTRY, July 11, L42-48

1 †Hans Nielsen	3 3 2 1 2	11	1
2 Dean Barker	1 2 2 0	5	1
3 Martin Dugard	3 3 F 2	8	
4 Simon Wigg	3 2 3 2 1	11	1
5 Alastair Stevens	0 1 0 F	1	1
6 §John Bostin	2 0 0 0	2	
7 Troy Butler	fx1 1 2	4	1

15...SWINDON, August 3, L44-46

1 †Hans Nielsen	3 1 1 3 3	11	1
2 Troy Butler	1 2 2 3	8	
3 Martin Dugard	3 2 2 2	9	
4 Simon Wigg	3 3 3 0 R	9	
5 Dean Barker	1 0 0 1	2	1
6 Alastair Stevens	3 0 0 1 1	5	1
7 John Bostin	0 0 N 0	0	

16...WOLVERHAMPTON, August 10, L40-50

1 †Hans Nielsen	2 3 3 3 2	13	
2 Troy Butler	0 0 1 1	2	
3 Martin Dugard	2 1 1 0	4	
4 Simon Wigg	3 0 3 0 1	7	1
5 Dean Barker	1 2 1 2	6	
6 Alastair Stevens	3 1 3 0 1	8	1
7 John Bostin	0 N 0 0	0	

17...KING'S LYNN, August 17, D45-45

1 †Hans Nielsen	**3 3 3 3 3**	**15**	
2 Troy Butler	1 1 F 2	4	1
3 Martin Dugard	1 3 R 2	6	
4 Simon Wigg	3 3 2 0 1	9	
5 Dean Barker	2 0 1 0	3	2
6 John Bostin	0 0 N 0	0	
7 Alastair Stevens	1 0 3 1 3	8	

18...READING, August 27, L43-46

1 Hans Nielsen	3 3 2 3 2	13	1
2 Troy Butler	0 1 0 3	4	
3 Martin Dugard	3 2 1 1	7	
4 Simon Wigg	3 2 0 1 0	6	
5 Dean Barker	2 0 1 0	3	1
6 John Bostin	fxN N N	0	
7 Alastair Stevens	3 2 1 1 0 3	10	2
8 §§Kieran McCullagh	0	0	

19...Reading, August 27, L43-47

1 †Hans Nielsen	3 1 3 3 3	13	
2 Troy Butler	2 0 2 2 1	7	2
3 Martin Dugard	3 1 1 1	6	
4 Simon Wigg	2 3 0 1	6	
5 Dean Barker	0 1 1 R	2	1
6 Kieran McCullagh	1 N 0 0	1	
7 Alastair Stevens	3 1 0 1 3	8	1

20...BRADFORD, September 5, W51-39

1 †Hans Nielsen	**3 3 3 2 3**	**14**	**1**
2 Troy Butler	F 2 1 2	5	2
3 Martin Dugard	3 3 2 3	11	
4 Simon Wigg	3 3 3 3 1	13	
5 Dean Barker	R 1 2 0	3	1
6 John Bostin	2 1 0 2	5	
7 Alastair Stevens	R R R R	0	

21...Swindon, September 8, W47-43

1 †Hans Nielsen	3 3 3 3 2	14	
2 Troy Butler	0 0 F N	0	
3 Martin Dugard	3 3 2 2 0	10	1
4 Simon Wigg	3 3 2 1	9	
5 Dean Barker	1 0 0 1	2	1
6 John Bostin	1 0 N 0	1	
7 Alastair Stevens	R 0 3 3 2 3	11	1

22...BELLE VUE, September 12, W50-40

1 †Hans Nielsen	3 1 3 3 2	12	1
2 Dean Barker	1 2 1 0	4	1
3 Martin Dugard	3 3 3 3 1	13	1
4 Simon Wigg	2 N 0 0	2	
5 Troy Butler	0 3 1 2	6	1
6 John Bostin	2 0 N 0	2	1
7 Alastair Stevens	3 1 1 2 1 3	11	

23...Wolverhampton, September 17, W46-44

1 †Hans Nielsen	**2 3 2 3 3 3**	**16**	**2**
2 Dean Barker	3 0 X 1	4	
3 Martin Dugard	fx3 3 2 0	8	
4 Simon Wigg	1 0 3 0	4	1
5 Troy Butler	2 2 2 1	7	2
6 John Bostin	0 0 T 0	0	
7 Alastair Stevens	1 1 2 3	7	

24...CRADLEY HEATH, September 21, W48-42

1 †Hans Nielsen	2 3 3 3 3 3	17	
2 Dean Barker	1 1 1 2	5	2
3 Martin Dugard	0 2 2 2	6	
4 Simon Wigg	2 2 1 2 2	9	3
5 Troy Butler	0 0 2 1	3	1
6 John Bostin	1 2 N fx	3	1
7 Alastair Stevens	2 R T 0 3	5	

25...Cradley Heath, September 22, W51-39

1 †Hans Nielsen	3 2 2 3 2	12	1
2 Dean Barker	F 0 0 1	1	1
3 Martin Dugard	**3 3 3 3 3**	**15**	
4 Simon Wigg	3 3 3 1	10	
5 Troy Butler	0 1 0 1	2	
6 John Bostin	0 0 N 1	1	
7 Alastair Stevens	3 1 2 1 3	10	

26...COVENTRY, September 28, W51-38

1 †Hans Nielsen	3 3 3 2 1 3	15	
2 Dean Barker	1 3 1 3 0	8	
3 Martin Dugard	3 3 2 1 2 2	13	2
4 Simon Wigg	*rider replacement*		
5 Troy Butler	1 fn0 N	1	
6 John Bostin	1 0 1 N 0 2	4	1
7 Alastair Stevens	3 1 fx2 1 3	10	1

27...Bradford, September 29, L44-46

1 †Hans Nielsen	3 2 2 2 2 3	14	1
2 Dean Barker	1 0 0 N	1	
3 Martin Dugard	0 3 1 0	4	
4 Chris Morton	*1 3 1 3 3 2*	*13*	*2*
5 Alastair Stevens	0 0 T T	0	
6 John Bostin	0 0 N 0	0	
7 Peter Ravn	*3 2 3 0 1 3*	*12*	*1*

28...SWINDON, October 3, W49-41

1 †Hans Nielsen	E 3 3 3 3 3	15	
2 Alastair Stevens	0 1 1 1 1	4	
3 Martin Dugard	3 3 3 R 3 2	14	1
4 Simon Wigg	*rider replacement*		
5 Troy Butler	1 0 2 0 2	5	2
6 John Bostin	0 0 N 0	0	
7 Dean Barker	1 2 1 3 1 3	11	
8 Kieran McCullagh	*did not ride*		

29...WOLVERHAMPTON, October 12, W49-41

1 †Hans Nielsen	3 2 2 2 1	10	1
2 Alastair Stevens	1 1 2 3	7	2
3 Martin Dugard	1 2 1 3 3	10	1
4 Leigh Adams	*3 3 2 0*	*8*	
5 Troy Butler	0 0 X N	0	
6 John Bostin	0 0 N 0	0	
7 Dean Barker	3 3 3 0 2 3	14	1

30...Coventry, October 13, L42-48

1 †Hans Nielsen	3 3 3 1 3 3	16	1
2 Alastair Stevens	0 1 0 T	1	
3 Martin Dugard	2 1 1 2 1	7	1
4 Joe Screen	*2 1 0 2*	*5*	*1*
5 Troy Butler	0 3 1 2 0	6	
6 John Bostin	1 0 T 0	1	1
7 Dean Barker	2 1 1 2	6	1

31...Bradford, October 20, L33-57

1 †Hans Nielsen	0 1 3 2 1	7	
2 Alastair Stevens	1 0 T 0	1	
3 Martin Dugard	2 2 2 1 0	7	
4 Chris Morton	*2 1 0 1 3 1*	*8*	*1*
5 Troy Butler	3 0 0 0	3	
6 Kieran McCullagh	0 0 T 0	0	
7 Dean Barker	3 1 1 2	7	1

32...Belle Vue, October 26, W49-40

1 Hans Nielsen	3 3 2 2 2	12	2
2 Alastair Stevens	0 1 1 0	2	1
3 Martin Dugard	3 3 3 R 3	12	
4 Sean Wilson	*3 3 1 3*	*10*	
5 Troy Butler	1 R 0 N	1	
6 Kieran McCullagh	F 0 N fx	0	
7 Dean Barker	3 2 2 1 1 3	12	1

'90 ROSTER

BARKER, Dean
B 2.8.1970, Isleworth, Middlesex. *Signed from Eastbourne.*

BUTLER, Troy Steve
B 22.9.1967, Melbourne, Australia.

DUGARD, Martin Robert
B 18.5.1969, Worthing, West Sussex.

DUGARD, Paul Charles
B 17.10.1971, Shoreham, W.Sussex.

HOWSE, Kevin
B 20.9.1963, Whitney, Oxon. *Local junior.*

McCULLAGH, Kieran
B 14.10.1972, Abingdon, Oxon. *Local junior.*

McCULLAGH, Sean Patrick
B 17.2.1969, Abingdon, Oxon. *Local junior.*

NIELSEN, Hans Hollen
B 26.12.1959, Brovst, Denmark.

PARKER, Wayne Martin
B 26.3.1971, Swindon, Wiltshire. *Local junior.*

PITTS, Kevin
B 6.6.1969, Crawley, West Sussex.

STEVENS, Alastair
B 15.10.1968, Aylesbury, Bucks. *Recalled from Poole.*

SURMAN, Jonathan Raymond (Jon)
B 20.12.1966, Aylesbury, Bucks.

WIGG, Simon Antony
B 15.10.1960, Aylesbury, Bucks.

JOHN BOSTIN – *See Cradley Heath.*

Todd is the Ace in the title pack

Track Data

Promoters: Pat Bliss and Bill Dore.
Address: Smallmead Stadium, Bennet Road, Reading, Berkshire.
Telephone: 0734-863161.
Clubcall: 0898 12 18 75.
Track Length: 307 metres.
Track Record: 58.1 secs, Per Jonsson (Reading), October 12, 1987, heat 1, Reading v Coventry (British League).

READING played their hand of poker to absolute perfection. While everyone else was rushing around gathering their cards to their chest for the start of the 1990 Sunbrite League game, the Berkshire club waited until the very last moment before showing their hand.

Then they revealed their Aces.

Off the bottom of the pack, they dealt themselves a pair of Scandinavian picture cards in the return of their Swedish twosome Per Jonsson and Jan Andersson. Jonsson, after his year's sabbatical, and Andersson breaking his self-imposed retirement to return to Smallmead.

Then they looked in the National League pack and, on the eve of their first match, twisted and came up with the Joker in the championship chase: Todd Wiltshire.

Other promoters had fought shy of signing the New South Walian. They had a variety of reasons. Some doubted his commitment to speedway and quoted the fact that he had jeopardised his World Championship chances by attending his sister's wedding. Others took the view that he wasn't physically hard enough or mentally tough enough to survive in the big school. And some reckoned that his gating, so sharp and productive at National League level, would be trumped by the extra competitiveness of the top Division.

Reading paid their dues and came up with the one rider who turned their seven cards into a winning hand!

Wiltshire's arrival eclipsed all else at Smallmead and it took a World Champion to finally overshadow him after one of the most impressive Sunbrite League debut seasons for a long time.

He began his League career with 14 points at Coventry, followed that up with paid 15 in the return and then slammed in another dozen points at home to Wolverhampton to make his mark. Those selfsame doubters predicted his downfall once he had moved out of the reserve position and into a full team place. He answered them at Belle Vue with 10 paid 11 and followed that up with a top-scoring double figure score at King's Lynn and showed his toughness later when he returned after a broken collar bone.

Wiltshire was the bonus – but it was no one-man title-winning show. Skipper Jeremy Doncaster benefited from his full season at Smallmead to take over as England's number one in the averages and collected the Overseas Championship on the way.

Jonsson was relegated to a third heat leader berth but still managed a near eight and a half point average despite taking a little while to settle back into the groove and veteran Andersson provided that second string support to his fellow Swede Tony Olsson and the reliable David Mullett.

The XXXX Racers had lost the services of Mitch Shirra before the season even started and were forced to track another Kiwi, Nathan Murray, as a token reserve.

Ironically, he was injured just as he began to look as if he might hold his own at number seven and was replaced by David Steen and that was the only obvious weakness throughout the Reading line-up. They realised it and when Mullett was sidelined with a broken foot five days before Olsson broke his thigh while guesting for Cradley Heath, they moved swiftly to prevent their season ending in disappointment – bringing Armando Castagna back into the fold to boost their successful double challenge.

And he was able to share in both the match that won the League title and the two legs of their Speedway Star Knock Out Cup Final.

Roll of Honour

Seasons in British League: 19 (1971-1973 [Tilehurst]; 1975-1990).
British League Record: Champions (3), 1973, 1980, 1990. Runners-up (1), 1972. Third (1), 1977.
Speedway Star Cup Record: Winners (1), 1990. Runners-up (2), 1973, 1977.
Best League Cup Season: Semi-finalists (Group winners), 1984.
Inter League Cup Record: Never competed in the competition.
Appearances: Jan Andersson, 443 (1980-1988, 1990).
Points: Jan Andersson, 4582.5 (1980-1988, 1990).
World Finalists: Jan Andersson (1980-81-82, 1984-85), John Davis (1980), Jeremy Doncaster (1989), Bengt Jansson (1977), Dave Jessup (1978), Per Jonsson (1987-88, 1990), Anders Michanek (1971-72-73, 1975), Tony Olsson (1989), Mitch Shirra (1983-84, 1986, 1989), Jiri Stancl (1980, 1982), Alois Wiesböck (1979), Todd Wiltshire (1990).
BLRC Finalists: Anders Michanek (1971-72-73, 1975), Dave Jessup (1976-77-78), John Davis (1979), Jan Andersson (1980-81-82-83-84-85-86-87-88), Bobby Schwartz (1982), Mitch Shirra (1983, 1989), John Davis (1986), Per Jonsson (1988), Jeremy Doncaster (1989-90), Todd Wiltshire (1990).

Star of 90
TODD WILTSHIRE
Reading

READING

01...Coventry, March 31, W48-42

1 †Jeremy Doncaster	2 2 3 0	7	
2 David Mullett	1 1 2 0	4	3
3 Per Jonsson	1 3 1 1	6	2
4 Tony Olsson	2 0 1 1	4	2
5 Jan Andersson	3 2 2 2 3	12	
6 §§Nathan Murray	1 0 N 0	1	
7 §Todd Wiltshire	3 2 3 3 2 1	14	

02...COVENTRY, April 9, W46-44

1 Jeremy Doncaster	*rider replacement*		
2 David Mullett	1 1 3 1 1	7	2
3 Per Jonsson	3 2 3 3 0 2	13	1
4 Tony Olsson	1 1 0 0	2	2
5 †Jan Andersson	2 2 2 1 1 3	11	
6 Nathan Murray	E 0 N 0	0	
7 Todd Wiltshire	3 1 2 3 2 2	13	2
8 David Steen	*did not ride*		

03...WOLVERHAMPTON, May 7, W47-43

1 †Jeremy Doncaster	3 3 1 3 3	13	
2 David Mullett	2 2 R R	4	2
3 Per Jonsson	R 0 3 0	3	
4 Tony Olsson	3 2 1 2	8	2
5 Jan Andersson	1 1 2 1 0	5	1
6 Nathan Murray	0 N N 2 0	2	
7 Todd Wiltshire	3 3 2 N 2 2	12	1

04...Wolverhampton, May 7, D45-45

1 †Jeremy Doncaster	1 2 3 1	7	
2 David Mullett	0 1 1 2	4	2
3 Per Jonsson	3 3 2 0 0	8	
4 Tony Olsson	1 2 2 3 2	10	1
5 Jan Andersson	3 3 1 1	8	1
6 Nathan Murray	1 N 0 N 0	1	1
7 Todd Wiltshire	2 2 0 N 1 2	7	2

05...Cradley Heath, May 12, L38-52

1 †Jeremy Doncaster	1 2 2 3 3 3	14	
2 David Mullett	0 0 T N	0	
3 Per Jonsson	1 1 R N	2	1
4 Tony Olsson	1 2 0 0	3	1
5 Jan Andersson	2 1 2 2 2 0	9	2
6 Nathan Murray	1 T N 0 2	3	
7 Todd Wiltshire	3 0 3 1 0 X	7	

06...CRADLEY HEATH, May 14, W57-33

1 †Jeremy Doncaster	**3 3 3 3 3**	**15**	
2 David Mullett	2 1 1 2	6	2
3 Per Jonsson	2 2 3 2 R	9	
4 Tony Olsson	2 2 2 0	6	1
5 Jan Andersson	1 0 3 1	5	2
6 Nathan Murray	2 1 N 1	4	2
7 Todd Wiltshire	3 1 3 2 3	12	2

07...Swindon, May 26, W50-40

1 †Jeremy Doncaster	1 3 3 3 3	13	1
2 David Mullett	2 2 2 0	6	2
3 Per Jonsson	3 2 3 1 2	11	1
4 Tony Olsson	0 3 F 2	5	1
5 Jan Andersson	2 0 3 3	8	
6 Todd Wiltshire	1 0 3 2 1	7	1
7 David Steen	0 0 N 0	0	

08...Bradford, June 2, L37-53

1 †Jeremy Doncaster	3 0 2 1 2	8	
2 Todd Wiltshire	0 3 1 X	4	
3 Per Jonsson	1 3 1 0	5	1
4 Tony Olsson	3 1 2 1 1	8	4
5 Jan Andersson	1 2 3 1 2	9	
6 David Mullett	2 0 0 T 1	3	
7 David Steen	0 0 N 0	0	

09...Belle Vue, June 22, L40-50

1 †Jeremy Doncaster	0 3 3 3 3 3	15	
2 Todd Wiltshire	1 1 3 2 3 R	10	1
3 Per Jonsson	0 0 1 T T	1	
4 Tony Olsson	1 2 0 0	3	
5 Jan Andersson	3 1 1 1 2	8	2
6 David Mullett	1 1 T N R	2	
7 Troy Smith	R N T F 1	1	

10...OXFORD, June 25, W51-39

1 †Jeremy Doncaster	0 3 3 3 3	12	
2 Todd Wiltshire	1 1 3 2	7	1
3 Per Jonsson	2 3 2 3 2	12	1
4 Jan Andersson	2 R 0 2	4	2
5 Tony Olsson	3 1 1 0	5	
6 Nathan Murray	2 0 N 1	3	2
7 David Mullett	3 1 2 0 2	8	1

11...King's Lynn, June 28, L44-46

1 †Jeremy Doncaster	1 F 2 3 3	9	1
2 Todd Wiltshire	3 3 2 3 0	11	
3 Per Jonsson	2 3 2 1	8	
4 Tony Olsson	2 3 2 0	7	
5 Andy Smith	*1 2 F 0*	*3*	*2*
6 David Mullett	2 1 2 0 R	5	
7 Nathan Murray	0 N 0 1	1	

12...KING'S LYNN, July 2, W57-33

1 †Jeremy Doncaster	**3 3 3 3 3**	**15**	
2 Todd Wiltshire	0 2 3 1	6	1
3 Per Jonsson	2 3 3 3 1	12	1
4 Jan Andersson	2 2 2 2	8	2
5 Tony Olsson	1 3 1 2	7	3
6 Nathan Murray	0 N 0 0	0	
7 David Mullett	2 3 1 2 1	9	1

13...Oxford, July 6, W48-42

1 Jan Andersson	2 2 1 0	5	
2 Per Jonsson	1 1 3 3 3	11	2
3 †Jeremy Doncaster	2 X 3 2	7	
4 Tony Olsson	1 2 0 2	5	2
5 Jimmy Nilsen	*2 3 3 1 2*	*11*	*2*
6 David Mullett	3 2 R N 2	7	
7 Nathan Murray	1 1 N 0 0	2	1

14...Cradley Heath, July 7, W47.5-42.5

1 Jan Andersson	0 1.5 3 0 1	5.5	
2 Todd Wiltshire	*rider replacement*		
3 †Jeremy Doncaster	1 2 2 3 3 2	13	
4 Tony Olsson	1 1 3 2 3	10	
5 Per Jonsson	3 3 3 1 2 0	12	1
6 David Mullett	2 R 1 0 N 2	5	1
7 Nathan Murray	1 N N 0 1	2	2
8 Lance Sealey	*did not ride*		

15...CRADLEY HEATH, July 9, L44-46

1 †Jeremy Doncaster	2 2 3 3 3	13	
2 Todd Wiltshire	1 1 2 2	6	3
3 Per Jonsson	2 3 2 R 0	7	
4 Jan Andersson	0 1 1 1	3	2
5 Tony Olsson	1 2 2 2	7	
6 Nathan Murray	E N N 0 0	0	
7 David Mullett	3 1 1 1 N 2	8	2

16...Bradford, July 21, L41-49

1 Jan Andersson	3 0 1 0 0	4	1
2 Bobby Ott	*2 1 1 1 3*	*8*	*3*
3 †Jeremy Doncaster	3 3 2 2 0 0	10	
4 Tony Olsson	0 0 T T	0	
5 Chris Morton	*1 1 2 3 3 2*	*12*	
6 David Mullett	2 0 T 2	4	
7 David Steen	1 1 T 1	3	2

17...BRADFORD, July 23, W56-34

1 Todd Wiltshire	3 3 2 3	11	
2 Jan Andersson	fx1 3 1	5	1
3 †Jeremy Doncaster	3 3 3 3 N	12	
4 Per Jonsson	**3 3 3 2 3**	**14**	**1**
5 Tony Olsson	1 0 1 1	3	
6 David Steen	0 1 N 1 1	3	
7 David Mullett	2 2 1 0 3	8	1

18...BELLE VUE, July 30, L44-45

1 Phil Crump	*0 1 1 N*	*2*	
2 Jan Andersson	1 3 1 0	5	1
3 †Jeremy Doncaster	3 2 2 2 1	10	1
4 Per Jonsson	1 3 3 3 2 3	15	
5 Tony Olsson	R 0 0 N	0	
6 David Steen	fx0 N N 2	2	1
7 David Mullett	3 1 2 T 1 0 3	10	2

19...Swindon, August 4, D45-45

1 Jan Andersson	2 3 3 2 2 2	14	1
2 Todd Wiltshire	*rider replacement*		
3 †Jeremy Doncaster	1 3 3 3 0	10	1
4 Tony Olsson	3 1 1 1 0	6	2
5 Per Jonsson	1 2 0 2 3 3	11	1
6 David Mullett	2 0 1 R 0	3	
7 David Steen	0 0 N 1	1	
8 Troy Smith	*did not ride*		

20...COVENTRY, August 6, W49-41

1 Leigh Adams	*1 2 0 0*	*3*	*2*
2 Jan Andersson	2 3 2 3 0	10	
3 †Jeremy Doncaster	3 3 0 2	8	
4 Per Jonsson	3 1 3 3 3	13	1
5 Tony Olsson	0 2 2 0	4	1
6 David Steen	2 N F 1	3	
7 David Mullett	1 2 1 1 3	8	3

21...KING'S LYNN, August 13, W57-30

1 Todd Wiltshire	*rider replacement*		
2 Jan Andersson	**3 3 3 2 3 2**	**16**	**2**
3 †Jeremy Doncaster	0 2 3 3 3 3	14	
4 Per Jonsson	2 2 3 E 2	9	3
5 Tony Olsson	3 0 2 2 2	9	2
6 David Steen	fx N N N	0	
7 David Mullett	N 2 1 2 0 3	8	2
8 Troy Smith	1	1	

22...Coventry, August 18, W47-43

1 Jan Andersson	3 3 3 3 2 R	14	
2 Todd Wiltshire	*rider replacement*		
3 †Jeremy Doncaster	2 3 N N N	5	1
4 Tony Olsson	3 3 R 1 0	7	
5 Per Jonsson	1 1 0 2 2 2	8	1
6 David Mullett	2 fx1 2 3 2	10	
7 David Steen	0 1 1 N 0 1	3	1
8 Troy Smith	*did not ride*		

23...WOLVERHAMPTON, August 20, D45-45

1 Jan Andersson	1 2 0 1	4	3
2 Jimmy Nilsen	*2 3 3 3 3*	*14*	
3 †Jeremy Doncaster	2 3 1 0	6	
4 Per Jonsson	3 3 3 2 1	12	
5 Tony Olsson	0 2 2 2	6	2
6 David Steen	1 0 0 1 0 1	3	
7 David Mullett	F N N N	0	
8 Christian Howell	0	0	

24...Oxford, August 27, W46-43

1 Jan Andersson	2 1 2 2 3 1	11	2
2 Todd Wiltshire	1 3 3 3 3	13	1
3 †Jeremy Doncaster	1 2 3 2	8	
4 Per Jonsson	R 3 0 2	5	1
5 Peter Ravn	*1 0 N N*	*1*	
6 Carl Stonehewer	*2 0 2 1 R 2*	*7*	*1*
7 David Steen	fx0 T 1	1	1

25...OXFORD, August 27, W47-43

1 Jan Andersson	1 3 2 2 0	8	2
2 Todd Wiltshire	0 2 3 3	8	1
3 †Jeremy Doncaster	2 2 1 2	7	
4 Per Jonsson	3 2 3 3 2	13	1
5 Glenn Doyle	*1 3 2 R*	*6*	*1*
6 David Steen	fx0 0 2	2	
7 Troy Smith	2 0 0 1	3	1

26...Wolverhampton, September 3, L42-48

1 Jan Andersson	1 1 0 N	2	
2 Todd Wiltshire	0 3 3 3 3	12	
3 †Jeremy Doncaster	2 3 1 3 1	10	
4 Per Jonsson	1 3 2 2	8	1
5 Armando Castagna	2 0 fx0	2	
6 Troy Butler	*3 1 2 1 N 0 fx*	*7*	*2*
7 David Steen	0 N N 0 1	1	

27...SWINDON, September 10, W59-31

1 Todd Wiltshire	3 2 3 3 3	14	
2 Jan Andersson	1 0 2 2	5	2
3 Per Jonsson	3 2 3 2 1	11	1
4 Armando Castagna	R 2 3 0	5	1
5 †Jeremy Doncaster	3 3 2 1	9	2
6 David Steen	0 0 T 2	2	1
7 Billy Hamill	*3 3 3 1 3*	*13*	

28...BELLE VUE, September 24, W61-29

1 Todd Wiltshire	3 3 2 1 3	12	1
2 Jan Andersson	2 0 3 3	8	1
3 Per Jonsson	2 2 2 3	9	1
4 Armando Castagna	3 2 2 3 0	10	2
5 †Jeremy Doncaster	2 3 3 1	9	1
6 David Steen	1 0 N 0	1	
7 Billy Hamill	*3 3 2 1 3*	*12*	*2*

29...SWINDON, October 1, W53-37

1 Todd Wiltshire	0 3 3 2 1	9	1
2 Jan Andersson	1 2 3 2	8	2
3 Per Jonsson	2 3 3 3 2	13	
4 Armando Castagna	2 2 R 1	5	3
5 †Jeremy Doncaster	3 3 2 2	10	1
6 David Steen	0 0 N E	0	
7 David Mullett	3 2 0 R 3	8	1

30...Belle Vue, October 12, L39-51

1 Todd Wiltshire	1 1 0 1	3	1
2 Jan Andersson	2 0 2 1	5	
3 Per Jonsson	2 1 0 3 3	9	1
4 Armando Castagna	E F fxT	0	
5 †Jeremy Doncaster	3 3 3 3 1 1	14	
6 David Mullett	2 1 2 1 T 2	8	1
7 David Steen	0 0 N 0 0	0	

31...BRADFORD, October 15, W54-36

1 Todd Wiltshire	3 2 3 3 2	13	
2 Jan Andersson	0 1 1 N	2	2
3 Per Jonsson	3 3 3 1 1	11	2
4 Armando Castagna	2 2 2 2	8	3
5 †Jeremy Doncaster	1 3 3 2	9	1
6 David Steen	0 1 0 1	2	
7 David Mullett	2 2 fx2 3	9	1

32...King's Lynn, October 21, L29-61

1 Todd Wiltshire	3 0 2 2 1 2	10	
2 Jan Andersson	1 3 R 0 0	4	
3 Per Jonsson	3 1 1 F	5	
4 David Mullett	1 1 F 0	2	1
5 †Jeremy Doncaster	0 2 3 1	6	
6 Christian Howell	0 T 0 1	1	
7 David Steen	1 0 T E 0	1	

'90 ROSTER

ANDERSSON, Jan Hakan
B 7.5.1955, Alingsas, Sweden.
Returned after one seasen absence.

CASTAGNA, Armando
B 22.9.1963, Arzignano, Italy.

DONCASTER, Jeremy
B 16.6.1961, Grimsby, Humberside.

HOWELL, Christian Eric
B 18.1.1974, Reading, Berkshire.
Local junior.

JONSSON, Per
B 21.3.1966, Stockholm, Sweden.
Returned after one seasen absence.

MULLETT, David John
B 27.6.1965, Folkestone, Kent.

MURRAY, Nathan
B 8.12.1966, Hamilton, North Island, New Zealand. *Released by Glasgow.*

OLSSON, John Tony
B 13.3.1965, Visby, Sweden.

SEABRIGHT, Mark
B 28.2.1969, Fordingbridge, Hampshire. *Local junior.*

SEALEY, Lance
B 8.3.1970, Swindon, Wiltshire.
Local junior.

SMITH, Troy Lee
B 21.7.1971, Swindon, Wiltshire.

STEEN, David Roscoe
B 12.3.1966, Maidstone, Kent.

WILTSHIRE, Todd William
B 26.9.1968, Sydney, Australia.
Signed from Wimbledon.

Robins find it a slippery perch on top

Track Data

Promoters: Ted Nelson, Bill Chandler and Ron Byford.
Address: Abbey Stadium, Blunsdon, Swindon, Wiltshire, SN2 4ND.
Telephone: 0793-721253.
Hotline: 0898 800 671.
Track Length: 359.6 metres.
Track Record: 64.8 secs, Hans Nielsen (Oxford), September 8, 1990, heat 1, Swindon v Oxford (Sunbrite League).

THERE were times when Swindon looked good enough to win their first League championship since 1967. And there were occasions when they might have struggled to win a match in the National League.

And that must have been galling for the management team who had invested heavily in the New Year by signing Australian Leigh Adams from National League kingpins Poole – hoping he would be the final piece in their title-winning ambitions.

For a short spell it looked more than possible as the Team Coastal Windows Robins blazed a merry trail at the top of the table with Adams slotting into his new role as efficiently as all those experts had predicted.

But Swindon's downfall wasn't attributable to the new boy. The biggest concern for manager Ron Byford was the below par performances from the Dane Brian Karger whose third place in the 1989 British League Riders' Championship Final should have heralded his arrival in the Big League of consistently high scorers.

No-one knew at the time but a nightmare start to the campaign was to turn into a nightmare season for the talented Karger who was to break his thigh in June and spend the rest of the summer out of competitive action in this county.

In four away League matches before his injury, Karger scored only 25 points – and a dozen of those were in a 45-45 draw at Coventry, Swindon's first away points of the season.

And it was to be their away form which prevented them mounting a serious championship challenge despite that bright and breezy start. They were the last Sunbrite League team to win away from home (as late as August) and they were also surprisingly vulnerable at Blunsdon, losing to Reading, Belle Vue, Oxford and, worst of all, struggling Cradley Heath in the last home meeting of the season.

Why? Other than Karger's early poor form and then long absence, they also had to do without skipper John Davis for spells when he was on the sidelines with a series of niggling injuries that reduced his effectiveness as both team captain and middle order scorer.

Andrew Silver, who began so well, lost his points-scoring way the longer the season wore on and the much-heralded comeback of Aussie veteran Phil Crump was far from a rip-roaring success.

Crumpie found it difficult to pick up the pace of the Sunbrite League after a three and a half season absence but his return certainly boosted gates at the Abbey Stadium and, like days of old, he was never beaten until the chequered flag.

There were, as is often the case, major pluses in the Swindon season for a team that is still basically one of the youngest in the country. Adams settled in well and scored nearly 250 points in his debut season and David Smart, who announced his retirement at the end of the year, was as good an English-born number seven as there was anywhere in the Sunbrite League.

It was also pleasing to see Jimmy Nilsen put the traumas of the previous couple of seasons behind him and not only reach a World Final again but also to lift his average closer to his best ever 1987 figure.

And former World Under 21 Champion Peter Nahlin continued his unobtrusive journey towards genuine heat leadership as he climbed 13 places up the Sunbrite League charts.

Perhaps everyone expected too much of Swindon: certainly they have the youthful core of a team that should be mounting a title challenge within the next season or so.

Roll of Honour

Seasons in British League: 26 (1965-1990).
British League Record: Champions (1), 1967. Third (3), 1966, 1981, 1987.
Best Speedway Star Cup Seasons: Semi-finalists (5), 1968, 1970, 1980, 1981, 1990.
Best League Cup Season: Fifth, 1986.
Inter League Cup Record: Runners-up (1), 1980.
Appearances: Martin Ashby, 425 (1965-1967, 1971-1979).
Points: Martin Ashby, 4288.5 (1965-1967, 1971-1979).
World Finalists: Jan Andersson (1978), Barry Briggs (1964-65-66-67-68-69-70, 1972), Mike Broadbank (1958, 1961-62, 1964, 1966), Arne Carlsson (1962), Phil Crump (1982), Peter Moore (1963), Jimmy Nilsen (1986-87, 1990), Bo Petersen (1984), Bob Roger (1957), Mitch Shirra (1987), George White (1957, 1959), Ian Williams (1957).
BLRC Finalists: Barry Briggs (1965-66-67-68-69-70-71), Martin Ashby (1972-73-74-75-76), Bob Kilby (1977), Phil Crump (1979, 1981, 1983-84), Scott Autrey (1980), Steve Bastable (1982), Bo Petersen (1985), Alan Grahame (1986), Jimmy Nilsen (1987, 1989-90), Mitch Shirra (1987), Brian Karger (1988-89), Andrew Silver (1990).
Other Honours: National League (Division One) Champions, 1957. National League (Division Two) Champions, 1956.

Star of 90
LEIGH ADAMS
Swindon

SWINDON

01...BELLE VUE, April 14, W55-35

1 Brian Karger	2 1 1 1	5	
2 Peter Nahlin	0 3 1 0	4	1
3 Andrew Silver	**3 3 3 2 2**	**13**	**2**
4 †John Davis	1 1 2 3	7	2
5 Jimmy Nilsen	2 0 3 3 3	11	
6 David Smart	2 1 N 2	5	2
7 §§Leigh Adams	3 1 2 1 3	10	

02...OXFORD, April 21, W57-31

1 Brian Karger	3 3 R 3 1	10	1
2 Peter Nahlin	2 2 1 3	8	2
3 Andrew Silver	2 3 3 1	9	1
4 †John Davis	fx2 2 2	6	2
5 Jimmy Nilsen	3 1 3 2 2	11	1
6 Leigh Adams	3 1 1 3	8	1
7 David Smart	1 0 2 2	5	2

03...Belle Vue, April 27, L42-48

1 Brian Karger	3 1 0 T	4	
2 Peter Nahlin	1 0 2 N	3	
3 Andrew Silver	2 3 3 1 3 3	15	
4 Leigh Adams	0 3 0 1	4	
5 †Jimmy Nilsen	1 0 3 0 1	5	
6 Glenn Doyle	*2 1 1 3 0*	*7*	
7 David Smart	1 1 0 2	4	2

04...WOLVERHAMPTON, April 28, W57-33

1 Brian Karger	3 3 1 3	10	
2 Peter Nahlin	2 2 2 3 2	11	3
3 Andrew Silver	2 2 2 2	8	1
4 †John Davis	1 1 1 1	4	1
5 Jimmy Nilsen	2 3 3 3 3	14	
6 Leigh Adams	3 0 0 3	6	
7 David Smart	2 0 0 2	4	2

05...Bradford, May 5, L41-49

1 Brian Karger	2 0 0 N	2	
2 Peter Nahlin	1 2 0 2 0	5	1
3 Andrew Silver	3 2 3 3 2	13	
4 Bobby Ott	*3 3 0 1*	*7*	
5 †Jimmy Nilsen	0 0 N R	0	
6 David Smart	1 0 1 1	3	1
7 Leigh Adams	2 2 1 3 0 3	11	1

06...Coventry, May 12, D45-45

1 Brian Karger	2 1 3 2 3	11	1
2 Peter Nahlin	1 2 0 N	3	1
3 Andrew Silver	1 2 1 2 2	8	3
4 †John Davis	3 0 0 1	4	1
5 Jimmy Nilsen	1 2 1 1	5	1
6 David Smart	1 0 N 1	2	1
7 Leigh Adams	3 2 3 2 0 2	12	

07...READING, May 26, L40-50

1 Brian Karger	3 3 2 2 1 N	11	
2 Peter Nahlin	0 1 1 1	3	1
3 Andrew Silver	2 2 1 0 1	6	1
4 †John Davis	3 1 0 0	4	
5 Jimmy Nilsen	1 0 1 T	2	
6 Leigh Adams	2 1 1 2 3 R	9	3
7 David Smart	3 0 N 2	5	1

08...Cradley Heath, May 28, L37-53

1 Brian Karger	1 1 2 2	6	1
2 Peter Nahlin	0 2 0 0	2	
3 Andrew Silver	1 2 2 0 1	6	
4 †John Davis	1 0 T N	1	
5 Jimmy Nilsen	3 2 3 0 1 3	12	
6 Leigh Adams	2 1 F 2 1 2	8	2
7 David Smart	1 0 T 1	2	2

09...CRADLEY HEATH, May 28, W46-44

1 Brian Karger	2 0 3 3 fx	8	
2 Peter Nahlin	1 1 2 0	4	1
3 Andrew Silver	2 3 3 3 1	12	
4 †John Davis	1 0 N N	1	
5 Jimmy Nilsen	3 1 fnN	4	
6 Leigh Adams	3 1 1 1 0 3	9	2
7 David Smart	1 1 2 1 2 1	8	2

10...COVENTRY, June 2, W64-26

1 Brian Karger	2 3 0 3	8	
2 Leigh Adams	1 2 3 3 3	12	2
3 Andrew Silver	**2 3 3 3 2**	**13**	**2**
4 Peter Nahlin	2 1 1 2	6	2
5 Jimmy Nilsen	3 3 3 1	10	
6 †John Davis	2 3 1 2	8	1
7 David Smart	1 1 2 3	7	2

11...KING'S LYNN, June 16, W59-31

1 Andrew Silver	2 2 2 3 3	12	2
2 †John Davis	1 3 2 3	9	1
3 Brian Karger	**3 3 3 3 2**	**14**	**1**
4 Billy Hamill	*2 R 3 2*	*7*	*1*
5 Peter Nahlin	1 1 2 2	6	3
6 David Smart	2 0 1 3	6	1
7 Joe Screen	*3 1 0 1*	*5*	*1*

12...BELLE VUE, June 23, L42-48

1 Leigh Adams	3 3 0 2 2 1	11	2
2 Brian Karger	*rider replacement*		
3 Andrew Silver	2 1 1 1 1	6	1
4 Peter Nahlin	2 1 2 3 R	8	1
5 Jimmy Nilsen	1 1 0 3 3 0	8	1
6 David Smart	0 1 0 0	1	1
7 †John Davis	1 2 2 3	8	
8 Matthew Cross	*did not ride*		

13...WOLVERHAMPTON, June 30, W57-33

1 Leigh Adams	2 1 0 2	5	2
2 Peter Nahlin	1 2 1 3 2	9	3
3 Andrew Silver	0 2 3 0	5	1
4 Per Jonsson	*2 3 1 3*	*9*	*2*
5 Jimmy Nilsen	3 2 2 3 3	13	1
6 †John Davis	**3 3 3 3**	**12**	
7 David Smart	2 2 0 R	4	1

14...Wolverhampton, July 2, L41-49

1 Leigh Adams	1 3 2 2 3 2	13	
2 Chris Morton	*0 0 N 0*	*0*	
3 Andrew Silver	0 0 1 T	1	
4 Peter Nahlin	2 2 0 0	4	1
5 Jimmy Nilsen	0 3 2 1 0	6	1
6 Paul Thorp	*3 1 3 0 3*	*10*	
7 †John Davis	2 2 1 2	7	2

15...BRADFORD, July 19, W50-40

1 Jimmy Nilsen	3 3 1 3 3	13	
2 David Smart	1 1 0 N	2	
3 Andrew Silver	2 1 2 1	6	2
4 Per Jonsson	*3 R 1 0*	*4*	*1*
5 Leigh Adams	0 3 2 2	7	
6 †John Davis	R 1 2 3	6	1
7 Peter Nahlin	3 3 3 1 2 R	12	2

16...Belle Vue, July 20, L36-54

1 Richard Knight	*1 3 3 3 0*	*10*	
2 David Smart	0 R T T	0	
3 Andrew Silver	1 1 0 1 1	4	
4 Glenn Doyle	*fx2 1 0 0*	*3*	
5 Neil Evitts	*E R 0 T*	*0*	
6 Peter Nahlin	**3 3 N 3 3 2 3**	**17**	**1**
7 †John Davis	1 1 N 0 N 0	2	

17...Oxford, August 3, W46-44

1† Jimmy Nilsen	2 2 3 3 1	11	1
2 Phil Crump	0 1 3 X	4	1
3 Andrew Silver	1 3 1 1	6	3
4 Paul Thorp	*0 3 0 0*	*3*	
5 Leigh Adams	2 1 2 2 2	9	
6 David Smart	2 0 N 2	4	1
7 Peter Nahlin	1 2 1 2 3	9	1

18...READING, August 4, D45-45

1 Jimmy Nilsen	3 2 3 2 0	10	
2 Phil Crump	0 1 0 0	1	1
3 Andrew Silver	1 3 3 3 1	11	1
4 †John Davis	R N N N	0	
5 Leigh Adams	2 1 2 1	6	
6 Peter Nahlin	3 2 2 1 1 3	12	3
7 David Smart	1 R 2 0 2	5	1

19...Bradford, August 11, L32-58

1 Andrew Silver	1 0 1 2	4	2
2 Tony Olsson	*2 1 R 2*	*5*	
3 Peter Nahlin	1 1 1 1 0	4	1
4 †Phil Crump	1 0 2 1	4	2
5 Leigh Adams	2 1 0 2 2	7	
6 David Smart	1 0 0 2	3	1
7 Stephen Davies	*2 0 2 1*	*5*	*1*

20...King's Lynn, August 18, W46-44

1 Jimmy Nilsen	**3 3 3 3 3**	**15**	
2 †John Davis	R N N N	0	
3 Andrew Silver	1 2 3 2 1	9	
4 Phil Crump	0 0 0 N	0	
5 Leigh Adams	3 2 2 0	7	
6 Peter Nahlin	3 2 N 2 2 1 3	13	2
7 David Smart	1 0 0 0 1 0	2	

21...BRADFORD, August 25, W46-44

1 Jan Andersson	*2 3 3 1 3 1*	*13*	*1*
2 Leigh Adams	*rider replacement*		
3 Andrew Silver	3 2 1 2 3 2	13	1
4 †Phil Crump	1 2 0 1 1	5	2
5 Bobby Ott	*fx1 2 1*	*4*	
6 Neil Collins	*1 2 0 2*	*5*	*2*
7 David Smart	2 2 0 1 1	6	3

22...King's Lynn, August 27, W55-35

1 Jimmy Nilsen	2 3 3 1 3	12	1
2 Phil Crump	3 2 R 2	7	2
3 Andrew Silver	2 3 3 3 1	12	
4 †John Davis	3 3 1 3	10	1
5 Leigh Adams	0 1 2 2	5	1
6 Peter Nahlin	2 1 2 0	5	1
7 David Smart	0 R 2 2	4	

23...KING'S LYNN, August 27, W59-31

1 Jimmy Nilsen	**3 3 2 3 3**	**14**	**1**
2 †John Davis	0 2 2 3	7	1
3 Andrew Silver	3 0 3 2	8	1
4 Phil Crump	2 1 2 2	7	3
5 Leigh Adams	**3 3 3 3 2**	**14**	**1**
6 Peter Nahlin	3 2 2 2	9	1
7 David Smart	0 0 0 0	0	

24...OXFORD, September 8, L43-47

1 Jimmy Nilsen	2 1 3 3 3	12	1
2 Peter Nahlin	1 2 2 1	6	1
3 Andrew Silver	2 2 1 0	5	
4 Phil Crump	2 1 0 0	3	1
5 Leigh Adams	0 2 1 2 1	6	
6 †John Davis	3 1 N 0 2	6	1
7 David Smart	2 1 1 N 1	5	4

25...Reading, September 10, L31-59

1 †Jimmy Nilsen	2 0 3 2 3 2	12	
2 Peter Nahlin	0 1 1 0	2	
3 Andrew Silver	E 1 1 1	3	1
4 Phil Crump	1 1 1 0	3	1
5 Leigh Adams	2 0 0 2 0	4	
6 David Smart	1 1 T 0 1	3	2
7 Peter Ravn	*2 2 0 0*	*4*	

26..Reading, October 1, L37-53

1 Jimmy Nilsen	3 1 3 2 0 3	12	
2 Peter Nahlin	2 R 2 fx1	5	2
3 Andrew Silver	3 1 1 1 3 0	9	1
4 †John Davis	1 1 1 T	3	
5 Leigh Adams	0 0 T 0 1	1	
6 Phil Crump	2 0 T 2	4	
7 David Smart	1 1 T 1	3	2

27...Oxford, October 3, L41-49

1 Jimmy Nilsen	3 3 3 1 0	10	
2 Peter Nahlin	2 2 2 2	8	3
3 Andrew Silver	2 2 R 1	5	1
4 †John Davis	fxN N N	0	
5 Leigh Adams	2 2 2 2 1	9	
6 David Smart	3 0 0 N 0 0 2	5	
7 Phil Crump	1 1 0 N 1 1	4	2

28...COVENTRY, October 6, W54-36

1 Jimmy Nilsen	3 3 2 3 2	13	
2 Peter Nahlin	1 1 2 1	5	1
3 Andrew Silver	2 2 2 2 1	9	2
4 †John Davis	3 3 2 1	9	1
5 Leigh Adams	1 0 3 1	5	1
6 David Smart	2 R 0 3	5	1
7 Phil Crump	3 0 3 2	8	1

29...Wolverhampton, October 8, L32-58

1 †Jimmy Nilsen	2 3 0 2 2 1	10	
2 Peter Nahlin	1 2 3 1 1 0	8	4
3 Andrew Silver	1 1 1 0	3	
4 Alastair Stevens	*1 1 0 T*	*2*	*1*
5 Leigh Adams	0 2 2 1 1	6	1
6 David Smart	0 T 0 0	0	
7 Phil Crump	2 0 T 1	3	

30...CRADLEY HEATH, October 13, L38-52

1 Jimmy Nilsen	3 2 2 3 2 2	14	
2 Peter Nahlin	2 1 2 0 0	5	2
3 Andrew Silver	1 1 fxT	2	
4 †John Davis	0 3 0 T	3	
5 Leigh Adams	1 2 2 1 1 0	7	2
6 David Smart	2 0 0 2	4	
7 Phil Crump	1 1 T 1	3	3

31...Coventry, October 20, W46-44

1 Jimmy Nilsen	3 2 3 3 3	14	
2 Peter Nahlin	2 1 2 2 0	7	3
3 Andrew Silver	3 0 3 1	7	
4 †John Davis	2 0 0 0	2	
5 Leigh Adams	1 1 1 0	3	1
6 David Smart	3 1 0 3	7	
7 Phil Crump	2 1 1 2	6	3

32...Cradley Heath, October 24, L42-48

1 Jimmy Nilsen	3 1 3 3 2	12	1
2 Peter Nahlin	1 2 3 1 2 1	10	2
3 Andrew Silver	1 R fxN	1	
4 †John Davis	2 3 0 T	5	
5 Leigh Adams	R 1 3 0	4	
6 David Smart	2 2 2 1 1 1	9	1
7 Phil Crump	1 0 N 0	1	1

'90 ROSTER

ADAMS, Leigh Scott
B 28.4.1971, Mildura, Victoria, Australia. *Signed from Poole.*

CAMDEN, Steven
B 19.6.1973, Oxford, Oxon.

CHESSELL, Martin
B 30.1.1970, Ludlow, Shropshire.

CROSS, Matthew John
B 26.8.1968, Taunton, Somerset.

CRUMP, Philip John
B 9.2.1952, Mildura, Australia. *Returned after a three-season retirement.*

DAVIS, John Harry
B 10.11.1954, Oxford, Oxon.

FREEMAN, Wayne
B 1.4.1969, Townsville, Australia. *First season Australian.*

KARGER, Brian
B 9.2.1967, Horsans, Denmark.

NAHLIN, Peter Jan Erik
B 1.5.1968, Eskilstuna, Sweden.

NILSEN Jimmy Øivind
B 19.11.1966, Stockholm, Sweden.

SILVER, Andrew George
B 13.1.1967, North London.

SMART, David John
B 28.12.1965, Swindon, Wiltshire.

WILSON, Darrin
B 17.10.1965, Hastings, New Zealand.

WITTS, Andrew Mark
B 13.3.1971, Swindon, Wiltshire.

Sam has the blues cure – Part Two

Track Data

Promoter: Chris Van Straaten on behalf of POWAR Limited.
Address: Ladbroke Stadium, Sutherland Avenue, Monmore Green, Wolverhampton WV2 2JJ.
Telephone: 0902-870400.
Clubcall: 0898 12 18 79.
Track Length: 280 metres.
Track Record: 57.73 secs, Ronnie Correy (Wolverhampton), August 27, 1990, Heat 1, Wolverhampton v Belle Vue (Sunbrite League).

THE fans turned nasty as Wolverhampton's season seemed to be heading for despair and disappointment. They barracked promoter Chris Van Straaten, believing that his loyalty to former skipper Sam Ermolenko had been misplaced.

Even Van Straaten himself would privately admit that he began to wonder if he had done the wrong thing in opting to start the season without a natural replacement for the still injured Californian.

And as the weeks, and matches, ticked by it looked, for all the world, that he had made a monumental blunder, particularly when Sam suspended one comeback after feeling the strain while racing in the American Final of the World Championship.

But all the heartache was forgotten on Saturday, June 23rd, at Dudley Wood Stadium. The Dianetics Wolves lost their Black Country derby by four points – but, for once, the result hardly mattered.

What did matter was that, in his comeback match after his long injury lay-off, Sam the Man won two of his five races and finished the night as top scorer with a dozen points.

He had proved a point not only to himself, but to everyone who wondered whether he could ever make a successful return after the shattering injuries which ended his 1989 season. The day that Ermolenko decided he was ready to race again, Wolverhampton were stone bottom, nine points adrift of the table toppers from Oxford.

By the end of the year they had overhauled every other team except Reading to claim the runners-up spot for the second year in a row and Ermolenko had scored nearly 300 points and averaged nearly nine points a meeting.

It was a truly remarkable revival for both the rider and the club and should have silenced all those vociferous critics who made life so uncomfortable for the management in less heady days.

There were other reasons to rejoice at Monmore Green. The powerful Goodyear Cubs, Wolverhampton's second team, had run away with the British League Division Two pennant, completed the double by winning the Knock Out Cup without losing a match, and unearthed an exciting prospect in teenager Wayne Carter who was given 17 matches in the Sunbrite League and the guarantee of a permanent team place in 1991.

He got his breaks through a variety of reasons including injuries which hit virtually every member of the first team squad. Ermolenko began the year on the sidelines, Jan Staechmann soon joined him and Lars Munkedal was ruled out for the season when he broke his leg.

Graham Jones damaged his back at Swindon towards the end of June and never totally recovered; Neil Collins was in and out of the medical room; and Carl Stonehewer, on loan from Belle Vue, also ended up out of racing, another injured back victim.

Even when Wolverhampton tried to plug the gaps they were thwarted by officialdom. After Bo Petersen's restricted stand-in spell as a replacement for Ermolenko, Van Straaten and team manager Peter Adams tried to recruit 1989 Swedish Champion Peter Karlsson. They were willing to do a two-for-two swap that would have given Carter a team place at the expense of Stonehewer after Belle Vue had turned down a name-your-price bid for their asset. But it was ruled that even though they were actually lowering their overall team average (and remember they were bottom of the League at the time!) they couldn't make the change without letting either Neil Collins, Graham Jones or Ronnie Correy go because Karlsson (assessed at six points a meeting) had to replace someone with a higher average!

Eventually, the figures worked out right and Karlsson made a belated second start to his Sunbrite League career and showed glimpses of real form, including a paid 11 at Belle Vue, a paid nine at Oxford and a paid 21 points in two guest appearances for Coventry.

Roll of Honour

Seasons in British League: 23 (1965-1980, 1984-1990).
British League Record: Runners-up (2), 1989, 1990. Third (1), 1986.
Speedway Star Cup Record: Runners-up (2), 1968, 1989.
League Cup Record: Fifth, 1985.
Inter League Cup Record: Runners-up (1), 1976.
Appearances: George Hunter, 195 (1972-1980).
Points: Ole Olsen, 2248 (1970-1975).
World Finalists: Ronnie Correy (1989-90), Sam Ermolenko (1986-87-88), Hasse Holmkvist (1968), Hans Nielsen (1980), Ole Olsen (1970-71-72-73-74-75), Petr Ondrasik (1980), Finn Thomsen (1977).
BLRC Finalists: Peter Jarman (1965), Peter Vandenberg (1966), Jim Airey (1967), Hasse Holmkvist (1968), James Bond (1969), Ole Olsen (1970-71-72-73, 1975), George Hunter (1974), Jim McMillan (1976-77), Hans Nielsen (1978-79-80), Peter Ravn (1984-85), Preben Eriksen (1986-87), Ronnie Correy (1988-89-90), Sam Ermolenko (1990).
Other Honours: Provincial League Champions, 1963.

Star of 90

RONNIE CORREY

Wolverhampton

WOLVERHAMPTON

01...Swindon, April 28, L33-57

1 Ronnie Correy	1 0 3 3 R T	7	
2 Jan Staechmann	*rider replacement*		
3 Bo Petersen	R 3 1 0 1 T	5	
4 †Graham Jones	3 3 2 0 0 R	8	
5 Neil Collins	fx2 1 2 2 1 1	9	
6 §Carl Stonehewer	1 0 T 0	1	
7 Lars Munkedal	0 1 1 1	3	
8 Wayne Carter	*rider replacement*		

02...Reading, May 7, L43-47

1 Ronnie Correy	F 3 3 1 2 1	10	2
2 Carl Stonehewer	1 0 T 0	1	
3 Bo Petersen	2 0 0 N	2	
4 †Graham Jones	E 3 3 2 3 2	13	1
5 Neil Collins	2 1 3 1	7	
6 Leigh Adams	*2 fx1 T N*	*3*	
7 Lars Munkedal	1 1 1 0 1	4	2
8 Wayne Carter	3	3	

03...READING, May 7, D45-45

1 Ronnie Correy	3 1 2 0 2	8	3
2 Greg Hancock	*2 2 3 3 3*	*13*	*1*
3 Bo Petersen	0 R 0 N	0	
4 †Graham Jones	fx0 3 3 1	7	
5 Neil Collins	2 3 R 2	7	
6 Wayne Carter	R 1 1 1	3	
7 Lars Munkedal	3 T 1 0 3	7	

04...BRADFORD, May 14, W53-37

1 Ronnie Correy	**3 3 3 3 3**	**15**	
2 John Jorgensen	*2 1 3 2*	*8*	*2*
3 †Graham Jones	3 3 3 3 0	12	
4 Bo Petersen	1 0 0 N	1	1
5 Neil Collins	2 1 2 1	6	
6 Mark Loram	*2 2 0 1 3*	*8*	*1*
7 Lars Munkedal	1 0 0 2	3	2

05...Coventry, May 26, L38-52

1 Ronnie Correy	2 3 3 R 1 2 1	12	1
2 Jan Staechmann	1 2 3 2 1	9	2
3 †Graham Jones	1 2 1 2 fx	6	1
4 Bobby Ott	*X 2 3 0 E*	*5*	
5 Bo Petersen	*rider replacement*		
6 Carl Stonehewer	2 0 0 X 0 3	5	
7 Lars Munkedal	fx N N N	0	
8 Wayne Carter	1	1	

06...OXFORD, May 28, W48-42

1 Ronnie Correy	3 2 3 3 3 1	15	1
2 Jan Staechmann	0 2 2 1 2	7	3
3 †Graham Jones	3 2 1 2 1	9	1
4 John Jorgensen	*3 1 3 1 2 2*	*12*	*1*
5 Bo Petersen	*rider replacement*		
6 Carl Stonehewer	2 0 1 0 2	5	1
7 Wayne Carter	F 0 N R	0	

07...KING'S LYNN, June 4, W51-39

1 Ronnie Correy	3 3 1 3 2	12	2
2 Jan Staechmann	2 2 3 2	9	2
3 Leigh Adams	*2 2 2 3 3*	*12*	*1*
4 Carl Stonehewer	0 1 3 F	4	1
5 †Graham Jones	1 2 2 0	5	1
6 Neil Evitts	*2 3 0 1*	*6*	*1*
7 Wayne Carter	0 1 0 2	3	

08...Bradford, June 16, L21-69

1 Jeremy Doncaster	*3 1 1 2 1*	*8*	
2 Jan Staechmann	1 0 0 0	1	
3 †Graham Jones	2 0 1 1 0	4	
4 §§Peter Karlsson	1 1 0 0	2	
5 Neil Collins	0 0 1 N	1	
6 Carl Stonehewer	1 1 0 1	3	
7 Wayne Carter	0 1 1 0 0	2	1

09...Cradley Heath, June 23, L43-47

1 Ronnie Correy	2 3 X 1 2	8	2
2 Jan Staechmann	0 1 2 2	5	
3 †Sam Ermolenko	2 3 2 2 3	12	
4 Graham Jones	2 2 X 1 2	7	1
5 Neil Collins	1 1 fnT	2	2
6 Carl Stonehewer	1 0 E 2	3	1
7 Wayne Carter	2 0 1 0 2 1	6	2

Correy lost to Pedersen for bonus point

10...CRADLEY HEATH, June 25, W47-43

1 Ronnie Correy	0 2 3 3 2	10	
2 Jan Staechmann	1 1 2 1	5	1
3 †Sam Ermolenko	1 1 1 R	3	3
4 Joe Screen	*1 2 2 1*	*6*	*2*
5 Graham Jones	2 3 1 1 1	8	2
6 Carl Stonehewer	3 2 2 2 2	11	1
7 Wayne Carter	1 0 N 3	4	

Correy lost to Pedersen for bonus point.

11...Swindon, June 30, L33-57

1 Ronnie Correy	3 1 3 1 2 1	11	1
2 Jan Staechmann	0 R T 2	2	
3 †Sam Ermolenko	1 3 3 0 R	7	1
4 Graham Jones	1 1 2 1 fn	5	1
5 Neil Collins	0 F 1 1	2	1
6 Carl Stonehewer	1 0 T 2 0	3	
7 Wayne Carter	0 2 0 1	3	1

12...SWINDON, July 2, W49-41

1 Ronnie Correy	**3 3 3 3 3**	**15**	
2 Jan Staechmann	2 2 2 1	7	2
3 †Sam Ermolenko	1 1 1 2 1	6	
4 Neil Collins	3 1 2 0	6	2
5 Neil Evitts	*1 2 3 1*	*7*	*1*
6 Carl Stonehewer	1 3 0 3 1	8	
7 Wayne Carter	fx0 N 0	0	

13...COVENTRY, July 9, W49-41

1 Kelly Moran	*3 3 1 2 3*	*12*	*1*
2 Jan Staechmann	2 R 2 0	4	1
3 †Sam Ermolenko	2 3 3 1 E	9	1
4 Neil Collins	1 1 1 3	6	2
5 Carl Stonehewer	2 0 2 0	4	
6 Joe Screen	*3 3 0 3 1*	*10*	
7 Wayne Carter	1 1 1 1	4	1

14...Belle Vue, July 13, L39-51

1 Ronnie Correy	X 3 3 2 1 2	11	
2 Jan Staechmann	2 F T N	2	
3 †Sam Ermolenko	2 3 3 2 3 F	13	1
4 Neil Collins	2 1 0 1	4	1
5 Paul Thorp	*0 0 1 T*	*1*	
6 Carl Stonehewer	1 3 1 1 1 0	7	1
7 Wayne Carter	0 N N 0 1	1	

15...Coventry, July 14, W47-42

1 Ronnie Correy	3 3 2 2 1	11	
2 David Mullett	*2 2 2 0*	*6*	*2*
3 †Sam Ermolenko	1 3 3 3 R	10	
4 Neil Collins	1 1 0 fn	2	
5 Per Jonsson	*3 3 2 0*	*8*	
6 Carl Stonehewer	2 2 1 1 2	8	2
7 Wayne Carter	1 0 N fx1	2	2

16...BELLE VUE, July 23, W53-36

1 Ronnie Correy	3 2 3 3 1 1	13	
2 Richard Knight	*0 3 1 2 2*	*8*	*1*
3 †Sam Ermolenko	**3 3 3 2 3 3**	**17**	**1**
4 Neil Collins	1 0 1 N 0	2	1
5 Graham Jones	*rider replacement*		
6 Carl Stonehewer	F 1 1 3 0 3	8	
7 Wayne Carter	3 0 N 2	5	1
8 Ade Hoole	*did not ride*		

17...BRADFORD, July 30, W48-42

1 Ronnie Correy	2 3 3 2 2 1	13	2
2 Graham Jones	*rider replacement*		
3 Neil Collins	2 2 1 2 0	7	2
4 †Sam Ermolenko	1 3 3 3 fx2	12	1
5 Carl Stonehewer	0 2 1 3 1	7	1
6 Sean Wilson	*1 1 2 3*	*7*	*2*
7 Wayne Carter	2 0 0 fx	2	
8 Ade Hoole	*did not ride*		

18...King's Lynn, August 4, D45-45

1 Ronnie Correy	3 3 3 3 2 3	17	
2 Peter Karlsson	fx0 N N	0	
3 †Sam Ermolenko	2 3 3 0 2 0	10	
4 Dean Barker	*0 1 1 0*	*2*	
5 Graham Jones	*rider replacement*		
6 Neil Collins	2 0 3 2 2 R	9	2
7 Carl Stonehewer	3 1 0 R 0 3	7	1
8 Wayne Carter	*did not ride*		

19...KING'S LYNN, August 6, W49-41

1 Ronnie Correy	3 0 3 3 F 3	12	
2 Graham Jones	*rider replacement*		
3 †Sam Ermolenko	X 3 3 3 3 2	14	1
4 Neil Collins	0 R 2 2	4	
5 Peter Karlsson	1 1 N 1	3	
6 Carl Stonehewer	1 2 2 1 1 2	9	3
7 Troy Butler	*2 1 1 0 3*	*7*	*1*
8 Ade Hoole	*did not ride*		

20...Oxford, August 10, W50-40

1 Ronnie Correy	3 1 2 3 3	12	1
2 Graham Jones	*rider replacement*		
3 †Sam Ermolenko	R 2 2 2 1 3	10	2
4 Wayne Carter	0 N 0 N	0	
5 Sean Wilson	*1 2 2 2 2 0*	*9*	
6 Carl Stonehewer	1 3 1 0 1 3	9	2
7 Neil Collins	2 3 0 3 2	10	1

21...Bradford, August 18, D45-45

1 Ronnie Correy	2 0 1 1	4	2
2 Peter Karlsson	3 1 2 2 0	8	
3 Graham Jones	1 2 3 0	6	1
4 Wayne Carter	0 0 N N	0	
5 †Sam Ermolenko	1 3 2 3 3 3	15	1
6 Carl Stonehewer	1 0 T 1 2	4	2
7 Neil Collins	2 2 1 0 3	8	1

22...Reading, August 20, D45-45

1 Ronnie Correy	3 0 2 3 0	8	1
2 Peter Karlsson	0 1 0 T	1	
3 Graham Jones	1 0 N N	1	
4 Billy Hamill	*2 2 1 1*	*6*	*1*
5 †Sam Ermolenko	1 1 2 3 3 2	12	2
6 Carl Stonehewer	2 1 0 2	5	2
7 Neil Collins	3 3 2 1 0 3	12	

23...BELLE VUE, August 27, W52-37

1 Ronnie Correy	**3 3 3 3 3**	**15**	
2 Peter Karlsson	1 2 0 1	4	1
3 †Sam Ermolenko	2 F 0 3 3 3	11	1
4 Graham Jones	*rider replacement*		
5 Jan Staechmann	0 0 3 2 N	5	1
6 Carl Stonehewer	2 1 3 2 fx	8	1
7 Neil Collins	3 E 1 1 3 1	9	
8 Stephen Morris	*did not ride*		

24...READING, September 3, W48-42

1 Ronnie Correy	3 0 3 1 2	9	1
2 Jan Staechmann	2 1 2 1	6	1
3 †Sam Ermolenko	3 2 2 3 R	10	
4 Billy Hamill	*3 R 3 2*	*8*	
5 Neil Collins	F 2 2 1	5	1
6 Alan Grahame	*2 0 1 1 3*	*7*	*2*
7 Peter Karlsson	1 0 N 2	3	2

25...Cradley Heath, September 8, L37-53

1 Ronnie Correy	0 1 T 2 0	3	
2 Jan Staechmann	1 0 2 1	4	
3 †Sam Ermolenko	2 3 X R 1 2	8	1
4 Sean Wilson	*3 2 1 0 0*	*6*	
5 Neil Collins	1 1 0 T	2	1
6 Wayne Carter	1 0 N 3	4	
7 Andy Hackett	*3 3 1 1 2*	*10*	*2*

26...COVENTRY, September 10, W46-44

1 Ronnie Correy	3 3 1 1 3 3	14	
2 Jan Staechmann	2 fx3 0	5	1
3 †Sam Ermolenko	**2 3 3 2 2**	**12**	**3**
4 Joe Screen	*1 2 2 F*	*5*	
5 Neil Collins	0 0 1 T	1	1
6 Stephen Davies	*2 3 0 1*	*6*	*1*
7 Wayne Carter	1 0 0 2	3	1

27...OXFORD, September 17, L44-46

1 Ronnie Correy	R 2 1 3 2	8	
2 Graham Jones	1 1 3 0	5	1
3 †Sam Ermolenko	2 3 2 2 1	10	2
4 Neil Collins	3 1 0 0	4	1
5 Jan Staechmann	0 2 1 1	4	1
6 Alan Grahame	*3 3 1 1*	*8*	*1*
7 Peter Karlsson	2 1 0 2	5	1

28...Belle Vue, September 21, D45-45

1 Ronnie Correy	0 1 3 3 1 2 3	13	
2 Graham Jones	*rider replacement*		
3 †Sam Ermolenko	1 3 3 1 2 3 X	13	1
4 Neil Collins	1 3 1 1	6	1
5 Jan Staechmann	0 0 N 0 T	0	
6 Andy Hackett	*0 1 0 3*	*4*	
7 Peter Karlsson	3 1 2 1 2	9	2

29...CRADLEY HEATH, October 1, W54-36

1 Ronnie Correy	**3 3 3 3 2**	**14**	**1**
2 Graham Jones	1 1 2 0	4	
3 †Sam Ermolenko	3 2 3 3 3	14	
4 Neil Collins	2 2 1 1	6	1
5 Jan Staechmann	0 1 2 2	5	2
6 Stephen Davies	*2 1 0 1*	*4*	*1*
7 Peter Karlsson	3 0 1 3	7	

30...King's Lynn, October 6, W47-43

1 Ronnie Correy	3 2 3 3 2	13	
2 Joe Screen	*1 0 2 1*	*4*	*1*
3 †Sam Ermolenko	2 2 3 2 0	9	1
4 Neil Collins	3 1 1 0	5	1
5 Jan Staechmann	2 2 0 0	4	1
6 Peter Karlsson	0 3 1 E	4	
7 Troy Butler	*1 1 3 3*	*8*	*1*

31...SWINDON, October 8, W58-32

1 Ronnie Correy	**3 3 3 3 3 3**	**18**	
2 Jan Staechmann	0 2 1 2	5	2
3 †Sam Ermolenko	**3 3 2 3 3 2**	**16**	**2**
4 Neil Collins	2 fx3 2 0	7	2
5 Graham Jones	*rider replacement*		
6 Roman Matousek	*3 2 1 0 2*	*8*	*2*
7 Peter Karlsson	1 0 F 3	4	
8 Wayne Carter	*did not ride*		

32...Oxford, October 12, L41-49

1 Ronnie Correy	2 2 1 2 1 0	8	1
2 Jan Staechmann	0 1 0 N	1	1
3 †Sam Ermolenko	2 3 3 3 3 2	16	1
4 Neil Collins	2 F 0 0	2	
5 Sean Wilson	*1 1 1 N*	*3*	*1*
6 Stephen Davies	*1 0 N 2*	*3*	*1*
7 Peter Karlsson	2 3 1 1 1	8	1

'90 ROSTER

CARTER, Wayne
B 19.12.1970, Halifax, W. Yorkshire.
COLLINS, Neil Jeffrey
B 15.10.1961, Partington, Greater Manchester.
COOPER, Shane
B 16.1.1969, Nantwich, Cheshire. *Loal junior.*
CORREY, Ronnie Dean
B 8.11.1966, Bellflower, Ca., U.S.A.
ERMOLENKO, Guy Allen (Sam)
B 23.11.1960, Maywood, Ca., U.S.A.
HOOLE, Adrian Leslie (Ade)
B 28.8.1970, Telford, Shropshire.
JONES, Graham Tudor
B 5.5.1963, Oswestry, Shropshire.
KARLSSON, Peter Gunnar
B 17.12.1969, Gullspång, Sweden. *Swedish newcomer.*
MORRIS, Stephen
B 22.12.1972, Wolverhampton, West Midlands. *Local junior.*
MUNKEDAL, Lars
B 3.3.1967, Copenhagen, Denmark. *Recalled from Edinburgh.*
PETERSEN, Bo
B 21.2.1958, Bolbro, Denmark.
STAECHMANN, Jan
B 5.6.1966, Kolding, Denmark.
STONEHEWER, Carl Bryan
B 16.5.1972, Manchester. *On loan from Belle Vue.*

1990 NATIONAL LEAGUE FINAL TABLE

Team	P	Home W	D	L	PtsF	PtsA	Away W	D	L	PtsF	PtsA	Pts
1 POOLE	32	16	0	0	970	564	13	0	3	809	720	58
2 Middlesbrough	32	16	0	0	966	567	6	2	8	735	800	46
3 Ipswich	32	13	2	1	906	626	9	0	7	768	761	46
4 Glasgow	32	13	0	3	934.5	598.5	6	0	10	709	821	38
5 Hackney	32	13	0	3	887	644	6	0	10	721	807	38
6 Berwick	32	15	0	1	941	584	3	1	12	634.5	899.5	37
7 Wimbledon	32	12	1	3	872	656	4	2	10	720	813	35
8 Stoke	32	11	0	5	839	691	5	1	10	734	798	33
9 Exeter	32	14	0	2	951	582	1	1	14	625	907	31
10 Peterborough	32	13	0	3	878	657	2	0	14	578	956	30
11 Eastbourne	32	12	0	4	828	702	3	0	13	598	934	30
12 Newcastle	32	11	0	5	802	731	3	0	13	676.5	855.5	28
13 Edinburgh	32	10	1	5	854.5	678.5	2	0	14	666	861	25
14 Arena Essex	32	9	1	6	797	729	3	0	13	583	945	25
15 Rye House	32	7	0	9	778	749	1	0	15	608	923	16
16 Long Eaton	32	7	2	7	778	758	0	0	16	594	939	16
17 Milton Keynes	32	5	0	11	724	804	1	0	15	562	966	12

1990 NATIONAL LEAGUE

All the Results

	ARENA ESSEX	BERWICK	EASTBOURNE	EDINBURGH	EXETER	GLASGOW	HACKNEY	IPSWICH	LONG EATON	MIDDLESBROUGH	MILTON KEYNES	NEWCASTLE	PETERBOROUGH	POOLE	RYE HOUSE	STOKE	WIMBLEDON
ARENA ESSEX		58-38	38-58	57-36	62-34	44-52	54-42	47-49	51-43	48-48	47-49	47-49	52-43	41-51	51-45	50-46	50-46
BERWICK	71-25		61-35	48-45	63-32	51-44	46-47	49-47	54-42	51-45	68-27	68-27	73-23	61-35	68-28	56-40	53-42
EASTBOURNE	39-56	58-38		62-34	66-30	53-42	51-45	46-49	49-47	42-54	56-39	49-46	53-43	35-61	61-34	54-42	54-42
EDINBURGH	67-29	46.5-49.5	60-36		66-29	43-52	40-56	31-64	71-25	45-51	66-30	56-40	62-34	53-43	51-45	49-47	48-48
EXETER	76-20	56-40	63-32	56-39		60-35	45-51	53-43	65-31	67-29	64-32	55-41	68-28	44-52	64-32	53-43	62-34
GLASGOW	74-22	60-36	66-30	53-43	61-35		54-42	62-33	74-22	57-39	63-32	51.5-44.5	64-32	46-49	60-36	45-51	44-52
HACKNEY	44-50	61-35	62-33	52-44	51-45	50-46		53-42	62-34	43-53	67-29	60-35	59-37	47-49	68-28	57-39	51-45
IPSWICH	70-25	48-48	63-33	56-40	50-46	56-40	48-47		55-41	60-36	65-31	60-36	63-33	44-51	67-28	48-48	53-43
LONG EATON	54-42	46-50	41-55	52-44	48-48	40-56	49-47	43-53		40-56	56-40	54-42	69-27	45-51	49-47	44-52	48-48
MIDDLESBROUGH	53-43	71-25	61-35	65-31	61-34	60-36	58-38	53-43	62-34		68-28	55-41	70-26	59-37	58-37	52-44	60-35
MILTON KEYNES	53-42	46-49	41-55	46-50	40-56	40-56	45-51	44-49	59-37	39-57		49-46	51-45	44-52	48-47	37-59	42-53
NEWCASTLE	55-41	50-46	51-45	54-42	55-41	45-50	44-52	47-49	50-46	48-47	63-33		55-41	45-51	51-44	50-46	39-57
PETERBOROUGH	67-29	64-32	74-22	53-43	50-46	67-29	61-35	41-55	52-44	50-46	59-37	51-45		29-67	57-39	46-49	57-39
POOLE	61-35	70-26	71-25	52-43	57-39	62-34	63-32	59-37	56-40	58-38	56-40	63-33	58-38		73-23	57-39	54-42
RYE HOUSE	46-49	52-43	62-33	43-52	55-40	46-49	50-46	44-52	56-39	59-37	51-45	39-57	47-49	36-60		45-49	47-49
STOKE	54-40	58-38	54-42	62-34	61-35	50-46	47-49	40-56	61-35	45-51	55-37	41-55	66-30	44-52	50-46		51-45
WIMBLEDON	61-35	55-41	66-29	50-46	61-35	54-42	52-41	49-47	62-34	48-48	62-33	57-39	46-49	47-48	47-49	55-40	

National League Roll of Honour

1968	1 BELLE VUE	2 Nelson	3 Middlesbrough
1969	1 BELLE VUE	2 Reading	3 Romford
1970	1 CANTERBURY	2 Eastbourne	3 Rochdale
1971	1 EASTBOURNE	2 Bradford	3 Ipswich
1972	1 CREWE	2 Boston	3 Peterborough
1973	1 BOSTON	2 Workington	3 Eastbourne
1974	1 BIRMINGHAM	2 Eastbourne	3 Boston
1975	1 BIRMINGHAM	2 Newcastle	3 Stoke
1976	1 NEWCASTLE	2 Ellesmere Port	3 Workington
1977	1 EASTBOURNE	2 Rye House	3 Ellesmere Port
1978	1 CANTERBURY	2 Newcastle	3 Rye House
1979	1 MILDENHALL	2 Rye House	3 Oxford
1980	1 RYE HOUSE	2 Newcastle	3 Middlesbrough
1981	1 MIDDLESBROUGH	2 Weymouth	3 Newcastle
1982	1 NEWCASTLE	2 Mildenhall	3 Ellesmere Port
1983	1 NEWCASTLE	2 Mildenhall	3 Crayford
1984	1 LONG EATON	2 Mildenhall	3 Stoke
1985	1 ELLESMERE PORT	2 Poole	3 Middlesbrough
1986	1 EASTBOURNE	2 Poole	3 Middlesbrough
1987	1 EASTBOURNE	2 Mildenhall	3 Milton Keynes
1988	1 HACKNEY	2 Poole	3 Eastbourne
1989	1 POOLE	2 Wimbledon	3 Berwick
1990	1 POOLE	2 Middlesbrough	3 Ipswich

The Records...

▲ THE National League was formed in 1968 as the British League Division Two with 10 founder members – Belle Vue, Berwick, Canterbury, Crayford, Middlesbrough, Nelson, Plymouth, Rayleigh, Reading and Weymouth – and was renamed the New National League in 1975. The following year the prefix *New* was dropped from the League's title and since then it has operated as the National League.

▲ *THE following venues have staged National League racing: Arena Essex, Barrow (Holker Street and Park Road), Belle Vue, Berwick (Shielfield Park and Berrington Lough), Birmingham (Perry Barr and Bordesley Green), Boston, Bradford (Odsal), Canterbury, Coatbridge, Crayford, Crewe, Doncaster, Eastbourne, Edinburgh, Ellesmere Port, Exeter, Glasgow (Blantyre, Craighead Park and Shawfield Park), Hackney, Hull, Ipswich, King's Lynn, Long Eaton, Middlesbrough, Mildenhall, Milton Keynes (Groveway and Elfield Park), Nelson, Newcastle, Newport, Oxford, Paisley, Peterborough, Plymouth, Poole, Rayleigh, Reading (Tilehurst), Rochdale, Romford, Rye House, Scunthorpe (Quibell Park and Ashby Ville), Stoke, Sunderland, West Ham, Weymouth, Wimbledon, Wolverhampton and Workington.*

▲ THE most successful National League side has been Eastbourne who have won the Championship a record four times, in 1971, 1977, 1986 and 1987. The least successful has been Long Eaton who have been wooden spoonists four times – 1970, 1983, 1986 and 1988. Long Eaton are also the only side to have finished bottom one season (1983) and won the title the next (1984).

▲ *THE most points gained by a championship winning side was 62 by Rye House in 1980 when they lost seven matches in a 38 match schedule.*

▲ THE most successful League season enjoyed by a club was in 1990 when the National League champions Poole, who only dropped six points from 32 matches, had a success percentage of 90.625% – ahead of Hackney in 1988 (90%) and Newcastle in 1976 (89.706%).

▲ *THE worst-ever season experienced by a National League team that completed a full season was that of Workington in 1980 when they won two and lost 36 matches in their 38 meeting schedule for a success percentage of 5.263. In 1987 Boston withdrew after completing only 16 of what would have been a scheduled 32 matches and at the time had gained only one point out of a possible 32 - a success rate of 3.125%.*

▲ MIDDLESBROUGH are the only club to have completed all 23 seasons of the National League at the same track. Berwick have been members of the National League for 23 successive seasons but were forced to withdraw from the 1981 competition after completing 26 of their scheduled League matches even though they were without a home track. They had been evicted from Shielfield Park at the end of the previous season and while seeking planning permission to build a new home at Berrington Lough, raced their home meetings at Barrow, Workington, Glasgow and Newcastle. They were forced to pull out following a protest by Edinburgh promoter Mike Parker when they moved to Glasgow. Despite their problems they won the National League Knock Out Cup that season, racing every home leg on a neutral track. Even though their last League match was on September 4, they raced a further four Cup matches after that date, including the final against Edinburgh.

Silver Helmet

STEVE SCHOFIELD led the National League averages for much of the season.

But you won't find his name among the Silver Helmet statistics.

By one of those strange quirks of fate he was never involved in a challenge throughout the 1990 summer – even though he was the rider most likely to succeed!

Only two tracks, Hackney and Edinburgh, missed out on a titfer challenge during a campaign in which the most successful defenders were Kenny McKinna (Glasgow) and David Bargh (Newcastle), both of whom survived four challenges.

The trophy certainly did the rounds with challenges at all but four of the 17 National League tracks – Stoke and Peterborough joining the two named above – and, in all, a dozen riders held the crown for a varying time.

Top gun Craig Boyce held it twice – beating winter holder Kenny McKinna in the first challenge of the season and then regaining it against Chris Louis in the middle of June.

The competition also threw up a couple of unlikely challengers: debutant Scott Humphries of Rye House and another relatively new signing Jon Cooper of Milton Keynes.

Winter holder 1989-1990: Kenny McKinna (Glasgow)

Kenny McKinna (Glasgow) lost to **Craig Boyce** (Poole), April 27.

Boyce beat David Blackburn at Berwick, April 28; Lost to **Kenny McKinna** (Glasgow), May 1.

McKinna beat Nigel Crabtree (Stoke), May 2; Steve Regeling (Exeter), May 9; Rob Tilbury (Arena Essex), May 23; David Norris at Ipswich, May 31; Lost to **Dean Standing** (Ipswich), June 3.

Standing beat Craig Hodgson (Peterborough), June 7; Andy Buck (Eastbourne), June 14; Forfeited title at Exeter through injury, June 18.

Chris Louis (Ipswich) beat Steve Regeling at Exeter, June 18; Lost to **Craig Boyce** at Poole, June 19.

Boyce beat Jens Rasmussen at Rye House, June 24; Eric Monaghan (Stoke), June 26; Lost to **David Bargh** at Newcastle, July 1.

Bargh lost to **Rob Tilbury** at Arena Essex, July 7.

Tilbury beat Steve Lawson (Glasgow), July 14; Lost to **Jens Rasmussen** at Rye House, July 22.

Rasmussen forfeited title at Eastbourne through injury, August 4.

Paul Woods beat Scott Humphries (Rye House) at Eastbourne, August 4; Lost to **Steve Lawson** at Glasgow, August 8.

Lawson lost to **Nigel De'ath** at Long Eaton, August 15;

De'ath beat Jonathon Cooper (Milton Keynes), August 29; Lost to **Darren Sumner** at Middlesbrough, August 30.

Sumner lost to **David Bargh** at Newcastle, September 2.

Bargh beat Peter Glanz (Milton Keynes), September 9; Gordon Kennett (Eastbourne), September 17; Steve Lawson at Glasgow, September 19; Chris Louis (Ipswich), September 23; Lost to **Andy Grahame** at Wimbledon, October 10.

Winter holder 1990-1991: Andy Grahame (Wimbledon).

NATIONAL SERIES

Qualifying Rounds

NATIONAL LEAGUE TABLE

	P.	W.	D.	L.	PtsF.	PtsA.	Pts.
1 POOLE	*26*	*23*	*0*	*3*	*1457*	*1036*	*46*
2 IPSWICH	*31*	*22*	*2*	*7*	*1630*	*1336*	*46*
3 MIDDLESBROUGH	*29*	*20*	*1*	*8*	*1542*	*1238*	*41*
4 GLASGOW	*31*	*18*	*0*	*13*	*1589.5*	*1377.5*	*36*
5 HACKNEY	*27*	*18*	*0*	*9*	*1388*	*1191*	*36*
6 BERWICK	*31*	*17*	*1*	*13*	*1527.5*	*1438.5*	*35*
7 WIMBLEDON	*28*	*15*	*2*	*11*	*1398*	*1280*	*32*
8 EXETER	*31*	*15*	*1*	*15*	*1537*	*1432*	*31*
9 STOKE	*30*	*15*	*1*	*14*	*1476*	*1394*	*31*
10 Peterborough	31	15	0	16	1429	1544	30
11 Newcastle	30	14	0	16	1395.5	1477.5	28
12 Eastbourne	30	13	0	17	1319	1552	26
13 Arena Essex	30	12	1	17	1304	1562	25
14 Edinburgh	30	11	1	18	1426.5	1444.5	23
15 Rye House	31	8	0	23	1340	1622	16
16 Long Eaton	31	6	2	23	1303	1670	14
17 Milton Keynes	31	6	0	25	1247	1714	12

As at Sunday, September 23, 1990

Exeter, Monday, October 1, First leg

EXETER 39			
1 †Steve Regeling	1 2 1 2	6	2
2 Steve Bishop	3 3 2 1	9	1
3 Richard Green	3 3 3 2	11	
4 Ian Barney	0 0 N N	0	
5 Colin Cook	3 3 2 1	9	
6 Mark Simmonds	0 2 1 0	3	2
7 Frank Smart	1 0	1	
POOLE 35			
1 Craig Boyce	2 3 3 3	11	
2 Rod Colquhoun	0 0 2 1	3	1
3 Tony Langdon	2 0 2 3	7	
4 Mark Lemon	1 1 0 0	2	1
5 †Alun Rossiter	1 1 3 2	7	2
6 Gary Allan	2 2 R 1	5	1
7 Justin Elkins	*did not ride*		
WIMBLEDON 34			
1 Nathan Simpson	1 0 0 1	2	2
2 Neville Tatum	2 1 1 2	6	
3 †Ray Morton	3 2 3 3	11	
4 Nigel Leaver	0 1 0 2	3	2
5 Andy Grahame	2 3 3 3	11	
6 Peter Chapman	1 0 0 N	1	1
7 Deon Prinsloo	0	0	

Poole, Tuesday, October 9, Second leg

POOLE 42			
1 Craig Boyce	3 3 2 3	11	
2 Rod Colquhoun	1 R 1 1	3	1
3 Tony Langdon	1 3 2 3	9	
4 Justin Elkins	0 1 1 0	2	1
5 †Alun Rossiter	1 3 1 3	8	1
6 Gary Allan	2 2 3 2	9	2
7 Mark Lemon	*did not ride*		
EXETER 33			
1 †Steve Regeling	3 2 3 3	11	
2 Steve Bishop	2 1 2 1	6	3
3 Richard Green	3 2 2 1	8	
4 Ian Barney	0 N 0 0	0	
5 Colin Cook	2 R 2 2	6	
6 Mark Simmonds	0 2 0 N	2	
7 Frank Smart	0 0	0	
WIMBLEDON 33			
1 Nathan Simpson	2 3 1 1	7	1
2 Neville Tatum	0 1 0 2	3	
3 †Ray Morton	2 1 fx2	5	
4 Nigel Leaver	1 0 3 R	4	1
5 Andy Grahame	**3 3 3 3**	**12**	
6 Peter Chapman	0 N 0 1	1	
7 Justin Pryor	1	1	

Wimbledon, Wednesday, October 17, Third leg

WIMBLEDON 52			
1 Nathan Simpson	2 1 3 1	7	2
2 Neville Tatum	3 2 2 3	10	1
3 †Ray Morton	**3 3 3 3**	**12**	
4 Nigel Leaver	2 1 2 R	5	2
5 Andy Grahame	**3 3 3 3**	**12**	
6 Peter Chapman	2 1 1 2	6	2
7 Peter Schroeck	*did not ride*		
POOLE 29			
1 Craig Boyce	1 3 2 2	8	
2 Rod Colquhoun	0 0 fx1	1	1
3 Tony Langdon	2 2 3 1	8	
4 Mark Lemon	0 0 0 0	0	
5 †Alun Rossiter	2 3 R R	5	
6 Gary Allan	1 2 2 2	7	2
7 Justin Elkins	*did not ride*		
EXETER 27			
1 †Steve Regeling	1 3 3 1	8	1
2 Steve Bishop	0 0 1 2	3	
3 Richard Green	3 2 1 3	9	
4 Ian Barney	1 0 0 0	1	
5 Colin Cook	N N N N	0	
6 Mark Simmonds	1 1 1 1	4	1
7 Frank Smart	0 0 0 2	2	

Aggregate:
WIMBLEDON 119 Poole 106 Exeter 99

Middlesbrough, Thursday, October 4, First leg

MIDDLESBROUGH 50			
1 Darren Sumner	**3 2 3 2**	**10**	**2**
2 David Cheshire	0 3 2 3	8	1
3 Rod Hunter	2 0 1 1	4	2
4 Paul Bentley	3 2 2 3	10	
5 †Jamie Luckhurst	2 3 3 0	8	1
6 Steve Wilcock	**3 2 2 3**	**10**	**2**
7 Duncan Chapman	*did not ride*		
GLASGOW 31			
1 †Steve Lawson	1 1 3 3	8	
2 Charlie McKinna	0 0 2 1	3	1
3 Shane Bowes	3 3 2 1	9	1
4 Jason Lyons	1 1 1 2	5	1
5 Phil Jeffrey	fx0 0 0	0	
6 Sean Courtney	2 2 1 1	6	
7 Geoff Powell did not ride			
BERWICK 27			
1 Mark Courtney	2 3 1 0	6	
2 Alan Rivett	1 1 0 N	2	1
3 David Blackburn	2 1 0 0	3	
4 †Rob Grant	0 0 N N	0	
5 Andy Campbell	1 3 1 0	5	
6 David Walsh	0 1 0 3	4	
7 Scott Robson	3 2 2	7	

Glasgow, Wednesday, October 10, Second leg

GLASGOW 50			
1 †Steve Lawson	**3 3 2 3**	**11**	**1**
2 Charlie McKinna	2 fx3 1	6	1
3 Shane Bowes	fx1 3 1	5	
4 Sean Courtney	**3 3 2 3**	**11**	**1**
5 Jason Lyons	2 E 2 2	6	2
6 Kenny McKinna	3 3 3 0	9	
7 Phil Jeffrey	2	2	1
BERWICK 33			
1 Mark Courtney	2 1 2 3	8	2
2 Scott Robson	1 2 3 0	6	1
3 David Blackburn	0 0 R 1	1	
4 †Rob Grant	2 2 3 3	10	
5 Andy Campbell	1 2 0 0	3	1
6 David Walsh	2 0 1 2	5	
7 Kevin Little	*did not ride*		
MIDDLESBROUGH 25			
1 †Darren Sumner	fx3 1 2	6	
2 Mark Crang	1 0 0 0	1	
3 Rod Hunter	1 R 0 2	3	
4 Paul Bentley	3 1 1 1	6	1
5 Duncan Chapman	0 3 F 1	4	1
6 Steve Wilcock	1 1 1 2	5	
7 James Grieves	*did not ride*		

Berwick, Saturday, October 12, Third leg

BERWICK 40			
1 Mark Courtney	3 2 R R	5	1
2 Scott Robson	1 3 3 2	9	
3 David Blackburn	1 0 2 1	4	1
4 †Rob Grant	2 1 1 3	7	1
5 Andy Campbell	2 0 0 1	3	1
6 David Walsh	**3 3 3 3**	**12**	
7 Kevin Little	*did not ride*		
GLASGOW 35			
1 †Steve Lawson	2 3 1 0	6	1
2 Charlie McKinna	0 1 2 2	5	
3 Shane Bowes	3 2 F 2	7	1
4 Jason Lyons	0 1 3 3	7	1
5 Kenny McKinna	1 3 2 2	8	
6 Sean Courtney	0 0 1 N	1	1
7 Phil Jeffrey	1	1	1
MIDDLESBROUGH 33			
1 †Darren Sumner	3 1 3 0	7	
2 Mark Crang	0 0 0 1	1	
3 Rod Hunter	1 3 3 R	7	1
4 Paul Bentley	2 2 fx2	6	1
5 Duncan Chapman	0 1 2 1	4	1
6 Steve Wilcock	2 2 1 3	8	1
7 Colin Smith	*did not ride*		

Aggregate:
GLASGOW 116 Middlesbrough 108 Berwick 100

Stoke, Tuesday, October 9, First leg

STOKE 47			
1 Louis Carr	**3 3 3 3**	**12**	
2 Mark Carlson	1 1 0 2	4	1
3 †Nigel Crabtree	2 3 2 1	8	2
4 Eric Monaghan	**3 2 3 3**	**11**	**1**
5 David Clarke	2 1 1 1	5	3
6 Chris Cobby	3 2 2 0	7	
7 Mark Pearce	*did not ride*		
IPSWICH 32			
1 Chris Louis	2 3 3 2	10	
2 Craig Hyde	0 N N 0	0	
3 Dean Standing	3 R 0 0	3	
4 Shane Parker	1 3 1 1	6	
5 †Alan Mogridge	0 3 2 fx	5	
6 Robbie Fuller	1 0 1 3	5	1
7 Darren Fitch	2 1	3	1
HACKNEY 29			
1 †Paul Whittaker	1 2 2 3 2	10	1
2 Shawn Venables	0 0 0 3	3	
3 Gary Tagg	0 fx0 1 2	3	2
4 Dave Hamnett	2 2 1 2 3	10	
5 Steve Schofield	*rider replacement*		
6 Roland Pollard	1 1 0 1	3	1
7 David Wolstenholme	0	0	

Ipswich, Thursday, October 11, Second leg

IPSWICH 44			
1 Chris Louis	**3 3 3 3**	**12**	
2 Darren Fitch	fx0 0 0	0	
3 Dean Standing	fx1 1 3	5	
4 Shane Parker	1 3 3 2	9	1
5 †Alan Mogridge	**3 2 3 3**	**11**	**1**
6 Robbie Fuller	1 3 2 1	7	1
7 Lawrence Hare	*did not ride*		
STOKE 35			
1 Louis Carr	2 2 2 1	7	1
2 Mark Carlson	3 1 0 R	4	1
3 †Nigel Crabtree	3 2 3 2	10	
4 David Clarke	1 0 1 fx	2	
5 Eric Monaghan	1 2 0 1	4	3
6 Chris Cobby	2 3 1 2	8	
7 Mark Pearce	*did not ride*		
HACKNEY 29			
1 †Paul Whittaker	1 3 1 3 1	9	1
2 Michael Warren	2 0 1 2 fx	5	
3 Gary Tagg	0 E 2 2 3	7	
4 Dave Hamnett	2 2 0 0 2	6	1
5 Steve Schofield	*rider replacement*		
6 Shawn Venables	0 0 1 0	1	1
7 Roland Pollard	1	1	

Hackney, Friday, October 12, Third leg

IPSWICH 38			
1 Chris Louis	3 2 3 2	10	
2 Darren Fitch	0 F 0 0	0	
3 Dean Standing	2 3 0 3	8	1
4 Shane Parker	3 2 2 X	7	1
5 †Alan Mogridge	2 3 3 3	11	
6 Robbie Fuller	0 0 0 2	2	1
7 Lawrence Hare	*did not ride*		
HACKNEY 35			
1 †Paul Whittaker	3 3 3 3 R	12	
2 Michael Warren	2 1 1 2 1	7	1
3 Gary Tagg	2 1 1 3 1	8	
4 Dave Hamnett	1 0 1 3 R	5	1
5 Steve Schofield	*rider replacement*		
6 Shawn Venables	fxF N N	0	
7 Roland Pollard	1 2	3	1
8 David Wolstenholme	*did not ride*		
STOKE 34			
1 Louis Carr	1 3 2 2	8	
2 Mark Carlson	0 1 1 N	2	1
3 †Nigel Crabtree	0 2 R 3	5	1
4 David Clarke	1 3 2 1	7	
5 Eric Monaghan	1 2 2 3	8	1
6 Chris Cobby	2 1 0 1	4	1
7 Mark Pearce	0	0	

Aggregate:
STOKE 116 Ipswich 114 Hackney 93

NATIONAL SERIES

The FINAL

GLASGOW won the first major trophy in their National League history by claiming the first ever National Series.

The competition was launched to try and add extra interest to the campaign and it certainly worked in that respect.

There was a nail-biting chase to fill the top nine places at the cut-off date of September 23 – it was actually extended – and 12 National League teams were involved practically to the deadline Sunday.

Stoke, praying that the weather was kind to them, grabbed the last qualifying place by beating Edinburgh on September 22, and that provided a convenient splitting into three qualifying groups for the final round of matches.

Avoiding tracks with the same race-nights, Hackney and Ipswich were included in the same group as Stoke.

In some ways the regional spread of the qualifiers was the tournament's only obvious weakness and there were grave doubts about the effort put into the final leg of their qualifier by double winners Poole who went into the last round at Wimbledon holding a 10 point lead which they surprisingly squandered.

Victory would have given the Echo Pirates a long and expensive trip to Scotland for the final itself once Glasgow had made sure of their place in the final at the expense of championship runners-up Middlesbrough and Berwick.

No-one could accuse the supporters of taking the competition lightly, however.

All three tracks in the final reported bumper attendances for their home leg and Glasgow, in particular, were more than happy with the gate for their meeting despite being forced to run in opposition to a major Sunday afternoon Scottish soccer game and seeing the rain come down in stair-rods in the hours before the first race.

Rain had partly wrecked the opening round of the final with referee Graham Brodie being forced to abandon the Wimbledon meeting after the Glasgow pairing of Shane Bowes and Sean Courtney had both fallen in the rain in abortive attempts to run a heat 14 which was eventually abandoned.

First round

Wimbledon, Wednesday, October 24

WIMBLEDON 31			
1 Nathan Simpson	2 2 3	7	1
2 Neville Tatum	3 1 2	6	2
3 †Ray Morton	R 0 2	0	
4 Nigel Leaver	3 3 3	6	
5 Andy Grahame	3 3 3	9	
6 Peter Chapman	0 2 1	3	1
7 Peter Schroeck	*did not ride*		
GLASGOW 25			
1 †Steve Lawson	1 3 2	6	1
2 Jason Lyons	2 0 1	3	1
3 Shane Bowes	3 1	4	1
4 Sean Courtney	fx 2	2	
5 Kenny McKinna	3 2 0	5	
6 Charlie McKinna	2 1 2	5	2
7 Phil Jeffrey	*did not ride*		
STOKE 15			
1 Louis Carr	1 0 3	4	
2 Mark Carlson	0 1 0	1	
3 Garry Stead	2 0 0	2	
4 David Clarke	fx 1 1	1	
5 †Eric Monaghan	1 0 0	1	1
6 Chris Cobby	2 3 1	6	
7 Jason Reed	*did not ride*		

Abandoned after 13 heats, result to stand after 12 races when all teams had an equal number of rides. Discount scores underlined.

Second round

Stoke, Saturday, October 26

GLASGOW 42			
1 †Steve Lawson	2 1 3 2	8	2
2 Jason Lyons	1 2 2 3	8	2
3 Shane Bowes	2 3 3 2	10	
4 Sean Courtney	0 0 N N	0	
5 Kenny McKinna	3 2 3 2	10	
6 Charlie McKinna	0 1 2 1	4	3
7 Phil Jeffrey	2 0	2	1
WIMBLEDON 38			
1 Nathan Simpson	3 R R 1	4	
2 Neville Tatum	2 1 1 3	7	1
3 †Ray Morton	3 2 0 3	8	
4 Nigel Leaver	1 1 3 1	6	1
5 Andy Grahame	**3 3 3 3**	**12**	
6 Peter Chapman	0 0 0 1	1	
7 Peter Schroeck	*did not ride*		
STOKE 28			
1 Louis Carr	3 2 1 2	8	1
2 Mark Carlson	0 3 R R	3	
3 Garry Stead	0 0 N 0	0	
4 †Eric Monaghan	1 3 0 1	5	
6 David Clarke	1 1 1 0	3	3
6 Chris Cobby	2 2 2 2	8	
7 Jon Hughes	1	1	

Third round

Glasgow, Sunday, October 27

GLASGOW 40			
1 †Steve Lawson	2 3 2 R	7	1
2 Jason Lyons	F 2 3 F	5	1
3 Shane Bowes	R 3 3 3	9	
4 Sean Courtney	2 2 2 0	6	2
5 Kenny McKinna	**3 3 3 3**	**12**	
6 Charlie McKinna	1 0 X fx	1	
7 Phil Jeffrey	*did not ride*		
WIMBLEDON 35			
1 Nathan Simpson	3 2 3 2	10	
2 Neville Tatum	N 1 2 1	4	3
3 †Ray Morton	2 2 1 1	6	2
4 Nigel Leaver	3 1 0 2	6	1
5 Andy Grahame	2 1 1 3	7	
6 Peter Chapman	0 0 0 1	1	
7 Peter Schroeck	1	1	
STOKE 32			
1 Louis Carr	3 1 1 3	8	
2 Mark Carlson	1 R 0 0	1	
3 Garry Stead	0 1 2 1	4	1
4 David Clarke	1 0 0 2	3	
5 †Eric Monaghan	3 3 2 2	10	1
6 Chris Cobby	0 2 1 3	6	2
7 Jon Hughes	*did not ride*		

Aggregate

GLASGOW 107 Wimbledon 104 Stoke 75

Roll of Honour

1990 1 GLASGOW 107
2 Wimbledon 104
3 Stoke 75

SUPERNATIONAL

THE Supernational was an end of season tournament run on a knock-out basis involving the top eight tracks in the National League.

It was abandoned after two seasons because of the problems of determining the top eight tracks when fixtures were postponed.

Roll of Honour

1982 NEWCASTLE 121 Ellesmere Port 71
1983 NEWCASTLE 100 Crayford 91

INJURY HIT POOLE IN CUP TRIUMPH

PIRATES BEAT ALL THE FATES

BRAVERY can come wrapped up in different guises. And Poole showed a collective bravery on their way to avenging last season's National League Knock Out Cup Final defeat against Berwick.

No-one would have given the Echo Pirates a prayer of reaching the final shoot-out for the second time in two seasons as the lights went out on their second round challenge at Berrington Lough, the track where they had lost the double only 12 months earlier. It was Saturday, July 21, and shortly after 7.30 p.m. and Poole seemed as far away from another Cup triumph as it is possible to be.

They had what had appeared a comfortable 16 point cushion from the first leg...but that was before fate intervened.

It was bad enough when they lost high-scoring Dane Tom Knudsen with a broken leg that was to keep him out for the rest of the season, after a heat two pile-up when he and fellow reserve Jon Gould had crashed heavily.

But, two races later another shunt involving Gould, saw skipper Alun Rossiter making the same ambulance ride to the Borders General Hospital with leg injuries.

That left Poole down to five fully fit riders, including the rookie Gould in his first ever cup-tie!

And that precious 16 point lead had already been halved to eight points as Berwick capitalised on their opponent's misfortune.

Poole manager Neil Street called his shell-shocked and possibly demoralised troops to a hastily convened team meeting and, somehow, instilled into them a willingness and eagerness to face the rest of the battle.

Inspired by the coaxing of Street and the brilliance of Craig Boyce, the Echo Pirates refused to succumb to the inevitable. They dropped a 5-1 in heat five which left the aggregate scores 64-60 and all of Northumbria was expecting Berwick to steamroller the opposition into submission.

But the overall scores never drew closer than four points and as Poole's confidence rose with each heat win so Berwick's resolve weakened and the Dorset club took 12 points from the last three heats to record one of their most famous victories of all time.

One can only imagine the reaction from Knudsen and Rossiter as they heard the news while waiting for further medical treatment!

Poole's win put them into the last eight but if they thought that the hard work was over they were to be disillusioned as they were to have to face both Hackney and Ipswich on their way to the final.

ROLL OF HONOUR

1968	CANTERBURY 112 Reading 80
1969	BELLE VUE 91 Crewe 45
1970	IPSWICH 80 Berwick 76
1971	IPSWICH 92 Crewe 64
1972	CREWE 89 Peterborough 67
1973	BOSTON 89 Workington 66
1974	BIRMINGHAM 81 Eastbourne 74
1975	EASTBOURNE 83 Workington 72
1976	NEWCASTLE 83 Berwick 72
1977	EASTBOURNE 98 Berwick 57
1978	EASTBOURNE 83 Rye House 73
1979	RYE HOUSE 92 Berwick 64
1980	BERWICK 79 Middlesbrough 76
1981	EDINBURGH 101 Berwick 89
1982	NEWCASTLE 118 Ellesmere Port 74
1983	EXETER 96 Weymouth 95
1984	HACKNEY 83 Berwick 72
1985	EASTBOURNE 83 Ellesmere Port 73
1986	EASTBOURNE 90 Mildenhall 64
1987	EASTBOURNE 100 Mildenhall 91
1988	HACKNEY 110 Wimbledon 82
1989	BERWICK 109 Poole 83
1990	POOLE 107 Middlesbrough 85

The third round survivors included the unlikeliest team of all. Milton Keynes, who hadn't won a tie since beating Stoke in the first round in 1979, drew fellow strugglers Rye House and a Kevin Jolly maximum helped them open up a first leg lead that they were able to defend successfully at Hoddesdon with a solid all-round team performance in which they provided only three heat winners but, more important, had the second placed rider in all but three of the 16 races.

They didn't get much further, however, being soundly thrashed by Middlesbrough home and away with Daz Sumner grabbing a 15 point maximum at Elfield Park, a track that had fast become one of his favourites.

In fact, it was Middlesbrough who looked the most comfortable Cup team of all once they had disposed of Edinburgh in another controversial tie in which the Monarchs lost out by a single point after Freddy Schøtt had been excluded for dangerous riding in heat 15 and his team-mate Carl Blackbird had fallen in the re-run to give the Bears a crucial 5-0 which meant they only had to share the points in the last race to squeeze through.

Once over that close call Middlesbrough never left it so late again, beating the Knights by 58 points and then bettering even that with the biggest win of the competition, licking Wimbledon 128-63 with a powerful 59-36 first leg win at Plough Lane where Sumner, Dave Cheshire and Rod Hunter all got into double figures.

While Middlesbrough were roaring through to their first Cup Final since 1980, the Echo Pirates were producing two more spell-binding performances after their rearguard action at Berwick. They won at Hackney in the third round where West German Peter Schroeck made his club debut and then completed the double over Ipswich with a brilliant display in which their top four scored a total of 46 points between them to compensate for struggling reserves Gary Chessell and Rod Colquhoun.

It meant that the teams who were to finish first and second in the National League also contested the Knock Out Cup – originally sponsored by travel firm Tee Mill but left without any backer when the company went into liquidation and left the National League as one of its creditors – and Poole drew first blood.

Craig Boyce's 21 point paid maximum helped them to an 18 point first leg lead and he was again in scintillating form in the return with a further 16 points from his six completed rides.

This time he had the backing from Gary Allan and Tony Langdon and Poole's up front strength was too much for Middlesbrough to combat. Poole provided seven of the 16 heat winners and were able to overcome the absence of Chessell, injured in the first leg, and blood teenager Justin Elkins for his first, memorable taste of Cup action.

Middlesbrough's chances of winning the Knock Out Cup for the first time despite being founder members of the National League in 1968, were gone. For Poole it was a different story as the double that had eluded them in 1989, was their's for the taking!

NATIONAL LEAGUE CUP

1st Round

First leg, Long Eaton, April 11

LONG EATON 57

1 Kevin Smart	2 1 1 2 1	7	1
2 Gary O'Hare	0 3 3 3 1	10	
3 †Richard Hellsén	2 3 3 2 3	13	1
4 Paul Fry	2 2 1 N 2	7	2
5 Jamie Habbin	3 3 0 3 1	10	
6 Nigel De'ath	2 1 2 0 0	5	3
7 Peter Lloyd	3 2 0	5	1

BERWICK 39

1 †Mark Courtney	3 1 2 2 1 3	12	1
2 Scott Robson	1 R 1 1 2 F	5	2
3 David Blackburn	3 2 3 3 3 2	16	
4 David Walsh	0 1 0 2 0 T	3	
5 Andy Campbell	1 0 T 1 0	2	
6 Alan Rivett	1 0 T 0 T	1	
7 Kevin Little	0 0 T	0	

Second leg, Berwick, April 14

BERWICK 62

1 Mark Courtney	3 3 2 1 2	11	2
2 Scott Robson	0 2 2 1 3	8	2
3 David Blackburn	1 2 3 3 3	12	2
4 David Walsh	1 2 3 2 3	11	2
5 †Rob Grant	2 3 2 2 1	10	2
6 Alan Rivett	3 2 3 fx	8	
7 Kevin Little	1 1 0	2	1

LONG EATON 33

1 Kevin Smart	2 0 2 0 0	4	
2 Jamie Habbin	1 1 3 0 1 2	8	2
3 †Richard Hellsén	3 1 R 0 3 2	9	
4 Gary O'Hare	0 0 T 1 1	2	
5 Paul Fry	3 1 3 0 fx0	7	
6 Nigel De'ath	2 0 1 T	3	
7 Peter Lloyd	0 0 T	0	

BERWICK win 101-90 on aggregate.

2nd Round

First leg, Ipswich, May 31

IPSWICH 60

1 Chris Louis	3 3 3 3 0	12	
2 Shane Parker	R 2 3 2 2	9	2
3 Dean Standing	2 3 3 0 2	10	1
4 †Alan Mogridge	2 2 2 2 1	9	4
5 David Norris	3 3 3 2 3	14	
6 Robbie Fuller	3 F 0 R	3	
7 Colin White	1 1 1	3	

GLASGOW 36

1 Kenny McKinna	2 0 0 3 1 3	9	
2 Phil Jeffrey	1 1 T 2 1	5	1
3 Charlie McKinna	1 0 0 0 N	1	
4 Shane Bowes	1 2 fxR 1 2	6	1
5 Sean Courtney	0 1 T 1 T	2	1
6 †Steve Lawson	2 1 1 3	7	
7 Jason Lyons	X 3 2 1 0	6	

Second leg, Glasgow, June 3

GLASGOW 54

1 †Steve Lawson	2 3 2 1 3	11	
2 Charlie McKinna	0 2 2 0 R	4	1
3 Kenny McKinna	2 3 3 3 2	13	1
4 Sean Courtney	3 1 1 F 1	6	1
5 Shane Bowes	2 3 2 2 3	12	2
6 Jason Lyons	F 1 2 1 2	6	2
7 Phil Jeffrey	2 0 N	2	

IPSWICH 41

1 Chris Louis	3 0 3 2 fx2	10	
2 Shane Parker	1 2 1 0 1	5	
3 Dean Standing	3 F 3 2 3 0	11	1
4 †Alan Mogridge	0 1 0 1 1 0	3	
5 David Norris	1 0 3 3 1	8	
6 Robbie Fuller	3 1 N T	4	
7 Colin White	E 0 T	0	

IPSWICH win 101-90 on aggregate.

2nd Round

First leg, Peterborough, June 1

PETERBOROUGH 48

1 Frank Andersen	2 1 3 2 3 3 2	16	
2 Mick Poole	*rider replacement*		
3 †Craig Hodgson	**3 3 3 3 3 3**	**18**	
4 Ian Barney	0 1 0 N N	1	
5 Nigel Flatman	R 2 R 2 1 1	6	
6 Phil Disney	3 F N 0 0 N 0	3	
7 Sean Barker	2 1 0 1 0	4	1
8 Darren Tupper	*did not ride*		

STOKE 48

1 Louis Carr	3 3 2 X 3	11	
2 Rob Woffinden	1 2 2 R 2	7	1
3 †Nigel Crabtree	1 2 3 2 2	10	1
4 Eric Monaghan	3 2 3 2 1	11	
5 Chris Cobby	1 0 1 1 0	3	1
6 Mark Carlson	1 2 0 1 1 1	6	2
7 Mark Pearce	0 fnN	0	

Second leg, Stoke, June 2

STOKE 65

1 Louis Carr	3 3 2 E 2	10	
2 Rob Woffinden	1 X N N N	1	
3 †Nigel Crabtree	**3 3 3 3 3**	**15**	
4 Eric Monaghan	3 3 3 2 1	12	1
5 Chris Cobby	1 2 0 2 2	7	3
6 Mark Carlson	3 2 1 3 1 3	13	2
7 Mark Pearce	2 2 0 1 2	7	4

PETERBOROUGH 31

1 Mick Poole	*rider replacement*		
2 Nigel Flatman	fx1 0 1 1 1	4	1
3 Frank Andersen	1 2 1 2 3 1 3	13	1
4 Sean Barker	0 0 2 0 0 0	2	
5 †Craig Hodgson	2 2 2 1 3 0 N	10	
6 Phil Disney	fx0 fnT N	0	
7 Darren Tupper	1 0 1 T 0 0	2	1
8 Richard Davidson	*did not ride*		

STOKE win 113-79 on aggregate

First leg, Arena Essex, June 2

ARENA ESSEX 41

1 †Rob Tilbury	3 2 0 3 2 1 2	13	
2 Martin Goodwin	*rider replacement*		
3 Simon Wolstenholme	1 1 2 1 1 T	6	1
4 Kevin Brice	1 2 2 1 1 1 0	8	2
5 Wayne Garratt	2 1 1 1 2 0	7	3
6 Kevin Teager	1 0 1 0	2	1
7 Adrian Stevens	3 2 0	5	
8 Robert Ledwith	*did not ride*		

NEWCASTLE 55

1 †Peter Carr	2 3 3 3 3	14	
2 Simon Green	R 0 3 2 3	8	1
3 David Bargh	**3 3 3 3 3**	**15**	
4 Paul Smith	X 0 0 F N	0	
5 Martin Dixon	3 3 2 R 2	10	1
6 Spencer Timmo	2 0 0 N	2	
7 Mark Thorpe	R 2 1 2 1	6	2

Second leg, Newcastle, June 3

NEWCASTLE 61

1 †Peter Carr	**3 3 3 3 3**	**15**	
2 Simon Green	0 2 2 F 1	5	2
3 David Bargh	2 3 3 3 3	14	
4 Paul Smith	2 0 0 N N	2	1
5 Martin Dixon	3 3 3 1 2	12	1
6 Spencer Timmo	1 0 N 0	1	
7 Mark Thorpe	3 2 3 1 2 1	12	2

ARENA ESSEX 35

1 †Rob Tilbury	2 2 1 2 2 3 2	14	
2 Martin Goodwin	*rider replacement*		
3 Simon Wolstenholme	1 1 1 2 0 0 1	6	1
4 Kevin Brice	0 1 1 N T	2	1
5 Wayne Garratt	1 1 0 2 1 R	5	1
6 Kevin Teager	2 0 1 2 0	5	2
7 Adrian Stevens	0 3 0 0	3	
8 Shaun Nicholls	*did not ride*		

NEWCASTLE win 116-76 on aggregate.

2nd Round

First leg, Edinburgh, June 3

EDINBURGH 51

1 Les Collins	fxN N N N	0	
2 Mick Powell	1 2 1 0 N	4	1
3 Freddy Schøtt	2 1 1 3 3	10	1
4 Michael Coles	3 1 1 R 3	8	1
5 Carl Blackbird	2 2 3 2 2	11	3
6 †Brett Saunders	R 3 0 1 2 1	7	1
7 Scott Lamb	3 3 3 0 2 0	11	

MIDDLESBROUGH 45

1 Darren Sumner	2 0 2 3 1 2	10	1
2 David Cheshire	3 3 0 2 3	11	1
3 †Jamie Luckhurst	F fxT N N	0	
4 Steve Wilcock	0 2 3 0 1	6	2
5 Rod Hunter	1 3 2 3 1	10	1
6 Max Schofield	2 1 T 1 N	4	
7 Duncan Chapman	1 1 2 0 0 0	4	1

Second leg, Middlesbrough, June 7

MIDDLESBROUGH 51

1 Darren Sumner	2 1 0 3 2	8	
2 David Cheshire	1 3 2 1 3	10	1
3 Steve Wilcock	0 3 3 1 3	10	
4 Paul Bentley	3 3 2 0 1	9	1
5 Rod Hunter	1 2 1 3 2	9	3
6 †Jamie Luckhurst	3 1 F 0	4	
7 Duncan Chapman	1 0 0	1	

EDINBURGH 44

1 Les Collins	3 1 3 2 2 3	14	
2 Mick Powell	0 0 T N N	0	
3 Freddy Schøtt	2 R 3 2 X 0	7	1
4 Michael Coles	2 2 2 0 T	6	1
5 Carl Blackbird	0 1 3 1 fx	5	2
6 †Brett Saunders	2 2 0 1	5	1
7 Scott Lamb	0 3 1 1 2	7	1

MIDDLESBROUGH win 96-95 on aggregate.

First leg, Exeter, June 4

EXETER 61

1 †Steve Regeling	3 3 3 3 2	14	
2 Steve Bishop	0 1 2 1 N	4	
3 Richard Green	2 2 3 1 2	10	3
4 Peter Jeffery	3 2 3 2 1	11	2
5 Mark Simmonds	2 0 0 N N	2	1
6 Colin Cook	2 1 3 2 1	9	2
7 Andy Sell	3 R 2 3 3	11	1

WIMBLEDON 35

1 Nathan Simpson	2 1 1 1 0 0	5	1
2 †Ray Morton	1 3 T 0 T	4	1
3 Neville Tatum	3 2 3 2 1 1	12	
4 Andy Grahame	0 0 2 3 2 3	10	
5 Nigel Leaver	1 1 0 0 0 0	2	
6 Deon Prinsloo	0 0 0 T	0	
7 Justin Pryor	1 0 1	2	

Second leg, Wimbledon, June 27

WIMBLEDON 62

1 Nathan Simpson	2 2 3 2 3	12	2
2 Neville Tatum	R 3 fx2 3	8	1
3 †Ray Morton	3 3 2 R 3	11	
4 Andy Grahame	**2 2 3 3 2**	**12**	**3**
5 Nigel Leaver	3 3 2 2 1	11	1
6 Deon Prinsloo	1 1 1 N	3	1
7 Justin Pryor	2 1 1 1	5	1

EXETER 33

1 †Steve Regeling	3 1 3 3 3 1	14	
2 Steve Bishop	1 0 T 1 N T	2	
3 Richard Green	2 fxN fx1 0	3	
4 Mark Simmonds	0 0 T 1 N	1	
5 Peter Jeffery	1 2 fx0 2 2	7	1
6 Colin Cook	3 1 2 T 0 0 0	6	1
7 Greg Daniels	fx0 T fx	0	

WIMBLEDON win 97-94 on aggregate.

2nd Round

First leg, Poole, June 5

POOLE 56

1 Gary Chessell	2 2 3 1 F	8	2
2 Gary Allan	1 3 2 2 1	9	3
3 †Alun Rossiter	fnN N N N	0	
4 Craig Boyce	2 3 3 2 3	13	
5 Tony Langdon	0 2 2 2 3	9	2
6 Tom Knudsen	3 3 2 3 1 N 1	13	
7 Rod Colquhoun	2 1 1 N 0 0 0	4	2

BERWICK 40

1 Mark Courtney	3 1 1 3 N 2 2	12	1
2 †Rob Grant	0 0 1 2 3 0	6	1
3 David Blackburn	*rider replacement*		
4 David Walsh	3 0 3 1 3 3 1	14	1
5 Andy Campbell	1 1 0 0 T 0 2	4	
6 Kevin Little	0 0 T 1 T	1	
7 Alan Rivett	1 2 0 0	3	
8 Steve Widt	*did not ride*		

Second leg, Berwick, July 21

BERWICK 50

1 Mark Courtney	3 2 1 2 2	10	1
2 Alan Rivett	0 1 3 2 fx	6	1
3 David Blackburn	3 1 3 3 2	12	
4 Andy Campbell	2 3 3 1 0	9	1
5 †Rob Grant	0 2 1 1 1	5	2
6 Kevin Little	2 2 0 N	4	2
7 Scott Robson	3 0 fx1	4	

POOLE 44

1 Rod Colquhoun	2 0 2 1 0 1	6	1
2 Gary Allan	1 1 3 1 2 2	10	3
3 †Alun Rossiter	N T T N N	0	
4 Craig Boyce	3 2 3 2 3 3	16	1
5 Tony Langdon	1 3 2 0 3 3	12	
6 Tom Knudsen	fnN N T	0	
7 Jon Gould	fxfxT X 0	0	

POOLE win 100-90 on aggregate.

First leg, Milton Keynes, June 5

MILTON KEYNES 56

1 Mark Lyndon	2 1 1 2 0	6	2
2 Peter Glanz	3 2 3 3 3	14	
3 †Kevin Jolly	**3 3 3 3 3**	**15**	
4 Andy Hines	1 1 2 1 1	6	2
5 David Clarke	2 3 1 0 2	8	2
6 Kieran McCullagh	2 1 0 0	3	1
7 Mark Blackbird	3 1 0	4	

RYE HOUSE 39

1 Roger Johns	fx0 1 1 2 3	7	2
2 Trevor O'Brien	fxT F 2 T 1	3	1
3 †Jens Rasmussen	E 2 3 3 3 X	11	
4 Glen Baxter	3 2 2 2 2 2	13	1
5 Linden Warner	0 1 0 T 1	2	1
6 Nigel Sparshott	0 0 T 0 T	0	
7 Wayne Baxter	1 2 0 0	3	

Second leg, Rye House, June 10

RYE HOUSE 51

1 Roger Johns	3 1 3 3 0	10	
2 Trevor O'Brien	0 3 N 1 2	6	
3 †Jens Rasmussen	3 3 2 3 3	14	
4 Glen Baxter	3 3 3 1 3	13	
5 Linden Warner	1 2 0 0 0	3	1
6 Nigel Sparshott	1 0 0 0 1	2	1
7 Wayne Baxter	0 3 0	3	

MILTON KEYNES 45

1 Mark Lyndon	2 1 1 1 2	7	1
2 Peter Glanz	1 0 2 3 3	9	1
3 †Kevin Jolly	1 2 2 2 2	9	1
4 Andy Hines	2 1 0 2 1	6	2
5 David Clarke	F 2 2 F 1	5	1
6 Kieran McCullagh	2 0 1 T	3	2
7 Mark Blackbird	3 2 1 F	6	1

MILTON KEYNES win 101-90 on aggregate.

NATIONAL LEAGUE CUP

2nd Round

First leg, Eastbourne, June 10

EASTBOURNE 40

1 †Gordon Kennett	2 1 2 fx 1 0	6	1
2 Justin Walker	0 T 1 2 1	4	1
3 Andy Buck	2 3 2 3 2 2	14	
4 Paul Woods	3 2 3 1 2 1	12	1
5 Tony Primmer	F 0 T 1 0	1	1
6 Keith Pritchard	2 F 0 0	2	
7 Darren Grayling	F T 1	1	

HACKNEY 56

1 †Andy Galvin	3 3 2 3 2	13	1
2 Michael Warren	1 1 3 0 3	8	
3 Steve Schofield	3 2 3 3 3	14	
4 Paul Whittaker	2 1 3 0 3	9	1
5 Gary Tagg	1 2 1 fx1	5	1
6 Tim Korneliussen	3 1 N 0 0 N	4	
7 Dave Hamnett	1 N 0 N 2	3	1

Second leg, Hackney, June 15

HACKNEY 64

1 †Andy Galvin	**3 2 3 3 3**	**14**	**1**
2 Michael Warren	1 3 2 1 3	10	1
3 Steve Schofield	**3 3 3 3 3**	**15**	
4 Paul Whittaker	3 2 3 2 2	12	2
5 Gary Tagg	1 0 1 2 2	6	2
6 Tim Korneliussen	E 1 0 0	1	
7 Dave Hamnett	3 3 0	6	

EASTBOURNE 32

1 †Gordon Kennett	2 3 2 2 1 1	11	
2 Justin Walker	F T 1 1 1	3	2
3 Andy Buck	2 fn T T N	2	
4 Paul Woods	2 1 1 0 0 R	4	1
5 Tony Primmer	fxN 2 0 1	3	
6 Keith Pritchard	1 1 0 1 2	5	1
7 Darren Grayling	2 0 0 2 0 0	4	

HACKNEY win 120-72 on aggregate.

3rd Round

First round, Milton Keynes, July 17

MILTON KEYNES 40

1 Peter Glanz	2 2 3 3 3 1	14	1
2 Andy Hines	1 0 2 1 2 2	8	1
3 †Kevin Jolly	3 3 0 0 1	7	1
4 Trevor Banks	1 2 0 0 T	3	
5 David Clarke	0 0 T T 2 2	4	
6 Mark Blackbird	0 0 T 0	0	
7 Thierry Hilaire	3 R 0 1	4	

MIDDLESBROUGH 56

1 Darren Sumner	**3 3 3 3 3**	**15**	
2 †Jamie Luckhurst	0 1 1 2 1	5	1
3 Rod Hunter	2 3 2 1 3	11	1
4 Paul Bentley	2 2 0 1 0	5	1
5 David Cheshire	3 1 2 2 0	8	1
6 Steve Wilcock	2 1 1 3	7	1
7 Duncan Chapman	1 1 3	5	2

Second leg, Middlesbrough, July 19

MIDDLESBROUGH 69

1 Darren Sumner	3 3 0 3 2	11	
2 David Cheshire	1 2 3 3 2	11	2
3 Rod Hunter	**3 3 3 3 3**	**15**	
4 Paul Bentley	2 3 2 1 1	9	3
5 †Jamie Luckhurst	3 2 3 1 2	11	2
6 Steve Wilcock	**3 2 2 3**	**10**	**2**
7 Duncan Chapman	R 1 1	2	

MILTON KEYNES 27

1 Peter Glanz	2 0 1 2 2 3	10	
2 Andy Hines	0 1 2 0 1	4	
3 †Kevin Jolly	1 R T T N	1	
4 Trevor Banks	0 1 2 0 0 T	3	
5 David Clarke	1 0 1 2 1 F	5	1
6 Mark Blackbird	2 1 0 R	3	
7 Thierry Hilaire	1 0 0 0	1	1

MIDDLESBROUGH win 125-67 on aggregate.

3rd Round

First leg, Wimbledon, July 18

WIMBLEDON 57

1 Nathan Simpson	3 3 3 1 2	12	2
2 Neville Tatum	2 1 2 2 3	10	2
3 †Ray Morton	2 3 3 1 2	11	1
4 Andy Grahame	3 2 3 2 3	13	1
5 Nigel Leaver	2 3 0 2 1	8	2
6 Peter Chapman	0 N 0 0	0	
7 Justin Pryor	1 0 1 1	3	1

STOKE 37

1 Louis Carr	*rider replacement*		
2 Rob Woffinden	fx1 R R T	1	
3 †Nigel Crabtree	R 3 2 3 2 3 3	16	
4 Eric Monaghan	X R 1 0 3 2 N	6	1
5 Chris Cobby	X 2 1 0 0	3	
6 Mark Carlson	3 0 1 2 0 1 1	8	2
7 Mark Pearce	2 1 T 0	3	1
8 Richard Davidson	*did not ride*		

Second leg, Stoke, July 21

STOKE 51

1 Louis Carr	3 3 3 3 2	14	
2 Rob Woffinden	1 0 N 0 0	1	
3 †Nigel Crabtree	2 2 2 2 2	10	3
4 Eric Monaghan	0 3 3 0 1	7	1
5 Chris Cobby	2 1 1 3 R	7	
6 Mark Carlson	1 0 3 fx3 1	8	
7 Mark Pearce	3 1 N	4	

WIMBLEDON 45

1 Nathan Simpson	2 3 0 3 1 0 3	12	
2 †Ray Morton	0 2 1 2 fx3	8	1
3 Neville Tatum	3 1 2 2 1 1 E	10	2
4 Andy Grahame	*rider replacement*		
5 Nigel Leaver	1 0 1 2 2 3	9	2
6 Peter Chapman	2 2 0 T 1	5	
7 Deon Prinsloo	X 1 T 0	1	
8 Troy Scott	*did not ride*		

WIMBLEDON win 102-88 on aggregate.

First leg, Ipswich, July 19

IPSWICH 61

1 Chris Louis	3 2 3 3 3 3 3	20	
2 David Norris	*rider replacement*		
3 Dean Standing	3 1 3 1 3 2	13	2
4 †Alan Mogridge	2 3 3 2 0 2	12	3
5 Shane Parker	1 3 2 1 2 3	12	2
6 Robbie Fuller	3 0 0 0	3	
7 Colin White	1 0 0	1	
8 Craig Hyde	*did not ride*		

NEWCASTLE 35

1 †Peter Carr	2 R 3 1 2 N	8	
2 Simon Green	0 1 2 0 T T	3	
3 David Bargh	1 3 R 2 2 1	9	2
4 Paul Smith	0 T T 0 N	0	
5 Martin Dixon	1 1 2 1 1 0	6	2
6 Ian Stead	0 0 T N 1 0	1	1
7 Mark Thorpe	2 2 2 1 E 1	8	1

Second leg, Newcastle, July 29

NEWCASTLE 54

1 †Peter Carr	E 3 3 2 1	9	
2 Simon Green	3 2 2 1 2	10	1
3 David Bargh	0 3 1 3 3	10	
4 Paul Smith	0 2 3 1 0	6	1
5 Martin Dixon	1 0 0 2 2	5	2
6 Ian Stead	3 3 2 1	9	2
7 Mark Thorpe	2 2 1 0	5	3

IPSWICH 41

1 Chris Louis	0 3 3 3 0 3 3	15	
2 David Norris	*rider replacement*		
3 Dean Standing	2 0 2 2 3 N 0	9	1
4 †Alan Mogridge	1 2 1 0 0 1 2	7	2
5 Shane Parker	3 1 0 N 2 0 0	6	
6 Craig Hyde	1 1 1 0	3	1
7 Colin White	0 T 1	1	1
8 Darren Fitch	*did not ride*		

IPSWICH win 102-89 on aggregate.

3rd Round

First leg, Hackney, August 10

HACKNEY 47

1 †Andy Galvin	X 2 1 1 0	4	1
2 Gary Tagg	2 fxN N N	2	
3 Steve Schofield	3 2 2 3 3	13	
4 Paul Whittaker	1 3 3 2 2	11	
5 Tim Korneliussen	0 1 0 N E	1	
6 Michael Warren	1 2 2 0 1 1	7	3
7 Dave Hamnett	2 3 0 0 3 1	9	

POOLE 48

1 Craig Boyce	3 3 0 3 2 2 3	16	
2 Gary Allan	X 2 1 fx1 0	4	
3 †Alun Rossiter	0 3 1 0 2 0	6	2
4 Tony Langdon	2 3 3 3 0 1	12	1
5 Tom Knudsen	*rider replacement*		
6 Gary Chessell	3 1 1 2 2	9	
7 §Peter Schroeck	0 N 1 N	1	

Second leg, Poole, August 21

POOLE 62

1 Craig Boyce	3 3 2 3 1 3	15	
2 Gary Allan	1 2 1 2 1 2	9	3
3 †Alun Rossiter	1 1 2 3 3	10	2
4 Tony Langdon	3 2 2 3 2	12	2
5 Tom Knudsen	*rider replacement*		
6 Gary Chessell	3 2 2 3	10	
7 Rod Colquhoun	2 0 1	3	2
8 Steve Langdon	1 2 fx	3	2

HACKNEY 33

1 †Andy Galvin	2 1 2 3 1 1	10	
2 Gary Tagg	0 0 1 fxN	1	
3 Steve Schofield	3 3 3 3 2 2	16	
4 Paul Whittaker	1 3 0 0 0 0	4	
5 Tim Korneliussen	0 0 T N R R	0	
6 Michael Warren	1 0 T R T	1	
7 Dave Hamnett	0 0 T 1	1	

POOLE win 110-80 on aggregate.

Semi Final

First leg, Wimbledon, August 22

WIMBLEDON 36

1 Nathan Simpson	0 1 fx1 0 0	2	2
2 Neville Tatum	1 2 1 2 0 3	9	
3 †Ray Morton	2 2 3 1 3 2	13	
4 Andy Grahame	1 0 1 3 fxT	5	
5 Nigel Leaver	0 2 0 T 1 2	5	1
6 Peter Chapman	2 F T T	2	
7 Justin Pryor	0 T 0	0	

MIDDLESBROUGH 59

1 Darren Sumner	2 1 3 2 3	11	1
2 David Cheshire	3 3 2 2 2	12	1
3 Rod Hunter	3 3 3 2 3	14	
4 Paul Bentley	2 fx3 1 1	7	2
5 †Jamie Luckhurst	3 3 0 1 0	7	1
6 Steve Wilcock	3 F 2 1	6	2
7 Dave Edwards	1 1 0	2	

Second leg, Middlesbrough, August 23

MIDDLESBROUGH 69

1 Darren Sumner	**3 3 3 3 3**	**15**	
2 David Cheshire	2 2 2 2 3	11	3
3 Rod Hunter	**2 3 3 3 3**	**14**	**1**
4 Paul Bentley	fx3 1 2 1	7	2
5 †Jamie Luckhurst	3 1 2 2 2	10	2
6 Steve Wilcock	**2 3 2 2**	**9**	**3**
7 Dave Edwards	3 0 0	3	

WIMBLEDON 27

1 Nathan Simpson	0 2 0 0 2 1 2	7	
2 Neville Tatum	1 2 1 1 1 1 1	8	1
3 †Ray Morton	1 1 3 3 0 N 1	9	
4 Andy Grahame	*did not ride*		
5 Nigel Leaver	1 0 0 1 0 0	2	1
6 Peter Chapman	0 0 T 0	0	
7 Justin Pryor	1 0 T 0	1	
8 Martin Jones	*did not ride*		

MIDDLESBROUGH win 128-63 on aggregate.

Semi Final

First leg, Poole, August 28

POOLE 60

1 Craig Boyce	3 2 3 3 3 3 1	18	2
2 Gary Allan	1 2 2 2 0 1	8	3
3 †Alun Rossiter	3 2 2 1 1 2	11	3
4 Tony Langdon	3 3 3 0 2 2	13	
5 Tom Knudsen	*rider replacement*		
6 Gary Chessell	3 2 1 2	8	2
7 Rod Colquhoun	2 0 0	2	1
8 Jon Gould	*did not ride*		

IPSWICH 36

1 Chris Louis	2 1 3 2 3 3	14	1
2 David Norris	0 0 1 3 0 1	5	
3 Dean Standing	0 F 0 N T	0	
4 †Alan Mogridge	1 1 3 1 0 0	6	1
5 Shane Parker	0 0 2 2 3 R	7	
6 Robbie Fuller	1 T 1 1 T	3	1
7 Craig Hyde	0 1 T	1	

Second leg, Ipswich, August 30

IPSWICH 47

1 Chris Louis	3 3 3 3 2	14	
2 Shane Parker	F 1 2 0 1	4	1
3 Dean Standing	2 0 2 1 0	5	1
4 †Alan Mogridge	2 2 3 1 1	9	2
5 David Norris	0 3 1 0 1	5	
6 Robbie Fuller	3 3 1 3 0	10	
7 Craig Hyde	0 N 0	0	

POOLE 49

1 Craig Boyce	2 1 1 1 2 3	10	1
2 Gary Allan	1 0 2 1 3 3	10	2
3 †Alun Rossiter	1 2 2 2 2 2 2	13	1
4 Tony Langdon	3 3 1 0 3 3 0	13	1
5 Tom Knudsen	*rider replacement*		
6 Gary Chessell	2 0 0 N	2	
7 Rod Colquhoun	1 0 0	1	1
8 Steve Leigh	*did not ride*		

POOLE win 109-83 on aggregate.

The FINAL

First leg, Poole, September 18

POOLE 62

1 Craig Boyce	**3 3 3 2 3 2 3**	**19**	**2**
2 Gary Allan	1 1 3 3 3	11	
3 †Alun Rossiter	1 2 1 3 3 3	13	2
4 Tony Langdon	0 2 2 2 2 2	10	4
5 Tom Knudsen,	*rider replacement*		
6 Gary Chessell	3 fnN N	3	
7 Rod Colquhoun	0 2 2 0 2 0	6	1
8 Justin Elkins	*did not ride*		

MIDDLESBROUGH 34

1 Darren Sumner	2 1 1 0 1 0	5	2
2 David Cheshire	0 0 1 T 2	3	
3 Rod Hunter	3 2 3 2 0 1	11	
4 Paul Bentley	1 1 1 1 1	5	
5 †Jamie Luckhurst	3 3 0 0 1 fx	7	
6 Steve Wilcock	1 0 T T	1	1
7 Dave Edwards	2 0 0	2	

Second leg, Middlesborugh, September 20

MIDDLESBROUGH 51

1 Darren Sumner	3 3 fx2 1	9	2
2 David Cheshire	1 2 3 1 F	7	1
3 Rod Hunter	3 1 2 R 3	9	
4 Paul Bentley	0 1 3 3 2	9	1
5 †Jamie Luckburst	1 2 2 2 0	7	1
6 Steve Wilcock	3 2 0 1 3	9	2
7 Dave Edwards	1 0 N	1	

POOLE 45

1 Craig Boyce	2 R 3 3 3 2 3	16	
2 Gary Allan	0 2 3 2 2 0 2	11	2
3 †Alun Rossiter	1 R 1 R 1	3	1
4 Tony Langdon	3 2 3 1 1 N	10	1
5 Tom Knudsen	*rider repalcement*		
6 Justin Elkins	F 1 N N 0	1	
7 Rod Colquhoun	2 0 1 0 1	4	2
8 Steve Leigh	*did not ride*		

POOLE win 107-85 on aggregate.

Sad Chick checks out on Hammers

Track Data

Promoters: Chick Woodroffe and Peter Thorogood.
Address: Arena Essex Sports Complex, A1306 Arterial Road, Purfleet, Essex, RM16 1NX.
Telephone: 0708-863443.
Hotline: 0898 800 694.
Track Length: 253 metres.
Track Record: 57.2 secs, Martin Goodwin (Arena Essex), July 9, 1988, heat 1, Arena Essex v Peterborough (National League).

CHICK WOODROFFE dropped his bombshell when it was least expected – at Arena Essex's penultimate meeting of yet another troubled season.

He told the club's loyal supporters that the whole shooting match was up for sale as ill health forced him to quit after seven hard seasons in the National League during which the Hammers had survived through good housekeeping policies rather than because of bountiful crowds at their Purfleet track.

No-one was better at balancing the books than Chick and his co-promoter Peter Thorogood who have warned long and hard about the financial penalties for promoters who paid out more than was coming in. Their philosophy was simple: They wouldn't get involved in the rat race to sign big names if it was going to bankrupt the club.

It was a policy which drew protests from a minority of their fans who sent off their complaining letters to the Speedway Press but Arena had the best answer of all: they were opening for the 1990 season.

Once again on practice day no-one knew for sure who would be wearing the club colours. Rob Tilbury had insisted throughout the winter that he wanted to move on. At first he fancied a crack in the Sunbrite League and, when there was little response from that exalted direction, he said he wouldn't mind joining another National League outfit.

By the time practice was over he had signed on the dotted line and Peter Thorogood knew the likely seven starters for the first match. Adrian Stevens, transfer-listed by King's Lynn, was one newcomer of whom much was expected. Kevin Brice was the second newcomer and, as had been the custom in recent seasons, no-one could be quite certain what he would deliver.

By the end of the season there was satisfaction from Brice's performances and deep disappointment of the lack of impact that Stevens had on the National League despite his years of experience.

Brice actually improved his overall average to near five points a meeting but Stevens struggled to maintain a figure around four points a match and the rider everyone believed could provide genuine heat leader back up to long-serving Martin Goodwin and exuberant Tilbury must have been as depressed as everyone else at his inability to score far more prolifically.

Once or twice he looked as if he could make the breakthrough – paid 12 in a win at Rye House and another dozen points in an away defeat against Milton Keynes – but his inability to cope with his own home track where he won only FOUR races all season – was his continued undoing.

Arena's season-long handicap was that they couldn't unearth that third high scorer to augment their top two and Goodwin's World Championship injury increased the pressure on the rest of the team to produce the points. In Arena's situation rider replacement was of little real use if they were to win matches.

They had two likely youngsters in Wayne Garratt and Troy Pratt. Each had spells when they looked more than capable of such status and both of them improved their seasonal points tally but they couldn't maintain the consistency needed to lift them out of their second string harness.

Pratt was hampered by injury and possibly he returned too soon, but he emphasised his potential with a 15 point maximum at Eastbourne and ended a season he began at reserve as number four in the averages. Garratt, also on loan from Cradley Heath, saw his average slip back marginally but was a better all round rider and soldiered on throughout the summer without ever dropping out of the team's top five.

The third of the club's young hopefuls, Simon Wolstenholme, spent most of the winter looking for a move but eventually agreed to stay on and must now be seeking far more from his season.

It was his third successive everpresent season but he slipped back to reserve and it could well be that he needs a change of scenery if he is to make real progression.

Roll of Honour

Seasons in National League: 7 (1984-1990).
Best National League Season: Fourth, 1986.
National League Cup Record: Semi-finalists, 1986, 1987.
National League Team Championship: Runners-up (2), 1986, 1987. Qualified (4), 1985, 1986, 1987, 1989.
Appearances: Martin Goodwin, 235 (1984-1990).
Points: Martin Goodwin, 2363.5 (1984-1990).
World Finalists: None.
NLRC Finalists: Alan Sage (1984), Neil Middleditch (1985), Andrew Silver (1986-87), Martin Goodwin (1988-89-90).

Star of 90
WAYNE GARRATT
Arena Essex

ARENA ESSEX

01...Long Eaton, April 4, L42-54

1 †Martin Goodwin	2 3 3 3 2 3	16	
2 Simon Wolstenholme	0 0 T 1 1 F	2	1
3 Rob Tilbury	1 1 1 2 2 1	8	2
4 §§Adrian Stevens	0 1 T N T	1	1
5 Wayne Garratt	2 2 1 0 2	7	1
6 §Kevin Brice	0 2 0 T	2	
7 Troy Pratt	2 0 2 2 fx	6	1

02...EXETER, April 7, W62-34

1 †Martin Goodwin	2 3 2 3 3	13	1
2 Simon Wolstenholme	1 2 1 3 3	10	3
3 Rob Tilbury	2 3 2 2 3	12	2
4 Adrian Stevens	3 0 0 1 2	6	1
5 Wayne Garratt	2 1 1 1 2	7	3
6 Kevin Brice	3 3 1 R	7	
7 Troy Pratt	2 2 3	7	1

03...PETERBOROUGH, April 21, W52-43

1 †Martin Goodwin	R 3 3 2 3	11	
2 Adrian Stevens	1 1 1 0 1	4	1
3 Rob Tilbury	3 2 3 3 3	14	
4 Simon Wolstenholme	2 2 1 1 0	6	2
5 Wayne Garratt	1 R 2 0 N	3	1
6 Kevin Brice	3 R R N	3	
7 Troy Pratt	2 2 2 3 2	11	3

04...Peterborough, April 22, L29-67

1 †Martin Goodwin	2 1 2 3 1 2	11	
2 Adrian Stevens	0 0 T 2 1	3	1
3 Rob Tilbury	1 1 2 0 R	4	
4 Simon Wolstenholme	0 0 0 N 0	0	
5 Wayne Garratt	1 2 1 1 R N	5	
6 Kevin Brice	1 0 0 T	1	
7 Troy Pratt	3 0 R 0 2	5	

05...LONG EATON, April 28, W51-43

1 †Martin Goodwin	3 1 3 3 3	13	
2 Adrian Stevens	0 0 T N N	0	
3 Rob Tilbury	1 X 1 2 3 3	10	
4 Simon Wolstenholme	X 3 3 0 1	7	
5 Wayne Garratt	fn 2 R 2 2	6	3
6 Kevin Brice	3 3 1 2	9	
7 Troy Pratt	F R 3 2 1 X	6	2

06...MIDDLESBROUGH, May 5, D48-48

1 †Martin Goodwin	3 3 3 2 3	14	
2 Adrian Stevens	1 0 N N N	1	
3 Rob Tilbury	2 2 1 3 0	8	1
4 Simon Wolstenholme	1 1 2 R 0	4	1
5 Wayne Garratt	F 2 0 1 2	5	
6 Kevin Brice	3 3 0 2 3	11	1
7 Troy Pratt	2 3 0 0 0	5	1

07...EASTBOURNE, May 12, L38-58

1 †Rob Tilbury	1 1 3 3 2 3 R	13	
2 Martin Goodwin	*rider replacement*		
3 Simon Wolstenholme	0 0 1 X 0 2 1	4	1
4 Adrian Stevens	1 0 1 N 1	3	
5 Wayne Garratt	0 3 2 3 0 1 2	11	2
6 Kevin Brice	2 3 0 1 0	6	
7 Troy Pratt	1 fx N N	1	1
8 Robert Ledwith	*did not ride*		

08...Glasgow, May 23, L22-74

1 †Rob Tilbury	3 1 2 1 1 1	9	
2 Martin Goodwin	*rider replacement*		
3 Simon Wolstenholme	N 0 1 N T	1	
4 Kevin Brice	0 1 0 0 0	1	
5 Wayne Garratt	1 1 0 1 1 0 2	6	
6 §Kevin Teager	1 0 1 F 1	3	
7 Adrian Stevens	0 1 0 0	1	
8 Robert Ledwith	0 0 1	1	1

09...Middlesbrough, May 24, L43-53

1 †Rob Tilbury	3 2 3 3 2 3 1	17	
2 Martin Goodwin	*rider replacement*		
3 Simon Wolstenholme	1 3 2 1 0 0	7	
4 Kevin Brice	3 0 1 3 0 0	7	1
5 Wayne Garratt	F 2 1 1 N 2 1	7	1
6 Kevin Teager	2 0 1 0 1 T	4	
7 Adrian Stevens	R 1 N	1	
8 Robert Ledwith	*did not ride*		

10...Berwick, May 26, L25-71

1 †Rob Tilbury	1 2 3 2 2 1 T	11	
2 Troy Pratt	*rider replacement*		
3 Simon Wolstenholme	0 0 1 0 1 R	2	
4 Kevin Brice	1 1 1 0 1 fx	4	
5 Wayne Garratt	0 fxT N T	0	
6 Kevin Teager	2 F 1 0	3	
7 Adrian Stevens	1 1 2 0 0	4	2
8 Robert Ledwith	0 F 1	1	

11...MILTON KEYNES, June 16, L47-49

1 †Rob Tilbury	**3 3 3 3 3**	**15**	
2 Kevin Teager	E 1 1 0 N	2	
3 Simon Wolstenholme	0 2 0 R N	2	
4 Kevin Brice	3 2 3 1 2	11	1
5 Wayne Garratt	2 1 R N N	3	2
6 Robert Ledwith	1 3 F 2 1	7	
7 Adrian Stevens	1 3 0 2 1 0	7	

12...RYE HOUSE, June 30, W51-45

1 †Rob Tilbury	3 3 2 2 3	13	1
2 Troy Pratt	2 1 E 3 3	9	1
3 Simon Wolstenholme	1 R 1 R N	2	1
4 Kevin Brice	2 2 0 R 0	4	1
5 Wayne Garratt	1 3 2 2 1	9	2
6 Kevin Teager	3 2 2 1 R	8	1
7 Adrian Stevens	2 2 0 2	6	1

13...Exeter, July 2, L20-76

1 †Rob Tilbury	1 N 1 T N N	2	
2 Martin Goodwin	*rider replacement*		
3 Troy Pratt	0 0 0 0 0 0	0	
4 Kevin Brice	2 R 1 1 1	5	
5 Wayne Garratt	0 2 0 1 1	4	
6 Simon Wolstenholme	1 1 1 1 1 1 R	6	1
7 Adrian Stevens	0 1 0 0 2	3	
8 Robert Ledwith	0 0	0	

14...NEWCASTLE, July 7, L47-49

1 †Rob Tilbury	3 2 3 1 2 3 3	17	1
2 Martin Goodwin	*rider replacement*		
3 Troy Pratt	1 2 0 2 2	7	1
4 Kevin Brice	R 0 0 N N	0	
5 Wayne Garratt	2 1 2 1 1	7	2
6 Simon Wolstenholme	3 2 1 2 0 1	9	1
7 Adrian Stevens	1 2 2 1	6	1
8 Kevin Teager	0 1	1	1

15...GLASGOW, July 14, L44-52

1 †Rob Tilbury	2 3 1 2 1 3 2	14	
2 Martin Goodwin	*rider replacement*		
3 Troy Pratt	0 3 2 0 2 3	10	
4 Kevin Brice	R 1 1 N 0	2	2
5 Wayne Garratt	2 2 2 2 R 0	8	1
6 Simon Wolstenholme	X 2 1 0 1	4	2
7 Adrian Stevens	1 3 2 0	6	
8 Robert Ledwith	*did not ride*		

16...Rye House, July 22, W49-46

1 †Rob Tilbury	3 3 2 3 1	12	
2 Simon Wolstenholme	1 fx 1 1 0	3	1
3 Troy Pratt	R 2 3 3 3	11	
4 Kevin Brice	fx 1 0 2 0	3	2
5 Wayne Garratt	3 2 1 1 1	8	
6 Chris Young	1 F N	1	
7 Adrian Stevens	3 2 3 2 1	11	1

17...WIMBLEDON, July 28, W50-46

1 Rob Tilbury	1 3 3 2 1	10	
2 †Martin Goodwin	3 2 3 1 3	12	1
3 Troy Pratt	1 2 2 3 3	11	1
4 Kevin Brice	2 2 0 0 N	4	
5 Wayne Garratt	0 0 2 1 0	3	
6 Simon Wolstenholme	2 2 1 1	6	2
7 Adrian Stevens	3 0 1 0	4	1

18...Eastbourne, July 29, W56-39

1 Rob Tilbury	3 fx 3 3 3	12	
2 †Martin Goodwin	**2 3 3 2 3**	**13**	**2**
3 Troy Pratt	**3 3 3 3 3**	**15**	
4 Kevin Brice	1 0 N N N	1	
5 Wayne Garratt	3 2 2 1 2	10	1
6 Simon Wolstenholme	2 F 0 0 1	3	
7 Adrian Stevens	0 1 fx 1 0	2	1

19...IPSWICH, August 4, L47-49

1 †Martin Goodwin	R 2 3 3 3 1	12	1
2 Kevin Brice	1 0 N 0 N	1	
3 Rob Tilbury	3 3 1 1 2 2	12	2
4 Wayne Garratt	0 0 1 N 2	3	
5 Troy Pratt	3 2 3 0 2 1	11	1
6 Simon Wolstenholme	3 2 0 R	5	1
7 Adrian Stevens	2 1 0	3	1

20...Milton Keynes, August 7, L42-53

1 †Martin Goodwin	2 3 3 1 1 2	12	1
2 Kevin Brice	1 0 0 N T	1	1
3 Rob Tilbury	2 2 3 R E 2	9	1
4 Troy Pratt	3 2 1 0 fx	6	
5 Wayne Garratt	0 1 0 fxN	1	1
6 Simon Wolstenholme	1 0 1 T	2	
7 Adrian Stevens	3 3 1 2 2 0	11	1

21...EDINBURGH, August 11, W57-36

1 †Martin Goodwin	0 3 3 3 3 3 3	18	
2 Kevin Brice	1 2 3 2 3	11	2
3 Rob Tilbury	N 3 3 3 3 3	15	
4 Wayne Garratt	X X X 2 2 2	6	3
5 Troy Pratt	*rider replacement*		
6 Simon Wolstenholme	3 fx0 fx	3	
7 Adrian Stevens	1 2 1 0 0	4	
8 Robert Ledwith	*did not ride*		

22...Ipswich, August 16, L25-70

1 †Martin Goodwin	2 0 0 1 2 1	6	1
2 Kevin Brice	0 2 1 2 1 1	7	
3 Rob Tilbury	1 1 1 0 T	3	
4 Wayne Garratt	3 1 2 1 1 0	8	1
5 Troy Pratt	fxT 0 T N	0	
6 Simon Wolstenholme	1 0 0 0	1	
7 Adrian Stevens	0 0 0 0	0	

23...Edinburgh, August 26, L29-67

1 †Martin Goodwin	2 2 1 F 1 2 2	10	1
2 Kevin Brice	1 R 2 2 1 3	9	1
3 Rob Tilbury	1 1 1 R R	3	
4 Wayne Garratt	1 1 2 1 0 1	6	2
5 Troy Pratt	*rider replacement*		
6 Simon Wolstenholme	1 0 0 0	1	
7 Adrian Stevens	0 0 0	0	
8 Robert Ledwith	R	0	

24...Newcastle, August 27, L41-55

1 †Martin Goodwin	3 0 2 2 0 1	8	
2 Kevin Brice	1 0 0 3 0 F	4	
3 Rob Tilbury	2 1 2 2 2 2 T	11	1
4 Wayne Garratt	2 2 3 0 2 1 3	13	
5 Troy Pratt	*rider replacement*		
6 Simon Wolstenholme	1 0 0 T 0	1	1
7 Adrian Stevens	2 1 1	4	1
8 Robert Ledwith	*did not ride*		

25...STOKE, August 30, W50-46

1 †Martin Goodwin	3 3 F 3 0	9	
2 Kevin Brice	1 1 0 2 2	6	
3 Rob Tilbury	3 3 2 3 2	13	
4 Wayne Garratt	2 3 3 1 2	11	
5 Troy Pratt	F F 1 2 0	3	1
6 Simon Wolstenholme	3 1 1 0	5	
7 Adrian Stevens	2 1 0	3	1

26...Stoke, September 2, L40-54

1 †Martin Goodwin	3 R 3 3 3 2	14	1
2 Kevin Brice	0 2 0 fxfx	2	
3 Rob Tilbury	3 1 1 1 3	9	1
4 Wayne Garratt	1 2 2 0 0 3	8	
5 Troy Pratt	0 0 3 0 0	3	
6 Simon Wolstenholme	2 0 T 1	3	
7 Adrian Stevens	0 1 T	1	

27...Hackney, September 7, W50-44

1 †Martin Goodwin	3 2 2 3 X	10	
2 Kevin Brice	1 1 2 1 1	6	2
3 Rob Tilbury	1 3 3 1 3	11	1
4 Wayne Garratt	1 2 3 2 fx	8	1
5 Troy Pratt	3 0 fxN N	3	
6 Simon Wolstenholme	3 1 2 0	6	1
7 Adrian Stevens	2 2 1 0 1	6	2

28...Wimbledon, September 12, L35-61

1 †Martin Goodwin	3 1 1 3 3 2	13	1
2 Kevin Brice	0 2 0 2 1	5	2
3 Rob Tilbury	0 3 2 F 0 3	8	
4 Troy Pratt	0 0 0 1 0	1	
5 Wayne Garratt	1 1 1 1 2 R	6	
6 Simon Wolstenholme	0 0 T T	0	
7 Adrian Stevens	1 1 T	2	

29...HACKNEY, September 13, W54-42

1 †Martin Goodwin	3 2 3 R 3	11	
2 Kevin Brice	0 1 2 2 3	8	2
3 Rob Tilbury	2 1 3 3 2	11	
4 Troy Pratt	2 1 2 2 1	8	2
5 Wayne Garratt	1 2 3 2 F	8	2
6 Simon Wolstenholme	3 1 0 0	4	1
7 Adrian Stevens	2 1 1	4	2

30...BERWICK, September 20, W58-38

1 †Martin Goodwin	2 3 2 1 3	11	1
2 Kevin Brice	1 1 2 0 2	6	2
3 Rob Tilbury	**3 3 3 3 2**	**14**	**1**
4 Wayne Garratt	2 2 1 2 2	9	2
5 Troy Pratt	0 1 2 2 3	8	2
6 Adrian Stevens	R 2 1 0	3	1
7 Simon Wolstenholme	2 3 2	7	1

31...Poole, October 2, L35-61

1 †Martin Goodwin	2 2 3 2 2 1	12	
2 Kevin Brice	0 1 T 1 0	2	2
3 Rob Tilbury	2 1 2 1 3 2	11	
4 Wayne Garratt	1 2 1 2 1 R	7	2
5 Troy Pratt	R 0 0 0 0	0	
6 Adrian Stevens	0 0 T T	0	
7 Simon Wolstenholme	3 0 0	3	

32...POOLE, October 6, L41-51

1 †Martin Goodwin	3 2 3 3 F	11	1
2 Kevin Brice	R 3 3 0 1	7	1
3 Rob Tilbury	2 1 1 0 R	4	2
4 Troy Pratt	R 2 0 0 1	3	
5 Wayne Garratt	R R 1 N 1	2	
6 Simon Wolstenholme	3 3 R 2 2 2	12	
7 Adrian Stevens	2 0 N	2	1

1990 ROSTER

BRICE, Kevin Neil
B 23.8.1958, Canterbury, Kent. *Signed from Rye House.*

GARRATT, Wayne Malcolm
B 30.10.1968, Halesowen, West Midlands. *On loan from Cradley Heath.*

GOODWIN, Martin
B 15.1.1960, Pembury, Kent.

LEDWITH, Robert Tience
B 10.11.1971, Forest Gate, London.

NICHOLLS, Shaun
B 30.11.1971, Ipswich, Suffolk. *Junior.*

PRATT, Troy Gavin
B 21.1.1968, Harlow, Essex. *On loan from Cradley Heath.*

STEVENS, Adrian Lawrence
B 15.7.1970, South Witham, Grantham, Lincolnshire. *Signed from King's Lynn.*

TILBURY, Robert (Rob) John Michael
B 5.4.1963, Canterbury, Kent.

WOLSTENHOLME, Simon
B 25.1.1971, Sheffield, South Yorkshire.

YOUNG, Christopher
B 6.6.1968, South Norwood, London.

KEVIN TEAGER - see Rye House.

Bandits can smile again says Terry

Track Data

Promoters: Terry Lindon and Dick Barrie.
Address: Berrington Lough, Near Ancroft, Berwick-upon-Tweed, Northumberland.
Telephone: 0289-87345.
Information Line: 0898 31 21 40.
Track Length: 253 metres.
Track Record: 55.1 secs, Andrew Silver (Arena Essex), July 4, 1987, Heat 1, Berwick v Arena Essex (National League).

TERRY LINDON ended his first season as a speedway promoter in the black – and that was some achievement at Berrington Lough, the most isolated outpost in the country. But, more important, he changed the aggressive face of Berwick as visiting teams, once again, began to enjoy their trips to the Borders.

He did it without destroying the club's prominent home record – even though they lost a long unbeaten record to Hackney they were the only visiting side to win at Berrington Lough – and they remained tough and uncompromising travellers as they stayed in the top six and only bowed out of the Knock Out Cup to eventual winners Poole.

Whereas in 1989, defeat against the Echo Pirates came in the final, this time around the two teams were drawn together in the second round after Berwick had accounted for Long Eaton yet again in the one and only first round tie.

Defeat against Poole was probably the low spot of the Berwick season (if you discount an awful showing in the Scottish Team Championship) as they had held the South Coast club to a 16 point first leg lead and still failed to make up the leeway even though Poole lost both skipper Alun Rossiter and potent reserve Tom Knudsen through injury without either of them completing a ride!

Lindon must also have quickly realised that in co-promoter Dick Barrie he had a shrewd market manipulator. Barrie advised two early moves into the transfer market and for the price of three seasons tickets he signed two riders, Steve Widt and Alan Rivett.

Widt, snapped up from Ipswich, made a reasonable number eight, but Rivett was a powerful acquisition whose points-scoring made a mockery of his £200 transfer fee. The Australianised Kiwi never missed a match, scored 224 League points, and finished fifth in the team charts ahead of the promising Scott Robson and skipper Rob Grant. How Exeter, who sold him so cheaply, must have wished they had insisted on a sliding scale payment in the deal.

David Blackburn survived a traumatic accident at Peterborough – from which he only survived because of the quick-thinking of the track and medical staff – and David Walsh developed as a true heat leader while everyone else marked time to provide another solid middle-order look.

Blackburn's return was the stuff of which Boys' Own stories were made in the post-war era. He missed nearly six weeks of racing but turned up unannounced on the night that the Federation Bandits were taking on Wimbledon, astonished the club management by not only riding but by winning his first three rides, surviving a fall and then going out to make it 12 points out of 15 in a courageous comeback.

He later had to return to Peterborough in the H.E.A.T. National League Team Championship but showed he had no hang-ups at all about the place although, overall, he was nowhere near the dominant force he had been before the accident. Some blamed it on the crash; others felt it was impending fatherhood!

Walsh, signed from Cradley Heath on a full-time contract at the beginning of the season, overtook Mark Courtney at the top of the scoring table but there was little to choose between them.

There were occasions when Courtney looked what he could possibly have been and that was the most naturally talented rider in the National League.

Save for that slip-up against Hackney, Berwick were almost as strong as ever on their own peculiar track but their away form (with one notable exception: a draw at Ipswich) was more suited to a team trying to avoid the wooden spoon than one with any silverware aspirations. Their only wins were, predictably, at Milton Keynes and Long Eaton and, perhaps inevitably, against Edinburgh!

Roll of Honour

Seasons in National League: 22 (1968-1980 [Shielfield Park]; 1982-1990 [Berrington Lough]).
National League Record: Third (1), 1989.
National League Cup Record: Winners (2), 1980, 1989. Runners-up (6), 1970, 1976, 1977, 1979, 1981, 1984.
National League Team Championship: Fourth (1), 1979. Qualified (7), 1979, 1980, 1984, 1985, 1987, 1989, 1990.
Appearances: Rob Grant, 377 (1978-1990).
Points: Steve McDermott, 3006 (1979-1988).
World Finalists: None.
NLRC Finalists: Roy Williams (1968), Maury Robinson (1969-70), Doug Wyer (1971), Doug Templeton (1972), Willie Templeton (1973-74), Graham Jones (1978-79), Wayne Brown (1980-81), Steve McDermott (1982-83, 1985-86), Bruce Cribb (1984), Rob Woffinden (1987), Mark Courtney (1988), David Blackburn (1989), David Walsh (1990).

BERWICK enter the 1991 Sunbrite League First Division – the first time they have competed in anything other than the National League (Second Division).

Star of 90
MARK COURTNEY
Berwick

BERWICK

01...MIDDLESBROUGH, April 7, W51-45

1 Mark Courtney	2 2 1 2 E	7	2
2 †Rob Grant	0 3 2 2 3	10	
3 David Blackburn	3 3 3 3 0	12	
4 David Walsh	2 2 3 1 3	11	1
5 Andy Campbell	1 1 1 0 2	5	2
6 §Alan Rivett	3 1 R 0 1	5	
7 Kevin Little	1 0 N F	1	

02...HACKNEY, April 21, L46-47

1 Mark Courtney	3 2 X 2 1	8	
2 Scott Robson	F 1 2 fnN	3	2
3 David Blackburn	3 3 3 3 2	14	
4 Andy Campbell	0 0 0 1 0	1	1
5 †Rob Grant	3 1 1 2 0	7	1
6 Alan Rivett	2 1 fx3 1 1	8	1
7 Kevin Little	E N 3 N 2	5	

03...POOLE, April 28, W61-35

1 Mark Courtney	3 X 2 2 2	9	2
2 Andy Campbell	1 3 2 1 3	10	1
3 David Blackburn	**3 3 3 3 3**	**15**	
4 David Walsh	1 1 3 3 3	11	1
5 †Rob Grant	2 3 1 2 X	8	1
6 Alan Rivett	3 2 0 0	5	1
7 Kevin Little	2 1 0	3	2

04...Wimbledon, May 2, L41-55

1 Mark Courtney	3 R 2 2 2 3	12	
2 †Rob Grant	0 2 T T T	2	
3 David Blackburn	2 3 2 R 0 1	8	
4 David Walsh	2 1 3 3 0 1	10	
5 Andy Campbell	0 0 1 3 0 0	4	
6 Alan Rivett	3 0 0 1 T	4	1
7 Kevin Little	1 R T	1	

05...Ipswich, May 3, D48-48

1 Mark Courtney	3 1 1 0 3	8	1
2 †Rob Grant	1 0 3 2 2	8	
3 David Blackburn	2 3 2 3 1	11	
4 David Walsh	2 3 2 3 2	12	1
5 Andy Campbell	0 0 0 0 N	0	
6 §Steve Widt	3 0 1 N	4	1
7 Kevin Little	2 1 1 1 R	5	3

06...Peterborough, May 4, L32-64

1 †Mark Courtney	2 1 3 1 1 1	9	1
2 Alan Rivett	0 0 0 2 0 2	4	
3 David Blackburn	3 1 fnN T	4	
4 David Walsh	fx1 1 0 1 0	3	
5 Andy Campbell	3 3 3 0 1 0	10	
6 Steve Widt	1 0 1 0	2	
7 Jason Straughan	0 R T N	0	

07...EASTBOURNE, May 5, W61-35

1 Mark Courtney	**3 3 3 3 3 3**	**18**	
2 Andy Campbell	0 2 2 2 1 3	10	3
3 David Blackburn	*rider replacement*		
4 David Walsh	3 3 3 3 1 2	15	1
5 †Rob Grant	1 2 1 3 2 2	11	1
6 Alan Rivett	3 1 1 0	5	
7 Kevin Little	1 1 F	2	1
8 Steve Widt	fx	0	

08...EXETER, May 12, W63-32

1 Mark Courtney	2 3 3 2 3 1	14	3
2 David Blackburn	*rider replacement*		
3 Andy Campbell	3 2 3 2 2 3	15	
4 David Walsh	2 2 2 3 1 2	12	2
5 †Rob Grant	3 1 2 1 1	8	3
6 Alan Rivett	3 1 2 3 2	11	2
7 Kevin Little	1 1 1 0	3	1
8 Steve Widt	*did not ride*		

09...Newcastle, May 13, L46-50

1 Mark Courtney	2 3 2 2 0 2 T	11	
2 David Blackburn	*rider replacement*		
3 Andy Campbell	0 2 1 3 2 1 1	10	1
4 David Walsh	3 2 2 3 2 2 3	17	1
5 †Rob Grant	0 R 0 1 1 T	2	2
6 Alan Rivett	3 0 1 1 0	5	1
7 Kevin Little	0 1 N	1	1
8 Steve Widt	*did not ride*		

10...ARENA ESSEX, May 26, W71-25

1 Mark Courtney	**2 3 2 2 3**	**12**	**3**
2 Alan Rivett	3 2 1 3 3	12	1
3 Andy Campbell	2 3 3 1 3	12	1
4 David Walsh	**3 3 3 3 2**	**14**	**1**
5 †Rob Grant	2 1 2 3 2	10	3
6 Kevin Little	E 3 2 2	7	2
7 Steve Widt	3 0 1	4	

11...LONG EATON, June 9, W54-42

1 Mark Courtney	3 2 3 2 3	13	1
2 Alan Rivett	2 1 3 2 3	11	3
3 Andy Campbell	2 3 1 0 3	9	
4 David Walsh	2 2 3 3 2	12	2
5 †Rob Grant	0 3 1 3 X	7	
6 Kevin Little	2 R 0 F F	2	
7 Steve Widt	0 N 0	0	

12...Milton Keynes, June 19, W49-46

1 †Mark Courtney	2 3 2 2 3	12	1
2 Alan Rivett	1 1 2 1 2	7	2
3 Andy Campbell	1 2 2 3 1	9	
4 David Walsh	**2 3 3 3 2**	**13**	**2**
5 Scott Robson	3 0 0 0 0	3	
6 Kevin Little	2 0 1 1 fx	4	2
7 Steve Widt	1 0 N	1	1

13...WIMBLEDON, June 23, W53-42

1 †Mark Courtney	3 3 1 2 0	9	1
2 Scott Robson	0 1 3 0 0	4	
3 David Blackburn	3 3 3 0 3	12	
4 David Walsh	1 2 1 3 3	10	2
5 Andy Campbell	0 3 2 2 2	9	1
6 Alan Rivett	3 2 0 1 F 3	9	1
7 Kevin Little	fx N N	0	

14...RYE HOUSE, July 7, W68-28

1 Mark Courtney	**3 3 3 2 3**	**14**	**1**
2 Alan Rivett	0 2 2 2 0	6	3
3 David Blackburn	R 2 3 3 3	11	1
4 David Walsh	3 3 fx N N	6	
5 †Rob Grant	**2 2 3 2 2**	**11**	**4**
6 Andy Campbell	2 2 3 3 2	12	1
7 Scott Robson	3 3 1 1	8	

15...Eastbourne, July 8, L38-58

1 Mark Courtney	2 2 1 2 2 2 1	12	1
2 Alan Rivett	0 2 0 T 1	3	1
3 David Blackburn	3 2 1 0 1 3	10	
4 David Walsh	*rider replacement*		
5 †Rob Grant	0 1 T N T	1	
6 Andy Campbell	2 0 R 3 0 2	7	
7 Scott Robson	0 1 2 1 1	5	2
8 Kevin Little	fx0	0	

16...Exeter, July 9, L40-56

1 Mark Courtney	0 1 1 0 2	4	1
2 Alan Rivett	2 2 2 3 2 3 1	15	1
3 David Blackburn	2 2 2 2 2 R	10	
4 David Walsh	*rider replacement*		
5 †Rob Grant	1 0 1 T N	2	2
6 Andy Campbell	1 1 2 1 1 2 1	9	4
7 Scott Robson	0 0 N	0	
8 Kevin Little	0 F	0	

17...Poole, July 10, L26-70

1 Mark Courtney	3 3 1 R 1 N 2	10	
2 Alan Rivett	F 0 T N N	0	
3 David Blackburn	1 1 0 0 1	3	
4 David Walsh	*rider replacement*		
5 †Rob Grant	0 0 1 2 0	3	
6 Andy Campbell	3 0 2 1 0 1 1	8	
7 Scott Robson	1 0 1 0 R	2	
8 Kevin Little	0 0	0	

18...NEWCASTLE, July 14, W68-27

1 Mark Courtney	2 3 2 3 2 3	15	2
2 Alan Rivett	3 1 2 0 2	8	3
3 David Blackburn	3 3 3 2 3 1 3	18	1
4 David Walsh	*rider replacement*		
5 †Rob Grant	1 1 1 2 2	7	2
6 Andy Campbell	**3 2 2 3 3**	**13**	**2**
7 Scott Robson	2 3 0 2	7	2
8 Kevin Little	*did not ride*		

19...Hackney, July 20, L35-61

1 Mark Courtney	2 1 3 2 2 N	10	1
2 Alan Rivett	0 2 0 1 T 1	4	2
3 David Blackburn	2 1 2 1 3 2	11	
4 David Walsh	F N N N T	0	
5 †Rob Grant	2 0 1 0 T	3	
6 Andy Campbell	3 0 2 0 0 1 1	7	
7 Scott Robson	0 0 T 0 0	0	

20...IPSWICH, July 28, W49-47

1 Mark Courtney	2 2 3 1 1	9	2
2 Alan Rivett	1 1 3 0 2	7	3
3 David Blackburn	3 3 1 2 1	10	
4 Andy Campbell	0 1 3 2 2	8	1
5 †Rob Grant	1 2 2 1 0	6	2
6 Scott Robson	3 1 0 2 3	9	1
7 Kevin Little	0 N 0	0	

21...Glasgow, July 29, L36-60

1 Mark Courtney	3 1 1 1 2 1 2	11	1
2 Alan Rivett	2 2 2 2 1 3	12	2
3 David Blackburn	R 0 1 2 0 1	4	
4 David Walsh	*rider replacement*		
5 †Rob Grant	F 0 0 1 0	1	1
6 Andy Campbell	1 1 0 3 1 1	7	1
7 Scott Robson	0 1 N	1	
8 Kevin Little	*did not ride*		

22...GLASGOW, August 4, W51-44

1 Mark Courtney	2 3 3 0 2 2 2	14	
2 †Rob Grant	0 2 2 0 0	4	2
3 David Blackburn	1 2 2 3 3 1	12	2
4 David Walsh	*rider replacement*		
5 Andy Campbell	2 3 1 1 2 2	11	3
6 Alan Rivett	R 0 R N	0	
7 Scott Robson	3 3 1 3 0	10	
8 Kevin Little	*did not ride*		

23...PETERBOROUGH, August 18, W73-23

1 Mark Courtney	**3 2 3 2 3**	**13**	**2**
2 †Rob Grant	R 3 3 2 2	10	2
3 David Blackburn	**3 3 3 3 3**	**15**	
4 David Walsh	3 2 1 3 2	11	3
5 Andy Campbell	2 3 2 2 1	10	2
6 Alan Rivett	3 1 2 3	9	1
7 Scott Robson	2 2 1	5	2

24...STOKE, August 25, W56-40

1 Mark Courtney	3 2 1 1 1	8	1
2 †Rob Grant	2 1 3 R 1	7	2
3 David Blackburn	3 3 3 2 2	13	
4 David Walsh	2 3 1 3 2	11	
5 Andy Campbell	1 2 0 1 1	5	4
6 Alan Rivett	3 2 1 0	6	1
7 Scott Robson	2 2 2	6	3

25...Rye House, August 26, L43-52

1 Mark Courtney	3 N 2 2 3	10	
2 †Rob Grant	1 1 1 0 N	3	1
3 David Blackburn	0 0 2 0 2	4	
4 David Walsh	2 1 2 1 1	7	3
5 Andy Campbell	3 2 0 2 0	7	
6 Alan Rivett	1 2 1 X	4	2
7 Scott Robson	2 1 2 3 fx	8	

26...Stoke, August 27, L38-58

1 Mark Courtney	2 2 2 2 1 1	10	1
2 †Rob Grant	1 R 1 T T	2	1
3 David Blackburn	1 3 1 2 R R	7	
4 David Walsh	0 3 fxF 3 0	6	
5 Andy Campbell	1 0 T 1 2	4	
6 Alan Rivett	2 1 0 3	6	1
7 Scott Robson	3 0 R	3	

27....MILTON KEYNES, September 8, W68-27

1 Mark Courtney	**3 3 2 2 2**	**12**	**3**
2 Alan Rivett	1 0 2 3 3	9	1
3 David Blackburn	fx3 2 3 3	11	1
4 David Walsh	**3 3 3 3 3**	**15**	
5 Andy Campbell	1 2 1 2 2	8	3
6 †Rob Grant	3 3 1 F	7	
7 Scott Robson	R 3 3	6	

28...Edinburgh, September 9, W49.5-46.5

1 Mark Courtney	3 3 3 2 2	13	
2 Alan Rivett	0 F 2 0 1	3	1
3 David Blackburn	3 2 3 2 1	11	
4 David Walsh	2 3 1 1 1	8	3
5 Andy Campbell	3 1.5 0 1 3	8.5	1
6 †Rob Grant	2 0 0 N	2	
7 Scott Robson	0 1 3 R	4	

29...Middlesbrough, September 13, L25-71

1 Mark Courtney	R 1 2 2 0 2	7	
2 Alan Rivett	1 0 1 T 0 1	3	
3 David Blackburn	1 3 1 0 1 R	6	1
4 David Walsh	fnT R T N	0	
5 Andy Campbell	fx0 1 0 1 1	3	
6 †Rob Grant	0 0 T 0	0	
7 Scott Robson	3 1 0 2 0	6	

30...Long Eaton, September 19, W50-46

1 Mark Courtney	3 3 3 1 2	12	1
2 Alan Rivett	0 1 1 1 0	3	
3 David Blackburn	E 1 1 3 N	5	
4 David Walsh	2 2 2 2 0	8	
5 Andy Campbell	1 1 1 2 1	6	5
6 †Rob Grant	2 1 0 0 N	3	1
7 Scott Robson	3 3 3 2 2	13	

31...Arena Essex, September 20, L38-58

1 Mark Courtney	3 3 0 0 0 N	6	
2 Alan Rivett	0 0 0 N N	0	
3 David Blackburn	0 2 0 T T	2	
4 David Walsh	3 2 3 3 1 1	13	
5 Andy Campbell	1 R 1 3 3 0	8	
6 †Rob Grant	1 0 T T 0	1	
7 Scott Robson	3 1 1 1 1 1	8	

32...EDINBURGH, September 29, W48-45

1 Mark Courtney	2 2 3 1 1	9	2
2 Alan Rivett	0 1 0 N 3	4	1
3 David Blackburn	3 3 1 0 0	7	1
4 David Walsh	3 2 3 2 2	12	
5 Andy Campbell	1 0 1 2 1	5	
6 †Rob Grant	3 0 0 N	3	
7 Scott Robson	2 3 1 2 R	8	1

1990 ROSTER

BLACKBURN, David Martin
B 7.1.1962, Coventry, West Midlands.

CAMPBELL, Andrew Neil
B 3.10.1959, Guildford, Surrey.

COURTNEY, Mark Vincent
B 25.3.1961, Braintree, Essex.

GRANT, Robert (Rob)
B 17.2.1959, Throckley, Northumberland.

LITTLE, Kevin
B 24.9.1972, Edinburgh, Scotland.

RIVETT, Alan
B 21.3.1956, Whangerei, New Zealand. *Signed from Exeter.*

ROBSON, Scott
B 15.8.1971, Sunderland, Tyne & Wear.

SMITH, Fraser Roy
B 23.11.1970, Bellshill, Scotland. *Local junior.*

STRAUGHAN, Jason
B 11.7.1970, Tweedmouth, Northumberland.

WALSH, David
B 29.8.1963, Sowerby Bridge, West Yorkshire. *Signed from Cradley Heath after being on loan in 1989.*

WIDT, Stephen
B 8.9.1967, Mount Isa, Australia. *Signed from Ipswich.*

Bold Eagles land on a rocky perch

Track Data

Promoters: Gareth Rogers.
Address: Arlington Stadium, Arlington Road West, Hailsham, East Sussex, BN27 3RE.
Telephone: 0323-841642.
Track Length: 302 metres.
Track Record: 57.05 secs, Martin Dugard (Eastbourne), July 25, 1987, heat 13, Eastbourne v Edinburgh (National League Knock-out Cup).

THERE was a familiar ring to Eastbourne's end of season farewells – with promoter Gareth Rogers again expressing serious doubts about the track's future.

Then suddenly everything looked so much brighter when Stadium owner Bob Dugard came galloping along in his guise of saviour, brandishing an application form and bank surety to join the 1991 Sunbrite League. Why, he even had the names of the seven riders he wanted in his new-look team and, all of a sudden, the future looked so much brighter for Arlington.

Fans should have known better. Nothing ever goes that smoothly at the East Sussex track and no sooner had Eastbourne officially applied to rejoin the Sunbrite League than they were once again biting their nails when the National League promoters had a rethink on their future, threw in their lot with Mervyn Stewkesbury's amalgamation plan – and, lo and behold, found four other tracks willing to make the jump before they got around to asking Eastbourne if they wanted automatic promotion.

Once again the Eagles were in the melting pot – with Dugard insisting it was First Division or bust. And in Rogers' case that meant only one decision as he didn't fancy the financial ruination option.

He admitted: "The message was clear from my own bankers. I couldn't afford another season in the Second Division no matter what it was called."

It hasn't been an easy promoting baptism for the former schoolteacher but at least he had learnt his lesson on how to deal with malcontent riders and supporters. He let those who were unhappy at Arlington move on and brought in a couple of signings who were more than happy to ride for the club.

Paul Woods, who had missed most of 1989 with a troublesome wrist injury and whose whole career was then put in the balance with an eye injury, was given medical clearance to make a comeback only a couple of weeks before the start of the new campaign and didn't hesitate to resume his career at the track where he had first made his name in the seventies.

He was joined by Australian Tony Primmer who had made impressive Arlington appearances for his previous club Milton Keynes. When Justin Walker found himself without a club after Peterborough had failed to pay a transfer fee instalment he also joined the Eagles to give them three new faces at the beginning of the season.

Unfortunately for them the most familiar name of all was missing from their team sheet in their first three League matches – skipper Gordon Kennett who damaged his shoulder in a pre-season practice session and didn't make his first appearance until the end of April.

By then Eastbourne had already lost heavily at Peterborough, Wimbledon and Hackney (tough matches all) and the message had got through that it was going to be a long, hard summer.

It was. Some surprising results (a 20 point away win at Arena Essex and a 17 point home defeat against the same opposition!) should have kept the fans on their toes but Eastbourne supporters, fed on a National League diet of titles and cups, didn't take too kindly to middle of the table fare and the hot summer enticed far too many to other Sunday afternoon attractions.

Team-wise the side was disrupted by a falling out (later patched up) with Darren Grayling and then the shock retirement in September of Andy Buck who was suffering from a viral infection.

But at least something good came out of the season with new Aussie Brian Nixon patiently awaiting his team chance and then making everyone wonder why he hadn't been given it earlier!

Roll of Honour

Seasons in National League: 16 (1969-1978; 1985-1990).
National League Record: Champions (4), 1971, 1977, 1986, 1987. Runners-up (2), 1970, 1974. Third (2), 1973, 1988.
National League Cup Record: Winners (6), 1975, 1977, 1978, 1985, 1986, 1987. Runners-up (1), 1974.
National League Team Championship: Runners-up (1), 1976. Third (3), 1977, 1987, 1988. Fourth (1), 1989. Qualified (7), 1976, 1977, 1978, 1986, 1987, 1988, 1989.
Appearances: Gordon Kennett, 329 (1970-1972, 1985-1990).
Points: Gordon Kennett, 3523.5 (1970-1972, 1985-1990).
World Finalists: Kelly Moran (1982), Kai Niemi (1980).
NLRC Finalists: Reg Trott (1969), Dave Jessup (1970), Malcolm Ballard (1971-72), Bobby McNeil (1973-74), Paul Gachet (1975), Steve Weatherley (1976), Colin Richardson (1977), Mike Sampson (1978), Gordon Kennett (1985-86, 1988-89-90), Martin Dugard (1987).
Other Honours: National League (Division Three) Champions, 1947.

Star of 90

GORDON KENNETT

Eastbourne

EASTBOURNE

01...Peterborough, April 13, L22-74

1 †Keith Pritchard	1 0 0 2 1 R 1	5	
2 Gordon Kennett	*rider replacement*		
3 Andy Buck	1 1 1 1 0 N T	4	
4 Paul Woods	0 1 1 0 0 2 T	4	2
5 §Tony Primmer	2 1 2 0 1 1 0	7	
6 Darren Grayling	1 0 T 1	2	
7 Steve Masters	R 0 T 0	0	
8 John Cook	0	0	

02...Wimbledon, April 25, L29-66

1 †Keith Pritchard	1 0 1 0 1 1 0	4	1
2 Gordon Kennett	*rider replacement*		
3 Andy Buck	2 1 2 1 2 1 2	11	
4 Paul Woods	0 2 2 0 1 0 1	6	
5 Tony Primmer	1 1 0 0 T	2	2
6 §Justin Walker	3 1 0 T N	4	
7 Steve Masters	2 0 T 0	2	1
8 John Cook	F	0	

03...Hackney, April 27, L33-62

1 †Keith Pritchard	fx0 0 N 1	1	
2 Gordon Kennett	*rider replacement*		
3 Andy Buck	2 1 3 2 1 2 2	13	1
4 Paul Woods	fx1 1 1 0 1 T	4	2
5 Tony Primmer	2 2 0 2 1 3 1	11	2
6 Darren Grayling	0 2 1 T 0 0	3	
7 Justin Walker	1 0 T	1	
8 Steve Masters	0	0	

04...LONG EATON, April 29, W49-47

1 †Gordon Kennett	3 2 3 2 3	13	
2 Keith Pritchard	1 0 2 1 3	7	1
3 Andy Buck	3 2 fx2 3	10	
4 Paul Woods	1 2 1 0 2	6	1
5 Tony Primmer	0 1 3 0 0	4	1
6 Justin Walker	2 1 0 N	3	
7 Darren Grayling	1 3 1 1	6	1

05...Berwick, May 5, L35-61

1 †Gordon Kennett	2 R 3 2 3 0	10	
2 Keith Pritchard	1 1 0 T 2 1	5	1
3 Andy Buck	2 1 2 2 1 3	11	1
4 Paul Woods	2 2 1 1 0 1	7	1
5 Tony Primmer	0 0 0 R T	0	
6 Justin Walker	2 0 0 T	2	
7 Darren Grayling	0 0 T	0	

06...MIDDLESBROUGH, May 6, L42-54

1 †Gordon Kennett	2 3 2 2 R	9	
2 Keith Pritchard	0 1 2 1 1	5	1
3 Andy Buck	3 2 2 1 3	11	1
4 Paul Woods	1 2 2 0 1	6	
5 Tony Primmer	0 F N 2 0	2	
6 Justin Walker	3 2 1 1 0	7	3
7 Darren Grayling	0 1 1	2	2

07...Arena Essex, May 12, W58-38

1 †Gordon Kennett	3 2 3 3 3	14	
2 Keith Pritchard	2 1 1 2 2	8	3
3 Andy Buck	2 3 2 1 R	8	
4 Paul Woods	3 2 1 0 2	8	3
5 Tony Primmer	2 3 2 3 3	13	1
6 Justin Walker	3 2 0 1	6	2
7 Darren Grayling	0 1 0	1	1

08...STOKE, May 13, W54-42

1 †Gordon Kennett	2 2 1 3 3	11	
2 Keith Pritchard	1 1 2 0 2	6	3
3 Andy Buck	3 3 2 1 3	12	1
4 Paul Woods	2 0 1 0 2	5	3
5 Tony Primmer	3 2 2 2 0	9	
6 Justin Walker	3 2 0 N	5	1
7 Darren Grayling	2 3 0 1	6	2

09...Stoke, May 19, L42-54

1 †Gordon Kennett	**3 3 3 3 3 3**	**18**	
2 Keith Pritchard	F 0 T 1 2	3	
3 Andy Buck	0 1 0 1 R T	2	
4 Paul Woods	3 2 0 3 1 1	10	
5 Tony Primmer	1 0 2 2 fx1	6	1
6 Justin Walker	F N T T	0	
7 Darren Grayling	2 1 0 T 0	3	

10...EXETER, May 20, W66-30

1 †Gordon Kennett	2 3 3 3 2	13	
2 Keith Pritchard	1 0 R 1 1	3	2
3 Andy Buck	**3 3 3 3 3**	**15**	
4 Paul Woods	2 2 3 2 1	10	3
5 Tony Primmer	3 1 2 2 2	10	4
6 Justin Walker	2 2 2 2	8	3
7 Darren Grayling	3 2 2	7	1

11...Ipswich, June 14, L33-63

1 †Gordon Kennett	3 3 0 1 R N	7	1
2 Justin Walker	fx0 T T T 0	0	
3 Andy Buck	3 2 1 2 0 1	9	
4 Paul Woods	1 2 1 2 1 2	9	
5 Tony Primmer	0 1 0 0 T	1	1
6 Keith Pritchard	2 0 0 2	4	
7 Darren Grayling	0 1 1 1	3	1

12...PETERBOROUGH, June 24, W53-43

1 †Gordon Kennett	1 3 2 3 3 3	15	1
2 Tony Primmer	0 3 2 2 3	10	1
3 Andy Buck	3 3 2 fx2	10	
4 Paul Woods	2 2 2 1 2	9	2
5 Justin Walker	1 T 1 2 0	4	2
6 Keith Pritchard	fnN N N	0	
7 Darren Grayling	2 0 1 1 1 0	5	2

13...Milton Keynes, June 26, W55-41

1 †Gordon Kennett	2 3 3 0 3	11	
2 Tony Primmer	1 2 3 2 2	10	4
3 Andy Buck	R 1 2 1 2	6	3
4 Paul Woods	3 3 3 1 1	11	
5 Justin Walker	R R N N 1	1	1
6 Keith Pritchard	2 2 3 E 3	10	
7 Darren Grayling	0 2 2 0 2	6	1

14...WIMBLEDON, July 1, W54-42

1 †Gordon Kennett	2 2 2 3 2	11	1
2 Tony Primmer	1 3 1 1 2	8	3
3 Andy Buck	3 2 2 2 3	12	
4 Paul Woods	2 2 1 2 0	7	2
5 Justin Walker	1 1 2 0 1	5	2
6 Keith Pritchard	3 2 1 3	9	2
7 Darren Grayling	2 0 0	2	1

15...BERWICK, July 8, W58-38

1 Gordon Kennett	3 3 1 3 3	13	
2 Tony Primmer	1 1 1 3 3	9	
3 Andy Buck	2 3 3 3 2	13	
4 Paul Woods	1 3 2 2 2	10	2
5 Justin Walker	3 0 0 fxN	3	
6 Keith Pritchard	3 0 2 X 1	6	2
7 Darren Grayling	1 3 0	4	

16...Long Eaton, July 12, W55-41

1 †Gordon Kennett	**3 3 2 3 3 3**	**17**	**1**
2 Tony Primmer	2 3 2 2 1 0	10	1
3 Andy Buck	1 3 2 2 2 2	12	1
4 Paul Woods	1 1 0 3 1 2	8	2
5 Justin Walker	*rider replacement*		
6 Keith Pritchard	2 2 1 0 3	8	2
7 Darren Grayling	0 0 N 0	0	
8 Steve Masters	*did not ride*		

17...GLASGOW, July 15, W53-42

1 †Gordon Kennett	3 3 3 3 3 2 3	20	
2 Justin Walker	*rider replacement*		
3 Andy Buck	F 2 1 1 1 N	5	1
4 Paul Woods	3 2 1 2 2 1	11	2
5 Tony Primmer	0 2 1 3 2 2	10	2
6 Keith Pritchard	2 E 1 2 1	6	3
7 Darren Grayling	0 1 N F	1	
8 Steve Masters	0	0	

18...Exeter, July 16, L32-63

1 †Gordon Kennett	1 2 1 3 3 2	12	
2 Justin Walker	*rider replacement*		
3 Andy Buck	1 3 3 2 3 T	12	
4 Paul Woods	0 0 1 1 1 0	3	
5 Tony Primmer	1 0 0 0 1 1	3	1
6 Keith Pritchard	2 0 F R	2	
7 Darren Grayling	fx0 0	0	
8 Steve Masters	0 0	0	

19...ARENA ESSEX, July 29, L39-56

1 †Gordon Kennett	F 1 0 0 T	1	1
2 Tony Primmer	fx1 T 1 3 1 2	8	3
3 Andy Buck	2 3 2 1 2 0	10	
4 Paul Woods	E 2 2 1 2 1 2	10	1
5 Justin Walker	*rider replacement*		
6 Keith Pritchard	3 2 R 1 1	7	1
7 Darren Grayling	1 2 0	3	
8 Darren Standing	fx0	0	

20...RYE HOUSE, August 4, W61-34

1 †Gordon Kennett	3 1 fnN N	4	1
2 Tony Primmer	2 2 2 2 2	10	3
3 Andy Buck	0 3 3 3 2	11	1
4 Paul Woods	3 3 2 2 3	13	1
5 Keith Pritchard	1 2 1 2 3	9	3
6 Darren Standing	2 1 fxN	3	
7 Darren Grayling	1 3 3 1 3 0	11	1

21...Glasgow, August 8, L30-66

1 Gordon Kennett	*rider replacement*		
2 Tony Primmer	1 3 1 0 3 2 0	10	1
3 Andy Buck	0 0 0 1 N	1	
4 Paul Woods	2 2 0 2 0 1 0	7	1
5 †Keith Pritchard	0 1 1 2 0 2	6	
6 Darren Standing	2 1 T T 1 0	4	
7 Darren Grayling	0 N T 0	0	
8 Justin Walker	0 2	2	

22...Middlesbrough, August 9, L35-61

1 Gordon Kennett	*rider replacement*		
2 Tony Primmer	1 3 2 0 1 3 3	13	2
3 Andy Buck	1 2 2 2 F 1 2	10	
4 Paul Woods	2 2 1 0 1 1 0	7	1
5 Keith Pritchard	1 1 0 1 E	3	1
6 Darren Standing	1 T 1 T T 0	2	1
7 Darren Grayling	0 0 N	0	
8 Justin Walker	R 0	0	

23...Edinburgh, August 10, L36-60

1 Gordon Kennett	*rider replacement*		
2 Tony Primmer	3 2 2 1 2 2 2	14	1
3 Andy Buck	1 R 0 1 N	2	1
4 Paul Woods	fx2 3 0 0 1 1	7	1
5 †Keith Pritchard	1 1 1 2 2 0 0	7	2
6 Darren Standing	2 1 T 1 0 1	5	1
7 Justin Walker	1 R T	1	1
8 Steve Masters	*did not ride*		

24...EDINBURGH, August 12, W62-34

1 Gordon Kennett	*rider replacement*		
2 Tony Primmer	**2 3 2 3 3**	**15**	**3**
3 Darren Standing	2 3 0 1 2	8	1
4 Paul Woods	3 3 3 2 0 2	13	
5 †Keith Pritchard	2 2 1 1 3 fx	9	3
6 §§Brian Nixon	2 3 F 1	6	1
7 Darren Grayling	3 3 3 2 0	11	

25...NEWCASTLE, August 26, W49-46

1 Paul Woods	2 1 1 1 3	8	2
2 †Gordon Kennett	3 3 F 2 3	11	
3 Andy Buck	2 3 3 3 1	12	
4 Tony Primmer	1 2 0 0 N	3	1
5 Keith Pritchard	2 1 1 1 R	5	1
6 Darren Standing	3 1 2 2 X	8	3
7 Darren Grayling	R 2 0	2	

26...IPSWICH, September 2, L46-49

1 †Gordon Kennett	3 3 1 1 2	10	1
2 Tony Primmer	0 2 1 0 1	4	2
3 Andy Buck	3 2 1 0 3	9	
4 Paul Woods	2 2 X 2 0	6	
5 Keith Pritchard	0 0 3 2 1	6	
6 Darren Standing	3 2 1 0 3	9	2
7 Justin Walker	R 2 N	2	

27...Rye House, September 9, L33-62

1 †Gordon Kennett	3 2 2 2 1	10	
2 Tony Primmer	1 1 1 1 R T	4	2
3 Andy Buck	0 2 R 0 fx	2	
4 Paul Woods	2 2 2 1 1 0	8	1
5 Keith Pritchard	1 1 0 1 2 2	7	2
6 Darren Standing	fxN T T	0	
7 Brian Nixon	X 2 0 T 0	2	

28...Poole, September 11, L25-71

1 †Gordon Kennett	2 2 3 2 2 2	13	
2 Tony Primmer	0 1 F 0 N	1	1
3 Andy Buck	1 1 0 0 N	2	
4 Paul Woods	1 0 1 1 1 0	4	1
5 Keith Pritchard	0 1 0 1 1	3	
6 Justin Walker	1 0 T 0	1	
7 Brian Nixon	0 0 T 1 R	1	

29...POOLE, September 16, L35-61

1 †Gordon Kennett	2 0 1 1 T	4	
2 Tony Primmer	1 3 2 0 1 0	7	1
3 Andy Buck	3 1 F 1 1	6	1
4 Paul Woods	2 2 1 0 1	6	
5 Keith Pritchard	1 1 R 0 2	4	2
6 Justin Walker	3 2 0 0	5	1
7 Brian Nixon	1 1 1	3	1

30...Newcastle, September 17, L45-51

1 †Gordon Kennett	3 2 1 2 3	11	2
2 Tony Primmer	1 3 3 2 3	12	
3 Justin Walker	1 1 0 N N	2	
4 Paul Woods	2 E 0 1 0	3	2
5 Keith Pritchard	3 2 2 1 1	9	
6 Brian Nixon	3 0 1 0 2 1	7	1
7 §§Scott Swain	1 0 0 0	1	

31...MILTON KEYNES, Sept 30, W56-39

1 †Gordon Kennett	3 2 3 3 3	14	
2 Tony Primmer	1 1 3 2 3	10	2
3 Keith Pritchard	3 2 3 fx1	9	1
4 Paul Woods	2 3 3 2 fx	10	1
5 Darren Standing	1 1 2 fnN	4	2
6 Brian Nixon	1 2 N 2	5	2
7 Darren Grayling	2 0 1 1 fx0	4	

32...HACKNEY, October 7, W51-45

1 †Gordon Kennett	2 3 3 3 3	14	
2 Tony Primmer	0 R 0 N N	0	
3 Keith Pritchard	2 3 2 2 1	10	1
4 Paul Woods	3 3 2 1 1	10	
5 Darren Standing	2 1 0 1 0	4	2
6 Brian Nixon	3 3 2 1 1	10	1
7 Darren Grayling	1 2 0 F	3	

1990 ROSTER

BUCK, Andrew Gordon (Andy)
B 25.5.1962, Peterborough, Cambs.

COOK, Jonathan Frank (John)
B 8.8.1965, Brighton, East Sussex.

GRAYLING, Darren
B 3.3.1972, Eastbourne, East Sussex.

KENNETT, Gordon William
B 2.9.1953, Bromley, Kent.

MASTERS, Steve
B 6.12.1970, Eastbourne, East Sussex.

NIXON, Brian
B 10.9.1962, Taree, Australia. *First season Australian.*

PRIMMER, Tony
B 11.4.1966, Maitland, Australia. *Signed from Milton Keynes.*

PRITCHARD, Keith Albert
B 19.7.1957, Ashford, Kent.

STANDING, Darren
B 20.6.1969, Southampton, Hampshire.

SWAIN, Scott
B 29.10.1971, Eastbourne, East Sussex. *Local junior.*

WALKER, Justin Lee
B 16.2.1971, Wordsley, West Midlands. *Signed on loan from Cradley Heath.*

WOODS, Paul
B 17.1.1959, Canterbury, Kent. *Signed from Rye House.*

Schøtt in the dark hits target

Track Data

Promoters: John Campbell and Doug Newlands.
Address: Powderhall Stadium, Beaverhall Road, Edinburgh, EH7 4JE.
Telephone: 031-556-3979.
Hotline: 0898 800 689.
Track Length: 312 metres.
Track Record: 61.6 secs, Mark Loram (Ipswich), September 29, 1989, Heat 6, Edinburgh v Ipswich (National League).

THANK Heaven for Freddy Schøtt. It wasn't the happiest of seasons for Edinburgh or their fans but at least it was bearable thanks to the discovery of the young Dane.

The Monarchs' management, whose season started dismally with their team backers Belmont Garages pulling out, had spotted Freddy's name in the overseas scorers but it wasn't until they read in the *Speedway Star* that he wanted to come over to England that they decided to make concrete moves.

And how grateful they were – for Schøtt was a shining beacon in an otherwise dimly lit year for the Scottish club. He came into Britain for his first taste of action and ended the season with more than 250 points and a near eight point average to become the first genuine Edinburgh discovery to have made heat leader status!

But he gave more than points to the team. He gave excitement to the fans as he never, ever gave up until the chequered flag and that was in marked contrast to some of his team-mates who seemed too willing to give up the chase once the first and second bends had been negotiated.

For a Dane he wasn't the sharpest of gaters but he more than made up for that with his willingness to mix it and soon became immensely popular with the fans.

Unfortunately for the club he was the only huge plus – although there were other meritorious performances from team members.

Les Collins maintained his ranking as number one, refused to let his own feelings about tyres affect his points-scoring but was never quite as effective as he had been in the previous couple of seasons although he is a long, long way from being on the slide as a regular points-piler.

Somehow Michael Coles coped with that horrendously long road journey from his home in deepest Devon and was another of the team who never knew the true meaning of being beaten. But even Edinburgh officials were privately asking how much longer he could afford to spend so much time behind the steering wheel on his way to and from meetings.

That was the good side of life at Powderhall. Now for the bad, or, conservatively, at least the not so good.

Skipper Brett Saunders had an absolute nightmare with machinery which lasted almost to the night he banged himself up at Ipswich. Ironically he was looking far more like his old self on that Southern trip. He had won his last four rides at Wimbledon on the Wednesday night and had 10 paid 11 from five outings at Ipswich when he was carted off to hospital with a ruptured spleen and seven broken ribs which kept him out for the rest of the season and saw him lose a tremendous amount of weight after surgeons patched him up again.

Mick Powell, a sensational first season newcomer in 1989, struggled at first as he tried to come back after that bad thigh fracture and then appeared to give up as he fell out with the team management and finally asked for a transfer insisting he would rather stay in Australia than return for a third season with the Monarchs.

And Carl Blackbird was probably the most expensive failure of the year. Edinburgh paid around £13,000 to buy his contract and also had to meet his personal terms and certainly got nothing like their moneysworth. It couldn't have helped that he was making the long trip from his Southern home and some might say that Edinburgh should have read the writing on the wall when he failed to turn up for his League debut after being approached to sign for Poole. The National League Management Committee ruled that he had to stay at Edinburgh – where he had signed a contract and ridden in a challenge match against Slangerup – and while he claimed he would give his all for the Scottish club he displayed nothing like the form that had taken him to England recognition not so long ago.

Scott Lamb, like Powell, ended the year on the list and despite a regular training school at Linlithgow there was still little sign of any home grown produce coming onto the market.

Roll of Honour

Seasons in National League: 14 (1977-1990).
Best National League Season: Fourth, 1981.
National League Cup Record: Winners (1), 1981.
National League Team Championship: Winners (1), 1981. Qualified (5), 1978, 1981, 1983, 1986, 1989.
Appearances: Dave Trownson, 374 (1977-1987).
Points: Dave Trownson, 3045.5 (1977-1987).
World Finalists: Jack Young (1950-51), Bernt Persson (1967).
NLRC Finalists: Bert Harkins (1977), Rob Hollingworth (1978), Neil Collins (1981), Dave Trownson (1982-83), Mark Fiora (1984), Les Collins (1986-87, 1989-90), Jamie Luckhurst (1988).
Other Honours: Provincial League Knock-out Cup Winners, 1961.

Star of 90

FREDDY SCHØTT

Edinburgh

EDINBURGH

01...HACKNEY, April 22, L40-56

1 Les Collins	2 2 3 3 3 1	14	
2 Michael Coles	1 F 2 0 3	6	2
3 †Brett Saunders	2 2 0 0 1	5	
4 Mick Powell	0 fxNTN	0	
5 Scott Lamb	1 3 2 1 1 0	8	
6 Mark Pearce	3 1 X 0	4	1
7 §§Freddy Schøtt	1 T 1 1 0	3	1

02...Milton Keynes, April 24, W50-46

1 Les Collins	**3 3 3 3 3 3**	**18**	
2 Michael Coles	0 1 2 2 2	7	3
3 †Brett Saunders	2 R 1 0 3	6	1
4 Scott Lamb	1 1 0 0 2	4	1
5 Mark Pearce	fx0 T N N	0	
6 §Anthony Boyd	0 1 NT	1	
7 Freddy Schøtt	3 3 3 0 1 3 1	14	

03...Long Eaton, April 25, L44-52

1 Les Collins	2 3 1 2 2 3	13	
2 Michael Coles	1 1 1 3 R	6	1
3 †Brett Saunders	2 2 1 2 0	7	1
4 Scott Lamb	2 1 0 0 T	3	1
5 Mark Pearce	3 fx1 N T 1	5	
6 Anthony Boyd	1 0 N T	1	
7 Freddy Schøtt	F 3 3 0 1 2	9	1

04...Middlesbrough, April 26, L31-65

1 Les Collins	3 3 2 1 2 2	13	
2 Michael Coles	0 0 T 3 1 0	4	
3 †Brett Saunders	0 1 1 0 0	2	
4 Scott Lamb	1 F 0 T T	1	
5 §Carl Blackbird	0 1 1 1 3 1	7	
6 Mark Pearce	1 0 0 T	1	
7 Freddy Schøtt	0 3 0 0	3	

05...IPSWICH, April 29, L31-64

1 Les Collins	1 0 1 1 1	4	
2 Michael Coles	0 1 1 0 2	4	
3 †Brett Saunders	1 1 2 0 E	4	1
4 Scott Lamb	0 1 R 0 0	1	1
5 Carl Blackbird	1 2 3 2 2 0	10	
6 Freddy Schøtt	2 2 0 1 2	7	1
7 Mark Pearce	1 T 0	1	1

06...RYE HOUSE, May 4, W51-45

1 Les Collins	2 2 3 2 3	12	
2 Mick Powell	0 1 N T N	1	1
3 †Brett Saunders	0 0 3 R N	3	
4 Michael Coles	1 1 R 1 1	4	2
5 Carl Blackbird	3 2 2 3 3	13	
6 Scott Lamb	1 1 2 3 1	8	
7 Freddy Schøtt	3 X 1 2 3 1	10	1

07...MILTON KEYNES, May 13, W66-30

1 Les Collins	**3 3 3 3 3**	**15**	
2 Mick Powell	0 2 1 1 0	4	1
3 †Brett Saunders	3 2 1 2 2	10	3
4 Michael Coles	1 3 2 0 1	7	1
5 Carl Blackbird	3 1 3 3 3	13	
6 Scott Lamb	2 1 3 2	8	1
7 Freddy Schøtt	3 3 3	9	

08...NEWCASTLE, May 25, W56-40

1 Les Collins	**3 3 3 3 2**	**14**	**1**
2 Mick Powell	F 1 0 N N	1	
3 Freddy Schøtt	2 1 3 1 3	10	1
4 Michael Coles	1 3 0 0 3	7	
5 Carl Blackbird	fx2 2 2 1	7	1
6 †Brett Saunders	3 1 3 2 2	11	2
7 Scott Lamb	2 2 1 1	6	2

09...LONG EATON, June 11, W71-25

1 Les Collins	**3 3 3 3 3**	**15**	
2 Mick Powell	0 1 1 2 2	6	2
3 Freddy Schøtt	**3 3 3 3 3**	**15**	
4 Michael Coles	2 3 1 2 1	9	2
5 Carl Blackbird	**3 2 3 2 2**	**12**	**3**
6 †Brett Saunders	**3 2 2 3 3**	**13**	**2**
7 §§Brian Mercer	1 N 0	1	

10...Rye House, July 1, W52-43

1 Les Collins	3 1 1 3 3	11	2
2 Michael Coles	0 2 1 2 2	7	2
3 Freddy Schøtt	1 2 3 2 3	11	1
4 †Brett Saunders	3 fx3 0 0	6	
5 Carl Blackbird	2 2 2 1 0	7	3
6 §§Nigel Alderton	1 N 0 N	1	1
7 Scott Lamb	2 2 0 2 3	9	

11...Hackney, July 6, L44-52

1 Les Collins	2 3 3 1 2 2	13	2
2 Mick Powell	0 0 N T T 0	0	
3 Freddy Schøtt	2 1 2 2 0 2	9	2
4 †Brett Saunders	1 2 1 3 2 T	9	2
5 Carl Blackbird	2 1 0 1 N	4	1
6 Michael Coles	2 2 1 T 3 0	8	
7 Scott Lamb	0 1 0	1	1

12...PETERBOROUGH, July 8, W62-34

1 Les Collins	2 2 fx3 3	10	
2 Mick Powell	0 0 fxN 1	1	1
3 Freddy Schøtt	**3 3 3 2 3**	**14**	**1**
4 †Brett Saunders	1 2 1 2 2	8	4
5 Carl Blackbird	3 3 2 3 0	11	
6 Michael Coles	3 2 2 3 2	12	2
7 Scott Lamb	2 2 2	6	2

13...Glasgow, July 11, L43-53

1 Les Collins	2 2 3 3 3 2	15	
2 Mick Powell	0 1 T N N	1	1
3 Freddy Schøtt	2 2 1 0 1	6	
4 †Brett Saunders	2 2 2 0 R	6	1
5 Carl Blackbird	fx0 3 1 0	4	
6 Michael Coles	2 1 3 1 3	10	1
7 Scott Lamb	1 0 X fx	1	1

14...WIMBLEDON, July 22, D48-48

1 Les Collins	0 3 0 3 3	9	
2 Mick Powell	1 2 0 N N	3	1
3 Freddy Schøtt	2 2 2 0 1	7	1
4 †Brett Saunders	2 2 1 1 0	6	1
5 Carl Blackbird	1 1 2 1 2	7	2
6 Michael Coles	2 1 1 1	5	4
7 Scott Lamb	3 3 2 1 2	11	1

15...POOLE, July 27, W53-43

1 Les Collins	3 3 1 3 2	12	1
2 †Brett Saunders	1 1 1 2 2	7	1
3 Freddy Schøtt	3 2 3 2 3	13	
4 Michael Coles	1 2 1 0 1	5	1
5 Carl Blackbird	0 1 3 fx1	5	1
6 Scott Lamb	3 2 1 2 1	9	4
7 Nigel Alderton	F 2 N	2	

16...Exeter, July 30, L39-56

1 Les Collins	2 2 2 3 0 2	11	1
2 Mick Powell	1 1 1 T 1	4	2
3 Freddy Schøtt	1 R T T N	1	
4 †Brett Saunders	3 2 1 1 1 1	9	1
5 Carl Blackbird	1 R R 0 1	2	
6 Michael Coles	1 3 1 3 1 3 0	12	
7 Scott Lamb	0 N 0	0	

17...Poole, July 31, L43-52

1 Les Collins	2 1 R 0 3	6	
2 Mick Powell	0 0 N N T	0	
3 Freddy Schøtt	2 2 0 0 N	4	1
4 †Brett Saunders	0 2 3 1 1 1	8	
5 Carl Blackbird	2 1 2 1 F	6	2
6 Michael Coles	3 3 3 1 2 3 2	17	
7 Scott Lamb	1 fx1	2	

18...GLASGOW, August 2, L43-52

1 Les Collins	2 3 3 1 2 2	13	2
2 †Brett Saunders	3 0 3 fx3	9	
3 Freddy Schøtt	3 1 1 2 X	7	
4 Michael Coles	1 2 1 0 0	4	1
5 Carl Blackbird	3 fx2 0 1	6	
6 Scott Lamb	3 0 0 0 T	3	
7 Mick Powell	0 1 N	1	

19...Newcastle, August 6, L42-54

1 Les Collins	1 2 2 1 1	7	
2 †Brett Saunders	0 1 3 1 X	5	2
3 Freddy Schøtt	3 3 2 2 3 0	13	
4 Michael Coles	R 1 0 0 0	1	1
5 Carl Blackbird	3 2 2 1 3	11	1
6 Scott Lamb	3 0 0 T	3	
7 Mick Powell	1 1 0	2	

20...EASTBOURNE, August 10, W60-36

1 Les Collins	2 2 1 3 0	8	1
2 †Brett Saunders	1 3 3 3 3	13	1
3 Freddy Schøtt	**2 2 3 3 3**	**13**	**2**
4 Michael Coles	3 0 3 F 3	9	
5 Carl Blackbird	0 1 2 2 2	7	3
6 Scott Lamb	3 3 3 1	10	
7 Nigel Alderton	R 0 0	0	

21...Arena Essex, August 11, L36-57

1 Les Collins	3 1 2 1 1	8	1
2 †Brett Saunders	2 2 2 1 0 2	9	2
3 Freddy Schøtt	3 fxN T T	3	
4 Michael Coles	2 2 0 0 1 0	5	1
5 Carl Blackbird	1 1 1 1 2	6	2
6 Scott Lamb	0 1 X 1	2	1
7 Nigel Alderton	2 1 0 F	3	

22...Eastbourne, August 12, L34-62

1 Les Collins	1 0 1 1 2 3	8	
2 †Brett Saunders	F 1 0 3 2	6	
3 Scott Lamb	0 2 3 2 1	8	
4 Michael Coles	0 2 0 1 0 1	4	
5 Carl Blackbird	1 1 0 1 3	6	2
6 Mick Powell	1 1 0 N	2	
7 Nigel Alderton	0 N T 0	0	

23...ARENA ESSEX, August 26, W67-29

1 Les Collins	0 3 1 2 3	9	1
2 †Brett Saunders	**3 2 3 3 3**	**14**	**1**
3 Freddy Schøtt	3 2 3 1 2	11	1
4 Michael Coles	R 2 3 3 F	8	1
5 Carl Blackbird	3 3 2 3 1	12	2
6 Scott Lamb	**3 2 3 2**	**10**	**2**
7 Mick Powell	2 1 0	3	1

24...Wimbledon, September 5, L46-50

1 Les Collins	1 0 1 2 2	6	2
2 †Brett Saunders	0 3 3 3 3	12	
3 Freddy Schøtt	3 3 2 fx2 0	10	1
4 Carl Blackbird	1 1 0 3 2 3	10	3
5 Michael Coles	2 2 1 0 1	6	
6 Scott Lamb	0 0 1 T	1	
7 Mick Powell	1 0 T	1	

25...Ipswich, September 6, L40-56

1 Les Collins	2 1 fx2 E 1	6	3
2 †Brett Saunders	1 2 3 3 1 fn	10	1
3 Freddy Schøtt	2 2 fxT T N	4	
4 Carl Blackbird	3 1 1 1 2 2	10	1
5 Michael Coles	1 0 2 0 2 1	6	
6 Scott Lamb	2 0 T fx	2	
7 Nigel Alderton	1 0 T 1 0	2	2

26...Peterborough, September 7, L43-53

1† Les Collins	3 3 1 2 1 3 N	13	1
2 Brett Saunders	*rider replacement*		
3 Scott Lamb	1 1 3 1 2 1	9	
4 Michael Coles	0 1 1 3 R 1	6	2
5 Carl Blackbird	2 2 2 2 1 2 0	11	3
6 Nigel Alderton	0 0 N T 0	0	
7 Mick Powell	1 0 3 0	4	
8 Rob Fisher	*did not ride*		

27...BERWICK, September 9, L46.5-49.5

1 †Les Collins	1 2 3 2 3 3 3	17	2
2 Scott Lamb	2 1 0 3 3 0	9	
3 Freddy Schøtt	*rider replacement*		
4 Michael Coles	1 2 0 1 0 0	4	1
5 Carl Blackbird	F 1 2 1 0 2	6	2
6 Mick Powell	1 0 1.5 2 2	6.5	1
7 Nigel Alderton	3 1 N	4	
8 Mike McLuskey	*did not ride*		

28...MIDDLESBROUGH, September 16, L45-51

1 †Les Collins	3 3 3 3 3 2 3	20	
2 Freddy Schøtt	*rider replacement*		
3 Carl Blackbird	1 0 2 1 1 1 2	8	
4 Michael Coles	0 2 0 2 1 2	7	1
5 Scott Lamb	1 0 1 0 1	3	2
6 Mick Powell	3 2 0 T 0	5	
7 Nigel Alderton	0 2 0	2	1
8 Mike McLuskey	*did not ride*		

29...Stoke, September 22, L34-62

1†Les Collins	3 3 2 2 3 2	15	1
2 Michael Coles	0 1 3 1 1	6	1
3 Carl Blackbird	1 1 2 1 2	7	
4 Freddy Schøtt	1 0 1 0 N	2	1
5 Scott Lamb	2 1 0 0 0	3	
6 Mick Powell	1 0 R 0	1	
7 Nigel Alderton	0 0 T 0	0	

30...EXETER, September 23, W66-29

1 †Les Collins	1 1 2 2 1	7	3
2 Michael Coles	2 3 3 3 3	14	
3 Carl Blackbird	1 3 1 2 3	10	1
4 Freddy Schøtt	3 3 1 3 3	13	
5 Scott Lamb	2 2 3 3 F	10	2
6 Mick Powell	**3 3 2 2**	**10**	**2**
7 Mike McLuskey	F 2 0	2	1

31...Berwick, September 29, L45-48

1 †Les Collins	3 3 3 1 3	13	
2 Michael Coles	1 1 1 0 X	3	1
3 Freddy Schøtt	1 3 2 3 3 3	15	1
4 Scott Lamb	2 1 0 T 0	3	1
5 Carl Blackbird	0 2 2 0 2	6	1
6 Mick Powell	1 0 0 N	1	
7 Nigel Alderton	F 2 2 fx	4	

32...STOKE, October 21, W49-47

1 †Les Collins	2 0 2 1 2	7	1
2 Michael Coles	1 1 3 3 2	10	1
3 Carl Blackbird	3 3 3 3 R	12	
4 Freddy Schøtt	3 3 fn3 0	9	
5 Scott Lamb	fx0 2 1 1	4	
6 Mick Powell	2 2 1 1 1 R	7	2
7 Mike McLuskey	0 0 N	0	

1990 ROSTER

ALDERTON, Nigel Anthony
B 14.1.1969, Cabarita, Victoria, Australia. *First season Australian.*

BLACKBIRD, Carl Ivan
B 26.3.1965, Peterborough, Cambs. *On loan from Reading.*

BOYD, Anthony Phillip
B 23.5.1971, Ashton-under-Lyne, Greater Manchester. *On loan from Stoke.*

COLES, Michael Timothy
B 11.8.1965, Exeter, Devon. *On loan from Exeter.*

COLLINS, Leslie
B 24.5.1958, Partington, Greater Manchester.

LAMB, Robert Scott
B 28.10.1966, Edinburgh, Scotland.

McLUSKEY, Michael
B 25.11.1964, Perth, Scotland.

MERCER, Brian
B 19.8.1961, Hawick, Scotland. *Junior.*

POWELL, Michael George
B 24.9.1969, Brisbane, Australia.

SAUNDERS, Brett Gavin
B 9.11.1961, Sydney, Australia.

SCHØTT, Frede (Freddy)
B 28.12.1970, Kolding, Denmark. *Newcomer from Denmark.*

TEMPLETON, Gilbert Muir
B 7.9.1962, Falkirk, Scotland.

ROB FISHER - See Peterborough.
MARK PEARCE - see Stoke.

Big barney over Colin's team place

Track Data

Promoter: Colin Hill.
Address: County Ground Stadium, Cowick Street, St. Thomas', Exeter, Devon.
Telephone: 0392-51478.
Hotline: 0898 800 625.
Track Length: 396 metres.
Track Record: 66.2 secs, Scott Autrey (Exeter), July 16, 1979, heat 6, Exeter v Belle Vue (British League).

COLIN COOK was heading for the old heave-ho when Exeter promoter Colin Hill decided to swoop onto the transfer market to sign Peterborough's out of sorts skipper Ian Barney.

The writing was on the wall for the 35-year-old veteran when he was relegated to the second half so that Barney could make his debut at home to Ipswich in the middle of June.

Yet Cook never missed another match, other than when he was late arriving for the National Series round at Wimbledon because of car troubles on his way.

He was given an unexpected reprieve when grass-tracker Andy Sell decided it was time to retire. Cook came back into the team at Hackney four days after Barney's first appearance, was second top scorer with 12 points and then grabbed successive paid maximums in the next two matches against Stoke and Arena Essex and there was no way he could be left out after that!

Sell never came back and Exeter began scouting elsewhere when Peter Jeffery broke his leg on August Bank Holiday afternoon as the Falcons went down to one of two home defeats.

As has been the custom for so many years there were two sides to Exeter. Near invincible around their own steeply-banked quarter mile home circuit. And, often, poor opposition on their travels.

This time around they lost their unbeaten home record in only their second match when Hackney were the victors, and their fans had to wait until the third from last away match for their sole victory (against Milton Keynes) although they did earn a draw at Long Eaton at the beginning of August which was rewarded with a subsequent challenge match booking.

Too few of the Exeter riders were able to consistently reproduce their home form away from the West Country although that is not a beef that could be directed towards their skipper Steve Regeling.

Only once all season was he out of double figures away from home – at Edinburgh in the penultimate match – and his sequence of paid scores (13-12-13-16-12-13-17-14-16-14-18-18-13-15-8-14) was the equal of any rider in the land. That included two six-ride maximums at Long Eaton and Newcastle and, generally, he was recognised as one of the Superstars of the National League the length and breadth of the country.

Rarely did he have the necessary support for Exeter to mount any real challenge in either major competition and too often he was left to fight a lone rearguard. Richard Green was as exciting as ever but less effective than he had been the previous season and even before his accident Jeffery had failed to make the progress expected with the contrast between his home and away displays being more and more marked.

Steve Bishop, in his sixth season with the club, has become a popular second string and in Cornish discovery Mark Simmonds the Falcons have a youngster who could develop much further as he showed signs, towards the end of the summer, that he hasn't yet been overtaken by the County Ground phobia.

Neither has loan signing Deon Prinsloo (from Wimbledon) who won a host of admirers in his short stay, so much so that Exeter made no secret of their desire to sign him outright. The biggest disappointment of all was Barney.

He struggled at Peterborough but was abysmal for his new club and it is to his credit that he stuck at it and not only saw out the season but indicated he would like to return in 1991.

Roll of Honour

Seasons in National League: 10 (1980-1983; 1985-1990).
Best National League Season: Fifth, 1989.
National League Cup Record: Winners (1), 1983.
National League Team Championship: Third (1), 1989. Qualified (2), 1982, 1989.
Appearances: Steve Bishop, 192 (1982-1983, 1985-1986, 1989-1990).
Points: Colin Cook, 1584 (1985, 1986-1990)).
World Finalists: Martin Ashby (1968), Scott Autrey (1976, 1978), Zdenek Kudrna (1979), Ivan Mauger (1973-74-75-76-77), Jan Verner (1978).
NLRC Finalists: Robert Maxfield (1980-81), Andy Campbell (1982), Keith Millard (1983), Steve Regeling (1988-89-90).
Other Honours: British League Champions, 1974. National League (Division Three) Champions, 1948. Provincial League Knock-out Cup Winners, 1962.

Star of 90
RICHARD GREEN
Exeter

EXETER

01...Arena Essex, April 7, L34-62

1 †Steve Regeling	3 3 3 R 3 1	13	
2 Steve Bishop	0 2 0 2 1 1	6	3
3 Richard Green	0 X 3 fx1	4	
4 Colin Cook	1 2 1 0 T	4	
5 Peter Jeffery	F 0 0 2 0	2	
6 Andy Sell	0 1 T 2	3	
7 Mark Simmonds	1 1 T R	2	

02...GLASGOW, April 30, W60-35

1 †Steve Regeling	3 3 3 2 3	14	
2 Steve Bishop	2 2 3 1 X	8	2
3 Richard Green	E 1 3 3 1	8	
4 Colin Cook	2 1 0 R N	3	1
5 Peter Jeffery	3 3 2 2 3	13	1
6 Andy Sell	3 R 3 fx	6	
7 Mark Simmonds	1 3 2 1 1	8	1

03...Rye House, May 6, L40-55

1 †Steve Regeling	3 R 3 fx3 3	12	
2 Steve Bishop	0 2 1 fx0 1	4	1
3 Richard Green	1 3 3 3 2 fx	12	
4 Colin Cook	1 1 0 T 0	2	
5 Peter Jeffery	3 0 2 2 0 1	8	1
6 Andy Sell	R N T T	0	
7 Mark Simmonds	1 0 1 T	2	

04...HACKNEY, May 7, L45-51

1 †Steve Regeling	R 2 3 0 2	7	
2 Steve Bishop	2 1 1 0 0	4	1
3 Richard Green	3 3 2 fxfx	8	
4 Colin Cook	2 1 1 2 N	6	3
5 Peter Jeffery	3 2 2 1 3	11	
6 Scott Pegler	N 0 N N	0	
7 Mark Simmonds	1 1 3 1 3 0	9	1

05...Glasgow, May 9, L35-61

1 †Steve Regeling	3 3 1 3 R 3	13	
2 Steve Bishop	0 0 0 1 0	1	
3 Richard Green	2 2 1 F N	5	
4 Colin Cook	1 2 0 0 1 0	4	
5 Peter Jeffery	0 1 3 3 2	9	1
6 Andy Sell	0 R T 1	1	
7 Mark Simmonds	2 0 T 0	2	

06...Middlesbrough, May 10, L34-61

1 †Steve Regeling	3 3 2 3 3 2	16	
2 Steve Bishop	0 1 T 1 2	4	
3 Richard Green	F 1 1 fx0	2	
4 Colin Cook	1 3 0 0 0	4	
5 Peter Jeffery	0 2 1 1 1	5	1
6 Andy Sell	1 0 0 1	2	1
7 Mark Simmonds	0 1 0	1	

07...Berwick, May 12, L32-63

1 †Steve Regeling	fx3 3 3 3	12	
2 Steve Bishop	R 0 T N T	0	
3 Richard Green	3 1 2 1 X 2	9	
4 Colin Cook	X 0 1 0 fx	1	
5 Peter Jeffery	1 1 0 2 3 F	7	
6 Andy Sell	2 0 0 1	3	
7 Mark Simmonds	0 0 0 fx	0	

08...Eastbourne, May 20, L30-66

1 †Steve Regeling	3 3 3 R 1 3	13	
2 Steve Bishop	0 0 1 T T	1	
3 Richard Green	1 1 1 0 1	4	1
4 Colin Cook	1 0 0 fx0	1	
5 Peter Jeffery	0 1 2 1 fxF	4	
6 Andy Sell	0 2 0 fn	2	
7 Mark Simmonds	1 0 T 1 3	5	

09...LONG EATON, May 21, W65-31

1 †Steve Regeling	1 3 3 3 3	13	
2 Steve Bishop	0 1 3 1 1	6	
3 Richard Green	3 3 3 2 1	12	1
4 Colin Cook	1 2 2 2 2	9	4
5 Peter Jeffery	**3 3 3 3 3**	**15**	
6 Andy Sell	2 1 2 3	8	1
7 Mark Simmonds	0 1 1	2	

10...MIDDLESBROUGH, June 11, W67-29

1 †Steve Regeling	3 3 2 3 2	13	
2 Steve Bishop	1 2 3 0 3	9	1
3 Richard Green	3 3 2 2 2	12	2
4 Peter Jeffery	1 3 3 2 1	10	2
5 Mark Simmonds	0 1 2 3 3	9	1
6 Colin Cook	**3 2 2 2**	**9**	**3**
7 Andy Sell	2 2 1	5	3

11...IPSWICH, June 18, W53-43

1 †Steve Regeling	3 2 3 3 3	14	
2 Steve Bishop	1 1 3 1 3	9	1
3 Richard Green	2 2 X 1 2	7	2
4 §Ian Barney	1 0 1 1 0	3	1
5 Peter Jeffery	2 3 3 2 3	13	
6 Mark Simmonds	1 0 N 1 0	2	
7 Andy Sell	3 0 2 fn	5	1

12...Hackney, June 22, L45-51

1 †Steve Regeling	3 3 3 2 3 2	16	1
2 Steve Bishop	1 0 T N 1	2	
3 Richard Green	1 1 1 0 0	3	2
4 Ian Barney	1 2 1 0 1	5	2
5 Peter Jeffery	3 fx2 1 1	7	
6 Colin Cook	1 2 1 2 3 3	12	
7 Mark Simmonds	0 0 T	0	

13...STOKE, June 25, W53-43

1 †Steve Regeling	3 2 2 2 3	12	
2 Steve Bishop	0 1 3 0 2	6	2
3 Richard Green	2 X 1 2 3	8	
4 Ian Barney	1 1 2 0 0	4	
5 Peter Jeffery	3 3 1 0 2	9	2
6 Mark Simmonds	0 1 2 N	3	1
7 Colin Cook	**3 2 3 3**	**11**	**1**

14...ARENA ESSEX, July 2, W76-20

1 †Steve Regeling	**2 3 3 3 3**	**14**	**1**
2 Colin Cook	**3 2 2 2 3**	**12**	**3**
3 Richard Green	**2 3 2 2 2**	**11**	**4**
4 Ian Barney	1 3 3 2 2	11	2
5 Peter Jeffery	**3 2 2 3 3**	**13**	**2**
6 Steve Bishop	2 3 1 R	6	1
7 Mark Simmonds	3 3 3	9	

15...Ipswich, July 5, L46-50

1 †Steve Regeling	3 3 3 2 3	14	
2 Richard Green	2 1 N T 2	5	1
3 Peter Jeffery	1 2 2 2 0 2	9	1
4 Steve Bishop	3 3 1 1 0	8	1
5 Colin Cook	0 2 0 3 1	6	2
6 Greg Daniels	R E 0 0	0	
7 Mark Simmonds	2 0 1 1 0	4	1

16...Peterborough, July 6, L46-50

1 †Steve Regeling	3 2 3 1 3 3	15	1
2 Richard Green	1 1 1 2 1 2	8	2
3 Peter Jeffery	2 fx2 2 1	7	1
4 Ian Barney	1 2 1 3 1 0	8	1
5 Colin Cook	E 0 R T 2	2	
6 Steve Bishop	1 3 1 T 1	6	1
7 Mark Simmonds	0 fxT	0	

17...BERWICK, July 9, W56-40

1 †Steve Regeling	**3 3 3 3 3**	**15**	
2 Colin Cook	1 F 0 1 0	2	
3 Richard Green	**3 2 3 3 3**	**14**	**1**
4 Ian Barney	N 0 0 0 N	0	
5 Peter Jeffery	**3 3 3 2 2**	**13**	**2**
6 Steve Bishop	3 1 3 1 1 fx	9	
7 Mark Simmonds	2 0 1	3	1

18...Stoke, July 14, L35-61

1 †Steve Regeling	3 fx3 1 3 3	13	1
2 Richard Green	2 3 2 0 2 1	10	2
3 Peter Jeffery	1 1 1 0 2	5	
4 Ian Barney	1 0 T 0 T	1	
5 Colin Cook	R 1 1 1 1	4	1
6 Steve Bishop	2 0 0 0	2	
7 Mark Simmonds	0 0 T 0	0	

19...EASTBOURNE, July 16, W63-32

1 †Steve Regeling	3 2 3 3 3	14	
2 Colin Cook	2 1 3 2 2	10	3
3 Richard Green	2 2 2 fxN	6	2
4 Ian Barney	2 1 1 0 1	5	2
5 Peter Jeffery	3 3 2 2 2	12	1
6 Steve Bishop	3 3 3 1 3	13	1
7 Mark Simmonds	N 2 1	3	2

20...Newcastle, July 22, L41-55

1 †Steve Regeling	**3 3 3 3 3 3**	**18**	
2 Colin Cook	1 1 1 0 2 2	7	1
3 Richard Green	1 F 1 0 fx	2	1
4 Ian Barney	2 2 0 0 T	4	
5 Peter Jeffery	1 1 2 1 2 1	8	2
6 Steve Bishop	1 1 T 0	2	
7 Mark Simmonds	0 0 T	0	

21...PETERBOROUGH, July 23, W68-28

1 †Steve Regeling	3 3 3 3 2	14	
2 Colin Cook	**2 2 3 2 2**	**11**	**4**
3 Richard Green	3 2 2 2 2	11	3
4 Ian Barney	1 2 0 X 0	3	1
5 Peter Jeffery	**3 3 3 3 3**	**15**	
6 Steve Bishop	3 1 3 3	10	
7 Mark Simmonds	2 1 1	4	2

22...EDINBURGH, July 30, W56-39

1 †Steve Regeling	**3 3 3 3 3**	**15**	
2 Colin Cook	0 2 3 2 R	7	2
3 Richard Green	2 3 2 2 2	11	2
4 Ian Barney	R R 0 N 0	0	
5 Peter Jeffery	2 3 1 3 3	12	
6 Steve Bishop	3 0 R N	3	
7 Mark Simmonds	2 2 0 2 2	8	3

23...Long Eaton, August 1, D48-48

1 †Steve Regeling	**3 3 3 3 3 3**	**18**	
2 Colin Cook	2 1 2 R 3	8	2
3 Richard Green	fx2 2 2 X 2	8	2
4 Ian Barney	0 0 1 1 1	3	
5 Peter Jeffery	2 1 3 0 fx3	9	
6 Steve Bishop	1 0 T T	1	
7 Mark Simmonds	0 1 T	1	

24...WIMBLEDON, August 6, W62-34

1 †Steve Regeling	**2 2 3 3 3**	**13**	**2**
2 Colin Cook	3 3 3 2 2	13	1
3 Richard Green	**3 3 3 3 3**	**15**	
4 Ian Barney	0 0 0 0 N	0	
5 Peter Jeffery	3 2 3 2 2	12	2
6 Steve Bishop	3 1 1 1	6	1
7 Mark Simmonds	1 F 1 1	3	

25...Wimbledon, August 8, L35-61

1 †Steve Regeling	2 2 3 3 1 1	12	1
2 Colin Cook	0 1 2 1 F 0	4	3
3 Richard Green	2 2 1 F N	5	
4 Ian Barney	0 2 T 2 0	4	
5 Peter Jeffery	1 1 2 1 1	6	1
6 Steve Bishop	2 0 0 1	3	
7 Mark Simmonds	1 fxT 0	1	1

26...NEWCASTLE, August 13, W55-41

1 †Steve Regeling	**3 3 3 3 3**	**15**	
2 Colin Cook	2 1 2 1 3	9	1
3 Richard Green	2 3 2 3 2	12	
4 Ian Barney	1 0 0 N N	1	1
5 Peter Jeffery	2 3 1 1 1	8	1
6 Steve Bishop	3 1 1 0 2	7	2
7 Mark Simmonds	2 1 0 0	3	2

27...POOLE, August 27, L44-52

1 †Steve Regeling	3 R 3 3 X	9	
2 Colin Cook	0 3 3 X 2 2	10	
3 Richard Green	3 3 2 2 1	11	
4 Ian Barney	0 1 3 0 T	4	
5 Peter Jeffery	2 3 0 fnN	5	
6 Steve Bishop	3 1 0 0 0	4	
7 Mark Simmonds	1 F 0 0	1	

28...MILTON KEYNES, September 3, W64-32

1 †Steve Regeling	R 3 3 3 3	12	
2 Steve Bishop	3 1 3 1 2	10	
3 Richard Green	3 2 3 fx2	10	2
4 Ian Barney	1 2 1 N 1	5	1
5 Colin Cook	**3 3 3 3 3**	**15**	
6 Mark Simmonds	2 2 3 1 1	9	3
7 §Deon Prinsloo	3 0 0	3	

29...Milton Keynes, September 4, W56-40

1 †Steve Regeling	**3 3 3 3 3**	**15**	
2 Steve Bishop	1 0 1 2 0	4	1
3 Richard Green	**3 3 3 2 3**	**14**	**1**
4 Ian Barney	3 0 1 0 N	4	
5 Colin Cook	2 3 3 3 0	11	1
6 Mark Simmonds	2 0 0 3 2	7	1
7 Deon Prinsloo	1 0 0	1	1

30...RYE HOUSE, September 10, W64-32

1 †Steve Regeling	**3 2 2 3 3 3**	**16**	**2**
2 Peter Jeffery	*rider replacement*		
3 Richard Green	3 3 2 2 3 1	14	2
4 Steve Bishop	1 2 1 1 1	6	2
5 Colin Cook	2 3 3 2 2 2	14	2
6 Ian Barney	2 1 1 1	5	1
7 Mark Simmonds	3 3 3 0	9	
8 Greg Daniels	0	0	

31...Edinburgh, September 23, L29-66

1 †Steve Regeling	3 1 F 2 1 T	7	1
2 Peter Jeffery	*rider replacement*		
3 Richard Green	2 2 2 3 1 2 2	14	
4 Steve Bishop	R R 1 1 0 0	2	
5 Colin Cook	R 0 T 0 N	0	
6 Ian Barney	1 0 0 0	1	1
7 Mark Simmonds	2 0 0 1	3	1
8 §Frank Smart	F 1 1	2	

32...Poole, October 14, L39-57

1 †Steve Regeling	3 2 1 3 3 1	13	1
2 Steve Bishop	0 0 1 2 2 0	5	2
3 Richard Green	2 1 2 2 1 2	10	
4 Ian Barney	1 N 0 N T	1	
5 Colin Cook	fx2 1 0 1 0	4	
6 Mark Simmonds	3 0 1 1	5	2
8 Frank Smart	1 0 T	1	

1990 ROSTER

BARNEY, Ian John
B 15.2.1961, Stamford, Lincolnshire.
Signed from Peterborough.
BISHOP, Steven
B 26.11.1963, Bristol, Avon.
COOK, Colin
B 29.8.1954, Southwold, Suffolk.
DANIELS, Greg
B 23.4.1964, Bridgwater, Somerset.
GREEN, Richard
B 16.8.1965, Wreningham, Norfolk.
JEFFERY, Peter Adrian
B 3.11.1966, Bideford, Devon.
PEGLER, Scott
B 3.8.1973, Exeter, Devon.
REGELING, Steven Grae
B 2.10.1959, Mount Isa, Australia.
SELL, Andrew (Andy)
B 26.3.1964, Bristol, Avon.
SIMMONDS, Mark Douglas
B 10.5.1971, Truro, Cornwall.
SMART, Frank Dean
B 27.10.1969, Perth, Australia
First season Australian.
DEON PRINSLOO - See Wimbledon.

A bridge too far for sharp Tigers

Track Data

Promoters: Peter McBride and Neil Macfarlane.
Address: Shawfield Stadium, Rutherglow Road, Glasgow, G73 1SZ.
Telephone: 041-613-1552.
Information Line: 0898 31 21 41.
Track Length: 332 metres.
Track Record: 65.4 secs, Chris Louis (Ipswich), 3.6.1990, Heat 1, Glasgow v Ipswich, National League Knock Out Cup; Andy Galvin (Hackney), 17.6.1990, Heat 1, Speedway Star National League Pairs Championship.

GLASGOW were one year shy of the biggest jump in their history...marching back into the First Division after an 18 year absence from the top flight.

Co-promoter Neil Macfarlane admitted as much when he declined the chance of being one of the four National League clubs to be nominated for membership of the new look Division One during the winter.

He knew that the average age of the 1990 squad was too old to give the Radio Clyde Tigers a realistic opportunity of taking the incumbents into the higher plane without having to break the bank to add the extra ballast needed to survive at a new level.

But he made the club's priorities obvious: "We want to get promotion at the end of 1991 when we should need to sign only two new riders to have a chance of staying in the First Division."

Glasgow has been one of the real success stories of recent years. Gone are the days when everyone dreaded a trip to the city and new owner Peter McBride successfully built on the sound foundations laid by his predecessors in the two previous seasons of speedway at Shawfield Park.

The track's growing status was reflected often during the summer. Initially when it was chosen as the venue for the launch of the city's Special Olympics; secondly when the National League took the Speedway Star Pairs Championship north of the border for the first time; and lastly in the final meeting of the season when the home side won the National Series ahead of fellow finalists Wimbledon and Stoke.

It provided a splendid finale to a campaign in which the Tigers had finished in a highest ever National League placing of fourth, qualified for the National League Fours for only the third time, and regularly attracted some of the biggest crowds in the country to their well-appointed home.

While a switch of race-day from Friday evening to Wednesday night (forced upon them by the stadium landlords) caused a significant drop in overall attendance figures it was not of such magnitude to cause any real concern and certainly maintained the club's status among the three best supported teams in the National League.

Yet there were real fears in the opening weeks of the season that the bubble had burst - on track if not off it. The Tigers lost their two opening away matches more heavily than they might have expected, then were beaten at home by Poole, suffered two more away defeats and after losing 45-51 at home to Stoke were anchored firmly at the wrong end of the table without a point from their first six matches. By then Macfarlane was ready to ring the changes. He had agreed terms with West German Tommy Dunker and decided to axe veteran Steve Lawson in a bid to inject some much-needed life into his lacklustre squad. The gamble on playing roulette with team places (they preferred to operate a squad system) had backfired badly and there was serious concern that things were going to go horrendously wrong.

Exeter's visit on May 9th produced a first home win of the season and, of even greater pleasure to the Shawfield fans, Lawson bounced back with his first double figure return of the season.

From that crucial moment on, the pendulum was swinging in the right direction and Lawson (and Glasgow) hardly ever looked back after that. Shane Bowes came on a bomb and ended the season as a worthy heat leader while young Jason Lyons survived a torrid baptism to climb into a top five berth before the end of his initial campaign.

With another young Aussie, Michael Carter, on his way and a firm bid in for Edinburgh's Mick Powell by Christmas, the Tigers are sharpening their claws for that promotion push!

Roll of Honour

Seasons in National League: 13 (1977-1981 [Blantyre]; 1982-1986 [Craighead Park]; 1988-1990 [Shawfield Park]).
Best National League Season: Fourth, 1990.
National League Cup Record: Quarter-finalists, 1983.
National League Team Championship: Qualified (3), 1980, 1988, 1990.
National Series: Winners (1), 1990.
Appearances: Steve Lawson, 436 (1978-1986, 1988-1990).
Points: Steve Lawson, 4910 (1978-1986, 1988-1990).
World Finalists: Jim McMillan (1972).
NLRC Finalists: Brian Collins (1977), Steve Lawson (1978-79, 1981-82, 1984-85-86), Jim McMillan (1983), Kenny McKinna (1988-89), Shane Bowes (1990).

Star of 90
SHANE BOWES
Glasgow

GLASGOW

01...Peterborough, April 16, L29-67

1 †Steve Lawson	2 1 2 0 R	5	
2 Charlie McKinna	1 0 2 1 2	6	2
3 Kenny McKinna	1 1 2 2 1	7	
4 Shane Bowes	2 1 0 1 2	6	
5 Phil Jeffrey	R 0 T 1 0	1	1
6 Martin McKinna	2 0 0 1	3	1
7 §§Jason Lyons	0 R 0 1	1	

02...Middlesbrough, April 19, L36-60

1 †Steve Lawson	2 0 2 2 3	9	
2 Charlie McKinna	1 1 2 1 1	6	2
3 Kenny McKinna	2 2 3 0 1	8	
4 Shane Bowes	2 2 F 1 R N	5	1
5 §Sean Courtney	0 1 2 1 0	4	1
6 Jason Lyons	1 0 T 0	1	1
7 Geoff Powell	2 1 0 0	3	1

03...POOLE, April 27, L46-49

1 †Steve Lawson	3 0 1 1 3	8	1
2 Charlie McKinna	2 3 3 2 1 3	14	1
3 Kenny McKinna	2 3 3 F 2	10	1
4 Shane Bowes	0 3 1 0 F	4	1
5 Sean Courtney	2 1 2 2 T	7	
6 Geoff Powell	0 0 0 N	0	
7 Jason Lyons	1 0 2 0	3	1

04...Exeter, April 30, L35-60

1 †Steve Lawson	0 0 T T T	0	
2 Charlie McKinna	1 2 1 2 2 2	10	1
3 Kenny McKinna	1 1 1 3 1 2	9	1
4 Phil Jeffrey	1 2 0 0 0	3	
5 Sean Courtney	0 0 2 1 0	3	
6 Martin McKinna	2 2 0 3 R 3	10	
7 Jason Lyons	0 E 0	0	

05...Poole, May 1, L34-62

1 †Steve Lawson	1 0 R 1 N	2	
2 Charlie McKinna	0 2 1 3 1 1	8	
3 Kenny McKinna	2 2 3 3 1 3	14	
4 Phil Jeffrey	2 2 0 0 N	4	
5 Sean Courtney	1 1 1 R 1 0	4	2
6 Martin McKinna	0 0 1 N	1	
7 Jason Lyons	1 0 T 0	1	

06...STOKE, May 2, L45-51

1 †Steve Lawson	2 2 0 1 1	6	1
2 Charlie McKinna	1 1 3 2 3	10	2
3 Kenny McKinna	3 3 2 1 0	9	
4 Sean Courtney	3 3 1 2 3	12	
5 Phil Jeffrey	1 R F 0 N	1	
6 Martin McKinna	F N F 0	0	
7 Jason Lyons	3 0 2 1 1	7	2

07...EXETER, May 9, W61-35

1 Charlie McKinna	1 1 1 2 1	6	3
2 †Steve Lawson	2 3 3 2 3	13	
3 Kenny McKinna	3 3 0 2 3	11	1
4 Sean Courtney	2 2 2 1 2	9	3
5 Shane Bowes	3 1 3 3 1	11	1
6 Geoff Powell	1 1 0 N	2	
7 Jason Lyons	3 2 2 2	9	2

08...ARENA ESSEX, May 23, W74-22

1 Charlie McKinna	0 3 3 3 3	12	
2 Phil Jeffrey	2 2 1 2 2	9	3
3 Kenny McKinna	**2 3 3 3 3**	**14**	**1**
4 Sean Courtney	**2 3 2 2 2**	**11**	**4**
5 Shane Bowes	3 2 3 2 F	10	2
6 †Steve Lawson	**3 3 2 3**	**11**	**1**
7 Jason Lyons	2 3 2	7	2

09...Newcastle, June 11, W50-45

1 †Steve Lawson	3 3 3 3 2	14	
2 Charlie McKinna	2 1 3 1 fx	7	1
3 Kenny McKinna	2 2 2 3 2	11	
4 Sean Courtney	2 2 2 0 0	6	1
5 Shane Bowes	1 3 fx2 0	6	2
6 Jason Lyons	fnN N N	0	
7 Phil Jeffrey	2 1 1 0 1 1	6	3

10...Stoke, June 23, L46-50

1 †Steve Lawson	2 2 2 0 2	8	
2 Charlie McKinna	1 1 3 1 3	9	3
3 Kenny McKinna	2 1 1 1 2	7	1
4 Sean Courtney	2 1 2 2 1	8	1
5 Shane Bowes	1 3 1 2 fx	7	2
6 Jason Lyons	1 3 0 1	5	
7 Phil Jeffrey	0 1 1	2	1

11...MIDDLESBROUGH, June 24, W57-39

1 †Steve Lawson	2 1 3 1 3	10	1
2 Charlie McKinna	1 2 3 2 2	10	2
3 Kenny McKinna	3 3 E 3 3	12	
4 Sean Courtney	2 1 2 0 0	5	1
5 Shane Bowes	1 3 3 2 fx	9	2
6 Jason Lyons	3 2 1 0 1	7	2
7 Phil Jeffrey	2 0 2	4	1

12...IPSWICH, June 27, W62-33

1 †Steve Lawson	1 3 3 3 3	13	
2 Charlie McKinna	0 2 3 2 0	7	2
3 Kenny McKinna	**3 3 3 3 3**	**15**	
4 Sean Courtney	3 2 3 2 1	11	2
5 Shane Bowes	1 3 X 2 2	8	2
6 Jason Lyons	fx 1 F 2	3	
7 Phil Jeffrey	3 2 0	5	1

13...RYE HOUSE, July 6, W60-36

1 †Steve Lawson	3 1 1 3 3	11	2
2 Charlie McKinna	1 2 2 2 2	9	2
3 Kenny McKinna	1 3 2 1 3	10	1
4 Sean Courtney	2 3 F N N	5	
5 Shane Bowes	1 2 1 3 2	9	3
6 Jason Lyons	3 2 1 F 3	9	
7 Phil Jeffrey	1 3 1 2	7	2

14...EDINBURGH, July 11, W53-43

1 †Steve Lawson	3 3 1 3 3	13	
2 Martin McKinna	1 0 fnN N	1	
3 Kenny McKinna	3 3 2 2 3	13	
4 Charlie McKinna	1 0 2 2 1	6	1
5 Shane Bowes	3 3 E 1 2	9	2
6 Jason Lyons	0 1 1 1 fx1	4	2
7 Phil Jeffrey	3 2 0 0 2	7	

15...Hackney, July 13, L46-50

1 †Steve Lawson	2 3 2 1 3 1	12	2
2 Jason Lyons	X 0 fx2 3	5	
3 Kenny McKinna	1 2 3 2 2	10	
4 Charlie McKinna	1 1 1 2 0	5	2
5 Shane Bowes	3 2 3 3 fx0	11	
6 Geoff Powell	1 1 T N	2	1
7 Phil Jeffrey	F 0 T 1	1	

16...Arena Essex, July 14, W52-44

1 †Steve Lawson	**3 3 3 3 3**	**15**	
2 Jason Lyons	1 0 2 1 2	6	
3 Kenny McKinna	1 R 3 3 1	8	1
4 Charlie McKinna	3 0 1 1 1	6	
5 Shane Bowes	1 3 3 2 2	11	1
6 Geoff Powell	3 1 0 N	4	
7 Phil Jeffrey	2 0 0 R	2	1

17...Eastbourne, July 15, L42-53

1 †Steve Lawson	1 0 3 3 3 2	12	1
2 Jason Lyons	2 3 F 2 0 0	7	1
3 Kenny McKinna	3 2 1 1 1	8	
4 Charlie McKinna	0 0 0 T 0	0	
5 Shane Bowes	1 3 2 0 3	9	
6 Geoff Powell	1 0 N T	1	
7 Phil Jeffrey	3 2 F 0	5	1

18...Milton Keynes, July 24, W56-40

1 †Steve Lawson	2 3 2 3 3	13	
2 Charlie McKinna	1 fx2 1 2	6	2
3 Kenny McKinna	3 E 2 1 2	8	1
4 Jason Lyons	0 1 2 1 2	6	3
5 Shane Bowes	E 2 3 3 3	11	
6 Geoff Powell	0 3 1 N	4	1
7 Phil Jeffrey	2 1 1 2 1 1	8	3

19...Wimbledon, July 25, L42-54

1 †Steve Lawson	3 2 1 1 3 1	11	1
2 Charlie McKinna	1 1 1 0 1	4	2
3 Kenny McKinna	2 1 2 3 2 0	10	
4 Jason Lyons	1 0 1 fx0	2	2
5 Shane Bowes	2 3 2 2 2	11	1
6 Geoff Powell	1 0 T T	1	
7 Phil Jeffrey	3 0 0	3	

20...Ipswich, July 26, L40-56

1 †Steve Lawson	1 1 1 3 3 N	9	1
2 Charlie McKinna	0 0 2 1 3 2	8	
3 Kenny McKinna	2 1 1 0 0 0	4	
4 Jason Lyons	0 fnN N N	0	
5 Shane Bowes	2 2 3 2 1 2	12	
6 Geoff Powell	2 0 1 0	3	1
7 Phil Jeffrey	3 0 1 fx	4	1

21...BERWICK, July 29, W60-36

1 †Steve Lawson	1 2 3 3 3	12	1
2 Charlie McKinna	0 3 3 1 0	7	
3 Kenny McKinna	**2 3 3 3 3**	**14**	**1**
4 Sean Courtney	2 0 N N N	2	1
5 Shane Bowes	3 3 2 2 2	12	2
6 Jason Lyons	3 3 2 R 0 2	10	1
7 Phil Jeffrey	2 1 0 0	3	1

22...MILTON KEYNES, August 1, W63-32

1 †Steve Lawson	3 E 2 3 1	9	2
2 Charlie McKinna	1 3 2 3 3	12	
3 Kenny McKinna	2 3 2 1 2	10	2
4 Sean Courtney	2 2 0 1 2	7	2
5 Shane Bowes	**3 3 3 3 3**	**15**	
6 Jason Lyons	2 3 2 R	7	1
7 Phil Jeffrey	F 2 1 0	3	2

23...Edinburgh, August 2, W52-43

1 †Steve Lawson	1 3 3 3 3	13	
2 Charlie McKinna	0 R 2 2 F	4	1
3 Kenny McKinna	2 2 3 3 2	12	1
4 Sean Courtney	0 2 1 1 1	5	2
5 Shane Bowes	2 3 2 2 3	12	1
6 Jason Lyons	2 1 0 1	4	1
7 Phil Jeffrey	1 1 X	2	2

24...Berwick, August 4, L44-51

1 †Steve Lawson	3 0 0 0 3	6	
2 Charlie McKinna	1 1 F 2 2	6	
3 Kenny McKinna	3 1 2 3 1 0	10	2
4 Sean Courtney	1 1 1 1 1	5	
5 Shane Bowes	0 3 3 3 0 3	12	
6 Jason Lyons	1 R T T	1	1
7 Phil Jeffrey	2 2 fx	4	1

25...EASTBOURNE, August 8, W66-30

1 †Steve Lawson	**3 3 3 3 3**	**15**	
2 Charlie McKinna	0 2 3 1 3	9	1
3 Kenny McKinna	2 3 2 0 3	10	1
4 Sean Courtney	1 1 2 2 1	7	3
5 Shane Bowes	3 2 3 3 1	12	
6 Jason Lyons	1 3 2 2	8	2
7 Phil Jeffrey	3 1 1	5	1

26...Long Eaton, August 15, W56-40

1 †Steve Lawson	3 1 2 1 3	10	2
2 Charlie McKinna	2 0 0 3 1	6	2
3 Kenny McKinna	3 1 3 1 2	10	1
4 Sean Courtney	2 1 0 2 1	6	
5 Shane Bowes	1 3 3 2 1	10	2
6 Jason Lyons	2 3 2 2	9	2
7 Phil Jeffrey	3 1 1	5	

27...PETERBOROUGH, August 19, W64-32

1 †Steve Lawson	1 2 3 3 3	12	
2 Charlie McKinna	3 1 2 1 3	10	2
3 Kenny McKinna	**3 3 3 3 3**	**15**	
4 Sean Courtney	3 3 0 2 fx	8	1
5 Shane Bowes	2 2 1 2 1	8	3
6 Jason Lyons	3 2 0 1	6	1
7 Phil Jeffrey	2 3 F	5	1

28...LONG EATON, August 31, W74-22

1 †Steve Lawson	**2 2 2 3 3**	**12**	**3**
2 Charlie McKinna	3 3 3 3 1	13	
3 Kenny McKinna	**3 3 3 2 3**	**14**	**1**
4 Sean Courtney	X 3 1 2 2	8	3
5 Shane Bowes	3 1 2 3 2	11	1
6 Jason Lyons	**3 2 2 3**	**10**	**2**
7 Phil Jeffrey	2 2 2	6	3

29...WIMBLEDON, September 9, L44-52

1 †Steve Lawson	3 0 3 2 3 2 0	13	
2 Shane Bowes	*rider replacement*		
3 Charlie McKinna	1 3 0 3 1 2	10	
4 Sean Courtney	3 2 2 1 0 1	9	1
5 Jason Lyons	2 0 2 0 0 0	4	1
6 Phil Jeffrey	3 1 1 1 1	7	1
7 Geoff Powell	1 fxN	1	
8 Martin McKinna	*did not ride*		

30...Rye House, September 16, W49-46

1 †Steve Lawson	2 2 2 2 2	10	1
2 Jason Lyons	0 0 3 3 3	9	
3 Shane Bowes	3 3 2 2 2	12	
4 Charlie McKinna	fx2 0 F 0	2	
5 Sean Courtney	1 1 2 1 1	6	3
6 Martin McKinna	1 0 N N	1	
7 Phil Jeffrey	3 2 2 1 1	9	3

31...NEWCASTLE, September 19, W51.5-44.5

1 †Steve Lawson	3 1 3 2 3	12	1
2 Charlie McKinna	1 2 3 1 3	10	
3 Shane Bowes	2 3 1 2 2	10	
4 Sean Courtney	3 1 1 1 1	7	2
5 Jason Lyons	0 3 2 F 1	6	1
6 Phil Jeffrey	2 fx1.5 0 2	5.5	1
7 Martin McKinna	1 0 N	1	1

32...HACKNEY, September 26, W54-42

1 †Steve Lawson	**3 3 3 3 3**	**15**	
2 Jason Lyons	1 0 3 1 0	5	
3 Shane Bowes	3 3 2 0 3	11	
4 Sean Courtney	1 1 1 1 1	5	1
5 Charlie McKinna	3 3 2 2 1	11	
6 Phil Jeffrey	2 2 2 1	7	2
7 Martin McKinna	0 0 0	0	

1990 ROSTER

BOWES, Shane Leonard
B 4.3.1969, Adelaide, Australia.
COURTNEY, Sean Joseph
B 5.9.1964, Braintree, Essex.
BRAILSFORD, Kenneth
B 7.3.1965, Kilmarnock, Scotland.
DUNKER, Tom
B 26.6.1969, Neumunster, West Germany. *Signed but refused permission to race by the National League Management Committee.*
GRIEVES, James Robert
B 28.9.974, Paisley, Scotland. *Local junior.*
JEFFREY, Philip Spencer
B 1.2.1965, Berwick-upon-Tweed, Northumberland.
LAWSON, Stephen Faulder (Steve)
B 11.12.1957, Workington, Cumbria.
LYONS, Jason Rodney
B 15.6.1970, Mildura, Australia.
McKINNA, Archibald Kenneth
B 21.10.1962, Glasgow, Scotland.
McKINNA, Charles Edward
B 25.6.1961, Glasgow, Scotland.
McKINNA, Martin
B 6.12.1965, Glasgow, Scotland.
POWELL, Geoffrey
B 22.3.1962, Workington, Cumbria.

Kestrels cop it without handy Andy

Track Data

Promoter: Dave Pavitt.
Address: Hackney Stadium, Waterden Road, London E15.
Telephone: 081-985-9822.
Hotline: 0898 800 694.
Track Length: 292.6 metres.
Track Record: 59.5 secs, Andy Galvin (Hackney), May 4, 1990, Heat 1, Hackney v Long Eaton (National League).

THERE'S an old saying in sport that one man doesn't make a team. That may be true but you will not find anyone at Waterden Road who would argue with a claim that one man's absence makes a losing team!

Facts to support the argument? In the 22 matches in which he completed his full quota of riders Andy Galvin was on the winning team no fewer than 17 occasions. And of the 10 meetings he didn't complete or missed through injury, only two were won!

Of course, it wasn't as simple as that as the HL1 Kestrels ended the season with another of their tall scorers, Steve Schofield, also on the sidelines on doctor's order, but there can be no disputing Galvin's immense contribution to the side's fortunes, as both a points-gatherer and also skipper.

He led the Londoners on a title assault reminiscent of their 1988 season in which they won both the National League championship and the Knock Out Cup as they fired on all cylinders, registering eight wins in a row before falling for the first time at Plough Lane where they lost, early on, the services of their young Danish reserve Tim Korneliussen.

He had been one or two foreigners imported at the beginning of the season. West German Uwe Gessner never lasted long enough to race in the League but Under 21 international Korneliussen looked, and scored like, a prized addition to the ranks.

He got eight on his home League debut, scored a cracking 11 paid 12 in a dramatic, controversial and rare away win at Berwick and then scored double figures again at home to Eastbourne.

He looked like one of the finds of the season but ended up as number eight after losing more than a stone in weight when he was laid low with food poisoning, an illness from which he never fully recovered.

Even though Hackney persevered with him for many months he was never to regain the form which highlighted his first few matches but there is no-one with any doubt that if he can return fully fit in 1991 he could become a consistently high scorer, particularly in the Second Division.

With Schofield as rich in points as ever, Galvin a potent if less rugged pack-leader and Paul Whittaker, who has yet to miss a National League match for Hackney since making his debut in 1984, registering regular double figures, the HL1 Kestrels were able to capitalise on the improved form of Gary Tagg and Michael Warren and give extended opportunities to Australian Dave Hamnett without relinquishing their ambitions of a second championship in three seasons.

Their defeat at Wimbledon was followed, immediately, by another at Peterborough but there was no great surprise in that. What did shake the faithful though was that another run of five successive wins should be ended by a two point reverse at Long Eaton of all places where Korneliussen failed to score and Galvin was restricted to seven, paid eight which was, at the time, his lowest return of the season.

Hackney's final position was fifth and included a total of 13 defeats, three of them at home. But closer examination shows they weren't too far away from the honours.

Of those three home defeats one was by a couple of points against champions Poole and the two others when they were without Galvin. And of the 10 defeats on their travels, three, including the afternoon that Galvin broke his thigh, were by fewer than half a dozen points.

And, just to show what might have been, Hackney went to Newcastle in their last match of the season without both Galvin and Schofield – and WON by eight points!

That became the unlikely prelude to a winter of drama and mystery over who would be the 1991 promoter – Dave Pavitt, Derek Howes, Malcolm Simmons and Terry Russell were all in the frame – in a script that would have done justice to any fiction writer.

Roll of Honour

Seasons in National League: 6 (1984-1986, 1988-1990).
National League Record: Champions (1), 1988.
National League Cup Record: Winners (2), 1984, 1988.
National League Team Championship: Third (3), 1985, 1986, 1990. Qualified (6), 1984, 1985, 1986, 1988, 1989, 1990.
Appearances: Paul Whittaker, 232 (1984-86, 1988-90).
Points: Andy Galvin 2152 (1984-86, 1988-90).
World Finalists: Dicky Case (1936), Morian Hansen (1936-37), Bengt Jansson (1967, 1971), Antonin Kasper (1983), Dag Lovaas (1974), Cordy Milne (1936-37), Zenon Plech (1975-76, 1979-80-81), Colin Pratt (1967), Finn Thomsen (1979-80).
NLRC Finalists: Barry Thomas (1984), Trevor Banks (1985), Malcolm Simmons (1986), Mark Loram (1988), Steve Schofield (1989-90).
Other Honours: National League (Division Two) Champions, 1938. Speedway Star Knock-out Cup Winners, 1971.

Stars of 90

TIM KORNELIUSSEN and ANDY GALVIN

Hackney

HACKNEY

01...MILTON KEYNES, April 6, W67-29

1 †Andy Galvin	3 3 3 2 fx	11	1
2 Michael Warren	1 0 2 2 2	7	2
3 Steve Schofield	**3 3 3 3 2**	**14**	**1**
4 Paul Whittaker	**3 3 3 3 3**	**15**	
5 Gary Tagg	2 2 1 2 3	10	3
6 §§Tim Korneliussen	3 1 1 3	8	
7 §§Dave Hamnett	1 0 1	2	

02...Berwick, April 21, W47-46

1 †Andy Galvin	2 3 fxF 2	7	1
2 Michael Warren	1 2 0 E 0	3	2
3 Steve Schofield	2 3 3 3 3	14	
4 Paul Whittaker	2 2 X 1 3	8	
5 Gary Tagg	1 1 X R 1	3	2
6 Tim Korneliussen	3 0 1 2 2 3	11	1
7 Dave Hamnett	1 0 N	1	

03...Edinburgh, April 22, W56-40

1 †Andy Galvin	3 2 2 2 2	11	3
2 Michael Warren	0 1 1 3 1	6	2
3 Steve Schofield	3 3 3 2 3	14	
4 Paul Whittaker	2 3 2 3 3	13	1
5 Gary Tagg	3 1 1 0 2	7	2
6 Tim Korneliussen	2 1 0 0 2	5	
7 Dave Hamnett	0 0 N	0	

04...EASTBOURNE, April 27, W62-33

1 †Andy Galvin	**3 3 3 3 3**	**15**	
2 Michael Warren	2 0 2 1 2	7	1
3 Steve Schofield	**3 2 2 3 3**	**13**	**2**
4 Paul Whittaker	3 3 0 0 2	8	1
5 Gary Tagg	0 1 3 2 0	6	1
6 Tim Korneliussen	3 1 3 3 1	11	1
7 Dave Hamnett	2 F N	2	1

05...LONG EATON, May 4, W62-34

1 †Andy Galvin	**3 3 3 3 3**	**15**	
2 Michael Warren	2 1 3 1 2	9	2
3 Steve Schofield	0 3 3 3 3	12	
4 Paul Whittaker	1 3 1 1 2	8	3
5 Gary Tagg	2 2 2 R 2	8	2
6 Dave Hamnett	3 3 0 3	9	
7 §Ian Humphreys	E 0 1	1	

06...Stoke, May 5, W49-47

1 †Andy Galvin	1 3 3 1 2	10	2
2 Michael Warren	fxT 1 1 3	5	
3 Steve Schofield	3 2 3 2 1	11	1
4 Paul Whittaker	2 2 3 2 2 3	14	1
5 Gary Tagg	1 2 1 0 2	6	3
6 Dave Hamnett	0 0 N N	0	
7 Ian Humphreys	2 0 fxX 1	3	

07...Exeter, May 7, W51-45

1 †Andy Galvin	3 3 3 2 1	12	1
2 Michael Warren	1 0 2 0 1	4	1
3 Steve Schofield	2 3 3 3 2	13	
4 Paul Whittaker	1 2 2 3 3	11	
5 Gary Tagg	0 R 1 1 1	3	2
6 Dave Hamnett	2 0 0 N	2	1
7 Ian Humphreys	3 1 R 2	6	1

08...NEWCASTLE, May 11, W60-35

1 †Andy Galvin	3 3 fx3 N	9	
2 Michael Warren	1 0 3 2 3	9	
3 Steve Schofield	**3 3 3 3 3**	**15**	
4 Paul Whittaker	1 2 3 2 3	11	1
5 Gary Tagg	3 1 1 0 2	7	2
6 Dave Hamnett	1 2 0 1	4	2
7 Ian Humphreys	2 1 1 1	5	

09...Wimbledon, May 23, L41-52

1 †Andy Galvin	3 2 2 2 2 2	13	2
2 Michael Warren	0 0 0 T 2	2	
3 Steve Schofield	3 3 3 3 1 3	16	
4 Paul Whittaker	0 2 0 0 3 0	5	
5 Gary Tagg	1 0 1 1 0 1	4	1
6 Tim Korneliussen	fnT T N	0	
7 Ian Humphreys	fx1 T 0	1	

10...Peterborough, May 28, L35-61

1 †Andy Galvin	2 3 0 2 R 2	9	
2 Michael Warren	1 0 0 1 1	3	2
3 Steve Schofield	2 3 1 2 3 3	14	
4 Paul Whittaker	2 1 1 1 R 1	6	2
5 Gary Tagg	E 0 0 T 1 0	1	
6 Tim Korneliussen	0 0 T T T	0	
7 Ian Humphreys	1 R N 1	2	

11...Milton Keynes, June 12, W51-45

1 †Andy Galvin	3 3 E 3 3	12	
2 Michael Warren	0 2 2 3 2	9	1
3 Steve Schofield	3 3 3 2 3	14	
4 Paul Whittaker	R 3 3 0 1	7	
5 Gary Tagg	3 1 2 1 0	7	2
6 Tim Korneliussen	1 0 N N	1	
7 Dave Hamnett	fx0 0 0 1 0	1	

12...EXETER, June 22, W51-45

1 †Andy Galvin	F 3 3 2 3	11	1
2 Michael Warren	2 0 2 fxF	4	
3 Steve Schofield	3 3 1 2 3	12	
4 Paul Whittaker	2 2 3 3 R	10	
5 Gary Tagg	F 1 0 1 2	4	3
6 Tim Korneliussen	2 2 1 2	7	2
7 Dave Hamnett	3 0 0	3	

13...RYE HOUSE, June 29, W68-28

1 †Andy Galvin	0 3 2 2 2	9	3
2 Michael Warren	1 2 3 3 3	12	1
3 Steve Schofield	**3 3 3 3 3**	**15**	
4 Paul Whittaker	3 3 1 3 3	13	
5 Gary Tagg	2 fx3 1 1	7	1
6 Tim Korneliussen	3 2 1 1	7	1
7 Dave Hamnett	2 1 2	5	2

14...EDINBURGH, July 6, W52-44

1 †Andy Galvin	**3 3 3 3 3**	**15**	
2 Gary Tagg	1 0 2 2 0	5	2
3 Steve Schofield	3 3 3 R 3	12	
4 Paul Whittaker	3 2 1 2 1	9	1
5 Tim Korneliussen	0 1 0 E N	1	1
6 Michael Warren	1 R 0 1	2	
7 Dave Hamnett	3 3 R 1 1	8	

15...GLASGOW, July 13, W50-46

1 †Andy Galvin	1 3 2 3 2	11	1
2 Gary Tagg	3 0 1 R 2	6	1
3 Steve Schofield	2 3 3 0 3	11	1
4 Paul Whittaker	2 2 1 1 3	9	
5 Tim Korneliussen	0 1 0 N 1	2	1
6 Michael Warren	2 3 0 1 F	6	1
7 Dave Hamnett	3 2 0	5	

16...Long Eaton, July 18, L47-49

1 †Andy Galvin	2 1 R 1 3	7	1
2 Gary Tagg	3 0 2 2 2 1	10	1
3 Steve Schofield	**3 3 3 3 3 3**	**18**	
4 Paul Whittaker	1 3 3 0 1	8	
5 Tim Korneliussen	0 0 N N N	0	
6 Michael Warren	1 T 0 N 2 0 T R	3	1
7 Dave Hamnett	0 1 N 0	1	

17...BERWICK, July 20, W61-35

1 †Andy Galvin	**3 2 2 2 2**	**11**	**4**
2 Gary Tagg	1 3 2 3 2	11	
3 Steve Schofield	**3 3 3 3 3**	**15**	
4 Paul Whittaker	**3 3 3 3 3**	**15**	
5 Tim Korneliussen	1 0 1 1 0	3	
6 Michael Warren	2 1 1 0	4	
7 Dave Hamnett	1 1 0	2	2

18...STOKE, July 27, W57-39

1 †Andy Galvin	**3 3 3 3 3**	**15**	
2 Gary Tagg	1 2 3 2 3	11	2
3 Steve Schofield	**3 3 3 3 3**	**15**	
4 Paul Whittaker	2 3 0 2 0	7	1
5 Tim Korneliussen	0 1 1 0 1	3	
6 Michael Warren	3 1 1 1	6	
7 Dave Hamnett	0 0 0	0	

19...Ipswich, August 2, L47-48

1 †Andy Galvin	3 3 2 2 0	10	
2 Gary Tagg	fn1 fx1 2	4	1
3 Steve Schofield	3 3 3 3 X	12	
4 Paul Whittaker	2 2 2 1 3	10	1
5 Tim Korneliussen	0 1 0 0 N	1	1
6 Michael Warren	2 2 0 2 0 3	9	1
7 Ian Humphreys	1 0 0	1	1

20...PETERBOROUGH, August 3, W59-37

1 †Andy Galvin	2 2 1 1 N	6	2
2 Gary Tagg	1 1 3 2 3	10	2
3 Steve Schofield	**3 3 3 3 2**	**14**	**1**
4 Paul Whittaker	3 3 2 2 3	13	
5 Tim Korneliussen	1 2 1 1 3	8	2
6 Michael Warren	3 1 1 1 1	7	
7 Ian Humphreys	1 0 0	1	

21...IPSWICH, August 17, W53-42

1 †Andy Galvin	1 3 3 2 1	10	1
2 Gary Tagg	0 2 3 1 3	9	1
3 Steve Schofield	3 3 X 3 3	12	
4 Paul Whittaker	3 2 1 3 0	9	
5 Tim Korneliussen	0 0 N N N	0	
6 Michael Warren	2 F 1 0 1 2	6	2
7 Dave Hamnett	3 1 2 1	7	

22...POOLE, August 31, L47-49

1 †Andy Galvin	2 3 0 1 0	6	1
2 Michael Warren	1 fx2 1 1	5	1
3 Steve Schofield	**3 3 3 3 3**	**15**	
4 Paul Whittaker	3 3 3 2 1	12	
5 Tim Korneliussen	0 1 1 1 0	3	
6 Ian Humphreys	0 0 N N	0	
7 Dave Hamnett	2 0 1 0 3	6	1

23...Rye House, September 2, L46-50

1 †Andy Galvin	3 fnN N N	3	
2 Tim Korneliussen	1 2 1 2 T	6	
3 Steve Schofield	3 2 3 3 3 3	17	
4 Paul Whittaker	3 2 3 2 1 3	14	
5 Michael Warren	2 0 0 F 0	2	1
6 Shawn Venables	1 1 1 0 0 T	3	2
7 Dave Hamnett	0 1 R fx0	1	

24...Poole, September 4, L32-63

1 Tim Korneliussen	0 0 T 0 N	0	
2 Michael Warren	1 1 2 F 1 R	5	
3 Steve Schofield	3 fx3 3 fx3	12	
4 †Paul Whittaker	1 2 0 2 1	6	
5 Dave Hamnett	0 1 T N 0	1	1
6 Ian Humphreys	1 1 T F	2	
7 Shawn Venables	0 2 1 2 1 fx	6	2

25...ARENA ESSEX, September 7, L44-50

1 Michael Warren	2 2 0 2 3 2 2	13	2
2 Andy Galvin	*rider replacement*		
3 Steve Schofield	fx3 3 T T N	6	
4 †Paul Whittaker	2 3 R 1 3 2 3	14	1
5 Tim Korneliussen	0 0 fxN T	0	
6 Shawn Venables	0 0 T 0 2	2	
7 Dave Hamnett	1 1 3 X 0 1 3	9	
8 §Roland Pollard	0	0	

26...Arena Essex, September 13, L42-54

1 †Paul Whittaker	2 3 3 1 0 1 2	12	
2 Michael Warren	1 0 3 2 0 1 0	7	2
3 Steve Schofield	3 3 3 R 3 2 3	17	
4 Andy Galvin	*rider replacement*		
5 Gary Tagg	0 2 F 1 1	4	1
6 Shawn Venables	1 R 1 T	2	
7 Dave Hamnett	R 0 0	0	
8 Tim Korneliussen	*did not ride*		

27...WIMBLEDON, September 14, W51-45

1 †Paul Whittaker	2 2 2 3 3 2	14	
2 Michael Warren	0 1 1 0 1 1	4	2
3 Steve Schofield	3 3 3 3 3 2 3	20	
4 Andy Galvin	*rider replacement*		
5 Gary Tagg	1 0 1 0 2	4	2
6 Tim Korneliussen	3 2 0 0 N 0	5	1
7 Dave Hamnett	2 0 N 2	4	1
8 Shawn Venables	*did not ride*		

28...Glasgow, September 26, L42-54

1 †Paul Whittaker	2 2 3 3 3 2	15	
2 Michael Warren	0 0 2 2 1 2	7	1
3 Steve Schofield	1 2 1 3 2 2	11	
4 Tim Korneliussen	fxT T T N	0	
5 Gary Tagg	2 fx0 N 0	2	
6 Shawn Venables	1 1 0 1 0	3	1
7 Dave Hamnett	3 0 1 0	4	1

29...Middlesbrough, September 27, L38-58

1 †Paul Whittaker	1 3 1 3 2 1 1	12	
2 Michael Warren	0 0 0 0 3 3	6	
3 Steve Schofield	1 3 2 3 2 3 3	17	
4 Andy Galvin	*rider replacement*		
5 Gary Tagg	0 1 0 0 T	1	1
6 Shawn Venables	0 F T 0	0	
7 Dave Hamnett	2 0 T 0	2	
8 Duncan Chapman	*0 0*	*0*	

30...MDDLESBROUGH, September 28, L43-53

1 †Paul Whittaker	2 2 2 2 1 3 0	12	1
2 Michael Warren	1 1 3 2 1 R	8	2
3 Steve Schofield	2 3 3 fxN N	8	
4 Andy Galvin	*rider replacement*		
5 Gary Tagg	0 0 2 fx3 1 3	9	1
6 Shawn Venables	2 F T N 0	2	
7 Dave Hamnett	fx0 T 3 0 1	4	
8 Roland Pollard	*did not ride*		

31...Eastbourne, October 7, L45-51

1 †Paul Whittaker	3 R fx3 3 3 2	14	
2 Michael Warren	1 2 2 1 1 R 3	10	
3 Steve Schofield	*rider replacement*		
4 Dave Hamnett	1 0 0 T N	1	
5 Gary Tagg	0 1 3 2 2 0 2	10	1
6 Shawn Venables	2 1 3 1 2 0	9	2
7 §§David Wolstenholme	fx1 T	1	
8 Roland Pollard	*did not ride*		

32...Newcastle, October 15, W52-44

1 †Paul Whittaker	3 3 3 3 3 3 2	20	
2 Michael Warren	0 1 2 1 0 2	6	
3 Steve Schofield	*rider replacement*		
4 Dave Hamnett	3 2 0 3 2 1	11	2
5 Gary Tagg	2 3 3 1 1 N	10	1
6 Shawn Venables	1 0 2 0 F	3	1
7 Roland Pollard	0 1 1	2	1
8 Tony Richardson	*did not ride*		

1990 ROSTER

GALVIN, Andrew Simon (Andy)
B 13.11.1965, Whitstable, Kent.
GESSNER, Uwe
B 19.8.1964, Bad Iburg, West Germany. *Only rode in early season challenges.*
HAMNETT, David John
B 12.6.1970, Waratah, Australia.
Newcomer from Australia.
HUMPHREYS, Ian
B 29.7.1963, Isleworth, Middlesex.
On loan from Arena Essex.
KORNELIUSSEN, Tim
B 28.1.1968, Aalborg, Denmark.
Newcomer from Denmark.
POLLARD, Roland Clive
B 23.8.1971, Lewisham, London.
Local junior.
SCHOFIELD, Steven
B 27.2.1958, Mitcham, Surrey.
TAGG, Gary Edward
B 7.2.1969, Wokingham, Berks.
VENABLES, Shawn
B 12.3.1969, Vancouver, Canada.
WARREN, Michael James
B 7.11.1966, Engfield, London.
WHITTAKER, Paul Joffre
B 23.3.1968, Folkestone, Kent.
WOLSTENHOLME, David
B 30.7.1973, Sheffield, West Yorkshire. *Junior.*
DUNCAN CHAPMAN - See Middlesbrough.
TONY RICHARDSON - See Newcastle.

Witches' gold dust washed up

Track Data

Promoters: John Louis and Mike Western.
Address: Foxhall Stadium, Foxhall Road, Ipswich,. Suffolk, IP4 5TL.
Telephone: 0473-623640.
Hotline: 0898 800 674.
Track Length: 300 metres.
Track Record: 58.9 secs, John Cook (Ipswich), October 10, 1985, heat 1, Ipswich v Oxford (British League).

THREE young Australians decided Ipswich's fate in a season which promised so much and yet produced so little of tangible reward.

■ Shane Parker, another gilt-edged prospect from Down Under who scored nearly 300 points in his debut season in the National League and was heading for heat leader status before the sheer longevity of a British season finally weighed him down.

■ Billy Lellman, a bright as a button discovery who found it so impossible to settle thousands of miles away from his home that he suffered severe depression and was advised to return home to Australia by doctors even before he had completed his first League match.

■ Damon Richardson, a comparative late arrival who completed only one National League match before being ruled out with injury that sidelined him from first team duty for the rest of the summer.

The Witches struck gold with Parker and might well have found themselves with two other 22-carat nuggets had fate not conspired against both Lellman and Richardson to such an extent that they contributed next to nothing to the campaign.

You always had the impression that Ipswich were one rider short of championship material, even in the heady days when they built up a commanding lead at the top of the table and seemed to be racing away with what would have been, astonishingly, their first-ever Second Division pennant.

They started off in unstoppable mood, racking up five successive wins (four of them away from home) before Berwick pulled off a surprise draw at Foxhall Heath. They picked up again after that temporary setback with another seven successive wins and when they travelled down to the West Country for vital matches on successive nights at Exeter and Poole they looked, for all the world, as the champions-elect.

Everything went wrong at the County Ground in a stormy meeting which ended with two of the youthful Witches being attended to in the Royal Devon and Exeter Hospital at Wonford.

David Norris, a forward-looking capture from Eastbourne, had damaged his back and Dean Standing (who, coincidentally had followed the same South to East Coast route 12 months earlier) was black and blue from a painful encounter with the steel fence.

Both missed the following night's short trip to Poole and Ipswich returned to East Anglia seething at the bruising treatment meted out by the fiery Falcons, their unbeaten record shattered and with no points out of four for their troubles.

Norris was to miss a huge chunk of the season while he made a slow recovery and, during his absence, Ipswich lost further away matches at Glasgow, Middlesbrough, and Berwick in succession.

While they remained on top of the table, it was obvious that Poole would overhaul them as they kept picking up points from their matches in hand.

Chris Louis, England's Golden Boy in the National League, did his best to stem the tide and there was always considerable back-up from skipper Alan Mogridge. But Standing had more poor scores than might have been expected, particularly in the closing weeks of the season, and, understandably, Parker was unable to maintain his high level of scoring throughout.

But it was the absence of another points-scorer at reserve which was Ipswich's eventual undoing although only in terms of winning titles.

They were certainly the most potentially exciting side in the land with a crop of youngsters that should have been the envy of every other promoter!

Roll of Honour

Seasons in National League: 5 (1969-1971; 1989-1990).
National League Record: Third (2), 1971, 1990.
National League Cup Record: Winners (2), 1970, 1971.
National League Team Championship: Fourth (1), 1990. Qualified (1), 1990.
Appearances: The late Peter Bailey, 100 (1969-1971).
Points: Chris Louis, 973 (1989-1990).
World Finalists: John Cook (1985), Ray Cresp (1961), Jeremy Doncaster (1987), John Louis (1972, 1974-75-76), Peter Moore (1958, 1960), Kai Niemi (1984-85), Gerd Riss (1987), Billy Sanders (1977, 1980, 1983-84), Dennis Sigalos (1982-83).
NLRC Finalists: Ted Spittles (1969), John Harrhy (1970), John Louis (1971), Mark Loram (1989), Chris Louis (1990).
Other Honours: British League Champions, 1975, 1976, 1984. Speedway Star Knock-out Cup Winners, 1976, 1978, 1981, 1984. Inter League Cup Winners, 1977.

Star of 90
SHANE PARKER
Ipswich
90

IPSWICH

01...Peterborough, April 6, W55-41

1 Chris Louis	**3 3 3 3 2**	**14**	**1**
2 Robbie Fuller	1 0 3 2 0	6	1
3 Dean Standing	R 0 3 3 3	9	
4 †Alan Mogridge	3 2 3 0 3	11	1
5 §David Norris	1 3 1 2 2	9	2
6 §§Shane Parker	R 1 0 1 2	4	
7 §§Colin White	1 1 N	2	

02...Milton Keynes, April 17, W49-44

1 Chris Louis	3 3 X 3 3	12	
2 Robbie Fuller	0 0 1 N 0	1	
3 Dean Standing	3 R 2 1 2	8	1
4 †Alan Mogridge	2 2 2 2 1	9	3
5 David Norris	1 3 3 2 R	9	1
6 Shane Parker	R R 1 3 3	7	1
7 Colin White	2 1 0	3	

03...RYE HOUSE, April 19, W67-28

1 Chris Louis	**3 3 3 3 3**	**15**	
2 Robbie Fuller	2 0 0 N 2	4	2
3 Dean Standing	2 3 3 2 2	12	2
4 †Alan Mogridge	**2 2 2 2 2**	**10**	**5**
5 David Norris	**3 3 3 3 3**	**15**	
6 Shane Parker	3 X fx 1 3	7	
7 Colin White	2 2 fx	4	1

04...Stoke, April 28, W56-40

1 Chris Louis	2 3 2 3 2	12	1
2 Robbie Fuller	0 0 0 N 2	2	
3 Dean Standing	1 3 1 3 1	9	1
4 †Alan Mogridge	3 2 3 0 3	11	1
5 David Norris	2 3 2 1 3	11	2
6 Shane Parker	3 2 1 2 1 1	10	3
7 Colin White	1 R N	1	

05...Edinburgh, April 29, W64-31

1 Chris Louis	3 3 3 1 3	13	
2 Robbie Fuller	2 0 0 1 0	3	1
3 Dean Standing	**3 3 3 3 3**	**15**	
4 †Alan Mogridge	**3 2 3 3 2**	**13**	**2**
5 David Norris	2 3 2 2 1	10	3
6 Shane Parker	3 2 2 fx 3	10	1
7 Colin White	0 0 N	0	

06...BERWICK, May 3, D48-48

1 Chris Louis	2 2 3 2 1	10	
2 Robbie Fuller	R N 0 N 0	0	
3 Dean Standing	3 1 3 2 3	12	1
4 †Alan Mogridge	1 2 3 1 0	7	2
5 David Norris	3 3 R 1 2	9	2
6 Shane Parker	fx R 1 2 1 3	7	1
7 Colin White	1 2 R	3	

07...MIDDLESBROUGH, May 7, W60-36

1 Chris Louis	2 3 0 3 3	11	
2 Robbie Fuller	0 N N 1 2	3	1
3 Dean Standing	**2 3 3 3 3**	**14**	**1**
4 †Alan Mogridge	0 2 2 R 2	6	2
5 David Norris	1 1 3 2 2	9	3
6 Shane Parker	**3 3 2 2 3 3**	**16**	**2**
7 Colin White	1 0 0	1	

08...Long Eaton, May 9, W53-43

1 Chris Louis	3 3 3 1 2	12	1
2 Robbie Fuller	0 0 3 0 3	6	
3 Dean Standing	2 0 3 3 1	9	
4 †Alan Mogridge	1 1 3 0 3	8	2
5 David Norris	2 2 0 2 3	9	1
6 Shane Parker	3 2 1 2 0	8	1
7 Craig Hyde	1 R N	1	

09...NEWCASTLE, May 10, W60-36

1 Chris Louis	3 3 3 2 3	14	
2 Robbie Fuller	1 1 1 E 3	6	
3 Dean Standing	1 1 2 3 2	9	1
4 †Alan Mogridge	3 3 3 1 2	12	2
5 David Norris	1 2 2 F 1	6	2
6 Shane Parker	3 2 3 2 2	12	2
7 Craig Hyde	1 F fx	1	

10...MILTON KEYNES, May 24, W65-31

1 Chris Louis	2 3 2 3 3	13	
2 Colin White	0 1 2 1 1	5	1
3 Shane Parker	**3 3 3 3 3**	**15**	
4 †Alan Mogridge	**3 3 3 2 2**	**13**	**2**
5 David Norris	**2 2 2 2 2**	**10**	**5**
6 Robbie Fuller	3 1 0 3	7	
7 §§Damon Richardson	1 0 1	2	

11...Rye House, May 27, W52-44

1 Chris Louis	3 2 2 2 3	12	
2 Shane Parker	2 1 3 1 2	9	3
3 Dean Standing	3 3 R 2 2	10	1
4 †Alan Mogridge	3 3 0 0 2	8	1
5 David Norris	E 2 3 3 R	8	1
6 Robbie Fuller	R 0 1 1	2	1
7 Colin White	2 1 0 0	3	

12...PETERBOROUGH, June 7, W63-33

1 Chris Louis	**3 3 3 3 3**	**15**	
2 Shane Parker	2 0 2 2 3	9	2
3 Dean Standing	**3 3 3 3 3**	**15**	
4 †Alan Mogridge	3 3 0 1 2	9	1
5 David Norris	1 2 2 2 2	9	3
6 Robbie Fuller	3 1 0 1	5	
7 Colin White	F 1 0	1	1

13...EASTBOURNE, June 14, W63-33

1 Chris Louis	2 3 3 3 3	14	
2 Shane Parker	1 1 3 2 3	10	2
3 Dean Standing	fx 3 3 3 2	11	1
4 †Alan Mogridge	2 2 3 1 E	8	1
5 David Norris	3 1 2 2 3	11	3
6 Robbie Fuller	3 2 0 1	6	
7 Colin White	1 2 0 R	3	1

14...Exeter, June 18, L43-53

1 Chris Louis	2 1 3 F 2	8	1
2 Shane Parker	0 2 1 T 1 1	5	1
3 Dean Standing	3 3 2 fnN N	8	
4 †Alan Mogridge	F 1 0 3 2 1	7	1
5 David Norris	3 3 2 2 fxT	10	1
6 Robbie Fuller	2 0 0 2 T 0	4	
7 Colin White	0 1 0	1	

15...Poole, June 19, L37-59

1 Chris Louis	3 2 1 3 2 1 1	13	4
2 Shane Parker	1 2 2 0 3 0 2	10	
3 Dean Standing	*rider replacemenet*		
4 †Alan Mogridge	2 X fx 2 1 2 2	9	
5 Robbie Fuller	0 1 1 T 1	3	1
6 Craig Hyde	1 T 0 0	1	
7 Colin White	0 0 0	0	
8 Steve Leigh	*1*	*1*	

16...Glasgow, June 27, L33-62

1 Chris Louis	2 1 2 1 3 0	9	1
2 Shane Parker	3 fx 1 2 1 1	8	1
3 Dean Standing	2 1 R 0 1	4	
4 †Alan Mogridge	2 2 0 1 0 2	7	
5 Robbie Fuller	0 1 0 1 0	2	1
6 §§Darren Fitch	1 0 T T	1	1
7 Colin White	2 0 T	2	

17...Middlesbrough, June 28, L43-53

1 Chris Louis	3 2 2 2 1 3	13	1
2 Shane Parker	1 0 1 1 3 0	6	2
3 Dean Standing	2 1 3 2 2 2	12	1
4 †Alan Mogridge	fx 2 2 3 2 F	9	1
5 Robbie Fuller	1 1 T 0 0 T	2	1
6 Darren Fitch	0 0 T T	0	
7 Colin White	1 T 0 T	1	

18...EXETER, July 5, W50-46

1 Chris Louis	1 3 3 2 1 1	11	3
2 David Norris	*rider replacement*		
3 Dean Standing	2 F 0 fnN N	2	1
4 †Alan Mogridge	2 2 3 3 2 3 2	17	
5 Shane Parker	0 1 X 1 3 3	8	1
6 Robbie Fuller	3 3 1 2 1 1	11	1
7 Colin White	1 0 0 0	1	
8 Darren Fitch	*did not ride*		

19...WIMBLEDON, July 12, W53-43

1 Chris Louis	3 3 3 3 2 2 3	19	
2 David Norris	*rider replacement*		
3 Dean Standing	1 2 2 1 3 3	12	2
4 †Alan Mogridge	0 3 3 2 1 1	10	2
5 Shane Parker	1 3 1 1 2 0	8	1
6 Robbie Fuller	1 2 1 0 0	4	1
7 Colin White	fx 0 N	0	
8 Darren Fitch	*did not ride*		

20...GLASGOW, July 26, W56-40

1 Chris Louis	3 3 3 3 3 1	16	
2 David Norris	*rider replacement*		
3 Dean Standing	3 2 3 2 2 1	13	1
4 †Alan Mogridge	1 2 2 1 2 3	11	2
5 Shane Parker	2 3 3 F 1 3	12	2
6 Robbie Fuller	1 1 fx N	2	
7 Colin White	fx 0 0 0	0	
8 Craig Hyde	2	2	

21...Berwick, July 28, L47-49

1 Chris Louis	**3 3 3 3 3 3**	**18**	
2 Colin White	0 0 1 T 1	2	
3 Dean Standing	2 3 1 3 2	11	1
4 †Alan Mogridge	2 2 2 2 0 0	8	2
5 Shane Parker	3 1 1 0 T	5	2
6 Craig Hyde	2 0 fx F F	2	
7 Darren Fitch	1 0 N	1	1

22...HACKNEY, August 2, W48-47

1 Chris Louis	1 2 3 3 2 3 1	15	1
2 David Norris	*rider replacement*		
3 Dean Standing	2 1 3 3 3 R	12	1
4 †Alan Mogridge	3 2 2 1 1 2	11	1
5 Shane Parker	0 1 0 1 fx 2	4	1
6 Robbie Fuller	3 1 R 1 1	6	1
7 Craig Hyde	fx N 0	0	
8 Darren Fitch	*did not ride*		

23...Arena Essex, August 4, W49-47

1 Chris Louis	3 1 3 3 3 1 3	17	
2 David Norris	*rider replacement*		
3 Dean Standing	0 3 2 2 2 0	9	1
4 †Alan Mogridge	1 3 1 1 0 0	6	3
5 Shane Parker	2 2 2 2 1 3	12	2
6 Robbie Fuller	1 1 2 0 E	4	1
7 Craig Hyde	0 1 N 0	1	
8 Darren Fitch	*did not ride*		

24...ARENA ESSEX, August 16, W70-25

1 Chris Louis	**3 3 3 3 3**	**15**	
2 David Norris	1 2 3 1 2	9	2
3 Dean Standing	**2 3 3 3 2**	**13**	**2**
4 †Alan Mogridge	X 3 3 2 2	10	2
5 Shane Parker	2 1 2 0 3	8	1
6 Robbie Fuller	**3 3 2 3**	**11**	**1**
7 Craig Hyde	2 2 0	4	2

25...Hackney, August 17, L42-53

1 Chris Louis	2 3 3 3 2 3	16	1
2 David Norris	3 1 fx R N	4	
3 Dean Standing	1 1 2 1 fx	5	2
4 †Alan Mogridge	2 2 2 0 2 2	10	1
5 Shane Parker	1 0 0 0 1	2	1
6 Robbie Fuller	1 0 T T	1	
7 Craig Hyde	0 2 2 0	4	

26...STOKE, August 23, D48-48

1 Chris Louis	3 3 2 2 3	13	1
2 Shane Parker	1 1 2 1 1	6	1
3 Dean Standing	1 0 1 0 0	2	1
4 †Alan Mogridge	1 fx 3 3 1	8	1
5 David Norris	2 3 1 1 1	8	
6 Robbie Fuller	1 2 2 3	8	
7 Craig Hyde	3 0 fx	3	

27...Eastbourne, September 2, W49-46

1 Chris Louis	2 3 2 3 3	13	1
2 Shane Parker	1 1 3 3 0	8	1
3 Dean Standing	1 fx N N N	1	
4 †Alan Mogridge	1 3 2 1 1	8	1
5 David Norris	3 fx 3 3 2	11	
6 Robbie Fuller	fx 1 0 2 2 0	5	
7 Craig Hyde	2 0 1 fx	3	1

28...EDINBURGH, September 6, W56-40

1 Chris Louis	**3 3 3 3 3**	**15**	
2 Shane Parker	0 1 1 0 1	3	1
3 Dean Standing	1 3 1 X 3	8	
4 †Alan Mogridge	2 3 3 2 fx	10	1
5 David Norris	0 0 2 3 2	7	2
6 Robbie Fuller	3 3 2 2 3	13	1
7 Craig Hyde	R N 0	0	

29...LONG EATON, September 13, W55-41

1 Chris Louis	**3 3 3 3 3**	**15**	
2 Shane Parker	0 1 2 0 0	3	
3 Dean Standing	1 3 1 1 3	9	2
4 †Alan Mogridge	3 3 1 2 2	11	3
5 David Norris	1 2 2 2 2	9	2
6 Robbie Fuller	3 2 0 2	7	
7 Craig Hyde	1 0 0	1	

30...Wimbledon, September 19, L47-49

1 Chris Louis	**3 3 3 3 3 3**	**18**	
2 Shane Parker	0 0 1 1 1	3	
3 Dean Standing	3 F 0 fx 1	4	1
4 †Alan Mogridge	2 2 3 E 2 1	10	1
5 David Norris	0 1 1 2 3 2	9	1
6 Robbie Fuller	2 1 T 0 T	3	
7 Craig Hyde	0 0 T	0	

31...Newcastle, September 23, W49-47

1 Chris Louis	3 3 2 2 3	13	
2 Shane Parker	0 1 1 0 1	3	2
3 Dean Standing	1 3 3 1 1	9	2
4 †Alan Mogridge	2 1 2 1 1	7	3
5 David Norris	3 2 1 2 2	10	1
6 Robbie Fuller	1 0 2 2 2	7	1
7 Craig Hyde	0 0 N	0	

32...POOLE, September 27, L44-51

1 Chris Louis	3 3 F 2 1	9	1
2 Shane Parker	0 0 0 2 3	5	
3 David Norris	3 fnN N N	3	
4 †Alan Mogridge	1 1 1 0 2	5	1
5 Dean Standing	2 3 3 2 1	11	
6 Robbie Fuller	3 2 2 1 fx 1	9	1
7 Craig Hyde	0 1 N 1 fx fx	2	1

1990 ROSTER

FITCH, Darren
B 10.10.1965, Ipswich, Suffolk. *Local junior.*

FULLER, Robert Ernest (Robbie)
B 13.3.1964, Ipswich, Suffolk.

HARE, Lawrence Charlton
B 23.12.1969, Elmsett, Nr. Ipswich, Suffolk. *Local junior.*

HYDE, Craig
B 14.2.1963, Bundaberg, Australia.

LELLMAN, William Leigh (Billy)
B 15.9.1970, Largs North, Australia. *First season Australian. Did not ride in the National League.*

LOUIS, Chrstopher
B 9.7.1969, Ipswich, Suffolk.

MOGRIDGE, Alan John
B 6.11.1963, London.

NORRIS, David Michael
B 20.8.1972, Eastbourne, East Sussex. *Signed from Eastbourne.*

PARKER, Shane Andrew
B 29.4.1970, Semaphore Park, Australia. *First season Australian.*

RICHARDSON, Damon Noel
B 10.4.1970, Adelaide, Australia. *First season Australian.*

STANDING, Dean Michael
B 20.6.1969, Southampton, Hampshire.

WHITE, Colin Peter
B 12.8.1972, Ilford, Essex. *On loan from Oxford.*

STEVE LEIGH - See Poole.

Loneliness of the long distance No 1

Track Data

Promoters: Roger Jones and Steve Yorke.
Address: Long Eaton Stadium, Station Road, Long Eaton, Nottinghamshire.
Telephone: 0602-731112.
Information Line: 0898 31 21 42.
Track Length: 336 metres.
Track Record: 62.27 secs, Kevin Smart (Long Eaton), June 27, 1990, Heat 1, Long Eaton v Eastbourne (National League). •Match abandoned after four heats.

RICHARD HELLSÉN has been around the British tracks for an eternity. He made his debut way back in the Autumnal days of October, 1973, alongside the likes of Ole Olsen, George Hunter, Tony Clarke, Bob Humphreys, Eddie Reeves, Arthur Price and Ray Bales, all of whom have long since retired.

In fact, of the 13 other riders who took part in that meeting at Wolverhampton the only rider who has seen any track action in the recent past was Malcolm Simmons who last rode 18 months or so ago.

Since that first competitive match in England, Hellsén has completed nearly 600 League and Cup meetings and, in his 40th year, would forgive anyone calling him a veteran.

Yet Hellsén still arrives at tracks looking forward to the races ahead as enthusiastically as any teenager embarking on a career. And even though he has only completed two seasons as a Long Eaton rider such has been his influence that it is hard to remember Station Road without him – and even more difficult to imagine what it will be like when he goes!

Promoter Roger Jones admits: "He has been a marvellous signing. He is the ideal team-man and someone that everyone can look up to."

He was an example to the rest of his team-mates but unfortunately for the Invaders there were too many occasions when the rest of the side's standards slipped way below those set by their team captain.

Once or twice during the season, Jones was forced to read the riot act with his team as mechanical problems rather than a lack of riding talent contributed to yet another season in which the East Midlands side struggled at the wrong end of the table.

Hellsén is certainly no longer the force he was but, even so, he scored a half a century more points than any of his team-mates (in four fewer matches) and average nearly one and a half points a meeting more than Nigel De'ath, second in the club charts. That, in a sentence, was Long Eaton's big problem. They had hoped that they would find someone to ease into the number one role but ended up relying on the stalwart Swede for the bulk of their points, particularly away from home where he was invariably top scorer.

Kevin Smart (signed from Poole), Nigel De'ath (on loan from Oxford) and junior Jon Bell all made their club debuts in the opening League match of the season and Jamie Habbin joined the newcomers' roll-call in the following meeting.

Smart bubbled on occasions (like when he smashed the track record and in the final match of the season when he scored the team's only full maximum of the season) but too often lost his sparkle; De'ath was potent on occasions when he was fully fit; but Bell disappeared from the team very quickly. Habbin was perplexingly inconsistent as he went up and down the scoring scales as adroitly as any concert pianist, spanning a zero at home to Rye House and a paid 15 point maximum at home to Milton Keynes! But at least he added some colour to the outfit with his shocking pink leathers and he also added a little youth to a team that inclined towards the elderly in some respects. Inconsistency is a good word to sum up several of the Long Eaton riders.

Gary O'Hare would always get somewhere between nought and 13 but there was never a way of telling which and Paul Fry was never a totally reliable scorer although he did certainly contribute more big scores and fewer low scores than in the past and looks more than capable of holding down a permanent heat leader role with a little bit of good fortune in the season ahead. Peter Lloyd was ruled out for much of the season after pulling his shoulder out of joint while warming up his bike at a grass-track meeting – a freak accident which prompted Roger Jones to call for a new look at the way speedway assets are used by grass track clubs – and Keith White called it a day after three last places in his opening League match.

His retirement, and niggling injuries, allowed for experimentation at reserve but, unfortunately for Jones, the most promising second halfer of all, Mark Blackbird, was unavailable as he was already out on loan to Milton Keynes!

Roll of Honour

Seasons in National League: 17 (1969-1974, 1979-1980, 1982-1990).
National League Record: Champions (1), 1984.
National League Cup Record: Semi-finalists, 1969.
National League Team Championship: Fourth (1), 1983. Qualified (1), 1983.
Appearances: Dave Perks, 190 (1979, 1983-1985, 1989).
Points: Dave Perks, 1831 (1979, 1983-1985, 1989).
World Finalists: Anders Michanek (1967), Ray Wilson (1967).
NLRC Finalists: Peter Wrathall (1969), Ken Vale (1970), Malcolm Shakespeare (1971), Roger Mills (1971-72), Geoff Bouchard (1973-74), Dave Perks (1979, 1983-84-85), Mike Sampson (1980), Alan Molyneux (1982), Mark Fiora (1986), Nigel Sparshott (1987), Keith White (1988), Richard Hellsén (1989-90).

Stars of 90

KEVIN SMART and RICHARD HELLSEN

Long Eaton

LONG EATON

01...ARENA ESSEX, April 4, W54-42

1 §Kevin Smart	3 3 3 3 2	14	
2 †Keith White	1 0 N 0 0	1	
3 Richard Hellsén	3 fx2 N N	5	
4 Gary O'Hare	1 2 3 1 1	8	1
5 Paul Fry	3 1 2 3 3	12	2
6 §Nigel De'ath	3 2 3 1 1 3	13	1
7 §§Jon Bell	1 F 0 0	1	

02...Newcastle, April 15, L46-50

1 Kevin Smart	2 2 2 1 2	9	1
2 Gary O'Hare	1 0 1 0 X	2	1
3 †Richard Hellsén	3 2 3 3 2 1	14	
4 §Jamie Habbin	2 2 3 R 3	10	
5 Paul Fry	0 1 2 1 F	4	3
6 Nigel De'ath	3 0 1 3	7	
7 Peter Lloyd	F 0 T	0	

03...Wimbledon, April 18, L34-62

1 Kevin Smart	2 1 F 1 1	5	
2 Gary O'Hare	0 0 T 2 1	3	1
3 †Richard Hellsén	2 1 2 1 1	7	1
4 Jamie Habbin	3 1 1 0 2 0	7	1
5 Paul Fry	2 2 2 0 2 0	8	1
6 Nigel De'ath	2 0 0 T	2	
7 Peter Lloyd	1 1 0	2	2

04...EDINBURGH, April 25, W52-44

1 Kevin Smart	3 3 3 0 2	11	
2 Gary O'Hare	R 1 2 2 1	6	1
3 †Richard Hellsén	1 2 2 3 3	11	1
4 Paul Fry	fx2 2 3 0	7	1
5 Jamie Habbin	1 R 3 1 1	6	
6 Nigel De'ath	2 0 3 3	8	1
7 Peter Lloyd	3 0 0	3	

05...Arena Essex, April 28, L43-51

1 Kevin Smart	2 0 0 1 0	3	
2 Gary O'Hare	1 1 0 N 1	3	1
3 †Richard Hellsén	2 2 X 1 1	6	2
4 Paul Fry	2 2 0 F 2	6	2
5 Jamie Habbin	3 3 1 2 0	9	
6 Nigel De'ath	2 3 2 2 3 3	15	
7 Peter Lloyd	1 0 N	1	1

06...Eastbourne, April 29, L47-49

1 Kevin Smart	2 3 2 1 1	9	1
2 Gary O'Hare	0 0 N 3 R	3	
3 †Richard Hellsén	0 1 2 1 2	6	
4 Paul Fry	2 1 0 3 R	6	1
5 Jamie Habbin	3 3 2 3 1	12	1
6 Nigel De'ath	3 3 fnN N	6	
7 Peter Lloyd	0 2 1 0 2	5	

07...NEWCASTLE, May 2, W54-42

1 Kevin Smart	1 2 2 3 3	11	2
2 Gary O'Hare	fnN N N N	0	
3 †Richard Hellsén	2 3 3 3 2	13	
4 Paul Fry	2 2 3 1 1	9	2
5 Jamie Habbin	3 3 1 0 1	8	1
6 Peter Lloyd	2 2 N 3 N 1 1 2	11	1
7 Mark Blackbird	1 1 0 R 0 N	2	2

08...Hackney, May 4, L34-62

1 Kevin Smart	F 0 2 1 0	3	1
2 Peter Lloyd	1 1 1 0 0	3	1
3 †Richard Hellsén	2 2 E 3 0 1	8	
4 Paul Fry	0 1 2 2 2 1	8	1
5 Jamie Habbin	3 2 0 0 T N	5	
6 Jon Roberts	1 0 2 T N 0	3	1
7 Mark Blackbird	2 1 T N 1	4	1

09...IPSWICH, May 9, L43-53

1 Kevin Smart	1 3 1 0 1	6	2
2 Gary O'Hare	2 1 2 2 2	9	
3 †Richard Hellsén	3 3 2 3 2	13	
4 Paul Fry	fx1 1 1 0	3	1
5 Jamie Habbin	3 2 0 2 0	7	1
6 Peter Lloyd	2 1 0 1 1	5	2
7 Jon Roberts	0 0 N	0	

10...STOKE., May 16, L44-52

1 Kevin Smart	2 1 1 0 2 0	6	2
2 Nigel De'ath	*rider replacement*		
3 †Richard Hellsén	3 3 2 3 1 3	15	
4 Paul Fry	0 1 0 2 2 1	6	
5 Jamie Habbin	3 3 2 3 0 0 1	12	
6 Peter Lloyd	2 1 0 N	3	
7 Gary O'Hare	0 0 2 0	2	1
8 Jon Roberts	*did not ride*		

11...Exeter, May 21, L31-65

1 Kevin Smart	2 0 2 2 0 2 1	9	1
2 Nigel De'ath	*rider replacement*		
3 †Richard Hellsén	2 2 R 0 2 2	8	
4 Paul Fry	3 2 1 0 T 1 0	7	
5 Jamie Habbin	0 1 T T 0	1	
6 Peter Lloyd	1 0 1 R 1 0	3	
7 Gary O'Hare	3 0 0 N	3	
8 Michael Howe	0	0	

12...Poole, May 22, L40-56

1 Kevin Smart	3 2 3 1 3 2	14	
2 Peter Lloyd	0 0 T 0 T	0	
3 †Richard Hellsén	1 3 3 1 3 3	14	
4 Paul Fry	2 0 F 1 0 0	3	
5 Jamie Habbin	R 2 3 0 fxN	5	
6 Michael Howe	0 1 T T 1	2	
7 Gary O'Hare	2 0 0	2	

13...Berwick, June 9, L42-54

1 Kevin Smart	1 1 2 2 0	6	1
2 Gary O'Hare	0 0 2 T 2	4	
3 †Richard Hellsén	3 3 2 3 1 1	13	1
4 Paul Fry	1 2 F 1 1	5	1
5 Peter Lloyd	3 1 1 0 2	7	1
6 §Jon Surman	3 fx1 0 1	5	2
7 Michael Howe	1 1 N	2	

14...Edinburgh, June 11, L25-71

1 Kevin Smart	2 1 2 2 0 1 2	10	
2 Nigel De'ath	*rider replacement*		
3 †Richard Hellsén	1 2 2 1 R R	6	
4 Paul Fry	1 R 0 1 1 N	3	1
5 Gary O'Hare	1 0 1 0 0 N	2	
6 Jon Surman	0 0 0 T 1	1	
7 Peter Lloyd	2 0 0 F	2	
8 Michael Howe	1	1	1

15...WIMBLEDON, June 13, D48-48

1 Kevin Smart	0 1 2 0 0 0	3	2
2 Nigel De'ath	*rider replacement*		
3 †Richard Hellsén	1 1 2 3 3 2 3	15	1
4 Paul Fry	3 2 2 2 3 3	15	
5 Gary O'Hare	1 1 F 0 N	2	1
6 Peter Lloyd	1 2 1 0	4	1
7 Jon Surman	3 3 0 2 1	9	
8 Michael Howe	*did not ride*		

16...EASTBOURNE, July 12, L41-55

1 Kevin Smart	0 0 T 1 1	2	
2 Nigel De'ath	1 1 T 1 2	5	
3 †Richard Hellsén	3 3 3 2 2 3	16	
4 Paul Fry	0 F 3 3 F R	6	
5 Jamie Habbin	2 1 1 0 N	4	
6 Gary O'Hare	3 2 0 0 1 1	7	2
7 Jon Surman	1 0 N	1	

17...HACKNEY, July 18, W49-47

1 Kevin Smart	1 0 N 1 0	2	1
2 Nigel De'ath	0 1 3 1 2	7	
3 †Richard Hellsén	2 2 3 3 2	12	
4 Paul Fry	2 2 2 2 2	10	2
5 Jamie Habbin	3 3 1 2 1	10	3
6 Gary O'Hare	3 0 1 0 0	4	1
7 Jon Surman	2 1 1	4	1

18...POOLE, July 25, L45-51

1 Kevin Smart	2 1 3 fnN	6	1
2 Nigel De'ath	1 2 2 1 2	8	1
3 †Richard Hellsén	3 2 3 2 1	11	
4 Paul Fry	2 3 3 3 2	13	
5 Jamie Habbin	0 2 0 0 0	2	1
6 Gary O'Hare	0 1 0 R	1	
7 Jon Surman	3 R 0 0 1	4	1

19...Peterborough, July 27, L44-52

1 Kevin Smart	1 0 2 1 3	7	
2 Nigel De'ath	3 1 1 1 0	6	2
3 †Richard Hellsén	3 3 3 3 2	14	
4 Paul Fry	3 2 2 0 R N	7	
5 Jamie Habbin	0 0 1 2 T	3	2
6 Gary O'Hare	2 0 fx1	3	
7 Jon Surman	1 1 2 0	4	1

20...EXETER, August 1, D48-48

1 Kevin Smart	1 3 3 1 0	8	
2 Nigel De'ath	0 1 1 2 1	5	2
3 †Richard Hellsén	3 3 2 2 R	10	
4 Paul Fry	1 2 1 3 2	9	
5 Jamie Habbin	3 fnN N N	3	
6 Gary O'Hare	3 2 0 2 1 2	10	3
7 Jon Surman	2 0 0 N 0 1	3	1

21...MIDDLESBROUGH, August 8, L40-56

1 Kevin Smart	1 2 0 0 N	3	
2 Nigel De'ath	0 1 2 T 2	5	1
3 †Richard Hellsén	2 3 3 2 2 3	15	
4 Paul Fry	0 2 0 1 N	3	
5 Jamie Habbin	1 R N 0 N	1	
6 Gary O'Hare	3 fx2 2 0 1 0	8	2
7 Jon Surman	2 1 T 1 1	5	2

22...Rye House, August 12, L39-56

1 Kevin Smart	0 1 2 1 2	6	2
2 Nigel De'ath	1 2 1 3 2	9	2
3 †Richard Hellsén	1 3 2 3 3 2	14	
4 Paul Fry	3 1 1 0 0 N	5	
5 Jamie Habbin	F 0 1 fxN	1	
6 Jon Surman	1 fxT 3 0	4	
7 Gary O'Hare	0 0 T 0	0	

23...Milton Keynes, August 14, L37-59

1 Kevin Smart	2 2 0 1 T	5	
2 Nigel De'ath	1 E 1 1 0 fx	3	1
3 †Richard Hellsén	3 fnN T N	3	
4 Paul Fry	3 0 2 0 T	5	
5 Jamie Habbin	1 1 0 fn0	2	
6 Gary O'Hare	2 0 3 2 0 2 1	10	
7 Jon Surman	1 2 2 0 1 1 2	9	4

24...GLASGOW, August 15, L40-56

1 Kevin Smart	0 2 3 1 0 0	6	1
2 Paul Fry	1 2 0 2 2 3 3	13	1
3 Richard Hellsén	*rider replacement*		
4 Nigel De'ath	0 3 2 1 3 R 2	11	
5 Jamie Habbin	3 2 0 1 0 3	9	1
6 †Gary O'Hare	R 0 R T	0	
7 Jon Surman	1 T 0	1	
8 Michael Howe	0	0	

25...MILTON KEYNES, August 29, W56-40

1 Kevin Smart	3 3 3 2 3	14	
2 Jon Surman	2 0 2 F 1	5	2
3 Nigel De'ath	3 0 0 0 3	6	
4 Paul Fry	3 1 0 fx1	5	
5 Jamie Habbin	**2 3 3 3 2**	**13**	**2**
6 †Gary O'Hare	3 2 3 2	10	1
7 §Duncan Chapman	1 1 1	3	1

26...Middlesbrough, August 30, L34-62

1 Kevin Smart	1 0 T 0 0	1	
2 Jon Surman	0 1 T 2 1	4	1
3 Nigel De'ath	3 2 2 1 1 1	10	1
4 Paul Fry	R 1 0 N N	1	1
5 Jamie Habbin	1 2 1 0 0	4	
6 †Gary O'Hare	3 1 0 2	6	1
7 Duncan Chapman	2 1 3 0 1 1	8	1

27...Glasgow, August 31, L22-74

1 Kevin Smart	1 2 1 1 0 1 1	7	
2 Richard Hellsén	*rider replacement*		
3 Nigel De'ath	0 0 1 3 1 2 0	7	
4 Paul Fry	2 1 0 1 0	4	
5 Jamie Habbin	1 0 T 0 T	1	1
6 †Gary O'Hare	1 0 T 0	1	
7 Jon Surman	0 1 0	1	
8 Duncan Chapman	0 1 0 0	1	

28...RYE HOUSE, September 12, W49-47

1 Kevin Smart	1 F 3 0 2	6	1
2 Nigel De'ath	2 2 3 2 2	11	1
3 †Richard Hellsén	2 2 3 3 2	12	1
4 Paul Fry	3 2 3 1 1	10	1
5 Jamie Habbin	fx0 N N N	0	
6 Gary O'Hare	2 3 1 1 0 0	7	1
7 Jon Surman	1 0 1 1	3	1

29...Ipswich, September 13, L41-55

1 Kevin Smart	2 0 3 3 3 1	12	
2 Nigel De'ath	1 1 3 2 1 0	8	2
3 †Richard Hellsén	3 2 0 1 1	7	
4 Paul Fry	0 2 1 0 T	3	1
5 Jamie Habbin	2 1 2 fx0	5	1
6 Gary O'Hare	0 fxT 3	3	
7 Jon Surman	2 0 1	3	

30...Stoke, September 16, L35-61

1 Kevin Smart	0 2 2 1 0 0	5	1
2 Nigel De'ath	1 1 3 2 3 1	11	2
3 †Richard Hellsén	1 2 1 1 2	7	1
4 Paul Fry	2 1 2 2 2 1	10	1
5 Jamie Habbin	0 0 1 0 T	1	1
6 Gary O'Hare	1 0 T 0	1	
7 Duncan Chapman	F 0 T	0	

31...BERWICK, September 19, L46-50

1 Kevin Smart	1 2 0 N T	3	2
2 Nigel De'ath	2 3 2 3 3 R	13	
3 †Richard Hellsén	2 3 2 3 3	13	
4 Paul Fry	F 2 3 E 1 1	7	
5 Jamie Habbin	3 0 2 0 T 3	8	1
6 Gary O'Hare	1 R 0 fxT	1	
7 Jon Surman	0 0 R 1	1	

32...PETERBOROUGH, Sept. 26, W69-27

1 Kevin Smart	**3 3 3 3 3**	**15**	
2 Nigel De'ath	1 2 2 2 3	10	2
3 †Richard Hellsén	3 3 2 3 1	12	
4 Paul Fry	1 2 2 2 2	9	4
5 Jamie Habbin	3 3 3 0 3	12	
6 Gary O'Hare	3 2 1 2	8	2
7 Jon Surman	2 1 0	3	2

1990 ROSTER

BELL, Jonathan Joseph
B 10.12.1969, Burleston, Warks.
DE'ATH, Nigel
B 19.5.1965, Bicester, Oxfordshire.
On loan from Oxford.
FRY, Paul
B 25.10.1964, Ledbury, Hereford & Worcester. *On loan from Cradley.*
GALVIN, Stafford Xavier
B 23.4.1964, Brisbane, Australia. *First season newcomer.*
HABBIN, James William (Jamie)
B 5.5.1966, Welwyn Garden City, Hertfordshire. *On loan from National League.*
HELLSÉN, John Richard
B 1.6.1951, Stockholm, Sweden.
LLOYD, David Peter Glyn
B 17.12.1962, Leamington Spa, Warwickshire.
O'HARE, Patrick Gary
B 14.9.1963, Manchester.
ROBERTS, Jonathon (Jon)
B 24.2.1970, Poynton, Cheshire.
SMART, Kevin Rodney
B 3.9.1963, Inglesham, Wiltshire.
Signed from Poole.
SURMAN, Jonathan Raymond (Jon)
B 20.12.1966, Aylesbury, Buckinghamshire. *On loan from Oxford.*
WHITE, Keith
B 27.8.1956, Hackney, London.
MARK BLACKBIRD - See Milton Keynes.
DUNCAN CHAPMAN - See Middlesbrough.
MICHAEL HOWE - See Milton Keynes.

Cheshire cat licks the cream

Track Data

Promoters: Tim Swales and Ken Knott.
Address: Cleveland Park Stadium, Stockton Road, Middlesbrough, Cleveland.
Telephone: 0642-211411.
Information Line: 0898 31 21 43.
Track Length: 302 metres.
Track Record: 61.1 secs, Darren Sumner (Middlesbrough), July 5, 1990, Heat 1, Middlesbrough v Stoke (National League).

ALMOST THERE. Middlesbrough could have adopted the old Andy Williams mid-sixties pop favourite as their own Cleveland Park theme tune.

They were almost there – in both the major National League competitions. They finished runners-up to Poole in the chase for the championship pennant and again it was their South Coast rivals who ended their hopes of winning the Knock Out Cup for what would have been, surprisingly, their first Cup victory in 23 seasons in the Second Division.

Frankly, there was never really a week or even a match when the Delta Taxi Bears would have fancied their chances of winning the League for the second time in their history. They were the team who came through at the death to snatch second place from pace-setters Ipswich with a last-gasp draw at Wimbledon in their last match of the season.

That was the first, and last time, they climbed into second place in the table and even so they still finished six wins short of the champions.

But they had far more realistic hopes of a KO Cup reward as they brushed aside Edinburgh (with only four points to spare in a controversial second leg on their own track), Milton Keynes (by a massive 53 points!) and Wimbledon on their way to only their second ever final.

It was the Wimbledon tie that raised hopes in the North East as they grabbed an unexpected 23 point first leg lead from a superb all-round performance at Plough Lane and followed that up with an even more comprehensive victory in the return match to actually claim an even bigger overall winning margin than against luckless Milton Keynes. If they could annihilate Wimbledon – why couldn't they beat Poole? So the argument went and even an 18 point away defeat in the opening leg of the final didn't totally destroy those fond hopes of glory.

But Poole proved they were the best team in the National League and even though Middlesbrough won the second leg they were never in sight of clawing back the deficit.

Even so it was a memorable finale to a season that began slowly but gathered momentum as the weeks ticked by. There had been some early doubts about the composition of the 1990 squad and when co-promoter Ken Knott revealed the major winter signing at a pre-season Supporters' Club function the name of David Cheshire as a replacement for the Newcastle-bound Martin Dixon went down like a lead balloon.

Later some of those same fans, who had been so lukewarm in their reception of the new boy, had the courage to offer Cheshire their apologies and his end of season average (7.11) was less than half a point below Dixon's 1989 figure and a similar percentage down on his 1990 mark.

Considering he had missed three seasons, Cheshire could be included among that growing list of comeback riders who had defied time.

In some ways the Middlesbrough fans could be forgiven their scepticism, particularly when they saw their team beaten at home by nearest rivals Newcastle in the early season Tyne Tees Trophy. At least that defeat was tempered – by the revelation that Rod Hunter had agreed to return to Britain and to ride not for his 1989 club the Diamonds, but for Middlesbrough. He made an enormous difference to the route the new season would take and actually improved on his previous season's figures, collecting a mammoth 10 point average.

Darren Sumner was impeccable on the slicker tracks, Paul Bentley maintained his improvement even if it wasn't at quite the expected pace, and skipper Jamie Luckhurst weighed in with solid scoring when he wasn't out of action with injury.

But the real bonus was the continued good form of evergreen Steve Wilcock who relished his 14th campaign in the club's colours and pushed his average up by nearly two points a meeting to lay the foundations for such a successful season.

Roll of Honour

Seasons in National League: 23 (1968-1990).
National League Record: Champions (1), 1981. Runners-up (1), 1990. Third (4), 1968, 1980, 1985, 1986.
National League Cup Record: Runners-up (2), 1980, 1990.
National League Team Championship: Winners (2), 1985, 1986. Third (2), 1981, 1982. Qualified (9), 1981, 1982, 1983, 1984, 1985, 1986, 1987, 1988, 1990.
Appearances: Steve Wilcock, 534 (1976-1987, 1989-1990).
Points: Steve Wilcock, 5016 (1976-1987, 1989-1990).
World Finalists: None.
NLRC Finalists: Allan Brown (1968), Graham Plant (1968), Terry Lee (1969), Tom Leadbitter (1970, 1975), Bruce Forrester (1971, 1973-74), Dave Durham (1972), Alan Emerson (1976-77), Steve Wilcock (1978-79-80-81-82-83-84-85), Mark Courtney (1986), Martin Dixon (1987-88), Rod Hunter (1990).
Other Honours: National League (Division Two) Champions, 1947.

Star of 90

ROD HUNTER

Middlesbrough

MIDDLESBROUGH

01...Berwick, April 7, L45-51

1 Darren Sumner	3 3 1 1 2 2	12	1
2 §David Cheshire	1 0 3 2 0	6	
3 †Jamie Luckhurst	2 1 2 fxfx3	8	
4 §Rod Hunter	3 2 3 3 1 N	12	1
5 Paul Bentley	E 1 N T 2 1	4	1
6 §§Paul Smith	2 0 0 0 T	2	
7 Duncan Chapman	0 0 T 1	1	1

02...GLASGOW, April 19, W60-36

1 Darren Sumner	3 1 0 2 2	8	1
2 David Cheshire	0 3 3 3 3	12	
3 †Jamie Luckhurst	0 3 3 1 3	10	
4 Paul Bentley	1 2 2 3 1	9	2
5 Rod Hunter	3 3 1 3 2	12	2
6 Steve Wilcock	3 3 0 2	8	1
7 Duncan Chapman	0 1 0	1	

03...EDINBURGH, April 26, W65-31

1 Darren Sumner	1 3 3 3 3	13	1
2 David Cheshire	2 2 3 2 2	11	2
3 †Jamie Luckhurst	2 2 0 1 2	7	2
4 Paul Bentley	2 1 3 2 1	9	3
5 Rod Hunter	3 2 2 3 3	13	1
6 Steve Wilcock	3 1 3 0	7	1
7 Duncan Chapman	2 1 2	5	1

04...RYE HOUSE, May 3, W58-37

1 Darren Sumner	3 3 2 3 3	14	
2 David Cheshire	1 2 3 1 3	10	2
3 †Jamie Luckhurst	2 1 1 1 1	6	1
4 Paul Bentley	2 2 2 1 0	7	3
5 Rod Hunter	**3 3 3 3 3**	**15**	
6 Steve Wilcock	2 3 X fx	5	
7 Duncan Chapman	F 1 0	1	

05...Arena Essex, May 5, D48-48

1 Darren Sumner	2 3 3 2 2 2	14	1
2 David Cheshire	0 0 1 T 2	3	
3 †Jamie Luckhurst	1 2 1 3 1	8	
4 Paul Bentley	2 1 2 3 F 1	9	2
5 Rod Hunter	3 3 1 1 3	11	1
6 Steve Wilcock	1 1 0 T 1	3	2
7 Duncan Chapman	0 F N	0	

06...Eastbourne, May 6, W54-42

1 Darren Sumner	3 3 3 0 2	11	1
2 David Cheshire	1 1 3 fx3	8	
3 †Jamie Luckhurst	0 2 3 1 2	8	
4 Paul Bentley	2 0 0 3 3	8	1
5 Rod Hunter	3 3 3 3 1	13	1
6 Steve Wilcock	2 0 0 2	4	1
7 Duncan Chapman	1 1 F	2	1

07...Ipswich, May 7, L36-60

1 Darren Sumner	3 3 0 1 1 N	8	1
2 David Cheshire	1 0 1 2 0	4	1
3 †Jamie Luckhurst	0 1 1 2 N	4	
4 Paul Bentley	3 1 2 fx1 fx	7	1
5 Rod Hunter	2 0 2 3 1 fn	8	2
6 Steve Wilcock	2 1 0 T 1 1	5	
7 Duncan Chapman	fx N T 0	0	

08...EXETER, May 10, W61-34

1 Darren Sumner	2 3 2 3 3	13	1
2 David Cheshire	1 2 3 3 3	12	2
3 †Jamie Luckhurst	3 fx N N N	3	
4 Paul Bentley	3 2 2 2 1	10	2
5 Rod Hunter	2 R 3 2 3	10	1
6 Steve Wilcock	2 2 fx2 0 2	8	3
7 Duncan Chapman	3 1 F 1	5	1

09...Rye House, May 20, L37-59

1 Darren Sumner	3 2 3 2 1 3	14	
2 David Cheshire	2 1 0 0 0 F	3	2
3 †Jamie Luckhurst	0 T T T T	0	
4 Paul Bentley	0 3 1fx 0 0	4	
5 Rod Hunter	2 1 3 fx3 2	11	
6 Steve Wilcock	1 2 0 T 0	3	
7 Duncan Chapman	0 1 T 1	2	

10...ARENA ESSEX, May 24, W53-43

1 †Darren Sumner	2 3 0 2 2	9	2
2 David Cheshire	0 1 2 2 1	6	
3 Steve Wilcock	2 3 2 1 2	10	1
4 Paul Bentley	2 1 2 3 3	11	1
5 Rod Hunter	1 3 3 3 3	13	1
6 Duncan Chapman	3 F 0 R	3	
7 §§Martin Jones	1 0 0	1	

11...Exeter, June 11, L29-67

1 Darren Sumner	0 0 0 1 0	1	
2 David Cheshire	2 2 0 3 1	8	
3 Steve Wilcock	1 0 0 0 N	1	
4 Paul Bentley	2 1 1 1 0 3	8	1
5 Rod Hunter	3 R 1 3 1 1	9	
6 †Jamie Luckhurst	1 1 T T	2	
7 Duncan Chapman	0 0 T 0 0	0	

12...Poole, June 12, L38-58

1 Darren Sumner	2 0 0 0 0 0	2	1
2 David Cheshire	3 2 3 3 1 3	15	
3 †Jamie Luckhurst	1 2 1 T 0	4	
4 Paul Bentley	1 2 0 2 0 1	6	1
5 Rod Hunter	2 1 1 1 3 2	10	1
6 Dave Edwards	1 0 T T	1	
7 Duncan Chapman	E 0 T	0	

13...WIMBLEDON, June 14, W60-35

1 Darren Sumner	1 2 2 R 3	8	2
2 David Cheshire	0 3 2 3 3	11	
3 Rod Hunter	**3 3 3 3 3**	**15**	
4 Paul Bentley	2 2 fx3 1	8	
5 Steve Wilcock	0 1 3 N 2	6	2
6 †Jamie Luckhurst	3 2 N 1 0 2 N	8	3
7 Duncan Chapman	2 0 N N 2	4	2

14...NEWCASTLE, June 21, W55-41

1 †Darren Sumner	3 1 3 3 3	13	
2 David Cheshire	2 0 1 1 3	7	1
3 Rod Hunter	2 3 3 3 2	13	
4 Paul Bentley	2 3 2 1 2	10	1
5 Steve Wilcock	1 1 1 1 1	5	3
6 Mark Crang	2 1 0 0 N	3	2
7 Duncan Chapman	3 0 E 1	4	

15...Glasgow, June 24, L39-57

1 †Darren Sumner	3 0 2 1 0 1	7	1
2 David Cheshire	0 2 1 3 2 fx	8	2
3 Rod Hunter	1 3 1 3 3 2	13	
4 Paul Bentley	3 2 R 1 1 2	9	
5 Steve Wilcock	0 0 0 T 1	1	1
6 Mark Crang	F 0 T T	0	
7 Duncan Chapman	1 0 T	1	

16...IPSWICH, June 28, W53-43

1 †Darren Sumner	2 2 1 3 2	10	1
2 David Cheshire	0 3 3 0 2	8	
3 Rod Hunter	**3 3 3 3 3**	**15**	
4 Paul Bentley	3 3 F 1 E	7	
5 Steve Wilcock	2 1 1 0 1	5	1
6 Mark Crang	3 1 R 0 1 1	6	2
7 Duncan Chapman	2 0 N fn	2	1

17...Peterborough, June 29, L46-50

1 †Darren Sumner	2 0 1 T 3	6	1
2 David Cheshire	3 3 2 3 2 2	15	1
3 Rod Hunter	3 3 1 1 3 3	14	1
4 Paul Bentley	2 1 1 T 0	4	
5 Steve Wilcock	1 0 0 N 0	1	1
6 Duncan Chapman	2 1 2 0 0	5	
7 Martin Jones	1 0 R	1	1

18...Milton Keynes, July 3, W57-39

1 †Darren Sumner	**3 3 3 3 3**	**15**	
2 David Cheshire	0 0 0 1 2	3	
3 Rod Hunter	3 2 3 2 3	13	
4 Paul Bentley	2 3 2 2 2	11	3
5 Steve Wilcock	3 1 0 E 2	6	1
6 Duncan Chapman	3 1 2 1 1 F	8	2
7 Mark Crang	1 0 N	1	

19...STOKE, July 5, W52-44

1 †Darren Sumner	3 1 2 2 1	9	
2 David Cheshire	1 3 F 0 N	4	
3 Rod Hunter	**3 3 3 3 3**	**15**	
4 Paul Bentley	2 3 1 1 3	10	1
5 Steve Wilcock	1 2 3 1 2	9	3
6 Mark Crang	2 0 N X	2	
7 Duncan Chapman	X 0 2 0 1	3	

20...POOLE, July 26, W59-37

1 Darren Sumner	3 3 1 3 3	13	
2 David Cheshire	2 2 1 0 3	8	2
3 Rod Hunter	3 2 2 1 3	11	1
4 Paul Bentley	2 2 1 2 0	7	3
5†Jamie Luckhurst	1 3 2 2 1	9	1
6 Steve Wilcock	2 2 1 1 2	8	5
7 Duncan Chapman	3 0 N	3	

21...Stoke, July 28, W51-45

1 Darren Sumner	2 1 3 3 2	11	
2 David Cheshire	0 3 3 2 2	10	1
3 Rod Hunter	2 3 3 0 2	10	1
4 Paul Bentley	2 0 0 1 0	3	
5 †Jamie Luckhurst	1 2 2 3 3	11	1
6 Steve Wilcock	3 0 2 0 1	6	2
7 Duncan Chapman	0 0 N	0	

22...MILTON KEYNES, August 2, W68-28

1 Darren Sumner	3 3 3 3 2	14	
2 David Cheshire	1 2 3 1 1	8	1
3 Rod Hunter	**3 3 3 3 3**	**15**	
4 Paul Bentley	2 2 X 2 1	7	4
5 †Jamie Luckhurst	**3 3 3 2 2**	**13**	**2**
6 Steve Wilcock	2 2 2 3	9	2
7 Duncan Chapman	1 0 1	2	1

23...Long Eaton, August 8, W56-40

1 Darren Sumner	**3 3 3 3 3**	**15**	
2 David Cheshire	2 1 3 1 3	10	1
3 Rod Hunter	3 3 3 3 2	14	
4 Paul Bentley	2 1 1 1 2	7	3
5 †Jamie Luckhurst	3 0 2 2 0	7	1
6 Steve Wilcock	1 0 1 0	2	
7 Andy Sumner	0 1 F	1	

24...EASTBOURNE, August 9, W61-35

1 Darren Sumner	3 3 3 3 2	14	
2 David Cheshire	0 0 3 2 F	5	1
3 Rod Hunter	**2 3 3 3 3**	**14**	**1**
4 Paul Bentley	3 2 1 2 1	9	2
5 †Jamie Luckhurst	0 1 3 2 1	7	2
6 Steve Wilcock	3 3 2 2	10	1
7 Andy Sumner	2 fxF	2	1

25...PETERBOROUGH, August 16, W70-26

1 Darren Sumner	**3 3 2 3 3**	**14**	**1**
2 David Cheshire	1 1 3 3 3	11	
3 Rod Hunter	**3 3 3 3 3**	**15**	
4 Paul Bentley	2 3 3 2 1	11	2
5 †Jamie Luckhurst	3 2 1 1 1	8	1
6 Steve Wilcock	**3 2 2 2 2**	**11**	**4**
7 Andy Sumner	F F N	0	

26...LONG EATON, August 30, W62-34

1 Darren Sumner	**3 3 3 3 3**	**15**	
2 David Cheshire	2 0 1 2 3	8	2
3 Rod Hunter	2 3 3 2 3	13	1
4 Steve Wilcock	**2 2 3 2 2**	**11**	**4**
5 †Jamie Luckhurst	**3 3 2 3 2**	**13**	**2**
6 Martin Jones	fx 0 0 N	0	
7 Dave Edwards	1 0 1 0	2	

27...Newcastle, September 2, L47-48

1 Darren Sumner	3 0 1 0 2	6	1
2 David Cheshire	0 1 2 2 2	7	1
3 Rod Hunter	fx3 2 3 1	9	1
4 Paul Bentley	2 2 1 1 1	7	2
5 †Jamie Luckhurst	1 fx2 E 2	5	1
6 Steve Wilcock	3 1 1 1 2 3	11	3
7 Dave Edwards	0 2 N	2	

28...BERWICK, September 13, W71-25

1 Darren Sumner	2 1 2 3 1	9	3
2 David Cheshire	3 2 3 3 3	14	
3 Rod Hunter	**3 3 3 3 3**	**15**	
4 Paul Bentley	3 3 1 2 3	12	1
5 †Jamie Luckhurst	**2 2 3 2 2**	**11**	**4**
6 Steve Wilcock	2 2 2 2	8	3
7 Dave Edwards	1 R 1	2	1

29...Edinburgh, September 16, W51-45

1 Darren Sumner	2 3 3 3 F	11	
2 David Cheshire	F 1 0 2 3	6	1
3 Rod Hunter	3 2 3 0 3	11	
4 Paul Bentley	2 1 0 2 1	6	2
5 †Jamie Luckhurst	3 3 2 2 0	10	
6 Steve Wilcock	2 1 0 1	4	1
7 Dave Edwards	1 1 1	3	1

30...HACKNEY, September 27, W58-38

1 Darren Sumner	3 2 1 1 0	7	1
2 David Cheshire	2 1 1 3 2	9	3
3 Rod Hunter	3 3 3 3 2	14	
4 Paul Bentley	2 2 1 2 2	9	2
5 †Jamie Luckhurst	1 3 2 2 1	9	3
6 Steve Wilcock	3 2 E 2 1	8	2
7 Dave Edwards	1 0 N 1	2	

31...Hackney, September 28, W53-43

1 Darren Sumner	3 1 2 2 2	10	1
2 David Cheshire	0 2 1 N 2	5	1
3 Rod Hunter	3 3 3 0 3	12	
4 Paul Bentley	1 1 0 1 1	4	3
5 †Jamie Luckhurst	3 2 3 2 2	12	1
6 Steve Wilcock	3 0 1 1 3	8	1
7 Dave Edwards	1 1 0	2	

32...Wimbledon, October 3, D48-48

1 Darren Sumner	1 1 2 1 0	5	1
2 David Cheshire	2 3 1 0 0	6	
3 Rod Hunter	2 2 1 0 N	5	
4 Paul Bentley	1 3 2 3 1	10	1
5 †Jamie Luckhurst	3 2 3 3 fx	11	1
6 Steve Wilcock	2 0 0 2 3	7	1
7 Dave Edwards	3 1 0	4	1

1990 ROSTER

BENTLEY, Paul
B 18.1.1968, Newcastle-upon-Tyne, Tyne & Wear.

CHAPMAN, Duncan
B 16.11.1971, Scarborough, North Yorkshire.

CHESHIRE, David
B 17.3.1966, Perth, Australia. *Signed from National League offices.*

CRANG, Mark
B 11.1.1966, Darlington, Co. Durham.
Signed on loan from Belle Vue.

EDWARDS, David
B 2.7.1968, Cessnock, Australia.

HUNTER, Roderick Norman (Rod)
B 25.4.1956, Melbourne, Australia.
On loan from Bradford.

JONES, Martin
B 3.5.1974, Bradford, West Yorkshire. *Local junior.*

LUCKHURST, Jamie Reginald
B 26.1.1965, Ashford, Kent.

SCHOFIELD, Max
B 10.3.1970, Leeds, West Yorkshire.

SUMNER, Andrew
B 31.7.1970, Stockport, Greater Manchester.

SUMNER, Darren Keith (Daz)
B 14.3.1968, Stockport, Greater Manchester.

WILCOCK, Stephen Byron (Steve)
B 24.1.1954, Dewsbury, West Yorkshire.

PAUL SMITH - See Newcastle.

It's a hard day's Knight for Terry

Track Data

Promoters: Terry Cheney.
Address: Elfield Park Stadium, Elfield Park, Milton Keynes, Buckinghamshire.
Telephone: 0908-270411.
Information Line: 0898 31 21 45.
Track Length: 265 metres.
Track Record: 55.4 secs, Darren Sumner (Middlesbrough), July 3, 1990, Heat 1, Milton Keynes v Middlesbrough (National League).

NO-ONE has fought longer or harder to keep speedway alive than Terry Cheney. But 1990 ended as it had begun – with Milton Keynes firmly anchored as the sport's wooden spoonists and the financial future of the track once again in serious doubt.

Somehow Cheney and his band of enthusiastic volunteers had managed to complete another season at Elfield Park and just about the only direction in which you couldn't see improvement was in the team's overall results.

Certainly the Stadium itself was far more conducive to attracting supporters by the end of October than it had been when the promotion were forced to cancel their planned opening meeting because they had still not complied with all the Speedway Control Board regulations governing track requirements.

Almost anyone who attended a meeting at Elfield Park in 1990 came away suitably impressed with the strides that had been taken as the management tried to turn it from a field into a pukka Stadium fit for professional sport. Sadly, though, the effort put into actually keeping the Stadium open seemed to detract from the equally important job of presenting professional speedway on track.

There is no doubt that Terry Cheney let himself down in that direction as he was called in front of the National League Management Committee yet again to explain some of his actions during the year and he also had an appearance before the Speedway Control Board after unwisely allowing one of his programme contributors to get too carried away with his comments over the Michael Lee affair.

Cheney was heavily fined for that indiscretion and only narrowly escaped the fate of his then partner Chris Rance who had his SCB promoting licence suspended!

There was also a crying need for the Knights to engage someone who could actually save them spending unnecessary money which went on a team rebuilding exercise which left them where they had been the previous year – stuck firmly at the foot of the National League.

In 1989, in their first season at their new home, Milton Keynes finished bottom of the table with only seven wins and two draws from a total of 34 League fixtures. In 1990 they had an even less impressive record, winning only five times in 32 matches and ending up with four points fewer than the previous season! That League position made a mockery of all Cheney's brave winter words when he promised fans something more than a struggle to stay open.

He unloaded unwisely and paid the penalty. Tony Primmer, one of the most exciting Aussie newcomers of '89, was allowed to move to Eastbourne and no amount of money could compensate for his rich promise. It is easy to say that Primmer demanded a move but there had to be something amiss for a rider of such obvious talent to be unhappy enough to be on his bike.

Peter Glanz was a shrewd signing, particularly when he had sorted out his early season problems; but Kevin Jolly was obviously an expensive capture who is on the downward spiral of his career rather than on the way up. That, in many senses, was the big problem at Elfield Park. Too many of the riders wearing Milton Keynes' colours were looking towards the end rather than the peak of their careers. Possibly that is where Cheney's own inexperience and naivete led him down the wrong track. A wiser sage in the ways and wiles of the sport might have been worth his weight in points and gold!

Thierry Hilaire amused and entertained but did very little by way of scoring points; Mark Lyndon decided he wanted to go mid-season; and he was later followed out by the promising David Clarke. Andy Hines, always a trier, took a premature retirement and was subsequently replaced by yet another rider who had seen perkier days in Rob Woffinden. At least there were some comforting signs that Cheney was beginning to learn his lesson. Mark Blackbird, on loan from Long Eaton, was a revelation given regular race activity; and Jon Cooper impressed from his late August debut but, by then, it was far too late to salvage anything, other than survival, from the season.

Roll of Honour

Seasons in National League: 13 (1978-1988 [Groveway], 1989-1990 [Elfield Park]).
National League Record: Third (1), 1987.
National League Cup Record: Quarter-finalists, 1979.
National League Team Championship: Third (2), 1983, 1984. Qualified (2), 1983, 1984.
Appearances: Keith White, 190 (1982-1987).
Points: Keith White, 1807 (1982-1987).
World Finalists: None.
NLRC Finalists: Andy Grahame (1979), Bob Humphreys (1981), Keith White (1982-83-84), Nigel De'ath (1985), Trevor Banks (1987), Troy Butler (1988).

Star of 90

PETER GLANZ

Milton Keynes

MILTON KEYNES

01...Hackney, April 6, L29-67

1 §Kevin Jolly	2 0 3 R N N	5	
2 Trevor Banks	0 1 1 2 0	4	
3 §Peter Glanz	N 1 0 0 1	2	1
4 †Andy Hines	0 0 T 1 1	2	1
5 David Clarke	1 2 0 1 0	4	
6 Mark Lyndon	2 2 2 2 1 1	10	
7 §Thierry Hilaire	0 0 N 0 2	2	

02...IPSWICH, April 17, L44-49

1 Kevin Jolly	2 3 F 3 0	8	
2 David Clarke	1 2 2 1 1	7	4
3 †Andy Hines	2 1 2 0 3	8	
4 Trevor Banks	3 1 3 0 2	9	1
5 Peter Glanz	0 2 0 1 1	4	
6 Mark Lyndon	3 0 0 N	3	
7 Thierry Hilaire	R 3 R 2	5	

03...EDINBURGH, April 24, L46-50

1 Kevin Jolly	1 3 2 2 F	8	2
2 David Clarke	2 2 1 1 1	7	2
3 †Andy Hines	1 3 1 1 2	8	1
4 Trevor Banks	3 2 3 3 1	12	
5 Peter Glanz	2 0 2 2 0	6	2
6 Mark Lyndon	1 E N N	1	1
7 Thierry Hilaire	2 0 2 0 0 0	4	1

04...NEWCASTLE, May 1, W49-46

1 Trevor Banks	2 2 2 3 0	9	2
2 Peter Glanz	1 3 3 3 R	10	1
3 Kevin Jolly	2 3 2 1 3	11	
4 †Andy Hines	0 1 2 1 1	5	2
5 David Clarke	1 2 3 0 2	8	1
6 Mark Lyndon	N 1 N N	1	1
7 Thierry Hilaire	3 0 2 fxR	5	1

05...Poole, May 8, L40-56

1 Kevin Jolly	3 1 2 1 1 2	10	2
2 David Clarke	0 0 T T 2 2	4	1
3 †Andy Hines	1 0 T T T	1	1
4 Trevor Banks	2 2 0 1 0 0	5	
5 Peter Glanz	1 0 3 0 0	4	1
6 Mark Lyndon	2 2 1 2 3	10	
7 Thierry Hilaire	0 2 3 1	6	

06...Stoke, May 12, L37-55

1 Trevor Banks	2 2 2 1 1 1	9	3
2 Peter Glanz	1 1 3 2 2 3	12	2
3 Kevin Jolly	2 fxT T T	2	
4 †Andy Hines	1 1 0 2 1 0	5	1
5 David Clarke	0 R 0 1 2 2	5	
6 Mark Lyndon	3 0 fxT 0 1	4	
7 Thierry Hilaire	R N T	0	

07...Edinburgh, May 13, L30-66

1 Trevor Banks	2 2 2 2 0 1 2	11	
2 Peter Glanz	1 0 0 2 2 3 1	9	1
3 Kevin Jolly	*rider replacement*		
4 †Andy Hines	0 0 0 T N	0	
5 David Clarke	2 1 1 1 2 1 0	8	1
6 Mark Lyndon	1 0 0 1	2	
7 §§Kieran McCullagh	0 0 T 0 0	0	
8 Muir Templeton	*did not ride*		

08...WIMBLEDON, May 15, L42-53

1 Trevor Banks	2 1 1 0 0	4	
2 Peter Glanz	1 3 3 0 3	10	1
3 Kevin Jolly	2 0 1 2 2	7	1
4 †Andy Hines	2 1 2 2 1	8	2
5 David Clarke	0 2 3 0 3	8	
6 Mark Lyndon	3 0 1 1	5	
7 Rob Fortune	R fx0	0	

09...Wimbledon, May 16, L33-62

1 Trevor Banks	3 1 1 1 0 0	6	
2 Peter Glanz	R fx0 R T	0	
3 Kevin Jolly	2 3 1 3 0 3	12	
4 †Andy Hines	2 2 0 1 1	6	
5 David Clarke	0 1 1 2 2 0	6	1
6 Mark Lyndon	2 0 T 1	3	1
7 Rob Fortune	0 0 T	0	

10...STOKE, May 22, L37-59

1 Peter Glanz	fxT T T N	0	
2 Trevor Banks	fnT T T N	0	
3 †Kevin Jolly	2 1 3 1 1 3	11	
4 Andy Hines	1 1 0 1 0 1	4	1
5 David Clarke	0 3 1 2 0 2	8	1
6 Mark Lyndon	1 2 N 0 2 2 1	8	1
7 §Mark Blackbird	1 0 3 0 2 0 0	6	1

11...Ipswich, May 24, L31-65

1 Peter Glanz	*rider replacement*		
2 Mark Lyndon	1 1 1 0 2	5	
3 †Kevin Jolly	3 2 2 1 2 1 0	11	
4 Andy Hines	1 0 2 3 1 1	8	
5 David Clarke	F 1 R R 1	2	1
6 Keiran McCullagh	0 0 T T	0	
7 Mark Blackbird	2 0 3 0 0	5	
8 §§Peter Byrne	0 0	0	

12...HACKNEY, June 12, L45-51

1 Trevor Banks	*rider replacement*		
2 Peter Glanz	2 1 3 1 3 1 R	11	1
3 †Kevin Jolly	1 2 2 R 0 T N	5	1
4 Andy Hines	1 1 1 0 2	5	2
5 David Clarke	2 0 2 2 2	8	
6 Mark Lyndon	3 1 2 R 3 1	10	2
7 Mark Blackbird	2 1 2 1	6	2
8 Kieran McCullagh	*did not ride*		

13...Peterborough, June 15, L37-59

1 Peter Glanz	1 0 3 3 2	9	
2 David Clarke	0 1 2 1 3	7	
3 †Kevin Jolly	1 2 1 1 1	6	2
4 Andy Hines	1 1 0 T N	2	1
5 Mark Lyndon	0 2 2 2 2	8	
6 Mark Blackbird	0 0 0 N	0	
7 Thierry Hilaire	1 3 1 Xfx X	5	1

14...Arena Essex, June 16, W49-47

1 Mark Lyndon	0 0 1 2 0	3	1
2 Peter Glanz	2 3 2 3 3	13	1
3 Kevin Jolly	2 2 1 2 2	9	2
4 †Andy Hines	1 3 2 3 1	10	
5 David Clarke	F 1 1 fxN	2	1
6 Kieran McCullagh	F F N N	0	
7 Mark Blackbird	2 1 3 2 1 3	12	1

15...BERWICK, June 19, L46-49

1 Peter Glanz	3 1 2 2 0	8	
2 David Clarke	0 3 3 1 3	10	1
3 †Kevin Jolly	2 1 3 1 2	9	3
4 Andy Hines	1 2 3 1 1	8	1
5 Mark Lyndon	0 0 N N N	0	
6 Mark Blackbird	3 3 2 R R fx	8	
7 Thierry Hilaire	fxfxfx3	3	

16...EASTBOURNE, June 26, L41-55

1 Peter Glanz	3 R 1 3 3 0	10	1
2 Trevor Banks	*rider replacement*		
3 †Kevin Jolly	1 1 1 2 0 3	8	2
4 Andy Hines	1 0 3 1 0 2	7	1
5 David Clarke	0 2 1 0 T 0	3	
6 Mark Blackbird	3 3 2 2 1	11	
7 Thierry Hilaire	1 X 0	1	
8 Kieran McCullagh	1	1	

17...MIDDLESBROUGH, July 3, L39-57

1 Trevor Banks	1 0 1 T 0	2	1
2 Peter Glanz	2 3 3 3 3 3	17	
3 †Kevin Jolly	2 2 1 2 1 1	9	
4 Andy Hines	fx2 2 0 N	4	
5 David Clarke	1 1 R R 0	2	1
6 Mark Blackbird	2 1 0 1 1	5	1
7 Thierry Hilaire	0 T 0	0	

18...Rye House, July 15, L45-51

1 Trevor Banks	2 2 2 0 2 1	9	1
2 Peter Glanz	0 1 1 2 3	7	2
3 †Kevin Jolly	R 2 2 2 0	6	1
4 Andy Hines	3 2 2 1 1 2	11	2
5 David Clarke	fx0 N T N	0	
6 Mark Blackbird	3 0 3 1 2 1	10	2
7 Thierry Hilaire	1 1 T	2	

19...GLASGOW, July 24, L40-56

1 Peter Glanz	3 3 X 3 fxF N	9	
2 Andy Hines	0 1 N 1 T	2	
3 †Kevin Jolly	2 2 3 3 2 3 1	16	
4 Trevor Banks	*rider replacement*		
5 David Clarke	2 1 0 2 0 0	5	2
6 Mark Blackbird	1 0 0 3 0 0	4	
7 Thierry Hilaire	3 R N 1	4	
8 Peter Byrne	0	0	

20...PETERBOROUGH, July 31, W51-45

1 Peter Glanz	2 3 3 2 3 3	16	1
2 David Clarke	1 2 2 3 3	11	3
3 †Kevin Jolly	N 2 3 3 3	11	
4 Andy Hines	0 3 1 0 0	4	1
5 Mark Blackbird	2 0 2 1 0	5	
6 Paul Atkins	2 1 F 1	4	
7 Thierry Hilaire	0 N T 0	0	

21...Glasgow, August 1, L32-63

1 Peter Glanz	2 fx3 3 2 3	13	
2 Mark Blackbird	0 1 0 1 R 1	3	
3 †Kevin Jolly	1 1 1 R N	3	1
4 Trevor Banks	*rider replacement*		
5 Andy Hines	0 0 1 N N	1	
6 David Clarke	3 0 2 2 2 0	9	
7 Thierry Hilaire	1 0 T F	1	
8 Paul Atkins	1 1 0 0	2	

22...Middlesbrough, August 2, L28-68

1 Peter Glanz	R R 0 0 N	0	
2 Mark Blackbird	2 1 1 2 2 1 R	9	1
3 †Kevin Jolly	1 1 1 T T	3	1
4 Trevor Banks	*rider replacement*		
5 Andy Hines	0 1 0 N N	1	
6 David Clarke	3 0 2 2 1 2 3	13	
7 Thierry Hilaire	0 0 T fx1 fx	1	
8 Paul Atkins	1 0 0	1	

23...ARENA ESSEX, August 7, W53-42

1 Peter Glanz	**3 3 2 3 3 3 3**	**20**	**1**
2 Trevor Banks	*rider replacement*		
3 †Kevin Jolly	0 3 2 R 2 3	10	2
4 Andy Hines	1 1 0 2 1	5	3
5 Mark Blackbird	2 2 2 3 1	10	
6 David Clarke	2 1 1 0 0	4	
7 Thierry Hilaire	fx3 1	4	
8 Paul Atkins	0	0	

24...LONG EATON, August 14, W59-37

1 Peter Glanz	3 fx3 3 3 1	13	
2 Trevor Banks	*rider replacement*		
3 †Kevin Jolly	0 2 1 3 2 2	10	3
4 Andy Hines	2 1 0 N N	3	
5 Mark Blackbird	R X 3 3 3 3	12	
6 Thierry Hilaire	3 1 3 2 3	12	1
7 David Clarke	F 2 2 1 3	8	2
8 Paul Atkins	1	1	

25...RYE HOUSE, August 28, W48-47

1 Peter Glanz	1 0 R 2 2 0	5	
2 Andy Hines	R 1 T 0 N	1	
3 Trevor Banks	*rider replacement*		
4 †Kevin Jolly	2 R 3 1 3 2	11	1
5 Mark Blackbird	1 3 3 2 0 2 2	13	3
6 §Rob Woffinden	3 2 0 3 3 N	11	
7 Thierry Hilaire	1 2 2 2 F	7	2
8 Jon Cooper	E N	0	

26...Long Eaton, August 29, L40-56

1 Peter Glanz	*rider replacement*		
2 Andy Hines	0 0 T 2 0	2	1
3 Rob Woffinden	0 2 1 3 2 0	8	1
4 †Kevin Jolly	1 1 1 1 1 2	7	3
5 Mark Blackbird	F 2 2 3 2 1 1	11	
6 Jon Cooper	2 1 2 3 3	11	1
7 Thierry Hilaire	F 1 fx	1	
8 Peter Byrne	0	0	

27...Exeter, September 3, L32-64

1 Peter Glanz	1 1 1 1 N	4	3
2 Thierry Hilaire	2 F 1 2 3 fx	8	1
3 †Kevin Jolly	1 2 2 R 2 T	7	
4 Mark Blackbird	0 0 0 2 2	4	
5 Rob Woffinden	2 1 2 2 R 1	8	
6 Jon Cooper	0 0 T F	0	
7 Peter Byrne	1 0 0	1	

28...EXETER, September 4, L40-56

1 Peter Glanz	2 2 3 R 0 N	7	
2 Thierry Hilaire	0 1 T N 1 1	3	3
3 Rob Woffinden	1 2 fxT N	3	1
4 †Kevin Jolly	1 2 2 1 1 1	8	2
5 Mark Blackbird	R 1 2 2 2	7	1
6 Jon Cooper	3 2 1 2 2 1	11	2
7 Peter Byrne	0 T 1 0	1	

29...Berwick, September 8, L27-68

1 Peter Glanz	2 1 1 1 R 1 1	7	1
2 Rob Woffinden	0 0 T 1 2	3	
3 Trevor Banks	*rider replacement*		
4 †Kevin Jolly	0 2 2 1 T N	5	
5 Mark Blackbird	2 2 0 0 1 1	6	
6 Jon Cooper	2 1 0 0 1 0	4	2
7 Thierry Hilaire	fx2 E fx	2	
8 §Michael Howe	0 0	0	

30...Newcastle, September 9, L33-63

1 Peter Glanz	2 2 3 2 3 2 1	15	
2 Rob Woffinden	0 1 T 1 1	3	
3 Trevor Banks	*rider replacement*		
4 †Kevin Jolly	0 1 0 N T	1	1
5 Mark Blackbird	1 1 2 1 R 1	6	1
6 Jon Cooper	1 0 1 1 3 2	8	
7 Thierry Hilaire	R 0 0 R	0	
8 Michael Howe	0 0	0	

31...POOLE, September 23, L44-52

1 Peter Glanz	3 2 3 R 3 0	11	
2 Thierry Hilaire	F fxN N T	0	
3 Mark Blackbird	2 2 1 1 2	8	
4 †Kevin Jolly	3 2 3 2 3 2	15	
5 Rob Woffinden	R N R T T	0	
6 Jon Cooper	3 1 1 1 1 1 1	9	4
7 Michael Howe	1 0 0 0	1	

32...Eastbourne, September 30, L39-56

1 Peter Glanz	2 2 1 2 2 1	10	2
2 Thierry Hilaire	X fxT 0 2	2	
3 Mark Blackbird	1 3 R N 1 3	8	
4 †Kevin Jolly	3 3 2 1 3 2	14	
5 Rob Woffinden	0 1 0 0 N	1	
6 Jon Cooper	3 R T R 1	4	1
7 Michael Howe	X R T 0	0	

1990 ROSTER

ALLAN, Glenn Stuart
B 20.7.1966, Hull, Humberside.
ATKINS, Paul George
B 28.8.1966, Chalfont St. Giles, Bucks.
BANKS, Trevor Charles
B 4.10.1955, Folkestone, Kent.
BLACKBIRD, Mark David
B 17.12.1970, Peterborough, Cambs. *On loan from Long Eaton.*
BYRNE, Peter John
B 5.5.1962, Toowoomba, Australia. *First season Australian.*
COOPER, Jonathon Paul (Jon)
B 23.7.1969, Ipswich, Suffolk. *On loan from Ipswich.*
FORTUNE, Robert James (Rob)
B 24.3.1963, Kidderminster, Hereford & Worcester.
GLANZ, Peter Lybaek
B 3.5.1962, Fredericia, Denmark. *On loan from Reading.*
HILAIRE, Thierry
B 1.6.1963, Suresnes, France. *Signed from Long Eaton.*
HINES, Anthony (Andy)
B 23.3.1957, Ipswich, Suffolk.
HOWE, Michael David
B 5.5.1973, Nottingham, Notts. *Signed from Long Eaton.*
JOLLY, Kevin Guy
B 29.1.1958, Eye, Suffolk.
McCULLAGH, Kieran
B 14.10.1972, Abingdon, Oxon. *On loan from Oxford.*
WILSON, Michael Leonard
B 11.4.1967, Hastings, New Zealand.
WOFFINDEN, Robert (Rob)
B 27.3.1962, Scunthorpe, Humberside. *On loan from Stoke.*
DAVID CLARKE - See Stoke.
MARK LYNDON - See Peterborough.
MUIR TEMPLETON - See Edinburgh.

Diamonds dig out a gem – again

Track Data

Promoter: Barry Wallace.
Address: Brough Park Stadium, The Fossway, Byker, Newcastle-upon-Tyne, NE6 2XJ.
Telephone: 091-276-0262.
Information Line: 0898 31 21 46.
Track Length: 330 metres.
Track Record: 63.5 secs, Chris Louis (Ipswich), September 23, 1990, Heat 1, Newcastle v Ipswich (National League); Mark Courtney (Berwick), October 7, 1990, Heat 1, Newcastle v Berwick (Autumn Trophy).

THERE must be something rejuvenating about the air that sweeps into Byker from the River Tyne. Whatever it is, it certainly works!

Newcastle had no right to expect Rod Hunter to make such a dramatically successful comeback in 1989 when they enticed him out of retirement.

And, having struck so lucky once, no-one in their right mind could have believed it would happen a second time when they took a gamble on re-signing David Bargh even though the New Zealander's weight had ballooned during a two-year absence from racing when he worked as a digger driver. When Bargh first announced that he was considering a comeback the noise from promoters clamouring for his signature was deafeningly silent. Coventry, who owned his contract, made it plain that he had no place in their 1990 plans and, other than Newcastle, the only other club to make any firm approach was Milton Keynes.

They soon dropped out of the race. And so would many another club when it became apparent that he wasn't going to be allowed to step down into the National League without a fight.

It was ruled that because his last Sunbrite League average (in 1987 remember) had been 7.46 he couldn't ply his trade with the Debmat Diamonds in the NL even though there was no Sunbrite League club particularly anxious to offer him a season's employment.

At one stage the whole affair got perilously close to the High Court with Bargh adamant that he would seek an injunction in his fight to ride again for his old club. Newcastle stuck with him even though there were times when many outside Brough Park questioned their loyalty to a rider who hadn't turned a wheel in anger for two and a half years.

Finally, as the season approached, Bargh was given permission to rejoin the club he had first joined as a 16-year-old in 1978, and even though he was handicapped by having only one engine for much of the season his form was an absolute revelation.

Hunter's comeback 12 months earlier had been quite remarkable. Bargh's was of epic proportions. The facts and figures support that. Rocket Rod had scored 427 points in 33 League matches for a club number one ranking of 9.283. Battler Bargh scored fewer points (363) in fewer matches (28) but took over at the top of the club charts with a 9.745 average. For the second year in a row the Diamonds had gambled and won the jackpot!

Bargh took only a match or two to get back into his stride and might have topped even his own impressive performances had he not been forced to fly home to New Zealand before the season had hardly got under way to see his seriously ill father. He missed three matches, returned on the morning of a meeting at Ipswich to score only two points but quickly slotted back into the groove with the first of five full maximums.

If only Newcastle had been able to afford to have kept both Bargh and Hunter then they might well have won their fourth National League championship – or at least mounted a genuine title challenge that would have inspired the Tynesiders to offer far more support than they did through the gate. Crowds, unfortunately, remained low enough to prompt new stadium owner Kevin Wilde – one of the promoting consortium – to warn of the consequences and for ex-promoter Richard Bailey to offer to take over the struggling club.

Bargh was the shining beacon but there were other bright spots. Simon Green began like a runaway train but got derailed; Peter Carr was still a potent scorer; Mark Thorpe flirted with both stardom and a lack of interest; Paul Smith had an up (11 points at both Long Eaton AND Hackney) and down (0 at home to Peterborough and at Berwick five nights later) start to his National League career and new signing Martin Dixon's season ended in September through injury.

Roll of Honour

Seasons in National League: 13 (1975-1983; 1986-1987; 1989-1990).
National League Record: Champions (3), 1976, 1982, 1983. Runners-up (3), 1975, 1978, 1980. Third (1), 1981.
National League Cup Record: Winners (2), 1976, 1982.
National League Team Championship: Winners (3), 1976, 1982, 1983. Runners-up (1), 1981. Qualified (7), 1976, 1977, 1978, 1979, 1981, 1982, 1983.
Appearances: Rod Hunter, 273 (1978-1983, 1989).
Points: Tom Owen, 2950 (1975-1982, 1987).
World Finalists: Brian Brett (1965), Ivan Mauger (1966-67-68), Anders Michanek (1970).
NLRC Finalists: Joe Owen (1975-76, 1982-83), Tom Owen (1977-78), Rod Hunter (1980, 1989), David Bargh (1981, 1990), David Blackburn (1987).
Other Honours: Provincial League Champions, 1964. English Cup Winners, 1939. National League Supernational Winners, 1982, 1983.

Star of 90

SIMON GREEN

Newcastle

NEWCASTLE

01...STOKE, April 8, W50-46

1 Peter Carr	*rider replacement*		
2 Simon Green	3 1 3 2 2 3	14	1
3 §†Martin Dixon	1 2 2 1 N 1	7	1
4 Mark Thorpe	0 1 1 3 1 1	7	2
5 David Bargh	3 3 3 3 0 2 2	16	
6 Gordon Whitaker	2 0 fxN	2	
7 §John Wainwright	1 0 0 1 2	4	2
8 David Nagel	*did not ride*		

02...LONG EATON, April 15, W50-46

1 †Peter Carr	3 3 0 3 N	9	
2 Simon Green	0 1 2 1 2	6	
3 Martin Dixon	2 3 3 2 2	12	2
4 Mark Thorpe	1 1 2 0 0	4	
5 David Bargh	3 3 0 3 3	12	
6 §Spencer Timmo	1 N 0 N 1	2	1
7 John Wainwright	2 1 0 1 1	5	2

03...WIMBLEDON, April 22, L39-57

1 †Peter Carr	0 2 2 R 3 3	10	
2 §Paul Smith	1 1 0 T 3 0	5	1
3 Simon Green	3 2 1 0 1 3	10	
4 Mark Thorpe	2 1 2 2 0 0	7	
5 Martin Dixon	0 0 1 N T	1	1
6 Spencer Timmo	2 1 N 0	3	1
7 John Wainwright	3 0 T T fx	3	

04...Milton Keynes, May 1, L46-49

1 †Peter Carr	**3 3 3 3 2 3**	**17**	**1**
2 Spencer Timmo	0 0 0 T T	0	
3 Martin Dixon	3 fx1 2 3 1	10	
4 Simon Green	3 2 1 1 2 2	11	2
5 Paul Smith	2 1 0 0 0	3	2
6 §§Jack Stevens	1 1 0 T	2	1
7 John Wainwright	2 0 1	3	

05...Long Eaton, May 2, L42-54

1 †Peter Carr	3 R 3 2 1 N	9	1
2 Spencer Timmo	fx1 T T 1	2	
3 Martin Dixon	3 fx2 2 0 3	10	
4 Simon Green	1 1 3 1 2 2	10	2
5 Mark Thorpe	0 T 0 N N	0	
6 Paul Smith	3 1 2 0 2 3 0	11	1
7 John Wainwright	0 X T 0	0	

06...Ipswich, May 10, L36-60

1 †Peter Carr	2 1 3 3 1 R	10	
2 Spencer Timmo	F 0 T T T	0	
3 Martin Dixon	3 2 1 1 3 0	10	
4 Simon Green	2 0 1 3 1 1	8	
5 David Bargh	fx2 0 fxN	2	
6 Paul Smith	2 0 2 0 0 2	6	1
7 John Wainwright	0 R T	0	

07...Hackney, May 11, L35-60

1 †Peter Carr	2 3 2 2 1 T	10	1
2 Spencer Timmo	F T E F 2 0	2	
3 Martin Dixon	R 2 0 1 0	3	
4 Simon Green	2 fx1 fxN T	3	1
5 David Bargh	0 2 3 fxN	5	
6 Paul Smith	3 1 2 2 0 1 2	11	1
7 John Wainwright	0 1 T R	1	

08...BERWICK, May 13, W50-46

1 †Peter Carr	3 3 1 3 2	12	1
2 Simon Green	1 2 fx2 3	8	1
3 David Bargh	**3 3 3 3 3**	**15**	
4 Mark Thorpe	1 0 0 0 0	1	1
5 Martin Dixon	2 1 2 1 0	6	
6 Paul Smith	2 N 1 3 0 1	7	
7 Steve Wicks	1 X N N	1	1

09...Edinburgh, May 25, L40-56

1 †Peter Carr	1 0 2 0 3 N	6	1
2 Simon Green	2 1 3 1 0 fx	7	
3 David Bargh	3 2 3 2 3 2	15	
4 Mark Thorpe	2 0 0 T 1	3	1
5 Martin Dixon	3 2 1 1 1 0	8	1
6 Paul Smith	1 0 T T 0	1	
7 John Wainwright	F fxT	0	

10...GLASGOW, June 11, L45-50

1 †Peter Carr	R 3 2 3 R 3	11	
2 Simon Green	1 0 T 1 2	4	1
3 David Bargh	N N 0 1 3 3	7	1
4 Paul Smith	0 0 0 N 1	1	
5 Martin Dixon	3 2 3 2 2 1	13	
6 Spencer Timmo	fx0 0 T	0	
7 Mark Thorpe	3 3 1 T 1 T 1	9	1

11...RYE HOUSE, June 18, W51-44

1 †Peter Carr	3 3 2 2 3	13	
2 Simon Green	fxR 2 0 F	2	
3 David Bargh	X 3 3 3 3	12	
4 Paul Smith	1 0 N 1 0	2	2
5 Martin Dixon	2 3 3 2 2	12	2
6 Spencer Timmo	1 1 N N	2	
7 Mark Thorpe	3 1 X 1 1 2	8	

12...Middlesbrough, June 21, L41-55

1 †Peter Carr	1 2 3 1 2 N	9	1
2 Simon Green	fx0 2 2 2 0	6	1
3 David Bargh	3 3 3 2 F 3	14	
4 Paul Smith	0 1 2 T 0 1	4	1
5 Martin Dixon	3 2 2 fx0 T	7	1
6 Steve Wicks	1 0 T 0 T 0	1	
7 Mark Thorpe	F N T	0	

13...POOLE, July 1, L45-51

1 †Peter Carr	3 0 0 3 R	6	
2 Simon Green	2 2 1 2 1	8	2
3 David Bargh	3 3 2 2 3	13	
4 Paul Smith	0 3 0 0 N	3	
5 Martin Dixon	3 2 2 1 0	8	2
6 John Wainwright	E 1 N N	1	
7 Mark Thorpe	2 1 0 0 2 1	6	

14...Arena Essex, July 7, W49-47

1 †Peter Carr	2 3 3 3 2	13	
2 Simon Green	1 2 1 1 2	7	2
3 David Bargh	**3 3 3 3 3**	**15**	
4 Paul Smith	1 0 0 0 0	1	
5 Martin Dixon	3 3 3 1 0	10	
6 John Wainwright	F R N F N 0	0	
7 Mark Thorpe	2 N F N 1	3	

15...Rye House, July 8, W57-39

1 †Peter Carr	2 3 2 3 2	12	1
2 Simon Green	fx2 1 fxN	3	1
3 David Bargh	R 3 3 3 2	11	
4 Paul Smith	3 1 0 R 3	7	1
5 Martin Dixon	2 2 3 2 fn	9	2
6 John Wainwright	fx0 N 1	1	
7 Mark Thorpe	3 2 3 2 3 1	14	2

16...PETERBOROUGH, July 9, W55-41

1 †Peter Carr	3 3 3 3 1	13	1
2 Simon Green	R 1 1 1 3	6	1
3 David Bargh	2 3 3 3 3	14	
4 Paul Smith	0 0 0 0 N	0	
5 Martin Dixon	3 2 2 2 2	11	2
6 John Wainwright	0 1 N N	1	1
7 Mark Thorpe	2 2 2 0 2 2	10	2

17...Berwick, July 14, L27-68

1 †Peter Carr	1 0 0 1 3 R	5	1
2 Simon Green	0 T 0 T N	0	
3 David Bargh	F 3 3 2 R X	8	
4 Paul Smith	0 0 T 0 N	0	
5 Martin Dixon	2 2 1 2 1 fx	8	
6 §Ian Stead	0 0 T 1	1	
7 Mark Thorpe	1 1 1 1 0 1	5	1

18...EXETER, July 22, W55-41

†Peter Carr	2 3 3 3 3 0	14	
2 Simon Green	0 2 2 2 2 3	11	2
3 David Bargh	*rider replacement*		
4 Paul Smith	0 0 0 N 1	1	
5 Martin Dixon	3 2 3 3 1 1 3	16	2
6 Ian Stead	2 2 N 0 1	5	2
7 Mark Thorpe	3 0 N 2 1 2	8	1
8 David Nagel	*did not ride*		

19...EDINBURGH, August 6, W54-42

1 †Peter Carr	3 2 3 3 3	14	
2 Simon Green	2 1 1 1 2	7	3
3 David Bargh	2 3 3 3 2	13	
4 Mark Thorpe	1 0 1 0 N	2	1
5 Martin Dixon	2 3 3 2 1	11	2
6 Ian Stead	0 0 0 N	0	
7 Paul Smith	2 2 0 1 2	7	2

20...Peterborough, August 10, L45-51

1 †Peter Carr	1 0 R T T 1	2	
2 Simon Green	0 2 X 3 2 3	10	
3 David Bargh	3 3 3 2 2 2	15	1
4 Mark Thorpe	2 1 2 1 N 3	9	1
5 Martin Dixon	1 2 1 1 0 0	5	3
6 Ian Stead	2 0 T T	2	
7 Paul Smith	0 1 1	2	

21...Exeter, August 13, L41-55

1 †Peter Carr	1 2 E 3 2 2	10	
2 Simon Green	0 1 0 1 R 1	3	2
3 David Bargh	3 2 3 3 2 3	16	
4 Mark Thorpe	0 0 T 0 T	0	
5 Martin Dixon	3 2 2 2 1 0	10	2
6 Ian Stead	1 0 T 0 1	2	
7 Paul Smith	0 0 T	0	

22...Poole, August 14, L33-63

1 †Peter Carr	2 1 R 3 T 1	7	
2 Simon Green	0 0 1 1 0 3	5	
3 David Bargh	3 2 3 3 0 2	13	
4 Mark Thorpe	0 0 0 1 N	1	
5 Martin Dixon	1 2 1 1 0	5	
6 Ian Stead	2 0 T 0	2	
7 Paul Smith	0 0 T 0	0	

23...Stoke, August 18, W55-41

1 †Peter Carr	2 fx3 2 R	7	
2 Simon Green	1 1 2 2 1	7	3
3 David Bargh	3 3 3 2 2	13	
4 Mark Thorpe	1 2 2 1 1	7	4
5 Martin Dixon	2 3 3 1 1	10	2
6 Ian Stead	2 0 N N	2	
7 Paul Smith	1 2 3 0 3	9	2

24...Eastbourne, August 26, L46-49

1 †Peter Carr	1 3 3 1 2 2	12	1
2 Simon Green	N N T N N	0	
3 David Bargh	3 2 3 2 3 2	15	2
4 Mark Thorpe	3 1 0 0 1	5	1
5 Martin Dixon	fxfx3 2 3	8	1
6 Ian Stead	fx0 N T 1	1	
7 Paul Smith	0 2 0 0 1 2	5	

25...ARENA ESSEX, August 27, W55-41

1 †Peter Carr	2 3 1 3 R	9	
2 Paul Smith	0 2 2 0 3	7	1
3 David Bargh	**3 3 3 3 3**	**15**	
4 Mark Thorpe	1 1 1 1 2	6	
5 Martin Dixon	3 3 3 1 2	12	1
6 Ian Stead	3 0 1 1 1	6	
7 John Wainwright	0 0 N	0	

26...MIDDLESBROUGH, Sept. 2, W48-47

1 †Peter Carr	2 2 3 1 3	11	
2 Simon Green	1 R 0 fxR	1	1
3 David Bargh	fx3 3 3 3	12	
4 Mark Thorpe	3 3 0 0 0	6	
5 Martin Dixon	fx2 3 2 0	7	2
6 Ian Stead	1 3 1 N	5	1
7 Paul Smith	2 3 0 1	6	

27...MILTON KEYNES, September 9, W63-33

1 †Peter Carr	**3 3 3 2 3**	**14**	**1**
2 Simon Green	1 2 3 2 2	10	2
3 David Bargh	3 3 fx3 3	12	
4 Mark Thorpe	3 2 3 3 2	13	1
5 Martin Dixon	2 fxN N N	2	1
6 Ian Stead	3 1 0 2 0	6	1
7 Paul Smith	2 1 2 1 0	6	1

28...EASTBOURNE, September 17, W51-45

1 †Peter Carr	2 2 1 2 2	9	2
2 Paul Smith	0 T 2 3 0	5	
3 David Bargh	**3 3 3 3 3 3**	**18**	
4 Simon Green	R F 3 3 1	7	1
5 Mark Thorpe	1 1 1 0 2	5	1
6 Ian Stead	2 2 0 2	6	1
7 Spencer Timmo	E 1 0	1	1

29...Glasgow, September 19, L44.5-51.5

1 †Peter Carr	2 2 2 3 2	11	1
2 Paul Smith	0 0 1 T fx	1	1
3 David Bargh	**3 3 3 3 3 3**	**18**	
4 Simon Green	2 1.5 fx1 fx	4.5	
5 Mark Thorpe	1 0 2 0 0	3	1
6 Ian Stead	0 0 N N	0	
7 Spencer Timmo	3 1 2 0 1	7	

30...IPSWICH, September 23, L47-49

1 †Peter Carr	1 2 3 3 3 2	14	1
2 Martin Dixon	*rider replacement*		
3 David Bargh	2 3 3 3 3 3 3	20	
4 Simon Green	1 2 1 1 F 0	5	1
5 Mark Thorpe	0 0 R 0 N	0	
6 Ian Stead	3 2 0 fx0	5	1
7 Paul Smith	2 0 1	3	1
8 Spencer Timmo	0	0	

31...Wimbledon, October 10, L39-57

1 †Peter Carr	1 1 1 1 1 3 3	11	
2 Simon Green	0 0 1 2 T 2 2	7	2
3 David Bargh	3 2 3 2 3 2 3	18	
4 Mark Thorpe	0 0 T T N	0	
5 Martin Dixon	*rider replacement*		
6 Ian Stead	1 0 0 fx	1	
7 Paul Smith	0 2 0 0	2	1
8 Spencer Timmo	0 0	0	

32...HACKNEY, October 15, L44-52

1 †Peter Carr	2 3 2 2 2 3	14	1
2 Simon Green	1 1 3 R 3 3	11	1
3 David Bargh	F 1 N T T	1	1
4 Paul Smith	1 0 0 T 0 0	1	
5 Mark Thorpe	0 2 1 1 2	6	
6 Ian Stead	3 2 2 0 1 1	9	1
7 Spencer Timmo	2 fxT	2	1

1990 ROSTER

BARGH, David Andrew
B 14.3.1962, Martinborough, New Zealand. *Signed from Coventry.*
CARR, Peter
B 22.1.1963, Preston, Lancashire.
DIXON, Martin
B 30.5.1961, Hartlepool, Cleveland.
GREEN, Simon Leslie
B 8.11.1969, Skipton, North Yorks. *Signed from Bradford.*
NAGEL, David Andrew
B 1.3.1973, Hexham, Northumberland. *Local discovery.*
RICHARDSON, Anthony (Tony)
B 20.7.1967, Bishop Auckland, Co. Durham.
SMITH, Paul
B 17.7.1970, York, North Yorkshire. *On loan from Belle Vue.*
STEAD, Ian Maurice
B 25.4.1964, Sheffield, South Yorkshire. *On loan from Stoke.*
STEVENS, Gregory Ronald (Jack)
B 24.9.1957, Newcastle, Australia. *First season Australian.*
TAAFFE, Ray
B 4.12.1966, Sydney, Australia. *Signed from Edinburgh.*
THORPE, Mark Andrew
B 26.3.1969, Christchurch, New Zealand.
TIMMO, Spencer
B 3.1.1966, Oxford, Oxfordshire. *On loan from Oxford.*
WAINWRIGHT, John
B 3.11.1969, Harlow, Essex. *Signed from Rye House.*
WHITAKER, Wayne Gordon
B 12.2.1966, Halifax, West Yorkshire.
WICKS, Steven
B 13.1.1968, Wallsend, Tyne & Wear.

The day the Panthers fell apart

Track Data

Promoters: David Hawkins.
Address: East of England Showground, Alwalton, Peterborough, PE2 0XE.
Telephone: 0733-233481.
Information Line: 0898 31 21 47.
Track Length: 347 metres.
Track Record: 62.4 secs, Mick Poole (Peterborough), October 6, 1989, Heat 1, Peterborough v Ipswich (Challenge); March 30, 1990, Heat 1, Peterborough v Long Eaton (Challenge).

PETERBOROUGH end every season with one of the best home records in the land. Few teams relish going to the East of England Showground where a fast motor and a strong heart are prerequisites for victory.

In the last three seasons you can count on the fingers of your two hands the number of defeats the Skoda Panthers have suffered on their home midden: two in 1988, four in 1989 and three in 1990.

Unfortunately for their faithful fans three of those defeats have, in turn, come in their opening home meeting of the new season and that has brought its own automatic confidence deflator with it!

No wonder promoter David Hawkins pleads: "I just hope the fixture list is more kind to us in the future."

It may be so out of necessity as the two teams who have dented the Panthers' home record before the season has really started have been Poole and Ipswich!

Defeat in the first home match of the season is never the ideal way to launch a fresh summer's challenge but, in Peterborough's case, that was the far from being their most disastrous evening.

No-one at Alwalton needs reminding of Wednesday, May 30th. The time was around 8.20. The place was Long Eaton's Station Road. And the event that changed the pattern of the entire season was heat six of the H.E.A.T. National League Team Championship in which Mick Poole hit the fence while trying to overtake fellow Aussie Rod Hunter.

He was carted off to hospital with a broken thigh and with that one split-second of misjudgement so snapped Peterborough's dream of remaining among the front-runners for the League crown.

They had set an early pace (mainly through getting in seven matches and five wins before the end of April) and actually led the table for a short spell but Poole's absence effectively ended their influence away from home.

In the only three matches they had raced before his accident, Peterborough had won two and the young Aussie had scored 40 points. In the remaining 13, the closest the Panthers ever came to victory was when they scored 45 points at Milton Keynes!

Poole's hospitalisation was followed by skipper Ian Barney's move to Exeter – he had been suffering the taunts of his own supporters and team-mate Craig Hodgson as he went through a dismal spell but ironically won four out of five races in his final team appearance – and a general period of unrest in which no-one could ever be sure of who was going to turn up wearing a Peterborough bib!

Mark Lyndon, an enigmatic New Zealander, arrived from Milton Keynes; former trials international Phil Disney had a brief on loan spell from Sunbrite League Bradford; Wayne Bridgeford made a splendid debut as number eight with two wins out of two; Mark Crang came on loan from Middlesbrough; and local juniors Paul Blackbird, Darren Tupper, Poole's younger brother Jack, Mark Jolly and Rob Fisher were pushed into emergency service without any apparent rhyme or reason to their selection other than the fact they were available at the time.

Bridgeford, at least, was given a reasonable run in the team and did enough to win a contract for 1991 although some of the others could feel a little peeved that they were dismissed so quickly and it was no surprise when Blackbird asked for a move to Milton Keynes after being discarded so prematurely.

Others were unhappy at the track. New signing Frank Andersen found it hard to settle in and had departed the scene before the end of the season even though, ostensibly, it was because he was suffering from a burnt arm.

Craig Hodgson's outspokenness (promoter Hawkins called it an attitude problem!) didn't help engender team spirit and the continual financial question marks over the track's long term future can hardly have contributed towards a happy atmosphere.

Roll of Honour

Seasons in National League: 21 (1970-1990).
National League Record: Third (1), 1972.
National League Cup Record: Runners-up (1), 1972.
National League Team Championship: Winners (4), 1977, 1978, 1988, 1989. Runners-up (1), 1985. Third (1), 1979. Qualified (10), 1976, 1977, 1978, 1979, 1981, 1982, 1985, 1987, 1988, 1989.
Appearances: Ian Barney, 339 (1980-1990).
Points: Ian Barney, 2505 (1980-1990).
World Finalists: None.
NLRC Finalists: Andy Ross (1970), Richard Greer (1971-72-73), Mike Lanham (1974), Brian Clark (1975-76), Dave Gooderham (1978), Nigel Flatman (1979), Andy Hines (1980, 1982), Ian Barney (1984, 1987-88), Kevin Hawkins (1985-86), Mick Poole (1989-90).

Star of 90

FRANK ANDERSEN

Peterborough

PETERBOROUGH

01...IPSWICH, April 6, L41-55

1 Mick Poole	2 2 2 R 3 R	9	1
2 †Ian Barney	0 3 2 0 1	6	
3 §Frank Andersen	3 1 0 1 0	5	1
4 Craig Hodgson	R 1 R 1 1	3	1
5 Scott Norman	2 2 2 2 1	9	
6 Nigel Flatman	3 2 N 1 1 T	7	2
7 Sean Barker	2 0 N N	2	1

02...Rye House, April 8, W49-47

1 Mick Poole	3 3 2 3 1 3	15	2
2 †Ian Barney	1 0 3 1 0	5	
3 Frank Andersen	0 1 1 2 1	5	2
4 Craig Hodgson	3 0 0 2 1	6	
5 Scott Norman	2 1 2 3 3	11	1
6 Nigel Flatman	2 1 N 2 2	7	
7 Sean Barker	0 N 0 T	0	

03...Wimbledon, April 11, W49-46

1 Mick Poole	3 2 3 2 3	13	
2 †Ian Barney	0 1 2 0 2	5	1
3 Frank Andersen	1 3 1 0 3	8	1
4 Craig Hodgson	0 1 0 1 1	3	1
5 Scott Norman	2 3 2 3 2	12	1
6 Nigel Flatman	3 2 N 0 0 1	6	1
7 Sean Barker	2 N 0 N	2	1

04...EASTBOURNE, April 13, W74-22

1 Mick Poole	**2 2 3 3 3**	**13**	**2**
2 Craig Hodgson	**3 3 3 2 3**	**14**	**1**
3 Frank Andersen	**3 3 3 2 3**	**14**	**1**
4 †Ian Barney	0 3 3 2 2	10	2
5 Scott Norman	3 2 2 3 1	11	2
6 Nigel Flatman	**3 2 N 2 2**	**9**	**3**
7 Sean Barker	2 0 N 1	3	1

05...GLASGOW, April 16, W67-29

1 Mick Poole	**3 2 2 3 3**	**13**	**2**
2 Craig Hodgson	0 3 3 3 R	9	
3 Frank Andersen	**2 3 3 2 2**	**12**	**3**
4 †Ian Barney	1 2 1 0 1	5	1
5 Scott Norman	**3 3 3 3 3**	**15**	
6 Nigel Flatman	**3 3 2 3**	**11**	**1**
7 Sean Barker	1 1 0	2	

06...Arena Essex, April 21, L43-52

1 †Mick Poole	2 3 R 1 2	8	2
2 Craig Hodgson	3 1 3 1 2	10	
3 Frank Andersen	fx 2 3 0 1	6	
4 Nigel Flatman	fx 1 1 2 1	5	2
5 Scott Norman	3 3 2 3 F	11	
6 Paul Blackbird	1 0 F 0	1	
7 Sean Barker	0 2 0	2	

07...ARENA ESSEX, April 22, W67-29

1 Mick Poole	**3 2 2 3 3**	**13**	**2**
2 Craig Hodgson	1 3 3 3 3	13	
3 Frank Andersen	2 3 0 2 1	8	2
4 †Ian Barney	2 3 1 2 1	9	2
5 Scott Norman	**3 2 3 3 3**	**14**	**1**
6 Nigel Flatman	2 3 1 2	8	1
7 Sean Barker	0 1 1	2	

08...BERWICK, May 4, W64-32

1 Mick Poole	**3 2 2 3 3**	**13**	**2**
2 Craig Hodgson	1 3 2 3 3	12	
3 Frank Andersen	1 X 3 2 2	8	3
4 †Ian Barney	1 2 2 2 2	9	4
5 Scott Norman	2 3 X 3 3	11	
6 Nigel Flatman	3 2 2 1	8	
7 Sean Barker	2 1 0	3	2

09...WIMBLEDON, May 11, W57-39

1 Mick Poole	F 3 2 3 2	10	
2 Nigel Flatman	2 0 0 0 2	4	1
3 Frank Andersen	2 2 3 1 2	10	2
4 †Ian Barney	1 3 3 1 1	9	2
5 Scott Norman	2 1 1 3 3	10	
6 Craig Hodgson	3 3 R 2 3	11	1
7 Sean Barker	1 2 N	3	

10...HACKNEY, May 28, W61-35

1 Mick Poole	3 3 2 3 2 2 3	18	1
2 Nigel Flatman	0 1 2 0 2	5	3
3 Frank Andersen	1 3 2 3 3 2	14	1
4 †Ian Barney	1 1 3 0 0	5	1
5 Scott Norman	*rider replacement*		
6 Craig Hodgson	3 3 2 2 3 1	14	2
7 Sean Barker	2 3 0	5	1
8 Darren Topper	*did not ride*		

11...Ipswich, June 7, L33-63

1 Frank Andersen	fx 1 1 1 1 2 1	7	1
2 Mick Poole	*rider replacement*		
3 †Craig Hodgson	1 0 2 3 2 2 1	11	
4 Scott Norman	2 2 3 1 R N	8	
5 Nigel Flatman	0 1 0 N N	1	1
6 §Phil Disney	1 1 T F 0	2	2
7 Sean Barker	2 2 R 0 0 0	4	
8 Paul Blackbird	*did not ride*		

12...MILTON KEYNES, June 15, W59-37

1 Frank Andersen	3 3 3 3 1	13	
2 Nigel Flatman	2 1 3 E 2	8	1
3 Craig Hodgson	2 3 2 2 3	12	
4 †Ian Barney	3 3 3 0 3	12	
5 Scott Norman	2 2 2 1 0	7	4
6 Phil Disney	3 fx 0 0 N	3	
7 Sean Barker	2 R 1 N 1	4	2

13...RYE HOUSE, June 22, W57-39

1 Frank Andersen	**3 3 3 3 3**	**15**	
2 Nigel Flatman	2 2 2 1 2	9	3
3 †Craig Hodgson	2 3 3 R 2	10	
4 Scott Norman	2 3 1 F 2	8	1
5 §Mark Lyndon	1 2 N 2 1	6	3
6 Phil Disney	3 N R F N	3	
7 Sean Barker	2 0 3 F N 1	6	2

14...Eastbourne, June 24, L43-53

1 Frank Andersen	2 0 3 0 3 2 R	10	1
2 Mick Poole	*rider replacement*		
3 †Craig Hodgson	3 2 R 3 3 2 3	16	
4 Scott Norman	3 1 2 1 0 1 1	9	
5 Nigel Flatman	fx F R T N	0	
6 Mark Lyndon	3 1 1 N 1 1	7	2
7 Sean Barker	1 N R F	1	
8 John Cook	*did not ride*		

15...MIDDLESBROUGH, June 29, W50-46

1 Frank Andersen	1 2 3 2 3 3 1	15	2
2 Mick Poole	*rider replacement*		
3 †Craig Hodgson	0 1 2 3 0 0 2	8	2
4 Scott Norman	0 2 3 3 2 2	12	1
5 Nigel Flatman	3 1 N 1 1	6	2
5 Mark Lyndon	3 2 R T 2 1	8	
7 Sean Barker	R 1 0 N	1	
8 Phil Disney	*did not ride*		

16...EXETER, July 6, W50-46

1 Frank Andersen	2 2 3 3 2	14	1
2 Mick Poole	*rider replacement*		
3 †Craig Hodgson	0 3 3 3 2 3	14	
4 Scott Norman	2 3 3 2 3 0 1	14	1
5 Nigel Flatman	0 0 R R 0	0	
6 Mark Lyndon	3 fn N N N	3	
7 Sean Barker	2 1 1 0 0 0	4	1
8 Paul Blackbird	1	1	1

17...Edinburgh, July 8, L34-62

1 Frank Andersen	1 0 3 0 0 1	5	
2 Mick Poole	*rider replacement*		
3 †Craig Hodgson	3 1 3 3 1 1 2	14	1
4 Scott Norman	2 1 R 2 1 1 0	7	
5 Nigel Flatman	0 1 T 0 N	1	
6 Mark Lyndon	1 0 1 0 3 1	6	1
7 Sean Barker	F N 1	1	
8 Paul Blackbird	F	0	

18...Newcastle, July 9, L41-55

1 Frank Andersen	2 3 3 1 1 0 3	13	1
2 Mick Poole	*rider replacement*		
3 †Craig Hodgson	1 3 2 3 2 1 1	13	2
4 Scott Norman	2 1 1 0 0 0	4	
5 Nigel Flatman	1 fx 2 2 0	5	1
6 Mark Lyndon	3 0 1 1	5	
7 Sean Barker	1 R 0	1	
8 Phil Disney	*did not ride*		

19...Exeter, July 23, L28-68

1 †Frank Andersen	1 0 2 1 3 1 3	11	1
2 Mick Poole	*rider replacement*		
3 Craig Hodgson	0 2 1 2 2 1	8	
4 Scott Norman	2 1 1 1 1 N 1	7	1
5 Nigel Flatman	0 R N T N	0	
6 Mark Lyndon	0 0 N R 1	1	
7 Sean Barker	1 R R 0 0	1	
8 Frank Smart	*0 0*	*0*	

20...Poole, July 24, L38-58

1 †Frank Andersen	3 1 2 1 2 2 2	13	1
2 Mick Poole	*rider replacement*		
3 Craig Hodgson	1 R 2 3 E 3 3	12	
4 Scott Norman	0 1 3 0 2 0 0	6	
5 Nigel Flatman	0 fx 1 1 T	2	1
6 Mark Lyndon	1 0 1 0 1	3	1
7 Sean Barker	2 0 0	2	
8 Paul Blackbird	*did not ride*		

21...LONG EATON, July 27, W52-44

1 †Frank Andersen	R 1 0 N N	1	1
2 Mick Poole	*rider replacement*		
3 Craig Hodgson	2 0 3 3 3 3	14	
4 Scott Norman	2 3 3 2 N 2	12	
5 Nigel Flatman	1 2 1 2 1	7	4
6 Mark Lyndon	3 2 2 1 1 2 1	12	2
7 Sean Barker	0 X R 0	0	
8 §Wayne Bridgeford	3 3	6	

22...Milton Keynes, July 31, L45-51

1 †Frank Andersen	3 2 2 2 2	11	
2 Nigel Flatman	0 1 1 1 2	5	2
3 Craig Hodgson	3 1 3 2 2	11	
4 Scott Norman	3 3 1 0 1	8	1
5 Mark Lyndon	1 1 0 1 1	4	2
6 Sean Barker	1 0 R N	1	
7 Wayne Bridgeford	3 2 0 0	5	1

23...Hackney, August 3, L37-59

1 †Frank Andersen	0 0 0 2 2 2 2	8	
2 Mick Poole	*rider replacement*		
3 Craig Hodgson	3 2 3 3 3 R	14	
4 Scott Norman	0 2 2 3 0 0	7	
5 Mark Lyndon	2 1 0 0 0 1	4	
6 Sean Barker	2 0 1 0	3	1
7 Wayne Bridgeford	F 0 1	1	1
8 Mark Jolly	*did not ride*		

24...NEWCASTLE, August 10, W51-45

1 †Frank Anderson	3 1 2 N N N	6	2
2 Mick Poole	*rider replacement*		
3 Craig Hodgson	2 2 E 3 2 1 3	13	1
4 Scott Norman	3 3 2 3 1 2	14	
5 Nigel Flatman	0 1 1 3 1	6	1
6 Mark Lyndon	3 0 N 3 3 0 0	9	
7 Sean Barker	1 0 N 0 N R 0	1	
8 Wayne Bridgeford	2	2	

25...Stoke, August 11, L30-66

1 Mark Lyndon	0 0 1 2 N 0 0	3	
2 †Mick Poole	*rider replacement*		
3 Craig Hodgson	1 2 3 3 1 1 R	11	1
4 Scott Norman	1 3 2 X 1 1 1	9	
5 Nigel Flatman	R 1 T N N	1	1
6 Wayne Bridgeford	0 1 T 1 0 1	3	
7 Sean Barker	2 F T 0 1	3	
8 §Jack Poole	0	0	

26...Middlesbrough, August 16, L26-70

1 Mark Lyndon	0 0 1 0 0 0	1	1
2 †Mick Poole	*rider replacement*		
3 Craig Hodgson	2 1 2 2 2 1 2	12	
4 Scott Norman	1 1 1 1 2 1 2	9	
5 Sean Barker	0 0 0 0 T	0	
6 Wayne Bridgeford	1 0 0 T 0	1	1
7 §Mark Crang	2 0 T 1 0	3	
8 Darren Tupper	*did not ride*		

27...Berwick, August 18, L23-73

1 Sean Barker	1 R R 0 F 1	2	1
2 †Mick Poole	*rider replacement*		
3 Craig Hodgson	2 2 1 3 2 T 2	12	
4 Scott Norman	1 1 1 1 1 0	6	
5 Mark Lyndon	0 0 N 0 N	0	
6 Mark Crang	N R N R T 1 0	1	
7 Wayne Bridgeford	1 0 1 0 fx	2	
8 Darren Tupper	*did not ride*		

28...Glasgow, August 19, L32-64

1 Sean Barker	0 0 1 1 2	4	1
2 †Mick Poole	*rider replacement*		
3 Craig Hodgson	2 1 3 1 2 1 2	12	1
4 Scott Norman	0 1 1 2 0 1	5	2
5 Mark Lyndon	1 2 0 R 0 T	3	
6 Darren Tupper	F 0 N N	0	
7 Wayne Bridgeford	1 0 0 3 2 2 F	8	
8 Muir Templeton	*did not ride*		

29...STOKE, August 31, L46-49

1 Frank Andersen	3 2 2 2 fx	9	1
2 †Mick Poole	*rider replacement*		
3 Craig Hodgson	2 3 3 3 3 2 3	19	1
4 Scott Norman	2 3 2 1 1 1	10	1
5 Sean Barker	1 0 0 0 N	1	1
6 Wayne Bridgeford	3 0 1 N 1 F 1	6	2
7 Mark Crang	0 1 N 0 0	1	
8 Darren Tupper	*did not ride*		

30...EDINBURGH, September 7, W53-43

1 †Mick Poole	2 2 3 3 2	12	1
2 Nigel Flatman	R N N N N	0	
3 Frank Andersen	2 3 1 3 3	12	1
4 Craig Hodgson	3 0 3 0 3	9	
5 Scott Norman	1 1 2 2 2	8	3
6 Wayne Bridgeford	3 3 1 N 0 0 0	7	1
7 Sean Barker	2 0 2 0 1	5	1

31...POOLE, September 14, L29-67

1 †Mick Poole	2 2 R 2 1 R	7	
2 Scott Norman	0 1 1 R 1	3	1
3 Frank Andersen	1 1 1 2 R 2	7	
4 Craig Hodgson	3 3 0 3 R 2	11	
5 Wayne Bridgeford	0 0 0 0 N	0	
6 Sean Barker	1 0 T T 0	1	
7 Mark Crang	0 T 0	0	

32...Long Eaton, September 26, L27-69

1 †Mick Poole	2 0 3 3 1 1	10	1
2 Frank Andersen	*rider replacement*		
3 Sean Barker	0 1 1 F 0 2	4	
4 Scott Norman	2 2 1 1 2 0	8	
5 Wayne Bridgeford	0 1 0 0 1 1 0	3	
6 Darren Tupper	0 0 T 0	0	
7 Mark Jolly	1 0 0	1	
8 Rob Fisher	1	1	

1990 ROSTER

ANDERSEN, Frank
B 24.2.1964, Kolding, Denmark.
Signed from Exeter.
BARKER, Sean
B 30.4.1969, Isleworth, Surrey.
BLACKBIRD, Paul Barry
B 17.12.1970, Peterborough, Cambs.
BRIDGEFORD, Wayne
B 20.10.1965, Warburton, Australia.
Signed from Rye House.
DISNEY, Phillip Anthony
B 25.11.1970, Halifax, West Yorks.
On loan from Bradford.
FISHER, Robert (Rob)
B 11.10.1968, Canada.
FLATMAN, Nigel William
B 30.3.1960, Felistowe, Suffolk.
HODGSON, Craig Stuart
B 8.7.1968, Adelaide, Australia.
JOLLY, Mark Victor
B 24.8.1967, Ipswich, Suffolk.
LYNDON, Mark David
B 15.3.1970, Christchurch, New Zealand. *Signed from Milton Keynes.*
NORMAN, Scott
B 21.7.1970, Adelaide, Australia.
POOLE, Matthew Wayne (Jack)
B 20.6.1973, Penrith, Sydney, Australia. *First season newcomer.*
POOLE, Michael Garth
B 27.11.1966, Sydney, Australia.
TUPPER, Darren
B 7.5.1962, Harlow, Essex.
IAN BARNEY – See Exeter.
ANTHONY BOYD - See Edinburgh.
JOHN COOK – See Eastbourne.
MARK CRANG - See Middlesbrough.
FRANK SMART – See Exeter.
MUIR TEMPLETON - See Edinburgh.

Poole pick up pieces – and the pots

Track Data

Promoters: Mervyn Stewkesbury and Peter Ansell.
Address: Poole Stadium, Wimborne Road, Poole, Dorset, BH15 2BP.
Telephone: 0202-681145.
Information Line: 0898 31 21 48.
Track Length: 371 metres.
Track Record: 64.4 secs, Chris Louis (Ipswich), August 7, 1990, Heat 1, Elfords Blue Riband.

BEAT the drums, sound the horns. Poole achieved what many thought was the impossible – and built an even better side out of the remnants of their 1989 title-winning side.

Leigh Adams, second in the averages, was gone to sample life in the Sunbrite League at Swindon. Alastair Stevens, number four in the charts, had been recalled by his parent track Oxford. And Kevin Smart, nominally number seven but with a six point plus average, had been sold to Long Eaton.

Any team missing the numbers two, four and seven from a championship winning squad would be facing problems building up a new team under the points limit but when those three riders had scored a massive 820 or so National League points between them it was a mountainous task.

Yet Poole not only did it, but also managed to reassemble a team that, mathematically, was even strong than its predecessor. And a side that added the National League Knock Out Cup to their collective silverware.

One major reason was that Australian Craig Boyce, who had actually outscored the more heavily publicised Adams in the previous campaign, was able to improve still further, marvellously adding more than a point a meeting to his already high average.

Points-wise he showed an even more marked acceleration and actually scored a further 88 points in one match less, an astronomical improvement at that high level.

There was also some extremely shrewd planning by the Poole management who persuaded Swindon to release Gary Chessell as part of the deal that took Adams to Blunsdon and then went back to the Wiltshire track to sign Dane Tom Knudsen.

Even though his season was to end with a broken leg, he was the key to continued success at Wimborne Road.

Tony Langdon, looking more and more like the third successive Poole Aussie to make the grade, was a much improved performer but early season results pinpointed a tail-end weakness in the Echo Pirates' line-up.

That gap was plugged in time for their opening match in the defence of their crown with Knudsen, unable to command a team place in the Sunbrite League, making a startling double figure debut at Glasgow.

His 11, paid 12 points, included a fall in his sixth and last ride but turned what would have been an inevitable defeat into a morale-boosting three point win at Shawfield Park. He won a race the following night even though Poole went down fairly heavily at Berwick but that was to be the only match in which he appeared that Poole lost!

Even though his season was cut short by a crash at Berwick in the Knock Out Cup, he had more than served his purpose. He had averaged more than 10 points a meeting from reserve (120 points in 11 matches) and helped Poole win 10 of those meetings. More important, by the time they were heavily involved in climbing up the table, he had been elevated to heat leader status which allowed the South Coast club to operate rider replacement for him in a dozen of their last fifteen matches, none of which were lost.

In all Poole were beaten only five times in a total of 40 League and Cup matches, twice at Berwick, twice at Middlesbrough and once at Edinburgh where they went down despite a six ride paid maximum from Boyce who went through the entire season without once being out of double figures!

But don't run away with the idea it was a one man band.

Alun Rossiter, Gary Allan and Tony Langdon all improved their averages considerably; new boys Chessell and Rod Colquhoun contributed points solidly; and, with an eye to the future, teenagers Mark Lemon and Justin Elkins look like gilt-edged prospects for tomorrow.

Roll of Honour

Seasons in National League: 6 (1985-1990).
National League Record: Champions (2), 1989, 1990. Runners-up (3), 1985, 1986, 1988.
National League Cup Record: Winners (1), 1990. Runners-up (1), 1989.
National League Team Championship: Runners-up (1), 1990. Fourth (1), 1988. Qualified (5), 1985, 1986, 1987, 1988, 1990.
Appearances: David Biles, 140 (1985-1988).
Points: Craig Boyce, 1341 (1988-1990).
World Finalists: Brian Crutcher (1952), Michael Lee (1983), Christer Löfqvist (1972), Malcolm Simmons (1975-76, 1978), Vaclav Verner (1982).
NLRC Finalists: Stan Bear (1985), Steve Schofield (1986, 1988), David Biles (1987), Leigh Adams (1989), Craig Boyce (1990).
Other Honours: British League Champions, 1969. National League (Division Two) Champions, 1952, 1955. National League (Division Three) Champions, 1957. Provincial League Champions, 1961, 1962.

Star of 90

ALUN ROSSITER

Poole

POOLE

01...Glasgow, April 27, W49-46

1 §Gary Chessell	R 2 0 1 N	3	
2 Gary Allan	1 0 1 N N	2	1
3 †Alun Rossiter	1 2 3 3 1	10	
4 Craig Boyce	3 2 3 3 2	13	
5 Steve Langdon	1 1 0 2 0	4	2
6 §Rod Colquhoun	3 1 0 2	6	2
7 §§Tom Knudsen	2 3 2 1 3 fx	11	1

02...Berwick, April 28, L35-61

1 Gary Chessell	fx0 2 0 0	2	
2 Gary Allan	2 2 0 1 2 1	8	2
3 †Alun Rossiter	1 2 2 1 2	8	
4 Craig Boyce	3 2 3 1 1	10	
5 Steve Langdon	0 1 0 N T	1	1
6 Rod Colquhoun	0 1 N N	1	1
7 Tom Knudsen	1 F 3 0 0 1	5	1

03...GLASGOW, May 1, W62-34

1 Gary Chessell	**3 3 3 2 2**	**13**	**2**
2 Gary Allan	2 1 2 2 2	9	3
3 †Alun Rossiter	1 3 2 2 2	10	1
4 Craig Boyce	3 3 2 3 3	14	
5 Steve Langdon	R 1 fx3 R	4	
6 Tom Knudsen	3 3 0 3	9	
7 Rod Colquhoun	2 0 1	3	2

04...MILTON KEYNES, May 8, W56-40

1 Gary Chessell	1 3 2 2 1	9	2
2 Gary Allan	2 1 1 0 1	5	
3 †Alun Rossiter	**3 3 3 3 3**	**15**	
4 Craig Boyce	**3 3 3 3 3**	**15**	
5 Tony Langdon	0 2 2 2 1	7	3
6 Rod Colquhoun	3 fx1 0	4	
7 Steve Langdon	1 0 0	1	

05...LONG EATON, May 22, W56-40

1 Rod Colquhoun	1 R 0 2 1	4	2
2 Gary Allan	2 2 1 2 2	9	1
3 †Alun Rossiter	2 3 3 2 fx	10	1
4 Craig Boyce	3 3 1 3 3	13	1
5 Tony Langdon	1 1 2 1 2	7	1
6 Tom Knudsen	3 3 1 1	8	1
7 Steve Langdon	1 2 2	5	1

06...MIDDLESBROUGH, June 12, W58-38

1 Gary Chessell	0 1 2 2 2	7	2
2 Gary Allan	1 2 3 2 3 2	13	1
3 Alun Rossiter	*rider replacement*		
4 †Craig Boyce	3 3 3 0 3	12	
5 Tony Langdon	fx1 2 3 3	9	1
6 Tom Knudsen	2 3 3 1	9	2
7 Rod Colquhoun	3 0 2	5	
8 Steve Langdon	R 1 1 1	3	1

07...IPSWICH, June 19, W59-37

1 Gary Chessell	2 fnN N N	2	
2 Gary Allan	R 3 2 3 3	11	
3 †Alun Rossiter	1 3 fx3 2	9	1
4 Craig Boyce	**3 3 3 3 3**	**15**	
5 Tony Langdon	1 0 2 0 3	6	1
6 Tom Knudsen	2 3 1 fn2 1 0	9	2
7 Rod Colquhoun	3 2 1 0 1	7	2

08...Rye House, June 24, W60-36

1 Gary Chessell	3 1 1 1 2	8	3
2 Gary Allan	1 2 2 2 2	9	1
3 †Alun Rossiter	3 2 3 3 2	13	
4 Craig Boyce	3 2 X 3 3	11	
5 Tony Langdon	2 0 3 2 1	8	3
6 Tom Knudsen	3 1 1 3	8	1
7 Rod Colquhoun	2 1 fx	3	1

09...STOKE, June 26, W57-39

1 Gary Chessell	1 0 N 2 N	3	2
2 Gary Allan	2 2 3 2 0	9	
3 †Alun Rossiter	2 1 2 1 3	9	2
4 Craig Boyce	2 3 3 3 3	14	
5 Tony Langdon	1 1 2 2 2	8	3
6 Tom Knudsen	3 1 2 1 2 2	11	4
7 Rod Colquhoun	0 2 N 1	3	1

10...Newcastle, July 1, W51-45

1 Gary Chessell	1 1 3 0 N	5	
2 Gary Allan	fx0 2 1 0	3	1
3 †Alun Rossiter	2 3 1 2 1	9	1
4 Craig Boyce	2 2 3 3 3	13	
5 Tony Langdon	1 0 1 N 2	4	1
6 Tom Knudsen	3 F T 3 3 1 3 2	15	2
7 Rod Colquhoun	1 N 1 T	2	

11...BERWICK, July 10, W70-26

1 Gary Chessell	1 2 2 1 1	7	3
2 Gary Allan	2 3 3 3 2	13	1
3 †Alun Rossiter	2 1 2 2 3	10	3
4 Craig Boyce	2 3 3 3 3	14	
5 Tony Langdon	1 2 2 3 2	10	4
6 Tom Knudsen	2 N 3 3 3	11	
7 Rod Colquhoun	0 3 2 N	5	1

12...RYE HOUSE, July 17, W73-23

1 Rod Colquhoun	1 2 2 2 2	9	4
2 Gary Allan	**3 3 3 3 3**	**15**	
3 †Alun Rossiter	3 3 3 1 3	13	
4 Craig Boyce	**3 3 2 3 3**	**14**	**1**
5 Tony Langdon	**2 2 3 3 2**	**12**	**3**
6 Tom Knudsen	3 2 1 2	8	2
7 Steve Leigh	2 0 0	2	1

13...PETERBOROUGH, July 24, W58-38

1 Gary Chessell	2 2 0 3 1	8	1
2 Gary Allan	1 3 3 3 2	12	1
3 †Alun Rossiter	3 1 2 1 N	7	1
4 Craig Boyce	3 3 3 E 3	12	
5 Tony Langdon	2 2 1 3 0	8	2
6 Steve Langdon	3 2 2 1	8	1
7 Rod Colquhoun	0 1 0 2 0	3	1

14...Long Eaton, July 25, W51-45

1 Gary Chessell	3 0 1 1 0	5	1
2 Gary Allan	fx1 3 2 3	9	
3 †Alun Rossiter	2 3 1 1 2	9	3
4 Craig Boyce	1 1 2 3 3	10	
5 Tony Langdon	3 3 0 2 3	11	
6 Steve Langdon	1 0 2 1	4	1
7 Rod Colquhoun	2 0 1	3	

15...Middlesbrough, July 26, L37-59

1 Gary Chessell	0 0 T 1 T 2	3	
2 Gary Allan	1 1 3 0 0 1	6	
3 †Alun Rossiter	0 1 T T 2	3	
4 Craig Boyce	3 3 3 2 3 1	15	2
5 Tony Langdon	0 0 3 3 R 0	6	
6 Steve Langdon	0 R T N	0	
7 Rod Colquhoun	1 1 2 0 0	4	1

16...Edinburgh, July 27, L43-53

1 Gary Chessell	0 3 F 1 2 0	6	
2 Gary Allan	2 0 3 1 1 T	7	1
3 †Alun Rossiter	1 2 fxT T	3	
4 Craig Boyce	**2 3 3 3 3 3**	**17**	**1**
5 Tony Langdon	3 fx0 2 0 0	5	
6 Rod Colquhoun	1 fx2 T	3	1
7 Steve Langdon	2 F fx	2	

17...EDINBURGH, July 31, W52-43

1 Gary Chessell	3 0 1 2 F	6	1
2 Gary Allan	1 1 2 R 2	6	
3 †Alun Rossiter	**3 3 3 3 3**	**15**	
4 Craig Boyce	3 3 3 3 2	14	
5 Tony Langdon	1 2 2 2 1	8	3
6 Steve Langdon	2 fx0 N	2	
7 Jon Gould	0 0 1 0	1	

18...Stoke, August 4, W52-44

1 Craig Boyce	N 3 3 3 2 3 2	16	1
2 Gary Allan	1 1 0 0 N 2	4	
3 †Alun Rossiter	2 3 3 3 0 1	12	
4 Tony Langdon	3 fx0 2 3 1	9	1
5 Tom Knudsen	*rider replacement*		
6 Gary Chessell	3 R 1 3 1 1 N	9	
7 Jon Gould	1 0 N 1	2	1
8 Steve Langdon	*did not ride*		

19...NEWCASTLE, August 14, W63-33

1 Craig Boyce	**3 3 3 3 3 3**	**18**	
2 Gary Allan	1 3 1 2 2 1	10	2
3 †Alun Rossiter	1 3 2 2 3 3	14	1
4 Tony Langdon	2 2 1 2 2 1 2	12	6
5 Tom Knudsen	*rider replacement*		
6 Gary Chessell	3 2 1 0 2	8	
7 Jon Gould	1 0 N	1	
8 Steve Langdon	*did not ride*		

20...Exeter, August 27, W52-44

1 Craig Boyce	2 3 X 3 1 3 N	12	
2 Gary Allan	1 2 2 1 1 1	8	2
3 †Alun Rossiter	2 1 2 1 2 2	10	3
4 Tony Langdon	1 1 2 1 3 3	11	2
5 Tom Knudsen	*drider replacement*		
6 Gary Chessell	2 0 2 2 3	9	
7 Rod Colquhoun	0 fn1 1	2	1

21...Hackney, August 31, W49-47

1 Craig Boyce	3 2 2 2 2 2 2	15	1
2 Gary Allan	E 1 0 3 1 fx	5	2
3 †Alun Rossiter	2 2 2 3 0 1	10	1
4 Tony Langdon	2 1 2 3 fx3	11	2
5 Tom Knudsen	*rider replacement*		
6 Gary Chessell	0 3 1 0 0 2	6	1
7 Rod Colquhoun	1 1 N	2	1
8 Steve Leigh	*did not ride*		

22...HACKNEY, September 4, W63-32

1 Craig Boyce	**3 2 3 3 3**	**14**	**1**
2 Gary Allan	2 3 fx1 3	9	1
3 †Alun Rossiter	1 3 0 1 2	7	
4 Tony Langdon	3 3 1 2 2	11	3
5 Gary Chessell	2 2 2 3 1	10	3
6 Steve Leigh	2 0 0 N	2	1
7 Rod Colquhoun	3 3 2 2	10	1

23...EASTBOURNE, September 11, W71-25

1 Craig Boyce	**3 3 3 3 3 3**	**18**	
2 Gary Allan	1 2 2 1 2 2	10	5
3 †Alun Rossiter	3 2 1 3 3	12	1
4 Tony Langdon	3 0 2 2 1	8	2
5 Tom Knudsen	*rider replacement*		
6 Gary Chessell	3 2 3 fx3	11	1
7 Rod Colquhoun	2 2 3 3 2	12	2
8 Steve Leigh	*did not ride*		

24...Peterborough, September 14, W67-29

1 Craig Boyce	3 2 3 3 1 N	12	
2 Gary Allan	1 1 1 2 2 3	10	4
3 †Alun Rossiter	3 3 N 3 2 3	14	1
4 Tony Langdon	2 2 1 3 3 3	14	1
5 Tom Knudsen	*rider replacement*		
6 Gary Chessell	3 0 1 2 1	7	2
7 Rod Colquhoun	2 2 3 2 1	10	2

25...Eastbourne, September 16, W61-35

1 Craig Boyce	**3 3 2 3 3 2**	**16**	**2**
2 Gary Allan	F 0 0 3 2 3	8	1
3 †Alun Rossiter	fx1 2 3 3 3	12	2
4 Tony Langdon	**3 3 2 2 2 3**	**15**	**3**
5 Tom Knudsen	*rider replacement*		
6 Gary Chessell	2 2 0 3 2	9	1
7 Rod Colquhoun	R 1 N	1	
8 §§Justin Elkins	fx	0	

26...Milton Keynes, September 23, W52-44

1 Craig Boyce	2 F 3 2 3	10	
2 Gary Allan	1 3 3 2 2	11	2
3 Alun Rossiter	3 3 2 3 3	14	
4 Tony Langdon	2 0 2 0 1	5	
5 Rod Colquhoun	1 3 1 1 0	6	2
6 §§Mark Lemon	E 0 1 1 N	2	1
7 Justin Elkins	2 N 2 F	4	1

27...WIMBLEDON, September 25, W54-42

1 Craig Boyce	fx3 3 2 3 3 3	17	
2 Gary Allan	2 1 2 3 0 2	10	3
3 †Alun Rossiter	0 3 0 3 1 2	9	2
4 Tony Langdon	1 2 1 0 2 1	7	
5 Tom Knudsen	*rider replacement*		
6 Justin Elkins	3 1 fxN	4	
7 Rod Colquhoun	1 2 1 3	7	1
8 Mark Lemon	*did not ride*		

28...Wimbledon, September 26, W48-47

1 Craig Boyce	3 0 2 3 3 2 2	15	1
2 Gary Allan	2 2 2 1 2 3 1	13	1
3 †Alun Rossiter	2 2 0 2 2 2 3	13	2
4 Tony Langdon	1 1 0 3 0 1 1	7	4
5 Tom Knudsen	*rider replacement*		
6 Justin Elkins	E fxN T	0	
7 Rod Colquhoun	fxfxN N	0	
8 Mark Lemon	*did not ride*		

29...Ipswich, September 27, W51-44

1 Craig Boyce	1 2 3 3 3 3 3	18	1
2 Gary Allan	2 3 0 2 2 2	11	2
3 †Alun Rossiter	1 2 0 1 1 2	7	1
4 Tony Langdon	fx0 3 3 3 fxN	9	
5 Tom Knudsen	*rider replacement*		
6 Mark Lemon	1 1 N N	2	2
7 Rod Colquhoun	2 0 T 2 fxfx	4	
8 Lawrence Hare	*did not ride*		

30...ARENA ESSEX, October 2, W61-35

1 Craig Boyce	3 3 2 1 3 3	15	1
2 Gary Allan	1 2 E 2 3 2	10	1
3 †Alun Rossiter	**3 3 3 3 3**	**15**	
4 Tony Langdon	3 R 3 2 2	10	2
5 Tom Knudsen	*rider replacement*		
6 Rod Colquhoun	2 1 3 1 1	8	1
7 Mark Lemon	1 1 F	2	2
8 Steve Leigh	0 0 1	1	

31...Arena Essex, October 6, W51-41

1 Craig Boyce	2 3 3 3 3 3 3	20	
2 Gary Allan	F R 2 2 R 3	7	
3 †Alun Rossiter	X N 3 3 2 2	10	1
4 Tony Langdon	2 2 1 1 1 2	9	5
5 Tom Knudsen	*rider replacement*		
6 Rod Colquhoun	1 R 2 R	3	1
7 Mark Lemon	F 1 1	2	1
8 Jon Gould	*did not ride*		

32...EXETER, October 14, W57-39

1 Craig Boyce	2 3 3 3 3	14	
2 Gary Allan	1 2 3 2 3	11	3
3 †Alun Rossiter	3 3 1 2 3	12	
4 Tony Langdon	**3 3 3 2 2**	**13**	**2**
5 Rod Colquhoun	2 1 0 R 1	4	1
6 Justin Elkins	2 1 0 N	3	
7 Mark Lemon	0 0 0 0	0	

1990 ROSTER

ALLAN, Gary Karl
B 21.6.1967, Manchester.
BOYCE, Craig
B 2.8.1967, Sydney, Australia.
CHESSELL, Gary
B 20.1.1965, Ludlow, Shropshire. *On loan from Swindon.*
COLQUHOUN, Rodney
B 28.2.1967, Mt. Warrigal, Australia. *Signed from Peterborough.*
ELKINS, Justin Mark
B 27.8.1974, Salisbury, Wiltshire. *First season newcomer.*
GOULD, John Lee
B 16.3.1967, Exeter, Devon
KNUDSEN, Tom
B 14.9.1968, Denmark. *On loan from Swindon.*
LANGDON, Anthony Michael (Tony)
B 20.6.1969, Brisbane, Australia.
LANGDON, Steve
B 4.5.1967, Brisbane, Australia.
LEIGH, Steven
B 26.7.1967, Romsey, Hampshire.
LEMON, Mark Ian John
B 12.2.1973, Brainsdale, Victoria, Australia. *First season newcomer.*
ROSSITER, Alun John
B 23.7.1965, Swindon, Wiltshire.
LAWRENCE HARE - see Ipswich.
PETER SCHROECK - see Wimbledon.

Broken arm, leg, wrist and hearts

Track Data

Promoters: Ronnie Russell and Barry Klatt.
Address: Rye House Stadium, Rye Road, Hoddesdon, Hertfordshire.
Telephone: 0992-450997.
Hotline: 0898 800 694.
Track Length: 257 metres.
Track Record: 58.6 secs, Jens Rasmussen (Rye House), August 26, 1990, Heat 13, Rye House v Berwick (National League).

EVERY season it seems to be the same old story at Hoddesdon. Come opening day and there's optimism in the air and talk of title challenges.

It was no exception. But this time the optimism had floated off down the River Lee before the ink had hardly dried on the new contracts and, once again, Rye House was plunged into despondency and despair.

There had been something of a winter clear-out with a new, but not necessarily younger look to the overall team strength, Paul Woods, 31, had gone to Eastbourne. Kevin Brice, 31, had moved across the Herts-Essex border to join Arena Essex. Peter Schroeck, 24, had been allowed to join Wimbledon. Kelvin Mullarkey, 39, had once again hung up his leathers. And Carl Chalcraft, after treading water for a couple of seasons, had drifted into retirement after being transfer-listed for most of the winter.

Replacing them were veterans Roger Johns from Wimbledon and Nigel Sparshott from Long Eaton who would, it was hoped, add the substance to a side with two fine heat leaders in Jens Rasmussen and Melvyn Taylor – and an abundance of young Aussie talent to fill the second string race-jackets.

It was a commendable ploy that was never given a chance to work properly. Mel Taylor smashed his arm up badly before the National League programme had even started; talented tail-ender Jamie Fagg landed in hospital with a broken leg before the end of May; Sparshott never looked capable of recapturing his old form and had a dreadful start to his new career; and Roger Johns was ruled out for four months of the season with a fractured scaphoid.

There was one appalling Sunday afternoon when virtually the whole of the Rockets' heat leader force was wiped out...and that was the club's first League match of what they thought was going to be a successful campaign!

Glen Baxter, destined to make enormous progress throughout the year, broke bones in his hand when he came down in a heat 12 crash against Peterborough and he was to be joined in hospital in Harlow by his skipper Jens Rasmussen, who suffered a suspected leg fracture in another incident in the following race.

With Taylor already out, it left the Rockets planning a daunting trip to Exeter without any of their top three and they became the first major victims of the bold National League decision to do away with guest riders for any reason.

In one fell swoop, Rye House had shown that there is always an exception to the rule and they were in such dire straits that National League headquarters were forced to agree that their match at the County Ground could be raced as a challenge fixture rather than force them to go through with what would have been a meaningless and unappealing one-sided contest.

They managed to fulfil their commitment with a couple of guest riders and, fortunately, the news wasn't quite as devastating as it first appeared with X-rays revealing that stalwart Rasmussen had not actually broken any bones. Baxter wasn't quite so fortunate but, on that occasion, he only actually missed a couple of League matches before returning to get a double figure return against Wimbledon.

The nightmare was far from over though. Six successive defeats (at home to Peterborough, Stoke and Wimbledon) saw the Rockets firmly rooted to the bottom of the National League but with something like a representative side (only Taylor was missing) they snapped out of the doldrums with victories over Exeter (easily) and Middlesbrough (even more comprehensively).

Then came the second major blow and that injury to Fagg just as he had swapped his number six race-jacket for Sparshott's number five.

He never made it back – but Linden Warner, Kevin Teager and that old warhorse Mullarkey did as the Rockets hit more troubles to end the season as they began...with a string of defeats.

Roll of Honour

Seasons in National League: 17 (1974-1990).
National League Record: Champions (1), 1980. Runners-up (2), 1977, 1979. Third (1), 1978.
National League Cup Record: Winners (1), 1979. Runners-up (1), 1978.
National League Team Championship: Runners-up (1), 1980. Fourth (1), 1982. Qualified (4), 1976, 1979, 1980, 1982.
Appearances: Bob Garrad, 421 (1976-1986).
Points: Bob Garrad, 3805 (1976-1986).
World Finalists: None.
NLRC Finalists: Brian Foote (1974-75), Ted Hubbard (1976, 1978), Kelvin Mullarkey (1977, 1980-81), Karl Fiala (1979), Bob Garrad (1982, 1984), Marvyn Cox (1983), Paul Woods (1986-87), Jens Rasmussen (1988-89-90).

Star of 90

GLEN BAXTER

Rye House

RYE HOUSE

01...PETERBOROUGH, April 8, L47-49

1 Glen Baxter	2 1 2 3 1 N	9	2
2 §Roger Johns	0 1 3 0 1 fx3	8	
3 †Jens Rasmussen	3 3 3 2 fnN	11	
4 §Nigel Sparshott	0 2 0 fn0	2	
5 Melvyn Taylor	*rider replacement*		
6 Jamie Fagg	3 2 2 0 1 2	10	2
7 Trevor O'Brien	1 1 fx3 fx2	7	
8 Wayne Bridgeford	*did not ride*		

02...Ipswich, April 19, L28-67

1 Jamie Fagg	R 0 fx0 0	0	
2 Roger Johns	1 1 1 3 2 2 0	10	
3 †Jens Rasmussen	3 2 2 1 F 1 1	10	
4 Melvyn Taylor	*rider replacement*		
5 Nigel Sparshott	0 1 0 1 0	2	1
6 §Wayne Bridgeford	0 N 0 T	0	
7 Trevor O'Brien	1 1 1 1 1 1	6	1
8 Colin Thorpe	*did not ride*		

03...STOKE, April 22, L45-49

1 Jamie Fagg	fx0 0 3 1	4	1
2 Roger Johns	2 2 2 2 2 1 3	14	1
3 †Jens Rasmussen	3 3 2 3 1 3	15	
4 Melvyn Taylor	*rider replacement*		
5 Nigel Sparshott	1 0 1 0 0	2	2
6 Wayne Bridgeford	2 1 T N	3	
7 Trevor O'Brien	R 1 1 3 R fx2	7	
8 Colin Thorpe	*did not ride*		

04...WIMBLEDON, April 29, L47-49

1 Glen Baxter	0 1 3 3 3 0	10	
2 Roger Johns	2 3 3 1 0 2 1	12	2
3 †Jens Rasmussen	3 3 1 1 R 3	11	
4 Melvyn Taylor	*rider replacement*		
5 Nigel Sparshott	1 0 1 3 0	5	
6 Jamie Fagg	3 0 0 3	6	
7 Trevor O'Brien	0 1 2 0	3	
8 Wayne Bridgeford	*did not ride*		

05...Middlesbrough, May 3, L37-58

1 Glen Baxter	2 0 3 2 2 2 2	13	1
2 Roger Johns	0 1 2 3 F 2	8	
3 †Jens Rasmussen	1 1 1 3 2 F	8	
4 Nigel Sparshott	0 2 0 0 N	2	1
5 Melvyn Taylor	*rider replacement*		
6 Jamie Fagg	1 0 0 N	1	
7 Trevor O'Brien	3 1 0 fxX 1	5	1
8 Wayne Bridgeford	*did not ride*		

06...Edinburgh, May 4, L45-51

1 Glen Baxter	3 3 2 X 2 0 0	10	
2 Roger Johns	1 2 fx1 1 0	5	1
3 †Jens Rasmussen	3 3 3 3 3 2	17	
4 Nigel Sparshott	0 1 0 N N	1	
5 Melvyn Taylor	*rider replacement*		
6 Jamie Fagg	2 fx1 1 2 2	8	1
7 Trevor O'Brien	X 2 2 0	4	1
8 Wayne Bridgeford	*did not ride*		

07...EXETER, May 6, W55-40

1 Glen Baxter	2 0 0 3 2 1	8	1
2 Roger Johns	1 2 2 0 1 fx	6	1
3 †Jens Rasmussen	3 3 3 1 3 2	15	1
4 Melvyn Taylor	*rider replacement*		
5 Nigel Sparshott	0 1 1 N 2	4	1
6 Jamie Fagg	3 2 2 1 3	11	3
7 Trevor O'Brien	2 3 2 2 2	11	2
8 Wayne Bridgeford	*did not ride*		

08...MIDDLESBROUGH, May 20, W59-37

1 Roger Johns	1 1 1 2 2	7	2
2 Melvyn Taylor	*rider replacement*		
3 †Jens Rasmussen	3 2 3 3 3 3	17	
4 Glen Baxter	0 3 3 2 3 2 1	14	1
5 Nigel Sparshott	1 0 N 2 1	4	1
6 Jamie Fagg	2 2 3 0 1 1	9	4
7 Trevor O'Brien	3 2 2 1	8	1
8 Wayne Bridgeford	*did not ride*		

09...IPSWICH, May 27, L44-52

1 Roger Johns	1 1 2 0 3 1 0	8	1
2 Melvyn Taylor	*rider replacement*		
3 †Jens Rasmussen	2 2 1 1 3 1 3	13	1
4 Glen Baxter	2 3 1 3 1 3 1	14	1
5 Jamie Fagg	fxfxN T T T	0	
6 Nigel Sparshott	3 1 0 2 0	6	2
7 Trevor O'Brien	1 fx2 0	3	
8 Linden Warner	*did not ride*		

10...Newcastle, June 18, L44-51

1 Roger Johns	2 1 2 0 2	7	1
2 Melvyn Taylor	*rider replacement*		
3 †Jens Rasmussen	3 2 3 2 3 1	14	
4 Glen Baxter	3 2 2 3 1 3 1	15	1
5 Linden Warner	0 0 N 0 0	0	
6 Nigel Sparshott	2 1 N 1	4	1
7 Trevor O'Brien	fx2 X fx1 F	3	1
8 §§Wayne Baxter	1	1	1

11...Peterborough, June 22, L39-57

1 Roger Johns	1 fnN N N	1	
2 Trevor O'Brien	R fx1 2 1 fx	4	2
3 †Jens Rasmussen	3 1 3 2 3 3	15	
4 Glen Baxter	3 2 2 2 3 1	13	
5 Linden Warner	0 1 N 0 0	1	1
6 Nigel Sparshott	0 0 T T 0	0	
7 Wayne Baxter	1 1 1 0 1 1	5	1

12...POOLE, June 24, L36-60

1 Trevor O'Brien	2 X 1 1 1 1 1	7	1
2 Melvyn Taylor	*rider replacement*		
3 †Jens Rasmussen	fx2 3 3 3 2 3	16	
4 Glen Baxter	1 3 3 2 2 0 0	11	
5 Linden Warner	0 fx0 0 0	0	
6 Nigel Sparshott	R 0 T 0	0	
7 Wayne Baxter	1 1 0	2	

13...Hackney, June 29, L28-68

1 Trevor O'Brien	2 1 X 0 2 R 1	6	2
2 Melvyn Taylor	*rider replacement*		
3 †Jens Rasmussen	3 1 1 2 2 1 2	12	
4 Glen Baxter	1 2 2 1 1 0 0	7	
5 Linden Warner	F 0 0 0 0	0	
6 Wayne Baxter	0 0 0 2	2	
7 Wayne Bridgeford	1 0 T	1	
8 Colin Thorpe	*did not ride*		

14...Arena Essex, June 30, L45-51

1 Trevor O'Brien	0 0 T 1 2	3	
2 Wayne Baxter	1 1 0 2 1	5	2
3 †Jens Rasmussen	3 2 3 3 3 3	17	
4 Glen Baxter	3 3 1 3 3 1	14	1
5 Linden Warner	X 1 0 1 0	2	
6 Wayne Bridgeford	1 0 1 2	4	
7 Colin Thorpe	0 0 T	0	

15...EDINBURGH, July 1, L43-52

1 Trevor O'Brien	1 1 3 0 3 1	9	2
2 Melvyn Taylor	*rider replacement*		
3 †Jens Rasmussen	2 3 3 1 3 2 1	15	1
4 Glen Baxter	1 3 3 1 0 2 2	12	1
5 Linden Warner	0 0 2 1 1 T	4	1
6 Wayne Baxter	3 0 fx0	3	
7 Wayne Bridgeford	N 0 0	0	
8 Colin Thorpe	*did not ride*		

16...Glasgow, July 6, L36-60

1 Trevor O'Brien	fx1 1 fx0 1 fx	3	
2 Melvyn Taylor	*rider replacement*		
3 †Jens Rasmussen	2 3 3 2 3 2 R	15	1
4 Glen Baxter	3 0 2 3 3 2 fn	13	
5 Linden Warner	F 0 0 N 1	1	
6 Wayne Baxter	0 0 T N 1	1	
7 Wayne Bridgeford	2 0 0 1 0	3	1
8 Kenny Brailsford	*did not ride*		

17...Berwick, July 7, L28-68

1 Trevor O'Brien	1 1 1 1 2 1 2	9	1
2 Melvyn Taylor	*rider replacement*		
3 †Jens Rasmussen	2 3 1 2 1 3 1	13	
4 Glen Baxter	N N T T N	0	
5 Linden Warner	E 0 0 F 0 0	0	
6 Wayne Baxter	0 1 0 1 1 0 1	4	1
7 Wayne Bridgeford	1 0 1 fx0 0	2	
8 Fraser Smith	*did not ride*		

18...NEWCASTLE, July 8, L39-57

1 Trevor O'Brien	1 2 2 1 1 2 1	10	1
2 Melvyn Taylor	*rider replacement*		
3 †Jens Rasmussen	3 3 3 2 3 2 3	19	
4 Kevin Teager	1 X 1 0 0 0	2	1
5 Linden Warner	0 1 1 1 0	3	1
6 Wayne Bridgeford	2 1 N 0	3	
7 Wayne Baxter	1 0 0 1	2	1
8 Colin Thorpe	*did not ride*		

19...MILTON KEYNES, July 15, W51-45

1 Trevor O'Brien	1 3 3 fxN 3 3	13	
2 Melvyn Taylor	*rider replacement*		
3 †Jens Rasmussen	**3 3 3 3 3 3 3**	**21**	
4 Kelvin Mullarkey	1 F R 0 N	1	1
5 Linden Warner	2 3 1 1 0 2	9	1
6 Kevin Teager	2 2 1 1 F 0	6	1
7 Wayne Baxter	0 0 N 1	1	
8 Colin Thorpe	*did not ride*		

20...Poole, July 17, L23-73

1 Trevor O'Brien	2 1 1 1 2 R 1	8	2
2 Melvyn Taylor	*rider replacement*		
3 †Jens Rasmussen	R R 1 1 T N	2	
4 Kelvin Mullarkey	R 2 R R N	2	
5 Linden Warner	1 0 0 1 1 0	3	
6 Kevin Teager	1 0 0 1	2	
7 Wayne Baxter	0 1 2 2 0 1 0	6	
8 Tony Kingsbury	*did not ride*		

21...ARENA ESSEX, July 22, L46-49

1 Glen Baxter	2 1 3 2 3 3	14	
2 Trevor O'Brien	0 3 2 2 2 2	11	3
3 †Jens Rasmussen	3 3 3 1 2	12	
4 Kelvin Mullarkey	fxN N N T	0	
5 Linden Warner	2 1 1 R 0	4	1
6 Kevin Teager	2 1 0 0 0 T	3	
7 Wayne Baxter	fx2 0 0	2	

22...Eastbourne, August 4, L34-61

1 Melvyn Taylor	1 R 2 1 2	6	
2 Trevor O'Brien	R 1 0 fxF 3	4	
3 †Jens Rasmussen	3 3 3 fnT	9	
4 Glen Baxter	2 2 0 N T	4	
5 Kelvin Mullarkey	0 1 T X 0	1	1
6 Kevin Teager	0 0 T 1 1	2	1
7 §Scott Humphries	3 2 1 0 1 0 1	8	1

23...LONG EATON, August 12, W56-39

1 Melvyn Taylor	3 2 3 1 3	12	1
2 Trevor O'Brien	2 1 3 2 fx	8	3
3 †Jens Rasmussen	3 3 E 3 3	12	
4 Glen Baxter	2 3 2 2 1	10	
5 Kelvin Mullarkey	1 R fxN 1	2	1
6 Scott Humphries	3 2 2 1 2 F	10	3
7 Wayne Baxter	2 0 N 0	2	1

24...Wimbledon, August 15, W49-47

1 Melvyn Taylor	2 3 2 2 0	9	1
2 Trevor O'Brien	1 1 0 1 1	4	3
3 †Jens Rasmussen	3 2 1 3 3	12	1
4 Glen Baxter	2 3 1 3 2	11	
5 Kelvin Mullarkey	1 1 N N N	2	1
6 Scott Humphries	2 0 2 0 2 0	6	1
7 Wayne Baxter	3 1 1 0	5	

25...BERWICK, August 26, W52-43

1 Melvyn Taylor	2 1 1 3 2	9	
2 Trevor O'Brien	F 3 2 3 3	11	
3 †Jens Rasmussen	**2 3 3 3 3**	**14**	**1**
4 Glen Baxter	0 3 3 1 0	7	
5 Kelvin Mullarkey	1 F 0 0 1	2	
6 Scott Humphries	3 3 0 1 2	9	1
7 Wayne Baxter	F 0 N	0	

26...Milton Keynes, August 28, L47-48

1 Melvyn Taylor	3 2 3 1 3	12	
2 Trevor O'Brien	2 1 0 1 0	4	2
3 †Jens Rasmussen	3 3 R 3 3	12	
4 Glen Baxter	3 2 3 0 1	9	
5 Kelvin Mullarkey	0 1 1 0 fx	2	1
6 Scott Humphries	2 2 1 1	6	1
7 Wayne Baxter	0 1 1	2	

27...HACKNEY, September 2, W50-46

1 Melvyn Taylor	2 3 2 2 2	11	
2 Trevor O'Brien	F 0 3 1 2	6	1
3 †Jens Rasmussen	2 3 3 3 2	13	
4 Glen Baxter	1 3 2 1 1	8	2
5 Scott Humphries	F fx1 1 1	3	2
6 Kelvin Mullarkey	2 0 1 fx	3	1
7 Wayne Baxter	3 2 1	6	1

28...EASTBOURNE, September 9, W62-33

1 Melvyn Taylor	2 3 3 2 2	12	2
2 Trevor O'Brien	0 1 3 2 3	9	1
3 †Jens Rasmussen	**3 3 3 3 3**	**15**	
4 Glen Baxter	**3 3 3 3 3**	**15**	
5 Scott Humphries	0 0 2 0 1	3	1
6 Kelvin Mullarkey	2 1 R 1	4	1
7 Wayne Baxter	3 0 1	4	

29...Exeter, September 10, L32-64

1 Melvyn Taylor	1 1 3 N 2	7	
2 Trevor O'Brien	0 0 1 1 2 0	4	1
3 †Jens Rasmussen	R 1 3 2 3 3	12	
4 Glen Baxter	2 0 0 0 T	2	
5 Scott Humphries	0 2 F 1 R F	3	
6 Wayne Baxter	0 0 T 1	1	
7 Kelvin Mullarkey	1 2 R	3	

30...Long Eaton, September 12, L47-49

1 Melvyn Taylor	3 3 R 2 R 3	11	1
2 Trevor O'Brien	fx1 2 2 1	6	
3 †Jens Rasmussen	1 3 2 3 3 3	15	
4 Glen Baxter	2 3 1 2 0	8	
5 Scott Humphries	1 0 0 T 1	2	1
6 Wayne Baxter	3 1 0 T	4	
7 Kelvin Mullarkey	0 R 1	1	1

31...GLASGOW, September 16, L46-49

1 Melvyn Taylor	3 2 3 3 3	14	
2 Wayne Baxter	1 1 1 1 2	6	1
3 Trevor O'Brien	X 3 0 3 3	9	
4 Glen Baxter	2 1 3 0 1	7	1
5 Scott Humphries	3 3 0 1 X	7	
6 Kelvin Mullarkey	2 fx0 fx	2	
7 Kevin Teager	N F 1	1	

32...Stoke, October 20, L46-50

1 Melvyn Taylor	3 2 3 3 3 2	16	
2 Trevor O'Brien	0 1 R 1 2	4	1
3 †Jens Rasmussen	2 3 3 3 3	14	
4 Glen Baxter	2 1 3 2 1	9	2
5 Scott Humphries	0 0 X 0 F	0	
6 Wayne Baxter	2 0 0 0	2	
7 Colin Thorpe	1 0 N	1	1

1990 ROSTER

BAXTER, Glen
B 15.12.1962, Adelaide, Australia.
BAXTER, Wayne
B 19.11.1964, Adelaide, Australia. *First season Australian.*
FAGG, Jamie Brian
B 25.7.1967, Dalby, Australia.
HUMPHRIES, Scott
B 31.7.1964, Sydney, Australia. *On loan from Wimbledon.*
JOHNS, Roger,
B 1.3.1954, Epsom, Surrey. *Signed from Wimbledon.*
KINGSBURY, Antony Harry (Tony)
B 1.12.1971, Hatfield, Hertfordshire. *Local junior.*
MULLARKEY, Kelvin John
B 29.3.1951, Chelmsford, Essex.
O'BRIEN, Trevor
B 17.11.1966, Tennent Creek, Australia.
RASMUSSEN, Jens
B 26.5.1959, Odense, Denmark.
SPARSHOTT, Nigel
B 2.9.1961, Swanley, Kent. *Signed from Long Eaton.*
TAYLOR, Melvyn Roy
B 26.4.1961, West Row, Suffolk.
TEAGER, Kevin Brian
B 21.7.1958, Tunstall, Suffolk.
THORPE, Colin Simon
B 23.3.1972, Birmingham, West Midlands.
WARNER, Linden
B 6.10.1961, Bury St. Edmunds, Suffolk.

KENNY BRAILSFORD -see Glasgow.
WAYNE BRIDGEFORD - see Peterborough.
FRASER SMITH - see Berwick.

A fitting tribute to Mr. Potter

Track Data

Promoter: The late Eric Stead and Ray Sant.
Address: Newcastle Stadium, Loomer Road, Newcastle-under-Lyme, Staffordshire.
Telephone: 0782-561575.
Information Line: 0898 31 21 49.
Track Length: 336.5 metres.
Track Record: 59.1 secs, Andrew Silver (Arena Essex), August 8, 1987, heat 1, Stoke v Arena Essex (National League).

NO-ONE will have happy memories of the Stoke season...even though it was a summer in which another piece of silverware was added to the collection.

Everything else was overshadowed by the shock death of promoter Eric Stead at a time when he was, typically, fighting to keep speedway at Loomer Road after a shock rental ultimatum from the landlords.

Eric's death stunned all speedway but his passing could not have been felt deeper than it was at the Potteries' track by those who had worked for and alongside him in recent years.

At least, in his last season in the sport, he had the satisfaction of holding the H.E.A.T. National League Team Championship trophy aloft after that memorable August Sunday afternoon when the Stoke Potters put behind them the depression of a disappointing League season.

Stoke has yet to win either the National League or its Cup competition but they had previously excelled in the Pairs competition with three victories in a span of only six years. They lost out in 1990 but then made amends with a surprise victory at Peterborough to put some gloss on what had, until then, been a decided lacklustre campaign.

Perhaps Eric, and Stoke fans, paid the penalty for being *too* loyal to his riders. While other promoters chopped and changed during the winter, Stoke began the new challenge with little more than cosmetic changes to their first team squad.

Australian Mark Carlson, who missed the whole of the 1989 season when he stayed at home, was signed on loan from Oxford and he was the only genuinely new face on parade for the first meeting of the year.

He had been a steady scoring second string with the Milton Keynes and could have been the missing link as he augmented the top six from the previous year: Nigel Crabtree, Eric Monaghan, Louis Carr, Chris Cobby, Rob Woffinden and promoter's son Ian Stead.

There was a nice rounded touch to the side. Plenty of experience but a collection of riders who weren't too long in the tooth to put themselves out when the going got a bit nasty!

Many would have fancied a bob or two on the Staffordshire side had they been allowed to bet on speedway. Those predictions seemed to be borne out when Stoke lost by only four points at Newcastle in their opening match and followed that up with a win at Rye House.

Even a home defeat by Ipswich was dismissed as, at that early stage, the East Anglians looked capable of going through the entire season without losing a single match. Another win at Glasgow to make it four points out of six away from home and everything looked rosy at Loomer Road.

Then the doubts began to creep in. Another home defeat – this time against Hackney – convinced most folk that the earlier defeat against Ipswich had not been something to be ignored and the full League season was to continue in such topsy-turvy fashion. Three home defeats in four matches (understandably to Poole, surprisingly to Middlesbrough and inexplicably to Newcastle) were followed by a stunning 48-48 draw at Ipswich and another equally praiseworthy success at Peterborough where Stoke became one of three visiting sides to win.

Only three teams (the top three) lost fewer away matches than the Potters but, at the other end of the scale, only four sides (the bottom four) had more defeats in front of their own fans.

Those statistics told their own story but, at the final retelling, count for nothing at all alongside the news of Eric Stead's death from a heart attack while awaiting a check up in a hospital in his native Sheffield.

Roll of Honour

Seasons in National League: 18 (1973-1990).
National League Record: Third (2), 1975, 1984.
National League Cup Record: Semi-finalists, 1987.
National League Team Championship: Winners (1), 1990. Runners-up (3), 1978, 1984, 1989. Fourth (3), 1977, 1980, 1985. Qualified (9), 1977, 1978, 1980, 1984, 1985, 1986, 1988, 1989, 1990.
National Series: Third (1), 1990.
Appearances: Nigel Crabtree, 231 (1984-1990).
Points: Nigel Crabtree, 2582 (1984-1990).
World Finalists: None.
NLRC Finalists: Mike Broadbank (1973-74), Alan Molyneux (1975), Les Collins (1976), Stuart Mountford (1977), Tony Lomas (1978), Ian Gledhill (1979), Tom Owen (1983-84-85), Paul Thorp (1986), Nigel Crabtree (1987, 1989), Graham Jones (1988), Eric Monaghan (1990).
Other Honours: National League (Division Three) Champions, 1949.

Star of 90
NIGEL CRABTREE
Stoke

STOKE

01...Newcastle, April 8, L46-50

1 Louis Carr	2 2 2 2 3	11	2
2 Rob Woffinden	0 0 2 T 0	2	
3 †Nigel Crabtree	3 2 2 3 3 3	16	
4 Eric Monaghan	2 3 1 3 0	9	
5 §Mark Carlson	1 1 0 0 0	2	1
6 Richard Davidson	0 0 N N	0	
7 Ian Stead	3 1 1 0 1	6	1

02...Rye House, April 22, W49-45

1 Louis Carr	3 3 1 3 3	13	1
2 Chris Cobby	1 2 1 2 2	8	1
3 †Nigel Crabtree	N 3 3 2 2	10	
4 Eric Monaghan	3 2 3 2 0	10	1
5 Mark Carlson	0 0 1 0 N	1	
6 Rob Woffinden	3 2 1 0 X 1	7	1
7 Ian Stead	R 0 0	0	

03...IPSWICH, April 28, L40-56

1 Louis Carr	3 1 2 1 0 1	8	1
2 Chris Cobby	1 0 T 0 T	1	
3 †Nigel Crabtree	3 1 3 3 2 2	14	
4 Eric Monaghan	1 2 3 2 3 0	11	
5 Mark Carlson	0 1 R T 0	1	1
6 Rob Woffinden	2 2 0 1 0	5	2
7 Ian Stead	0 T 0	0	

04...Glasgow, May 2, W51-45

1 Louis Carr	3 2 2 3 2 0	12	2
2 Chris Cobby	N 1 1 0 1	3	2
3 †Nigel Crabtree	2 3 3 3 3	14	
4 Eric Monaghan	2 2 3 3 2	12	
5 Mark Carlson	0 1 1 0 N	2	1
6 Rob Woffinden	F 2 0 T 2 2	6	1
7 Ian Stead	1 1 0	2	2

05...HACKNEY, May 5, L47-49

1 Louis Carr	3 3 3 3 1	13	
2 Chris Cobby	2 1 3 R 2	8	1
3 †Nigel Crabtree	1 0 2 3 fx	6	1
4 Eric Monaghan	3 1 2 1 0	7	
5 Mark Carlson	0 0 N 0 3	3	
6 Rob Woffinden	3 2 1 1 0 fx	7	1
7 Ian Stead	1 2 N	3	1

06...Wimbledon, May 9, L40-55

1 Louis Carr	fx 0 3 3 2 2	10	
2 Mark Carlson	2 1 2 0 T 1	6	1
3 †Nigel Crabtree	3 1 3 2 1 3	13	1
4 Eric Monaghan	1 0 3 2 1 0	7	
5 Chris Cobby	0 0 0 T 0 0	0	
6 Rob Woffinden	2 1 T T T	3	
7 Richard Davidson	fx N 1	1	1

07...MILTON KEYNES, May 12, W55-37

1 Louis Carr	**3 2 3 3 3**	**14**	**1**
2 Mark Carlson	0 3 1 2 2	8	1
3 †Nigel Crabtree	**3 3 3 3 3**	**15**	
4 Eric Monaghan	3 3 3 1 2	12	1
5 Chris Cobby	2 0 1 R 0	3	1
6 Rob Woffinden	F 1 2 0	3	1
7 Richard Davidson	X 0 0	0	

08...Eastbourne, May 13, L42-54

1 Louis Carr	3 3 1 1 0 0	8	
2 Mark Carlson	F T 0 T 0	0	
3 †Nigel Crabtree	1 3 3 3 1 2	13	1
4 Eric Monaghan	0 1 2 3 3 1	10	
5 Chris Cobby	1 1 2 2 3 1	10	3
6 Rob Woffinden	1 0 0 T	1	
7 Richard Davidson	0 fx T	0	

09...Long Eaton, May 16, W52-44

1 Louis Carr	3 1 N 2 2	8	3
2 Mark Carlson	1 2 1 1 1	6	1
3 †Nigel Crabtree	fx 3 3 3 2	11	
4 Eric Monaghan	2 2 3 3 3	13	
5 Chris Cobby	0 1 0 N 0	1	1
6 Rob Woffinden	3 0 1 1 3	8	
7 Mark Pearce	1 2 2 0	5	

10...EASTBOURNE, May 19, W54-42

1 Louis Carr	2 3 1 3 0	9	
2 Mark Carlson	1 2 1 0 1	5	3
3 †Nigel Crabtree	2 3 2 fx N	7	1
4 Eric Monaghan	X 1 1 2 2	6	2
5 Chris Cobby	2 2 3 2 2	11	1
6 Rob Woffinden	3 3 1 3 3	13	
7 Mark Pearce	1 2 0	3	

11...Milton Keynes, May 22, W59-37

1 Louis Carr	3 2 3 3 3 3	17	
2 Mark Carlson	2 0 2 2 3	9	2
3 †Nigel Crabtree	*rider replacement*		
4 Eric Monaghan	3 3 1 3 3 2 2	17	2
5 Chris Cobby	2 1 0 0 1 0	4	1
6 Rob Woffinden	3 2 1 2 1	9	2
7 Mark Pearce	0 3 0	3	
8 Richard Davidson	*did not ride*		

12...GLASGOW, June 23, W50-46

1 Louis Carr	3 2 3 0 fx	8	
2 Rob Woffinden	0 0 2 0 N	2	
3 †Nigel Crabtree	3 2 3 3 3	14	
4 Eric Monaghan	**3 3 3 3 3**	**15**	
5 Chris Cobby	0 0 2 1 1	4	1
6 Mark Carlson	3 0 0 2	5	
7 Mark Pearce	2 R 0 0	2	1

13...Exeter, June 25, L43-53

1 Louis Carr	1 2 F 2 1 1	7	2
2 Rob Woffinden	2 0 1 R 1	4	
3 †Nigel Crabtree	3 3 3 1 1 R	11	
4 Eric Monaghan	2 3 3 3 3 2	16	
5 Chris Cobby	0 1 T T 1	2	
6 Mark Carlson	2 0 T 0	2	
7 Mark Pearce	1 0 0	1	1

14...Poole, June 26, L39-57

1 Louis Carr	3 2 0 3 R 1	9	
2 Rob Woffinden	R 0 0 T T	0	
3 †Nigel Crabtree	3 3 1 R 1 R	8	
4 Eric Monaghan	3 3 3 3 3 0	15	
5 Chris Cobby	0 0 T 0 N	0	
6 Mark Carlson	2 1 1 0 1	5	
7 Mark Pearce	1 0 N 1	2	1

15...Middlesbrough, July 5, L44-52

1 Louis Carr	2 3 1 3 2 0 2	13	
2 Rob Woffinden	R 0 3 1 3 0	7	1
3 †Nigel Crabtree	2 2 2 2 3 2 1	14	
4 Eric Monaghan	*rider replacement*		
5 Chris Cobby	0 1 1 0 0	2	1
6 Mark Carlson	3 1 N 1 0 2	7	2
7 Mark Pearce	1 N 0 T	1	
8 Jeff Law	*did not ride*		

16...EXETER, July 14, W61-35

1 Louis Carr	1 2 3 2 N	8	2
2 Rob Woffinden	0 3 0 2 3	8	1
3 †Nigel Crabtree	3 3 3 2 3	14	
4 Eric Monaghan	3 2 3 3 1	12	1
5 Chris Cobby	2 1 2 1 0	6	4
6 Mark Carlson	3 2 2 2 2	11	3
7 Mark Pearce	1 1 0	2	

17...Hackney, July 27, L39-57

1 Louis Carr	2 2 2 2 2 1	11	1
2 Mark Carlson	0 0 1 1 2	4	2
3 †Nigel Crabtree	2 1 3 1 R 2	9	
4 Eric Monaghan	3 2 2 1 1 2	11	2
5 Chris Cobby	1 R 0 T N	1	
6 Richard Davidson	1 0 T 0	1	1
7 Mark Pearce	2 0 T 0	2	

18...MIDDLESBROUGH, July 28, L45-51

1 Louis Carr	3 1 3 2 1	10	1
2 Mark Carlson	1 2 1 1 3	8	
3 †Nigel Crabtree	3 3 1 2 F	9	
4 Eric Monaghan	3 2 2 1 3	11	1
5 Chris Cobby	0 0 1 0 1	2	1
6 Mark Pearce	2 1 1 0 F	4	
7 Richard Davidson	1 0 N	1	1

19...POOLE, August 4, L44-52

1 Louis Carr	2 2 2 3 fx fx	9	
2 Mark Carlson	fx 0 2 N T	2	
3 †Nigel Crabtree	3 2 R 1 2	8	
4 Eric Monaghan	2 2 2 1 3 3	13	
5 Rob Woffinden	R N 0 N 0	0	
6 Chris Cobby	3 1 1 1 0 T	6	2
7 Mark Pearce	2 1 1 2	6	3

20...PETERBOROUGH, August 11, W66-30

1 Louis Carr	3 2 3 2 2	12	2
2 Mark Carlson	2 0 2 2 3	9	2
3 †Nigel Crabtree	**3 3 3 3 3**	**15**	
4 Eric Monaghan	3 1 3 3 3	13	1
5 Chris Cobby	2 2 0 2 2	8	3
6 Richard Davidson	1 1 0 N	2	
7 Mark Pearce	3 0 2 2	7	2

21...NEWCASTLE, August 18, L41-55

1 Louis Carr	3 2 2 1 3 3	14	
2 Mark Carlson	0 1 1 T 0	2	1
3 †Nigel Crabtree	R R 0 0 R 3	3	
4 Eric Monaghan	3 3 1 1 0 2	10	2
5 Chris Cobby	0 2 T 3 2 0	7	1
6 §§Jon Hughes	0 1 N T	1	
7 Mark Pearce	3 1 0 T	4	

22...Ipswich, August 23, D48-48

1 Louis Carr	fx 2 3 2 fx	7	1
2 Mark Carlson	2 1 1 N 0	4	1
3 †Nigel Crabtree	3 X 2 0 3	8	
4 Eric Monaghan	3 3 3 3 2	14	
5 §David Clarke	0 1 0 1 2	4	1
6 Chris Cobby	2 2 3 0 2 2	11	1
7 Mark Pearce	0 0 N	0	

23...Berwick, August 25, L40-56

1 Louis Carr	R 1 0 N N	1	
2 Mark Carlson	1 0 0 T T	1	
3 †Nigel Crabtree	F 3 3 1 2 3	12	
4 Eric Monaghan	3 2 2 3 3 3	16	1
5 David Clarke	0 X 3 0 fx	3	
6 Chris Cobby	0 0 2 0 2	4	2
7 Mark Pearce	1 1 1 0	3	

24...BERWICK, August 27, W58-38

1 Louis Carr	fx 2 3 3 2	10	1
2 Mark Carlson	3 0 2 1 2	8	1
3 †Nigel Crabtree	2 2 3 R 3	10	1
4 Eric Monaghan	**3 3 3 2 3**	**14**	**1**
5 David Clarke	2 1 2 1 1	7	2
6 Chris Cobby	1 3 N 0	4	
7 Mark Pearce	0 1 3 1	5	1

25...Arena Essex, August 30, L46-50

1 Louis Carr	2 2 2 1 3	13	1
2 Mark Carlson	0 1 3 1 1 1	7	1
3 †Nigel Crabtree	2 2 2 2 3 3	14	
4 Eric Monaghan	3 2 R 3 R 1	9	
5 David Clarke	1 0 1 R T	2	
6 Chris Cobby	1 0 T T	1	
7 Mark Pearce	0 0 T	0	

26....Peterborough, August 31, W49-46

1 Louis Carr	1 1 2 3 3	10	1
2 Mark Carlson	0 2 0 N N	2	
3 †Nigel Crabtree	2 3 3 2 3 2	15	1
4 Eric Monaghan	3 2 3 0 1 2	11	1
5 David Clarke	0 0 N 0 N	0	
6 Chris Cobby	2 0 T 1 3	6	
7 Mark Pearce	1 1 T 1 2 fx	5	4

27...ARENA ESSEX, September 2, W54-40

1 Louis Carr	1 2 2 2 fx	7	3
2 Mark Carlson	2 3 2 1 2	10	2
3 †Nigel Crabtree	2 3 1 1 1	8	3
4 Eric Monaghan	3 3 3 3 X	12	
5 David Clarke	2 R 0 2 2	6	1
6 Chris Cobby	3 0 1 3	7	
7 Mark Pearce	1 1 2	4	1

28...WIMBLEDON, September 8, W51-45

1 Louis Carr	0 1 0 1 1	3	1
2 Mark Carlson	1 2 3 2 3	11	
3 †Nigel Crabtree	3 0 3 3 3	12	
4 Eric Monaghan	**3 3 3 3 3**	**15**	
5 David Clarke	N R 1 0 2	3	1
6 Chris Cobby	3 N 1 2 1 0 0	7	
7 Jon Hughes	0 0 N N	0	

29...LONG EATON, September 16, W61-35

1 Louis Carr	**3 3 3 2 2**	**13**	**2**
2 Mark Carlson	2 1 0 0 N	3	1
3 †Nigel Crabtree	3 3 3 3 R	12	
4 Eric Monaghan	**3 3 3 3 3**	**15**	
5 David Clarke	1 0 0 1 N	2	
6 Chris Cobby	3 2 2 2 3	12	2
7 Mark Pearce	2 1 0 1	4	2

30...EDINBURGH, September 22, W62-34

1 Louis Carr	2 2 2 3 1	10	2
2 Mark Carlson	1 3 1 3 2	10	2
3 †Nigel Crabtree	3 2 3 2 1	11	1
4 Eric Monaghan	3 2 3 2 3	13	1
5 David Clarke	0 0 N 1 3	4	1
6 Chris Cobby	3 2 3 1 3	12	1
7 Mark Pearce	2 0 0	2	1

31...RYE HOUSE, October 20, W50-46

1 Louis Carr	E 2 1 2 0	5	1
2 Mark Carlson	1 1 1 2 1	6	3
3 †Nigel Crabtree	1 3 N N N	4	
5 Eric Monaghan	3 3 2 1 3	12	1
5 David Clarke	1 X 1 1 2	5	1
6 Chris Cobby	2 3 3 2 2 3	15	1
7 Mark Pearce	R 2 R R 1	3	1

32...Edinburgh, October 21, L47-49

1 Louis Carr	3 2 3 R 2 2 3	15	1
2 Mark Carlson	0 1 1 1 2 1	6	2
3 Nigel Crabtree	*rider replacement*		
4 Eric Monaghan	2 0 1 T N	3	
5 David Clarke	1 3 2 F fx F T	6	1
6 Chris Cobby	3 2 2 X 2 3 3	15	1
7 §§Garry Stead	1 0 N 1	2	
8 Jon Hughes	*did not ride*		

1990 ROSTER

CARLSON, Mark
B 24.10.1965, Gold Coast, Australia. *On loan from Oxford.*

CARR, John Louis
B 28.1.1960, Preston, Lancashire.

CLARKE, David John
B 25.3.1969, Rugby, Warwickshire. *Signed from Milton Keynes.*

COBBY, Christopher Robert
B 18.8.1969, Stoke-on-Trent, Staffordshire.

CRABTREE, Nigel Robin
B 15.3.1960, Halifax, West Yorkshire.

DAVIDSON, Richard William
B 30.4.1964, Paraparaumu, New Zealand.

HUGHES, Jonathan
B 18.12.1969, Burton-on-Trent, Staffordshire.

LAW, Jeffrey
B 11.3.1963, Bradford, West Yorkshire. *Stand-in junior.*

MONAGHAN, Eric
B 31.10.1957, Whiteley, Greater Manchester.

PEARCE, Mark Andrew
B 25.1.1968, Townsville, Australia.

REED, Jason Scott
B 10.10.1969, Hinckley, Leicestershire.

STEAD, Garry
B 5.1.1972, Meltham, West Yorkshire.

IAN STEAD - see Newcastle.
ROBERT WOFFINDEN - see Milton Keynes.

The missing links that hit the Dons

Track Data

Promoters: Peter Brown and Don Scarff.
Address: Wimbledon Stadium, Plough Lane, London SW17 0BL.
Telephone: 081-946-5361.
Hotline: 0898 800 694.
Track Length: 286 metres (1165 metres, 4 lap race).
Track Record: 56.4 secs, Nathan Simpson (Wimbledon), October 3, 1990, Heat 1, Wimbledon v Middlesbrough (National League).

WIMBLEDON came within a whisker of joining the 1990 Sunbrite League. And, when the final decision was made to stay put for another season in the National League, the Montine Dons not only lost their chance to attract the world's best to Plough Lane...they also lost the man who had turned them into the most talked about team in the country!

For Russell Lanning's first decision after talks that would have taken the Londoners back into the top flight, had broken down was to refuse a new contract.

Plough Lane – and Wimbledon – was never the same once he had left. The buzz had gone out of the club's publicity machine and while Lanning had never actually won a trophy while at the track he had given the club an identity of its own and certainly made them an attraction wherever they went.

You can't help but wonder what Lanning might have done with the team that his successors managed to assemble despite losing Australian Todd Wiltshire who was to confound all his critics by going on to finish third in his debut World Final.

Lanning had discovered Wiltshire with a little help from the family's Australian connections with Down Under journalist Peter White and he had turned him into a figure of some controversy.

Some felt his reputation had been overblown but he proved them all wrong. The only sadness was that he wasn't able to do it in Wimbledon's famous red and yellow and their decision to accept nomination to the 1991 Sunbrite League came too late to keep Lanning.

As soon as it was obvious that the New South Walian wasn't going to hang around for another season, Wimbledon moved swiftly and agreed a deal with Oxford to sign surplus to requirements Andy Grahame on a loan agreement.

It was an inspired decision and Grahame quickly endeared himself to his new public with a rattling good maximum in the Maslens Classic, the opening night of the new season.

He was a tower of strength from that moment onwards and crowned his own season by becoming the first Wimbledon rider to win the National League Riders' Championship Final. But that was just about the only honour that came the Dons' way as they slipped out of the top six in the National League; suffered a surprise home and away defeat to Middlesbrough in the semi-final of the Knock Out Cup and didn't mount any serious challenge for either the Team or Pairs Championships.

Exactly why their only taste of success came in finishing runners-up in the National Series (and could argue they might have won had not their home leg been curtailed by the weather) is hard to explain.

They had retained five of their 1989 side and should have been as strong with Grahame replacing Wiltshire and three or four riders fighting for Roger Johns' vacant position.

But, for some reason, things never gelled and while Simpson upped his average, Neville Tatum, Ray Morton and Nigel Leaver all went in the opposite direction.

Could it have been Lanning's influence?

Roll of Honour

Seasons in National League: 6 (1985-1990).
National League Record: Runners-up (1), 1989.
National League Cup Record: Runners-up (1), 1988.
National League Team Championship: Fourth (1), 1987. Qualified (3), 1985, 1987, 1990.
National Series: Runners-up (1), 1990.
Appearances: Roger Johns, 182 (1985-1989).
Points: Roger Johns, 1763 (1985-1989).
World Finalists: Bob Andrews (1960-61-62, 1964), Barry Briggs (1954-55-56-57-58-59), Cyril Brine (1950-51), Mike Erskine (1950), Sverre Harrfeldt (1963), Trevor Hedge (1970), Ron How (1957-58-59, 1961-62-63), Vic Huxley (1936), Edward Jancarz (1977, 1979, 1981-82), Tommy Jansson (1973, 1975), Dave Jessup (1982), Benny Kaufman (1938), Wilbur Lamoreaux (1937-38), Reg Luckhurst (1965), Leo McAuliffe (1963), Cyril Maidment (1961), Geoff Mardon (1953-54), Peter Moore (1956), Ronnie Moore (1950-51-52-53-54-55-56, 1958-59-60-61-62, 1969, 1971), Kai Niemi (1982), Norman Parker (1949, 1951), Wal Phillips (1936), Geoff Pymar (1938), Ernie Roccio (1951).
NLRC Finalists: Mike Ferreira (1985), Jamie Luckhurst (1986), Kevin Jolly (1987-88), Todd Wiltshire (1989), Andy Grahame (1990).
Other Honours: National League (Division One) Champions, 1954, 1955, 1956, 1958, 1959, 1960, 1961. National Trophy Winners, 1938, 1950, 1951, 1953, 1959, 1960, 1962. National League (Division One) Knock-out Cup Winners, 1962. Speedway Star Knock-out Cup Winners, 1968, 1969, 1970.

Star of 90
NEVILLE TATUM
Wimbledon

WIMBLEDON

01...PETERBOROUGH, April 11, L46-49

1 Nathan Simpson	1 1 1 2 2	7	2
2 Nevile Tatum	2 2 3 3 3	13	
3 †Ray Morton	3 2 2 3 1	11	
4 §Andy Grahame	3 3 3 1 0	10	1
5 Nigel Leaver	1 X 2 0 0	3	1
6 Jim Dormer	X F 0 N	0	
7 §Peter Schroeck	R 1 1 0	2	1

02...LONG EATON, April 18, W62-34

1 Nathan Simpson	1 3 2 0 2	8	2
2 Neville Tatum	**3 2 3 3 3**	**14**	**1**
3 †Ray Morton	**3 3 3 2 2**	**13**	**2**
4 Andy Grahame	1 2 3 3 3	12	1
5 Nigel Leaver	0 3 1 3 3	10	
6 §§Deon Prinsloo	3 R F N	3	
7 Peter Schroeck	0 1 1 0	2	

03...Newcastle, April 22, W57-39

1 Nathan Simpson	3 3 1 2 2	11	1
2 Neville Tatum	2 2 3 3 2	12	2
3 †Ray Morton	0 3 3 2 1	9	1
4 Andy Grahame	3 3 2 3 1	12	2
5 Nigel Leaver	1 1 3 1 2	8	1
6 Peter Schroeck	1 0 N 1	2	1
7 Deon Prinsloo	0 2 1 0	3	

04...EASTBOURNE, April 25, W66-29

1 Nathan Simpson	**3 3 3 3 2**	**14**	**1**
2 Neville Tatum	**2 2 3 2 3**	**12**	**3**
3 †Ray Morton	3 3 3 3 fx	12	
4 Andy Grahame	**3 3 3 2 3**	**14**	**1**
5 Nigel Leaver	0 2 2 2 3	9	3
6 Deon Prinsloo	F 1 fx2	3	1
7 Peter Schroeck	1 0 1	2	

05...Rye House, April 29, W49-47

1 Nathan Simpson	3 3 3 1 2	12	2
2 Neville Tatum	1 2 3 2 1	9	2
3 †Ray Morton	2 2 2 fx1	7	1
4 Andy Grahame	2 1 2 2 3	10	1
5 Nigel Leaver	0 2 1 2 2	7	1
6 Deon Prinsloo	2 1 N E 0 fx	3	1
7 Peter Schroeck	1 N fxN 0	1	1

06...BERWICK, May 2, W55-41

1 Nathan Simpson	2 2 2 2 2	10	
2 Neville Tatum	1 1 1 0 3	6	3
3 †Ray Morton	**3 3 3 3 3**	**15**	
4 Andy Grahame	3 3 3 1 0	10	1
5 Nigel Leaver	1 1 fx1 2	5	1
6 Deon Prinsloo	fxN 2 1	3	1
7 §Peter Chapman	2 1 2 1	6	

07...STOKE, May 9, W55-40

1 Nathan Simpson	3 2 1 3 1	10	1
2 Neville Tatum	R 3 F 3 3	9	
3 †Ray Morton	fxN N N N	0	
4 Andy Grahame	2 3 2 2 3	12	2
5 Nigel Leaver	3 2 1 2 2	10	2
6 Peter Chapman	3 N 2 fx	5	
7 Deon Prinsloo	1 2 1 3 1 1	9	2

172

08...Peterborough, May 11, L39-57

1 Nathan Simpson	3 1 2 2 1 2 3	14	
2 Neville Tatum	1 0 3 R 0	4	
3 Ray Morton	*rider replacement*		
4 Andy Grahame	3 2 3 2 0 0	13	
5 Nigel Leaver	0 1 1 R 1	3	
6 †Peter Chapman	2 1 1 0 1 0	5	1
7 Deon Prinsloo	0 R N	0	
8 Justin Pryor	*did not ride*		

09...Milton Keynes, May 15, W53-42

1 Nathan Simpson	**3 3 3 3 2**	**14**	**1**
2 Neville Tatum	0 0 2 2 0	4	1
3 †Ray Morton	3 2 1 1 0	7	
4 Andy Grahame	3 2 2 1 3	11	2
5 Nigel Leaver	1 3 3 3 1	11	
6 Peter Chapman	F 0 N N	0	
7 Deon Prinsloo	2 1 1 0 2	6	1

10...MILTON KEYNES, May 16, W62-33

1 Nathan Simpson	2 1 2 1 2	8	3
2 Neville Tatum	fx2 3 3 3	11	
3 †Ray Morton	**3 3 2 3 N**	**11**	**1**
4 Andy Grahame	3 3 2 3 3	14	
5 Nigel Leaver	1 2 fx2 1	6	3
6 Peter Chapman	3 1 R N	4	
7 Deon Prinsloo	1 2 3 0 2	8	1

11...HACKNEY, May 23, W52-41

1 Nathan Simpson	1 1 3 2 1	8	3
2 Neville Tatum	2 2 3 2 3	12	1
3 †Ray Morton	2 3 0 N N	5	
4 Andy Grahame	3 3 2 3 3	14	
5 Nigel Leaver	2 1 1 1 2	7	2
6 Peter Chapman	3 N N N	3	
7 Deon Prinsloo	fx0 fx1 1 1	3	

12...Long Eaton, June 13, D48-48

1 Nathan Simpson	3 3 2 3 1	12	1
2 Neville Tatum	2 0 R 1 3	6	2
3 †Ray Morton	3 3 3 2 0	11	
4 Andy Grahame	2 3 2 1 2	10	
5 Nigel Leaver	R 0 E 1 2	3	1
6 Deon Prinsloo	0 0 1 1 1	3	1
7 §§Justin Pryor	2 0 1	3	

13...Middlesbrough, June 14, L35-60

1 Nathan Simpson	2 3 3 1 1 2	12	2
2 Neville Tatum	3 0 0 2 1 0	6	
3 †Ray Morton	R 1 T T T	1	
4 Andy Grahame	3 2 0 2 0 0	7	
5 Nigel Leaver	1 1 2 1 1 1	7	2
6 Deon Prinsloo	fx0 1 0	1	1
7 Justin Pryor	fx1 T	1	

14...Berwick, June 23, L42-53

1 Nathan Simpson	2 R 2 2 3 1	10	1
2 Neville Tatum	1 1 fx1 1	4	3
3 †Ray Morton	1 2 3 0 1	7	
4 Andy Grahame	3 2 0 3 1 2	11	
5 Nigel Leaver	2 1 2 1 2 F	8	3
6 Deon Prinsloo	fx0 T T	0	
7 Justin Pryor	2 0 T	2	

15...Eastbourne, July 1, L42-54

1 Nathan Simpson	3 3 3 1 1 1	12	
2 Neville Tatum	0 F 2 3 0	5	1
3 †Ray Morton	1 R 0 0 2	3	
4 Andy Grahame	**3 3 3 3 3 3**	**18**	
5 Nigel Leaver	R 0 0 1 1 0	2	
6 Deon Prinsloo	0 1 T T	1	
7 Justin Pryor	1 0 T	1	

16...Ipswich, July 12, L43-53

1 Nathan Simpson	2 0 2 1 1 0	6	1
2 Neville Tatum	0 2 2 3 3 2	12	
3 †Ray Morton	3 0 2 R 1	6	1
4 Andy Grahame	2 3 1 3 fxT	9	
5 Nigel Leaver	1 R 0 T T 2	3	1
6 Peter Chapman	3 1 1 N T	5	1
7 Justin Pryor	2 0 N 0	2	1

17...Edinburgh, July 22, D48-48

1 Nathan Simpson	2 3 3 3 3 2 2	18	2
2 †Ray Morton	3 0 1 0 3 3	10	1
3 Neville Tatum	3 R 3 3 2 3	14	
4 Andy Grahame	*rider replacement*		
5 Nigel Leaver	fx0 1 0 0 1	2	1
6 Peter Chapman	1 1 2 fx	4	
7 Deon Prinsloo	0 fxfx	0	
8 Troy Scott	*did not ride*		

18...GLASGOW, July 25, W54-42

1 Nathan Simpson	2 3 3 1 3	12	
2 †Ray Morton	fx2 3 R 3	8	1
3 Neville Tatum	3 2 3 2 1	11	
4 Andy Grahame	3 3 3 0 2	11	1
5 Nigel Leaver	0 0 0 1 3	4	1
6 Peter Chapman	R 1 N 2 F	3	1
7 Deon Prinsloo	2 1 N 2	5	2

19...Arena Essex, July 28, L46-50

1 Nathan Simpson	2 1 3 0 2 3	11	
2 †Ray Morton	0 3 2 3 0 2	10	1
3 Neville Tatum	3 N 1 1 1 1	7	2
4 Andy Grahame	3 3 fxN T	6	
5 Nigel Leaver	1 F 2 3 2 2	10	
6 Peter Chapman	1 1 T T	2	
7 Deon Prinsloo	0 fx0 T 0	0	

20...Exeter, August 6, L34-62

1 Nathan Simpson	1 1 1 0 0 0	3	1
2 †Ray Morton	0 3 2 1 2 3	11	
3 Neville Tatum	2 1 2 2 1 1	9	
4 Andy Grahame	2 R T T T	2	
5 Nigel Leaver	1 2 R 1 0 2	6	2
6 Peter Chapman	2 R N 1 0	3	1
7 Justin Pryor	0 N 0 T	0	

21...EXETER, August 8, W61-35

1 Nathan Simpson	1 3 3 2 2	11	2
2 Neville Tatum	3 1 1 fx2	7	1
3 †Ray Morton	3 3 1 3 3	13	1
4 Andy Grahame	**3 3 3 3 3**	**15**	
5 Nigel Leaver	2 0 2 0 2	6	3
6 Peter Chapman	3 1 R 3	7	
7 Justin Pryor	F F 2	2	

22...RYE HOUSE, August 15, L47-49

1 Nathan Simpson	3 3 3 3 1 3	16	1
2 Neville Tatum	0 1 2 2 3	8	2
3 †Ray Morton	2 fx3 fx2	7	
4 Andy Grahame	3 2 2 3 2 1	13	
5 Nigel Leaver	fx0 0 1 1	2	1
6 Justin Pryor	1 0 N 0	1	
7 Deon Prinsloo	0 N 0	0	

23...EDINBURGH, September 5, W50-46

1 Nathan Simpson	3 2 3 3 0	11	
2 Neville Tatum	2 1 1 2 1	7	3
3 †Ray Morton	2 3 2 1 3	11	
4 Andy Grahame	3 2 2 1 1	9	1
5 Nigel Leaver	0 1 3 0 2	6	2
6 Peter Chapman	3 1 0 0	4	1
7 Justin Pryor	2 0 0	2	1

24...Stoke, September 8, L45-51

1 Nathan Simpson	2 1 2 1 0	6	3
2 Neville Tatum	3 2 fx1 2	8	1
13 †Ray Morton	1 3 R R N	4	1
4 Andy Grahame	2 3 3 2 2	12	
5 Nigel Leaver	0 1 1 2 0	4	
6 Peter Chapman	2 2 N 2 2 1 1	10	1
7 Justin Pryor	1 N N 0	1	1

25...Glasgow, September 9, W52-44

1 Nathan Simpson	2 3 1 2 2 2	12	2
2 Neville Tatum	0 1 2 0 3	6	
3 †Ray Morton	2 3 2 3 2 3	15	1
4 Andy Grahame	1 3 3 3 3	13	
5 Nigel Leaver	0 T 1 1 1	3	1
6 Peter Chapman	2 fxT 0 R	2	
7 Justin Pryor	0 N 1	1	1

26...ARENA ESSEX, September 12, W61-35

1 Nathan Simpson	2 2 2 2 1	9	2
2 Neville Tatum	1 1 3 3 3	11	2
3 †Ray Morton	3 2 0 R 1	6	2
4 Andy Grahame	**2 3 3 3 3**	**14**	**1**
5 Nigel Leaver	3 F 2 2 2	9	1
6 Peter Chapman	3 2 3 0	8	1
7 Justin Pryor	2 1 1	4	1

27...Hackney, September 14, L45-51

1 Nathan Simpson	3 2 3 2 1 3	14	
2 Neville Tatum	1 1 2 1 3	8	3
3 †Ray Morton	1 0 2 2 1	6	
4 Andy Grahame	3 3 2 2 3 1	14	
5 Nigel Leaver	0 1 1 0 0	2	2
6 JIm Dormer	0 T 0 N	0	
7 Justin Pryor	1 0 T 0	1	

28...IPSWICH, September 19, W49-47

1 Nathan Simpson	2 3 2 3 0	10	1
2 Neville Tatum	1 2 2 3 2	10	2
3 †Ray Morton	1 3 2 0 3	9	1
4 Andy Grahame	3 1 2 1 2	9	1
5 Nigel Leaver	1 2 1 1 F	5	1
6 Peter Chapman	3 2 0 0 0	5	
7 Justin Pryor	1 0 N	1	

29...Poole, September 25, L42-54

1 Nathan Simpson	1 3 2 R 0	6	
2 Neville Tatum	3 R 1 0 0	4	
3 †Ray Morton	2 1 2 2 1	8	2
4 Andy Grahame	2 2 3 3 3 2	15	
5 Nigel Leaver	0 1 1 1 0	3	2
6 Peter Chapman	2 3 N 0 T 1	6	
7 Justin Pryor	0 N 0	0	

30...POOLE, September 26, L47-48

1 Nathan Simpson	1 3 1 0 0	5	
2 Neville Tatum	0 1 3 N 1	5	
3 †Ray Morton	3 3 2 2 1	11	
4 Andy Grahame	**3 3 3 3 3**	**15**	
5 Nigel Leaver	0 1 1 1 0	3	1
6 Peter Chapman	3 0 2 0 F	5	1
7 Justin Pryor	2 1 0	3	1

31...MIDDLESBROUGH, October 3, D48-48

1 Nathan Simpson	3 3 2 1 1 2	12	3
2 Neville Tatum	fx1 3 R 3	7	
3 †Ray Morton	X R T N N	0	
4 Andy Grahame	2 2 3 3 2 3	15	
5 Nigel Leaver	fxfx2 1 2 2	7	1
6 Peter Chapman	0 3 1 1 1	6	1
7 Justin Pryor	1 N 0	1	

32...NEWCASTLE, October 10, W57-39

1 Nathan Simpson	3 3 3 1 1	11	1
2 Neville Tatum	2 1 3 1 0	7	1
3 †Ray Morton	0 2 2 3 1	8	
4 Andy Grahame	3 3 3 3 2	14	
5 Nigel Leaver	2 2 1 2 0	7	3
6 Peter Chapman	3 1 1 1	6	1
7 Justin Pryor	2 2 0	4	2

1990 ROSTER

CHAPMAN, Peter Bryan
B 5.2.1966, Boston, Lincolnshire. *On loan from Peterborough.*
DORMER, James (Jim)
B 13.8.1963, Forest Gate, London.
GRAHAME, Andrew George
B 10.9.1957, Birmingham, West Midlands. *On loan from Oxford.*
LEAVER, Nigel Paul
B 28.9.1965, Walsall, West Midlands.
MORTON, Raymond Paul
B 19.6.1968, London.
PRINSLOO, Deon
B 24.4.1972, Gwelo, Zimbabwe. *First season newcomer.*
PRYOR, Justin
B 6.12.1970, Waratah, Australia. *First season newcomer.*
SCHROECK, Peter Engnaz
B 18.9.1966, Aschaffenburg, West Germany. *Signed from Rye House.*
SCOTT, Troy
B 18.11.1968, Broken Hill, New South Wales, Australia. *First season newcomer.*
SIMPSON, Nathan Vincent
B 15.3.1969, Slough, Berkshire.
TATUM, Neville
B 21.7.1965, Epsom, Surrey.
MARTIN JONES - See Middlesbrough.

AVERAGES National League

No.	Rider	Track/s	M.	R.	Pts.	BP.	TPts.	Average	1989	Up/Down
1	Craig Boyce	Poole	32	178	456.0	13	469.0	10.539	11	10
2	Steve Schofield	Hackney	30	159	409.0	6	415.0	10.440	1	-1
3	Chris Louis	Ipswich	32	175	433.0	18	451.0	10.309	12	9
4	Steve Regeling	Exeter	32	173	430.0	11	441.0	10.197	6	2
5	Rod Hunter	Middlesbrough	32	164	393.0	17	410.0	10.000	14	9
6	David Bargh	Newcastle	28	149	358.0	5	363.0	9.745		
7	Mick Poole	Peterborough	13	71	154.0	16	170.0	9.577	18	11
8	Andy Grahame	Wimbledon	31	159	364.0	15	379.0	9.535		
9	Andy Galvin	Hackney	23	111	238.0	24	262.0	9.441	2	-7
10	Jens Rasmussen	Rye House	31	180	416.0	6	422.0	9.378	13	3
11	Gordon Kennett	Eastbourne	25	128	286.0	9	295.0	9.219	10	-1
12	Eric Monaghan	Stoke	31	166	364.0	18	382.0	9.205	24	12
13	Steve Lawson	Glasgow	32	160	334.0	21	355.0	8.875	20	7
14	Melvyn Taylor	Rye House	11	56	119.0	5	124.0	8.857	39	25
15	Alun Rossiter	Poole	31	159	324.0	28	352.0	8.855	34	19
16	Martin Goodwin	Arena Essex	22	123	260.0	12	272.0	8.846	25	9
17	David Walsh	Berwick	24	118	237.0	23	260.0	8.814	41	24
18	Les Collins	Edinburgh	32	176	362.0	25	387.0	8.795	15	-3
19	Tom Knudsen	Poole	11	55	104.0	16	120.0	8.727		
20	David Norris	Ipswich	23	111	205.0	37	242.0	8.721	57	37
21	Darren Sumner	Middlesbrough	32	164	331.0	23	354.0	8.634	36	15
22	Mark Courtney	Berwick	32	174	341.0	34	375.0	8.621	7	-15
23	Nigel Crabtree	Stoke	30	158	330.0	10	340.0	8.608	5	-18
24	Nathan Simpson	Wimbledon	32	174	335.0	39	374.0	8.598	52	28
25	Kenny McKinna	Glasgow	28	145	293.0	17	310.0	8.552	4	-21
26	Shane Bowes	Glasgow	28	143	274.0	29	303.0	8.476	70	44
27	Richard Hellsén	Long Eaton	28	146	300.0	8	308.0	8.438	19	-8
28	Paul Whittaker	Hackney	32	178	354.0	14	368.0	8.270	46	18
29	Dean Standing	Ipswich	30	148	278.0	27	305.0	8.243	31	2
30	Peter Carr	Newcastle	31	165	324.0	16	340.0	8.242	23	-7
31	Louis Carr	Stoke	32	171	318.0	32	350.0	8.187	49	18
32	Rob Tilbury	Arena Essex	32	173	335.0	16	351.0	8.116	33	1
33	Tony Langdon	Poole	29	158	260.0	58	318.0	8.051	60	27
34	Alan Mogridge	Ipswich	32	174	299.0	51	350.0	8.046	40	6
35	Craig Hodgson	Peterborough	31	184	351.0	15	366.0	7.957	47	12
36	Freddy Schøtt	Edinburgh	28	133	245.0	17	262.0	7.880		
37	Frank Andersen	Peterborough	27	149	260.0	29	289.0	7.758	28	-9
38	Richard Green	Exeter	32	164	285.0	33	318.0	7.756	37	-1
39	Jamie Luckhurst	Middlesbrough	25	114	194.0	26	220.0	7.719	53	14
40	Peter Jeffery	Exeter	27	139	247.0	21	268.0	7.712	54	14
41	David Blackburn	Berwick	26	134	246.0	7	253.0	7.552	8	-33
42	Glen Baxter	Rye House	26	149	267.0	14	281.0	7.544	35	-7
43	Gary Allan	Poole	32	173	283.0	42	325.0	7.514	55	12
44	Martin Dixon	Newcastle	27	139	231.0	30	261.0	7.511	42	-2
45	Ray Morton	Wimbledon	31	145	255.0	17	272.0	7.503	22	-23
46	Neville Tatum	Wimbledon	32	163	268.0	36	304.0	7.460	30	-16
47	Paul Bentley	Middlesbrough	31	159	243.0	48	291.0	7.321	87	40
48	Kevin Jolly	Milton Keynes	31	160	258.0	30	288.0	7.200	27	-21
49	David Cheshire	Middlesbrough	32	161	261.0	27	288.0	7.155		
50	Brett Saunders	Edinburgh	25	127	198.0	27	225.0	7.087	29	-21
51	Carl Blackbird	Edinburgh	29	153	236.0	34	270.0	7.059		
52	Peter Glanz	Milton Keynes	30	162	262.0	22	284.0	7.012	32	-20
53	Nigel De'ath	Long Eaton	23	117	186.0	19	205.0	7.009	78	25
54	Steve Wilcock	Middlesbrough	30	137	190.0	50	240.0	7.007	93	39
55	Scott Norman	Peterborough	31	177	285.0	21	306.0	6.915	50	-5
56	Charlie McKinna	Glasgow	32	164	249.0	34	283.0	6.902	71	15
57	Andy Buck	Eastbourne	28	147	241.0	12	253.0	6.884	26	-31
58	Sean Courtney	Glasgow	24	116	160.0	34	194.0	6.690	38	-20
59	Tony Primmer	Eastbourne	32	169	236.0	46	282.0	6.675	79	20
60	Gary Chessell	Poole	23	109	156.0	25	181.0	6.642		
61	Colin Cook	Exeter	31	153	215.0	38	253.0	6.614	62	1
62	Shane Parker	Ipswich	32	171	243.0	38	281.0	6.573		
63	Andy Campbell	Berwick	32	175	250.5	37	287.5	6.571	51	-12
64	Paul Woods	Eastbourne	32	181	246.0	37	283.0	6.254		
65	Alan Rivett	Berwick	31	145	188.0	36	224.0	6.179	128	63
66	Gary Tagg	Hackney	28	143	179.0	41	220.0	6.154	89	23

LEGEND

The 1990 National League averages listed are taken from the official referee's marked programmes.

Reading from left to right the figures list the following: overall ranking; rider; track or tracks; matches; rides; points; bonus points; total points; calculated match average (out of 12.000), 1989 ranking; and movement up or down the rankings.

The calculated match average is taken by dividing the total number of points scored by the number of rides and multiplied by four.

Riders are only given an overall ranking if they rode in a minimum of six National League matches during the 1990 season.

▲ Statistics are supplied courtesy of Derek Smithson, official statistician to the National League and we thank him for all his co-operation in ensuring the complete accuracy of the statistics.

AVERAGES National League

No.	Rider	Track/s	M.	R.	Pts.	BP.	TPts.	Average	1989	Up/Down
67	Kevin Smart	Long Eaton	32	163	227.0	22	249.0	6.110	68	1
68	Rod Colquhoun	Poole	29	109	134.0	32	166.0	6.092	125	57
69	Michael Coles	Edinburgh	32	169	223.0	32	255.0	6.036	59	-10
70	Nigel Flatman	Peterborough	25	101	121.0	31	152.0	6.020	81	11
71	Paul Fry	Long Eaton	32	166	222.0	27	249.0	6.000	73	2
71	Jon Cooper	Milton Keynes	8	38	47.0	10	57.0	6.000	139	68
73	Roger Johns	Rye House	11	64	86.0	9	95.0	5.938	44	-29
74	Simon Green	Newcastle	30	158	201.5	33	234.5	5.937	107	33
75	Phil Jeffrey	Glasgow	29	115	133.5	36	169.5	5.896	90	15
76	Chris Cobby	Stoke	31	145	181.0	32	213.0	5.876	77	1
77	Trevor Banks	Milton Keynes	12	60	80.0	8	88.0	5.867	67	-10
78	Rob Grant	Berwick	29	124	149.0	31	180.0	5.806	56	-22
79	Wayne Garratt	Arena Essex	32	164	205.0	33	238.0	5.805	76	-3
79	Jason Lyons	Glasgow	32	133	162.0	31	193.0	5.805		
81	Scott Robson	Berwick	22	91	119.0	13	132.0	5.802	85	4
82	Darren Standing	Eastbourne	11	41	47.0	12	59.0	5.756	100	18
83	Jamie Fagg	Rye House	9	42	49.0	11	60.0	5.714	119	36
84	Jamie Habbin	Long Eaton	28	125	161.0	17	178.0	5.696	69	-15
85	Troy Pratt	Arena Essex	25	119	150.0	18	168.0	5.647	114	29
86	Keith Pritchard	Eastbourne	32	159	186.0	38	224.0	5.635	80	-6
87	Mark Blackbird	Long Eaton/Milton Keynes	25	136	175.0	16	191.0	5.618	141	54
88	Mark Carlson	Stoke	32	144	166.0	34	200.0	5.556		
89	Brian Nixon	Eastbourne	7	29	34.0	6	40.0	5.517		
90	Scott Lamb	Edinburgh	31	132	158.0	23	181.0	5.485	72	-18
91	Nigel Leaver	Wimbledon	32	165	181.0	43	224.0	5.430	83	-8
92	Trevor O'Brien	Rye House	32	179	209.0	33	242.0	5.408	129	37
93	Peter Chapman	Wimbledon	21	81	99.0	10	109.0	5.383	96	3
94	Michael Warren	Hackney	32	169	196.0	30	226.0	5.349	130	36
95	Steve Bishop	Exeter	32	144	167.0	23	190.0	5.278	65	-30
96	Andy Sell	Exeter	10	32	35.0	6	41.0	5.125	86	-10
97	David Clarke	Milton Keynes/Stoke	35	174	191.0	30	221.0	5.080	84	-13
98	Mark Thorpe	Newcastle	29	134	148.0	21	169.0	5.045	94	-4
99	Robbie Fuller	Ipswich	31	135	153.0	17	170.0	5.037	102	3
100	Ian Barney	Peterborough/Exeter	31	138	147.0	26	173.0	5.014	48	-52
101	Andy Hines	Milton Keynes	26	115	121.0	21	142.0	4.939	61	-40
102	Kevin Brice	Arena Essex	32	145	156.0	23	179.0	4.938	109	7

DEBUTANTS

The averages of riders who made their debut in the 1990 National League were:

Tom Knudsen (Poole & Denmark)	8.727
Freddy Schøtt (Edinburgh & Denmark)	7.880
Shane Parker (Ipswich & Australia)	6.573
Jason Lyons (Glasgow & Australia)	5.805
Brian Nixon (Eastbourne & Australia)	5.517
Adrian Stevens (Arena Essex & England)	4.471
Tim Korneliussen (Hackney & Denmark)	4.429
Dave Hamnett (Hackney & Australia)	4.275
Paul Smith (Middlesbrough/Newcastle & England)	4.000
Justin Elkins (Poole & England)	4.000
Jack Stevens (Newcastle & Australia)	4.000
Rob Fisher (Peterborough & England)	4.000
Phil Disney (Peterborough & England)	3.636
Deon Prinsloo (Wimbledon/Exeter & Zimbabwe)	3.622
Wayne Baxter (Rye House & Australia)	3.571
Mark Lemon (Poole & Australia)	3.500
Justin Pryor (Wimbledon & Australia)	3.378
Nigel Alderton (Edinburgh & Australia)	2.750
Darren Fitch (Ipswich & England)	2.667
Damon Richardson (Ipswich & Australia)	2.667
Garry Stead (Stoke & England)	2.667
Colin White (Ipswich & England)	2.552
Frank Smart (Exeter & Australia)	2.400
Brian Mercer (Edinburgh & Scotland)	2.000
David Wolstenholme (Arena Essex & England)	2.000
Martin Jones (Middlesbrough & England)	1.333
Scott Swain (Eastbourne & England)	1.000
Peter Byrne (Milton Keynes & Australia)	0.444
Kieran McCullagh (Milton Keynes & England)	0.000
Darren Tupper (Peterborough & England)	0.000
Matthew Poole (Peterborough & Australia)	0.000

CHART TOPPERS

The top rider from each nation represented in the 1990 National League was:

Craig Boyce (Poole & Australia)	10.539
Steve Schofield (Hackney & England)	10.440
David Bargh (Newcastle & New Zealand)	9.745
Jens Rasmussen (Rye House & Denmark)	9.378
Kenny McKinna (Glasgow & Scotland)	8.552
Richard Hellsén (Long Eaton & Sweden)	8.438
Thierry Hilaire (Milton Keynes & France)	3.745
Deon Prinsloo (Wimbledon & Zimbabwe)	3.622
Peter Schroeck (Wimbledon & West Germany)	2.824

BYE-BYE BOYS

The following riders appeared in at least six matches in the 1989 National League but did not ride in the 1990 National League:
Todd Wiltshire (Sunbrite League), Mark Loram (Sunbrite League), Leigh Adams (Sunbrite League), Preben Eriksen (retired), Malcolm Simmons (retired), Alastair Stevens (Sunbrite League), Malcolm Holloway (retired), David Jackson (stayed in Australia), Dave Perks (retired), Lars Munkedal (Sunbrite League), Paul Evitts (retired), Ian M. Stead (retired), Barry Thomas (retired), Derek Richardson (retired), Carl Chalcraft (retired), Derrol Keats (retired), Gary Rolls (retired), Carl Baldwin (retired), Max Schofield (British League Division Two), Wayne Ross (retired), Lee Pavitt (retired), Anthony Hulme (retired), Nick Floyd, Glenn Allan.

AVERAGES National League

No.	Rider	Track/s	M.	R.	Pts.	BP.	TPts.	Average	1989	Up/Down
103	Mark Simmonds	Exeter	32	115	118.0	23	141.0	4.904	150	47
104	Rob Woffinden	Stoke/Milton Keynes	25	110	122.0	12	134.0	4.873	101	-3
105	Justin Walker	Eastbourne	21	65	62.0	16	78.0	4.800	91	-14
106	Mark Lyndon	Milton Keynes/Peterborough	31	140	148.0	19	167.0	4.771	92	-14
107	Scott Humphries	Rye House	11	58	57.0	11	68.0	4.690	105	-2
108	Jon Surman	Long Eaton	19	76	70.0	18	88.0	4.632	117	9
109	Gary O'Hare	Long Eaton	31	131	129.0	20	149.0	4.550	75	-34
110	Adrian Stevens	Arena Essex	32	119	112.0	21	133.0	4.471		
111	Tim Korneliussen	Hackney	23	84	82.0	11	93.0	4.429		
112	Mark Pearce	Edinburgh/Stoke	27	91	79.0	20	99.0	4.352	146	34
113	Simon Wolstenholme	Arena Essex	32	142	131.0	21	152.0	4.282	97	-16
114	Dave Hamnett	Hackney	28	102	95.0	14	109.0	4.275		
115	Darren Grayling	Eastbourne	25	92	85.0	13	98.0	4.261	151	36
116	Steve Langdon	Poole	11	39	34.0	7	41.0	4.205		
117	Peter Lloyd	Long Eaton	14	56	49.0	9	58.0	4.143	108	-9
118	Ian Stead	Stoke/Newcastle	21	73	64.0	11	75.0	4.110	112	-6
119	Mick Powell	Edinburgh	23	78	64.5	15	79.5	4.077	63	-56
120	Paul Smith	Middlesbrough/Newcastle	31	138	119.0	19	138.0	4.000		
	Justin Elkins	Poole	5	12	11.0	1	12.0	4.000		
	Jack Stevens	Newcastle	1	3	2.0	1	3.0	4.000		
	Rob Fisher	Peterborough	1	1	1.0	0	1.0	4.000		
121	Kevin Little	Berwick	16	48	34.0	12	46.0	3.833	154	30
122	Shawn Venables	Hackney	9	40	30.0	8	38.0	3.800		
123	Thierry Hilaire	Milton Keynes	25	94	78.0	10	88.0	3.745	156	30
124	Dave Edwards	Middlesbrough	8	23	18.0	3	21.0	3.652	134	7
	Phil Disney	Peterborough	3	11	8.0	2	10.0	3.636		
125	Deon Prinsloo	Wimbledon/Exeter	20	74	55.0	12	67.0	3.622		
126	Wayne Baxter	Rye House	22	84	66.0	9	75.0	3.571		
127	Geoff Powell	Glasgow	10	28	21.0	4	25.0	3.571	123	-7
	Mark Lemon	Poole	5	16	8.0	6	14.0	3.500		
128	Duncan Chapman	Middlesbrough/Long Eaton	27	87	64.0	12	76.0	3.494		
129	Steve Widt	Berwick	6	15	11.0	2	13.0	3.467		
130	Nigel Sparshott	Rye House	12	48	32.0	9	41.0	3.417	113	-21
131	Justin Pryor	Wimbledon	18	45	30.0	8	38.0	3.378		
132	Wayne Bridgeford	Rye House/Peterborough	20	80	60.0	7	67.0	3.350	138	2
133	Kevin Teager	Arena Essex/Rye House	11	52	37.0	5	42.0	3.231	111	-26
	Steve Leigh	Poole	3	9	5.0	2	7.0	3.111	144	
134	Martin McKinna	Glasgow	8	25	17.0	2	19.0	3.040	95	-43
135	Sean Barker	Peterborough	32	119	74.0	16	90.0	3.025		
	Roland Pollard	Hackney	2	4	2.0	1	3.0	3.000		
136	Ian Humphreys	Hackney	10	33	22.0	2	24.0	2.909	132	-8
	Robert Ledwith	Arena Essex	5	14	9.0	1	10.0	2.857		
	Peter Schroeck	Wimbledon	5	17	9.0	3	12.0	2.824	125	
137	Kelvin Mullarkey	Rye House	13	47	25.0	8	33.0	2.809	86	-55
138	Nigel Alderton	Edinburgh	11	32	18.0	4	22.0	2.750		
139	Mark Crang	Middlesbrough/Peterborough	9	31	17.0	4	21.0	2.710		
140	Spencer Timmo	Newcastle	13	37	21.0	4	25.0	2.703	116	-28
	Darren Fitch	Ipswich	3	6	2.0	2	4.0	2.667		
	Jon Roberts	Long Eaton	2	6	3.0	1	4.0	2.667		
	Damon Richardson	Ipswich	1	3	2.0	0	2.0	2.667		
	Garry Stead	Stoke	1	3	2.0	0	2.0	2.667		
	Gordon Whitaker	Newcastle	1	3	2.0	0	2.0	2.667	133	
141	Colin White	Ipswich	19	58	33.0	4	37.0	2.552		
142	Craig Hyde	Ipswich	16	47	25.0	4	29.0	2.468	153	7
143	John Wainwright	Newcastle	13	39	19.0	5	24.0	2.462	143	-4
	Paul Atkins	Milton Keynes	5	13	8.0	0	8.0	2.462		
	Frank Smart	Exeter	2	5	3.0	0	3.0	2.400		
	Mike McLuskey	Edinburgh	2	5	2.0	1	3.0	2.400		
	Jon Gould	Poole	3	9	4.0	1	5.0	2.222		
144	Linden Warner	Rye House	12	60	27.0	5	32.0	2.133		
	Andy Sumner	Middlesbrough	3	8	3.0	1	4.0	2.000	136	
	Paul Blackbird	Peterborough	3	6	2.0	1	3.0	2.000	131	
	Steve Wicks	Newcastle	2	6	2.0	1	3.0	2.000	152	
	Anthony Boyd	Edinburgh	2	4	2.0	0	2.0	2.000		
	Colin Thorpe	Rye House	2	4	1.0	1	2.0	2.000		
	Brian Mercer	Edinburgh	1	2	1.0	0	1.0	2.000		
	Chris Young	Arena Essex	1	2	1.0	0	1.0	2.000		
	David Wolstenholme	Hackney	1	2	1.0	0	1.0	2.000		
145	Richard Davidson	Stoke	7	17	5.0	3	8.0	1.882		
146	Michael Howe	Long Eaton/Milton Keynes	9	19	6.0	1	7.0	1.474		
	Martin Jones	Middlesbrough	3	9	2.0	1	3.0	1.333		
	Mark Jolly	Peterborough	1	3	1.0	0	1.0	1.333		
	Steve Masters	Eastbourne	5	10	2.0	1	3.0	1.200	142	
	Jon Bell	Long Eaton	1	4	1.0	0	1.0	1.000		
	Jon Hughes	Stoke	2	4	1.0	0	1.0	1.000		

AVERAGES National League

No.	Rider	Track/s	M.	R.	Pts.	BP.	TPts.	Average	1989Up/Down
	Keith White	Long Eaton	1	4	1.0	0	1.0	1.000	58
	Scott Swain	Eastbourne	1	4	1.0	0	1.0	1.000	
	Peter Byrne	Milton Keynes	5	10	2.0	0	2.0	0.800	
	Kieran McCullagh	Milton Keynes	4	9	1.0	0	1.0	0.444	
	Darren Tupper	Peterborough	2	5	0.0	0	0.0	0.000	
	Greg Daniels	Exeter	2	5	0.0	0	0.0	0.000	
	Jim Dormer	Wimbledon	2	5	0.0	0	0.0	0.000	126
	Rob Fortune	Milton Keynes	2	5	0.0	0	0.0	0.000	97
	Jason Straughan	Berwick	1	2	0.0	0	0.0	0.000	
	John Cook	Eastbourne	2	2	0.0	0	0.0	0.000	
	Matthew Poole	Peterborough	1	1	0.0	0	0.0	0.000	
	Scott Pegler	Exeter	1	1	0.0	0	0.0	0.000	
	Listed below are the averages of those riders who rode for more than one club								
	Ian Barney	Exeter	21	88	72.0	13	85.0	3.864	
		Peterborough	10	50	75.0	13	88.0	7.040	
	Mark Blackbird	*Long Eaton*	*2*	*8*	*6.0*	*3*	*9.0*	*4.500*	
		Milton Keynes	*23*	*128*	*169.0*	*13*	*182.0*	*5.688*	
	Wayne Bridgeford	Peterborough	12	54	44.0	6	50.0	3.704	
		Rye House	8	26	16.0	1	17.0	2.615	
	Duncan Chapman	*Long Eaton*	*4*	*15*	*12.0*	*2*	*14.0*	*3.733*	
		Middlesbrough	*22*	*70*	*52.0*	*10*	*62.0*	*3.543*	
	David Clarke	Milton Keynes	24	124	149.0	22	171.0	5.516	
		Stoke	11	50	42.0	8	50.0	4.000	
	Mark Crang	*Middlesbrough*	*5*	*17*	*12.0*	*4*	*16.0*	*3.765*	
		Peterborough	*4*	*14*	*5.0*	*0*	*5.0*	*1.429*	
	Michael Howe	Long Eaton	5	8	5.0	1	6.0	3.000	
		Milton Keynes	4	11	1.0	0	1.0	0.364	
	Mark Lyndon	*Milton Keynes*	*15*	*62*	*73.0*	*7*	*80.0*	*5.161*	
		Peterborough	*16*	*78*	*75.0*	*12*	*87.0*	*4.462*	
	Mark Pearce	Edinburgh	5	15	11.0	2	13.0	3.467	
		Stoke	22	76	68.0	18	86.0	4.526	
	Deon Prinsloo	*Exeter*	*2*	*6*	*4.0*	*1*	*5.0*	*3.333*	
		Wimbledon	*18*	*68*	*51.0*	*11*	*62.0*	*3.647*	
	Paul Smith	Middlesbrough	1	4	2.0	0	2.0	2.000	
		Newcastle	30	134	117.0	19	136.0	4.060	
	Ian Stead	*Newcastle*	*16*	*58*	*53.0*	*7*	*60.0*	*4.138*	
		Stoke	*5*	*15*	*11.0*	*4*	*15.0*	*4.000*	
	Kevin Teager	Arena Essex	5	25	21.0	2	23.0	3.680	
		Rye House	6	27	16.0	3	19.0	2.815	
	Rob Woffinden	*Milton Keynes*	*8*	*34*	*37.0*	*2*	*39.0*	*4.588*	
		Stoke	*17*	*76*	*85.0*	*10*	*95.0*	*5.000*	
	Listed below are guest appearances by riders who helped out short-handed tracks								
	Steve Leigh	Ipswich	1	1	1.0	0	1.0	4.000	
	Duncan Chapman	Hackney	1	2	0.0	0	0.0	0.000	
	Frank Smart	Peterborough	1	2	0.0	0	0.0	0.000	

BEST OF BRITISH

The ten best-placed British born riders in the 1990 National League averages (with their 1989 rankings) were:

1 Steve Schofield (Hackney)	*2*	10.440
3 Chris Louis (Ipswich)	*9*	10.309
3 Andy Grahame (Wimbledon)	–	9.535
4 Andy Galvin (Hackney)	*2*	9.441
5 Gordon Kennett (Eastbourne)	*8*	9.219
6 Eric Monaghan (Stoke)	*15*	9.205
7 Steve Lawson (Glasgow)	*11*	8.875
8 Melvyn Taylor (Rye House)	*26*	8.857
9 Alun Rossiter (Poole)	*22*	8.855
10 Martin Goodwin (Arena Essex)	*16*	8.846

The following riders (with their 1989-1990 rankings) are no longer in the National League Top Ten British charts:

Kenny McKinna (Glasgow)	*3-18*	8.552
Nigel Crabtree (Stoke)	*4-16*	8.608
Mark Courtney (Berwick)	*5-15*	8.621
David Blackburn (Berwick)	*6-28*	7.552
Mark Loram (Sunbrite League King's Lynn)		
Les Collins (Edinburgh)	*10-12*	8.795

▲ ***The statistics which appear in this section relate to National League matches only and do not include Knock Out Cup or the end-of-the-season National Series. Full details of these competitions are given elsewhere in the 1991 Speedway Yearbook.***

FOREIGNERS

Foreign riders - not born in the British Isles or Commonwealth - are now allowed to compete in the National League on a British ACU licence. Their 1990 averages were as follows:

Jens Rasmussen (Rye House & Denmark)	9.378
Tom Knudsen (Poole & Denmark)	8.727
Richard Hellsén (Long Eaton & Sweden)	8.438
Freddy Schøtt (Edinburgh & Denmark)	7.880
Frank Andersen (Peterborough & Denmark)	7.758
Peter Glanz (Milton Keynes & Denmark)	7.012
Tim Korneliussen (Hackney & Denmark)	4.429
Thierry Hilaire (Milton Keynes & France)	3.745
Deon Prinsloo (Wimbledon & Zimbabwe)	3.622
Peter Schroeck (Wimbledon & West Germany)	2.824

The top rider from each nation represented in the 1990 National League was:

Craig Boyce (Poole & Australia)	10.539
Steve Schofield (Hackney & England)	10.440
David Bargh (Newcastle & New Zealand)	9.745
Jens Rasmussen (Rye House & Denmark)	9.378
Kenny McKinna (Glasgow & Scotland)	8.552
Richard Hellsén (Long Eaton & Sweden)	8.438
Thierry Hilaire (Milton Keynes & France)	3.745
Deon Prinsloo (Wimbledon & Zimbabwe)	3.622
Peter Schroeck (Wimbledon & West Germany)	2.824

INDIVIDUAL MEETINGS
National League

MASLENS CLASSIC
Wimbledon, Wednesday, March 28
Andy Grahame 15, Jens Rasmussen 11, Chris Louis 10, Andy Galvin 10, Steve Schofield 9, Ray Morton 8, Nigel Leaver 8, Tony Primmer 8, Nathan Simpson 7, Craig Boyce 7, Kevin Jolly 6, Neville Tatum 6, Rob Tilbury 5, Paul Whittaker 3, Paul Woods 3, Andy Buck 3. *Reserves:* Peter Schroeck 1 (1), Jim Dormer 0 (1).

Roll of Honour
1990 - Andy Grahame.

ESSEX CHAMPIONSHIP
Arena Essex, Saturday, June 9
Jens Rasmussen 13, Steve Schofield 12, Rob Tilbury 12, Paul Woods 12, Gordon Kennett 11, Wayne Garratt 11, Kevin Brice 7, Kevin Teager 7, Simon Wolstenholme 7, Adrian Stevens 7, Paul Whittaker 6, Robert Ledwith 5, Andy Buck 5, Scott Norman 2, Brian Nixon 1. *Reserves:* Shaun Nicholls 2 (4), Tommy Palmer 0 (3).

Roll of Honour
1984 - Bob Garrad; 1985 - Mike Ferreira; 1986 - Martin Goodwin; 1987 - Gordon Kennett; 1988 - Mark Loram; 1990 - Jens Rasmussen.

MERCURY INVITATION CHAMPIONSHIP
Rye House, Sunday, July 29
Steve Schofield 15, Jens Rasmussen 13, Andy Galvin 12, Nigel Crabtree 11, Glen Baxter 11, Nathan Simpson 10, Neville Tatum 8, Eric Monaghan 8, Paul Whittaker 7, Melvyn Taylor 7, Nigel Sparshott 5, Scott Humphries 4, Linden Warner 4, Kevin Teager 2, Trevor O'Brien 1, Wayne Baxter 1. *Reserves:* Colin Thorpe 1 (4), Garry Thompson 0 (3).

Roll of Honour
1990 - Steve Schofield.

ELFORDS' BLUE RIBAND
Poole, Tuesday, August 7
Chris Louis 14, Alun Rossiter 13 (+3), Steve Regeling 13 (+2), Craig Boyce 12, Tony Langdon 10, Steve Schofield 9, Gary Allan 9, Frank Andersen 8, Shane Parker 6, Jens Rasmussen 5, Freddy Schøtt 5, Melvyn Taylor 4, Andy Grahame 4, Neville Tatum 3, David Blackburn 3, Andy Galvin 1. *Reserves:* Gary Chessell 1 (2), Jon Gould 0 (1).

Roll of Honour
1970 - Barry Briggs; 1971 - Ole Olsen; 1972 - Ray Wilson; 1973 - Anders Michanek; 1974 - Ole Olsen; 1975- Malcolm Simmons; 1976 - Malcolm Simmons; 1977 - Malcolm Simmons; 1978 - Malcolm Simmons; 1979 - Bobby Schwartz; 1980 - Dave Jessup; 1981 - Bruce Penhall; 1982 - Bobby Schwartz; 1983 - Erik Gundersen; 1984 - Mitch Shirra; 1985 - Stan Bear; 1986 - Kevin Smith; 1987 - Melvyn Taylor; 1988- Steve Schofield; 1989 - Steve Schofield; 1990 - Chris Louis.

STAR OF ANGLIA
Ipswich, Thursday, August 9
Chris Louis 14, Dean Standing 11 (+3), Steve Schofield 11 (+2), Nigel Crabtree 10, Andy Galvin 10, Martin Goodwin 9, Eric Monaghan 9, Alun Rossiter 9, Freddy Schøtt 8, Jens Rasmussen 8, Shane Parker 6, Neville Tatum 6, Peter Jeffery 4, Melvyn Taylor 3, Carl Blackbird 2, Rob Tilbury 0. *Reserve:* Robbie Fuller 0 (1).

Roll of Honour
1979 - John Louis; 1980 - Ole Olsen; 1981 - Kenny Carter; 1982 - Bo Petersen; 1983 - Dennis Sigalos; 1984 - Hans Nielsen; 1985 - Hans Nielsen; 1987 - Hans Nielsen; 1989 - Chris Louis; 1990 - Chris Louis.

HL1 SOUTHERN RIDERS' CHAMPIONSHIP
Hackney, Friday, August 24
Steve Schofield 15, Chris Louis 14, Tony Langdon 11, Paul Woods 9, Nathan Simpson 8, Jens Rasmussen 7, Alun Rossiter 7, Neville Tatum 7, Martin Goodwin 6, Melvyn Taylor 6, Steve Regeling 6, David Norris 6, Andy Galvin 5, Rob Tilbury 5, Peter Jeffery 4, Andy Buck 4.

Roll of Honour
1969 - Colin Pratt; 1970- Terry Betts; 1971 - Terry Betts; 1975 - Tommy Jansson; 1976 - John Louis; 1984 - Jamie Luckhurst; 1985 - Jamie Luckhurst; 1986 - Martin Dugard; 1987 - Andy Buck; 1988 - Andy Galvin; 1989 - Chris Louis; 1990 - Steve Schofield.

HILLSIDE TROPHY
Peterborough, Monday, August 27
Steve Regeling 13 (+3), Neville Tatum 13 (+2), Craig Hodgson 11, Frank Andersen 10, Jens Rasmussen 10, Glen Baxter 9, Nigel De'ath 8, Scott Norman 8, Carl Blackbird 8, Ian Barney 7, Melvyn Taylor 7, Les Collins 6, Peter Glanz 3, Wayne Bridgeford 3, Alan Mogridge 1, Sean Barker 0. *Reserves:* Craig Hyde 2 (3), Rob Fisher 1 (3).

Roll of Honour
1989 - Richard Hellsén; 1990 - Steve Regeling.

CRAIG FEATHERBY MEMORIAL
Milton Keynes, Tuesday, September 18
Steve Regeling 15, Steve Schofield 14, Peter Glanz 12 (+3), Kevin Jolly 12 (+2), Mark Blackbird 10, Nathan Simpson 10, Rob Tilbury 9, Tony Primmer 8, Mark Carlson 7, Richard Hellsén 7, Thierry Hilaire 4, Les Collins 4, Rob Woffinden 3, Michael Howe 3, Mick Poole 0, Paul Blackbird 0. *Reserves:* Jason Gage 1 (6), Steve Reynolds 0 (3).

Originally postponed, July 10 because of stadium vandalism.

Roll of Honour
1983 - Kenny Carter; 1984 - Keith White; 1985 - Neil Middleditch; 1986 - Alastair Stevens; 1987 - Andrew Silver; 1988 - Andy Galvin; 1989 - Les Collins; 1990 - Steve Regeling.

†Craig FEATHERBY (B 12.5.1960, Norwich – D 16.9.1983). The son of former rider Clive Featherby, he made his debut for Milton Keynes in 1981 after previous experience with Boston and Long Eaton. He died after a crash at Peterborough during heat six of the Knights' National League match. In all he rode in 67 League and Cup matches for the club, scoring more than 600 points.

SUPERNATIONAL MARATHON
Arena Essex, Saturday, September 29
Abandoned after 12 heats, rain. *Scorers at the time: Ray Morton 9, Paul Whittaker 7, Martin Goodwin 6, Dean Standing 6, Kevin Brice 6, Jamie Luckhurst 6, Nathan Simpson 6, Alan Mogridge 5, Troy Pratt 4, Rob Tilbury 4, Paul Woods 4, Wayne Garratt 3, Neville Tatum 3, Simon Wolstenholme 2, Adrian Stevens 1, Gary Tagg 0. Re-staged October 20. See later for Results and Roll of Honour,*

EAST MIDLANDS CHAMPIONSHIP
Long Eaton, Wednesday, October 3
Nigel Crabtree 15, Eric Monaghan 14, Paul Fry 12, Shane Parker 12, Melvyn Taylor 8, Nigel De'ath 8, Martin Goodwin 8, Jens Rasmussen 8, Richard Hellsén 7, David Blackburn 7, Kevin Smart 6, Gordon Kennett 4, Tony Primmer 4, Steve Regeling 3, Mark Blackbird 1, Peter Glanz 0. *Reserves:* Duncan Chapman 2 (3), Stafford Galvin 1 (2).

Roll of Honour
1967 - Anders Michanek; 1968 - Ray Wilson; 1969 - Barry Briggs; 1970 - Ray Wilson; 1971 - Anders Michanek; 1978 - Steve Bastable; 1989 - Eric Monaghan; 1990 - Nigel Crabtree.

FORK RENT 16 LAPPER
Ipswich, Thursday, October 4
1 Craig Boyce 23, 2 Alan Mogridge 21, 3 Paul Whittaker 19, 4 Eric Monaghan 16, 5 Shane Parker 15, 6 Chris Louis 13, 7 Martin Goodwin 13, 8 Nathan Simpson 8. *Qualifying scorers:* Boyce 11, Goodwin 11, Neville Tatum 9, Louis 9, Monaghan 8, Whittaker 7, Mogridge 7, Parker 7, Dean Standing 5, Simpson 4, Louis Carr 4, Tony Langdon 3, Jens Rasmussen 3, Glen Baxter 2, Jamie Habbin 2, Nigel Flatman 2. *Reserves:* Darren Fitch 2 (1), Craig Hyde 2 (1). *16 Lap Final:* Mogridge, Whittaker, Boyce, Parker, Monaghan, Simpson (R), Louis (R), Goodwin (fx).

Roll of Honour
1979 - Joe Owen; 1980 - Billy Sanders; 1981- Phil Crump; 1982 - Phil Crump; 1983 - Kenny Carter; 1984 - Phil Crump; 1985 - Kenny Carter; 1986 - Hans Nielsen; 1987 - Jan O. Pedersen; 1989 - Andy Galvin; 1990 - Craig Boyce.

BERWICK £3,500 BONANZA
Berwick, Saturday, October 13
David Walsh 15, Steve Regeling 13, Freddy Schøtt 10, Chris Louis 10, Shane Bowes 10, Kenny McKinna 9, Eric Monaghan 9, Andy Campbell 9, Andy Grahame 7, Rod Hunter 7, David Blackburn 7, Les Collins 4, Dean Standing 3, David Bargh 2, Mark Courtney 2, Scott Robson 2. *Reserves:* Rob Grant 1 (3), Kevin Little 0 (1).

Roll of Honour
1990 - David Walsh.

CHAMPIONSHIP OF SUSSEX
Eastbourne, Sunday, October 14
Alan Mogridge 13, Chris Louis 12 (+3), Gordon Kennett 12 (+2), Ray Morton 10, Neville Tatum 10, Richard Hellsén 10, Shane Parker 9, Nathan Simpson 8, Dean Standing 8, Jamie Habbin 6, Paul Woods 6, Brian Nixon 5, Tony Primmer 4, Darren Standing 2, Mark Blackbird 1, Keith Pritchard 0. *Reserves:* Darren Grayling 4 (4), Warren Mowat 0 (1), Scott Swain 0 (1).

Roll of Honour
1969 - Martyn Piddock; 1970 - Richard May; 1972 - Allan Emmett; 1973 - Roger Johns; 1976 - Steve Weatherley; 1985 - Jamie Luckhurst; 1986 - Neil Middleditch; 1987 - Nigel Crabtree; 1989 - Dean Standing; 1990 - Alan Mogridge.

SUPERNATIONAL MARATHON
Arena Essex, Saturday, October 20
1 Alan Mogridge, 2 Nigel Leaver, 3 Dean Standing, 4 Nathan Simpson, 5 Ray Morton, 6 Carl Blackbird, 7 Rob Tilbury, 8 Kevin Brice (N). *Qualifying scorers:* Mogridge 12, Simpson 11, Leaver 10, Tilbury 10, Morton 9, Standing 9, Blackbird 8, Brice 8, Wayne Garratt 8, Neville Tatum 7, Paul Whittaker 6, Paul Woods 6, Gary Tagg 5, Adrian Stevens 5, Simon Wolstenholme 4, Troy Pratt 2.

Roll of Honour
1984 - Andrew Silver; 1985 - Gordon Kennett; 1986 - Martin Goodwin; 1987 - Andrew Silver; 1988- Martin Goodwin; 1989 - Martin Goodwin; 1990 - Alan Mogridge.

STADIUM TROPHY
Ipswich, Thursday, October 25
Alan Mogridge 22, Shane Parker 21, Chris Louis 21, Dean Standing 19, Paul Woods 12, Darren Standing 10, Michael Warren 9, Robbie Fuller 8. *Qualifying scorers:* Dean Standing 16, Louis 15, Parker 14, Mogridge 14, Woods 10, Darren Standing 10, Fuller 8, Warren 7, Peter Chapman 6, Chris Cobby 5, Darren Fitch 3, Mark Blackbird 0. *Reserve:* David Norris 0 (1). *Final:* Mogridge, Parker, Louis, Dean Standing. *Eliminated semi finalists:* Warren, Woods, Fuller (F), Darren Standing.

Roll of Honour
1970 - John Harrhy; 1990 - Alan Mogridge.

NENE TROPHY
Peterborough, Friday, October 26
Mark Blackbird 14, Les Collins 12, Alan Mogridge 11, Richard Hellsén 10, Scott Norman 9, Nigel Flatman 9, Wayne Bridgeford 8, Anthony Boyd 4, Sean Barker 4, Melvyn Taylor 3, Rob Fisher 1, Carl Blackbird 1. *Reserves:* Darren Tupper 4 (5), Arron Bonnet 0 (1).

Originally postponed October 19, waterlogged track.

Roll of Honour
1990 - Mark Blackbird.

PAIRS MEETINGS

BEST PAIRS
Long Eaton, June 6
1 Paul Fry 17 & Jon Surman 6(1) = 23; 2 Richard Hellsén 17 & Matthew Cross 6 (1) = 23; 3 Gary O'Hare 15 & Paul Atkins 6 (3) = 21; 4 Kevin Smart 16 & Mark Lyndon 2 = 18; 5 Mark Carlson 13 & Shawn Venables 3 = 16; 6 Peter Lloyd 11 & Jim Dormer 4 (1) = 15; 7 Michael Howe 5 & Stuart Parnaby 5 (1) = 10. *Reserve:* Stafford Galvin 0 (2). Run-off: Fry, Surman, Cross, Hellsén (fx).

ECHO CLASSIC PAIRS
Poole, July 3
1 POOLE A 38 (Craig Boyce 22 (1) & Alun Rossiter 16 (2)); 2 EXETER 32 (Steve Regeling 23 & Richard Green 9 (2)); 3 HACKNEY 30 (Steve Schofield 21 (1) & Andy Galvin 9 (2)); 4 POOLE B 26 (Gary Allan 13 (1) & Tony Langdon 13 (1)); 5 STOKE 26 (Eric Monaghan 14 & Louis Carr 12 (3)); 6 LONG EATON 17 (Richard Hellsén 11 & Kevin Smart 6); 7 WIMBLEDON 16 (Nathan Simpson 12 & Neville Tatum 4 (1)). *Reserves:* Tom Knudsen 4 (1), Steve Leigh 0 (1).

INVITATION PAIRS
Middlesbrough, July 12
1 Steve Wilcock 15 (2) & Mark Thorpe 19 (2) = 34; 2 Darren Sumner 20 (2) & Andy Sumner 12 (1) = 32; 3 Simon Green 14 (2) & Jamie Luckhurst 13 (1) = 27; 4 Martin Dixon 22 & Mark Crang 4 (1) = 26; 5 Rod Hunter 22 & Duncan Chapman 4 = 26; 6 Les Collins 22 & Martin Jones 2(1) = 24; 7 Paul Bentley 9 & Dave Edwards 11 (2) = 20. *Reserve:* Tony Richardson 0 (3).

STAR PAIRS
Arena Essex, July 21
1 Rob Tilbury 15 & Adrian Stevens 8 (3) = 23; 2 Martin Goodwin 12 (2) & Troy Pratt 11 (1) = 23; 3 Steve Schofield 14 & Ian Humphreys 6 = 20; 4 Wayne Garratt 10 & Kevin Brice 8 (1) = 18; 5 Jens Rasmussen 14 & Wayne Baxter 0 = 14; 6 Dean Standing 12 & Colin White 2 (1) = 14; 7 Gordon Kennett 12 & Darren Grayling 2 = 14.

DIAMOND REUNION PAIRS
Newcastle, August 19
Postponed, torrential rain.

DEVON PAIRS CHAMPIONSHIP
Exeter, October 15
1 Richard Green 23 & Rob Woffinden 13 (2) = 36; 2 Steve Regeling 23 & Frank Smart 10 = 33; 3 Michael Coles 19 (1) & Ian Barney 9 = 28; 4 Les Collins 16 & Trevor O'Brien 11 (1) = 27; 5 Steve Bishop 15 (3) & Nigel Leaver 12 (1) = 27; 5 Colin Cook 21 & Thierry Hilaire 5 = 26; Kevin Smart 4 (1) & Mark Simmonds 19 = 23. *Reserves:* Greg Daniels 3 (2), Dixie Knight 3 (2).

BILLY SANDERS MEMORIAL PAIRS
Ipswich, October 18
1 Paul Whittaker 23 & Gary Tagg 14 (5) = 37; 2 Chris Louis 21 (2) & Alan Mogridge 15 (2) = 36; 3 Dean Standing 16 (3) & Shane Parker 15 (2) = 31; 4 Steve Regeling 22 & Colin Cook 7 (1) = 29; 5 Martin Goodwin 18 & Troy Pratt 6 = 24; 6 Eric Monaghan 9 (1) & David Clarke 8 (1) = 17; 7 Kevin Smart 13 & Richard Hellsén 0 = 13. *Reserve:* Darren Fitch 0 (7).

Roll of Honour
1988 - Peter Ravn; 1990 - Paul Whittaker and Gary Tagg.

†William Robert (Billy) SANDERS (B 9.9.1955, Sydney – D 23.4.1985). One of Australia's finest riders throughout the seventies and eighties, he joined Ipswich in 1972 when he was only 16 and spent all but three years of a 14 season career with the Witches. In all he rode in 403 official matches for the club, scoring more than 3,700 points for a career average of fractionally above 9 points a meeting. He committed suicide on April 23, 1985, because of personal and marital problems.

ONE of British speedway's oldest competitions – the Scottish Open Championship – was a victim of the end-of-season weather.

The Edinburgh promotion twice scheduled the event but on each occasion the elements intervened and forced its postponement.

It is the first time since 1982 that the Championship has not been staged North of the Border.

For the record we list the Roll of Honour for the competition.

STELRAD SCOTTISH OPEN CHAMPIONSHIP
Edinburgh, Sunday. October 28
Postponed, waterlogged track. Not re-staged. *Originally postponed, October 6, waterlogged track.*

Roll of Honour
1949- Jack Young; 1950 - Jack Young; 1951 - Jack Young; 1952 - Dick Campbell; 1953 - Tommy Miller; 1960 - Doug Templeton; 1961 - Trevor Redmond; 1962 - Doug Templeton; 1963 - Maurie Mattingley; 1964 - George Hunter; 1965 - Arne Pander; 1966 - Bill Landels; 1967 - Barry Briggs; 1968 - Martin Ashby; 1969 - Reidar Eide; 1970- Ivan Mauger; 1971 - Ivan Mauger; 1972 - Ivan Mauger; 1973 - Ivan Mauger; 1981 - Wayne Brown; 1983 - Steve Lawson; 1984 - Mitch Shirra; 1985 - Jamie Luckhurst; 1986 - Les Collins; 1987 - Neville Tatum; 1988 - Steve Lawson; 1989 - Todd Wiltshire.

POLE-AXED

NATIONAL League tracks Ipswich and Exeter took advantage of the new liberalism in Eastern Europe - by undertaking week-end tours of Poland.

And even though they lost all three challenge matches the two clubs made plenty of friends and Witches' young star Chris Louis was invited to join Unia Tarnow for the 1991 Polish League season.

Exeter's second meeting - an individual event - saw team-mates Steve Regeling and Richard Green face each other in a run-off for second place after Green had been the only rider to beat eventual winner Tomasz Gollob on the 374 metre Bydgoszcz track.

Saturday, July 7
STAL RZESZOW 54 (Janusz Stachyra 13:1, Jacek Rempala 11, Piotr Podrzycki 7:2. Robert Kuzdzal 7, Romuald Janusz 6, Janusz Slaczka 5:1, Giorgi Petranov 3, Krzysztof Nurzynski 2:1)
IPSWICH 36 (Chris Louis 11:2, Alan Mogridge 9:2, Craig Hyde 5:1, Robbie Fuller 4:1, Shane Parker 4:1, Dean Standing 2, Colin White 1)

Sunday, July 8
UNIA TARNOW 48 (Robert Kuzdzal 12, Jacek Rempala 10, Janus Stachyra 8:1, Piotr Styczynski 5:2, Romuald Janusz 5, Slawomir Tronina 3:2, Piotr Lesniowski 3, Piotr Zieba 2:1)
IPSWICH 42 (Chris Louis 14, Alan Mogridge 14, Craig Hyde 6, Colin White 4, Dean Standing 3:1, Shane Parker 1, Robbie Fuller 0)

Saturday, October 6
UNIA LESZNO 57 (Roman Jankowski 13:1, Slawomir Rypien 0, Zenon Kasprzak 12:1, **Zbigniew Krakowski 11:4**, Dariusz Lowicki 4, Piotr Pawlicki 14, Roman Mitura 1:1, Piotr Grycha 2)
EXETER 32 (Steve Regeling 11, Rob Woffinden 1, Richard Green 10, Ian Barney 0, Steve Bishop 3:1, Mark Simmonds 5:1, Deon Prinsloo 2, Frank Smart 0)

GRAND PRIX SPONSOR
Bydgoszcz, Sunday, October 7
Tomasz Gollob 14, Richard Green 13 (+3), Steve Regeling 13 (+2), Ryszard Dolomosiewicz 12, Andrej Korolev 8, Jacek Wozniak 8, Steve Bishop 8, Jacek Krzyzaniak 7, Deon Prinsloo 7, Mark Simmonds 6, Oleg Budzko 6, Valeri Sokolov 6, Waldemar Cieslewicz 5, Ian Barney 4, Rob Woffinden 1, Frank Smart 0. *Reserve:* Jacek Gollob 1 (1).

TESTIMONIAL MEETINGS

DOUG WYER FAREWELL
Edinburgh, Sunday, April 8
1 Les Collins 19 (3) & Joe Screen 18 (2) = 37; 2 Kelly Moran 22 (2) & David Cheshire 13 (1) = 35; 3 Chris Morton 14 (2) & Steve Lawson 14 = 28; 4 Sean Wilson 18 & Jason Lyons 7 (2) = 25; 4 Brett Saunders 15 (1) & Gary Havelock 10 (1) = 25; 6 Michael Coles 15 (1) & Paul Thorp 8 = 23; 7 Sean Courtney 12, Scott Lamb 0 & *reserve* Mike McLuskey 4 = 16.

Douglas WYER (B 16.8.1947, Nottingham). He began riding at Sheffield in 1969 and had spells with Berwick, Doncaster, Halifax and Birmingham before joining Edinburgh in 1986. An ex-England international and 1976 World Finalist, he retired after fracturing his thigh in a crash at Middlesbrough in the National League Team Championships on June 9, 1988.

GEOFF POWELL TESTIMONIAL
Glasgow, Wednesday, July 18
GLASGOW 53 (Steve Lawson 8:1, Charlie McKinna 11:1, Kenny McKinna 14, Geoff Powell 5, Shane Bowes 7:2, Jason Lyons 3:2, Phil Jeffrey 5:1) **HEROES 42** (Les Collins 5:1, Scott Lamb 6:1, Mick Powell 5:1, Freddy Schøtt 12, Mike McLuskey 0, Brett Saunders 12, Michael Irving 2).

Geoff POWELL made his National League debut for Glasgow in 1981 but has only been an automatic choice for the Tigers in one of his 10 seasons – in 1986 when he was an everpresent in 40 official matches. In all he has ridden in only 160 matches, scoring 510 points at an average of 3.85.

KEITH WHITE FAREWELL
Long Eaton, Wednesday, August 22
LONG EATON 26 (Nigel De'ath 1, Mark Blackbird 7, Paul Fry 10, Gary O'Hare 8) **STOKE 25** (Ian Stead 3, Louis Carr 7, Rob Woffinden 5, Mark Carlson 10) **LEICESTER 24** (Steve Regeling 11, Peter Carr 4, Colin Cook 6, Jon Surman 3) **NATIONAL LEAGUE SELECT 20** (Steve Schofield 11, Peter Glanz 0, Tony Primmer 6, Trevor Banks 3). *Reserves:* Nigel Sparshott 1 (2), Paul Blackbird 0 (2)

Keith WHITE announced his retirement after the opening National League match of the season after an 18 season career which began at Peterborough in 1972 and saw him ride for Crewe, Birmingham, Milton Keynes and Long Eaton in Division Two and Leicester, Hackney and Coventry in the British League. A former Inter Continental Finalist (1977) he rode in more than 650 matches throughout his career.

CHALLENGE MATCHES National League

HL1 TROPHY
First leg, Thursday, March 15
IPSWICH 55 (Chris Louis 12, Billy Lellman 7:3, Dean Standing 8:2, Alan Mogridge 8:3, David Norris 9:1, Shane Parker 9:1, Craig Hyde 2:1)
HACKNEY 41 (Andy Galvin 12:1, Michael Warren 3, Steve Schofield 16, Paul Whittaker 8:1, Gary Tagg 0, Tim Korneliussen 2, Uwe Gessner 0).
Second leg, Friday, March 16
HACKNEY 51 (**Andy Galvin 15**, Michael Warren 4:1, **Steve Schofield 15**, Paul Whittaker 7:1, Gary Tagg 2:1, Tim Korneliussen 4:1, Uwe Gessner 4)
IPSWICH 45 (Chris Louis 11, Billy Lellman 3, Dean Standing 5:1, Alan Mogridge 7:4, David Norris 9:1, Shane Parker 9:2, Colin White 1:1)
Ipswich win 100-96 on aggregate.

LONEX CUP
First leg, Friday, March 23
HACKNEY 62 (**Andy Galvin 13:2**, Michael Warren 5:1, **Steve Schofield 13:2**, **Paul Whittaker 15**, Gary Tagg 3:1, Tim Korneliussen 11, Uwe Gessner 2)
ARENA ESSEX 34 (Martin Goodwin 7, Simon Wolstenholme 5:1, Rob Tilbury 6:2, Adrian Stevens 0, Wayne Garratt 5, Kevin Brice 8:1, Troy Pratt 3)
Second leg, Saturday, March 24
ARENA ESSEX 43 (Martin Goodwin 4, Simon Wolstenholme 12:1, Rob Tilbury 9, Adrian Stevens 6:1, Wayne Garratt 1, Kevin Brice 4:1, Troy Pratt 7:1)
HACKNEY 52 (Andy Galvin 10:2, Michael Warren 6, Steve Schofield 11, **Paul Whittaker 15**, Gary Tagg 3, Tim Korneliussen 6:2, Dave Hamnett 1)
Hackney win 114-77 on aggregate.

TYNE TEES TROPHY
First leg, Thursday, March 29
MIDDLESBROUGH 45 (Darren Sumner 14, Steve Wilcock 9:2, Jamie Luckhurst 4, Paul Bentley 10, David Cheshire 3:2, Paul Smith 3, Max Schofield 2:1)
NEWCASTLE 51 (*Rider replacement for Peter Carr*, Simon Green 14:1, Martin Dixon 16, Mark Thorpe 5:1, David Bargh 10:2, Gordon Whitaker 3, John Wainwright 3:2)

Second leg, Sunday, April 1
NEWCASTLE 52 (*Rider replacement for Peter Carr*, Simon Green 12:1, Martin Dixon 15:2, Mark Thorpe 4, David Bargh 15, Gordon Whitaker 3:2, John Wainwright 3)
MIDDLESBROUGH 44 (Darren Sumner 12, Steve Wilcock 1, Jamie Luckhurst 2, Paul Bentley 8:3, David Cheshire 8, Paul Smith 13, Max Schofield 0)
Newcastle win 103-89 on aggregate.

PRIDE OF LONDON
First leg, Friday, March 30
HACKNEY 50 (**Andy Galvin 15**, Michael Warren 4:1, Steve Schofield 14, Paul Whittaker 7:2, Gary Tagg 2, Tim Korneliussen 6:1, Dave Hamnett 2:1)
WIMBLEDON 46 (Nathan Simpson 7:1, Neville Tatum 10:1, Ray Morton 7, Andy Grahame 14:1, Nigel Leaver 6:4, Jim Dormer 0, Peter Schroeck 2)
Second leg, Wednesday, April 4
WIMBLEDON 55 (Nathan Simpson 6, Neville Tatum 5:2, Ray Morton 11:3, **Andy Grahame 15**, Nigel Leaver 10:2, Peter Schroeck 5, Jim Dormer 3)
HACKNEY 41 (Andy Galvin 10, Michael Warren 4:1, Steve Schofield 14:1, Paul Whittaker 8:1, Gary Tagg 0, Tim Korneliussen 5:1, Dave Hamnett 0)
Wimbledon win 101-91 on aggregate.

TUNNEL TROPHY
First leg, Saturday, March 31
ARENA ESSEX 46 (Martin Goodwin 10:1, Simon Wolstenholme 6:1, Rob Tilbury 13:1, Adrian Stevens 3, Wayne Garratt 2:1, Kevin Brice 7:1, Troy Pratt 5:1)
EASTBOURNE 50 (Keith Pritchard 12:1, *rider replacement for Gordon Kennett*, Andy Buck 13:1, Paul Woods 9:1, Tony Primmer 13:2, Darren Grayling 2, Steve Masters 1:1)

Second leg, Sunday, April 1
EASTBOURNE 50 (Keith Pritchard 13:1, *rider replacement for Gordon Kennett*, Andy Buck 10:1, Paul Woods 9:3, Tony Primmer 13:2, Darren Grayling 3, Steve Masters 2:1)
ARENA ESSEX 46 (Martin Goodwin 15, Simon Wolstenholme 3:1, Rob Tilbury 12, Adrian Stevens 4, Wayne Garratt 5:1, Kevin Brice 0, Troy Pratt 7)
Eastbourne win 100-92 on aggregate.

SPRING CLASSIC
First leg, Saturday, March 31
BERWICK 59 (Mark Courtney 11:2, Scott Robson 9:2, David Blackburn 12:2, Rob Grant 9:2, David Walsh 10:1, Alan Rivett 8, Kevin Little 0)
EDINBURGH 37 (Les Collins 13:1, Michael Coles 4:1, Brett Saunders 8, Scott Lamb 6, Phil Jeffrey 2, Mark Blackbird 1:1, Mark Pearce 3:1)

Second leg, Sunday, April 1
EDINBURGH 45 (Les Collins 12:1, Michael Coles 6:1, Brett Saunders 8:1, Scott Lamb 7, Phil Jeffrey 2:2, Mark Blackbird 7:2, Mark Pearce 3)
BERWICK 51 (Mark Courtney 16, Scott Robson 0, David Blackburn 12, Rob Grant 4:2, David Walsh 10:2, Alan Rivett 9, Kevin Little 0)
Berwick win 110-82 on aggregate.

EASTER TRIANGLE
First leg, Friday, April 13
HACKNEY v ARENA ESSEX v RYE HOUSE
Postponed, waterlogged track.
First leg, Saturday, April 14
ARENA ESSEX 18 (Martin Goodwin 4:1, Adrian Stevens 4:1, Rob Tilbury 2:1, Kevin Brice 3, Wayne Garratt 2, Simon Wolstenholme 3:1, Troy Pratt)
HACKNEY 21 (Andy Galvin 6, Michael Warren 1, Paul Whittaker 5, Gary Tagg 2:1, Steve Schofield 6, Tim Korneliussen 1, Dave Hamnett)
RYE HOUSE 8 (Jamie Fagg 1, Roger Johns 0, Jens Rasmussen 5, Nigel Sparshott 0, *rider replacement for Melvyn Taylor*, Trevor O'Brien 2, Shaun Nicholls)
Abandoned after eight heats.

Second leg, Sunday, April 15
RYE HOUSE 39 (Trevor O'Brien 9:2, Roger Johns 15:1, Jens Rasmussen 10:1, Nigel Sparshott 3:1, *rider replacement for Melvyn Taylor*, Jamie Fagg 2:1, Wayne Bridgeford)
HACKNEY 38 (Gary Tagg 2, Paul Whittaker 9, **Andy Galvin 12**, Michael Warren 3, Steve Schofield 11, Tim Korneliussen 1, Roland Pollard)
ARENA ESSEX 31 (Martin Goodwin 6, Adrian Stevens 0, Rob Tilbury 7, Kevin Brice 3:2, Wayne Garratt 2:1, Simon Wolstenholme 6, Troy Pratt 7:1)
Aggregate: Hackney 59, Arena Essex 49 Rye House 47

EASTER TROPHY
First leg, Friday, April 13
POOLE 50 (Gary Chessell 7:1, Gary Allan 8:2, Alun Rossiter 8:1, Craig Boyce 13:1, Tony Langdon 2:1, Steve Langdon 5:1, Rod Colquhoun 7)
EXETER 46 (Steve Regeling 12:2, Steve Bishop 13:1, Richard Green 1, Colin Cook 8:1, Peter Jeffery 5:1, Andy Sell 6:1, Mark Simmonds 1:1)

Second leg, Monday, April 16
EXETER 56 (Steve Regeling 13:1, Steve Bishop 9:2, Richard Green 12:1, Colin Cook 2, Peter Jeffery 11, Andy Sell 6:1, Mark Simmonds 3:2)
POOLE 40 (Gary Chessell 9, Gary Allan 3:1, Alun Rossiter 10, Craig Boyce 12:1, Steve Langdon 0, Steve Leigh 0, Rod Colquhoun 6:3)
Exeter win 102-90 on aggregate.

SCOTTISH TEAM CHAMPIONSHIP
Edinburgh, first leg, Friday, June 15
GLASGOW 49 (**Kenny McKinna 12**, Charlie McKinna 5:2, **Steve Lawson 12**, **Sean Courtney 8:4**, Shane Bowes 2:1, Jason Lyons 9, Phil Jeffrey 1:1)
EDINBURGH 41 (Les Collins 8:1, Carl Blackbird 8:1, Freddy Schøtt 6:2, Scott Lamb 6, Mick Powell 4, Brett Saunders 9:1)
BERWICK 18 (Mark Courtney 3, Kevin Little 1, Andy Campbell 7, Jason Straughan 1:1, Rob Grant 2, Alan Rivett 2:1, Steve Widt 2)

Glasgow, second leg, Wednesday, August 22
GLASGOW 47 (Steve Lawson 9, Jason Lyons 6:1, Kenny McKinna 10:1, Charlie McKinna 6:2, **Shane Bowes 12**, Sean Courtney 4:1)
EDINBURGH 37 (Les Collins 7, Scott Lamb 5:1, Freddy Schøtt 9, Carl Blackbird 3:3, Brett Saunders 7, Michael Coles 6:2, Mick Powell 0)
BERWICK 24 (Mark Courtney 4, Scott Robson 1, David Blackburn 4:1, Alan Rivett 6, Andy Campbell 1, David Walsh 8, Kevin Little 0)

Berwick, third leg, Friday, September 14
GLASGOW 44 (Steve Lawson 5, Jason Lyons 7:1, Charlie McKinna 9, Phil Jeffrey 5:3, Shane Bowes 10:1, Sean Courtney 7:2, Martin McKinna 1)
BERWICK 41 (**Mark Courtney 12**, Alan Rivett 4:2, David Blackburn 8, Rob Grant 0, Andy Campbell 7:1, David Walsh 8:2, Scott Robson 2)
EDINBURGH 23 (Les Collins 7, Mick Powell 3, Nigel Alderton 3, Scott Lamb 6:3, *Mark Thorpe 3*, Mike McLuskey 1)
Aggregate: Glasgow140 Edinburgh 101 Berwick 83

HERTS-ESSEX CUP
First leg, Saturday, August 18
ARENA ESSEX 53 (Martin Goodwin 10:1, Kevin Brice 7:2, Rob Tilbury 17, Wayne Garratt 12:4, *rider replacement for Troy Pratt*, Simon Wolstenholme 4, Adrian Stevens 3:1)
RYE HOUSE 43 (Melvyn Taylor 8:2, Trevor O'Brien 6:1, Jens Rasmussen 12:1, Glen Baxter 11, Kelvin Mullarkey 1, Scott Humphries 3, Wayne Baxter 2:1)

Second leg, Sunday, September 16
RYE HOUSE 49 (Melvyn Taylor 19, Trevor O'Brien 9:1, *rider replacement for Jens Rasmussen*, Glen Baxter 13:3, Scott Humphries 6:2, Kelvin Mullarkey 1:1, Wayne Baxter 1)
ARENA ESSEX 47 (Martin Goodwin 13, Kevin Brice 2, Rob Tilbury 9:3, Wayne Garratt 1, Troy Pratt 8, Simon Wolstenholme 9, Adrian Stevens 5:1)
Original staging on Sunday, August 19, postponed, waterlogged track.
Arena Essex win 100-92 on aggregate.

CHALLENGE MATCHES
National League

SCOTTISH CUP

First leg, Sunday, September 2
EDINBURGH 50 (Les Collins 6:1, Brett Saunders 9:1, Freddy Schøtt 14, Carl Blackbird 9:1, Michael Coles 5:2, Scott Lamb 3:1, Mick Powell 4)
GLASGOW 46 (Steve Lawson 13, Charlie McKinna 0, Kenny McKinna 10:1, Sean Courtney 2:1, Shane Bowes 8:1, Jason Lyons 5:2, Phil Jeffrey 8:1)
Second leg, Wednesday, October 3
GLASGOW 55 (Steve Lawson 16:1, Charlie McKinna 8:3, Shane Bowes 10:2, *rider replacement for Kenny McKinna*, Sean Courtney 11:3, Jason Lyons 7, Phil Jeffrey 3, James Grieves 0)
EDINBURGH 40 (Les Collins 13, Michael Coles 1, Carl Blackbird 6, Freddy Schøtt 13:1, Scott Lamb 2:1, Mick Powell 4, Nigel Alderton 1:1)
Glasgow win 101-90 on aggregate.

AUTUMN TRIANGLE

Hackney, first leg, Friday, September 21
HACKNEY 47 (**Paul Whittaker 13:2**, Michael Warren 11, **Steve Schofield 15**, Gary Tagg 8:3, Tim Korneliussen 0, *rider replacement for Andy Galvin*, Dave Hamnett 0)
RYE HOUSE 32 (Melvyn Taylor 9, Trevor O'Brien 2, *rider replacement for Jens Rasmussen*, Wayne Baxter 4:1, Glen Baxter 11, Scott Humphries 6:1)
ARENA ESSEX 29 (Martin Goodwin 9, Kevin Brice 2, Rob Tilbury 8, Adrian Stevens 0, Wayne Garratt 6:1, Troy Pratt 3:1, Simon Wolstenholme 1:1)

Arena Essex, second leg, Saturday, October 13
ARENA ESSEX 47 (Martin Goodwin 10:1, Kevin Brice 7:2, Rob Tilbury 11, Adrian Stevens 3:2, Wayne Garratt 8:1, Troy Pratt 6:3, Simon Wolstenholme 2:1)
RYE HOUSE 31 (Melvyn Taylor 8, Trevor O'Brien 1, Jens Rasmussen 9, Scott Humphries 3, Glen Baxter 9, Wayne Baxter 1)
HACKNEY 30 (Paul Whittaker 10, Michael Warren 5:1, Gary Tagg 10:1, Dave Hamnett 4:1, *rider replacement for Andy Galvin*, Roland Pollard 1:1)

Rye House, third leg, Sunday, October 14
HACKNEY 41 (Gary Tagg 11, Dave Hamnett 9:2, Paul Whittaker 14, Michael Warren 4:1, *rider replacement for Andy Galvin*, Roland Pollard 3:2)
RYE HOUSE 35 (Melvyn Taylor 7, Trevor O'Brien 4, **Jens Rasmussen 12**, Scott Humphries 3, Glen Baxter 7, Wayne Baxter 2:1)
ARENA ESSEX 31 (Martin Goodwin 5, Kevin Brice 2, Rob Tilbury 9, Adrian Stevens 1:1, Wayne Garratt 4:2, Troy Pratt 10, Simon Wolstenholme 0)
Aggregate: Hackney 118 Arena Essex 107 Rye House 98.

AUTUMN TROPHY

First leg, Saturday, September 22
BERWICK 22 (Mark Courtney 5, Alan Rivett 0, *rider replacement for David Blackburn*, David Walsh 7:1, Andy Campbell 5:1, Rob Grant 2:1, Scott Robson 3)
NEWCASTLE 20 (Peter Carr 3:1, Simon Green 3, David Bargh 6, Mark Thorpe 2, *Rod Hunter* 3, Ian Stead 2, Paul Smith 1)
Abandoned after seven heats, generator failure, scores to stand.

Second leg, Sunday, October 7
NEWCASTLE 43 (Peter Carr 9:2, Simon Green 11:1, David Bargh 8:1, Mark Thorpe 4, *Rod Hunter 5*, Ian Stead 2, Paul Smith 4)
BERWICK 53 (Mark Courtney 9:2, Kevin Little 1, David Blackburn 9:2, David Walsh 13, Andy Campbell 6:1, Rob Grant 3:1, Scott Robson 12:1).
Berwick win 75-63 on aggregate.

ANGLIA-HERTS TROPHY

First leg, Friday, September 28
PETERBOROUGH 57 (Mick Poole 16, *rider replacement for Frank Andersen*, *Carl Blackbird 15*, Scott Norman 8, Nigel Flatman 4:2, Wayne Bridgeford 9:3, Sean Barker 5:2)
RYE HOUSE 39 (Melvyn Taylor 7, Trevor O'Brien 4:1, Jens Rasmussen 8:1, Glen Baxter 10:1, Scott Humphries 8, Wayne Baxter 2:1, Kelvin Mullarkey 0)
Second leg, Sunday, October 7
RYE HOUSE 60 (Melvyn Taylor 11:1, Trevor O'Brien 8:1, **Jens Rasmussen 15**, Glen Baxter 12:2, Scott Humphries 6:1, Colin Thorpe 5:1, Wayne Baxter 3:2)
PETERBOROUGH 36 (*Martin Goodwin 13:1, rider replacement for Mick Poole, Troy Pratt 8:1*, Scott Norman 5, Nigel Flatman 0, Wayne Bridgeford 9:1, Sean Barker 1:1, Anthony Boyd 0)
Original staging, Sunday, September 30, postponed, waterlogged track.
Rye House win 99-93 on aggregate.

TWO LEG CHALLENGES

First leg, Wednesday, March 21
LONG EATON 53 (Kevin Smart 7, Keith White 2:2, Richard Hellsén 12, Gary O'Hare 10, Paul Fry 8:1, Nigel De'ath 11:3, Peter Lloyd 3:1)
MILTON KEYNES 42 (Kevin Jolly 8, Mark Lyndon 15, Peter Glanz 6, Andy Hines 3:2, Trevor Banks 4, Thierry Hilaire 3, Glenn Allan 3)

Second leg, Tuesday, April 3
MILTON KEYNES 45 (Kevin Jolly 6:1, Andy Hines 5, Peter Glanz 8, Trevor Banks 10:1, Mark Lyndon 8:1, Thierry Hilaire 6:2, Mike Wilson 2)
LONG EATON 50 (Kevin Smart 3, Keith White 3:1, Richard Hellsén 6:1, Gary O'Hare 8, Paul Fry 7:2, Nigel De'ath 15, Peter Lloyd 8)
Long Eaton win 103-87 on aggregate.

First leg, Friday, March 23
PETERBOROUGH 59 (Mick Poole 8:2, Nigel Flatman 9:2, **Frank Andersen 15**, Ian Barney 10:1, Scott Norman 9:3, Justin Walker 7:1, Sean Barker 1:1)
MILTON KEYNES 37 (Kevin Jolly 12, Mark Lyndon 11:2, Peter Glanz 3:1, Andy Hines 3, Trevor Banks 2, Thierry Hilaire 4, Glenn Allan 2)

Second leg, Tuesday, March 27
Postponed, track licence not issued.

First leg, Sunday, March 25
EDINBURGH 54 (Les Collins 15, Michael Coles 7:2, Brett Saunders 11, Scott Lamb 8:2, Phil Jeffrey 4, Mark Blackbird 4:1, Mark Pearce 5)
GLASGOW 42 (Steve Lawson 9, Shane Bowes 12, Kenny McKinna 7:2, Sean Courtney 2:1, Charlie McKinna 9, Geoff Powell 2, Jason Lyons 1)

Second leg, Wednesday, April 4
GLASGOW 53 (Steve Lawson 6, Martin McKinna 3, Kenny McKinna 14, Charlie McKinna 7:4, Sean Courtney 10, Geoff Powell 4, Jason Lyons 9:1)
EDINBURGH 43 (Les Collins 17, Michael Coles 5:1, Brett Saunders 7:1, Scott Lamb 7, Phil Jeffrey 1, Mark Blackbird 5, Mark Pearce 1)
Edinburgh win 97-95 on aggregate.

First leg, Wednesday, March 29
LONG EATON 42 (Kevin Smart 3, Keith White 4:1, Richard Hellsén 6, Gary O'Hare 6:3, Paul Fry 10:1, Nigel De'ath 10:3, Peter Lloyd 3)
PETERBOROUGH 54 (Mick Poole 15:2, Nigel Flatman 4:1, Frank Andersen 12:1, Ian Barney 14, Scott Norman 5:1, Justin Walker 2:1, Sean Barker 2)

Second leg, Friday, March 30
PETERBOROUGH 55 (Mick Poole 14:1, Nigel Flatman 2, Frank Andersen 10, Ian Barney 11:3, Scott Norman 12:2, Justin Walker 3, Sean Barker 3)
LONG EATON 40 (Kevin Smart 5, Keith White 3:2, Richard Hellsén 13, Gary O'Hare 1:1, Paul Fry 7, Nigel De'ath 5:1, Peter Lloyd 6:2)
Peterborough win 109-82 on aggregate.

First leg, Saturday, March 31
STOKE 54 (Louis Carr 7:1, Chris Cobby 10:2, Nigel Crabtree 11:1, Eric Monaghan 13:1, Mark Carlson 0, Rob Woffinden 9:1, Ian Stead 4:2)
MILTON KEYNES 42 (*Rider replacement for Kevin Jolly*, Trevor Banks 11:2, Peter Glanz 10, Andy Hines 1, Mark Lyndon 14:2, Thierry Hilaire 5, Glenn Allan 1)

Second leg, Tuesday, April 10
MILTON KEYNES 40.5 (Kevin Jolly 5:1, Andy Hines 7.5, Peter Glanz 4:1, Trevor Banks 13, David Clarke 1:1, Mark Lyndon 7, Thierry Hilaire 3:1)
STOKE 55.5 (Louis Carr 8:1, Chris Cobby 2, Nigel Crabtree 13, **Eric Monaghan 15**, Mark Carlson 7:4, Rob Woffinden 10.5:1, Ian Stead 0)
Stoke win 109.5-82-5 on aggregate.

First leg, Thursday, May 17
MIDDLESBROUGH 56 (Darren Sumner 3:2, David Cheshire 10, Jamie Luckhurst 4:1, Paul Bentley 14, Rod Hunter 10:2, Steve Wilcock 8:2, Duncan Chapman 7:1)
PETERBOROUGH 39 (Mick Poole 15:2, rider *replacement for Frank Andersen*, Craig Hodgson 4, Ian Barney 2, Scott Norman 15, Paul Blackbird 0, Sean Barker 3:1)

Second leg, Friday, May 18
PETERBOROUGH 55 (Mick Poole 0, Nigel Flatman 12:1, Craig Hodgson 13, Ian Barney 7:2, Scott Norman 12:1, Paul Blackbird 4:1, Sean Barker 7)
MIDDLESBROUGH 40 (Darren Sumner 0, David Cheshire 3, Steve Wilcock 5:1, Paul Bentley 8:1, Rod Hunter 13, Martin Jones 4, Duncan Chapman 7:1)
Middlesbrough win 96-94 on aggregate.

Thursday, March 22
IPSWICH 64 (Chris Louis 15, Billy Lellman 4:1, Dean Standing 13:1, **Alan Mogridge 11:4**, David Norris 11, Shane Parker 8:1, Colin White 2:1)
POOLE 32 (Gary Chessell 9, Gary Allan 7:2, Craig Boyce 7:1, *rider replacement for Alun Rossiter*, Tony Langdon 0, Steve Langdon 9:1, Rod Colquhoun 0)

Thursday, March 22
MIDDLESBROUGH 54 (Darren Sumner 13:1, **Steve Wilcock 13:2**, Jamie Luckhurst 6:1, Paul Bentley 7:2, David Cheshire 6:1, Paul Smith 5, Max Schofield 4:1)
LONG EATON 42 (Kevin Smart 1, Keith White 7:1, Richard Hellsén 13:2, Gary O'Hare 8, Paul Fry 3:1, Nigel De'ath 10, Peter Lloyd 0)

CHALLENGE MATCHES National League

Sunday, March 25
NEWCASTLE 34 (Peter Carr 3:1, Simon Green 6:1, Martin Dixon 10:1, Mark Thorpe 4:1, David Bargh 6:1, Gordon Whitaker 4:1, John Wainwright 1:1)
IPSWICH 62 (Chris Louis 11:1, Robbie Fuller 4, **Dean Standing 15**, **Alan Mogridge 14:1**, David Norris 10:3, Shane Parker 7:2, Colin White 1)

Sunday, March 25
RYE HOUSE 57 (Melvyn Taylor 11:1, Roger Johns 8:3, Jens Rasmussen 7, Nigel Sparshott 2:1, Glen Baxter 13:1, Jamie Fagg 8:1, Trevor O'Brien 8:1)
POOLE 37 (Gary Chessell 13, Gary Allan 6, Craig Boyce 12:1, *rider replacement for Alun Rossiter,* Tony Langdon 2:2, Rod Colquhoun 2, Steve Langdon 2:1)

Monday, March 26
EXETER 72 (Steve Regeling 14:1, Steve Bishop 13:2, Richard Green 14:1, Colin Cook 8:3, Peter Jeffery 10:3, Andy Sell 8:3, Mark Simmonds 5:1)
LONG EATON 24 (Kevin Smart 6, Keith White 0, Richard Hellsén 8, Gary O'Hare 4, Paul Fry 1, Nigel De'ath 5, Peter Lloyd 0)

Thursday,. March 29
IPSWICH 48 (Chris Louis 14, Robbie Fuller 0, Dean Standing 7:1, Alan Mogridge 6:1, David Norris 5:1, Shane Parker 14, Colin White 2)
KANGAROOS 48 (Leigh Adams 11, Glen Baxter 6:1, Steve Regeling 11:1, Scott Norman 6:1, Mick Poole 10:1, Jamie Fagg 4:1, Steve Widt 0)

Sunday, April 1
RYE HOUSE 38 (Melvyn Taylor 3, Roger Johns 6:2, Jens Rasmussen 8:1, Nigel Sparshott 1, Glen Baxter 11, Jamie Fagg 6:1, Trevor O'Brien 3:2)
IPSWICH 57 (Chris Louis 12:1, Robbie Fuller 0, Dean Standing 8:2, Alan Mogridge 7:3, **David Norris 15**, Shane Parker 15:1, Colin White 0)

Monday, April 2
EXETER 61 (Steve Regeling 14, Steve Bishop 11:2, Richard Green 11:1, Colin Cook 3:3, Peter Jeffery 10:1, Andy Sell 5:2, Mark Simmonds 7:2)
STOKE 35 (Louis Carr 5:1, Chris Cobby 2, Nigel Crabtree 10, Eric Monaghan 13, Mark Carlson 1, Rob Woffinden 4:1, Ian Stead 0)

Saturday, April 7
STOKE 59 (Louis Carr 12:2, Chris Cobby 1:1, **Nigel Crabtree 13:2**, Eric Monaghan 14, Mark Carlson 4, Rob Woffinden 14:1, Ian Stead 1)
LONG EATON 37 (Kevin Smart 3:3, Paul Fry 11:1, Richard Hellsén 11, Gary O'Hare 7, Keith White 1:1, Nigel De'ath 4, Peter Lloyd 0)

Monday, April 9
EXETER 59 (Steve Regeling 9:1, **Steve Bishop 14:1**, Richard Green 9, Colin Cook 4:1, Peter Jeffery 12:1, Andy Sell 8:1, Mark Simmonds 3:1)
RYE HOUSE 37 (*Andy Galvin 11:2*, Roger Johns 3, *Frank Andersen 12:1, rider replacement for Jens Rasmussen,* Nigel Sparshott 1:1, Jamie Fagg 3, Trevor O'Brien 7:1)
**Fixture was originally scheduled as a National League match but changed to a challenge when Rye House had all three heat leaders injured the previous afternoon.*

Sunday, April 15
EASTBOURNE 32 (*Chris Louis 8:1*, Keith Pritchard 4:1, Andy Buck 9, Paul Woods 2, Tony Primmer 4, Darren Grayling 3, Steve Masters 2:1)
WIMBLEDON 63 (Nathan Simpson 10:1, Neville Tatum 13, Ray Morton 13, Andy Grahame 13, Nigel Leaver 10:2, Dean Prinsloo 0, Peter Schroeck 4:1)

Sunday, April 22
EASTBOURNE 50 (*Steve Regeling 13*, Keith Pritchard 8:1, Andy Buck 8:1, Paul Woods 6, Tony Primmer 8:1, Darren Grayling 4:1, Justin Walker 3:2)
POOLE 46 (Gary Chessell 13:1, Gary Allan 4:1, Alun Rossiter 6:1, Craig Boyce 10, Steve Langdon 3, Steve Leigh 1, Rod Colquhoun 9:1)

Sunday, May 20
NEWCASTLE 51 (Peter Carr 15, Simon Green 5:1, David Bargh 12, Mark Thorpe 5, Martin Dixon 11:3, Paul Smith 2, John Wainwright 1)
KANGAROOS 45 (Mick Poole 11:1, Scott Norman 8:2, Craig Boyce 13, Mick Powell 0, Craig Hodgson 4, Shane Bowes 3:2, Jason Lyons 6:2)

Milton Keynes, Tuesday, August 21
WHITE KNIGHTS 39 (Peter Glanz 7:2, Thierry Hilaire 8, Kevin Jolly 7:1, Jon Cooper 7:1, Mark Blackbird 4, Paul Blackbird 2:1, Paul Atkins 4)
BLACK KNIGHTS 56 (Jon Surman 7:1, Andy Hines 10:2, Tony Primmer 9:2, David Clarke 7:2, **Mark Carlson 15**, Peter Byrne 1:1, Kieran McCullagh 7)

Wednesday, September 5
LONG EATON 52 (Kevin Smart 7:2, Nigel De'ath 10:1, Richard Hellsén 7:1, Paul Fry 10, Jon Surman 4:2, Gary O'Hare 11:1, Duncan Chapman 3:1)
EXETER 44 (Steve Regeling 15, Mark Simmonds 5, Richard Green 7, Steve Bishop 3, Colin Cook 10, Ian Barney 4, Deon Prinsloo 0)

Thursday, September 6
MIDDLESBROUGH 65 (Darren Sumner 11:1, David Cheshire 7:1, Rod Hunter 5, Paul Bentley 9:3, Jamie Luckhurst 7:1, **Steve Wilcock 11:1**, Dave Edwards 2:1, Mark Crang 8, Martin Jones 0, Andy Sumner 5:1)
NEWCASTLE 54 (Peter Carr 6:1, Simon Green 9:2, David Bargh 16, Mark Thorpe 3:1, Martin Dixon 8:1, Ian Stead 0, Paul Smith 5, John Wainwright 2, Steve Wicks 2, David Nagel 3:2)

Monday, September 17
EXETER 54 (Steve Regeling 13:1, Ian Barney 0, Richard Green 7:1, Steve Bishop 8:1, Colin Cook 12:2, Mark Simmonds 7:1, Deon Prinsloo 7:1)
NATIONAL LEAGUE SELECT 35 (David Blackburn [Berwick] 2:1, Michael Coles [Edinburgh] 13, Frank Andersen [Peterborough] 3, Rob Woffinden [Stoke] 5:1, Alan Rivett [Berwick] 6, Frank Smart [Exeter] 1, Mark Lemon [Poole] 5)

Friday, October 5
HACKNEY PAST & PRESENT 35 (*Rider replacement for Steve Schofield,* Paul Whittaker 11:1, Gary Tagg 3, *Chris Louis 6:1, Alan Mogridge 7:1*, Dave Hamnett 6, Michael Warren 2)
AUSTRALIAN SELECT 31 (Todd Wiltshire 8, Shane Parker 0, Glen Baxter 0, Tony Langdon 4:2, Craig Boyce 8, Tony Primmer 5:1, Scott Humphries 6:1)
Abandoned after 11 heats, rain.

Wednesday, October 10
LONG EATON 57 (Kevin Smart 4:2, Nigel De'ath 12:1, Richard Hellsén 8:1, Paul Fry 13, Jamie Habbin 6:4, **Mark Blackbird 12**, Jon Surman 2:1)
SIMMONS SELECT 39 (Les Collins [Edinburgh] 16, Gary O'Hare [Long Eaton] 3, Louis Carr [Stoke] 7, Mark Carlson [Stoke] 6:1, Eric Monaghan [Stoke] 6:1, Jon Hughes [Long Eaton} 1, Stafford Galvin [Long Eaton] 0)

Thursday, October 11
MIDDLESBROUGH v EDINBURGH, ***cancelled, waterlogged track.***

40TH ANNIVERSARY MEETING

Wednesday, May 23
LONG EATON 42 (Kevin Smart 9, *rider replacement for Nigel De'ath,* Richard Hellsén 10:1, Paul Fry 7, Gary O'Hare 1:1, Dave Perks 4, Peter Lloyd 6:1, Jon Roberts 5:2)
EX-LEICESTER 42 (Steve Regeling 12, Colin Cook 2, Les Collins 12, *Mark Courtney, did not arrive*, Eric Monaghan 9:1, Jon Surman 5:2, Michael Howe 2)

CHARITY MEETING

Sunday, October 21
NEWCASTLE 45 (Peter Carr 11, Simon Green 5, *Andy Smith* 9, Paul Smith 5:2, *Kelvin Tatum 10:1*, Ian Stead 3, Ray Taaffe 2)
JOE OWEN'S JETS 33 (Gary Havelock [Bradford] 8, Rob Grant [Berwick] 3, David Walsh [Berwick] 6, Paul Bentley [Middlesbrough] 0, Paul Thorp [Bradford] 10, Duncan Chapman [Middlesbrough] 3, Steve Wicks [Newcastle] 3)
Original staging, Sunday, June 24, postponed, waterlogged track.

FOUR TEAM TOURNAMENTS

Arena Essex, Saturday, September 8
RYE HOUSE 40 (Melvyn Taylor 11, Trevor O'Brien 5, **Jens Rasmussen 12, Glen Baxter 12**) **ARENA ESSEX 28** (Wayne Garratt 8, Kevin Brice 6, Rob Tilbury 9, Simon Wolstenholme 5) **IPSWICH 14** (Alan Mogridge 3, David Norris 8, Robbie Fuller 3, Craig Hyde 0) **PETERBOROUGH 14** (Craig Hodgson 7, Scott Norman 3, Wayne Bridgeford 2, Sean Barker 2)

Peterborough, Friday, September 21
PETERBOROUGH 29 (Mick Poole 7, Craig Hodgson 10, Wayne Bridgeford 5, Scott Norman 7)
EXETER 28 (Steve Regeling 10, Ian Barney 5, Richard Green 7, Colin Cook 6) **STOKE 28** (Louis Carr 6, Eric Monaghan 10, David Clarke 4, Chris Cobby 8) NATIONAL **LEAGUE SELECT 11** (Anthony Boyd [Stoke] 1, Carl Blackbird [Edinburgh] 6, Mark Blackbird [Milton Keynes] 0, Sean Barker [Peterborough] 3, Mark Jolly [Peterborough] 1)

MARTIN HEWLETT MEMORIAL TROPHY

Exeter, Monday, August 20
EXETER 32 (**Steve Regeling 15**, Ian Barney 2, Colin Cook 8:2, Mark Simmonds 7:1) **SWINDON 24** (Phil Crump 13, Wayne Freeman 2:1, Steve Camden 1:1, David Smart 7, Mark Lemon 1) **EXPRESS & ECHO RANGERS 22** (Peter Jeffery 5:1, Steve Bishop 6:1, Richard Green 11, Frank Smart 0)

†Martin John HEWLETT (B 6.2.1962, Swindon – D 15.9.1982) made his British League debut for his local club Swindon in 1979 and spent the two following seasons at National League Exeter, where he quickly developed into a heat leader. He was recalled by Swindon in 1982 and collapsed with a brain haemorrhage on the centre green after racing against Birmingham on September 11, 1982, and died in hospital four days later. In all he rode in 121 matches for the two clubs, scoring more than 700 points. He was a hugely popular rider with supporters.

JUNIOR Scene

WOLVERHAMPTON totally dominated British League Division Two racing – with arguably one of the finest all-round teams the junior league has ever seen.

While their squad may have lacked an out and out Superkid in the mould of major 1989 discovery Joe Screen, there was a marvellous balance about the Goodyear Cubs and in teenager Wayne Carter they nourished and encouraged a youngster who is destined for a full-time Sunbrite League team berth in 1991. Carter relished his role as skipper of the Monmore Green outfit and after showing promising form as a stand-in for the senior side turned down the opportunity of a guaranteed National League place to stay with the juniors as they chased the Cup and League double.

Wolverhampton had wrapped up the league title well before the final weeks of the season and gained maximum bonus points from their 16 matches.

Their only League defeats were at Belle Vue, early in April, and at King's Lynn at the beginning of October when the title chase was over. They had ample revenge for those reverses – beating both Belle Vue and King's Lynn home and away en route to a place in the Knock Out Cup Final.

Unfortunately that competition ended in controversy and near farce. The Goodyear Cubs held an eight-point lead from the first leg when they went to Odsal for the return in what was to be Bradford's final meeting of the season. Heat four provided all the drama with referee Angus McLeod finally having to abandon the race after one rider fell, one was lapped and two others failed to complete the course thinking the race had been stopped.

Arguments raged for 15 or 20 minutes by which time the threatening fog had descended on the huge bowl making it impossible to see from one side of the track to the other. Eventually the second leg was abandoned and re-run a couple of weeks later at Cradley Heath where Wolverhampton completed the double.

1990 British League Division Two Final Table

	M.	W.	D.	L.	PtsF	PtsA	BP	Tpts
Wolverhampton	32	26	4	2	723	417	16	72
Reading	32	20	2	10	637	505	12	54
King's Lynn	32	19	2	11	620	526	11	51
Bradford	32	15	1	16	588	554	8	39
Swindon	32	13	2	17	578	562	6	34
Belle Vue	32	12	3	17	553	578	6	33
Cradley Heath	32	12	1	19	500	635	6	31
†Oxford	32	10	1	21	481	662	4	23
Coventry	32	9	0	23	449	690	3	21

†Two points deducted for fielding an ineligible rider

Roll of Honour

1987	1 SHEFFIELD	2 Bradford	3 Coventry
1988	1 BRADFORD	2 Belle Vue	3 Sheffield
1989	1 BELLE VUE	2 Oxford	3 Swindon
1990	1 WOLVERHAMPTON	2 Reading	3 King's Lynn

BRITISH LEAGUE DIVISION TWO KNOCK OUT CUP

Preliminary Round

Coventry 19 Oxford 17
Oxford 25 Coventry 11
OXFORD win 42-30 on aggregate.

First round

Kings Lynn 26 Reading 10
Reading 25 King's Lynn 10
KING'S LYNN win 36-35 on aggregate.
Cradley Heath 17 Bradford 19
Bradford 19 Cradley Heath 17
BRADFORD win 38-34 on aggregate.
Oxford 19 Swindon 17
Swindon 29 Oxford 7
SWINDON win 46-26 on aggregate.
Wolverhampton 24 Belle Vue 12
Belle Vue 7 Wolverhampton 29
WOLVERHAMPTON win 53-19 on aggregate.

Semi final

King's Lynn 16 Wolverhampton 20
Wolverhampton 28 King's Lynn 8
WOLVERHAMPTON win 48-24 on aggregate.
Bradford 28 Swindon 8
Swindon 18 Bradford 18
BRADFORD win 46-26 on aggregate.

FINAL

Wolverhampton 22 Bradford 14
†Bradford 11 Wolverhampton 24
WOLVERHAMPTON win 46-25 on aggregate.
†Original staging of the second leg was abandoned with Bradford leading 10-8 because of fog and re-staged at Cradley Heath.

Roll of Honour

1987 BRADFORD 91 Sheffield 87
1988 CRADLEY HEATH 102 Reading 77
1989 BELLE VUE 99 Swindon 78
1990 WOLVERHAMPTON 46 Bradford 25

BRITISH LEAGUE DIVISION TWO

All the Results

	BELLE VUE	BRADFORD	COVENTRY	CRADLEY HEATH	KING'S LYNN	OXFORD	READING	SWINDON	WOLVERHAMPTON
BELLE VUE		23-13 17-16	21-14 16-18	18-18 17-19	19-14 17-19	16-20 19-16	17-19 09-25	19-16 25-09	20-15 18-18
BRADFORD	20-16 16-20		26-10 26-10	22-14 22-14	23-12 †06-28	20-16 27-09	15-21 21-15	20-16 27-09	18-18 11-25
COVENTRY	25-11 11-25	13-23 19-17		17-18 06-27	09-27 21-15	23-13 17-19	19-17 12-24	10-26 09-27	10-25 16-20
CRADLEY HEATH	12-24 17-16	12-23 23-13	24-10 23-13		20-16 11-25	14-22 24-12	08-28 09-25	11-24 24-12	15-21 06-30
KING'S LYNN	21-15 21-15	19-17 14-22	22-14 30-06	29-07 20-16		20-16 21-15	28-08 26-10	25-11 14-22	16-20 21-15
OXFORD	24-12 19-16	18-17 07-29	10-26 10-26	19-16 15-21	18-18 17-19		19-16 15-20	19-17 12-24	11-24 09-26
READING	19-16 24-12	28-08 23-13	24-11 29-07	18-17 22-14	18-18 28-08	15-21 20-16		26-10 22-14	18-18 16-20
SWINDON	15-21 18-18	18-17 24-12	25-11 16-20	29-07 13-21	15-21 22-14	24-12 28-07	22-14 17-19		12-21 18-18
WOLVERHAMPTON	24-12 23-13	20-15 23-13	28-07 26-09	26-10 28-08	28-08 25-11	20-16 27-09	23-12 22-14	23-13 23-12	

JUNIOR Scene

Belle Vue

Joe Screen	4	12	35	1	36	12.00
Richard Musson	31	89	200	13	213	9.57
Mike Lewthwaite	11	28	59	2	61	8.71
Max Schofield	12	34	57	7	64	7.53
Scott Smith	*20*	*64*	*88*	*11*	*99*	*6.19*
Richard Smith	22	67	55	13	68	4.06
Steve Cope	1	3	2	1	3	4.00
Mike Hampson	16	47	36	3	39	3.32
Bobby Grahame	*10*	*33*	*21*	*0*	*21*	*2.55*
Dean Child	*1*	*3*	*0*	*0*	*0*	*0.00*

Bradford

Bryan Larner	24	69	140	9	149	8.64
Phil Disney	25	75	141	14	155	8.27
Stuart Parnaby	32	97	191	14	205	8.45
Simon Bean	14	44	40	9	49	4.45
Dean Child	*16*	*52*	*48*	*7*	*55*	*4.23*
Nigel Douglas	14	44	28	6	34	3.09
Steve Parnaby	1	1	0	0	0	0.00

Coventry

Andy Phillips	1	3	9	0	9	12.00
Jason Gage	1	3	7	0	7	9.33
Andy Meredith	27	75	102	14	116	6.19
Lee Coleman	*31*	*89*	*125*	*11*	*136*	*6.11*
Darren Etheridge	3	10	13	1	14	5.60
Rob Homer	*5*	*14*	*17*	*2*	*19*	*5.43*
Paul Bromwich	21	63	78	4	82	5.21
Chris Clarence	27	85	72	15	87	4.09
Dean Child	*1*	*5*	*5*	*0*	*5*	*4.00*
Andy Witts	*8*	*25*	*19*	*1*	*20*	*3.20*
Matthew Powell	3	7	2	1	3	1.71

Cradley Heath

Mark Robinson	22	62	118	7	125	8.06
Scott Smith	*14*	*45*	*76*	*8*	*84*	*7.47*
David Haynes	31	94	132	12	144	6.13
Rob Homer	*18*	*55*	*58*	*9*	*67*	*4.87*
Mark Meredith	31	100	99	19	118	4.72
Bobby Grahame	*1*	*3*	*3*	*0*	*3*	*4.00*
Steve Griffiths	4	12	8	3	11	3.67
Dean Scott	2	7	2	0	2	1.14
Aaron Hill	1	3	2	0	2	2.67
Morgan Hughes	1	3	2	1	3	4.00
Gary Frankum	1	3	0	0	0	0.00

King's Lynn

Roger Horspool	32	95	203	16	219	9.22
Tom Grinstead	32	94	156	28	184	7.83
Emerson Fairweather	10	30	45	10	55	7.33
Lee Farthing	10	31	46	9	55	7.10
Darren Spicer	24	76	93	17	110	5.79
Martin Cobbin	20	61	77	11	88	5.77

▲ BRITISH League Division Two statistics were prepared by Peter Morrish, official statistician to the Sunbrite British League.
▲ Statistics read, from left to right, matches, rides, points, bonus points, total points and an average out of a maximum of 12 points per meeting.

Oxford

Paul Dugard	19	57	158	0	158	11.09
Kevin Pitts	12	34	59	10	69	8.12
Kieran McCullagh	12	38	56	3	59	6.21
Steve Masters	9	29	40	1	41	5.66
Jon Armstrong	1	3	3	1	4	5.33
Sean McCullagh	23	71	79	9	88	4.96
Lance Sealey	*8*	*24*	*23*	*3*	*26*	*4.33*
Lee Coleman	*1*	*3*	*3*	*0*	*3*	*4.00*
Rob Fisher	1	3	3	0	3	4.00
Wayne Parker	14	39	29	3	32	3.28
Kevin Howse	25	74	28	9	37	2.00
Derrol Santos	1	3	0	0	0	0.00
Mark Woods	1	2	0	0	0	0.00

Reading

David Steen	27	80	188	6	194	9.70
Troy Smith	32	90	138	32	170	7.56
Christian Howell	32	100	155	18	173	6.92
Lance Sealey	*29*	*88*	*129*	*18*	*147*	*6.68*
Mark Seabright	8	27	27	9	36	5.33

Swindon

Peter Byrne	1	3	7	1	8	10.67
Matthew Cross	28	81	191	10	201	9.93
Martin Chessell	21	66	121	8	129	7.82
Wayne Freeman	15	47	73	14	87	7.40
Steve Camden	25	78	95	21	116	5.95
Andy Witts	*11*	*32*	*38*	*10*	*48*	*5.05*
Darren Boulton	5	18	17	5	22	4.89
Anthony Blake	6	22	17	0	17	3.09
Brett Wakeling	4	12	6	2	8	2.67
Darrin Wilson	2	6	8	2	10	6.67
Mike Courage	1	3	1	0	1	1.33
Frank Smart	1	3	1	0	1	1.33
Rob Camden	1	2	0	0	0	0.00
Dean Scott	*1*	*3*	*0*	*0*	*0*	*0.00*

Wolverhampton

Carl Stonehewer	11	33	82	7	89	10.79
Wayne Carter	30	87	210	20	230	10.57
Ade Hoole	32	100	183	25	208	8.32
Stephen Morris	31	100	172	32	204	8.16
Shane Cooper	21	63	72	19	91	5.78
Shawn Venables	1	4	4	1	5	5.00

Top Ten Averages

1 Paul Dugard	19	57	158	0	158	11.09
2 Carl Stonehewer	11	33	82	7	89	10.79
3 Wayne Carter	30	87	210	20	230	10.57
4 Matthew Cross	28	81	191	10	201	9.93
5 David Steen	27	80	188	6	194	9.70
6 Richard Musson	31	89	200	13	213	9.57
7 Roger Horspool	32	95	203	16	219	9.22
8 Mike Lewthwaite	11	28	59	2	61	8.71
9 Bryan Larner	24	69	140	9	149	8.64
10 Stuart Parnaby	32	97	191	14	205	8.45

(Minimum qualification: 6 matches)

THE National League, the one-time forerunners in giving young lads their speedway fling, again slipped backwards in their attitude towards juniors.

They quite wisely abandoned the formula that was used in 1989 – it produced a League table based on percentage success with Rye House staging 37 junior League matches and Berwick only 10 – and which caused so much confusion.

But instead of reverting to a genuine National Junior League they introduced a system of three regional Junior Divisions and couldn't even complete those totally successfully.

The Southern Section, which included only six tracks, was never finished as Hackney and Wimbledon had one uncompleted match.

Some tracks did take advantage of the whole operation.

How else can you explain the presence in the Hackney team on one occasion of Danish Under 21 international Tim Korneliussen? Or, for that matter, how does the Frenchman Thierry Hilaire come to ride in a couple of junior matches for Milton Keynes?

There also appeared to be no ruling on who could ride for whom. Scotland's Muir Templeton turned out for Berwick, Edinburgh and Glasgow and, in the same Northern Section, Paul Gould wore the colours of Edinburgh, Middlesbrough and Newcastle!

If Junior League racing is to be treated seriously then more discipline must be introduced to the League set-up and stringent regulations must be introduced and adhered to.

▲ In the team statistics in this Section riders who appeared for more than one team are in italics.

JUNIOR Scene

1990 NATIONAL JUNIOR LEAGUE FINAL TABLES AND AVERAGES

Central

	M	W	D	L	PF	PA	Pts
Stoke	**10**	**9**	**0**	**1**	**193**	**105**	**18**
Rye House	10	3	3	4	152	145	9
Milton Keynes	10	4	1	5	144	148	9
Ipswich	10	4	1	5	145	152	9
Long Eaton	10	3	2	5	131	165	8
Peterborough	10	2	3	5	120	170	7

IPSWICH

Craig Hyde	3	9	19	1	20	8.89
Darren Fitch	9	22	43	5	48	8.73
Colin White	5	13	28	0	28	8.62
Andrew Mountain	9	20	25	4	29	5.80
Lawrence Hare	3	8	10	1	11	5.50
Jason Gage	*8*	*19*	*19*	*2*	*21*	*4.42*
Adrian Mountain	1	3	1	1	2	2.67
Damon Richardson	1	1	0	0	0	0.00

LONG EATON

Jon Roberts	2	6	18	0	18	12.00
Duncan Chapman	2	6	14	0	14	9.33
Mark Lemon	1	3	7	0	7	9.33
Stafford Galvin	8	23	40	4	44	7.65
Keith Stanley	4	8	10	1	11	5.50
Andy Meredith	5	11	12	2	14	5.09
Aaron Hill	2	5	4	2	6	4.80
Jon Bell	2	6	7	0	7	4.67
Chris Storey	7	16	12	2	14	3.50
Michael Howe	*3*	*8*	*6*	*1*	*7*	*3.50*
Jason Gage	*1*	*2*	*1*	*0*	*1*	*2.00*
Mark Jolly	*1*	*2*	*0*	*0*	*0*	*0.00*

MILTON KEYNES

Mark Blackbird	3	7	20	1	21	12.00
Thierry Hilaire	2	5	15	0	15	12.00
Paul Blackbird	*1*	*2*	*5*	*1*	*6*	*12.00*
Mark Jolly	*3*	*8*	*19*	*2*	*21*	*10.50*
Peter Byrne	7	20	30	9	39	7.80
Kieran McCullagh	7	19	33	2	35	7.37
Michael Howe	*3*	*8*	*10*	*2*	*12*	*6.00*
Glenn Allan	3	8	8	0	8	4.00
Mike Wilson	1	4	2	0	2	2.00
Steve Reynolds	4	6	2	1	3	2.00
Mark Taylor	1	1	0	0	0	0.00

PETERBOROUGH

Wayne Bridgeford	*1*	*3*	*9*	*0*	*9*	*12.00*
Anthony Boyd	*1*	*2*	*6*	*0*	*6*	*12.00*
Trevor Eadon	1	2	4	1	5	10.00
Jon Cooper	1	2	5	0	5	10.00
Paul Blackbird	*5*	*15*	*34*	*0*	*34*	*9.07*
Phil Disney	1	3	5	0	5	6.67
Mark Meredith	2	3	3	1	4	5.33
Mark Jolly	*8*	*22*	*24*	*4*	*28*	*5.09*
Darren Tupper	10	23	23	5	28	4.87
Matthew Poole	2	5	5	0	5	4.00
Rob Fisher	4	9	2	0	2	0.89
Paul Wood	3	6	0	0	0	0.00

RYE HOUSE

Wayne Baxter	10	30	69	5	74	9.87
Wayne Bridgeford	*6*	*14*	*27*	*0*	*27*	*7.71*
Colin Thorpe	9	24	35	5	40	6.67
Garry Thompson	3	6	5	1	6	4.00
Tony Kingsbury	10	23	15	2	17	2.96
Grahame Baxter	1	2	1	0	1	2.00

STOKE

Richard Davidson	9	27	71	5	76	11.26
Jon Hughes	10	29	69	9	78	10.76
Garry Stead	10	24	35	9	44	7.33
Jason Reed	3	6	9	1	10	6.67
Andy Torkington	4	8	7	1	8	4.00
Kevin Makin	1	2	2	0	2	4.00
Andy Hutton	1	2	0	0	0	0.00

Northern

	M	W	D	L	PF	PA	Pts
Middlesbrough	**8**	**7**	**0**	**1**	**159**	**79**	**14**
Edinburgh	8	5	0	3	128	110	10
Newcastle	8	4	0	4	114	125	8
Berwick	8	4	0	4	112	124	8
Glasgow	8	0	0	8	81	156	0

BERWICK

Colin Smith	3	9	17	1	18	8.00
Muir Templeton	*1*	*2*	*4*	*0*	*4*	*8.00*
Jason Straughan	7	21	37	2	39	7.43
Michael Lowrie	5	12	16	3	19	6.33
Fraser Smith	8	20	21	8	29	5.80
George Hislop	6	12	13	4	17	5.67
Steve Widt	2	4	4	0	4	4.00

EDINBURGH

Nigel Alderton	7	19	41	3	44	9.26
Mike McLuskey	6	17	36	2	38	8.94
Anthony Boyd	*3*	*8*	*15*	*0*	*15*	*7.50*
Dave Stevens	4	9	10	4	14	6.22
Brian Mercer	7	17	19	4	23	5.41
George Wells	2	4	3	2	5	5.00
James Grieves	1	3	3	0	3	4.00
Muir Templeton	*1*	*2*	*1*	*0*	*1*	*2.00*
Paul Gould	*1*	*2*	*0*	*0*	*0*	*0.00*

GLASGOW

Michael Irving	8	22	44	1	45	8.18
Shaun Bickley	1	3	5	0	5	6.67
Jason Lyons	1	3	4	0	4	5.33
Muir Templeton	*6*	*15*	*14*	*0*	*14*	*3.73*
Andrew Nielson	4	9	5	3	8	3.56
Robert Thomson	4	6	3	0	3	2.00
Paul Coward	1	2	1	0	1	2.00

MIDDLESBROUGH

Mike Carter	1	2	5	1	6	12.00
Duncan Chapman	7	17	44	6	50	11.76
Dave Edwards	8	21	50	6	56	10.67
Max Schofield	1	3	8	0	8	10.67
Martin Jones	5	15	34	5	39	10.40
Andy Sumner	1	3	4	2	6	8.00
Paul Coward	2	4	4	2	6	6.00
Tony Richardson	3	6	5	2	7	4.67
Dean Child	2	4	3	0	3	3.00
Paul Gould	*1*	*3*	*2*	*0*	*2*	*2.67*
Steve Crome	1	2	0	0	0	0.00

NEWCASTLE

Ray Taaffe	6	18	36	3	39	8.67
Steve Wicks	5	15	29	1	30	8.00
Jack Stevens	1	2	3	0	3	6.00
Paul Gould	*1*	*2*	*2*	*1*	*3*	*6.00*
David Nagel	8	19	24	3	27	5.68
Chris Readshaw	8	17	16	3	19	4.47
Steve Newton	1	2	2	0	2	4.00
John Endecot	1	1	1	0	1	4.00
Craig Rathbone	1	2	1	0	1	2.00

Southern

	M	W	D	L	PF	PA	Pts
Poole	**10**	**6**	**0**	**4**	**160**	**129**	**12**
Arena Essex	10	6	0	4	150	140	12
Hackney	9	5	0	4	146	118	10
Eastbourne	10	5	0	5	136	163	10
Wimbledon	9	4	0	5	135	130	8
Exeter	10	3	0	7	124	171	6

ARENA ESSEX

Nick Floyd	1	2	3	1	4	8.00
Shaun Nicholls	10	24	36	6	42	7.00
Robert Ledwith	10	28	48	1	49	7.00
Tommy Palmer	9	22	29	9	38	6.91
Chris Young	10	24	34	6	40	6.67

EASTBOURNE

Steve Masters	4	11	20	3	23	8.36
Brian Nixon	7	20	40	0	40	8.00
Scott Swain	5	13	23	1	24	7.38
Warren Mowat	10	26	31	5	36	5.54
Jason Green	5	12	10	2	12	4.00
John Cook	7	16	12	1	13	3.25

EXETER

Deon Prinsloo	*2*	*5*	*12*	*0*	*12*	*9.60*
Frank Smart	6	16	34	0	34	8.50
Wayne Freeman	2	6	11	1	12	8.00
Steve Hone	3	8	9	3	12	6.00
Mark Simmonds	2	5	7	0	7	5.60
Scott Pegler	5	14	16	2	18	5.14
Steve Brennan	7	15	16	3	19	5.07
Greg Daniels	8	19	15	2	17	3.58
Jonathan Blake	1	3	2	0	2	2.67
Paul Hay	1	2	1	0	1	2.00
Philippe Berge	1	3	1	0	1	1.33
Anthony Blake	*1*	*2*	*0*	*0*	*0*	*0.00*
Alan Spencer	1	0	0	0	0	0.00

HACKNEY

Tim Korneliussen	1	2	5	1	6	12.00
Dave Hamnett	4	12	30	2	32	10.67
Shawn Venables	6	17	34	2	36	8.47
Roland Pollard	9	22	38	3	41	7.45
David Wolstenholme	7	16	26	3	29	7.25
Simon Phillips	3	7	6	0	6	3.43
Ricky Sandford	5	11	6	1	7	2.55
Mark Unicombe	1	2	1	0	1	2.00

POOLE

Steve Leigh	10	27	51	8	59	8.74
Mark Lemon	10	26	45	5	50	7.69
Justin Elkins	10	27	48	3	51	7.56
Anthony Blake	*3*	*6*	*5*	*3*	*8*	*5.33*
Jon Gould	7	13	11	2	13	4.00

WIMBLEDON

Deon Prinsloo	*5*	*15*	*35*	*3*	*38*	*10.13*
Justin Pryor	9	26	57	2	59	9.08
Jim Dormer	4	10	16	3	19	7.60
Garry Sweet	6	13	14	1	15	4.62
Troy Scott	9	18	13	3	16	3.56
Julian Hardy	1	2	0	0	0	0.00
Dean Scott	2	3	0	0	0	0.00

Roll of Honour

NATIONAL JUNIOR LEAGUE

1988	1 POOLE	2 Stoke	3 Milton Keynes
1989	1 HACKNEY	2 Middlesbrough	3 Eastbourne

NATIONAL JUNIOR REGIONAL LEAGUES

Central

1990	1 STOKE	2 Rye House	3 Milton Keynes

Northern

1990	1 MIDDLESBROUGH	2 Edinburgh	3 Newcastle

Southern

1990	1 POOLE	2 Arena Essex	3 Hackney

▲ NATIONAL LEAGUE junior statistics were prepared by Derek Smithson, official statistician to the National League.
▲ Statistics read, from left to right, matches, rides, points, bonus points, total points and an average out of a maximum of 12 points per meeting.

JUNIOR Scene

RICHARD MUSSON, the 17-year-old starlet from Yorkshire, was excluded for unfair riding in his opening race in the 1990 British League Division Two Riders' Championship.

But he refused to be rattled by referee Paul Ackroyd's decision and simply went out and won his next four rides – and waited for the opposition to crumble!

One by one, his chief rivals for the crown dropped points and after all qualifiers – based on their League averages – had taken four rides, Musson was joint leader with Reading's Troy Smith and Wolverhampton's Wayne Carter who were also on nine points. Carter dropped another point in his last outing and had to be content with a run-off for third place, but Smith grabbed the race win that forced a decider for the title and the £150 winner's cheque. Musson, on his home Belle Vue track, snatched an early lead and never looked like making another mistake as he became the third Ace in a row to take the crown.

BRITISH LEAGUE DIVISION TWO RIDERS' CHAMPIONSHIP

Belle Vue, Sunday, September 9

Richard Musson 12 (+3), Troy Smith 12 (+2), Ade Hoole 11 (+3), Wayne Carter 11 (+2), David Steen 10, Roger Horspool 10, Phil Disney 8, Mark Robinson 8, Andy Meredith 7, Stuart Parnaby 5, David Haynes 5, Tom Grinstead 4, Richard Smith 2, Kevin Howse 1, Lee Coleman 0, Christian Howell 0. *Reserve:* Stephen Morris 4 (2).

Roll of Honour

1984 - Lawrie Bloomfield; 1985 - Jamie Habbin; 1987 - Mark Loram; 1988 - Paul Smith; 1989 - Carl Stonehewer; 1990 - Richard Musson.

CROWNCRAFT SOUTH WEST JUNIOR CHAMPIONSHIP

Exeter, Monday, September 24

Scott Swain 14, Frank Smart 13, Mark Lemon 13, Deon Prinsloo 12, Wayne Freeman 11, Robert Ledwith 11, Brian Nixon 7, John Cook 7, Anthony Blake 7, Steve Brennan 5, Greg Daniels 5, Warren Mowat 5, Stafford Galvin 4, Steve Masters 4, Tommy Palmer 1. *Reserve:* Alan Spencer 1 (4).

Roll of Honour

1987 - Peter Jeffery; 1989 - Mark Simmonds; 1990 - Scott Swain.

STARS OF TOMORROW

Friday, October 19, Hackney

Cancelled, waterlogged track.

Roll of Honour

1988 - Shawn Venables; 1989 - Darren Grayling.

Individual

CHRIS PRIME MEMORIAL TROPHY

Newcastle, Sunday, May 6

Steve Wicks 4 (2), Scott Smith 4 (2), Richard Musson 3, Mark Crang 3, Phil Disney 3, Stuart Parnaby 3, Dave Edwards 2, Anthony Boyd 2, Glenn Allan 2, Dean Child 1, Jason Straughan 1, Mike McLuskey 1 (2), Tony Richardson 0, David Nagel 0, Jack Stevens 0, Steve Widt 0. *Reserves:* Peter Byrne 1, Chris Readshaw 0 (2). ***Meeting abandoned after five heats, rain. All riders except where indicated had one ride.***

Roll of Honour

1978 - Tom Owen; 1979 - Alan Emerson; 1980 - Robbie Blackadder; 1981 - David Bargh; 1982 - Rod Hunter; 1983 - Steve McDermott; 1984 - John Louis; †1985 - Charlie McKinna; 1986 - Dave Perks; 1987 - Nigel Crabtree; 1989 - Duncan Chapman. †Held at Berwick.

†Christopher Younger PRIME (B 25.3.1960, Hull - D 3.4.1978) suffered fatal injuries during his first National League ride for Newcastle against Mildenhall in what was only his third league outing for the Diamonds.

OXFORDSHIRE BL2 CHAMPIONSHIP

Oxford, Friday, June 29

Paul Dugard 15, David Steen 11 (+3), Matthew Cross 11 (+2), Lee Coleman 11 (+1), Martin Chessell 10, Kevin Pitts 9, Troy Smith 9, Andy Meredith 7, John Cook 6, Wayne Parker 6, Steve Camden 4, Ade Hoole 4, Sean McCullagh 4, David Haynes 3, Kevin Howse 2, Rob Homer 2. *Reserves:* Chris Storey 4 (2), Kieran McCullagh 0 (1).

FUTURE CHAMPIONS CHASE

Edinburgh, Friday, June 29

1 Dave Edwards 2 Max Schofield 3 Anthony Boyd 4 Peter Byrne. *Losing semi-finalists:* Ray Taaffe, Mike McLuskey, Richard Davidson, Nigel Alderton, Michael Howe, Brian Mercer, Stafford Galvin, Jason Straughan. *Losing quarter finalists:* Fraser Smith, Peter Leckie, Paul Gould, George Wells, Andy Nielson, Stuart Coleman, Grant Blackie, David Nagel. *Qualifying scorers:* Michael Howe 9, Nigel Alderton 8, Richard Davidson 8, Peter Byrne 8, Dave Edwards 8, Max Schofield 7, Anthony Boyd 5, Jason Straughan 5, Ray Taaffe 5, Mike McLuskey 5, Brian Mercer 5, Andy Nielson 4, Stafford Galvin 3, Paul Gould 3, George Wells 2, David Nagel 1, Peter Leckie 1, Fraser Smith 1, Stuart Coleman 1, Grant Blackie 0, Robert Thomson, reserve, 0 (1).

ARTHUR NUTLEY MEMORIAL TROPHY

Sunday, July 22, Eastbourne

Scott Humphries 15, Brian Nixon 12, Scott Swain 11.5, Steve Masters 11, Warren Mowat 10, Roland Pollard 10, Garry Sweet 8, Darren Boulton 8, John Cook 6.5, Michael Howe 5, Jon Cooper 5, Jon Bell 5, Mark Bruton 5, Rob Fisher 3, Jason Green 1, Brett Wakeling 0. *Reserve:* Daniel O'Brien 1 (4).

†Arthur NUTLEY was Eastbourne team manager from 1979 to his death in November, 1985.

STARS OF TOMORROW

Berwick, Saturday, August 11

Mike McLuskey 15, Jason Straughan 13, Frank Smart 13, Colin Smith 13, David Nagel 9, Greg Daniels 8, Brian Mercer 8, Tony Bright 7, Michael Lowrie 7, Steve Widt 6, Fraser Smith 5, Andrew Nielson 4, Muir Templeton 3, George Hislop 3, Robert Thomson 1, Steve Reynolds 0, *Reserve:* Craig Rathbone 2 (4).

Roll of Honour

1970 - Jim Gallacher; 1971 - Malcolm McPhie; 1972 - Wattie Robertson; 1973 - Robin Dixon; 1974 - Vic Harding; 1975 - Peter Waite; 1976 - Jon Bower; 1977 - Ian Darling; 1978 - Rob Grant; 1979 - Neil Farnish; 1980 - Paul Henderson; 1982 - Martin McKinna; 1983 - Peter Erskine; 1984 - Jackson Irving; 1985 - Jackson Irving; 1987 - Steve Wicks; 1990 - Mike McLuskey.

FRANK BARNEY MEMORIAL TROPHY

Peterborough, Friday, August 24,

Wayne Bridgeford 15, John Wainwright 12, Roger Horspool 11, Mark Crang 10, Craig Hyde 10, Darren Spicer 10, Mark Meredith 9, Stafford Galvin 8, Paul Blackbird 8, Matthew Poole 6, Mark Jolly 6, Jon Bell 4, Rob Fisher 4, Darren Tupper 3, Colin Thorpe 1, Tony Kingsbury 1. *Reserve:* Paul Wood 1 (3).

†Frank BARNEY was the father of Exeter's Ian Barney and a long-time official at Peterborough. He died in July, 1990.

BRETT ALDERTON MEMORIAL TROPHY

Milton Keynes, Tuesday, September 11

Paul Blackbird 14, Robert Ledwith 12, Kieran McCullagh 10 (+3), Shawn Venables 10 (+2), Colin White 10 (+1), Peter Byrne 10 (N), Richard Davidson 9, Anthony Boyd 9, Tommy Palmer 8, Roland Pollard 7, Mark Jolly 6, Darren Fitch 5, Stafford Galvin 3, Troy Scott 2, Kevin Howse 2, Michael Howe 0. *Reserves:* Steve Reynolds 2 (2), Chris Storey 0 (2).

Roll of Honour

1982 - Bo Petersen; 1985 - Carl Blackbird; 1987 - Trevor Banks; 1988 - Mark Loram; 1990 - Paul Blackbird.

†Brett ALDERTON (B 3.12.1963, Sydney, Australia – D 21.4.1982) was the son of ex-rider Denis. He came to Britain in 1981 and established himself in the Milton Keynes' National League side. He suffered severe head injuries when he crashed in a trial at King's Lynn on April 17, 1982, and died four days later without regaining consciousness at Cambridge's Addenbrooke Hospital. His heart was used in a transplant operation at the city's Papworth Hospital. He rode in 34 matches for Milton Keynes, scoring 125 points.

Challenges

Milton Keynes, Tuesday, May 29

MILTON KEYNES 39 (**Mark Blackbird 12**, Kieran McCullagh 11, Peter Byrne 9, Glenn Allan 7, Andrew Mountain 0)
RYE HOUSE 26 (Wayne Baxter 11, Colin Thorpe 7, Wayne Bridgeford 4, Graham Barker 2, Tony Kingsbury 2)
LONG EATON 18 (Michael Howe 8, Matthew Cross 6, Chris Storey 3, Jon Bell 1, Stafford Galvin 0)
ARENA ESSEX 12 (Chris Young 5, Tommy Palmer 3, Robert Ledwith 2, Nick Floyd 1, Shaun Nicholls 1)

Peterborough, Friday, October 5

LONG EATON 28 (Stafford Galvin 5, Keith Stanley 8, Jon Bell 11, Chris Storey 4) **ARENA ESSEX 26** (Chris Young 4, Shaun Nicholls 7, Tommy Palmer 6, Robert Ledwith 9) **IPSWICH 24** (Rob Fisher 11, Colin Thorpe 7, Andrew Mountain 2, Adrian Mountain 4) **PETERBOROUGH 15** (Matthew Poole 8, Anthony Boyd 3, Mark Jolly 4, Scott Birland 0)

Eastbourne, Sunday, October 21

EASTBOURNE 39 (Steve Masters 14, Jason Green 2:1, Scott Swain 12, Warren Mowat 5, John Cook 1:1, Mark Bruton 4, Daniel O'Brien 1:1)
NATIONAL JUNIOR LEAGUE SELECT 57 (Roland Pollard [Hackney] 10:4, Ricky Sandford [Hackney] 13, Tommy Palmer [Arena Essex] 3, Steve Leigh [Poole] 7:1, Justin Elkins [Poole] 13, **Paul Dugard [Oxford] 11:1,** Tony Bright [Eastbourne] 0)

SUBSCRIBERS

The following were subscribers to the 1991 Speedway Yearbook.

A1	James Easter, Travel Plus
A2	Evening Echo, Poole
A3	Tony Millard, Phonesport Ltd
A4	Pat Foley, Speedwaycall
A5	Mike Bennett, MBI Video
A6	Coal Products Limited
A7	Dallfield Construction
A8	Trevor Hedge
A9	Don Godden
A10	Coastal Windows
1	BSPA (Rugby)
3	Maurice Ducker
4	Mervyn Stewkesbury
5	Alan Hodder
6	Derek Smithson
7	Myra Clarke
8	Colin Pratt
9	Philip Rising
10	Mike Patrick
11	Peter White
12	Gareth Parry
13	Richard Frost
14	John Hipkiss
15	Bryn Williams
16	Dick Barrie
17	Bob Dugard
18	David Williams
19	Tony Lethbridge
20	Neil Macfarlane
21	John Eglese (SCB)
22	Ivan Mauger
23	Barry Briggs
24	Peter Morrish
25	John Richardson
26	Michael Wright
27	Richard Haddow
28	Edward McGurk
29	Charles McKay
30	Trevor John Mundon
31	Barry Bowles - ACU Referee
32	George D. Sheridan
33	Stephen Rowland
34	Paul Eggett
35	Michael Gardner
36	Tracey Cator
37	Jack Bailey
38	Frank Marsh
39	Bob Tasker
40	Neil Girdham
41	Keith Hookham
42	Peter Robinson
43	James Sutherland
44	Rosemary Mellers
45	Michael C. Tandy
46	David Whurr
47	Eileen Ann Large
48	Dave Day
49	Jerry Harrison
50	Andrew Townshend
51	Bob Boardman
52	Kurt Willems
53	Derek J. Hosie
54	Stan Vatcher
55	John & Rosemary Edwards
56	Vic Butcher
57	Paul Church
58	Chiefy Lee
59	Lisa Jayne Matthews
60	Marcus Ayton
61	David J. Carter
62	Brian A. Pearson
63	Paul McNess
64	Shaun Dixon
65	Peter Gardner
66	Raymond John Brewer
67	Andrew Bayliss
68	Ann Oehl
69	Len Webster
70	Julie Porter
71	Brian John Deakin
72	Robert Drew
73	Charles Clark
74	Peter Wing
75	John Clifford Hurrell
76	Nicholas Gardner
77	Patrick J. Mitchell
78	Reg Miles
79	Paul Miles
80	Richard Smethurst
81	David Ward
82	Dawson A. Moss
83	John Henry Hilton
84	Sharon J. Fisher
85	Colin James Salisbury
86	Steve Brown
87	Kelvin Thompson
88	Philip Kent
89	Mr. David Styles
90	Timothy Cole
91	Paul Reynolds
92	R.A. Beaven
92	Rebecca Jarvis
93	Bill Playle
94	Keith Stanley
95	Patricia A. Palmer
96	Karen Hughes
97	Paul Carrington
98	Paul Frankum
99	Fiona & Ross Calder
100	Sales Family
101	Kirsty & Simon Colven
102	Tracy White
103	Martyn Neil Green
104	David Shadbolt
105	Nigel Whitworth
106	Sarah Booth
107	Peter Alan Scully
108	Paul Stephen Jaques
109	Paul & Rosie Brown
110	Barrie J. Wood
111	John Tredwell
112	Steven Williams, MCSP, SRP
113	Mark Cooper
114	Gary Crapper
115	Colin Marshall
116	Mr. J. Phillips
117	Peter & Ann Foster
118	Mr. Ian Bellingham
119	Neil Charles Reynolds
120	Adrian Howell
121	Robert Burton
122	Jeff Lukomiak
123	"H"
124	Michael Piggins
125	Nicholas Jennings
126	David Macdonald
127	J.G. Baldwin
128	Ray Allen
129	Alan Marriott
130	David Hood
131	L.A. Perry
132	David Greaves
133	Graham & Lisa
134	John Rogers
135	Kevin Stuart Rutter
136	Mike Noble
137	Roy Nuttall
138	Michael J. Aris
139	Nigel John Palmer
140	David Habbin
141	Dave & Lynda Hutchinson
142	Mel Homer
143	Chris Knights
144	James Edward Gooderham
145	V. Verner
146	Terry Hunt
147	Stephen Carpenter
148	Barry Hyne
149	David W. Stimpson
150	Frank Billington
151	K. Hammond
152	Mick Richardson
153	Sharon Horn
154	Stephen Arthur Hopkins
155	Anthony Taylor
156	Claire Vockins
157	Robin Dennis
158	J.H. Woods
159	Gail Hood
160	Mike Hunter
161	Andrew John Carr
162	S. Brownhill
163	James Charles Purchase
164	Mike 'Mimmo' Moseley
165	Sudden Sam's No 1 Fan
166	A.V. Barwick
167	Clive Alec Hervé
168	Robert I. Hipkiss
169	Colin Roy Pheasant
170	Michael Hodson
171	Andrew Downing
172	Terry P. Lewis
173	A. John Moore
174	Janet & Gerry Shoesmith
175	Carole Smith
176	Stanley Simpson
177	Alison J. Blunn
178	Alan Hickson
179	Clive Tyers
180	Malcolm Preen
181	Claire Elston
182	David Bartlett
183	Pauline McConnell
184	David Coulson
185	Roger Airey
186	Steve "Peptalk" Allen
187	James Hartley
188	E.V. Walder
189	John Oughton
190	Ken Taylor
191	Gary Bird
192	M.R. Gary Marshall
193	Steven Clarke
194	Dave Bone
195	Jim Alexander
196	Helen Cresswell
197	Graham Burrows
198	David Mainwaring
199	Mike Shaw
200	Nadia Wells
201	Mike Treadwell
202	Michael Stockham
203	Malcolm Owen
204	Phil Edwards
205	R. E. Bursill
206	Krister Svensson
207	Rob Brading
208	Paul Fiddes
209	P. Cadman
210	Geoff Ledger
211	Kevin Grant
212	Mark Harrison
213	Mr. B.W. Coe
214	Martyn Price
215	Graham F. Russell
216	Dave Farthing
217	Rob Lyon
218	A.P. Reeder
219	Jayne Higgins
220	Paul Dodgson
221	Helen & Steve Marsh
222	David Jones
223	David Adam
224	Brian E. Dolbear
225	Steve Clements
226	Mr. John L. Readman
227	Sam Fowler
228	Glynn Shailes
229	Joseph Allan Green
230	Anonymous
231	Nigel Platt
232	Graham Roger Pigney
233	Fred Morrow
234	Alan Beckett
235	Roy Cutting
236	Ken Weaver
237	Keith Williamson
238	James McEnroe
239	Ailsa & Sharon Fergie
240	G.S. Rowland
241	Graham Driver
242	Sarah-Jane Brown
243	Eileen Aston
244	Adrian Bell
245	Garry Chance
246	John Vaughan
247	Bobby & Carol Ott
248	Graham Flint
249	Ian Smith
250	Mr. Paul M. Markham
251	Bryan Alan Utley
252	Paul Reynolds
253	David Kinvig
254	Darren Evans
255	R. Hemsley
256	Moira & Frederick Furness
257	Lars Ström
258	Derek Richardson
259	Ian R. Willis
260	Jeremy Frosdick
261	Dave Baker
262	Mr. Brian Pears
263	S.C. Manton, 23.9.1990
264	Christine Fleming
265	Simon Wise
266	Mark & Deb Harvey
267	Graham E. Andrews
268	Carolyn Martin
269	Leslie O'Keeffe (Wimbledon Speedway)
270	Graham Smith
271	Ron D. Whittaker
272	Peter & Deirdre Cuckow
273	David Bottle
274	H.H. Loader
275	Mike Nicholls
276	Mrs. K. Lillington
277	Ivy Flatman
278	Jeff Brown
279	David Wright
280	Paul Cureton
281	Wendy J. Onion
282	Ivan Jeary
283	Glenn M. Hirst
284	Geoff Shelton
285	Stephen Blay
286	Tony Webb
287	Alison & Steve Royall
288	Bryn Williams
289	David Cullen
290	Anthony Brown
291	Dawn & Peter Gardner
292	Jason Hargreaves
293	T.A. Griffiths
294	John Bone
295	Hayley Broughton
296	Matthew Belcher
297	Kevin Neil Meynell
298	David Keeler
299	Brian Burford
300	Anonymous
301	Clive Aiken
302	Peter Charles Scaife
303	Andrew Hibbs
304	B.B.D. 134. N.L.M.831.
305	Christopher Mark Weston
306	David Wildman
307	Terry Foster
308	Gav Rackham
309	Sarah Jayne Ashford
310	Wayne Nation
311	Kevin Faithfull
312	Peter Forster
313	Roland Payne
314	John William Rolfe
315	Andrew Pinfield
316	Keith James Halliwell
317	Graham L. Smith
318	Robin Sarjant
319	David Sarjant
320	Paul Gillham
321	Justin White
322	Gary Steptoe
323	Paul L. Jeffries
324	David Woodley
325	Steve Park
326	Peter Amass
327	Thomas Elwood
328	Bridget Brockman
329	J. R. Oliver
330	Reginald Melhuish
331	John C. Vine
332	John Charles Smith
333	Darrell Aspery
334	Michael Stuart Brereton
335	Jeffrey Wilson
336	John Bonner
337	Sheila Cronin
338	Peter Robinson
339	David Morrell
340	Timothy Hadley Rowe
341	Howard Beaumont
342	J. J. McCormack
343	Mark Hawkes
345	J. Shackel
346	Graham Jarvis
347	Gary Thompson
348	Terry Townsend

SUBSCRIBERS

349	*Clive Cockrill*	*387*	*Aileen Mitchell*
350	*John Paul Humphrey*	*388*	*Mike Hunter*
351	*Mark Rendell*	*389*	*Dave Butler*
352	*David Armstrong*	*390*	*Trevor James*
353	*Neil Reynolds*	*391*	*Dawson Moss*
354	*Robert T. Bamford*	*392*	*John Boynton*
355	*Marianne Batten*	*393*	*Mags Young*
356	*Laurence Rogers*	*394*	*Tyrone Leslie Clapp*
357	*Mark Fulton*	*395*	*John Lord*
358	*Terry Catley*	*396*	*Barry Mobley*
359	*Peter & Kelli Titcombe*	*397*	*Graham Farnham*
360	*Bernard Le Bargy*	*398*	*Jane Marie Wirdman*
361	*Peter J. H. Carless*	*399*	*Jeff Bone*
362	*Darrin Worth*	*400*	*David Huw Jones*
363	*Gary Hicks*	*401*	*Richard Crowley*
364	*William John West*	*402*	*Kerry R. Pringle*
365	*Andrew Shurey*	*403*	*Jonathan Crawford*
366	*Lex & David Selby*	*404*	*D. R. Howarth*
367	*Carol Garland*	*405*	*Paul Wilkes*
368	*Philip John Allen*	*406*	*Ben Henshaw*
369	*Lee Whitmore*	*407*	*Master Arron Burke*
370	*Peter Pearson*	*408*	*Steve Chaloner*
371	*Mr. K. R. Muir*	*409*	*Kenneth Craig McCurdy*
372	*Ian Shepherd*	*410*	*Andy Marlow*
373	*D. A. Donaldson*	*411*	*Terry Delaney*
374	*Tracey Knights*	*412*	*Robert Peasley*
375	*No Entry*	*413*	*Stan Ward*
376	*Alan Swift*	*414*	*Linda & Diane Smith*
377	*Kevan Faultey*	*415*	*Robin Driscoll*
378	*Len Piper*	*416*	*John Hill*
379	*Neil Howard Southam*	*417*	*Peter Gudgeon*
380	*Gordon Wm. Rowlatt*	*418*	*Philip A.H. Longdon*
381	*John Hutton*	*419*	*Dr. Tim Sharrock*
382	*Kristian Austin – Peterborough mascot*	*420*	*Pete Sweetman*
		421	*Nigel Hillsdon*
383	*Sally Prodger*	*422*	*Bob Edwards (Cradley Heath statistician)*
384	*W. A. Giles*		
385	*Cheryl Tucker*	*423*	*Steve Clarke*
386	*Stephen Griffiths*	*424*	*David Nagel*

ACKNOWLEDGEMENTS

No book of this nature will ever be possible to compile without the help and assistance of so many people.

We acknowledge that help and assistance which we have had from so many different sources in speedway in both Great Britain and the rest of the world.

We have endeavoured to include all those who have helped in any way in the list that follows but no doubt we have inadvertently omitted some. To those we offer our apologies and assure them any oversight does not lessen our gratitude to them.

Pete Ansell, Dick Barrie, Peter Brown, Myra Clarke, Danmarks Motor Union (Denmark), Jørgen Dorscheus, James Easter, John Eglese (Speedway Control Board), Evzen Erban, FIM, Silvia Franc, Mike Gregory, Peter Gudgeon, Heinz Hausmann, David Hawkins, John Hipkiss, Alan Hodder, Nicola Horton (ACU), Roger Jones, Tony Lethbridge, John Louis, Neil Macfarlane, Ivan Mauger, Tony Millard, Peter Morrish, Norges Motorsykkelforbund (Norway), Sarah Oakes, Sharon Pace, Mike Patrick, Wladyslaw Pietrzak, Philip Rising, Ronnie Russell, Steve Sant, Angela Sharpe, Derek Smithson, Mervyn Stewkesbury, Suomen Moottoriliitto r.y. (Finland), Tim Swales, Dave Trownson, Peter White, Bryn Williams and Bo Wirebrand.

We also acknowledge the following publications whose archive material has, once again, been of considerable assistance: Bahnsport Aktuell (West Germany), Bahnsport Handbuch (1976-1980), Danmarks Motor Sports Kalender (Various), FIM Annuaire (Various), FIM Bulletin (1990), International Speedway Service Handbook (1984-1986), Kouzlo levych zatacek (Czechoslovakia), Motor Bladet (Denmark), Motor Cycle News (Great Britain), Peter White's Speedway World (Australia), PZM Informator (Various), PZM Wyniki Sportu Zuzlowego (1968-1980), Race & Touring (Sweden), Speedway Star (Great Britain), Speedway Yearbooks (1977-1982, 1986, 1990), Sportowiec Magazyn Ilustrowany (Poland), SVEMO Motorkalender (Various), Vom Dirt-Track Zum Speedway (East Germany), Who's Who of World Speedway (1976).

We would also like to thank all those supporters who showed their confidence in both our 1990 Speedway Yearbook and in this subsequent edition by becoming Subscribers.

LEGEND

Throughout the 1991 Speedway Yearbook the same abbreviations have been used in all sections.

Riders making guest appearances are automatically printed in *italic* type and riders who were unbeaten in a meeting are printed in **bold** type.

In the respective Club sections the following symbols have been used.

† Captain § Club & Test debut

§§ Debut in that respective League.

DOWN UNDER

As is the tradition Australia and New Zealand staged a series of 1991 World Championship qualifying rounds in 1990. Listed below are the results of those meetings which were held before January 1, 1991.

NORTHERN TERRITORY
Tennant Creek, Saturday, November 17
Wayne Bridgeford 15, Glen Baxter 14, Trevor O'Brien 13, Robbie Wark 11, Kelvin Willis 11, Danny Wark 5, Mark O'Cass 5, Wayne Lorymer 5, Stuart Cassidy 4, Dean Pierce 4, Kerrin Giezendanner 4, Tony Hardacre 2, Marcus Gray 2, Wally Bondarefe 1, Michael Clauson 1, Shane Cramp 0.

QUEENSLAND
Mackay, Saturday, December 1
Troy Butler 15, Darren Winkler 13, Alan Rivett 13, Wayne Baxter 11, Peter Christopher 11, John Reid 10, Stafford Galvin 8, Terry Keyse 7, Clinton Butler 5, Wayne Kennedy 5, Gary Richards 4, Craig Hyde 4, Steven Butler 4, Gary Davey 3, Brian Ward 2, Craig Jung 2, Kevin Winton, reserve, 2.

VICTORIA
Mildura, Sunday, December 23
Leigh Adams 15, Jason Lyons 14, Phil Crump 11, Mark Lemon 11, Cory Alderton 10, Nigel Alderton 10, Jason Hawkes 10, Matt McWilliam 8, Anthony Keys 6, Jodey Mason 5, Glen Bowles 5, Gavin Sedgeman 4, Justin Thomas 3, Paul Wheatland, reserve, 3, Reece Davison, reserve, 2, Rick Mason 1, Nigel Tremelling 1, Darren Wade 1.

NEW SOUTH WALES
Newcastle, Wednesday, December 26
Craig Boyce 15, Todd Wiltshire 14, Stephen Davies 13, Chris Watson 11, Rod Colquhoun 11, Mick Poole 10, Sean Willmott 8, Scott Humphries 8, Tony Primmer 8, Mark Unicomb 5, Jamie Plumb 4, Matthew Poole 3, Mick Holder 3, Darren Etheridge 3, Dave Hamnett 2, Tim Hunter 2.

WESTERN AUSTRALIA
Claremont, Perth, Friday, December 28
Glenn Doyle 30, David Cheshire 28, Michael Carter 22, Glyn Taylor 20, Guy Wilson 20, Ross Townson 15, Lewis Russell 11, Steve O'Leary 9, Marshall McDiarmid 9, Lee Redmond 8, Frank Smart 8, Col Burn 5, Steve Johnston, reserve, 0.
Riders had five races each, scoring 6-5-4-3-2-1.

SOUTH AUSTRALIA
Murray Bridge, Saturday, December 29
Shane Parker 15, Damon Richardson 11, Brett Tomkin 11, Neil Perry 10, Darrell Branford 9, Ross Noble 8, Steve Graetz 8, Barry Golding 7, Scott Norman 7, Troy Norvill 6, Garry Fischer 6, Paul Cooper 5, Mark Mitchell 3, Matthew Anchor 3, Ivan Clothier 1.
▲ ***The top two scorers from the six State Championships automatically qualified for the Australian Final at Alice Springs on January 27, to be joined by the top four scorers from a further qualifying round at the same track eight days earlier.***

SOUTH ISLAND (New Zealand)
Christchurch, Saturday, December 15
Mark Lyndon 15, Mark Thorpe 14, Justin Monk 12, Mark Jamieson 10, Jacqui Mauger 9, Dean Sullivan 9, John Tuffley 8, Darrin Hopewell 8, Nicholas Young 8, Rhys Hamburger 6, Ricky Bennett 6, Michael Hollow 5, Peter Hollow 3, Donald McDonald, reserve, 2, Andy Walker 1, Mason Taylor 1.
▲ *Jacqui Mauger, the niece of former World Champion Ivan Mauger, became the first lady rider ever to qualify from a World Championship round.*

WESTERN AUSTRALIAN OPEN CHAMPIONSHIP
Claremont, Perth, Saturday, December 8
Glenn Doyle 29, Glyn Taylor 26, *Andy Smith 23,* Guy Wilson 20, Michael Carter 18, David Cheshire 16, *Rob Woffinden 13,* Frank Smart 13, Lewis Russell 13, Mick Hartnett 7, Steve O'Leary 7, Col Curn 7, Chris Lee 6, Ross Townson 6, Marshall Diarmid 5, Steve Johnson 3, Lee Redmond, reserve, 3, Steve Lee, reserve, 3.
▲ *Although originally scheduled as the qualifying round of the World Championship the meeting's status was amended because of the presence in the line-up of two English riders.*

BILLY SANDERS MEMORIAL AUSTRALIAN OPEN
Brisbane, Friday, December 28
1 Todd Wiltshire 9, 2 Leigh Adams 7, 3 Sam Ermolenko 4, Troy Butler 4. *Qualifying scorers:* Butler 12, Ermolenko 12, Wiltshire 11, Adams 11, Andy Smith 11, Phil Crump 10, Craig Boyce 9, Gary Allan 8, Mick Poole 7, Alan Rivett 7, Rinat Mardanshin 7, Darren Winkler 5, Stephen Davies 5, Steve Langdon 2, Craig Hodgson 2, Rod Colquhoun 1.

A touring party from the Soviet Union made a successful visit to Australia at the end of the 1990 season and listed below are the results of all those meetings.

Darwin, Australia, Saturday, November 3
NORTHERN TERRITORY 32 (Wayne Bridgeford 9, Glen Baxter 6, Trevor O'Brien 5, Wayne Baxter 4, David Jackson 4, Brent Nott 4, Wayne Lorymer 0) **SOVIET UNION 57** (René Aas 12, Rinat Mardanshin 11, Mikhail Starostin 10:2 Rif Saitgareev 8, Viktor Gaidym 7:3, Vladimir Trofimov 6:1, Grigori Harchenko 3:2).

Alice Springs, Wednesday, November 7
NORTHERN TERRITORY 33 (Glen Baxter 8, Brent Nott 7:1, Trevor O'Brien 7, Wayne Bridgeford 6, Kelvin Willis 4, Wayne Baxter 1, Robbie Wark 0) **SOVIET UNION 57** (Oleg Kurguskin 14, Starostin 12:1, Mardanshin 9:2, Saitgareev 7, Harchenko 6:1, Aas 5:2, Gaidym 4:2, Andrej Korolev 0).

Townsville, Friday, November 9
NORTH QUEENSLAND 36 (Peter Christopher 8:2, Gary Richards 8, Gary Davey 8, John Reid 6, Terry Keyes 4:1, Paul de Bona 1, Rod Heathcote 1) **SOVIET UNION 54** (Kurguskin 12:2, Mardanshin 11:3, Starostin 9, Aas 7:1, Harchenko 7, Gaidym 6:1, Saitgareev 2).

Cairns, Saturday, November 10
NORTH QUEENSLAND 38 (John Reid 16, Gary Richards 9, Peter Christopher 7:1, Terry Keyes 2:1, Gary Davey 2, Ken McKenzie 1, Mark Pearce 1) **SOVIET UNION 52** (Mardanshin 14, Harchenko 9:1, Aas 9, Gaidym 7:2, Starostin 6:1, Kurguskin 5, Korolev 2).

Mackay, Friday, November 16
CENTRAL QUEENSLAND 45 (Tony Langdon 17, Troy Butler 14, Alan Rivett 5, Peter Christopher 5, Clinton Butler 2, John Reid 2, Gary Davey 0) **SOVIET UNION 45** (Mardanshin 11, Kurguskin 11, Starostin 9, Saitgareev 4, Gaidym 4, Aas 4, Trofimov 2).

Rockhampton, Saturday, November 17
CENTRAL QUEENSLAND 42 (Tony Langdon 13, Troy Butler 10, Darren Winkler 9, Clinton Butler 4, John Reid 3, Glen Tregea 2, Alan Rivett 1, Peter Christopher 0) **SOVIET UNION 48** (Mardanshin 10, Kurguskin 10, Saitgareev 9, Aas 8, Trofimov 5, Starostin 4, Gaidym 2).

Brisbane, Saturday, November 24
SOUTH QUEENSLAND 41 (Troy Butler 17, Alan Rivett 9:1, Steve Langdon 6:1, Darren Winkler 3:1, Mark Carlson 3:1, Clinton Butler 2, Mick Powell 1) **SOVIET UNION 49** (Mardanshin 10, Kurguskin 8:2, Saitgareev 8:1, Trofimov 7, Aas 6, Starostin 5:1, Harchenko 5:1).

Nambour, Saturday, December 1
YOUNG AUSTRALIA 40 (Phil Crump 12, Rod Colquhoun 8:1, Scott Humphries 7, Mark Lemon 5, Jason Lyons 4:1, Mick Holder 3:1, Cory Alderton 1) **SOVIET UNION 50** (Mardanshin 14, Saitgareev 9, Kurguskin 7:1, Gaidym 7, Trofimov 5:3, Starostin 5, Harchenko 3:1).

Newcastle, Saturday, December 8
NEW SOUTH WALES 49 (**Todd Wiltshire 15**, Craig Boyce 10:2, Stephen Davies 8:1, Mick Poole 8, Sean Willmott 4:2, Chris Watson 4, Darren Etheridge 0) **SOVIET UNION 41** (Mardanshin 13:1, Kurguskin 7:1, Saitgareev 7, Aas 5, Gaidym 4:2, Starostin 3:1, Trofimov 2:1).

Hobart, Tasmania, Saturday, December 15
AUSTRALIAN SELECT 47 (**Phil Crump 15**, Alan Rivett 9:1, Rod Colquhoun 8, Mick Poole 5, Troy Butler 5, Stephen Davies 4, Jason Lyons 1) **SOVIET UNION 43** (Starostin 11:2, Saitgareev 10:1, Mardanshin 7, Kurguskin 6:1, Aas 6, Gaidym 3, Trofimov 0).

North Arm, Adelaide, Friday, December 28
SOUTH AUSTRALIA 53 (Shane Bowes 13, Shane Parker 8, Scott Norman 8, David Norris 7, Brett Tomkin 7, Damon Richardson 6, Dennis Löfqvist 4) **SOVIET UNION 37** (Kurguskin 11, Saitgareev 10, Starostin 8, Aas 3, Harchenko 3, Gaidym 2, Korolev 0).

Mildura, Sunday, December 30
PHIL CRUMP'S YOUNG AUSSIES 46 (Leigh Adams 11, Phil Crump 10, Mark Lemon 8, Jason Lyons 8, Cory Alderton 6, Shane Bowes 3, Nigel Alderton 0) **SOVIET UNION 43** (Starostin 10, Kurguskin 9, Saitgareev 6, Gaidym 6, Harchenko 5, Aas 5, Mardanshin 2).

Perth, Tuesday, January 1, 1991
WESTERN AUSTRALIAN 148 (Andy Smith 31, Glyn Taylor 28, Glenn Doyle 27, David Cheshire 26, Michael Carter 22, Guy Wilson 9, Rob Woffinden 5) **SOVIET UNION 100** (Kurguskin 25, Saitgareev 22, Aas 18, Harchenko 17, Gaidym 10, Mardanshin 8, Starostin 0).
Scoring 6-5-4-3-2-1.

Albany, Saturday, January 5, 1991
WESTERN AUSTRALIA 51 (Doyle 18, Taylor 12, Cheshire 9, Smith 7, Carter 3, Woffinden 2, Wilson, did not ride) **SOVIET UNION 57** (Starostin 16, Saitgareev 15, Kurguskin 12, Gaidym 6, Trofimov 4, Aas 2, Mardanshin 2).

▲ ***Full details of the 1991 Swedish tour of Australia will be given in the 1992 Yearbook.***

1991 DIARY DATES

WORLD PAIRS
Holders: Denmark

Qualifying Round (Wiener-Neustadt, Austria, Sunday, April 7): Austria, Bulgaria, Finland, Holland, Norway, Soviet Union, Yugoslavia.

Semi Final 1 (Pardubice, Czechoslovakia, Sunday, June 16): Australia, Czechoslovakia, England, Hungary, Sweden, two qualifiers from qualifying round.

Semi Final 2 (Pocking, Germany, Sunday, June 16): Denmark, Italy, New Zealand, United States of America, Germany, two qualifiers from qualifying round.

WORLD FINAL (Poznan, Poland, Saturday, July 20): Poland, three qualifiers from Semi Final 1 and Semi Final 2.

▲ *The World Pairs reverts to four-rider heats.*

WORLD JUNIOR CHAMPIONSHIP
Holder: Chris Louis

Qualifying Round 1 (Norden, Germany, Sunday, May 26)

Qualifying Round 2 (Targovishte, Bulgaria, Sunday, May 26)

Qualifying Round 3 (Wolfslake, Germany, Sunday, May 26)

Qualifying Round 4 (Elgane, Norway, Sunday, May 26)

Semi Final 1 (Tcherkessk, Soviet Union, Sunday, June 30)

Semi Final 2 (Natschbach-Loipersbach, Austria, Sunday, June 30)

WORLD FINAL (Coventry , England, Sunday, September 29)

WORLD INDIVIDUAL CHAMPIONSHIP
Holder: Per Jonsson

Preliminary Round 1 (Ljubljana, Yugoslavia, Sunday, May 5).
Preliminary Round 2 (Neustadt-Donau, Germany, Sunday, May 5).
Preliminary Round 3 (Wroclaw, Poland, Saturday, May 5).
Preliminary Round 4 (Wiener-Neustadt, Austria, Sunday, May 5).
Qualifying Round A (Miskolc, Hungary, Sunday, June 2):
Qualifying Round B (Pfaffenhofen, Germany, Sunday, June 2)
Qualifying Round C (Neubrandenburg, Germany, Sunday, June 2)
Qualifying Round D (Czestochowa, Poland, Saturday, June 1)
British Final (Coventry, Sunday, May 19)
Commonwealth Final (King's Lynn, England, Sunday, June 2): 10 qualifiers from British Final; 4 qualifiers from Australia; 2 qualifiers from New Zealand.
Continental Semi Final 1 (Slany, Czechoslovakia, Sunday, June 23)
Continental Semi Final 2 (Lonigo, Italy, Sunday, June 23)
Scandinavian Final (Brovst, Denmark, Sunday, June 23): 6 qualifiers from Denmark; 5 qualifiers from Sweden; 2 qualifiers from Norway; 2 qualifiers from Finland. Sixteenth qualifier to be decided by a race-off between one rider from Denmark, Finland, Norway and Sweden.
Overseas Final (Bradford, England, Sunday, June 23): 12 qualifiers from Commonwealth Final; 4 qualifiers from North American Final.
Semi Final 1 (Abensberg, Germany, Sunday, August 18)
Semi Final 2 (Rovno, Soviet Union, Sunday, August 11)
Semi Finals will be drawn with qualifiers from the Continental Semi Finals (14), Scandinavian Final (9) and Overseas Final (9).

WORLD FINAL (Gothenburg, Sweden, Saturday, August 31): *8 qualifiers from each Semi Final.*

WORLD TEAM CUP
Holders: United States of America

Group D, Round 1 (Leipzig, Germany, Sunday, April 21): Bulgaria, East Germany, Holland, Yugoslavia.

Group D, Round 2 (Krsko, Yugoslavia, Sunday, April 28): Bulgaria, East Germany, Holland, Yugoslavia.

Group C, Round 1 (Lonigo, Italy, Sunday, May 19): Austria, Italy, Norway, Poland, Winners Group D.

Group C, Round 2 (Tarnow, Poland, Sunday, May 26): Austria, Italy, Norway, Poland, Winners Group D.

Group B, Round 1 (Diedenbergen, Germany, Sunday, July 7): Finland, Hungary, West Germany, Winners Group C.

Group B, Round 2 (Debrecen, Hungary, Sunday, July 14): Finland, Hungary, West Germany, Winners Group C.

Group A (Pardubice, Czechoslovakia, Sunday, August 25): Australia, Czechoslovakia, Sweden, Winners Group B.

WORLD FINAL (Vojens, Denmark, Saturday, September 14): Denmark, England, United States of America, Winners Group A.

WORLD LONG TRACK CHAMPIONSHIP
Holder: Simon Wigg

Qualifying Round (Ludwigslust, Germany, Saturday, April 27)
Semi Final 1 (Scheeßel, Germany, Sunday, July 14)
Semi Final 2 (Pfarrkirchen, Germany, Sunday, June 30)
Semi Final 3 (Jubek, Germany, Sunday, June 30)
WORLD FINAL (Marianske-lazne, Czechoslovakia, Sunday, July 28)

▲ The World Long Track Championship reverts to six-rider heats.

CHAMPIONS CUP
Holder: Hans Nielsen

FINAL (Elgane, Norway, Sunday, June 9).

All dates and venues are subject to alteration .